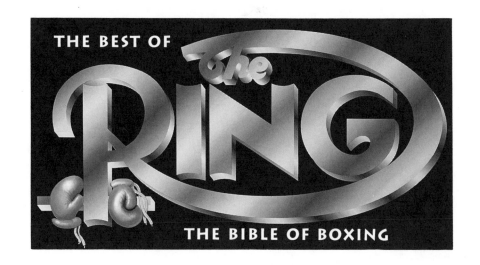

THE BEST OF

# the RING

THE BIBLE OF BOXING

Edited by Stanley Weston

Bonus Books, Inc., Chicago

Library of Congress Catalog Card Number: 91-77022

International Standard Book Number: 0-929387-68-6

**Bonus Books, Inc.**
160 East Illinois Street
Chicago, Illinois 60611

*Printed in the United States of America*

## ADVERTISING DISCLAIMER

All advertisements included in this book are for illustrative purposes only. Any information contained in the advertisements, including prices, addresses, and other general information may no longer be valid and is printed for the enjoyment of the reader only. THE RING and Bonus Books are not responsible for the fulfillment of any product ordered.

THE BEST OF

**RING**

THE BIBLE OF BOXING

# Contents

# Preface

Every day, *The Ring* receives inquiries from boxing fans the world over. It's been that way for almost three-quarters of a century. Sometimes, a fan needs to have an old-time memory refreshed. Other times, he needs a bet settled. Whatever the reason, *The Ring* gets questions.

—"What was the name of that heavyweight champion who went to college?"

—"What was Benny Leonard's father's first name?"

—"How many fights apiece did Jake LaMotta and Ray Robinson win in their series?"

—"Did any heavyweight champion have Indian blood?"

When someone has a boxing question, he invariably turns to *The Ring*. And since *The Ring* has been published longer than any sports magazine in existence, it enjoys a unique position of authority.

*The Ring* was founded by Nat Fleischer in 1922. He reigned as Editor and Publisher until his death in 1972, at age 84. A tireless dynamo—15- to 20-hour workdays were the rule, not the exception—Fleischer made time to author approximately 65 books, all involving the sport that fascinated him since he was a boy growing up on New York's teeming East Side.

Fleischer was a fanatical collector of boxing memorabilia, as well as a master archivist. He acquired vast photo collections and countless scrapbooks, many of which were the life's work of dedicated fans from all over the world. One such bonanza was purchased from a London dealer in 1936, the collection of a departed Welshman who had managed to fill 631 huge scrapbooks with newspaper clippings, magazine articles, programs, and ticket stubs. The earliest piece was a contemporary article detailing the historic 1805 fight between Tom Cribb and Bill Richmond.

Fleischer didn't stop adding to *The Ring's* massive picture and text files till the day he died. A few years before his passing, Fleischer told a *New York Times* columnist, "My best guess is that we have a collection of at least a million and a half boxing pictures, dating back to Roman times. As for the text, who knows? We add about half a dozen file cabinets every year. If I said 10 million fight reports and personality pieces, I don't think I'd be too far off."

These treasure chests of instantly available data has made *The Ring* supreme in its field and earned the magazine its international reputation as "The Bible of Boxing." One can easily understand why *The Ring* is an immortal champion in its own right by simply glancing through the collection of articles in this book, carefully selected from issues covering the magazine's long life span. It will also explain why, when a fan in Nigeria wants to know what shoe size Primo Carnera wore, he asks *The Ring*.

# Like Father Like Son

## A Story About Theodore Roosevelt and His Love for Boxing

### By CLARENCE RIORDAN

"LIKE Father, Like Son" is an adage as old as the hills. Down in San Juan, on the hill where the mansion of the Governor of Porto Rico is situated, there is a young man who not only in appearance, but in practically every move he makes, reminds his intimate friends of his illustrious dad. The young man is none other than Theodore Roosevelt.

The smile, the handshake and the energy put into his work is not the only reminder of his father. There is still a greater resemblance—his love for athletics. I was a great admirer of President Roosevelt and knew him well when he was Police Commissioner of New York City and later Governor of the Empire State. I was present many times with him at Jack Coopers' gymnasium where he would don the mitts and show his ability as a boxer.

Hence when I chanced to be in Porto Rico recently on the day Theodore Roosevelt made his bow as Governor, I made certain to pay my respects to the son of the great Teddy. The day following the inauguration, I learned that the newly appointed Governor had put in a strenuous early morning workout in calesthenics and then a few days later he went a step further and put on the gloves for a little tilt with the island's leading boxing trainer and champion, Frankie O'Ben.

Naturally the papers went strong for this, some printing first page headlines on the Governor's athletic ability. To the Islanders, it was a big surprise to think that a Governor could find time to take a little exercise during his recreation period and to one paper, it seemed rather a shock to learn that Theodore Roosevelt, the Governor of Porto Rico, was an ardent boxing enthusiast.

* * *

If the fellow who wrote that piece had been a New Yorker, he would have known better, for New York fight followers have often seen the Roosevelt family sitting in the first row in Madison Square Garden, directly behind the radio announcer. Those in the vicinity of the Roosevelts can vouch for the statement that there are no more ardent rooters at a good fight than the Oyster Bay celebrities, especially the fair sex of the family.

To New Yorkers, the news emanating from Porto Rico about Roosevelt's interest in boxing does not arouse any surprise. But if a statement were published that Theodore Roosevelt, Governor of Porto Rico, shuns boxing and thinks it degrading, that would immediately be regarded as a big news item.

The reason? Well, all of the Roosevelt boys were brought

*Theodore Roosevelt, when he held the office of Vice-president of the United States*

up on an athletic diet. All were taught the manly art of self defense when at school. Each had often heard his dad preach on the benefits of boxing. Therefore, when after spending his first week as Governor, Teddy announced that he had hired Porto Rico's best trainer, Frankie O'Ben for his sparring mate, the son of the former president was simply following in the footsteps of his illustrious father.

* * *

The late Theodore Roosevelt was a remarkable man. His life had been full of varied episodes and thrilling adventures. He made his mark as an all-around athlete, a ranchman, a soldier, a hunter and a politician, but boxing was his hobby. Never was there a child who gave less promise of strength and hardihood than Theodore Roosevelt. As a boy, the late president was referred to as a chicken-chested kid, so delicate was he that he was not permitted to play in strenuous games with other lads.

But like the son who holds the Governor's rein over Porto Rico today, Theodore Roosevelt had grit, determination and the courage of the fighting man. As a newspaper man who was assigned to politics on a New York paper, I had occasion to interview Roosevelt when he occupied the Police Commissioner's office and later when he went to Albany as head of New York State. I recollect distinctly an occasion when, with half dozen other scribes, we cornered Teddy after an appeal had been made to him by the Law and Order Society to stop a fight in the old Garden and he had refused, and asked for his reasons for not taking any action.

"BECAUSE I can see nothing wrong in boxing so long as the law is obeyed." was his reply. "Boxing is a great sport. Too bad our schools don't take it up. If they did, we would have more courageous young men and less ruffians."

With that he shifted his weight to the other foot, and told us a little story of his early life and how he overcame his physical ailment. He remarked that he loved a good scrap because he admired the fighting spirit in any man. When I learned that Roosevelt, the Porto Rican governor, was sparring with a professional boxer, for exercise. I couldn't help but think of the career of his dad. I went through my clippings, for I've kept a morgue for many years, and from there I drew out a story I had written many years ago on "Roosevelt and Boxing."

* * *

"I made my health, what it is today," said he, at our interview years ago. "When I found that, physically I was not the equal of other boys, I determined to make myself as stout and able a fighting man as my Norse ancestors. When only a boy, I was sent to Moosehead Lake to rid myself of asthma. I was brought up by a maiden aunt who felt that the change of air would help my ailment and also build me up. While en route, I became acquainted with three boys who took a keen delight in teasing me. One, in particular, every now and then would thrash me until my pride was hurt and I decided I would learn to defend myself so that I could retaliate if ever the occasion again arose.

"Upon my return home, I told my father what had happened, and he willingly consented to have me take up boxing. An instructor, Tom Long, an ex-prize fighter, was engaged and for two years he trained me. At the end of that period I won his lightweight amateur tournament and I felt elated at having mastered the sport. From then on, I took a keen delight in doning the gloves with my friends. I also took up wrestling at which I became proficient. Before I left school to enter college, I had learned considerable about both sports.

"Many of the boys at school ridiculed my sailor suit and thanks to my boxing lessons, every fellow who called me a dude was forced to take his medicine. It wasn't long before I no longer was molested, for the boys all learned that I wasn't afraid of a fair-stand-up fight.

"When I went to Harvard, I joined the boxing and wrestling teams. I sparred a great deal, and also was on the track team. It didn't make any difference to me that I seldom came in first, for I got more good out of my boxing and wrestling exercises than those who beat me, because I immensely enjoyed it and never injured myself.

* * *

"WHEN I became a member of the New York State Legislature, there was considerable commotion up at Albany by a faction that was opposed to boxing and other strenuous sports. I took issue with them. Like my father who believed that a fair, stand-up fight would do a boy a lot of good, I arose and defended boxing. I surprised, yes, and even shocked many mothers when I said:

"The boy that won't fight is not worth his salt. He is either a coward or constitutionally weak. I have taught my boys to take their own part and fight their way whenever they must. Cowardice is not in their makeup. I do not know which I should punish my boys for quicker—for cruelty or flinching. Both are abominable.

"I have never been able to sympathize with the outcry against boxing. The only objection I have to prize fighting as at present conducted is the crookedness that has attended its commercial development, but this can be easily eradicated. Outside of this, I regard boxing, professional and amateur, a healthful, vigorous sport that develops courage, keenness of mind, quickness of eye and a spirit of combativeness that fits the boy for every task that might confront him in the aver-

age lifetime. It is not half as brutalizing or demoralizing as many forms of big business and of legal work carried on in connection with such business."

* * *

THAT little talk drew heaps of comment in the next day's papers, but it did not phase the great Roosevelt. He was a born fighter, just as is his son, the Governor of Porto Rico. When the elder Roosevelt went to Harvard, he was not long in making known his prowess with the mitts. One day, while practicing in the gymnasium, he was approached by the class bully, who asked for a little set-to. Roosevelt was quick to oblige and with the gloves on, they stepped to the center to prepare for the proceedings. Teddy's opponent was anxious to beat him, and while in the act of shaking hands, he whipped over a terrific right to Roosevelt's jaw, which not only jarred the future president, but shocked him by this piece of unsportsmanship.

The students were quick to observe this foul work and immediately cries of shame and foul rent the air. Roosevelt, however, stood his ground. He smiled and raised his hand to curb the hissing. Then, to the astonishment of all, he politely held out his right hand for his opponent to grasp and to the discomforture of his rival, he stood in this position until the latter complied with the chivalry and courtesy of ring combat.

With that accomplished, Teddy, according to the person who told me this story, sailed into the bully and hammered him all over the ring. Never again did he try to slip one over on Roosevelt or any other member of the boxing fraternity. Throughout the remainder of their college days, Teddy and the fellow he whipped were the greatest of pals.

* * *

When he was governor of New York, Roosevelt, as his son recently did in Porto Rico, hired

*Tex Rickard, Theodore Roosevelt and Walter P. Chrysler at the Tunney dinner in 1928*

# Like Father, Like Son

a professional fighter to spar with him. The billiard room on the third floor of the Executive Mansion was fitted up as a gymnasium, and here the Governor spent an hour a day in wrestling, bag punching, boxing and rope skipping.

When he was Police Commissioner, he refused to stop the Choynski-Maher battle in Madison Square Garden. Teddy sneaked into the Garden, saw the fight, enjoyed every moment of the affair, and when the contest was over, he ordered that no arrests be made.

"It was one of the greatest bouts I ever saw," were Teddy's words to the newspapermen who interviewed him at headquarters the following morning. "I can see no harm in such exhibitions.

"Why stop it and make arrests? In my opinion, it is far better for a man to know how to protect himself as these fellows did last night than it is to be forced to resort to the use of firearms, knives or clubs."

ONE day Roosevelt put on the gloves with Billy Edwards, one time lightweight champion of the world. Edwards smiled as he faced the slender young student. He actually feared to strike a blow for fear he might injure the collegian. But when the gong sounded, and before Edwards realized it, young Teddy slipped by a left hook and crashed a straight left to Edwards' right eye and closed it.

It was accomplished so quickly and so suddenly, that the professional was completely taken off his guard. Edwards became furious and then tore into his opponent and almost had Teddy out when the bell sounded. However, Roosevelt took the beating courageously. He had lived up to his motto and even against such a renowned professional, he showed no signs of fear.

It was while in the White House where he had Mike Donovan, Jack Cooper and others box, fence and wrestle with him, that Roosevelt received an injury which blinded his left eye. While boxing with a young artillery captain, the captain struck Roosevelt a heavy blow that broke some blood vessels and throughout the remainder of his life, though few knew it, the left eye was useless.

The Governor of Porto Rico may never reach the heights of his illustrious dad, but he is following the footsteps of Theodore Roosevelt as a great lover of outdoor life. He is an ardent follower of all sports, especially boxing.

Here is one case "Like Father, Like Son."

*As Police Commissioner, Theodore Roosevelt refused to stop the Joe Choynski (above) — Peter Maher fight at the Garden.*

# GRUDGE FIGHTS

By WILBUR
WOOD

*Corbett, downed by Fitz's solar plexus blow, is counted out*

come into the sock market has killed off the grudge spirit so prevalent in the misty days of long ago when the satisfaction of having whipped a hated rival was about all even the victor had to show for his efforts when it was all over.

* * *

*P*ROBABLY there is more than a grain of truth in that statement. Certainly, some of the so-called fights foisted upon the suffering public nowadays look more like necking parties than grudge battles. Probably it is rather difficult for a boxer to work up a venomous hatred of his opponent when he bears in mind that the other fellow is helping him collect a young fortune for an hour's work.

Yet the grudge fight is by no means extinct. We had one of them only last September, when Jack Sharkey knocked out Tommy Loughran with a punch

'*I*T'S a grudge fight!"
Those four words constitute the shortest and best ballyhoo a fight can have. Fortunate is the promoter who lands one.

Farther back than the memory of even the oldest fan reaches, the grudge fight has held a peculiar fascination for the genus customer. The boys figure, and rightly, that when they see two boxers engaged in seeking personal satisfaction upon each other they are going to get their money's worth and something to spare. There seems to be a keener pleasure, as far as the customer is concerned, when he believes the fighters are peeved at each other than is the case when it is merely a matter of business, with no hard feeling between the combatants.

One of the oldest of the ballyhoo gags is to dress up a strictly business battle as a grudge fight. Sometimes that trick works, but, not often. There is something about a genuine grudge fight that cannot be counterfeited well enough to fool the fans.

Oldtime followers of the Queensbury art will tell you that grudge fights are dying out; that the big money which has

to the side of the forehead. Those two lads had petted a smoldering dislike for each other over a period of years until it grew to the point where it overshadowed even dollars and cents.

*Gene Tunney, listening to Dave Barry tolling off the "long" count*

# and THEIR FASCINATION

## Sharkey-Maloney, Dempsey-Tunney, Mitchell-Corbett, Ryan-McCoy Battles, History Makers

Sharkey seems to have been generously inoculated with the grudge germ. It is a fact that almost every one of the Boston gob's good showings has been made in a grudge fight.

It is no secret that when Sharkey enters the ring with a personal dislike of the fellow in the other corner, he is twice as good a fighter as when he looks upon his opponent as just another fighter.

For that reason the gob's handlers make earnest efforts to arouse in him a strong feeling against his opponent. When Sharkey either develops that feeling of his own accord or has it instilled into his mind, he is certain to put up a great battle.

Sharkey's best battles have been those against Harry Wills, Jimmy Maloney, Jack Dempsey and Tommy Loughran. He looked like a great fighter in all of them, even though he did lose to Dempsey on what is written into the records as a knockout but which many who were in a position to see what happened and were not blinded by prejudice, will insist to their dying days was a foul, or series of fouls, by Dempsey.

SHARKEY came by his hatred for Maloney naturally enough. Jimmy is of the South Boston Irish, their idol. Sharkey came up the fistic ladder contemporaneously with Maloney. To say that it irked the Boston Irish for this "Polock," as they contemptuously referred to Sharkey, an American citizen of Lithuanian descent, to have the crust to dispute with Maloney for heavyweight supremacy, is putting it mildly.

It got under Sharkey's none too thick skin, naturally enough, to be booed by Boston crowds even when he made a good fight. It irked him mightily to find himself unpopular, whereas Maloney, the favorite, winning or losing, remained the idol of Beantown fandom regardless of how he fared.

Sharkey's feeling against Maloney was accentuated by their first meeting in Boston, which Jack won on a foul in the ninth round. He was convinced that Jimmy deliberately hit him below the belt. When they met a second time, Sharkey received the decision, but still he was not satisfied. He wanted a knockout over his Boston rival and in 1927 he got it, before a huge crowd in New York.

"I'm going to beat up that big boy before I knock him out," Sharkey told his friends before they entered the ring. That is just what he did. Jack probably could have flattened Jimmy in two rounds that night, but he held off the finishing punch until he had given the Irishman a humiliating pasting. Sharkey looked like a great fighter that night.

* * *

THOSE who were fortunate enough to wager a few simoleons on Sharkey the night he boxed Loughran, played the hunch that the gob would turn in one of his good fights because he was brimming over with feeling against Tommy. Loughran, ordinarily a sweet-tempered young man, was just as bitter against Sharkey.

But for that mutual dislike, the fight probably would have consisted of fifteen rounds of dully scientific boxing. The grudge consideration made a brief but spectacular combat. Sharkey, as you will admit, if you were there, never looked better.

Grudge fights may be rarer in these days of important money than they were in the earlier times, but it so happens that the most expensive bout of all times, that between Tunney and Dempsey at Soldiers' Field in Chicago, was a super-grudge fight.

It is no secret that Gene and Jack each took into the ring that night a burning dislike for the other, though each had a high regard for the fistic prowess of his opponent.

Tunney made no secret of his feeling against the things that Dempsey represented in the fight game and Dempsey was just as intolerant of Tunney's ideas.

Many of the things that they said about each other in the presence of intimate friends are unprintable. When it came to putting the rap on each other, in private, they finished even up.

Tunney's dislike for Dempsey was intensified by the tremendous popularity which Dempsey acquired after being dethroned by the Marine. When both were introduced from the Madison Square Garden ring some weeks after their first joust, Dempsey was given one of the most tremendous ovations ever accorded a fighter. Tunney, a native New Yorker, introduced as champion of the world for the first time in his own bailiwick, was greeted with jeers and jibes.

*Jack Sharkey taking a count in bout with Jimmy Maloney*

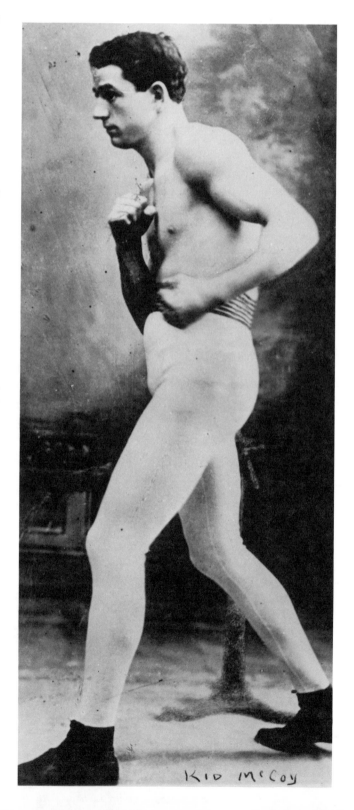

*Tommy Ryan (above) and Kid McCoy (right) are famous for their grudge fights.*

# Grudge Fights and Their Fascination

Added to all that, Tunney secretly envied Dempsey's punch, so lacking in his own pugilistic makeup. The fact that he had been dethroned by the last man in the world he would have cared to have push him off his perch, fanned Dempsey's feelings.

Nor was this feeling confined to the fighters themselves. Fans the country over took sides and many were the fights that resulted between members of the two factions after that never-to-be-forgotten seventh round when the so-called "long count" by Dave Barry enabled Tunney to escape a knockout. The argument still is going on. That one round strained many a friendship.

\* \* \*

*M*ANY things bring about grudge fights. Usually a neighborhood rivalry is the cause. Two lads from the same neighborhood will start in the sock market at about the same time and move up the ladder side by side. Inevitably there are arguments between their friends, with the result that each is steamed up against the other.

Sometimes a casual training bout in a gymnasium is the foundation of a grudge fight. One boxer will get the idea that the other is trying to show him up in the gym.

Other grudge fights arise from the rivalry between managers. And sometimes the grudge has no more reasonable basis than the mere fact that one fighter "doesn't like the other guy's looks."

Jim Corbett, for all that he was known as Gentleman Jim and supposedly was above such things, engaged in grudge fights with Charlie Mitchell and Bob Fitzsimmons.

Corbett's rows with Mitchell outside the ring did much to keep the readers of sports pages interested. The trouble between Mitchell and Corbett centered around the Englishman's belief that Corbett had beaten him out of a deserved fight with Sullivan; had, in fact, stepped in and grabbed the title when Mitchell was all set to take it over.

Sullivan and Mitchell had boxed a 39-round draw in Chantilly, France, in 1888, and thereafter the Englishman was certain that all he had to do to take over the championship was to get the Boston Strong Boy inside the ropes again. But Corbett beat Mitchell to it.

After dethroning Sullivan, Corbett appeared in an act at Miner's Bowery Theater in New York. Egged on by newspaper men who scented a good yarn, Mitchell decided to go to the theater with his protege, Frank P. Slavin of Australia, and publicly challenge Gentleman Jim.

Mitchell and Slavin caught up with Corbett and his manager, Jim Brady, in the bar room at the theater. Corbett was not disposed to have any trouble but Mitchell cussed him out and accused him of stealing the Sullivan match which rightfully should have been his (Mitchell's).

\* \* \*

*W*ORDS followed words, as so often is the case. Finally Mitchell bellowed out that he could whip Corbett and so could his protege, Slavin. The Englishman accompanied this statement with a swing aimed at Corbett's chin.

Then the fun began. In the general melee one of Corbett's sympathizers, Fatty Langtry, just missed Mitchell's head with a wine bottle. While the mixing was going on Slavin laughed but took no part in the fracas. He was in a mellow mood, having imbibed rather freely.

\* \* \*

*S*O Slavin, dressed in a Prince Albert coat, striped trousers, spats and a beaver hat and carrying a gold headed cane, leaned against the wall, viewing the hectic doings with an amused and tolerant eye. In the midst of the row, as Slavin reached over to the lunch counter for another piece of cheese, somebody hit him on the jaw with a blackjack.

Down went the Australian. He got up, dusting off his fancy togs and remarking, still with a benign tolerance: "That was a bloody good shot, old top, but, I say, don't let me get started; there's trouble enough here now."

Somebody had turned in a riot call and while the ruckus was going on at top speed, a squad of cops and detectives dashed in and flattened everyone they could get at.

Mitchell and Slavin escaped by a side door and passersby on the street were treated to the sight of a half dozen cops chasing Mitchell and Slavin up the Bowery for several blocks until the fighters finally hopped into a cab and got away.

Corbett vowed that he never would rest until he had got Mitchell in the ring and given him the beating of his life. They met in Jacksonville, Fla., in January, 1894, with Corbett scoring a knockout in the third round. Those who saw the fight will tell you that Corbett more than paid off the Englishman.

Fitzsimmons chased Corbett for a long time in an effort to land a fight and the sight of the Cornishman became extremely obnoxious to Gentleman Jim. Fitz walked into the dining room of Green's Hotel in Philadelphia one morning, while Corbett was eating breakfast and began to abuse him. In the verbal war which followed Corbett heaved the water bottle at Fitz's head, narrowly missing him, and a general engagement followed.

Later, while they were training for their fight at Carson City, Nev., they met on the road one morning. Fitz, according to the story, offered to shake hands but Corbett refused, saying there would be time for that when they met in the ring. It was in that fight that Fitz knocked out Corbett in the fourteenth round with his famous solar plexus punch.

\* \* \*

*S*PACE is lacking here to list the many bitter grudge fights of the last thirty years. Even the younger generation of ring fans will recall many of them, such as the series between Steve (Kid) Sullivan and Pepper Martin, between Carl Duane and Frankie Jerome. Also, there was the battle between Sid Terris and Ruby Goldstein for East Side lightweight supremacy, with Terris getting up off the floor to knock out his rival in the first round.

A case where rivalry between managers communicated itself to the boxers was the joust at Scranton in which Pete Latzo took the welterweight honors from Mickey Walker.

Paddy Mullins, Latzo's manager, was overjoyed at this victory over one of Jack Kearns' stable, as Kearns and Dempsey for years had ducked a fight with Harry Wills, Mullins' heavyweight entry.

If space permitted much could be written about the grudge fights between Tommy Ryan and Kid McCoy and between other famous Queensberry characters.

The reformers may be able to find some ammunition to use against the sport in grudge fights, but the fact remains that such encounters are the delight of the customers.

# Along the Great Fite Way
## By Ed Sullivan

OUT at Gus Wilson's magnificent training camp at Orangeburg, N. Y., the other day, Tom Kennedy, heavyweight of the Jeffries era, movie star and now manager of Ace Hudkins, the Nebraska Wildcat, was reminiscing about the old days with Gus Wilson and Johnny Dundee while grouped about them sat Hudkins, Pierre Charles, Al Singer and some other youngsters taking it all in with attentive and appreciative ears.

**"You hear a lot about psychology in the ring and how it often wins fights,"** mused Kennedy, shaking off the polo coat which he had brought on from Hollywood to house his huge frame. **"I want to tell you about a bit of psychology that I tried only to have it explode right in my face.**

"I was in France years ago, taking it easy with the wife, when I got a cable from Hull, England, asking me to fight a local heavyweight over there. The dough was good so I cabled right back, packed my bags and with the wife, started for Hull.

"Now Hull, England, is actually an Irish town. It developed that the fellow I was to fight was one Con O'Kelly, yes, the father of the Con O'Kelly who was over here last year fighting the modern heavies.

"I got a good hand as I got into the ring but when Con O'Kelly came down the aisle, the place went crazy.

*"I figured I'd pull some psychology on this local idol. I turned my back to him as he entered, figuring I'd scare him to death by ignoring him. As I stood there with my back to him, I was laughing to myself as I pictured him staring at me and marvelling at my calmness.*

"Finally, having given him enough, I turned around.

"My Lord! I almost collapsed on my chair. Looking at me, glaring at me, was a giant 6 feet 4 inches high and weighing about 230 pounds. If I grinned, it was a sickly grin. I had never seen such a monster and when he stripped, the chills ran up my back. He had arms like steel bands. His chest was the chest of a Jeffries. I thought of my psychology and wished I had seen him coming instead of turning my back, for I might have been able to get out an away.

"My legs were numb but I was thinking fast like a guy does who's scared stiff. As we came to the center of the ring for instructions, I doped it out. I'd have to beat him before the fight if I was to beat him at all. What to do? I had it. Setting myself as the referee talked about rules, I let fly with all my strength and plunked Con right in the stomach. As he sagged to the floor, I asked the referee casually: 'That kind of a blow won't be called foul, will it?' The referee was so dazed he could only nod 'no'. O'Kelly, relaxed when he was struck, hardly was able to get back to his chair. He never recovered from it.

**"I knocked him out in the third. My second piece of psychology was better than the first and thank God for that for O'Kelly was certainly a monster."**

* * *

## A Dead Man Knocked Out Fitzimmons

YOU won't find it in the record books but Bob Fitzsimmons, immortal Ruby Robert, was knocked out in one round at Syracuse, N. Y., in 1893, in the prime of Fitzsimmons'

pugilistic life. A dead man knocked him out and Fitzsimmons was tried for manslaughter and almost convicted.

Pull up your chairs, imagine that you are seated in the Friars' Club, on West 48th Street, New York City, while Fred Block, man-about-town and secretary of the Jewish Actors' Guild tells the strangest story ever told. Seated at the table as Block unfolds the weird yarn are Jimmy Elliott, Jack Pulaski, of Variety and myself.

**Fred Block is the chap who chartered the Friars' special train to the Sharkey-Scott fight. He handled Fitzsimmons on his eastern tour, he took Corbett to England, he handled Terrible Terry McGovern when Terry was uplifting the drama with "The Bowery after Dark." As a kid, he saw Corbett beat mighty John L. Sullivan at New Orleans.**

Block, although he is only 55 years old, is deeply steeped in the lore of the ring and the glamour of some of its great personalities.

"It was at Syracuse, N. Y., Nov. 19, 1893, that it happened," recalled Block. "I was touring the hinterlands with the Bob Fitzsimmons Specialty Company and we were routed into the Salt City.

"Fitzsimmons was featuring his boxing act and he had two spar mates along, a fine big Australian by the name of Con Riordon and an American fighter by name, Joe Dunphy. Fitz had brought Riordon along with him from Australia, was genuinely fond of him and had asked me to room with Riordon to see if I could make him stop drinking.

"That afternoon I had taken Riordon out for a walk before the matinee. A pair of new shoes were hurting him as he walked along and stopping, he cut the toe of one of them open. 'That dam booze is even leaking out of my feet', he kidded. I was to remember those words.

* * *

## Fitz Thought It Was Double-Cross

"RIORDON, that afternoon, was the first to go on with Bob. Halfway through the round, Fitz clipped him in the belly and he sagged to the floor. He seemed to be stupefied from drink so instead of slowing up the act, Fitz called Dunphy into the ring with him and we dragged Riordon to the wings and propped him on a chair.

"Just as Fitz and Dunphy were mixing it, there was a crash from the wings. Involuntarily all of us, including Fitzsimmons, turned to look and we saw Riordon slipping to the floor. His head had struck the chair and that was the noise we heard.

*"Before Fitzsimmons could turn back, Dunphy sneaked in a right-hand punch and Fitz went down as though he had been struck by a pole-axe. He was out cold and in a frenzy, I rang down the curtain.*

"As Bob came to, his only thought was that Riordon and Dunphy had deliberately framed him. His first words, muttered, were: 'Wait until I get that double-crossing b—— in the ring with me tonight.' He meant Riordon.

"But he never got Riordon into the ring with him. Riordon was dead. They had counted the last ten over the poor fellow as he slipped from the chair.

"Syracuse was in an uproar. This was murder, they shouted Fitzsimmons was jailed and brought to trial for manslaughter. The reformers were after him hot and heavy.

"Fred House, later Magistrate House of New York City, saved him. We brought House up from New York to defend Bob and he did a masterful job. Expert testimony proved Riordon died from the blow on his head as it hit the chair.

**"The testimony that freed Fitz, however, came from the dead fighter's lips. 'That dam booze is even leaking out of my feet,' Riordon had said jokingly on the afternoon of the tragedy. That testimony, from the lips of the dead fighter, was strong enough to win the case."**

\* \* \*

## When Jack Johnson Proved His Courage

JUST as Primo Carnera, the "Walloping Wop", was seating himself on his stool at the Garden for his sensational American debut against Big Boy Peterson, of Chicago, a big colored man charged down the aisle to Carnera's corner.

It was Jack Johnson, former heavyweight champion of the world. Johnson, who has been packing them in at the Canton Palace, Broadway and 50th Street restaurant as leader of his own colored jazz band, had taken the night off to see Carnera in his first fight because Li'l' Artha had taken a fancy to the huge fellow from watching him at Stillman's gym.

**"I hope," sneered a ringsider, "that Carnera shows more heart than Johnson showed while he was fighting."**

The dapper fellow sitting next to him turned on him.

"Say listen, Mister," he barked, "don't let anyone tell you Johnson didn't have plenty of heart. He proved it to me one night at Paris, France, and proved it so convincingly I never questioned his courage again.

"Johnson, that night, was fighting Battling Jim Johnson, an American negro, who was all arms like Elbows McFadden. In the second round Johnson let go with a hook. His forearm must have landed right on Battling Jim's elbow for Jack's arm was broken twice, clean.

"When he came back to the corner, he was pale as your shirt-front. 'I'se broke my arm,' he told me. 'Don't touch it, it hurts somethin' awful.'

**"For twenty rounds, with his title at stake, Jack Johnson kept on fighting and earned a draw with one hand. When he got back to the dressing room, he fainted dead away from pain. The doctor who set the arm wouldn't believe Johnson had fought with it. 'It ees not pozzible for a man to stand such pain,' he said.**

"So never think Jack Johnson didn't have heart aplenty."

The dapper man relaxed. He was Dan McKetrick, the American who introduced boxing to France.

\* \* \*

## Carnera Greater Card Than Louis Firpo

THIS Carnera, the "Walloping Wop", took Broadway completely by storm in his American debut at Madison Square Garden, thousands being turned away from his fight with Peterson because fire department officials found the huge arena jammed tight as a drum before 9 o'clock.

Opposed to Peterson, a second-rate heavyweight, and despite the fact that the New York fight writers insinuated that Peterson had been selected to take a 'dive', the fight fans stormed to the Garden and battled to get in to see Carnera in action.

There has never been a gate attraction to equal this huge fellow, who weighs 269 pounds in fighting condition, stands six feet six inches tall and incongruously enough wears baby-pink underwear.

His dressing room, after his spectacular one-round knockout of Peterson, was the tip-off as to his drawing power.

**There you found William Bolitho, the literary gentleman who writes on profound topics for the New York World; Maurice Chevalier, French movie idol; Jack Johnson, Johnny Dundee, Matchmaker Tom McArdle, Assistant**

District Attorney Gene Finnegan and a host of others. It was the kind of dressing room gathering reserved for a Dempsey.

The papers may scorn and scoff at Carnera but the people at large, not so sophisticated, want to see this modern giant. The people are intrigued by his mammoth proportions and they flock to gape at his huge shoulders, his mastodonic feet, his huge hands.

*He is the greatest drawing card in the ring to-day and if the million-dollar gates inaugurated by Dempsey are to return, Carnera is the foundation upon which they will have to be built. He alone has sufficient color to beguile that sort of money.*

## He Is as Fast as a Huge Cat

DESPITE his tremendous bulk and girth, the "Walloping Wop" is as fast in his movements as a huge cat. Those size 16 feet glide in and out with the soft tread of a panther.

Whether or not Peterson had any thought of fight was unimportant. Carnera swept out of his corner and was on top of the Chicagoan before Big Boy knew what had overwhelmed him.

Carnera is a straight puncher, avoiding the round-house swing of the novice for the deadly short, straight blow.

**It is in clinches that his terrific strength is most deadly. Tearing his arms loose by sheer power, he flails that right hand back and forth in a clubbing uppercut that sprawled Peterson on the floor as though he had been ejected from a cannon.**

Leo P. Flynn and Dan Morgan, two canny veterans, watched him and were eloquent. "He's the next world's champion," said Flynn. "He's your next million dollar gate," said the more practical Mister Morgan.

\* \* \*

## That Chicago Black Doesn't Scare Easily

JACK O'KEEFE, manager of Tuffy Griffiths, has another great fighter in Larry Johnson, the colored light-heavyweight whose knockout sock has stirred up the light-heavy division once bossed by Tommy Loughran.

They say negro fighters are not game. Johnson, born, believe it or not, in Ripley, Okla., is as game as a pebble.

Before his fight with the slugging Fred Lenhart, Spokane, Wash., knockerout, I was chatting with Johnson in his dressing room when one of his handlers came up and spoke to him.

**"I was just in Lenhart's dressing room, Larry," said the handler. "He says it will be all over in two rounds and to tell you that." Larry snickered: "That white boy is wrong as hell," he cracked calmly. "Instead of TWO rounds, it will go just one round and he won't be there when it ends."**

Lenhart, as if to fulfill his prediction, had all the better of the early rounds. Johnson, after dropping him five times with right hand shots high on the jaw, finally nailed him right on the button in the seventh and they carried Lenhart out, heels first.

O'Keefe picked up Johnson for $50 in Chicago when the negro paralyzer was looking for coffee and cakes. He'll make a fortune with him.

\* \* \*

## Delaney Has $200,000 to Live On

JACK DELANEY is not as sad as he might be over the news that a shortened right arm will prevent his contemplated come-back to the ring which treated him so handsomely in return for a few good fights and a lot of bad ones.

Delaney has at least $200,000 over and above all taxes on his dough.

*The Rapier of the North can buy plenty of beer, his favorite drink, with that sort of money.*

# When White Hopes

## How Luther McCarty Was Exploited

### By Prof. BILLY McCARNEY

*McCarty, the Cowboy*

*Luther McCarty as he appeared for his bout with Arthur Pelkey*

the two, the German is the outstanding heavyweight and were he not embroiled in the troubles that have beset him, long ago he would have cleaned up every contender. I have been associated with some of the world's greatest fighters, have managed and seconded the leaders in fisticuffs, and feel qualified to say that in Max Schmeling, boxing has the greatest prospect since Jack Dempsey polished off big Jess Willard. In fact, in the German lad, we have a second Dempsey. In his ring actions, his strength, his shiftiness and his punching power, Schmeling is a ringer for the man whose colorfulness and fighting ability made him the greatest of all modern ring attractions.

\* \* \*

*I* WAS one of the originators of the "White Hope" tournaments which flourished after Jim Jeffries was whipped by Jack Johnson and the world was seeking a white man to dethrone the negro. While waiting for the return of Schmeling and his ultimate battle with the winner of the Miami Beach contest to decide the world's heavyweight championship, I cannot help but think of the stirring "White Hope" days which were no different from what is going on at present except for the fact that no negro now holds the helm.

It was back in the period between 1910 and 1915 that every overgrown small town lad who thought he had any ability, was signed by big and small time managers, placed in the hands of trainers, with the dethroning of Jack Johnson as the chief objective. From the most unheard of places there came prospective heavyweight champions. They loomed on the fistic horizon from far off sections which were scarcely visible to the naked eye.

Some came on and begged for a chance because they saw big money ahead. Others were sent along by big moneyed men who thrived on the publicity they were getting. Still others were grabbed up by good judges of fighters from the mines, the lumber camps and the farms. Most of them came quickly and hit the trail back home even quicker.

Through a strange coincidence I managed the first "White Hope," Carl Morris, and I also managed the best of all the big fellows drawn to boxing by a desire of the white race, discovered by me in a period when the air was full of "white hopes," and in my judgment the best heavyweight prospect of all time, was this other fighter, Luther McCarty.

Luther McCarty came along at the right time. He was to develop a man to whip Johnson. The peer of all "white hope" expectations and the country still labored under the impression that any man, strong, brawny, tall, muscular and virile, could make the grade and bring back the heavyweight championship to the white race.

But to bring such a fellow to the front, was not an easy

*T*HE battle for recognition among the white heavyweights is on in full swing. From all parts of the world, England, Belgium, Germany, Italy, Argentina and America, the huskies are striving for the title left vacant by Gene Tunny's retirement. I may have more than an outside interest in the outcome of this battle royal when I say there are only two outstanding figures in the heavyweight ranks to-day, Jack Sharkey of Boston and Max Schmeling of Germany, but even if this were not the case, I still would stand by the above remark.

Furthermore, I will go a step beyond this by declaring that of

# Were The Rage—

task. There were too many false alarms in the field and, with my knowledge of ballyhoo, I decided upon a scheme which I knew would take the attention of the fight public from the rest of the boys and throw it on my hope, Luther McCarty.

I decided to make of Luther a picturesque, colorful character. I prepared a grand stage setting and the newspaper men, novelists and fight promoters throughout the country aided my cause. Having been an advance man on other occasions, I knew the rounds pretty thoroughly, and alive to the occasion, I gripped the public pulse with the story of this Western cowboy giant, the new "White Hope" who would whip any man in the universe.

\* \* \*

*L*UTHER had one thing, size. He had another, strength. He possessed a third great fighting asset—a fighting heart and last but not least, he was clever and a terrific hitter. What more did I want? There was all the material any press agent would deem sufficient to put his man over, but I wanted still more. His physical

Luther McCarty knocking out Al Kaufman

appearance was not sufficient, thought I, to keep him above all others in the public limelight. He must have added color—something about which the scribes could get special stories.

That was my aim and I soon hit upon an idea. The press agent—the ballyhoo man, got busy. I got Luther to dress in a cowboy makeup. I had photos taken of him swinging a lariat, riding a broncho, wearing buckskin, a red handkerchief and a sombrero.

Here now was a picturesque character, the kind around which the boys could write a colorful yarn. Press agenting was still in its infancy at the time, but our ballyhoo tactics were far more impressive than the cut and dried stuff of to-day. My plan worked. Reams and reams of publicity were obtained and almost overnight, Luther McCarty became the most talked of "White Hope" in America.

Of Luther's rise to fame and his untimely death, much has already been written, but of his family, little has been said. He came from American-Scotch parents. I took McCarty from his home, Driftwood Creek, Wild Horse Canon, Hitchcock County, Nebraska, in 1910, and worked secretly with him for almost a year before I started him on his career. While the East, particularly New York, was singing the praises of Al Palzer, Tom O'Rourke's fine heavyweight, and the Pacific Coast was shouting the praises of Charley Miller, the Fighting Motorman, a tremendously big and powerful fellow, Jim Flynn of Pueblo, the Fighting Fireman, suddenly ended the hopes of Miller with a knockout. Likewise he had checked the career of Carl Morris, leaving Al Palzer the leading, outstanding young white heavyweight at the time that I decided to launch the drive for Luther McCarty.

With Luther's name never before having graced the prints of any big town newspaper, I suddenly shot him into the front ranks by having him knock out Morris in the little town of Springfield, Mo. Soon after that, while we were passing through Ohio, where I was exploiting him, Luther read of the appearance in the villages of a street fakir of the old school, who looked and dressed like an Indian. He became eager

and noticing that he seemed worried, I asked him the cause. He told me he knew this fakir and asked if I would try to find him and report on his general appearance.

To ease his mind, I took a carriage and went to the nearby village. There, standing on the curb near a grocery store, was an Indian, tall and massive, and grouped about him was a troupe of performers.

There was a woman who did some acrobatic stunts; a man who bent heavy iron bars over his knee and broke heavy chains; a girl who permitted herself to be chained and then got out of the entanglement without outside help; a snake charmer; two ponies drawing an elaborately decorated wagon, a greyhound and several dogs of apparently mixed breed. The fakir also had a tent spread out and on this tent was printed:
"White Eagle, The Medicine Man"

\* \* \*

*T*HE Indian sold a concoction which he labelled "snake oil". When the performance was over, he stood before the entrance of the tent, and holding a bottle in his hands, he elucidated on the value of this medicine as a cure for toothache, rheumatism, gout, headache, aching muscles, and almost anything in the way of ills, and the crowd he drew and the sales he made, were convincing proof that those who gathered believed in its remedies.

I went back to the hotel and told Luther what I had seen. When I described the Indian, and told what he sold and of the circus performance, Luther fairly leaped off his chair. He made a dive for the door. I halted him and asked him what was wrong.

"Nothing," he replied. "Let me alone. I'll be back soon," and with those words, he threw open the door, rushed down the street, leaped on his horse and flew away in the direction I had given him.

He missed the road, however, and returned without having seen the Indian.

Some months later, we came

*Luther McCarty (right) squares off against Arthur Pelky.*

# When White Hopes Were the Rage—

into southern Ohio and there the country paper again had a story of the travelling circus and the Indian Medicine Man. Luther didn't wait to have me find out where they were, but this time he went down to Police Headquarters where he met the chief and asked whether he could be directed to the street fakir who was touring Ohio with his circus.

"I would like to know where I can find the Indian Medicine Man, White Eagle, he calls himself, and he sells 'rattlesnake oil,'" said Luther.

"I'm sorry," replied the chief. "He was here four days ago, but has left us. I don't know where he is, but if you seek his arrest for any crime he's committed, we'll get him for you."

"No," answered Luther, "don't go after him. He hasn't committed any crime. White Eagle is my father. He dresses like an Indian to help his sales

of rattlesnake oil. I haven't seen him for a long time. I've made some money since becoming a fighter and I would like to help him. If I can find him, I'll have him quit the rough circus road. I can take care of him now and that's why I'm anxious to find my dad."

That was the first I had heard of Luther's father and his make-up and the incident proved to me that Luther's heart was in the right spot. He showed me then that he took his fighting seriously and that he appreciated what the game was doing for him.

If Luther had not met his untimely death at the hands of Arthur Pelky, in my opinion he would have beaten Jack Johnson and brought back the heavyweight crown to the white race. He was a great fighter—a wonderful prospect, and the greatest white hope of all time.

*Take away McCarty's cowboy outfit and you still had a man with tremendous size.*

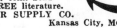

# On the Verge

## Dr. W. A. Walker Analyzes the Fighters' Temperament at Weighing-in Time

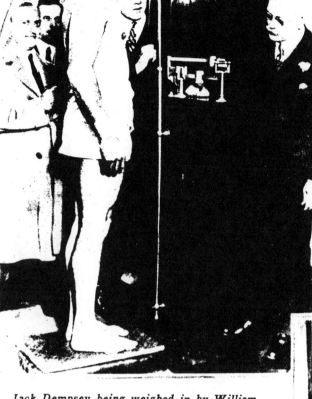

*Jack Dempsey being weighed in by William Muldoon for fight with Luis Firpo. Here he is in prime condition, ready to be unleashed for action*

*I*T was at the Yankee Stadium. Dr. William Walker, chief of the New York medical advisors of the State boxing commission was sitting in a little dressing room waiting for Tommy Loughran and Jack Sharkey to arrive. They were to be weighed in that afternoon for their heavyweight elimination bout.

Dr. Walker, with William Muldoon, the Grand Old Man of Boxing, looking on, was preparing his papers for the physical examination required of all boxers in the Empire State, when in walked genial Bert Stand, secretary to the commission, with the announcement that Sharkey was ready and at the call of the doctor.

Sharkey was ushered into a large room where the official scales were placed and around which a flock of newspaper photographers, motion picture cameramen and newsreel picture artists were in waiting to snap the proceedings. Jack got on the scales and Muldoon set the bar. The photographs taken, Sharkey was then asked to enter the little room where Dr. Walker had previously been, there to be examined.

I had noticed that although Sharkey outwardly attempted to be in a jovial mood, his muscles were tense, his eyes were fixed, he seemed to be extremely nervous and was eager to have it all over with. I asked Dr. Walker if that did not indicate perfect condition for the Bostonian, and he remarked:

"Come into that room after I'm through with the examination. I'll then explain fully just what each reaction indicates in the condition of the man."

\* \* \*

I was present at the weighing-in of Gene Tunney for his fight with Jack Dempsey in Philadelphia, for the Dempsey examination at Chicago and the Dempsey and Firpo tests and numerous other examinations of famous boxers for world-famous battles, hence was eager to study from close range the man who may shortly wear the crown which Gene Tunney abdicated.

I accepted Dr. Walker's offer and if ever there was any doubt in my mind of the accuracy of such a minute physical examination in gauging the condition of the men who are to engage in an important bout, I can safely say that such doubt quickly passed away.

Dr. Walker, who during his eight years with the New York State Boxing Board has examined more famous gladiators than any other physician, turned to me when both Sharkey and Loughran had left the room, and said:

"Sharkey will win the fight and possibly by a knockout. He is in perfect condition. Never saw him better. His whole body vibrates with energy. His eyes are sparkling.

*Luis Firpo receives blood pressure test for bout with Dempsey*

His pupil reflexes indicate a high-strung condition, which in Sharkey's case, is a sign of physical perfection. He is irritable—a sure sign of trouble ahead for Loughran. He is highly nervous, eager to be unleashed—a sign that he'll tear into Loughran and fight as he did against Jack Dempsey.

"In the words of the layman, he is primed for quick action and a sure killing. His pupils dilated and contracted very quickly—a sign of keenness of eye, fine vision, sure measurement of his man. He is 100 per cent perfect and no matter how good Loughran is, Jack will go him one better."

\* \* \*

*T*HOSE were Dr. Walker's words to me, taken in my interview in an effort to test the true meaning of those required physical examinations of a boxer on the eve of his battle.

Were they convincing? I should say one hundred per cent.

I asked Dr. Walker for his opinion on Loughran and he informed me that Tommy was rather sluggish compared to his rival, carried excess baggage around the back and that the

# of Battle

### By NAT FLEISCHER

energy which Tommy always had shown in the past, especially for his battles with Braddock and Lomski was missing.

There was an expert opinion worth a thousand times that of the average newspaper boxing expert. What, thought I, would the gamblers give to be in a position to obtain Dr. Walker's figures and his full report in bouts where considerable sums were being wagered? I approached Dr. Walker and queried him on this point and he smilingly replied:

"They've beaten you to it. Jim Farley and Bill Muldoon are never caught asleep. At the time of the Firpo-Dempsey battle, the commission asked me to release my complete chart to you boys for publication and I obeyed. What was the result? The gamblers got busy and used my report as they would a race chart and when the commission was apprised of the situation, they decided never again to make the examination figures public. All I am permitted to do now is to tell the newspaper boys in what condition I found the fighters, but I don't discuss the technical examination."

\* \* \*

*A*ND with that, Dr. Walker delved into the conditions of various types of fighters during the weighing-in procedure and from him, I learned the following interesting facts:

The smaller the fry and the less the ring experience, the less nervous the boys are and the less energy is expended.

A fighter of exceptional ability, the fellow who ranks among the leaders in his profession, no matter what his class, the more high strung he will appear on the eve of a fight. Such a chap shows considerable pent-up energy, is very irritable and is eager to get over with the proceedings. He shows every evidence of fine training. In other words, he is primed for battle and like a thoroughbred horse, is tearing at the reins to get into action.

The finer the condition of the fighter, the keener his eyes. He will show quick pupilary reflexes—they will dilate and contract without a single sign of sluggishness.

Jack Dempsey of the modern boys, exemplified more than any other fighter, the high-strung type. He was extremely fidgety and otherwise displayed the

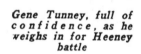

*Gene Tunney, full of confidence, as he weighs in for Heeney battle*

*Jack Sharkey on afternoon of contest with Dempsey*

\* \* \*

symptoms of a highly nervous person.

Benny Leonard ran him a close second. When Benny Leonard was well trained, he was the most irritable fellow that ever entered a ring.

Jack Dempsey and Gene Tunney were directly opposite. Both were equally irritable. Both were highstrung. Tunney, however, had marvelous control over his nervous system. He was able to hide what the other fellow showed openly. In Gene's case, only the medical man could see through his sham. Dr. Walker was able to detect all these symptoms yet the scribes all wrote about Gene's extreme calmness.

\* \* \*

Luis Firpo was exactly the other extreme. He showed absolutely no nervous energy signs. He was calm to the extreme. He was almost unaware that an examination was taking

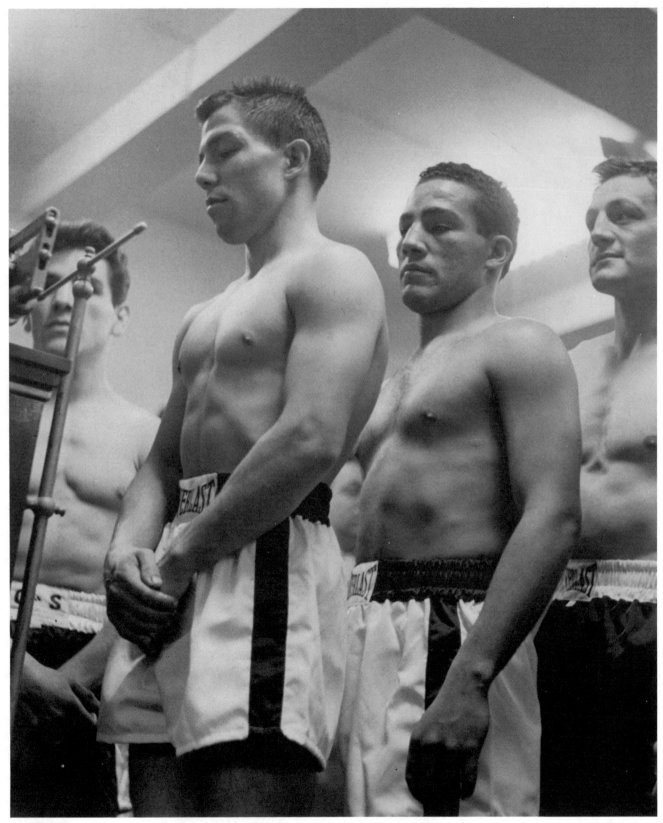

*Club fighters tend to be calmer than top flight fighters during weighing-in time. (Photo not from original article.)*

place to determine how fit he was to pit his strength against the world champion. He showed a lack of sensitiveness and, with it, the sluggishness that would indicate an inability to detect openings and take proper advantage of the opportunities that might present themselves to him.

Everything that happened in that fight with Dempsey was indicated in the physical examination. His reaction to the various tests showed him to be a man of gigantic strength, tremendous lung power, and heaps of vitality, but with a lack of brain power, slow thinking and lacking initiative. This I noted through the sluggishness of all his reflexes. They didn't react to any kind of impulse. His was a slow motion action toward the stimulus, but he had the brute strength and that figured to make up for some of his other defects.

The preliminary boy shows the same excitement or nervousness that the well trained athlete displays, but in the case of the latter, it is there because of his fine training while with the raw novice, it is displayed because of his fear and is not a reaction due to his training.

The mental condition also plays an important part. It has

*Dempsey, worried from constant dodging of process servers, looks anything but the Manassa Mauler when weighing in for his first fight with Tunney*

a marked effect on a high-strung fighter. The more high-strung, the greater the strain and the greater the physical defect. That is why a highly nervous fighter will invariably take a two-hour rest before his fight. He will sleep off some of this strain in order to be able to effect a complete coordination of mind and muscle when he enters the ring.

A striking example of nerves was recently displayed in the Jack Berg and Tony Canzoneri scrap at the Garden. Berg, in the dressing room several moments before entering the ring, was a source of deep aggravation to his handlers. He was unable to stand still for a minute, fidgeting around restlessly, moving around, shadow boxing and altogether presenting a nervous spectacle. He is all nerves just before entering the ring but once he steps inside the ropes, his position becomes relaxed. The amount of energy he expends while in action is responsible for this vibration.

He is merely a bundle of nerves tensed for action and waiting for the spark to release the fire. Once the fighting gets under way he is attuned to his task and the rapidity of his delivery of punches can be laid to relaxation while punching with both hands.

# Dempsey Monthly Contributor to The Ring

WITH the annual ranking of the fighters of the world in the February issue, Jack Dempsey, former world's heavyweight champion, started a series of articles for THE RING which the publisher hopes will continue for many years.

In this issue you will find an interesting and informative article by Dempsey in which he discussed the aftermath of the Miami fight and says some straight from the shoulder things about Schmeling.

In the next issue Dempsey will talk about the winner of the fight at Miami, and will have something to tell you about Primo Carnera, the mastodon of the maulers.

Is Carnera just another Dunkhorst, or is he to be reckoned with in the heavyweight situation?

Is Carnera a contender, or must we get ready to consign him to the fistic junk pile along with so many other battlers of exceeding bulk?

Do not fail to get THE RING for April—and for all the months thereafter, for Jack Dempsey promises some unusual articles for this magazine.

# RICKARD

*Tex Rickard when he promoted his first fight*

*I* WAS sitting comfortably in the observation car of the special train that took a gang of seventy-eight newspapermen from Miami to New York after the Sharkey-Scott fizzle. There were many veteran scribes and quite a number of newcomers in the group. Some of the boys just knew the late Tex Rickard by name and fame; others had little more than a mere interviewing acquaintance with the world's greatest sports promoter, and still others had been quite intimate with him.

As is usual in trips of this sort, especially a trip that was bringing the boys back from a battle that cost the Madison Square Garden Corporation a loss of between $30,000 and $35,000, the discussion drifted into the promotion field.

"What could you expect with a ham like Scott as one of the headliners?" was the remark of a well-known scribe who was trying to prove his point that nobody could do any better with a man like Scott as one of the selling points.

"I don't care how poor a drawing card Scott is, and I admit that the public has no use for him as a fighter," replied another of the audience, "but I'd wager my last dollar that if Tex Rickard were the promoter of this fight, he would have put it over with a bang regardless of Scott."

* * *

"*Y*OU'RE entitled to your opinion," shot back the first party, "but let me tell you that I've reported fights for more than fifteen years and I've never come across a so-called headliner who commanded less respect among the public for his fighting ability than did Scott. That Miami fight, in drawing $190,000, drew just about $50,000 more than anyone ever expected it would gross, Tex or no Tex."

And with that the reminiscences started. The air was full of comparisons. The promotion field was scanned and when all was over, the one point that was settled was the fact that there isn't a man in the boxing game today who compares with Tex Rickard. We'll go still further and say that it will take many years, years after I'm gone and those who were arguing in that train have passed into the Great Beyond before another Tex Rickard will be seen in action.

He was the last of the quaint picturesque Westerners—cowboy, gold hunter, gambler, promoter—a man with so great a personality that he attracted attention wherever he went. The greatest showman on earth—a fellow who could sell anything.

He was a cowboy, and a mighty good one, because he lived in a cowboy country where men are fearless dare-devils who would take a chance at anything just for the fun of doing it.

Gold hunter, because he lived among a rough and ready, daring crowd whose every move was one of prospecting along one line or another.

Gambler, because he lived among the men whose day and night dream was the hope that they could run one of their shoestrings into a million dollars.

Promoter, well, because that might have been an accident of chance, or possibly an opportunity

* * *

*A*CTUALLY, the business of promoting was wished on Tex because his partners in a Goldfield gambling house, "were too busy to handle a boxing bout." As Rickard was the front man, whose business was to mix and mingle with the crowd to get the customers for the roulette wheels, he was the man who looked best for a promotion job.

Goldfield asked Tex's partner, Kid

*Rickard as he looked when he signed Jeffries and Johnson*

*Below—The big time promoter at the time he left New York to negotiate for winter boxing in Miami just two weeks before his death*

# in Retrospect

An Appreciation of the
Great Promotor's Skill,
Two Years After His
Death

By
HYPE IGOE

*Jack Kearns, Dempsey and Rickard, the trio that made fistic history in a long association which had a vital bearing on boxing not only in America but the world over*

*The Dempsey-Carpentier fight at Boyle's Thirty Acres, Jersey City, on July 2, 1921, marked the true crest of Rickard's uncanny ability as a promoter*

posed bout than Tex Rickard. In that, he has no master now that he is gone, and no equal is in sight.

I happened to be in Tex's office the day that Luis Firpo entered and Tex first laid eyes on the Argentine. Luis had just collected $125 for a fight in Jersey City with Sailor Maxsted. He had knocked Maxsted

Kieley, to assume command, but the Kid wanted Tex to sub for him and so it went. He told the mob to nominate Tex and Tex it was to whom the task of putting Goldfield on the map was delegated. That's the story of how Tex Rickard entered the field of fight promotion in which he gained fame and fortune and became an international figure, the greatest sports promoter the world has ever known.

* * *

*I*F Tex were alive today, he would never have lost money on the Sharkey-Scott affair, because he would never have staged it. But, if he had arranged that card, he could have done nothing more than did Frank Bruen to put it over, and he would have taken his loss with the same smile that Bruen did for, to the Garden, it was worth a loss to get Scott out of the way and pave the path for the Sharkey-Schmeling affair, a sure $1,000,000 house.

They said of Rickard when he entered the promotion field that he knew nothing about boxing, just as they say about Frank Bruen. Nothing is farther from the truth in both cases. When Tex was elected to handle the Nelson-Gans affair at Goldfield, he sent his name roaring to undying fame like some strange comet. Even when he was green and just starting his career in the ring racket, Tex was a great judge of boxing. I never knew a man who was quicker to sense a great match, to foresee the dramatic possibilities of a pro-

kicking like a sea-crab and Tex had sent for Luis. It was that sense of the dramatic that had appealed to Tex—the big fellow possessing a wallop. Luis arrived and Tex spoke to him through an interpreter. Firpo had sold himself as soon as Tex laid his peepers on him. Tex's cold discerning eyes were drinking in Firpo's shaggy frame like rare wine.

Firpo arose to depart. Tex halted him at the door, swung him around so that he could look at his back. There was Tex with a beaming countenance. I saw Tex mentally whip a tape measure all over Firpo. He was making comparisons and felt satisfied he had found what he was looking for. When Luis left, up spoke Tex:

"God, what a man! Hype, he and Dempsey will make the greatest fight you ever seed. He's the nearest thing to Jeffries I ever looked at. I never seed such a neck. It will be the greatest fight in the world. Hype, that's the boy for me," and with that he slapped me on the back and laughed. I never saw Tex so happy as then.

* * *

*T*HAT was picking them. That was *knowing* fighters and fights. Subsequent events proved Rickard's value as a promoter and judge. If Tex were alive today, he would do with Primo Carnera what he did with Firpo. He never would permit Primo to get away from him. He never would permit the giant Italian showman to

*Dempsey (hat in hand) promised Rickard (with cane) that he would carry Carpentier a few rounds so that fans would get their money's worth.*

# Rickard in Retrospect

travel through the sticks. He'd have him right here in the Metropolitan district where by this time he would have primed Carnera for a gigantic outdoor bout. A showman—that was Tex Rickard.

A fascinating devil, too. One simply couldn't help but like poor 'ole Tedge. Enemy or friend, if Tex wanted you to like him, he had a way all his own to win his point and once you got through with him, you were one of his admirers.

For a strangely successful man, Tex Rickard was the least boastful of any fellow I've ever met.

An interview with him seldom got you anywhere. He would talk about anything and everything but himself. But when you least expected it, when you caught him in the proper mood, there was no better story-teller than Tex Rickard.

His tales were most delightful. They were tales of the Wild West, of the Yukon gold rush, of the frontier fights. and so on—the kind that caused that red corpuscle to reach the red-hot point. He never gave himself any the better of it. Always his friends—his associates in those hectic gold rush days—they were the fellows who came in for the greater portion of the yarns.

\* \* \*

*I* KNEW Tex as probably few others did and to me, he was the fairest man that ever lived. In the twenty years I knew him, I don't know of one lie that he told me. When he tried to hide a story to prevent a coup and I questioned him about it, he would sometimes say:

"Hype, between you and me, but not for publication, the story is true. But publicity now will hurt me and the Garden, Hype."

And that is why I always respected him. He had confidence in his friends and his friends shared such confidence with him.

I was often told many of his big promotion secrets beforehand but, true to my trust, I never betrayed Tex. When he said: "Now, Hype, don't go putting nothing of that in the papers," it remained a secret with me.

Rickard was always "good copy" for any newspaperman. The kind of "copy" which he furnished is no longer available for there is none in the field who compares with him and that is why good fight stories are so scarce nowadays.

Jim Jeffries was Rickard's idol. He loved Jack Dempsey, but he thought more of Jeffries as a fighter than any battler that ever graced the roped arena. We argued the point one day, and Tex most emphatically informed me that it was his opinion that Jeffries would have knocked out Dempsey.

It was a never-ending argument with us. I always insisted that Jack Dempsey, with his two great, punishing hands, could have whipped Jeff at his best, but you couldn't convince Tex of that. When I challenged Tex with the remark that no one-handed heavyweight ever lived who could whip the Manassa Mauler, Tex would shoot back:

"Hype, you're crazy. You didn't know the Jeffries I knew. You only think you did. Say, that feller was the man-killer of the modern heavyweights. The strongest, greatest puncher in the game. You never seed an athlete in all the world like Jeffries. Boy, what I would have given to see the real Jeffries tackle Jack Johnson!"

Yet they say that Tex Rickard was not sentimental. Can you beat it?

Here we have Jack Dempsey, the man who made Tex Rickard rich, the man who enabled Tex to reap international fame and fortune, the idol of the fight world. playing second fiddle to the fellow Rickard promoted years ago.

Dempsey was the cornerstone of Tex Rickard's monument, Madison Square Garden, yet Tex wouldn't change his mind about the prowess of Jack and Jim.

\* \* \*

*D*EMPSEY made $10,000,000 for Tex and his organization, and Tex would admit that there never was a more colorful fighter in the game than Dempsey, but when it came to fighting, that was a horse of another color with Tex. To him, the greatest of all heavyweights was his friend, Jim Jeffries, and no amount of argument could alter that opinion.

It makes no difference whether Dempsey makes a come-back. He may draw another million-dollar gate, but one thing you and I never again will see, will be a pair like Tex and Jack. Thanks to Rickard and Dempsey, we've "seed everything" in the promoting line. There's nothing new left.

# IT'S A LONG ROAD

## Overenthusiasm and Greed— Chief Obstacles to Success in Ring

*Eddie Hanlon of California, a bulldog scrapper whose strength was sapped at an early age.*

JAMES J. JEFFRIES won the heavyweight championship of the world after having engaged in about a dozen fights. But James J. Jeffries, whether he believed it or not, was something of a prize ring prodigy.

Champions are not made over night.

This is an axiom of the ring, but one that many managers fail to heed. Just recently Jeffries brought out a young heavyweight named Al Morro, a burly chap in whom Jeff saw himself recreated.

"If I could win a heavyweight championship, without any great experience, this fellow ought to be able to do it too," Jeff reasoned. So he sent the youngster along at too fast a pace and in consequence, young Mr. Morro ran into several thumpings.

Unfortunately, the over-confidence of managers in the ability of their proteges, or a desire to make money too quickly, has ruined many promising fighters.

I remember a fine-looking young sailor named Andy Schmader who boxed at the old National Athletic Club in Philadelphia ten years or more ago. Schmader was a finely put up boy, with a natural instinct for the game and a good right hand. He knocked out a number of second-raters around the Quaker City and seemed to be pointed for bigger things.

Over night he became a drawing card. He was offered a reasonably large sum to fight Bill Brennan, then one of the best heavyweights of his time. Naturally, there could be but one ending to such a battle. Andy

was beaten into a bloody pulp before being knocked out and that finished him.

Something happens to the soul stuff of youngsters who are overmatched, and they seldom overcome the effects of the beating they get. Schmader did not. He went down hill rapidly and never appeared in big-time competition any more.

Take Bulldog Eddie Hanlon as a prime example of what rushing can do to a youngster. Hanlon started to fight when he was sixteen. He was pitted against the greatest lightweight to be found. Because he was brave and never knew when to quit, he was often the recipient of severe beatings and was worn out before he was twenty-one. His sturdy body should have been able to stand up under the rigors of the ring for many years, but because he tried to weather them before he had matured, his career was cut in half.

* * *

*Max Baer of California, a fine prospect who will make good if handled properly.*

IT seems to me that this also applies to Kid Chocolate who was such a sensation in New York rings some eighteen months ago. The Cuban Negro started boxing when he was hardly more than a child. He engaged in one hundred and seventy bouts without a single defeat, and then was outslugged by Jack Kid Berg in a furious battle last Summer.

They say the body beating that Berg gave Chocolate started the latter on the downward grade. His subsequent defeat at the hands of Fidel La Barba and Bat Battalino have been laid to the door of the beating that he got at the hands of the Whitechapel Cockney.

It seems to me that the cause goes deeper than this. Chocolate didn't take half the thumping against Berg that Eddie Hanlon did in any one of his fights. Certainly his youth should be able to assimilate that. His sudden slipping from form was due to the fact that he fought too often before he had gained his full strength. Normally, you wouldn't think that a chap was being rushed when he didn't get his first chance at

# TO BOXING *PEAKS*

## By JACK KOFOED

a championship until he had engaged in one hundred and seventy battles. Would you?

But those one hundred and seventy matches were crowded into a few years. Chocolate fought almost continuously, once and sometimes twice a week. That took something from him that probably never will return. They said he was another Dixon but, when his big chances came, he failed to grasp them.

\* \* \*

*T*HE fact that a boy seems naturally fitted for a career in the prize ring is no excuse for pushing him too fast. Nothing takes the place of experience, and experience cannot be gained too quickly without paying an exorbitant price. Jeffries is always cited as an example of how far a man can go in a few fights, but Jeffries is one of the rare exceptions to an almost unalterable rule. To balance his success, a thousand failures, with every one laid at the door of too much haste, can be cited.

Now Bombardier Billy Wells may be something of a laughing stock when great fighters are mentioned. He had an unfortunate weakness in that he was unable to stand up under a stomach bombardment. But Wells, who was as fine a physical specimen as the ring ever saw, was also one of those fellows who was brought along too quickly. Perhaps this had something to do with his failure.

His experience was limited to Army boxing and a few professional bouts when he was tossed into a match with an English champion, Gunner Moir. The Gunner knocked him out in three rounds with a left hook to the body, and it may be that a sense of inferiority was planted in Wells' heart then and there. Perhaps that sense of inferiority was as great a handicap as any physical weakness.

And don't forget Joe Rivers, the Mexican lightweight, who might have become one of the immortals had he been brought along at a slower pace. Joe was only nineteen when he engaged in twenty-round battles with Johnny Kilbane, Joe Coster, Ad

*Kid Chocolate, a great feather-weight prospect who seems to have shot his bolt.*

Wolgast, Joe Mandot and others just as good.

By the time he was twenty-one Rivers had passed the peak of his ability. He was just a burnt-out youngster.

\* \* \*

*I* LOOK with doubt upon the methods used in ballyhooing Max Baer. This young California heavyweight is as superb a physical specimen as I have ever seen. He looks better than Jack Dempsey did at a similar stage in his career. Baer is handled by Frankie Burns, who used to be a great lightweight himself back on the Coast. But Burns' idea is very similar to that of Jeffries.

*Jim Jeffries (left), and his pupil, Al Morro. Morro was pitted against too good talent from the start with the result that he has failed to make good.*

*Joe Rivers, the Mexican lightweight, had the makings of a great one. By age twenty-one Rivers was burnt out.*

# It's a Long Road to Boxing Peaks

He apparently sees no need of spending much time building Max up. He seems to feel that if the California Catamount is going somewhere, he can just as easily beat the good ones as the tank artists.

Burns would have been willing to put Max into the ring with Jack Sharkey in the New York *American's* Christmas Fund Show, but the Commission would not stand for it. The Commission was absolutely right, too. Then Max was pitted against Ernie Schaaf for his Metropolitan debut.

Frankie Burns has Baer's best interest at heart but Dempsey had a long period of apprenticeship, and so did Fitzsimmons and all the other great fighters with the exception of Jeffries, and that apprenticeship is exactly what Max needs. Natural speed and punch and an instinct for the game is not enough.

Those assets must be sharpened in the fire of combat, and the fire must not be so hot as to shrivel the youngster in its blasting heat. It is undoubtedly true that a boy can be given too long a diet of set-up. He gets so used to them that when stiff opposition is offered he doesn't know what to do. His fibre is softened.

Ruby Goldstein is an excellent example. Against the tank artist and third-raters, Goldstein looked like another Benny Leonard. He had everything. But tough fellows like Ace Hudkins and Jimmy McLarnin just hung him over the ropes.

* * *

*E*XACTLY that sort of training harmed Young Stribling. Had his schedule been progressively better; that is to say, had he worked up from the stumble-bums of his earlier days, he might have been a champion long ago. But even when he was occasionally filling in with first line fighters, Billy's main diet consisted of those self-same pushovers. It did Stribling no good at all.

It is obvious then that there is a middle path between rushing a young fighter and carrying him too long on easy opposition. The former is ruinous not only to his morale but to his body and mind as well. The latter never gives him a chance to improve.

Bobby Jones, the greatest of all golfers, says that all he learned about the competitive game was due to matches he lost. In a lesser degree this is true of the youthful fighter. He learns best in bouts in which he is extended. Knocking a rival out with a punch teaches him nothing. Nor does a bout in which he is outclassed.

English managers have killed off many prospective stars by permitting half grown boys to engage in fifteen and twenty round fights. The New York Commission sought to curb a similar practice here by forbidding any boxer who has not attained his majority from going more than six rounds. This is a sound rule, but is partly nullified by managers declaring their proteges are two or three years older than they really are when applying for licenses.

So, I suppose promising kids will be ruined just so long as the men who direct their affairs are greedy or over enthusiastic. There isn't anything to do about it, but it is a shame that the Hanlons and the Schmaders and others like them should fall short of success through no real fault of their own, but because of the zealousness or greed of those guiding their careers.

*Eddie Hanlon as he looked when he was the 112-pound champion of the Pacific Coast.*

# Corbett
# Sharkey as

*Carnera Bout with Maloney*
*Added to Difficulties*
*of Situation*

*A scene in the recent Maloney-Carnera battle at Miami Beach.*

IT seems to me that the difficulties of boxing keep multiplying themselves. Of course, when everything is ironed out we will have our old prosperity and our old interest, and perhaps a great champion whose abilities will fit right into the traditions of the heavyweight title. But right now we are making progress rather slowly, and treading uncertain paths.

You know, I figured the Carnera-Maloney engagement in Miami to clarify things a little. But with the big Italian getting a hair-line decision, and many experts figuring the Bostonian the winner, it looks as if we slid backward in that fight.

Maloney cannot be counted a contender. He had his chance, and he blew it. But there may be possibilities in Carnera, after all. You must admit that he is comparatively inexperienced, and that considering his background, he has done pretty well. It seems impossible to hurt the giant, and a man of that type may be the answer to the 1931 prayer among the heavyweights.

Naturally, I am not overjoyed at the development of conditions which made it possible for a Schmeling to become champion, and for a Carnera to be spoken of seriously. I come of a school that demanded high skill in its title holders. They had to fight their way through a tough campaign, and accidental champions were almost unheard of. We had upsets. But not freaks.

However, I am not living in the past and I am not blind to the fact that times have changed, and with them the public taste has changed.

\* \* \*

NO one sport moves along its own peculiar lines. We travel in cycles, in trends. Years back we were strong for science. The sporting writers stressed that point. We had scientific fighters, scientific ball players, scientific jockeys. In every sport skill was the chief asset.

But man does not live and thrive by skill alone. Thousands of years ago—say in the Stone Age—we had no skill. It was all brute strength. A man lived by strength. He got his meat by strength. He got his wife that way.

As the ages proceeded we became more refined. But every now and then the race goes back for a while to the era of power. I like to think that this is the chief trouble with boxing right now, and that we will return to the age of skill within the next few years.

I see evidences of a revulsion of feeling in baseball, which I always have followed very closely. I was a pretty good player, and could have gone into the National League, in which my brother Joe was a famous pitcher for the great Baltimore Orioles. During the Summer, when I am in New York, I attend the games of the Giants religiously, as in addition to my intense interest in baseball, I am a John J. McGraw fan.

With the development of Babe Ruth in 1920 we went from the finer points of baseball into slugging. Science was dropped, the ball was changed to cater to the new trend.

Now the ball is being experimented with to cut down the hitting, and managers are turning to the more subtle specialties of baseball.

That's the way it is going to be in boxing. You tire of a steady steak diet, just as you tire of cream puffs. We must strike the happy medium.

\* \* \*

THAT medium, it seems to me, ought to be arrived at through Jack Sharkey. Now, there's a heavyweight who should be champion. He has skill, he can hit, he has ambition, he lives cleanly, he stresses his position as a citizen and his debt to his family. He embodies, to me, all the points that go to make the real title holder, and yet he isn't the champion.

If I were younger, and I were welcome in that camp, I would take hold of Sharkey and make a champion out of him.

Jack is of the emotional type. That has produced many great fighters, but they must be kept within emotional bounds. They must be guided every minute, in and out of the ring.

Sharkey is the one boxer now before the public eye who comes within the old-fashioned requirements. He is shifty and he boxes with some of that craftiness and style that marked out the school that was pushed into the background by the rise of the White Hopes.

I think the White Hopes hurt boxing more than any other class of any other period. Incidentally, I managed one of those White Hopes myself, Tom Cowler, the Australian. Now, there was a boxer. But the rising tide of power engulfed him and his style.

Sharkey marks a return of old precepts in the ring, and it would do the game a lot of good if a man of that type came back among the champions.

# Still Visions Champion

## As told by
### JAMES J. CORBETT
*(former heavyweight champion)*
### *to* DANIEL M. DANIEL

Sharkey should have beaten Schmeling. But the Bostonian let his emotion run riot. I think that experience will eradicate that fault. In fact, I am inclined to believe, and predict, that it has done this already, and that another Sharkey fight will show us a new fighter.

*Jack Sharkey, wno, according to Corbett, is the one boxer who comes within the old-fashioned requirements of heavyweight fighters.*

\* \* \*

THE contest with Maloney in Miami left Carnera's true abilities and position very much up in the air. Some experts tell me that the Venetian has tremendous possibilities. Others say he is a pusher and is so muscled that he never will be anything but that.

Some say he is fast, others decry his ungainliness. I don't remember when there was so much conflicting opinion on an outstanding heavyweight, that is, outstanding in so far as public attention is concerned.

Back in the old days we never took those big boys too seriously. The clever, skillful fighter never had to fear the big, lumbering man, who most often lacked experience, and was eliminated from public interest before he could develop know-how.

Take Ed Dunkhorst, for example. He was something of a Carnera about a generation ago. The Syracuse Freight Car, I think they called him. Well, Fitzsimmons mingled with this giant and what Bob did to him was a caution. Dunkhorst almost was killed by the wily Fitz.

Then there was Plaacke, the Dutch giant. Another Carnera type. It was Kid McCoy who finished this foreign "threat" in Philadelphia. Plaacke was a joke. McCoy was up to all the tricks in the game and he pointed to Plaacke's shoe string, indicating that it was untied. Plaacke stopped to see what was the trouble, and then they carried him out.

I fancy that men of the Fitzsimmons and McCoy type, if around now, would have no trouble at all in punching the Carneras and the Schmelings right out of the ring.

However, do not get the impression that this is the wail of the old timer, crying for the "good old days."

The situation surely is muddled to-day. But, as we know, it's always darkest before the dawn.

*When Sharkey lost his big chance—the fight with Max Schmeling for the world's crown.*

# Unusual

Jack Madden Turned a Cartwheel,
Loughran Walked Dazed Across
the Ring; O'Brien's Head Rested in
a Pail of Saw Dust; Jim Stewart
was Balanced Across the Top Rope

BOXERS who have received knockout blows have performed queer acrobatic feats. When Jess Willard hit Soldier Kearns a right uppercut on the chin in the eighth round of a bout in New York City, December 27, 1912, the Soldier fell on the ropes and hung there like a wet dish-rag.

Kid McCoy hit Peter Maher on the jaw in the fifth round of a bout at Coney Island, January 1, 1900. The Irish champion fell on his side and with one hand under his chin, lay there gazing like a cherub while the referee counted ten over him. Maher was so comfortable that he did not wish to be disturbed and he complained loudly when his seconds shook him and helped him to his corner.

Other boxers have executed remarkable feats after the receipt of the punch soporific, but it remained for Jack Madden, a New York bantam, to turn a cart-wheel after receiving a thump on the head that brought to an abrupt close a bout with Jimmy Barry.

The contest was staged at the Empire A. C., Maspeth, October 21, 1895, and was the outgrowth of much vociferous argumentation on the part of the two bantams.

Barry had laid claim to the bantam title by reason of numerous victories over his rivals in the West, and when Casper Leon questioned the validity of the Chicagoan's claim a match was made which was fought at Lamont, Ill., September 15, 1894. The battle was contested with skin gloves, the terms calling for a finish fight and the weight was 112 pounds.

Barry stopped Leon in the twenty-eighth round and rightly regarded this victory as clinching his title of bantam champion of America.

* * *

BUT about this time there arose an argument over the question of weight, Madden and his friends insisting that the limit of the class was, through usage, 105 pounds. Therefore, Madden claimed to be the 105 pound champion of America, and said he was content to permit Barry to hold the 112 pound honors.

However, Madden intimated that if Barry was able to make 105 pounds he could have a battle for the crown at those figures. Madden stood 4 feet 11 inches tall and could make 100 pounds and retain his strength. He was a clever boxer and a good ring general, but not a destructive hitter.

Barry stood 5 feet 2 inches tall, his legs being very short and slender, but the upper part of his body was like a middleweight's. He was a miniature Fitzsimmons. His arms were long and muscular and his chest measurement remarkable for a boy of his size. Barry was not a clever boxer, but he was a cool, heady fighter and his punches had triphammer force.

Barry accepted Madden's challenge with celerity and came East at once to train. On the night set for the contest Barry scaled a trifle below 105 pounds, much to the chagrin of the Maddenites, who were confident the Chicagoan would have difficulty in making the weight. Furthermore, Barry seemed vigorous and active and in condition to do his best.

The bout drew a large crowd to the Maspeth arena and there was considerable betting, with Barry a 9 to 10 favorite.

There was plenty of Madden money in sight, as it was predicted Madden would win by his cleverness, despite the fact that Casper Leon's science had availed nothing against the combativeness and hitting power of the red-headed chap from the Windy City.

* * *

WHEN the men entered the ring and squared off for the first round Madden, using all his speed and skill, danced about, tapping Barry with light lefts to the face and keeping out of hitting distance.

Barry studied his man for the first round and then in the second session he began to hook wicked lefts and savage right swings at his opponent.

At the close of the third round Barry had not landed a blow of any consequence and Madden had scored all the points. His supporters were jubilant and offered even money on their man. When Barry came out for the fourth round there was a dangerous glitter in his blue eyes and he prepared to cut loose with his heavy armament.

Madden, who owing to his success in the preceding rounds had become over-confident, danced in and out, jabbing and hooking with great success. The New Yorker then decided to do still greater execution, and, stepping in, let fly a left for the face and unhooked a right for the body. The left reached Barry's face, but the right never got as far as the mark, for Barry unloosed a right smash that crossed Madden's left and landed on the left side of Madden's head above the ear.

The effect on the New Yorker was spectacular. The force of the blow sent him over on his right shoulder, his feet performing a complete circle, so that when he finally landed he lay on his right side, where he was counted out. Madden was completely stunned by the blow on the head and required considerable attention before he recovered.

Barry ventured the suggestion that he could claim the 105 and 112 pound championships, but just to show that he was not fussy about a few pounds Barry met Sammy Kelly in a twenty round bout at the Broadway A. C. on January 30, 1897, at 116 pounds. The bout resulted in a draw, but had Kelly received the decision he would have won the bantam title.

* * *

THERE are many cases of peculiar knockouts. About three years ago Jose Lombardo, Panamaian featherweight, assumed a most unconventional pose when he was knocked

# Knockouts

By CHARLEY HARVEY

out by Louis Kid Kaplan in the Garden of New York. The Panama fighter was knocked through the ropes between the strands with the bottom rope locked under his knees, that alone preventing him from going out on the concrete. In that position he remained while he was counted out.

Another remarkable position taken by a fighter who was knocked out, was that in which Jim Stewart, a giant heavyweight of two decades ago, found himself when he fought Jim Barry at the old Palace A. C. in 1908. In the fourth round Barry connected with a stinging right to the chin and put Stewart to sleep. It did even more than that—it landed Jim on the top rope like a sack of flour and there he lay, perfectly balanced, while the referee counted over him.

So delicately was he balanced, that even the referee, Jim Bagley, was amazed and would have helped Jim, had not the rules prevented him from doing so. The crowd expected that Jim would tumble from his lofty position at any moment and all hands were considerably relieved when the count was completed and Stewart was carried to his corner. He remained unconscious for almost half an hour.

Soldier Kearns figured in a second peculiar knockout the night that he fought One Round Davis, a 210 pounder at the Fairmount A. C. of New York. The Soldier, who could hit with the force of the kick of a mule, crashed two beautiful right hand wallops to Davis' chin. Davis went over backward so hard that his feet flew up to where his head had been a moment before and had not the ropes protected him, he would probably have suffered a broken neck. But his knees rested against the top rope, and there he remained, unconscious, while being counted out. Billy Joh was the referee in that contest.

* * *

DAN MORGAN, who handled the affairs of Knockout Brown, tells a story about Brown's fight with Kid Goodman back in 1910, in which Brown clouted the Kid so hard that he dropped his hands at his side and through some peculiar movement, he became so entangled in the ropes that he stood helpless while Brown landed the deciding punch to the chin. That punch put Goodman into dreamland, yet he was on his feet while the fatal ten was tolled off. He could not fall because of his position against the ropes.

Those who saw the fight between Philadelphia Jack O'Brien and Stanley Ketchel at the old Pioneer Club well remember the peculiar position of O'Brien in the final seconds of that fight. Ketchel hit Jack so hard that he fell backward, his head landing in a pail of saw dust. Were it not for the fact that the bell sounded at the count of eight, Jack would have been counted out, for he couldn't budge, so helpless was he.

And still another strange knockout was that in which both Willie Lewis, now a referee, and Sailor Burke, now the owner of a taxi stand in Brooklyn, were the principals. Each connected with a telling punch at the same time, and both went down. Referee Joh started to count over Lewis with one hand and Burke with the other. At seven, Lewis staggered to his feet while Burke remained down and Willie won the fight by a knockout, although immediately after gaining the verdict, he fell again to the canvas.

Then there was the knockout of Tommy Loughran by Jack Sharkey in which Tommy, after being hit on the temple, was unconscious to his surroundings and walked along the side of the ropes asking for a place to sit down. He was escorted to his corner and the fight was awarded to Sharkey on a knockout.

Also the fight between Al Singer and Jimmy McLarnin, in which Singer, knocked to the canvas, tried repeatedly to raise himself while rubbing his neck but couldn't get his muscles to coordinate and was counted out. Another in which Singer figured was the bout with Battalino in which Al tried to run out of the ring after being knocked down.

* * *

MANY famous knockouts have been recorded in recent years and to tell of each peculiar one, would take more pages than are printed in this magazine.

A number of years ago two fights took place that have seldom been equalled for short finishes. One was fought at Carson City, Nev., March 17, 1897, as a preliminary to the historic Corbett-Fitzsimmons fight. The contestants were Dal Hawkins and Martin Flaherty of Lowell. They were in the pink of condition, and the spectators looked forward to a great battle, as both men were among the leading lightweights in the country at that time.

When the gong rang they rushed at each other. Hawkins crossed a right the first crack out of the box and copped Flaherty on the point of the jaw. He went to the floor with a thud and the referee began counting. The count was finished before Flaherty came to. The knockout punch was delivered in less than four seconds after the first bell rang. That battle goes on record as one of the shortest in the history of the prize ring.

Another fight that is still often spoken of as the shortest on record was fought at Buffalo, N. Y., between Maxey Haugh and Tommy Kelly, the "Harlem Spider." Haugh was neither clever nor a good ring general, nor anything else, but he had a wallop like the kick of a government mule.

The men ran at each other and Haugh uppercut the Spider on the jaw. He went down and was counted out. The timekeeper's stop watch showed that the finishing punch was delivered in a fraction less than six seconds after the fight began.

Another was back in 1907, up at Port Jervis, New York, where a fight was staged at a place called Hickory Grove between a Negro, George Nevins and a white boy, Billy O'Brien, tutored by Tom Sharkey. With the clang of the gong, the Negro leaped from his corner, swung his right and raised O'Brien off the floor. Billy fel backwards and landed with his head out of the ring. While in this position, and one leg caught in the ropes, he was counted out.

# How They Got

### By CLARENCE GILLESPIE

THERE are many fighters who owe their fistic experience to mere accident, and naturally the source of their start is a matter of no little interest to the large army of fight followers all over the world. Jim Jeffries might have been an obscure boilermaker but for the fact that he was twitted into taking up the profession because a Negro once reflected on his pugilistic prowess. Jeffries was a mere lad in his teens at the time, with no other thought than being a mechanic, or possibly owner of a boiler factory some day.

Jeffries always was a husky fellow, strong, vigorous and possessed of muscle. He recently told the story of how he became a fighter with considerable pride.

"I liked to box as long as I can remember," he said recently. "The sport used to have a great fascination for me. Many a time I used to sneak off in some quiet spot and have a tilt with the gloves with my brother Jack. Dad, who was always of a Puritanical turn of mind, was naturally opposed to me doing any boxing.

"He thought it was vulgar, and whenever he caught Jack and myself with the gloves enjoying a friendly bout he used to take me to task and chide me. Now I have a great respect for my father, but I could not see any harm in the exercise. But he pleaded so long that I finally made up my mind that I would obey his wishes and quit. And I did.

"But before long a fellow by the name of Hank Griffin came to town. Griffin, as you are aware, is a Negro, and he had the reputation of being strong and clever. Some folks looked upon him as a bully. They said that he was anxious to pick a quarrel. At any rate it was not very long before I came across Griffin, and we had it out.

"I can recall, as if it were but yesterday, how I left the factory with the best intentions in the world. Griffin thought that he was invincible and I said to myself that if he was he had to show me. So a match between us was arranged. There was nothing on the side. It was simply to show this fellow up that I consented to meet him.

"We fought with small gloves and I won in less than fifteen rounds. Whew! It was certainly a slashing bout, and I made a hit with my chums by bringing the Negro to his level. I guess you know the rest after that. I got tired of working in the factory and went to San Francisco.

"There I made the acquaintance of Billy Delaney. Delaney was handling Jim Corbett then and was looking for some good man to assist Corbett in training for his fight with Bob Fitzsimmons. Delaney thought that I would make a good workout partner for Corbett and I took the job. I got a lot of experience at the training camp, the kind one cannot obtain in the gymnasium."

* * *

PETER JACKSON became a fighter after he had learned, through a battle with the chief mate of a ship on which Peter was employed, that he possessed a great left hand and that he could hold his own against any man. The officer, a German, was a cruel man who flogged the deck hands at the least provocation and took great delight in inflicting severe punishment on the Negroes of his crew.

One day the German battered a young boy into insensibility. When Jackson came on the scene and saw that the German had used an iron bar on the lad's legs, he decided to risk imprisonment on a charge of mutiny, by offering to whip the officer if he would agree to fight like a man; without other than the use of nature's weapons, the bare fists.

Peter was well liked by the captain who disregarded the officer's charge against Peter and consented to referee the mill.

Jackson not only avenged himself for the many insults he had suffered at the hands of the German, but avenged the beatings his mates had received. He beat the German so badly that the officer quit the ship during their stay at Sydney.

A report of Peter's prowess was brought to Larry Foley, owner of a saloon and boxing club, and Larry sent for Peter and offered to give him some assignments. Jackson accepted, and so well did he perform, that he gained the respect of his great teacher who launched Peter on a professional fighting career. One night Foley pitted Peter against a bully and Peter won in such quick order that Foley was amazed and delighted.

"You'll do, Peter," he remarked. Thereafter he was tutored for a time by Foley and in a few years, Peter became one of the world's most renowned heavyweights. Peter lived up to his Australian reputation when he fought in this country and in Europe.

* * *

TERRY McGOVERN credited Billy Newman with giving him his first start. Newman, as ring devotees will recall, ran the old Polo A. C., at 155th street and Eighth avenue, and was the first promoter to realize the possibilities of cheap boxing in New York. Newman used to give weekly shows, the affairs being held on Saturday nights.

Newman was always on the watch for new talent and one day received a visit from McGovern. Terry was a mite of a lad, undeveloped and green. He went on with a novice and did so well that Newman gave him a couple of more chances. Soon McGovern made a local reputation.

When Newman ran shows in Yonkers, McGovern figured in many bouts and when the boxing scene shifted to Brooklyn, McGovern was in evidence at most of the shows. Terry's first real opportunity came when he fought George Monroe at Coney Island. He knocked Monroe out and then became a protégé of Sam Harris, who was managing Monroe at the time. The combination was a great success and before long McGovern became a champion and the most noted boxer of his day.

Joe Gans was a clerk in a fish market in Baltimore when he became imbued with a desire to seek fame in the ring. Gans did not have the least knowledge of fisticuffs when he entered the ring for the first time. In those days battles royal between four Negroes were popular. Little "boogies" or colored lads just itched for the chance of going on in the preliminary bouts.

Some of them rarely got any pay for their efforts. But it was different with Gans. He had a following and the management decided to compensate him to the extent of $5 for his services.

The lightweight champion earned every cent he made in his first fight. He waded in, swinging his arms in any old way. One after another of his opponents flopped, knocked dead to the world and in a few weeks Gans had established himself as one of the best battle royal exponents in the South. Gans picked up a lot of points about boxing and very soon was proficient. Success came, and in two years he was close to the top.

* * *

TOM SHARKEY learned his boxing when he was a sailor aboard a man-o'-war.

Jack Sharkey entered the field of pugilism after taking the measure of a sailor who had attacked him over an argument involving ice cream.

Gene Tunney was lured into the ring through his need for money. He was financially embarrassed and having gained a knowledge of fighting as an amateur, he went into the professional field when he found that he could gain a livelihood more readily in that profession than by returning to the work of a clerk which

# Their Start

*Many Champions of the Roped Square Found Their Way into Pugilism Through an Accident—Defeat of a Town Bully Was the Beginning of Jeffries' Career*

he had held prior to his enlistment in the Marines during the World War.

Jack Dempsey's start was made in the mines of Colorado. After the leader of a gang of bullies had repeatedly dropped chunks of dirt on Jack's head, Jack decided that he would have it out with him and beat him so severely with a few punches, that he never thereafter was molested. That victory gave him confidence and when he found himself stranded, he decided to make boxing pay his way.

\* \* \*

THE parents of John L. Sullivan had designed him for the priesthood. But the Boston strong boy had other intentions. He went to work in a tinsmith's shop in Roxbury. Sullivan was an athlete and fond of baseball. Sullivan's love of baseball was so great that he often played hookey instead of going to work. For this he was repeatedly reproached by the foreman.

One day Sullivan got in a row with the foreman and wound up by knocking him through the window. Mike Donovan, who is now boxing instructor at the New York A. C., was the manager of a club in Boston. Sullivan drifted to that city and spent many nights in the club watching ambitious fighters try their skill. Eventually Sullivan thought that he could do well with the gloves and put them on just for the fun of the thing.

Sullivan, with his strength and natural ruggedness, had no trouble in beating his men. He liked the sport so well that he concluded that it was more profitable and congenial than being housed in a shop all day, and became a pugilist.

Nonpariel Jack Dempsey, Jack McAuliffe and Jack Skelly used to work side by side in the same boiler factory in Brooklyn. They were all fond of boxing, and Dempsey and McAuliffe used to perform in the open lots.

Dempsey seemed to care more for wrestling and was found more on the mat than he was in the ring. McAuliffe got his chance when Billy Madden gave an amateur boxing tournament in New York. He was so successful that he became a professional. He has since boasted that he never trained in the real sense of the word after he left the amateur field.

Dempsey did so well at grappling that one day John Shanley, now dead, wanted to know why Dempsey did not become a boxer. Dempsey declared that he never had the chance, but the opportunity came when Shanley matched him for $200 a side against an "unknown." Dempsey knocked his rival out in jig time, and his career as a full-fledged pugilist began from that hour.

Gus Ruhlin worked in a printing shop before he became a pugilist. He began by whipping town bullies and wound up by becoming an enthusiastic football player. Ruhlin's first test was when he fought Steve O'Donnell, who was traveling around the country meeting all comers.

\* \* \*

JIM CORBETT entered the boxing profession through an accident. He became a member of the Olympic A. C. of San Francisco because of his fine achievements on the baseball field. One day he entered the gymnasium of the club and watched Prof. Walter Watson, the club's instructor, teach several members the mysteries of the art of self defense.

Corbett, after a while, thought that he could do as well if not better than the members and asked for a chance to put the gloves on with Watson. Corbett, although he acknowledged

that he did not know the first rudiments of boxing, made such a surprisingly fine showing that Watson became enthusiastic and volunteered to take Corbett under his wing then and there.

In just three months, Watson had coached his pupil so well that he won the amateur heavyweight and middleweight championships of California. After this Corbett's progress in the ring was comparatively easy.

A fragment from a piece of iron which lodged in his head gave Battling Nelson his first inspiration to become a pugilist. The Dane was employed in a machine shop in a suburb of Chicago, with fighting far from his thoughts. He was always a tough youngster and had a lot of narrow escapes from death.

After an accident had sent Nelson to the hospital he was lying on his cot reflecting on what he would do when he became well. Nelson concluded that returning to the shop would be distasteful to him. He wanted something more ambitious, and then and there hit upon the idea of becoming a pugilist.

"I don't know just how the thought seized me," explained Nelson afterward. "It just came over me. I told myself that if I ever recovered I would go into the ring. I said that being hit on the head with a piece of iron was worse than being struck with a glove and that if I could stand the iron I certainly could stand the punch. So I took the sport up."

\* \* \*

ABE ATTELL says that a cartoon of a fighting exhibition in San Francisco gave him his first idea of taking up the profession. Attell thought that it would be a fine thing to have his own picture in the paper some day and butted into one of the preliminary bouts in San Francisco.

Jack O'Brien of Philadelphia was a natural born fighter. His father's hayloft was his favorite stamping ground and all the boys in the neighborhood felt the sting of Jack's knockout blows.

George Dixon began life in a photograph gallery. Dixon made the acquaintance of a modern Job Trotter while delivering orders. He met another Negro from whom he tried to glean some important information. The Negro deceived him and Dixon made up his mind that if he ever met the fellow again he would give his a thrashing.

Fate brought the pair together again, and the featherweight kept his word with such dispatch that the Negro never deceived anyone else afterward. Dixon's success prompted him to take up boxing, and before long the colored boy startled the sporting world with his wonderful ring achievements.

Jem Mace helped Bob Fitzsimmons to become a fighter. The Cornishman worked as a blacksmith and when the retired English heavyweight champion appeared in Australia and held an amateur boxing tournament Fitzsimmons was one of the first to volunteer.

Fitz, with his long, lanky frame, had no trouble in making the required weights in two classes, and the manner in which he won convinced both Mace and himself that fighting and not blacksmithing was his forte. So Fitz deserted the bellows and the anvil for the glamour of the ring.

\* \* \*

BENNY LEONARD attributes his start in boxing to the success of Leach Cross. Here is what Benny says:
"In the yard back of a little pool

# How They Got Their Start

parlor at No. 131 Avenue C, New York City, the youth of our neighborhood gathered daily and there they often discussed the greatness of Leach Cross, our idol. I got so het up over his ability, that I began to practice sparring in an effort to imitate Leach. After a month's practice, Buck Areton, who fought under the name of Willie Grant, took me in hand and got me my first fight with a lad named Mickey Finnegan which I won in three rounds. That was the beginning of a most successful career."

Tony Canzoneri came up from the amateurs as did Frankie Genaro and Jackie Fields, other world champions.

Tommy Loughran was a newsboy before he took up fighting. Joe Dundee was a banana vendor and Johnny Dundee says that it was James J. Corbett who gave him his start in fisticuffs. And this is the way

that Johnny explains it to us:

"I was working in my father's fish market in West 42nd Street when Jim Corbett stopped in an automobile in front of the stage entrance of the American Theatre where he was playing in 'The Burglar and the Lady.' That was back in 1910. When Corbett came out of the car, I was standing near the curb, with mouth wide open, my eyes popping out of my head, so eager was I to see the former champion. He got out of the car, looked at me, and asked me to stand guard over his car until he returned.

"What a thrill I got! I got into the car, sat in the front seat while waiting for the show to end, and I had only one thought in mind—how I would like to be a champion like Corbett. That started me on my desire to become a boxer and shortly after, I became a full-fledged fighter!"

Ernie Schaaf received his start in the Navy; Jackie Berg, after he had won a street fight in the Whitechapel district of London; and Jess Willard, after he went gunning for a swindler who had relieved him of a considerable sum of money. Jimmy McLarnin came up from the amateurs and Maxie Rosenbloom made his way from a farm in Connecticut through the amateurs.

Stanley Ketchel was a tray juggler in a western restaurant when he got into a scrap with one of the help and handed him such a terrific lacing that Maurice Thompson, who saw him, took him in tow and made a fighter out of him. Leach Cross learned how to fight by running the gauntlet of sticks and stones every time he went from his home to school through an Irish district.

# A Corner in the Fistic Market

## By EDDIE BORDEN

SURPRISES and new faces were thrust upon the public last month, some with unexpected suddenness and as a result, interest in boxing increased. Ernie Schaaf and Tommy Loughran came through with two remarkable comeback attempts. Ernie proved his recovery from a slump by putting Stanley Poreda away in the sixth round in the Garden and showing the form that stamped him as a serious heavyweight contender last season. Loughran turned the tables on King Levinsky by giving him a boxing lesson in Philadelphia. Another big upset was furnished when Kid Tunero, coming Cuban middleweight, whipped Marcel Thil in an overweight match in Paris and although the title was not affected in any way, it placed Tunero among the middleweight aspirants.

Ben Jeby, New York middleweight, claimed the American title through his twelve-round knockout over Frank Battaglia. This was an important middleweight contest and the winner of a Jeby-Thil match, if such is arranged, will be the undisputed champion of the entire world. Eddie Murdock, veteran middleweight, scored a surprise victory over Jackie Fields and is entitled to some consideration for his showing. Young Peter Jackson gained the lightweight championship of the Pacific Coast through his ten-round kayo over Bobby Pacho. Tommy Paul occasioned a surprise when he defeated Fidel La Barba and Freddy Miller in turn upset the dope when he banged out a win over Paul.

In the heavyweight class Primo Carnera turned in a win over Jack League and kayoed Jack Spence in one round. Walter Neusel stopped Reggie Meen in six rounds. Larry Gains disposed of Paul Hoffman in six rounds. Unknown Winston disposed of Ted Sandwina in two rounds and Jim Darcy in one. Hans Birkie drew with Walter Cobb and defeated Jim Braddock. Cobb whipped George Godfrey. Braddock triumphed over Martin Levandowski and Martin kayoed Bob Olin in five rounds. Tony Shucco whipped Sam Ward.

Red Barry stepped into the limelight with a victory over Isadoro Gastanaga. Lee Ramage whipped Tuffy Griffiths. Jose Santa stopped Jim Maloney in the fourth round and Maloney finished Leo Mitchell in seven heats. Tiger Jack Fox whipped Frankie Simms and Larry Johnson. Al Ettore disposed of George Panka in three rounds. Frank Cawley finished Bill Higgins in two rounds. Les Kennedy drew with Dewey Kimrey and

whipped Bob Godwin. Charley Massare kayoed Henry Gerken in two rounds, Arthur Huttick in three and defeated Joe Barlow. Abie Feldman finished Red Boyette and Mike Balaban in one round each and whipped Johnny Rousseau. Tony Cancela scored over Leonard Dixon. Dick Daniels won over Tommy Pruett. Yustin Sirutis finished Chris Karchi in four rounds. Fred Lenhart whipped Tom Patrick. Tony Poloni won over Jack Silva. Jack Roper disposed of Wally Hunt in one round. Vincent Parrile kayoed Casimir in four rounds and Maxie Pink disposed of Mickey Taylor in six.

In the light-heavyweight division, Maxey Rosenbloom continued to elude all opposition. During the month he defeated Billy Jones and Chuck Burns. Bob Godwin won from Eric Lawson. George Manley scored over Pat Hayward. Owen Phelps won over Roscoe Manning. Young Firpo scored over Leo Lomski. Bob Olin whipped Paul Marque. Al White kayoed Dan Ladner in four rounds. Trader Horn finished Joe Petronis in two sessions.

Kid Tunero gets credit for middleweight honors in scoring over Marcel Thil. Ben Jeby clinched the American rights to the middleweight title by stopping Frank Battaglia in twelve rounds. Sammy Slaughter kayoed Henry Firpo in one round and Norman Conrad in ten. Vince Dundee defeated Franta Nekolny. Gorilla Jones kayoed Young Stuhley in four rounds and drew with Tommy Freeman. Jack Rosenberg drew with Paulie Walker and lost to Young Terry. Lou Brouillard has outgrown the welterweight ranks and in the future will combat the 160-pounders. He scored over Horatio Velha.

Paul Pirrone defeated Rosy Kid Baker. Rudy Marshall won over Leo Larrivee. Paul Delaney whipped Mickey Bishop. Billy Ketchell scored over Billy Angelo and kayoed Johnny O'Keefe in four rounds. Frank Goosby scored Johnny Roberts in the second round. Frankie O'Brien disposed of Tait Littman in two sessions. Solly Krieger whipped Jimmy Evans. Joe La Grey beat Freddy Fiducia. Millio Millitti kayoed Joe Robinson in two rounds and Freddy Polo finished Joe Grady at the same distance. Eddie Flynn finished Tommy Jones in four heats.

Jackie Fields lost a bout to Eddie Murdock over the welterweight limit. Billy Petrolle has been restored to the welterweight because of his announced intention to continue fighting. Numerous complaints were received because Billy was omitted from the ratings but it was not through any oversight. It was our opinion that Petrolle would retire after the Canzoneri bout but we were wrong. Baby Joe Gans won over Harry Devine. Eddie Kid Wolfe whipped Jose Estrada. Bep Van Klaveren defeated Phil Rafferty. Eddie Ran scored over Jay Macedon. Joey Goodman whipped Tony Stetz. Billy Holt won from Manuel Quintero.

Freddy Steele outpointed Leonard Bennett. Jimmy Phillips won over Tony Rock. Murray Brandt drew with Prince Saunders. Tommy King won from Cerefino Garcia. Eddie Holmes defeated Gordon Donahue and Charley Hudson.

Heading the lightweight class is Wesley Ramey with his victory over Tony Herrera. Eddie Cool won over Lew Massey. Tracey Cox whipped Jack Purvis. Young Peter Jackson stepped into the elite class with his ten-round kayo over Bobby Pacho. Harry Dublinsky defeated Prince Saunders and kayoed Frank Bojorski in eight rounds. Jack Portney drew with Wildcat O'Connor and whipped Frankie Hayes. Santiago Zorilla was beaten by Willard Brown and kayoed by Steve Haliako in three rounds. Steve also finished Joe Hall in five rounds.

Battling Gizzy stopped Louis Di Santis in four rounds. Joe Ghnouly kayoed Benny Garcia in five rounds and whipped Cecil Payne. Payne was also beaten by Abie Miller. Ray Miller won from Johnny Datto. Frankie Klick scored over Paola Villa and Louis Jallos. Roger Bernard defeated Young Geno. Johnny Lucas whipped Pat Igo. Patsy Pasculli kayoed Al Ridgway in three rounds. Johnny Bonito whipped Paris Apice and Jack Rose disposed of Al Casimini in four sessions.

In the featherweight division, Tommy Paul, after whipping Fidel La Barba, ran second to Freddy Miller in a later bout. Baby Arizmendi scored over Archie Bell. Johnny Pena drew with Varias Milling. Paul Dazzo whipped Johnny Mitchell. Abie Miller stopped General Padilla in six rounds. Nel Tarleton kayoed Leon Mestre in six rounds.

Among the bantams, Pete Sanstol scored over Benny Schwartz and Jimmy Mack. Mack defeated Matty White and stopped Billy Landers in six rounds. Joe Tieken whipped Eugene Huat. Jimmy Thomas won from Frankie Jarr. Ross Fields whipped Mose Butch. Dick Welsh defeated Johnny Edwards. Ernie Maurer disposed of Tuffy Tarzan in four rounds and Nick Scalba whipped Johnny Mauro.

Ginger Foran, of England, defeated Proxille Gyde, European champion, in the only important flyweight bout of the month.

The eight leading prospects of the month are:
Flyweight—Rafael Valdes, Cuba.
Bantamweight—Ernie Galiano, Elizabeth, N. J.
Featherweight—Mike Belloise, New York City.
Lightweight—Al Le Pore, Caldwell, N. J.
Welterweight—Joe Lyons, Buffalo, N. Y.
Middleweight—Jimmy Beeson, New Orleans, La.
Light-Heavyweight — Joe Jordan, Memphis, Tenn.
Heavyweight—Carl Camp, Portland, Ore.

# GIANTS NOT SO HOT!

## Ring Records Prove Size and Heft Do Not Indicate Ability

### By JACK KOFOED

JACK SHARKEY backed against the ropes. He unleashed a smashing right that landed flush on Primo Carnera's jaw. The Gargantuan Italian smiled his snaggle-toothed smile . . . . came close . . . . whipped in a right uppercut. His flying fist plu-unked against Sharkey's chin. The champion fell on his face. His big, smoothly muscled body hardly stirred while the referee counted him out. He had been beaten in the first defense of his title that he had attempted.

There was an immediate blah-blah from observers about the difference in the size of the men. People who had called Carnera a circus freak prophesied there would be no one to beat him in years. They harped on his 265 pounds. They forgot that two years before Sharkey beat him handily. They did not remember that inept Jim Maloney had suffered no damage at Primo's hands in two ten-round bouts.

The Italian's rise to the heavyweight championship of the world was due not to size alone . . . . but to his vast improvement in boxing and hitting.

In most cases tremendous bulk has been a handicap rather than an asset in the prize ring. Go back a few years . . . . and take a look-see at Herr Jan Plaacke, the Dutch blubber man, and Ed Dunkhorst, who was called "The Human Freight Car."

These fellows scaled close to three hundred pounds in weight. Kid McCoy, who was hardly more than a middle-weight, took on Plaacke in the Hollander's American début. I don't believe there ever was a fight in which there was such a disparity in weight.

McCoy, pale,

**THE COLOSSUS OF THE RING**

*Charles Freeman, the giant of giants, who was 6 feet 10 inches tall and scaled 323 pounds. Freeman fought only twice and then called it "quits." On both occasions he tackled William Perry, the "Tipton Slasher." In the first bout they fought 70 rounds to a draw and in the return engagement the American proved his superiority. Shortly after, Freeman died from dissipation.*

cold, sneering, came from his corner at the sound of the bell to meet Jan's lumbering attack.

He stopped for a moment, glanced to the floor. Then he pointed, and said: "Your shoe lace is untied."

Plaacke looked down, and the tricky McCoy buzzed a terrific corkscrew punch to the Dutchman's chin. It dazed Jan so badly that he never recovered . . . . and the Kid cut him into ribbons with laughing ease.

Dunkhorst was a better fighter than Plaacke, but Bob Fitzsimmons, a light-heavyweight, finished Ed's career with a whirl of hard, accurate blows. The three hundred pounds each of the big men carried meant nothing against the speed and accuracy of the smaller fellows.

I am not convinced that Primo Carnera deserves to rate with the really great heavyweight champions of the past. He has yet to prove how good he is. Neither am I sure that the mammoths are so dangerous that they deserve a special "Dreadnaught" class and should not be allowed to fight average heavyweights.

Here are the records of twenty of the biggest men who have seen action in the modern ring:

Size, of course, is an index neither of stamina nor resistance to punishment. Not long ago little Joe Walcott, who was called "The Giant Killer" expressed the wish that he was in his prime and could meet Primo Carnera.

"That big fellow's got a lantun jaw," said Walcott, "an' how I loved to crack them lantun jaws. They always fold up."

So far, of course, no one has hit Carnera on the chin hard enough to lay him among the sweet peas, though Sharkey did drop

## The Case Against the Big 'Uns

| | Weight | Fights | K.O. | Won | W-F | Draw | N. Dec. | L-F | L | K. by | Losing Ave. |
|---|---|---|---|---|---|---|---|---|---|---|---|
| Jan Plaacke ....... | 300 | 24 | 14 | 6 | 0 | 1 | 0 | 0 | 1 | 2 | .125 |
| Ed. Dunkhorst ..... | 285 | 32 | 16 | 7 | 0 | 2 | 0 | 1 | 2 | 4 | .219 |
| Ray Impelletiere ... | 270 | 11 | 11 | 0 | 0 | 0 | 0 | 0 | 0 | 0 | .000 |
| Primo Carnera ..... | 265 | 77 | 60 | 10 | 2 | 0 | 0 | 1 | 4 | 0 | .061 |
| Jose Santa ........ | 265 | 54 | 35 | 9 | 0 | 1 | 1 | 0 | 3 | 5 | .148 |
| Jess Willard ...... | 250 | 37 | 19 | 4 | 0 | 1 | 7 | 1 | 3 | 2 | .167 |
| Carl Morris ....... | 235 | 73 | 36 | 9 | 8 | 1 | 10 | 4 | 1 | 4 | .123 |
| George Godfrey.... | 230 | 95 | 72 | 9 | 1 | 0 | 3 | 4 | 5 | 1 | .105 |
| Vittorio Campolo ... | 235 | 23 | 14 | 2 | 0 | 1 | 0 | 0 | 3 | 3 | .261 |
| Arthur DeKuh ..... | 220 | 60 | 33 | 10 | 1 | 1 | 3 | 1 | 7 | 4 | .200 |
| Elzear Rioux ...... | 220 | 34 | 18 | 10 | 0 | 1 | 0 | 1 | 3 | 1 | .148 |
| Jim Jeffries ....... | 220 | 21 | 11 | 7 | 0 | 2 | 0 | 0 | 0 | 1 | .047 |
| Tom Cowler ....... | 220 | 71 | 25 | 15 | 2 | 0 | 11 | 1 | 7 | 10 | .253 |
| Al Palzer ......... | 220 | 14 | 5 | 2 | 0 | 0 | 6 | 0 | 1 | 4 | .357 |
| Luis Firpo ........ | 220 | 36 | 25 | 3 | 1 | 0 | 7 | 0 | 0 | 1 | .028 |
| Walter Cobb ...... | 220 | 51 | 27 | 9 | 0 | 0 | 15 | 1 | 4 | 5 | .186 |
| Fred Fulton ....... | 220 | 93 | 57 | 5 | 2 | 1 | 19 | 3 | 1 | 5 | .086 |
| Marcel Nilles ..... | 220 | 46 | 15 | 14 | 3 | 2 | 0 | 0 | 3 | 9 | .228 |
| Harry Wills ...... | 220 | 94 | 42 | 18 | 0 | 2 | 26 | 1 | 1 | 4 | .064 |
| Bombardier Wells .. | 215 | 41 | 30 | 3 | 0 | 0 | 0 | 0 | 0 | 8 | .195 |
| | 972 | 564 | 136 | 20 | 17 | 96 | 19 | 49 | 71 | .143 |

him for a count of nine in their first meeting. You'll notice the only ones who have not had "ten" counted over them are Carnera and the young Impelletiere. The latter hasn't met a puncher of any consequence as yet, so must be temporarily discounted.

Jeffries was the real iron man of the group. He never would have been knocked out had he not elected to come out of retirement. That blazing July day in Reno saw a tired man slaughtered on the accomplished fists of one of the great heavyweights, Jack Johnson. But I, for one, do not believe the Boilermaker would have been whipped by the Galveston black had he been the fighter he was five years before.

Of this group of giants Jeff was undoubtedly the best . . . . and his greatness was in a measure due to his speed as well as his uncanny ability to withstand punishment and a devastating punch with either hand. Carnera also has unusual speed for so big a man . . . . but most of the big fellows were slow of foot and clumsy in action.

Next to Primo, Willard was the biggest of the heavyweight champions. He possessed a certain degree of boxing skill and a fine right uppercut . . . . but lacked interest in the game and a fighting heart. No man ever suffered a more terrific beating than the Tall Pine of the Potawattomie took at Dempsey's hands. His ribs were broken . . . . his cheek bone fractured . . . . his body crushed by the Mauler's deadly fists.

Luis Angel Firpo was the most colorful of the giants . . . . and what a right hand he had! If it landed he had a chance with any man that ever lived. But he couldn't box and certainly was not a smart ringman. Jimmy DeForest tried to teach him to use his left, which was a mistake . . . . for Luis was right-hand crazy and wild with a desire to slug.

These three . . . . and the Negroes, Harry Wills and George Godfrey, were the only giants who amounted to anything. Because their skins were black, the latter were shunted aside and never given a real chance to win the title. Whether or not they could have done so is problematical. With all the ballyhoo that was raised about the never-never match between Dempsey and Wills I am certain Jack would have torn Harry's body to shreds and knocked him out inside of four rounds.

Godfrey had speed and a punch and boxing skill, but an inferiority complex regarding white men. I would rate him behind Wills in all-around ability.

The others? . . . . Well, they are nowhere.

I was in Tex Rickard's office when the great promoter wired expense money for Vittorio Campolo to come to the United States. The South American was enormously tall and rangy and a hitter, and Tex was enthusiastic about him. But he was allowed to rust . . . . to lose whatever prospects he had in inaction. Tommy Loughran gave one of the greatest exhibitions of his career when he outboxed Campolo in every one of the ten rounds they fought. Vittorio lashed away with terrific rights . . . . but succeeded in only punching the atmosphere full of holes. His career was definitely finished when Carnera knocked him out.

Arthur DeKuh, built along the same lines as Campolo, was frequently beaten. The thick-set Cobb was also a mark for the accurate hitters, and Jose Santa, who is taller than Carnera and just as heavy, has been bumped over quite frequently.

The most knocked out of the mammoths was Tom Cowler, who was called "The Man Mountain" and Marcel Nilles, a Frenchman. They were targets at one time or another for every rising young heavyweight in the game. What good did their size do them? Not a thing. Almost stationary on their pedals . . . . lacking in defensive skill . . . they took what came until they passed out.

It is interesting to note in these statistics that twenty men, averaging some 230 pounds, were knocked out 71 times and lost 49 decisions. That should explode the myth of their invulnerability, shouldn't it?

Of course, their triumphs were scored principally by the knockout route. Few had any real boxing skill, but with their great bulk they naturally had hitting power to spare.

Carnera had stopped approximately 78 per cent of his rivals . . . . but we can take that with a grain of salt, since so many of them were on the made-to-order plan. Godfrey comes next with a K. O. average of 75 . . . . Followed by Firpo with 70, Santa 65, Fulton and Campolo 61 each.

Fulton was the enigma of the big fellows. Tall and lanky, a good boxer and a hard hitter he failed deplorably in

*Al Palzer, who has the worst losing percentage among the better known Giants of the Squared Circle.*

# Giants Not So Hot!

all of his big tests. He was none too keen about fighting and his chin had some of the brittle element of glass. Very few fighters have been dusted off as quickly as Fulton was when he faced Dempsey in the Harrison (N. J.) ball park. That defeat seemed to quench whatever spark was in Fred. Before that the Minnesota plasterer had been considered a real championship prospect. Afterward he was just another fighter . . . . and a not too successful one.

He was stopped by a lot of lesser lights after the Dempsey joust.

It seems to me that I have proven a good case against the big fellows. The really great fighters of history seldom scaled over 200 pounds. All necessary dynamite and power can be packed into that amount of muscle. More usually slows the lads up.

Dempsey, Fitzsimmons, Corbett, Sullivan, Tunney, Johnson, Sharkey and Schmeling were not in the super-dreadnaught class . . . . but would you care to pit any of the giants, except Jeffries, against those fellows in their prime?

*Vittorio Campolo's career was finished when he was beaten by another giant, Primo Carnera.*

# Facts and Figures

## Interesting Data Concerning the Heavyweight Championship Battles from Paddy Ryan to Max Baer

### By LANK LEONARD

FISTIC facts and figures are now in order. When the atmosphere is full of fight talk, the average fan likes to have argumentative matter dished out to him so that he can keep up with the Jones family. The Baer-Braddock battle and the Louis-Carnera tilt have aroused unusual interest in the heavyweight division, hence to aid those who like to turn back the pages of ring history and discuss the championship fights of the past, let's dig in a bit ourselves and review items worth while.

The first American heavyweight champion was a negro slave—Tom Molyneaux .... He went to England in 1810 to fight Tom Cribb, the British champion, and was beaten in thirty-three rounds. .... He met Cribb again one year later, but lost on that occasion in eleven rounds, Cribb breaking his jaw .... Molyneaux died in Galway, Ireland, in 1818 .... Jacob Hyer was the first white man to be recognized as an American champion .... He claimed the title after beating Tom Beasley in 1816. ...

His son, Tom, followed in his footsteps and also won the American title .... Tom, like his father, retired undefeated, hanging up his ring togs in 1849 .... From that time on until the rise of John L. Sullivan, the title was tossed back and forth between England and America. ...

John Morrissey, John Heenan, Joe Coburn, Mike McToole, Tom Allen, Jem Mace, Johnny Dwyer, Joe Goss, and Paddy Ryan successively claimed the crown. ... It was after Ryan had beaten Goss, who claimed the English title, that Sullivan came to the front by defeating Ryan. ... And with the coming of Sullivan came the modern era of boxing.

This fight between Schmeling and Sharkey was the second one in which a champion was proclaimed without having defeated a champion. ... Marvin Hart was the first to claim the honor in that manner, Jeffries, then retired, naming Hart as his successor in 1905. ... The fight in which Carnera won the title was the seventh in which a foreign boxer fought for the title on American soil since Sullivan lost the crown. ... Charley Mitchell, Tommy Burns, Carpentier, Firpo, Heeney and Max Schmeling were the others. ... Only three of that group successfully scaled the heights .... Burns, Schmeling and Carnera. Fitz was an Englishman by birth but had been raised in Australia and was a naturalized American when he fought for the title. ... Burns was born in Canada, and his real name was Noah Brusso.

\* \* \*

THE longest modern heavyweight contest was between Johnson and Willard, 26 rounds. ... The shortest was between Dempsey and Firpo, two rounds. ...

Heavyweight title bouts since the passing of the bare-knuckle era have been staged in New Orleans, Jacksonville, Carson City, Coney Island, San Francisco, Reno, Los Angeles, Colma, Las

FIRPO HELPED MAKE RING HISTORY — HE WAS A FEATURED STAR IN THE SHORTEST AND MOST THRILLING HEAVYWEIGHT TITLE BOUT ON RECORD.

AND DON'T LET 'EM SHORTCHANGE YOU EITHER!

THE JOHNSON-WILLARD FIGHT WAS THE LONGEST-26 RDS. JOHNSON CLAIMS HE HAD AGREED TO GO "OUT" IN THE 10TH ROUND BUT KEPT FIGHTING UNTIL THE MONEY HE HAD BEEN PROMISED WAS GIVEN TO HIS WIFE AT THE RINGSIDE.

I CAN LICK ANY MAN IN THE HOUSE.

JOHN L. SULLIVAN WAS THE MOST PICTURESQUE OF ALL THE CHAMPIONS.

-ON THE WHISKERS BIG BOY!

THE FIRST WHITE AMERICAN CHAMPION, JACOB HYER, HID HIS CHIN BEHIND A BEARD.

LANK LEONARD——*

DEMPSEY WAS THE GREATEST BOX OFFICE ATTRACTION —$7,000,000 WAS ALL HE DREW AS CHALLENGER AND CHAMPION!

Vegas, Toledo, Benton Harbor, New York, Jersey City, Shelby, Philadelphia, and Chicago. ...

Four were fought outside the United States, one at Sydney, Australia; one at Paris, one at Havana and one at Rome. ... The greatest throng to ever witness a title match was jammed into the Soldiers' Field stadium at Chicago .... 150,000. ... And they paid a record sum at the gate .... $2,685,600. ...

Looking over the records of American and world heavyweight champions, you'll find that John L. Sullivan took part in more fights after whipping Paddy Ryan with bare knuckles for the American title in 1882 than any of his successors. Sullivan fought thirteen times before knocking out Ryan in seven rounds .... During nine months in 1883, John L. toured the United States, offering $1,000 to any man who could stay four rounds with him, and proceeded to knock out

# Facts and Figures

fifty with his "terrible right." The names of those victims never have been included in Sullivan's ring record, but there is no doubt as to the truth of his remarkable performances in bouts with "unknowns" who tried to win his offer. . . .

The record of the "Boston Strong Boy" shows that he had participated in twenty-six "regular fights" after stopping Ryan, up to the battle with Corbett on September 7, 1892, at New Orleans, which was his first and only defeat. . . . The activity of Corbett as the champion, covering a period of four and one-half years, was confined to four bouts, with Mitchell, Courtney, Sharkey and Bob Fitzsimmons. Gentleman Jim stopped Mitchell in two rounds and Courtney in six, each lasting one minute while the first moving pictures of a championship battle were taken at Edison's laboratory in Jersey. Corbett boxed a four-round draw with Tom Sharkey before losing the title to Fitzsimmons at Carson City, Nev., in 1897. . . .

Fitzsimmons was inactive, except for vaudeville engagements, during 1898, but a year later he defended the world title for the first time and was put away by Jeffries in eleven rounds. Jeffries ruled the heavyweight division for seven years, during which he fought ten times, beating all comers, including Fitz, in a return match, Corbett twice, Sharkey, Jack Munroe and others. . . .

Jeffries retired from the ring, unbeaten, in 1905 and handed his title to Marvin Hart after the latter had knocked out Jack Root. . . . Hart was recognized as champion for only eleven months when Tommy Burns beat him on a referee's decision in twenty rounds. Burns was the title holder for three and one-half years. He indulged in ten battles before Jack Johnson whipped him in 1908. . . .

Johnson, as the heavyweight king, had five fights in 1909 and then met Jeffries at Reno on July 4, 1910. Jeffries, though idle for five years, was induced to return to the ring to "regain the championship for the white race," but hard training for three months finally shattered his nervous system and Johnson stopped him in the fifteenth round. . . .

For seven years Johnson reigned as world champion until Jess Willard stowed him away in twenty-six rounds at Havana in 1915. Although Willard wore the crown for four years, he appeared in the ring twice,—in a ten-round no-decision bout with Frank Moran in the old Garden, which was easily won by the champion, and in his losing fight with Jack Dempsey at Toledo on July 4, 1919. . . .

Dempsey, who lost his title to Gene Tunney in the Sesqui-Centennial Stadium in Philadelphia, held the crown for more than seven years, during which time he defended his title in only six championship fights and collected several million dollars. Tunney retired, undefeated, after twice whipping Dempsey and also defeating Heeney.

There you are mates! Now let some of those wise birds try to stick you!

*The fifty men John L. Sullivan knocked out during a nine-month stretch in 1883 are not listed in his official record.*

# The Fall of the Mighty!

*Max Schmeling, in Great Comeback, Causes Fistic Sensation of the Age—His Right Hand Smashes Explode Myth of the "Superman." German May Be First to Regain Heavyweight Title*

### By NAT FLEISCHER

SUPER-MEN of the ring? Are there any such animals? For some time, like thousands of other ardent fight followers, I had thought that at last we had discovered such a fighter in Joe Louis, the Detroit Brown Bomber, but after the severe shellacking the Negro received at the hands of Max Schmeling in their great international struggle at the Yankee Stadium on June 19, the myth' has been thoroughly exploded. Henceforth, regardless of how great a fighter might appear in the early stages of his career, as had Louis up to the time of the German massacre, it behooves us all to refrain from designating a ring warrior in the "super" class until after his retirement.

The alibis given by the sporting fraternity after Joe's downfall were unnecessary, for not by the widest stretch of imagination could one honestly have given Schmeling other than a mere fighting chance to whip the Bomber, all angles weighed. Never in the history of modern pugilism has there been so thorough an upset as that in the Schmeling-Louis battle, in which more than ninety-nine per cent of fight experts and Johnny Public picked Joe to win.

The uncertainties of the fight game were never more in evidence than in that contest. With everything but experience against him, Schmeling came in the Stadium ring on the long end of 8 to 1 odds, with the sympathy of the spectators alone in his favor. A public execution, that's what the fight looked like before the sound of the opening gong, but with that clang came a series of shocks that culminated in the utter rout of the enemy within the roped square, the supposedly invincible Bomber, and the consternation of an army of onlookers.

\* \* \*

INSTEAD of the battle ending "when and how" Louis chose to do so, it went into the twelfth round, with Joe on the receiving end of nine of the rounds. So thorough and masterly a job did Schmeling perform, that the spectators sat in their seats dumbfounded at what they were witnessing. Instead of the Detroit Killer acting the part of the executioner, it was the German Schlager who was astounding all hands by bringing about the greatest fistic upset in modern history. And why the greatest?

Because never before in so important a contest was the almost unanimous pre-fight verdict so overwhelmingly in favor of the man who failed to live up to expectations!

The contest, which marked the first professional setback of the loser, ended in 2.29 of the twelfth round, with sixty thousand fans looking on in amazement. Not since the memorabe day when Jim Corbett shocked the fistic world by taking the title by the K.O. route from the great John L. Sullivan at New Orleans had such a jolt been meted out to the fight public. Schmeling, the thirty-year-old ring veteran, confident that he had located Louis' weakness when Joe had fought Paulino, went into the fray undismayed, unlike all of the gladiators who had faced the Brown Bomber previously. Afraid? Not Schmeling.

He said he wasn't scared because he knew how to whip Joe, and he proved to the skeptics, including yours truly, that he meant just what he had said.

In taking his first defeat and his first knockdowns as a pro, Louis at least answered the critics who said he couldn't take it. He took it, and how! He absorbed enough punishment to have laid low the average pugilist half a dozen times. Staggered time and again, he kept on his feet and fought back, at times even making Schmeling hesitate to follow up when it appeared that one more solid right would end the fray.

The left side of Joe's face began to puff at an early stage of the battle and when the fight was ended, it appeared that the Bomber had a double cheek, so swollen was it. Under his left eye was a mouse, but in general appearances Schmeling was no better off. His left eye was completely closed and the blood was visible on his lips.

\* \* \*

ALTHOUGH the bout was subject to boycott attacks during the last week of training, the German received a wild ovation when he had completed his "come-back" feat. The gathering arose almost in unison as Joe lay prostrate on the canvas, and let out lusty cheers for the dark-skinned German who had done what appeared on the surface to be the impossible.

The crowd was fully prepared for what took place in the twelfth

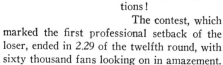

round. The indications that a fistic miracle might take place appeared on the horizon in the fourth round when Schmeling had scored the first knockdown. In that session, after Louis had assumed a lead in the first three rounds, Schmeling crossed a terrific right hook to Joe's chin. He quickly laced over a second shot and staggered the Bomber. Then came a flurry of flying fists, each connecting to the mark with sharpshooting accuracy, and down went Joe. He made an attempt to support himself on the upper strand, but lost the hold and sank to the mat, where he remained only for a short count of three.

But that knockdown stirred Schmeling on to victory. It proved to him what he had so often said at his training camp: "I know Louis' weakness. He is wide open to a right and I'll beat him with that punch." And true to his prediction, Herr Max set about the task with a vengeance. He went right hand crazy, and how those punches landed! Sitting at the ringside, one could hear the thud above the din as right after right went crashing against Joe's unsupported chin. For a fighter who had been acclaimed by fistic followers as the most finished of fighters of recent years, the Bomber displayed a lamentable weakness in defense. If anyone had tried to convince me a few weks ago that Louis could be copped so readily and so steadily with a right, I would have ridiculed him. Yet that's exactly what was happening!

\* \* \*

THAT fourth round was the beginnng of the end for the "Super-Man." The idol who had replaced Jack Dempsey as the magnet, slowly but surely from that fourth round, was nearing the end of his reign. He seemed not only to be wobbly, but in a daze. He acted in the next three rounds just as he did when he was so severely criticized by the scribes during the first fortnight of his training. It was a lackadaisical Joe Louis who was tossing punches at his foe. He was in a complete fog. The power behind those punches of his that had floored Baer, Levinsky, Carnera, Retzlaff and Paulino seemed gone. They were tame blows compared to the dynamite rights that were landing flush on his chin with regularity, round after round.

The German Schlager, the Teuton who had won the world championship on a foul from Jack Sharkey and lost the crown to him in a disputable decision, once more had reached the heights. He again was the man whom we praised to the skies back in 1929 and 1930. He had regained all his cunning. He had planned the battle as he figured it should be to enable him to overcome the Negro, and here he was on the brink of victory and certainly would not let the opportunity slip from him.

At times following the fourth session it seemed that Schmeling, with his left eye rapidly closing and body punches weakening him, might drop the advantage which he was gaining and that Louis would pile up enough points as the bout progressed to pull the chestnuts out of the fire. But no such thing happened.

A more determined, courageous, battling Schmeling never faced an opponent than was Schmeling as that fight continued. To him, as he expressed it after the bout, "the defeat of the widely heralded Bomber meant more than all the money he was getting for his triumph." It meant additional glory. It meant a chance to fight again for the world championship, with an excellent opportunity to be the first man to regain the world laurels in that division. It would place his name in the fistic archives as the man who not only came back, but annihilated the most-talked-of fighter in recent years. What a setting! And did he make good? Yes, with a vengeance.

\* \* \*

WE must doff our cap to the Black Uhlan. His was an exceptionally difficult task and he emerged with flying colors. From the seventh round to the last, the crowd sensed the change and the rooting then was for the German. The underdog was coming through and he was to have his just share of attention. They were watching a new-born Schmeling—the man who was unawed by the cold, expressionless features of the Detroit Annihilator. At last they were viewing a fight against Louis in which the opponent was not afraid of the Big Black Man.

It was the Schmeling who had risen to the heights when he fought an uphill battle against Johnny Risko in the Garden, the bout that really started him on the road to fame. It was a rejuvenated Schmeling, a man who had made up his mind that he would not be offered as a sacrifice and was out to show the world that he had not come to America merely to obtain some more of our money to carry home to the Fatherland.

He fought, in my opinion, the greatest battle of his long career. He remembered that three years ago, almost to the day, the referee had stopped his fight with Max Baer to save the Uhlan from further punishment, and how sweet must have been his victory as he avenged that defeat by an American by turning back Baer's conqueror in a most devastating manner? The brown embalmer, who, it was reckoned, would annihilate his foe, was himself embalmed in a manner that left the entire fight world gasping in amazement.

When the bout was over and Max was interviewed by the scribes, he repeatedly kept saying that he knew from the first time he had seen the Louis-Baer pictures that Joe was a target for a right and that he could therefore whip the Detroiter.

"I know I must land it, and when I do, I win," he said. "I practice, and I practice, over and over again before I come here and then I do it again in my camp, until I feel I am ready for Joe, and I find him more easy to be hit than I had expected. But Joe is a good fighter. He will be back, but he must first learn how to protect himself against a right."

\* \* \*

AND what Schmeling remarked goes doubly for me. I won't relegate Joe to the has-been class. I still think he is a great fighter, and he'll prove it after he gets a rest and starts a comeback. He'll come back—you can bet your last dollar on that. And when he does, he'll be as effective as he was against the boys he met previously to Schmeling. Joe has learned his lesson and he'll overcome the handicaps with proper coaching.

Regardless of what happened in the Schmeling bout, Louis was a great fighter before that fight and he'll be great again. Make no mistake about that. His reputation cannot be destroyed overnight, just by one adverse decision. He proved that he was a superb boxer and a puncher of the extraordinary type against Baer, Levinsky, Retzlaff, Paulino and Carnera, and even though the claim is made that each of those was scared out of his wits when tossed against the Bomber, the fact remains that every good asset of a great fighter was in evidence on the side of Louis against those men.

\* \* \*

WHY then the sudden change? Well, there are several things that might answer that enigma. For one, I blame married life. I have always been a member of that school that frowns on a fighter still in his prime becoming a benedict. The fun that Louis got out of life in the last six months didn't do him any good. It softened him and made him work like a beaver for four weeks in the hot sun at Lakewood to condition himself.

He is of the type who needs work, and the long layoff following his married life, with the enjoyment that goes with riches, proved detrimental to his welfare, so far as his fighting was concerned. The boys who "covered" his camp often remarked that, but the impression given by his handlers was that Louis was just a big, overgrown boy who figured he would have little difficulty in hurdling the last big obstacle to his climb to a titular fight, and that's where they erred.

Then the weight problem seemed to handicap Joe. He should have scaled at least 202 instead of the 198. He came in too fine and that was obvious from the start. We do not offer these to take away any credit from Schmeling for his marvelous victory, for such is farthest from our aim, but there must be some reason for Joe's complete reversal of form, and the above is my answer.

\* \* \*

EXPERIENCE mastered youth. Schmeling knew just what to do when he had Joe going and, quick as a flash, he went after his prey. He even outsmarted Louis in the very things we all

# The CELEBRATION

*Joe Jacobs, manager of Schmeling (extreme left), and Joe Malone, one of Max's trainers, cheering the victory as Schmeling, Donovan, Blackburn and others rush to Louis' aid after the knockout.*

*Schmeling, left eye closed, greets the cheering thousands as Harry Balogh, the announcer, holds up Max's hand in token of victory.*

*Schmeling and his manager and handlers. Left to right—Joe Malone, Jacobs and Max Machon (upper row), and Doc Casey sitting next to Max.*

thought the Bomber was supreme. Schmeling won the crowd by the manner in which he stepped in for what was expected to be his slaughter. That terrible right hand sock of Schmeling did more than batter down the man who previously had petrified his opponents by his mere presence. It proved that when the Bomber was hard hit, he didn't know how to fight his way out of the difficulty. It was unbelievable, but it was true!

In fact, I'm of the opinion that had Schmeling not been too deliberate, he could have ended the fight in the fourth or fifth round. But he still had respect for Joe's prowess and he decided not to press his advantage except by stages. A Dempsey killer would have sent Joe to sleep after that first knockdown. But the German sensed that he had the fight in hand immediately after Joe had hit the resin dust and he wasn't in a hurry to lose the golden opportunity by taking any needless chances.

The thrills experienced in the Louis-Carnera, Louis-Baer, and Baer-Carnera battles were nothing to be compared to those of the Schmeling-Louis mill. There was drama, and plenty of it, in that battle that was not on view in the others. It was the drama caused by the upset that made the last-named so thrilling an affair. The swirl of punches, the clamor of the fight throng, the suddenness with which the changes took place, the realization that a white man will continue to rule the fistic world for some time to come—all added to the drama.

\* \* \*

*B*Y his victory, Schmeling emerges on top of the list as the contender for the heavyweight championship bout with Braddock and such a bout, which is certain to be staged this fall, will now outdo in attendance and in receipts a possible Braddock-Louis affair. Why? Because, if Louis had conquered Schmeling as was expected, then the average fan would have conceded Braddock just as little chance to retain his crown as was given to Schmeling for the Louis contest. Now, however, things are different. The situation has changed. Braddock against Schmeling is certain to be a great fight, with the chances of each almost on a par. In fact, there were thousands who had viewed Max's victory over the Bomber, who left the Yankee Stadium thoroughly convinced that the German cannot miss setting ring history by being the first to regain the heavyweight championship. Of course, that remains to be seen, but suffice to say that not in years will two more evenly matched heavyweights be pitted against each other than in the case of Schmeling against Braddock, if such a fight takes place.

\* \* \*

*A*N analysis of Louis' downfall reveals little more than that he had hurt his thumbs in the early rounds and that he had no defense for a right. As for the sprained thumbs, that was most unfortunate, but as for the defense, I blame Joe's handlers for not having perfected it. When a fighter is called a "superfighter" and is listed by the great majority as the most finished ringman in years, it seems rather strange that such a flaw should not have been corrected.

In my many broadcasts on the fight during the seven weeks of training, I repeatedly called attention to the fact that Schmeling was tuning up on a right hook and a right uppercut, and that it behooved Louis to prepare a defense for those punches. In fact, I said only a day before the fight that the only things in Schmeling's favor were experience and one of the finest right hands a heavyweight has possessed in many years. Yet, like hundreds of others who had seen Joe rise from nowhere to world fame, I couldn't conceive that these would be sufficient to bring about Joe's downfall. That's the way of the fight game.

\* \* \*

*A*S for the details of the fight, that has been told so thoroughly in every language throughout the world that it is needless for me to repeat them. For the benefit of our army of readers who keep THE RING for record purposes, however, I'll review the story of the rounds.

For the first three rounds the battle was one of wits, with each striving to force the other into an opening and Louis pressing his man around the ring. He kept jabbing his left into Max's face with regularity. Schmeling kept backing away the major portion of the first three rounds, stolidly refusing to be drawn into an offensive move. Several times he took sturdy lefts to the face without a whimper and his eye began to redden and the crowd began to toss its sympathy for the man who they expected would soon be put out of his misery.

Then came the turn of the tide. In that hectic fourth round, in which Joe Louis hit the canvas for the first time in his pro career, Schmeling seemed almost as astounded at what he had accomplished as did the thousands of eyes that were focussed on the gladiators.

The hitherto invincible Brown Bomber, somewhat dazed, struggled to his feet at the count of three and from that point to the finish of the fight it was apparent that his rival not only had "the mere fighting chance" that is accorded to every fighter regardless of ability but that his stood out so prominently as to astound the onlookers. When that round was over it was with difficulty that Louis found his way to his corner.

In the fifth round, the end became apparent more so than at any time of the fight except the actual windup, when Schmeling caught his rival with a perfect clout on the chin three seconds after the round had ended. Neither the referee nor the fighters had heard the bell and so powerful was that punch that it made Louis' legs take a rubber appearance and befuddled Joe's brains to such extent that he never came out of the stupor.

\* \* \*

*T*HAT punch was the turning point of the fight. In my opinion, it ended every chance that Joe had of coming through to triumph. In the eighth round Louis twice fouled Schmeling with powerful left-hand swings that brought an agonized look to the German's face and sharp warning from Referee Donovan. There could be no doubt that the blows were unintentionally delivered, but hurt the German they did.

From that time on to the very finish the Detroit Negro showed little enthusiasm for his work, his punches lacked steam, his eyes had the daze of one whose brain was not functioning and his legs failed to hold up under the strain. At times he wobbled around the ring and on several occasions, while Max kept shooting right after right with high frequency, it seemed that Joe would topple over under the force of impact plus his own poor mental and physical condition but, game to the core, he stuck it out and staggered to his corner. Schmeling was in complete command from the fifth through the final round even though at times he was kept extremely busy blocking lefts.

\* \* \*

*S*CHMELING'S edge became wider and wider as the bout progressed and his rights landed harder and harder with each successive punch. Again and again he rocked the Balmer until in the twelfth he sensed the kill and he went after him as only the hunter does. With all of the fight gone out of the Brown Bomber, Schmeling unleashed an avalanche of rights to the jaw and finally mowed down his opponent in a neutral corner. Joe attempted to hold himself on the ropes, but with that hold released, he fell on his stomach, took a position as one fast asleep, and as ten was counted over him, he turned face upward, his face with an appearance of blankness, his eyes bleary and his body limp.

It was the end of a perfect night for Max Schmeling. He had succeeded where others had failed. He had earned for himself a niche in the fistic hall of fame.

A new king has risen in the form of the rejuvenated Black Uhlan of the Rhine. And with it came an added revival of interest in the heavyweights. No longer will it be necessary for Jack Dempsey to stage heavyweight white hope tournaments. No longer will the public be worrying, at least for a time, when the Negro race will again assume supremacy in the heavyweight ranks. The man upon whom his race had looked with favor fell down in the crucial test and with his fall ascended the Man Who Had Come Back.

# "Louis Bubble Has Burst,"

## By JAMES J. BRADDOCK
### (Heavyweight champion of the world)
### (Written exclusively for The Ring)

THE day after Max Schmeling, whose great comeback has stirred the fistic world just as did my unexpected victory over Max Baer, a triumph that enabled me to win the world heavyweight crown, the Editor of THE RING invited me to write an article for his magazine on my reactions before, during and after the big fight. Though signed to an agreement to write only for King Features, I couldn't turn down a magazine that has done and still does so much for boxing, so here goes.

Being the heavyweight champion of the world, gave me a greater interest in the Schmeling-Louis battle than anybody else. I realized that in the winner of that contest, I would have the man who would face me in the next battle for the crown. Therefore I watched the training of Louis and Schmeling with keenest interest. Never did I pay such attention to two fighters as I did to that pair.

With my manager, Joe Gould, I went to see each of the fighters four times at their respective camps, and on each occasion, I made a minute study of every action in the ring. I watched the footwork, the breathing, the attack and the defense and I tried to analyze the good and bad points. I tried, particularly, to find out what were the faults of each and I can truthfully say that what Schmeling had discovered about Louis' faults, I had found and so had Jack Johnson.

I might add, for it is not giving away any secret, that on several occasions Johnson and I trained together, our aim being for me to develop an attack that would take full advantage of Joe's shortcomings. That's why, when Schmeling took Joe into camp, I felt like kicking myself because I wasn't Joe's opponent instead of Max, for I knew and felt it within me, that I could have duplicated Max's feat and done it in quicker time.

* * *

THROUGHOUT the training period of Max and Joe, I couldn't help but feel that which ever way the bout went, I would be getting a fine opponent, a good drawing card and a good fighter for my first defense of the heavyweight title and that's why I was eager for a stirring battle.

Never for a moment did I think that Schmeling was a mark for Louis. If you RING readers followed my series of articles in the Hearst papers during the last week of training, you will bear me out in my statement that I repeatedly called attention to the fact that Schmeling might furnish a huge surprise and that age meant nothing in this case, no more than it did in mine when I fought Baer.

I thought that Louis would win, because of his splendid work in his professional fights. But I couldn't see what most critics said before the fight, that Louis would win in a round, because I saw in Schmeling an improved fighter, a man who was full of determination, a courageous battler who feared no man, and under such conditions, I couldn't understand why he wasn't given at least a fighting chance. Here is what I said:

"Against a fighter like Schmeling, who has two talented feet, a quick-thinking brain and a solid heart, Louis is going to find something new in opponents. Carnera never had any legs. Baer was scared stiff before the fight, as he himself has so often said. But Max is different. He isn't any older than I was when I beat Baer. He's in the best of condition. He's not afraid and I know he has the legs. With those in his favor, just watch Schmeling. He may furnish the biggest surprise of the year."

* * *

WELL, I don't want to brag and say "I told you so," because I didn't. I picked Louis to win, but said it would be a hard-fought battle. I remarked that Schmeling had a powerful right which he'd use often and land accurately, and said that I saw him use this often enough in training to convince me that he would do considerable damage with it.

So you see that I had discovered something worth while and my only wish before the fight was that I could take Schmeling's place, so confident was I that I could beat Joe after my study of him at the camp at Lakewood. I repeatedly told that to my manager. But since that couldn't be, I felt content to watch the fight at the Yankee Sadium and pick out pointers for my coming battle, and what I saw has again convinced me that the championship will remain in America at least for another year.

To me it makes little difference now, because in either Max or Joe, I have an opponent who will attract a good gate, and I'm candid to say that is a most important factor with me right now.

My feelings during the fight naturally were a little different from what they were prior to the battle because there in the ring I was seeing the men who were fighting for the chance to meet me. I didn't care who won, but because of the expert opinion which placed Louis in the "Superman" class, I told my manager that I hoped Joe would win so that I could get the chance to break that myth.

On the day of the fight I said to Gould: "Joe, something tells me that I may not get that chance I'm looking for. I hope I'm wrong, because I'll show him up if ever I get him in the ring."

"What are you worrying about," replied Gould. "You'll take Schmeling as easily as you will Louis."

Of course I realized that such talk was a manager's talk, but now that the fight is over, let me say that I think Joe is correct. I think Schmeling will find it far more difficult to hit me with a right than he did Joe. I've got a perfect defense for that kind of a blow, whereas Louis had none.

* * *

BEFORE the big fight, I was somewhat pushed into the background by the scribes because everything in boxing was written only on Louis. It was Louis this and Louis that, and I couldn't blame the scribes for that. Naturally at times it was mighty discouraging to think that I was the world champion, yet Louis got the bulk of the headlines in boxing, but I thought, as did my manager, that it was best for the sport to have it so.

After all, I, as champion, was looking forward to a million-dollar gate when I defended my crown, and how could I expect such a gate if the man who was being groomed for me wasn't kept continuously in the spotlight?

But it was tough on me, and just as tough on Joe Gould and my family. They all thought that I, being the champion, should always be the man of the hour and they couldn't understand the Louis angle, but being a fighter, I could.

And now that the Louis bubble has burst and that the "Superman" myth has exploded, I feel like a new man. Not that I liked to see Joe lose. On the contrary; he's a fine fellow and I think he's a great asset to boxing, but I'm happy because, as has already been remarked by many scribes, I have gained in magnitude as much as has Schmeling through his unexpected victory over Louis.

Until that knockout was scored, Jimmy Braddock was just the champion. He was the man whom Louis would meet in September and from whom Joe would take the title. Of course, the newspaper boys didn't consult me in making that statement. They didn't ask me whether I would submit or whether I would fight back hard to keep my crown, but now—well, things are different and I feel differently as a result. I not only am Jimmy Braddock, the champion, but I am the world title-holder who will be called upon to prevent the crown from passing overseas. If you don't think that that makes a big difference, well, then you've got another guess coming.

I'm thrilled at the thought of it. If I had made up my mind to fight against Louis as I had never fought before, I assure you RING readers that the feeling now is doubly so. It will be America against Germany now. In what an enviable position that places me!

I now can realize the feelings of John L. Sullivan when he

# Writes BRADDOCK

*Heavyweight Champion, in Exclusive Article, Admits He Feared Negro Heavyweight and Now Sees His Title Tenure Secure*

faced a foreigner. With him such a battle was one in which he called into action every ounce of energy because he realized that America, the land of his birth, was eagerly watching him. And that's the way I now feel and think.

Flag waving, you might say. No, it is not that—just a plain desire to keep America in front. What an incentive!

It's a thrill, boys, and I assure you that it will stir me on as never before. I know that when I meet Schmeling there'll be an army of scribes who'll favor Max because of what he has just accomplished, but to them I now say, don't be so hasty. The conditions are a little different and what I did against Baer, I'm confident I can do in my fight with Schmeling.

I called the turn on Louis months ago. As I have already said, I practiced a short right with Jack Johnson for almost a year in the hopes that I'd meet Louis and be the first to blast that "Superman" reputation, and I really regret that I didn't get the chance instead of Schmeling.

\* \* \*

LOUIS always looked to me like a sucker for a short right, if one would stand up and give it to him as did Schmeling, and I have noticed something about Schmeling which will enable me to halt his rise when he meets me. I know that Schmeling has told the newspaper

*James J. Braddock world heavyweight champion who comments on Louis's failure.*

boys that he has planned a battle for me that will bring him the title in September if we meet, but I think he'll have another guess coming.

He says that he had his plans all set when he came here and thought that he would get the bout with me, but instead found that Louis was to be his opponent, and that from a study of the moving pictures of my fight with Baer, he knows that he can beat me. Well, we'll cross that bridge when the time comes for us to face each other in ring action. I think I'll shock him the same as he shocked Louis. Wait and see!

\* \* \*

OF course, we must rate Schmeling as a great fighter, but his style is such that it is made to order for me. Perhaps the motion pictures have taught Max something about the "weakness" which he declares he has discovered in me, but I have likewise

discovered Max's faults. In a fight for the heavyweight title, the contestants cannot be regarded in the same light as those who meet in ordinary combat because of the gigantic stakes involved. And it is for that reason more than any other that a champion and challenger make such a close study of each other's styles, faults and good points.

I have heard Max say that I will not be ready for such a tough assignment in September as he will be, but to that I must say that, while from outward appearances it would seem that I have been an extremely idle fighter, I have left nothing undone to keep myself in perfect physical condition and even now, while I am giving this story to THE RING, I am in hard training at Loch Sheldrake, where I did my conditioning work for my fight with Baer. The day following Schmeling's victory, my training began in earnest, and I can assure my friends that Jimmy Braddock will retain his crown for America when he meets Max Schmeling.

# Dempsey Sees Louis

*Jack Writes, for The Ring, That Weaknesses Exposed by Negro in Schmeling Fight, and Beating He Took, Enshroud Joe's Future in Doubt*

*Jack Dempsey, who predicts that Louis will never again be as great as he was prior to the Schmeling bout.*

WHAT effect will the knockout of Joe Louis by Max Schmeling have on the Negro's future? That's what most of the fight fans are asking, because that thought is uppermost in their minds right now. When a fighter is a raw novice, just starting his career and suddenly finds himself on the mat, with the referee counting ten over him, the reaction varies according to the temperament of the boxer. If he is a high strung lad, full of pride, he may never again don a pair of mitts.

But if he is of the type that doesn't get easily discouraged and realizes through sound reasoning that the best of men might suffer a K.O. and that it's no disgrace, he'll get back into action with a vim and soon fight his way back into the top flight rank.

That is what must be considered in the case of Joe Louis. Is he going to take his knockout too seriously? Is he of the type that cannot forget? Will he bemoan his fate? Will he be shy of flying fists in his eagerness to avoid getting clouted as he was in his fight with Schmeling? Will the army of hero worshippers, especially those of his own race who idolized him, desert him in his most trying hour?

Those are vital questions that must be answered before we can discuss with any accuracy Louis' future. I should know, because I went through the mill just as did hundreds of others of the best fighters of all time. They are of such importance that it behooves Messrs. Black and Roxborough, Joe's mentors, to study each carefully and find the answer so as best to serve their charge.

* * *

ON the night before the Louis-Schmeling battle and immediately following that fight, my tavern, Dempsey's Restaurant on the corner of 50th Street and 8th Avenue, opposite Madison Square Garden in New York, was jammed to the walls with fight fans from all parts of the world and in my capacity as host, I naturally came in contact with the fans and heard many fine arguments. Every question which I have put into print here, is one that came up some time or other during the discussions in my place following the fight.

Trevor Wignall, England's greatest sports writer, was among those who questioned the possibility of Louis ever being as good as he was. "That beating about the head which Joe received," said Trevor, "won't do him any good."

"Nor those knockdowns," said Max Waxman, my business manager who formerly handled two champions, Joe and Vince Dundee, and knows a fighter when he sees one.

And I agree with them. I believe that Joe Louis had reached his highest point in professional boxing prior to the Schmeling bout and that from now on, he'll never improve. Why, you might ask, since I picked Joe to win in five rounds.

Well, because when I saw how readily Schmeling shot over his powerful right and scarcely ever missed, I realized for the first time that Joe's weakness had been found and that henceforth, no fighter possessing any "guts," would hesitate to mix it with Louis in which case he'll be plenty hit by rights. I don't care how good a fighter might be, once his immunity from punishment becomes a thing of the past, it's just too bad for him.

* * *

THEN again that terrible licking he received from Max won't do him any good. You can't readily forget those wallops. I remember my fight with Gunboat Smith on the Coast when I was still a kid just coming along. The Gunner hit me with all he had and had me fighting purely from instinct for I was out on my feet, and when I came to in my dressing room and was told by Jack Kearns that I had won, I couldn't believe it.

But that was the least part of my worries—trying to figure how I had done it. It was the Gunner's punches that gave me my real worries, and for some time after that fight I just couldn't get going properly because of the thought of those blows.

But in the case of Louis, it is far different. He had reached the highest point a fighter could attain other than to win a title. Reams were written about his greatness. Ed Van Every wrote a story on "Louis, Man and Super-fighter," and many novelties of all kinds were manufactured to depict Joe's rise. And then suddenly, as out of a clear sky, came the thud that landed him in the resin and the lights went out for him.

Can you imagine what such a downfall meant to a lad of Louis's schooling—a boy who had come up from nowhere, just as I did, to win fame and fortune and the acclaim of the fistic fans! Just think of that and you'll soon have a conception of what I mean when I try to prove that Joe will have a tough time to live that down and therefore a mighty tough time to make the expected comeback that the boxing writers predict.

* * *

FOR the good of boxing—I hope Joe does make a decided comeback. I hope that it comes so quickly that he'll surprise us just as we were surprised by his defeat. I hope that by this time next year, his rehabilitation will have been so complete that he will be the leading contender for the world heavyweight title.

That's what I wish for Joe because neither I, nor any fight follower, can get away from the fact that Joe Louis brought boxing back into its own after four lean, meagre years. His rise brought an end to the fistic depression and his popularity was so worldwide, that it helped the sport to recover in far quicker time than had been anticipated.

But I still think that the going is to be mighty rough because of the licking he took. What is the reaction to the Schmeling victory? Most favorable. Whereas prior to that triumph Louis stood almost alone as the attraction in boxing with scarcely any good cards to arrange unless he was the topliner, now there are at least half a dozen such good bouts in the market. Thus, overnight, my pal Max Baer remembers the picture as an extremely valuable prospect.

Where a few weeks ago he wasn't worth a grain of salt as a top line attraction, now he can name his own figures for a return

# Comeback Not Easy

## By JACK DEMPSEY
*(Former world heavyweight champion)*

bout with Louis because such a fight in New York will draw thousands of dollars more than did the Louis-Schmeling shindig. Why such a statement, you might ask. Because the antagonism that had been shown by those opposed to Nazism, would not interfere with the gate and because thousands of persons who refused to see Schmeling and Louis clash, will go miles to see Louis and Baer in a comeback.

What amused me most during the many weeks of preparation and ballyhoo for the big fight, were the statements of the writers calling attention to the perfect human machine in Louis. There never was a fighter who could be called perfect and I don't believe there ever will be. We are all human and we all at times make our mistakes. I made plenty and so did every good fighter I ever knew. Louis was no exception as his bout with Schmeling proved.

Of course it is a very simple matter for one to tell after a fight what precautions should have been taken and how the battle plan should have been mapped, but we cannot always foresee what the other fellow is likely to do. A punching like that which Louis received from Max never did any one any good. No matter how young one might be, punishment of that kind always leaves its mark. That's why I fear for Louis' future, but I hope I'm wrong. I hope he'll give me as much a surprise as I received when he was knocked out.

* * *

OF course, different fighters take defeat differently. Some brood over it to such an extent that they never are the same again. Others regard it in the light of experience, in which case such a defeat as Louis suffered at the hands of Schmeling won't affect him as much as it would otherwise. Still others have a certain amount of fear instilled into them as a result of a decisive defeat, and those lads are absolutely passé so far as their future in the ring is concerned.

I don't know to which class Louis belongs, but if we are to listen to his trainers and managers, then the Schmeling victory won't work so hard on Joe. It is their contention, as it is that of Louis, that Joe will be better than ever because he has learned a lesson on defense and that when he makes his comeback, he'll know how to protect himself against a right. I hope for Joe's sake, and for the best interests of boxing, of which I am still part and parcel despite the Dempsey Restaurant which I own opposite Madison Square Garden, that such will be the case. Box-

*Joe Louis, who according to Dempsey, will be a mark for any fighter who is fearless as was Schmeling and can throw a good right.*

ing needs Joe Louis just as much as the Brown Bomber needs the wholehearted support of those who idolized him before his downfall.

Unfortunately, in most cases in boxing, the fan fails to stand by a fallen idol. The fickle fight followers usually like to travel with a winner only, but I'm mighty glad to say that in my travels through the South, where I went with my manager, Max Waxman, to referee fights and wrestling matches throughout the month following Louis' defeat, I was elated at the fine write-ups and comment passed on Louis' defeat. The average fan I found to be very much in favor of giving Joe the full benefit of his great strides prior to the Schmeling defeat. That is as it should be. One triumph doesn't make a fighter and one doesn't break him.

The fact that my opinion is different from others in re Joe's comeback should have no bearing on the Bomber's status. We all have a right to our honest opinion, and as I said before, mine is that Joe will have a mighty tough time because if he meets fearless opponents from now on, he'll be a target for right-hand punches, and it won't be so easy for him to perfect his defense against those at this stage.

* * *

I HAVE been asked by many scribes whether the defeat of Louis would halt my heavyweight white hope tournaments. My answer is an emphatic no. Why should it?

First, I want to say that my tournaments are not white hope tourneys. They are heavyweight tournaments in which novices who have not been engaged in more than four pro fights are permitted to enter and there is no discrimination, no color line drawn. If they were white hope bouts, then certainly no Negroes would be permitted to enter, yet such is not the case.

Up in Canada recently we had the finals of the Montreal tourney, but unfortunately, the lad who looked like the best bet, a fast, two-fisted boy named Thiery, showed best until the final bout when I had to disqualify him for fouling. Thus he lost THE RING novice heavyweight belt which my pal, Nat Fleischer, presented to the winner, but I'll have him and the winner come to New York to compete in my finals next October or November in Madison Square Garden.

Nat, who was to have gone to France on June 20 to see the finals of the French tourney in which

4000

*Harry Balough, the announcer, holds up Joe's hand in token of victory. Joe's handlers rush into the ring and surround him, and the Bomber, expressionless, stands motionless while the voice of the announcer echoes over the mikes through the stadium.*

*Joe finally laughs! Yes, he's happy, and why shouldn't he be? Didn't he make good? He holds up three fingers to indicate to the photographers the round in which he triumphed while Jack Blackburn, his trainer, looks on.*

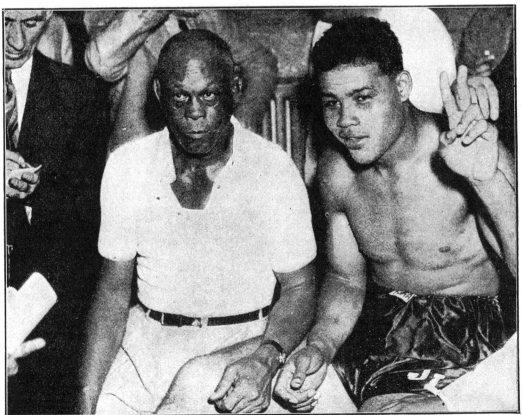

# IN OUR QUESTION BOX

By NAT FLEISCHER

M. H. McIntosh, Victoria, Australia

Q.—I am five feet three inches and weigh 122 pounds, clothed. My chest is 36½ inches normal and 40 inches expanded. Waist 26 inches, reach 68, age 16 years nine months and neck 15⅜. Are my measurements good for a boxer? Did Stanley Ketchel ever fight Jack Johnson and what was the result? I am exercising with the assistance of the six body building books published by the Jowett Institute of Physical Culture. Will these exercises slow me down and bind my muscles for boxing? I also have Super Physique barbell course by Siegmund Klein. Should I use this course in conjunction with the Jowett course or finish the latter before commencing Super Physique?

**A.—The measurements are perfectly up to the standard and you are developed nicely but the ability is the most important feature. You have to have a natural gift for the sport or else the most perfect physique in the world will not help a bit. Jack Johnson knocked out Ketchel when they fought. Finish one course before you start the next. It will not interfere with boxing exercises.**

Pat London, Portland, Ore.

Q.—I have noticed that there was very little publicity on the Louis-Braddock title bout. Was it because the majority of the papers are sympathetic with the Nazis and wish to suppress it or is it just accidental?

**A.—I am afraid you are mistaken about the publicity as the fight received nation wide publicity and certainly did not lack for space in the papers. Sentiment in spots favored Schmeling. The Nazi situation had nothing to do with the Braddock-Louis fight.**

Ed Malone, Seagroves, Texas

Q.—I am sixteen years of age, 5 feet 8½ inches tall and weigh 150 pounds. I have a reach of 72 inches. What will my approximate height, weight and reach be at my full development?

**A.—You will probably reach the 6 foot mark and scale in the vicinity of 190 pounds and your reach should increase from six to eight inches.**

A Ring Reader

Q.—Can exercising develop a chicken breast? If so will you please give me some chest exercises? Can bow legs be straightened? How? I weigh 147 pounds and am 5 feet 10 inches tall. How much will I weigh when I am 25 years old? I am sixteen now.

**A.—Questions relative to chicken breast and bow legs should be answered by your physician. He can give you the remedy. You will probably pass the six foot mark and scale about 175 pounds.**

Mabel Thompson, Chicago, Ill.

Q.—Are the reports about the estrangement of Joe Louis and his wife true?

**A.—Absolutely not. Joe ridicules such reports. He and his wife are happily married and the only reason she was not present at either his training camp or the fight, was because Joe and his mentors thought it best not to have her at either.**

Charles Phillips, Albany, N. Y.

Q.—How can one gain weight?

**A.—Get my book, "Training for Boxers," and read chapter on same. To gain weight one should eat starchy foods. Foods recommended most by physicians are: eggs, milk, cheese, cereals, beef, steaks. The latest issue of "Training for Boxers" contains several features not contained in the first issue.**

Peter Z. Narlo, Spokane, Wash.

Q.—What is a newspaper decision? If John Henry Lewis retires from the light-heavyweight throne and Tiger Jack Fox is rated the best light-heavyweight, would that make him champion? Al Morse of Spokane, thinks that Fox is a much cleverer and a more terrific hitter than Joe Louis. Is that true?

**A.—Newspaper decisions are rendered when the state does not allow an official decision and the sporting writers give their opinion as to who won the fight in the newspapers. If Lewis retires, an elimination tournament will be started with Fox as one of the entries if he decides to try for the title. The difference between F x and Louis can never be settled unless they meet in ring combat. Louis has a much better record but Fox has been coming in fine fashion.**

Arthur Sommers, New Haven, Conn.

Q.—What is the difference between a hook and a jab?

**A.—A jab is a straight blow landed by sticking out either the right or the left hand either for face or body. A hook is a blow which is delivered with a slight curvature of the arm.**

Matt Forinseca, Boston, Mass.

Q.—Did Johnny Dundee ever hold the world lightweight championship?

**A.—No, he held the featherweight title.**

Thomas Fulda, Milwaukee, Wis.

Q.—Is Joe Louis the youngest to win a world heavyweight title?

**A.—Yes. No other heavyweight king was less than 24 years old. Joe is only 23.**

Alice Farrington, Jersey City, N. J.

Q.—Some papers say that Jimmy Braddock is 31. Others say he is 32. My boy friend says that he is a member of a club where the boys insist that Jimmy is 36. Which is correct?

**A.—When Jimmy celebrated his birthday at his training camp at the Golfmore Country Club recently, he said he was 31. But he was born in 1905, which makes his age 32. That is correct.**

Arthur Ziminsky, Milwaukee, Wis.

Q.—What is the best rub down? I would like one that doesn't irritate the skin.

**A.—The one I use is Athleto, a splendid rub down that is neither irritating nor has a strong odor. I have found it the ideal rub down, better than any I have used. I didn't know about it until recently when it was called to my attention in a RING "ad." I have been using it ever since following any strenuous exercises. I can heartily recommend it to RING readers. Boxers and wrestlers, in particular, will find it an excellent rub down, soothing and beneficial.**

Thomas Horan, Philadelphia, Pa.

Q.—In making a fist, is it proper to place the thumb on top of the first finger?

**A.—No. You'll find this fully explained in "How to Box." Close your four fingers tightly, doubling the fingers into the palm of your hand, and bend the first joint of your thumb across the back of the second bone of the first two fingers. That gives you security against a possible fracture of the thumb.**

Gene Arlin, Philadelphia, Pa.

Q.—In limbering up exercises, on what should I lay most stress?

**A.—On abdominal exercises to get the most benefit out of your workout, use all kinds of exercises in which there is body bending to strengthen the muscles of the abdomen. Side stretching is also excellent.**

No letters will be answered by mail unless a self-addressed, stamped envelope is enclosed.

Michael Foster, Kansas City, Mo.

Q.—I have tried hard to master light bag punching but cannot make any headway. Can you inform me what is wrong with me?

**A.—No, I cannot unless I see you in action. The secret of light bag punching is two fold—getting the bag the proper height and proper timing. The bag should be about on a level with your chin so that you can hit straight and without looping your punch. Constant practice is necessary with straight out punching until such time as you are able to gauge the return of the ball and pace yourself accordingly.**

**Get the latest revised edition of "Training for Boxing" and you'll find a chapter highly illustrated on "Bag Punching."**

Ralph J. Falvo, Hawaii

Q.—I would like to know if Baby Arizmendi ever was the featherweight champion, and if so, what year?

**A.—Arizmendi won the New York State Featherweight Title in 1933 when he defeated Mike Belloise but his claims were given little recognition as Freddy Miller was the rightful champion at that time.**

RING Reader, Springfield, Vt.

Q.—What were Tommy Farr's most important bouts to date and how did he come out in them?

**A.—Max Baer, Bob Olin, Tommy Loughran and Walter Neusel were the leading opponents that Farr faced. He whipped Baer, Olin, Loughran and kayoed Neusel in three rounds.**

Mike Consello, Milwaukee, Wis.

Q.—When Bob Fitzsimmons and Peter Maher met at Langtry, was that fight for the championship?

**A.—No. At the time, Corbett had not fought for several years except in a four round draw with Tom Sharkey at the Woodward Pavilion of San Francisco and an exhibition for the movies against Peter Courtney in Edison's laboratory at East Orange, N. J., and Fitz, finding it impossible to get Corbett into the ring, claimed the title. Corbett, in turn, to avoid Fitz, had announced his retirement and "passed" the title to Peter Maher. Of course this was all tommyrot, and no one but Corbett and Maher took it seriously.**

**Hence when Fitz knocked out Maher in one round at Langtry—in fact, one punch—the Cornishman claimed the world honors. That fight took place on February 21, 1896 but it was not until St. Patrick's Day of the following year that Fitz actually clinched the world honors when he knocked out Corbett with the famed solar plexus punch at Carson City, Nevada.**

Dick Miller, Spencer, Iowa

Q.—I am 17 years old, 5 feet 5½ inches tall and weigh 120 pounds. Can you give me any idea as to my size at the age of 21?

**A.—You will possibly reach the 5 feet 9 inch mark and scale between 145 to 150 pounds.**

C. I. Arnheim, Brooklyn, N. Y.

Q.—I wish to obtain an A.A.U. boxing card to take part in amateur boxing. Where can I obtain same? What are the requirements? I wear glasses, have weak eyes. Is it possible to obtain an A.A.U. card with same? What has happened to Art Lasky? Will I ever be a heavyweight? I am 18 years old, weight 140 pounds.

**A.—You can obtain a card at the A.A.U. office, 291 Broadway, N.Y.C. You will be subjected to a physical examination and it is inadvisable to begin boxing with that handicap. Lasky has fully recovered his eyesight but cannot box any longer. You will probably reach the middleweight measurements but hardly that of a heavyweight.**

RING Reader, Australia

Q.—Could you please tell me the height and weight of Braddock, Baer and Schmeling?

**A.—Braddock 6 feet 3 inches, weight 197. Baer is 6 feet 2 1/2 inches and weighs 210. Schmeling is 6 feet 1 inch and weighs 192 pounds.**

"Cyclone" Thompson, Dallas, Texas

Q.—Is it true that Jem Mace fought a draw of only one round that lasted more than an hour? Could such a thing be possible?

**A.—Yes, it was possible in the bare-knuckle days when they fought under the London Prize Ring rules which stipulated that a round lasted until one of the contestants went down. On May 24, 1866, Mace clashed with Joe Goss at Longfield Court and after the bout had gone an hour and five minutes with neither taking a fall, the bout was declared a draw. A few months later, Mace beat Goss in 21 rounds lasting 31 minutes. They fought in a 16-foot ring near London.**

De Vdatte, Danilo Revuelta Ortez

Q.—In your Universal Boxing Course, advertised in THE RING, do you have any Spanish translations of this course?

**A.—No. Only in the English language.**

Segundo Valente, Buenos Aires, Argentina

Q.—Do you sell any back copies of THE RING, and if so, what is the price of them?

**A.—Back numbers of THE RING can be obtained if they are in stock. The price varies from 25 cents for the current years to 60 cents for much earlier issues.**

Felix Marino, Detroit, Mich.

Q.—What were some of the plays in which James J. Corbett appeared?

**A.—He made his theatrical debut in "Sport McAllister" at the Bijou of New York on June 26, 1892. Then he opened in "Gentleman Jack" at Elizabeth, N. J., on October 3, 1892. Later he appeared in "The Cadet" and several other plays.**

# Comeback Not Easy

boys from all over France had competed, but had to postpone the trip until the fall because of the postponement of the Schmeling-Louis bout, will bring back from Paris, England and Ireland the best heavyweights of those countries to compete against our best heavyweight novices.

So you see that Louis' defeat will have nothing to do with my tournaments. They will go on in the hopes that some day I'll uncover from among the army of competitors from all over the world, at least one real prospect that will pay me for all the trouble I've gone through to help boxing with my tournaments.

When Nat goes abroad, he'll attend the Paris, British and Irish one-night finals and select the boys who will make the trip to America for me.

# Movies and Johnson

## Schmeling Tells How He Developed Idea That Louis' Stance Made Negro Easy For Righthander

THERE is no doubt in my mind that, having knocked out the great Joe Louis, whom so many experts had called even greater than Jack Dempsey, I am destined to be the first man to regain the world's heavyweight championship. To my mind, I never should have lost the title when I did. But there is no use in raking up old stories and old probabilities. Let us confine ourselves to the glorious present, with its glorious developments.

The editor of THE RING Magazine has asked me to tell my ideas and reactions on the Louis fight, and to make you acquainted with the various reasons underlying the so-called upset—the defeat of the negro.

First let me say that this is not an article composed of boasting. The Louis fight was the most severe test of my career in the ring. Joe has tremendous possibilities. He has much to learn, especially as regards stopping a righthand punch. If he will disregard his defeat, pick up more courage than ever and set himself to perfecting those points which I exposed as weak, he will come back a very formidable contender.

If Louis worries over his defeat or his friends give him shabby treatment, he never will be good again. He might take heart from my own experience. No matter what setbacks I got—and the Philadelphia fight with Hamas was a discouraging one—I never listened to any analysis of myself and I never lost faith in Schmeling.

I knew that a strong resolution is the greatest asset in the ring, and I am confident that the title will be mine again. Louis must make up his mind that he is a great fighter, and then he must correct those things which I showed up as bars to his being a great fighter.

* * *

I SAY that I did not listen to analysis of myself as a fighter. Please do not get from this the idea that I had what you Americans call the swelled head and that I did not care to learn about myself. What I mean is that I was not going to let anybody run down Max Schmeling to Max Schmeling.

Before I go into discussion of the Louis fight, let me tell you that one of the things too much neglected in fight preparation is the motion picture.

The motion picture affords a great chance to the boxer to study the fine points of other fighters—of acknowledged masters. It also gives you a chance to study the weak points of your future opponent.

Louis had a fight with Paulino. I knew Paulino had a good right hand. I wanted to see how Louis reacted to it. That fight, through the pictures, taught me considerable. I cannot recommend the use of pictures too highly to other boxers.

Now, there is another thing I would like to talk about. In the July issue of THE RING, there was a story by Jack Johnson, maybe the greatest defensive fighter we ever have had, and certainly a master.

Johnson is an honest critic. Johnson is a negro. You

might have expected him to go crazy about Louis. So many whites did so. But Johnson saw Louis with the expert eye of a man who knew a lot about fighting.

Johnson criticized Louis's style. He said that with his peculiar side stance, Louis would be easy to hit for a man who had a good right and the faculty to study the thing out.

* * *

WELL, I read THE RING. The article struck me as being just what I had studied out for myself. I discussed it with Max Machon, my trainer. I said to Max, Johnson has an important message in this story. I know that the way Louis stands, I will not find it difficult to hit him with my right by crossing the punch over the negro's left as he shoots it from that sideways stance.

With this discovery I worked hard at Napanoch, and it turned out splendidly.

You know, when Louis misses a punch he is off balance. The Paulino fight showed that. Johnson's article verified my impression.

I worked out all these problems and they did a remarkable thing for my morale as well as my technical preparation for the fight. I knew I had him. I knew that when we weighed in. When I laughed and joked at that time, I did not put on an act. I never was so sure of a thing in my life, as I was that I had the secret of Louis's weakness and the secret of how to win from him. Louis said, "What is that guy joking about?" You know, when he said that he was worried. I sensed it. I said to myself, "Max, this man is afraid of you."

You know, in the fourth round I knew I had the fight. I could feel Louis wilting under my gloves. He was taking a beating mentally and physically. After all, in spite of all the panegyrics over him, he is not a very experienced fighter and he is only twenty-two years old.

* * *

WHEN I landed in New York for the fight, I said to the reporters that while money was a useful thing, and very necessary, indeed, I would not have come just for the money—that I had made the trip with the intention of beating Louis and regaining the title.

You know, I got some terrible writeups that day and the next. I was ridiculed. The writers seemed to think I would not last two or three rounds and that financial necessity had driven me to possible suicide. But when I said that I had come not alone for money but for victory, I was in absolute earnest.

Now I have shown that what I said was true, and that my ambition to be the first to regain the title is likely to be realized. I say this with no idea of calling Mr. Braddock a poor champion. Only too well do I know that your Mr. Braddock is a clever man and a great fighter. I know how, out of necessity, he fought back from terrible poverty to get the Baer fight—and the title. I am not trying to give the impression that Braddock is

# Article Aided Max

By

MAX SCHMELING

what you call a cheap champion. But I will beat him.

When I won the heavyweight championship, Nat Fleischer, editor and publisher of THE RING Magazine, gave to me a handsome belt. I also got a belt from the National Boxing Association. It was wonderful. I have these belts in my trophy room in my place in Germany, and no visitor leaves without seeing these belts. I intend to add to them another belt, because Mr. Fleischer told me before I left New York that if I did win from Braddock, he would give me another and more splendid trophy. Mr. Fleischer, please put in an order for that belt now because I am going to keep you to your word.

Not only that. I think that when I fight Braddock, I will go into the ring the favorite.

\* \* \*

**B**UT to go back to the Louis fight. You know, the day after the fight some motion picture people came to my room and they wanted me to pose for pictures and say something about the fight.

They gave me some written questions to answer, and had I answered them, I would have made a conceited fool out of myself. They asked me if the foul punch hurt me and if Louis hit me low on purpose. I refused because only a coward would hit foul on purpose, and after my fight with him I can tell you decisively that this negro certainly is far from a coward.

Those movie people gave me other questions to answer, and they all were in bad taste. Finally, Mr. Fleischer wrote out some more questions to be accepted by myself, and I very gladly and willingly replied over the movietone.

The first question was: What were my reactions in the first three rounds of the fight?

I replied, "After the first round I had no doubts. I could read every move Louis was about to make."

The second question was; Did you at any time think that Louis was dangerous?

I said, "Surely I did. I regarded him as very dangerous even when he was just about to be knocked out. I was taking no chances on a cross-up. I knew if he could get set to hit me right I would be hurt badly."

In this connection I want to say that because I knew

*The smile of a victor. Max Schmeling, happy over his defeat of the hitherto invincible Brown Bomber.*

Louis to be very dangerous at all times, I did not care to press my advantage in the early rounds.

\* \* \*

**S**OME of the writers said the next day that Jack Dempsey would have followed up my advantage in the fourth round and ended the fight then and there.

Well, that may be so. Dempsey was a wonderful fighter. But may I not at this time say that every boxing writer in America had warned me that Louis was a superman—that he was a killer, that nobody could hope to stand up against him? Did not even the experts who took me to task for not finishing Louis in the fourth warn me before the fight—day after day—that I would be very fortunate to last two rounds with the negro?

Now, having seen and

# Movies and Johnson Article Aided Max

read and taken heed, why should I have been criticized for having believed all these warnings to have been the truth, and taken the proper precautions? Surely, we should have some consistency.

Let me now analyze Joe Louis as a fighter. He can be hit with a right hand. That is sure. I proved it.

He has the most beautiful left jab I ever have seen. It is artistic, perfect.

He has no best punch. His straight left, which he planted often in my face, and his good right, which he caught me with on several occasions to my discomfort, are on a par.

Louis hits harder than any other fighter I have met. He always is dangerous.

Now I will sit back for a while and congratulate myself that neither the left nor the right got me down, and that now nothing can stand in my way to become the champion again.

# HALL OF FAME
## *Jack Johnson*

## JACK JOHNSON

JACK JOHNSON was the first Negro to hold the world heavyweight championship. He was born March 31, 1878, in Galveston, Texas. Johnson began his career in 1899 and fought for twenty-seven years, until 1926.

Known as "Li'l Artha," he is considered one of the finest defensive boxers of all time. He won the world heavyweight title from Tommy Burns on December 26, 1908 in Sydney, Australia, the police stopping the bout in the fourteenth round when Burns was a badly beaten fighter. The fight grossed the then startling figure of $131,000.

The following year, in 1909, Johnson defended the title against Stanley Ketchel, middleweight champion. In the twelfth round Ketchel dropped Johnson and the latter quickly got up and knocked out the middleweight king.

On July 4, 1910, Jim Jeffries came out of a six year retirement to try to regain the heavyweight title at Reno, Nevada, but Johnson easily knocked him out in fifteen rounds.

He successfully defended his title against Jim Flynn in 1912 and then went to Europe, where he remained for several years. During that time he took on Andre Spoul and Frank Moran in title bouts and won.

Johnson lost the title when he was knocked out by Jess Willard in twenty-six rounds on June 27, 1914 in Havana, Cuba. For the remainder of his career he fought mainly in Spain and Mexico and remained unbeaten.

# PITTSBURGH FISTIC STAR

*Billy Conn, Conqueror of Teddy Yarosz, Risko, and Dundee,*
*Rates High in the Middleweight Ranks*

### By PAUL BEELER

HIS last five fights grossed sixty thousand dollars. During the past six months he has decisively licked three former world's middleweight champions. He is only nineteen years old. His name is Billy Conn, and he is eminently worthy to carry on Pittsburgh's tradition as the home of great middleweights.

The most skeptical of critics have been won over. They are unanimous in stating that Conn will be the Smoky City's fifth world's champion in the middleweight division, a fighter who is more than likely to be even greater than the other four men who wore the 160-pound toga—Frank Klaus, George Chip, Harry Greb and Teddy Yarosz.

Just what sort of a lad is this Conn? Who is this new sensation in the fistic world?

He was born and raised in Pittsburgh's East End. His father was born and raised in the same neighborhood. Billy is named for his dad and is the oldest of five children. Billy Conn, Sr., is of Irish descent, and Billy, Jr.'s, mother was born in Ireland, which makes the youngster one of those rare specimens of modern fisticuffs, a genuine, dyed-in-the-wool, fighting Irishman.

\* \* \*

THE story of Billy Conn's rise in the fight game reads like a piece of fiction. From the time Billy left Sacred Heart School out on Center Avenue in the East Liberty section of Pittsburgh, boxing was his first love. He hung around the historic Lyceum Gymnasium day after day, watched the fighters train, and occasionally put on the gloves with some of the boys in training there.

One afternoon, he approached Johnny Ray, the greatest lightweight ever turned out in Pittsburgh, and told him he would like to be a fighter. "O.K., kid, put 'em on and get in there and I'll look you over," was the answer.

Billy obliged and from then on, there came about one of the greatest combinations in the boxing game. Johnny Ray, the astute, cagy, clever master boxer, and the ambitious, husky, brainy kid who absorbed every iota of knowledge passed on to him, did what he was told and literally lived and dreamed boxing twenty-four hours a day.

Johnny Ray developed his pupil systematically. "From the very first time I saw Billy hold up his hands, I knew he was going to be a great fighter," was Ray's comment the other day. "I never allowed him to fight as an amateur. He spent two years in the gymnasium, doing what I told him, and he has been thoroughly grounded in every fundamental of boxing. When I thought he was ready, he was started against the proper kind of opposition and gradually brought along, meeting better opponents each time, until he has faced them all in his class with results that are now a matter of record."

*Billy Conn, Pittsburgh middleweight, who is contender for world title.*

Billy Conn is the best managed fighter in the game. Johnny Ray handles the fighting end of the business and what Johnny doesn't know about boxing has never been discovered. John McGarvey, for years Pittsburgh's outstanding promoter, the man who operated fifteen years without a single losing show, and who knows all there is to know about the financial end of the fistic game, handles Conn's business.

\* \* \*

LET'S examine the young man's record, for in the last analysis, the book is the answer to any fighter. Who has he fought and who has he beaten?

After being carefully nursed along during 1935, boxing a lot of "Leftover McSweeneys" and others of that caliber, with an occasional adverse decision here and there, but with the win side of the ledger predominating, Conn was turned loose last year. Big game was the policy of the Ray-McGarvey company, and from the first day of January, 1936, up to the writing of this article, Billy Conn has won every fight in which he has engaged.

He was fed stiffer opposition as he went along. The opponents kept getting tougher and tougher, but Billy answered every question with a triumph.

Coming down the stretch in the waning days of 1936, Fritzie Zivic was matched with the East End Irishman. The fight was a local "natural." Duquesne Garden was jammed to the doors and the police had to battle the crowd who tried to storm the doors after the house was sold out. Conn took down the verdict after a gruelling battle.

Starting out in 1937, Conn was matched with the first of three former world's middleweight champions, Eddie (Babe) Risko. Risko had just lost a close one to Freddie Steele and the fans and newspapers in Pittsburgh were loud in their denunciation of what they considered a bad bit of matchmaking on the part of Messrs. McGarvey and Ray. "Billy will be killed! He won't last a round! Risko's too big and strong! You're ruining a great prospect!" were the blasts fired at the Conn directors.

Billy won all the way against Risko, made every post a winning one, and came down through the tenth round under wraps.

\* \* \*

TO give the fans and experts more cause for concern, Conn was then matched with Vince Dundee, ex-champ of the 160-pound class, who was in the midst of an impressive comeback campaign. The result was the same as in the Risko fight. Billy was out in front from gong to gong, made Dundee fight the way he wanted him to, and won going away. The sharpshooters took an awful licking in this one, with Billy on the short end.

Oscar Rankins, the rugged, hard-hitting red-headed Californian, who had won himself a great

*After beating three former world champions, nineteen-year-old Conn has his sights set on Freddie Steele.*

# Pittsburgh Fistic Star

big spot in the hearts of local fans by his deadly hitting prowess, was next in line. Rankins knocked Conn down in the second round with a sock on the chin that would have felled a horse. It was right here that Billy answered the question, "Can he take it?" He did. He took nine, got up and proceeded to give Mr. Rankins a boxing lesson for the remainder of the engagement.

Following the Rankins bout, the heat was on for a fight between Conn and Teddy Yarosz. Teddy had held the middleweight title. For years, he had been the prize box office attraction in Pittsburgh. No matter who Ted fought, the fans flocked to the purchase window and the Polish kid, who was born on the North Side, had long been the answer to every promoter's prayer.

Teddy had fully recovered from the knee injury that cost him the championship. He had stepped into Madison Square Garden and whipped Solly Krieger, Hebrew windmill and pride of Gotham. He went into Boston, Lou Brouillard's own backyard, and decisively trimmed the stocky Frenchman,

knocking him clear out of the ring in the tenth round. Yarosz was definitely and positively back! He was a fourteen-carat cinch to fight Steele for the title he formerly held, he was rated Number 1 challenger and, under the capable training of Ray Arcel, was in the greatest condition of his entire career.

The set-up was perfect. Two local boys, both middleweights, in the middleweight capital of the world, each with thousands of followers, one Polish and one Irish.

The boys met at Forbes Field, June 30, and the gate grossed close to $30,000. The result was the same as in all of Conn's previous fights. Billy was awarded the decision and completed his third victory over ex-champions of the middleweight class. That's all there was to lick. There aren't any more former middleweight champions hanging around, or Conn would be right on their tails.

\* \* \*

*W*HAT is Conn's style of fighting? He is the perfect fighter. In other words, he is a fighter's fighter. He does everything right. His boxing is O.K. He makes no mistakes, fights strictly according to Hoyle and the teachings of Johnny Ray, and has the finest defense of any boxer in the game, at any weight.

His left jab and hook are beautiful to watch, his right to the body carries plenty of authority and he is that rare combination, a great boxer who is, at the same time, aggressive. Billy carries the fight to his opponent and his only apparent weakness is an inclination to lose his head and "pitch" when hit hard by his opponent.

The plans for the future involve only one objective, a crack at Freddie Steele and the middleweight title. The match will draw more in Pittsburgh than anywhere else in the country. The Steel City is "middleweight minded" and the boys will cut up plenty of money if the bout is held here during the present season.

Billy Conn has the frame to grow into a light-heavyweight and probably a heavyweight. He has every qualification to get to the top in any division in which he fights. As a matter of fact, the heavier classes would be softer for Billy than the middleweight division, as his boxing ability would carry him over the slower moving big fellows with ease.

*Referee Houck steps in before classy Billy Conn can do any more damage to Gus Dorazio.*

# "What For That Fat Little Man Call Me a Bum?"

THE RING'S Globe Trotter brings you the news and the oddities of the game. To be sure, there are many oddities. For example, Tony Galento. The sport seems to have a yen for the odd rather than the mechanically perfect. That appears to explain the Galento situation.

The writer has just returned to New York from a swing through the South and into Texas and Oklahoma. He found there—not keen enthusiasm over Joe Louis as the heavyweight champion, but laughing speculation over Two-Ton Tony, and the hope that he would be able to make a real contest of his match with Louis in New York.

"Wouldn't it be funny if this fat-belly knocked Joe loose from the title!" sums up the conversation we heard on the subject.

Not that anybody really felt Galento could beat Louis, or even give the champion a respectable contest.

But in boxing, the sentiment of the public usually is with the underdog. That is especially true in this time, when the country—yes, the whole world—is so full of underdogs. And then, there is another vital factor.

*Joe Louis, angered by Galento's reference to the champ as a bum, demanded that his managers get Two-Ton Tony as an opponent. That's why the match was made.*

Louis is a fine fighter. It may be that after he has finished, his name will be set down among the great champions. But right now he is not what you could call a popular titleholder. He does nothing to make himself popular. He trains, he fights, he goes back into his shell, and then there is another match, and the newsreels show Joe doing something unspectacular, saying next to nothing, and not looking especially clever or alert while saying it.

The Black-Roxborough combination has not sold Joe Louis to the American public as a colorful fighter, as a dramatic champion, as a man loaded with human interest. This failure traces to the type of material with which they have to work.

* * *

LET us go back a way. John Lawrence Sullivan. A great fighter, but perhaps a greater figure than he deserved to be rated. Why? Because he had something out of the ring. John L. drank a lot. But he always was doing something. He always was moving among the people.

"Set them up for the house!" shouted Sullivan, and the populace went wild. He went around the country meeting all comers, he was close to the people, he did some "acting" on the stage, he always was making stories for the lads of the press.

Then came Jim Corbett. A smiling figure, a boon to the sport, a gentleman, a scholar, a bank clerk with gloves on. He was clever, skilled in handling not only fighters but the public. He was sure of himself, a suave man, an easy talker—a fine actor, too. He, truly, was a colorful champion.

After Corbett, Bob Fitzsimmons. The one-time blacksmith with the solar plexus punch. Ruby Robert. His actions, his speech, his love of fun and practical jokes—yes, and his tremendous hitting power, especially considering his freak build below the waist—yes, put him down among the drama guys.

Jim Jeffries, the Boilermaker, and his crouch. Well, here the situation begins to break down a little. Jeff was a great fighter, in a plodding sort of way, but he was not a really colorful champion until, in the sere and the yellow, he entered the ring with Jack Johnson in Reno. Then the drama slopped over, and Jim went down in the books as a Hollow Shell.

* * *

JACK JOHNSON. With the great smile. With the great defensive skill. With his goings on in this country, his forced shipment to countries abroad, his dashing about in bizarre cars, the Galveston roustabout, the talk of many continents. Yes, Jack was colorful.

Then Jess Willard. No, not colorful, at all, except for his size.

After Jess the human interest angle took a tremendous jump. Jack Dempsey, the Manassa Mauler, became the champion of the world. Dempsey, who had hopped freights, who had been a harvest hand, a miner—king of them all.

From the start, Dempsey made himself a dramatic, colorful fighter. The picture into which he went hurtling with his victory over Willard in Toledo in 1919 was conducive to the development of a great figure, if only he had the personality to

## Tony's Beer-Hoisting Picture and Louis' Question Made Galento Match for World's Heavyweight Championship

### By DANIEL M. DANIEL

*Two-Ton Tony Galento, the beer-guzzler from New Jersey.*

help. Jack had all of that. Tex Rickard, a great promoter, and the era of easy money and million dollar gates assisted nobly.

Dempsey, Gene Tunney, the Marine who was to marry an heiress—colorful, certainly. Jack Sharkey and Max Schmeling—well, not so hot. Carnera—colorful because of his size. Max Baer had the grandest chance of all, but he did not like to fight.

And so on we came to Jim Braddock, who sent the drama of the heavyweight championship skyrocketing. The man who had been a janitor, the man who had gone on relief, rose to the pinnacle. One of the greatest stories in the history of the ring.

Then Joe Louis. Joe slept, he read the funnies, then he knocked out somebody, and the cycle was started all over again. Sleep, the funnies, the phonograph—and a fight and sleep once more.

\* \* \*

IN the Louis-Galento match there is a multiplicity of interesting angles. For example, Joe's real hate of the Two-Ton guy. Galento, eager to develop publicity, urged on by one of the cleverest buildup organizations in the history of the ring, derided himself, but dragged Louis and all the other fighters into his derision. Said Louis:

**"What for that fat little man want to call me a bum?"**

That was one of the most valuable sentences in all the annals of pugilism. It set up a personal angle, which is a very rare thing in the ring today.

We of a skeptical age do not know how much of that personal antagonism of the old days really was on the level. Corbett's offer to fight Fitz in the bar at Green's Hotel in Philadelphia; Sullivan's whippersnapper vendetta with Corbett, and some of those other vendettas of the long ago read fine, but we sometimes think they were products of the early ballyhoo factory.

But in the Louis-Galento situation there is animus. Not on the part of Galento. We doubt if he could harbor real animus against anybody, as he is one of the zaniest of the ring zanies—a cap-and-bells guy wandered into the squared circle, a court jester, whose very appearance is a laugh. Certainly nobody will set up Tony as a model for the 1939 Gladiator. He is fat and pudgy, his language is fun and frolic and he will do anything to get publicity.

Only recently there was shown around the country a newsreel in which Galento dressed as a Spanish caballero. He strummed a gee-tar; he even went so far as to attempt to sing. The newsreel was funny. It helped along the buildup, the question:

"Can this bird really fight?"

\* \* \*

THE rise of Galento from nothing at all to a match for the world's heavyweight championship has many elements which are even more dramatic, certainly more incredible, than those which stood out in the development of Jim Braddock into Baer's successor.

Galento himself admits he is no great fighter. But he insists on painting every other heavyweight with the same brush.

Two-Ton Tony is no recent development. He has been in and out of the ring for the last twelve years.

Jack Dempsey had him, and could not see any material with which to work even in a picture which begged for human interest in the heavyweight class. Jack laughs at the whole thing, and, of course, derides the idea that Galento can fight.

"Galento goes around telling folks that I threw him over be-

cause he would not sell my whisky," chuckles Dempsey. "Well, that's plain bunk. I just could not see in Galento what other people appear to have discovered in him."

But—Jack still insists Galento is no scrapper. But millions of people think he is a fighter. They say he never has been knocked unconscious, that he is strong as a bull, can take it and dish it out. Behind it all is the human appeal, though. Human appeal rather than the appeal of a true fighter.

Galento got started as a bad fighter. He became a bouncer in a Newark place. He went back to fighting, then he retired. Galento could see little in himself, others saw less. But then clever men got hold of the Italian. Clever men. They saw a world steeped in worry and trouble seeking something or some one for a big laugh. They saw folks tired of the humdrum and the commonplace. They saw Galento—and got an idea.

\* \* \*

YOU will recollect how Galento broke into the New York papers. Pictures showing the fat man hoisting big steins of beer in his café in Newark.

Two-Ton became the merry Falstaff of the boxing ring. Managing editors saw those beer hoistings. They asked, "Whoinell is this bird?" Thy called in their sports editors and asked, "How come we did not think of this first?"

Said the S.E.: "Why, Mr. Gimfuss, this guy is a stumblebum. He can't fight a lick. It's all a gag."

Said the M.E.: "It may be a gag, but it's good stuff. Think up some variation of this, and send over a cameraman."

The cameramen flocked to Galento's place. So did the public. Business boomed. The clever men behind Tony developed their idea as they went along. Success came faster, bigger, than they ever had dreamed.

Into the situation pranced the nimble and adroit brain of Harry Mendel, whose part in the buildup has been ignored. Harry is a clever man who once was a sports writer in Newark. He became the aide of John Chapman, the mahout of the bike riding business. Harry handled fights from time to time, ran scraps in the old Velodrome in Newark.

# What For—

Well, Harry started to make Galento clever. Mendel wrote reams of snappy sayings, silly cracks, primordial philosophy and Rabelaisian riot, much of which found its way into the sports pages as having been uttered by the really slow-witted Galento.

"This guy certainly is funny," said the fans. The situation was cooking splendidly!

* * *

WHILE all this was going on in New Jersey, Joe Louis was reigning as heavyweight champion of the world. He was eating, sleeping, reading the funnies, and sleeping some more.

The public is not especially interested in the out-of-the-ring doings of a fighter who eats, sleeps and reads the funnies. It admires skill in the ring, but it wants a fillip to this mechanical adroitness. In short, it got a little tired of the non-acting champion and was all too eager to grasp at the comedy-relief which emanated from the Association for the Forcing of a Galento Match on Louis.

Galento kept pushing over third raters —and making wise cracks out of the brain of Harry Mendel.

The New York Boxing Commission had suspended Galento for those beer hoisting pictures. This august body, sometimes serene in its mental lucubrations, decided that a guy like Galento, who will pose for beer hoisting pictures, is not a good example to the growing American boy.

Into the picture came another factor, about which little is said. Louis is the second Negro heavyweight champion. The white race arrogates unto itself too many superlatives in a ring which has developed so many great Negro fighters, and which today has its Henry Armstrong in addition to Louis.

The promoters will tell you that it is not good for the heavyweight class to have a Negro champion, that too many folks do not like to see a Negro holding the title.

Personally, we think that is mainly hooey. Folks will go to see a fighter no matter what color his skin may be, just so long as he can fight. But we cannot overlook the importance of the fact that Louis is a Negro in the growth of the Galento buildup.

* * *

IT has been the contention of this magazine that Galento has not shown enough fighting skill and a record sufficiently impressive to warrant his being matched with Joe Louis.

It has been the contention that Galento has not done anything to merit a big outdoor fight with Louis, at big, outdoor prices.

But the public seems to want this fight, even if it does go only two rounds. The building up process has worked so well. And there is another angle.

The fight fan says: There should be a Louis fight this Summer. If it isn't Galento, it should be Nova. He is not ready, and we don't want to kill off a potential champion.

If it isn't Galento, it should be Baer. And he got such a plastering from Joe that the fans would not go for it again. Besides, we need Baer for Nova.

If it isn't Galento, should it be Farr? No. Farr has been licked by everybody, Nova included—and by Louis, as well.

If it isn't Galento, it would be some other fighter who would not last any longer than Two-Ton. Galento at least would inject some fun into a too-serious picture.

So you have the New York commission relenting. You have Mike Jacobs changing his mind—that is, if he really did not have the Galento match in his noggin all the time. You have the public accepting, you have the Louis vendetta angle, you have the results of perhaps the most astonishing ballyhoo in the entire history of the knuckle industry.

And so we say, if that's the way it is, let's get it over with!

* * *

AS a matter of fact, is this Galento match so much worse, let us say, than the Dempsey affair with Georges Carpentier?

The Gallic Orchid Man was much too small and light for Jack. But Rickard saw the big chance. Carpentier had fought in the World War. The memories of that struggle were fresh in the public mind.

So Carp was built up into a great opponent for the American mauler. It was the Battle of the Century.

Carpentier was hidden away at Manhasset, Long Island, in a training camp which was closed to the writers. The wily Jack Curley, handling the Frenchman, knew that if the experts glimpsed the Orchid Man in action and knew he scaled little more than 165 pounds, they would deride the match into a flop.

So reams and reams of ballyhoo were unfurled. To be sure, Carp hit Jack once, pretty hard. But just once. It was no fight; over in three heats. Could have been over in the first but Tex had begged Dempsey to carry the Orchid Man and give the fans a little run for their dough.

Yes, the Association for the Construction of Galento certainly can point the finger at fistic history. And so we will let Time and the Destinies—and Faith, Hope and Charity, as well—handle this situation as Galento hoists more beer and the slow-thinking Joe Louis asks again:

**"What for that fat little man want to call me a bum?"**

*Dr. William Walker examines Louis as challenger Galento looks on. Both fighters were pronounced fit for their fight.*

# The Mighty Atom

## By R. B. COZENS

### (By Special Correspondence from Sussex, England)

IF you are one of those little sawed-off guys, five feet nothing, with arms and legs like broomsticks, don't get that inferiority complex, don't get scared and envious of your lusty brethren, the men with brawn and muscle. Just listen to this story about a little chap who conquered the world. Let me present you, Jimmy Wilde.

Jimmy Wilde was the smallest fighter who ever stepped inside a British ring, BUT HE WAS THE BEST. No other fighter born in Great Britain has such a splendid record as THE TERROR FROM TYLORSTOWN.

Including fights in boxing booths, Jimmy Wilde made 864 appearances in the ring, and only lost four bouts in his whole career. In return fights, he reversed two of these decisions.

When he was flyweight champion of the world, Jimmy never weighed more than 100 pounds. In every contest, except one, Jimmy had to give away weight, and remember, he fought the best flyweights and bantams in the world.

Maybe you would be interested in the physical measurements of this Little Marvel, the tiny mite with a hammer in each glove. Here they are:

Height 5 feet 2½ inches; reach 68 inches; chest (normal) 32½ inches; chest (expanded) 34½ inches; neck 12¾ inches; thigh 15½ inches; waist 22 inches; calf 10¼ inches; ankle 8¼ inches; biceps 10¾ inches; forearm 10¾ inches; wrist 6½ inches.

If you study these measurements, you sure will agree that so far as physique was concerned, Jimmy was the cat's whisker. His forearm was sizeable; he had a good reach for a flyweight, but gosh, there can't be many lads in the whole wide world who cannot give Jimmy plenty of inches.

Let me make it quite clear. Jimmy was tiny, but he was tough. Yes, sir. He never had a serious illness in his life. He had worked in the coal mines in Wales as a youth, where you must be tough to keep your job. Those thin arms and legs were like iron, he was always in training.

Yes, Jimmy was small, but he had a fighting heart second to none. He fought hard, he loved a fight, he gave no quarter, and he expected none. Jimmy always fought to the last gasp; he had the iron in his soul.

* * *

JIMMY WILDE was born at 8 Station Road, Pontygwaith, Tylorstown, Wales, in 1892. The son of a miner, he went into the mines with other boys.

Married at the early age of 18—(he has two sons who are about twice as big as their father)—he promised his wife that he would give up fighting. But the lure of the ring was too strong, and he was soon the greatest attraction in Jack Scarrott's boxing booth.

As a booth fighter, Jimmy used to take on men weighing as much as 12 stones, and the result was always the same. Spectators used to protest at Jimmy being matched with brawny 170-pounders, and I guess it must have been a strange sight to watch a weedy little fellow weighing about 90 pounds (Jimmy's weight in his

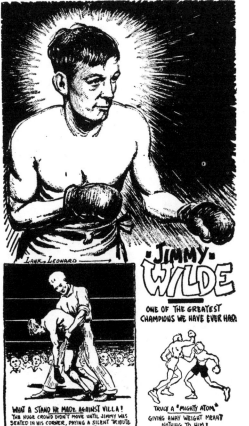

WHAT A STAND HE MADE AGAINST VILLA! THE HUGE CROWD DIDN'T MOVE UNTIL JIMMY WAS SEATED IN HIS CORNER, PAYING A SILENT TRIBUTE TO ONE OF ENGLAND'S BRAVEST HEARTS

JIMMY WILDE
ONE OF THE GREATEST CHAMPIONS WE HAVE EVER HAD.

TRULY A "MIGHTY ATOM" GIVING AWAY WEIGHT MEANT NOTHING TO HIM!

early days)—squaring up to a big-muscled miner nearly twice his weight. But the spectators never protested twice. Jack Scarrott used to offer the big fellow £1 if he could last three rounds, but nobody ever won that £1.

Jimmy first came into prominence in the professional ring in 1912 when he beat Billy Padden for the paperweight championship of England. He then proceeded to beat up all the small guys he could find. His first defeat was in 1915 when Tancy Lee, a dour little Scot, beat Jimmy in 17 rounds for the Flyweight Championship of Great Britain. Jimmy was suffering from a severe cold when he fought Lee and his backers and manager,

Ted Lewis, wanted him to call it off. Jimmy insisted on carrying on with the fight and experienced the bitterness of defeat.

Jimmy was always sure that he could lick Tancy Lee and a second battle took place in 1916. Jimmy was in great form on this occasion and he walloped Tancy all over the ring. In the 11th round, Tancy's seconds threw in the towel.

Prior to his second fight with Tancy Lee, Jimmy had won the Flyweight Championship with a spectacular victory over Joe Symonds who gave in after 12 smashing rounds.

Nineteen sixteen was Jimmy's lucky year, for it was then that he got on top of the world. Just before Christmas, he met the Zulu Kid (recognized as the flyweight champion of the U.S.A.) for the world title at the Holborn Stadium, London. Zulu Kid was clever, but Jimmy's terrific punching was too much for him, and he was knocked out in the 11th round.

* * *

IN 1918, a month after the Armistice, an Inter-Allied boxing tournament was held at the Royal Albert Hall, London, and in a three-round contest, Pal Moore, leading U.S.A. bantam, was given the decision over Jimmy after a sparkling scrap. The decision nearly caused a riot and a return contest was inevitable.

In 1919, C. B. Cochran promoted this "needle" fight at Olympia and Gene Corri was referee. The fight was fast and furious. Round after round was fought at a great pace, both men going all-out. In the 15th round Jimmy's nose came into contact with Pal's head, and the blood flowed from a severe cut. The last round provided the spectators with thrills galore and at the end Corri raised Jimmy's arm as the winner. A great fight.

In the same year, Jimmy outpointed Joe Lynch, who later became World Bantam Champion. They fought 15 rounds at the National Sporting Club, London. In fairness to Lynch it must be recorded that many thought the smart and likeable American was entitled to the decision.

Jimmy then went on tour in the U.S.A., where he took part in 11 contests and raked in a record pile of dough. He knocked out Mike Ertle in three rounds; Micky Russell in seven rounds; Bat Murray in eight rounds and again in two rounds, and Bobby Dyson in one round. He was given newspaper decisions over Johnny Asher, Patsy Wallace (twice), Frankie Mason and the

Zulu Kid, but lost a newspaper decision to Jack Sharkey. Contract difficulties prevented a return match with Sharkey.

Returning to Great Britain in 1920, Jimmy practically retired and did no fighting for seven months. He had beaten all the leading flyweights and most of the bantams, except Jack Sharkey. However, in January 1921 he was offered a contest with Pete Herman, ace American bantam, at the Royal Albert Hall, London, 20 rounds at 118 pounds.

Owing to a misunderstanding, Herman took the ring weighing about 121 pounds. Jimmy's manager, Ted Lewis, wanted to call the match off, as Herman was overweight and as strong as a featherweight. There was considerable argument, and the crowd got very restless. The fans had good reason for being in a bad temper, because a star preliminary bout between Battling Levinsky and Bombardier Billy Wells had been postponed owing to Levinsky having an injured hand.

The Prince of Wales (now the Duke of Windsor) was present, and stepped into the ring to make an appeal for order.

Notwithstanding this appeal, I fancy there would have been trouble if Jimmy had not sportingly agreed to see it through. But for once, Jimmy was not sure of success, because he insisted on the M.C. announcing to the great crowd that all bets were off. There was little in it during the first five rounds, but Pete was in great form and in the 17th round the referee stopped the fight and awarded the dicision to the American on a technical knockout.

Many people left the hall in tears, so great was the affection of the British sporting public for the Mighty Atom.

\* \* \*

*A*FTER this fight Jimmy decided to retire. He was nearly 30 years of age and had been fighting for 12 years. But Fate decided that Jimmy was to have one more scrap before he hung up his gloves, a fight that nearly cost him his life.

In June 1923, in New York City, Jimmy faced Pancho Villa, fierce little Filipino, for the world title. The little Welshman had received a tempting offer, and although he had been idle for so long, he was confident that no flyweight could rob him of his title.

Wilde's greatest stand, one that will never be forgotten by the throng that witnessed his downfall, was in his bout with Villa. Greater in defeat than ever he was in victory, was the phrase used by almost every sports writer who reported that battle.

The bravest little man who ever held a title in England, went down with flying colors in the seventh session, and not since the time that Battling Nelson was counted out on his feet in California, has a champion passed more gloriously. From the second round to the finish Wilde was badly whipped, yet Jimmy stood his ground and despite terrific punishment, remained game to the last, merciful interception by Referee Patsy Haley calling a halt to the proceedings.

A punch, landed on Wilde at the end of the second round after the bell had sounded, dropped Jimmy and it was the turning point of the battle. That blow ended whatever chances Wilde had against his aggressive brown opponent. It was a foul, and in England would have resulted in Villa's disqualification, but only a warning was administered by the referee in America. Jimmy had to be pushed out for the third round, and from then to the finish he took a severe beating.

*Pete Herman, who halted Wilde in England in seventeen rounds.*

Jimmy never recovered from that beating and never fought again.

\* \* \*

*J*UST a few more snapshots. In 1918 Wilde met the leading British featherweight, Joe Conn, at the Chelsea Football Ground, Stamford Bridge, London, in a 20-round contest. This was one of the greatest open-air fights ever staged in Britain.

Most of the wise boys thought that Jimmy was flying too high in tackling a first class feather. Conn was clever and had a real knockout punch. J. T. Hulls was the referee. Quite a lot of dough was wagered on the result, and the wiseacres opined that a good big man would always beat a good little man. The old saying is true, but the exception proves the rule, and Jimmy was the exception.

During the opening rounds, Conn boxed well at long range and Jimmy's lips and eye were cut. Many thought Jimmy was a beaten man.

Jack Goodwin, an old-time boxer and first class trainer, who trained Conn and was in his corner, has said that Wilde was licked by the fifth round, but Conn threw the fight away by over-confidence. Jimmy has stated that he knew he could not knock out a man like Conn in jig time and that his plan was to keep the fight going for several rounds, missing, and not punching with full force until Conn had weakened.

You can have it which way you like, but from the fifth round onwards, Conn spent a lot of time covering up, a rather peculiar procedure against a much smaller man. In round 10, Jimmy floored Conn six times and in the 12th round the fight was stopped after the Mighty Atom had punched his opponent all over the ring.

Just think of it, 100 pounds stopping 126 pounds, and the bigger fellow a top-notcher! In my opinion, this was Wilde's greatest performance.

In 1919 Jimmy had the unique experience of fighting a man smaller than himself. This was a French boy named Husson, who tipped the scales at 90 pounds. Husson was very speedy and elusive and for several rounds evaded Jimmy's attempts to land a K.O. The crowd was tickled at the spectacle and a wag advised Jimmy to get a butterfly-net. However, in the seventh round, the Welshman stopped the little tormenter with a dig in the stomach.

In 1916, the Mighty Atom paid a visit to Jack Scarrott's boxing booth and was offered £40 by genial Jack for an exhibition. In three and one-half hours Jimmy knocked out 19 opponents, all sizes, the majority in the first round. He then had a breather for half an hour and the booth was cleared.

A fresh audience was quickly forthcoming and in the next half hour Jimmy brought the fans to their feet with four more spectacular knockouts. As a knockout artist, he had no equal.

\* \* \*

*D*URING his career Jimmy fought the best. Make no mistake about that. If you inspect his record you will notice the names of many champions who had to yield to the little man from Wales. Here are some of them:

Young Jennings (ex-flyweight champion), Bouzoni, Young Baker, Alf Mansfield, Young Symonds (ex-bantam champion), Sid Smith (ex-flyweight champion), George Cullen, Johnny Best, George Clark, Johnny Hughes (ex-bantam champion), Tommy Harrison, Sam Kellar, Tommy

# The Mighty Atom

Noble (ex-bantam champion and well known in America), Art Edwards, Joe Lynch (ex-world bantam champion), Pal Moore and many others.

He never had any boxing tuition. He was just a natural fighter. His father-in-law, an old knuckle fighter, gave him much useful advice, but Jimmy was no orthodox or textbook boxer. His skill was acquired in the hard school of experience.

Where Jimmy differed from other fighters, was in his uncanny sense of anticipation and his ring generalship. Cool as an iceberg, Jimmy never allowed his opponent to fluster or confuse him. Wilde has more knockouts to his credit than any other flyweight or bantamweight the world has ever seen, and doctors and experts were always puzzled as to where Jimmy obtained his tremendous punching powers.

I think the secret lay in his wonderful timing. His hits were crisp and well directed, but that does not explain his great strength and stamina considering his low weight. Strength and stamina are not always associated with good muscular development. A man may be thin or even skinny, but that does not mean that he is a weakling. Fitzsimmons was lanky and wiry, but strong as an ox. Often outweighed, he proved far stronger than his opponent. In the same way, Wilde was tough, though a skinny lad.

\* \* \*

WITH tapering body and broad shoulders, with an anemic look that was quite deceiving, this little Welsh scrapper with his pallor and outward appearance of fragility, proved anything but a weakling when once in ring attire. Wilde's strength and his hitting power, considering his size and weight, were simply amazing. He was a highly skilled boxer and the power of his punches was almost magical.

Wilde always believed in avoiding any tactics that would reduce his stamina, hence instead of blocking the blows of his opponents, he had a knack of sidestepping an inch or two when the delivery was made and invariably got out of their range. The only time in his entire career where this method could not be used with effect was in his bout with Pancho Villa, but in that contest Jimmy met a boy who was just coming while Wilde, the champion, had already seen his best days.

His sense of distance was uncanny. He could stand within range of a blow when it started but when an opponent let it loose, a little jerk of the head or the body and the punch landed in space.

Always on his toes, his body executing a wavelike motion, his gloves resting on his hips without a semblance of a guard, his knees slightly bent, he proved a bewildering subject for any opponent. He always kept his man guessing, feinted him into knots and then connected with his terrific right, said to be the heaviest punch ever delivered by a fellow his weight. These are the qualities which Jimmy Wilde possessed and which enabled him to take his rank among the truly great—the Supermen.

Jimmy was a great fighter. He had the right mentality. He feared no man, and above all, he had an unshakeable confidence in himself, the sure sign of a real champion.

Jimmy was sure that he could lick anybody near his weight.

So remember, lads, even if you are small and thin, do not despair if you do not put on muscle and weight. Remember Jimmy Wilde, the greatest little fighter the world has ever seen, who was the idol of millions of men, women and children in Great Britain, the little fellow with the heart of a lion, the man who always fought against odds and came out on top.

Jimmy is alive and well today. He made quite a pile of money with his fists and was shrewd enough to provide for the future. He is president of the National Union of Boxers and has written a book entitled "Fighting Was My Business," a graphic account of his fighting career.

## RING NEWS FROM SOUTH AFRICA
### By BERT COHEN

THE Laurie Stevens-Phil Zwick encounter was unavoidably postponed as Zwick, suffering from a heavy cold, was unfit. Despite the postponement and a temperature of zero on the night of the fight, which was held in the open-air at Wanderers Stadium, a splendid crowd of nine thousand was present.

Zwick put up a courageous display but was outclassed by the Empire champ. Attacking from the start, Laurie was seldom in trouble and again displayed his amazing stamina by finishing as fast as he started.

Zwick provided the high light of the battle by dropping Stevens in the fifth with a corking right. Temporarily dazed, Stevens wisely took advantage of the count, rising only at eight. Zwick rushed in but the South African, fully recovered, drove him back with a ferocious body attack. Zwick took this, his solitary round, by only a shade. Of the remaining rounds, Stevens won seven, while two were even.

In the eighth, ninth and tenth, Lauie meted out terrific punishment, but the American, his face a gory mass, valiantly lasted out the scheduled ten rounds. Stevens was a clear victor on points, but Phil was a gallant loser. The large crowd left well satisfied by the boys' display. Weights: Stevens, 9 st. 9½ lbs.; Zwick, 9 st. 5½ lbs.

In the chief supporting bout, Dave Katzen, rising young fighter, wrested the South African bantamweight championship from Alec Knight. Though lacking Knight's punch, Katzen boxed with superb skill to win clearly. Watch out for this boy.

Les Van Rooyen, South African welter champ, boxed a draw with Len McLoughlin over six rounds; while Nick Swart (flyweight) shaded Scotty Fraser, also over six rounds.

Negotiations are still proceeding for a world's lightweight title match here in December.

The scheduled match between Laurie Stevens and Louis Botes, Natal lightweight champ, took place. Botes is a fighter of considerable experience, having fought some of the best men at his weight in England, while he has gone the full distance against Wesley Ramey and Aldo Spoldi. Nevertheless, he proved no match for the Empire champion, the ferocity of whose attack overwhelmed him. After the second round, Laurie scored almost at will and after Botes had been sent down to the canvas three times for long counts, the unequal contest was stopped in the fourth round. Weights: Stevens, 9 st. 9 lbs.; Botes, 9 st. 6½ lbs.

On the 24th of June, Stevens was married. His honeymoon embraces a tour of England, to be followed by a trip to U. S. A., where he will visit relatives in Los Angeles.

JOTTINGS—Willie Smith, the featherweight champ, fights Maurice Holtzer in Johannesburg on August 29 . . . . Freddie Miller sails shortly for the Union, He, too, will fight Smith . . . . Ben Foord, South African heavy, fights Jack Peterson next month for the Empire title . . . . The South African Olympic boxing team is: S. R. ("Robey") Leibbrandt, light-heavyweight; E. Peltz, middleweight; T. Hamilton-Brown, lightweight; Charlie Catterall (Empire champ.), featherweight; A. Hannan, bantamweight; A. Passmore, flyweight . . . . Watch out for them when the finals are fought.

# PRECIOUS SECONDS

### By CLARENCE GILLESPIE

A FEW weeks ago in Madison Square Garden, a large gathering of fight fans received the thrill that comes but seldom in boxing—that of a champion possessing extraordinary fighting qualities being sent to the canvas by the challenger. It was the fight between Henry Armstrong and Fritzie Zivic, in which the Pittsburgher gained the world welterweight crown by handing the title-holder a severe beating in the final sessions of their fifteen-round mill.

The fight was over. A new champion had been crowned. The crowd was making its exit from the House that Tex Built. Here and there, while the Garden help was trying to clear the building to close for the night, small gatherings stood discussing with a degree of fervidness the falling of a great title-holder.

I stood with Billy Gibson, manager of several former champions, in the Garden entrance.

"Great fight, wasn't it," he remarked. "How many champions have you seen knocked out in your day, or knocked down and on the verge of a knockout, Clarence?" he continued.

Off hand, I couldn't answer. As former Sports Editor of the old *Police Gazette,* I had seen too many to be able to keep tab, but I countered with the query, "Bill, did you ever give a thought to the many times you've seen a second separate a challenger from a title, or a champion from a knockout?"

"I never did," replied Gibson, as we started reminiscing. Here we had just seen a great little battler, one of the best of all time, the only title-holder to hold three crowns at one time, take a shellacking from his challenger, and saved from a knockout by just a few seconds.

*  *  *

I WONDER how many of you who are reading this article have ever thought of the many times your heart throbbed as it did when Armstrong was floored in the fifteenth round by Zivic and you experienced the thrill that comes when a champion is put away!

How many of you have experienced the thrill that comes when a champion is dropped and just as the referee had reached the final second, up came the title-holder to save himself from a kayo?

How many times have you seen the champ floored and get to his feet with only one second separating him from a knockout, then lashing out, had put the challenger to sleep?

Precious seconds—yes, that's what they are in boxing. One second often stands between the championship and a lost cause. One second often has kept a contender to his usual diet of ham-and—when, had Fate not decreed it, he could have leaped into the big money ranks.

I've seen many such contests and I daresay so have the majority of RING readers.

"One-two-three-four-five-six—"

The referee's arm rises and falls as the timekeeper bellows the count, pounding on the edge of the ring platform. The champion writhes on the floor. The challenger, tense, paws at the canvas in a neutral corner.

"Seven-eight-nine—"

The champion struggles to his feet

and the challenger rushes in for the kill. He leaves himself wide open and is impaled on a wildly thrown right hand. His body stiffens and he hits the floor. No need for a count

His seconds drag him to his corner, spray him with water. They revive him.

In his dressing room he mutters through bruised and swollen lips:

"I had him down. One second more and I'd have been champion of the world! What a break I got!"

*  *  *

ONE second more! Yes—the gripping drama of the ring is written in seconds. A second, even a split second, can mean the difference between glorious success and ignominious failure.

At the Polo Grounds on the night of September 14, 1923, in the greatest of all heavyweight fights, the destiny of Luis Angel Firpo was altered by the tick of a watch in the hands of the timekeeper.

Five times Firpo had been dropped by Jack Dempsey with a crowd of 90,000 roaring in hysteria.

Five times he had dragged himself to his feet.

Dempsey bore in for a knockout and Firpo sent him whirling through the ropes with a desperate thrust of his ponderous right hand. Still dazed from the effects of Dempsey's punches, Firpo rocked on his heels as Dempsey squirmed about in the laps of startled newspapermen at the ringside, striving to get back into the ring.

"One-two-three-four—"

Unless Dempsey could get back within ten seconds, Firpo would be the heavyweight champion of the world, master of millions!

And at six, Dempsey crawled back, rushed into a clinch, further weakened Firpo with his fearful body punches—then knocked him out in the second round.

*Benny Leonard going through the ropes in fight with Charley White.*

*Stanley Ketchel, who, after having floored Johnson, was knocked out with next wallop, delivered by the champ.*

Four years later Dempsey was to miss, by only a few seconds, the distinction of being the only former heavyweight champion ever to recapture the title. At Soldier Field, Chicago, in September of 1927, in that never-to-be-forgotten seventh round, Dempsey flattened Gene Tunney with a series of punches culminating in a left hook to the jaw—and wasted five precious seconds arguing with Referee Dave Barry when the referee ordered Dempsey to a neutral corner.

It may be that if Dempsey had gone to a neutral corner immediately, Tunney would have gotten up at nine—although the dazed look on his face as he sprawled on the canvas was evidence to the contrary. It may be that if he had gotten up, then he could have kept away from Dempsey—but the five seconds Dempsey frittered away in snarling, senseless argument effectively disposed of whatever chance he had to win.

\* \* \*

THIRTEEN years before Firpo, Stanley Ketchel came within a second of the heavyweight championship at Colma, California, when his murderous right dropped Jack Johnson in the twelfth round.

"One-two-three-four-five—"

The conqueror of Jeffries, the ogre of the ring, lay huddled on the floor, a writhing black hulk on the square of bleached canvas. Over him, the handsome Pole stood grimly waiting—waiting to drop him again if he should get up.

"Six-seven-eight-nine—"

Johnson was up! Ketchel lunged in—and the black crushed him with one blow, a right uppercut that ripped the teeth from his jaws and stripped him of his senses.

\* \* \*

CHARLIE WHITE, left hook artist from Chicago—Charlie with the high brow of the intellectual that belied his sluggishness of thought—was within four seconds of the lightweight championship on a summer afternoon in 1920 at Benton Harbor, Mich. For six rounds Benny Leonard had outboxed him, outpunched him, outgeneraled him, and had him poised for a knockout—and in the seventh round, White's deadly left hook had flashed and Leonard had been hit out of the ring.

"One-two-three-four—"

White had shaken off the fog enveloping his brain. The lightweight championship was at arm's length now! His left hook had done it! Leonard, the champion, was out of the ring! The title—but at six Benny climbed back into the ring and in the ninth round, White was stretched on the floor.

\* \* \*

LEONARD had another close call one night in 1921 in the old Madison Square Garden in New York. It was in his bout with Ritchie Mitchell, idol of Milwaukee. Leonard had stopped him once in seven rounds but Mitchell wasn't convinced. One more crack at the title, he wanted. He got it that night in the Garden—and the title hung, for an instant, on the thread of chance and swung tantalizingly close to him.

When the bell rang to start the fight, Leonard, cool, contemptuous of Mitchell, walked straight out to meet him, stabbed him with a left to the face and followed with a right, aimed at the jaw. It was high and struck Mitchell on the left cheek bone but it dropped him.

Ritchie, almost in a panic, tried to get up and his seconds bawled at him to take a count of nine. At nine, he rose and Leonard nailed him again. Again he went down, to roll over and come up at six.

Leonard was on him and, with a right to the jaw, dropped him a third time. Mitchell struggled to free himself from the canvas.

The count roared on. Leonard, grinning broadly, acknowledged the plaudits of the crowd. Mitchell, plainly, was through.

But at nine, Mitchell got up. He weaved about, almost ready to fall again and Leonard, his guard low, closed in. From somewhere, Mitchell pulled a left hook that thudded against Leonard's chin. The champion hit the canvas, his face pale, his eyes popping.

*Johnny Dundee, who was saved by two seconds from a kayo at the hands of Eddie Wallace.*

In his corner Bill Gibson shrieked:

"Shake your head, Benny! Shake your head!"

"One-two-three-four-five—"

Mitchell, his left eye closed, blood trickling from his nose and mouth, his head buzzing from the champion's punches, lurched against the ropes.

"Six-seven—"

Slowly at first, then more rapidly, Leonard began to shake his head. The light of understanding came back into his face and he winked at the frantic Gibson.

"Eight-nine—"

But Leonard was up. Now he was fencing for an opening. Now he was stabbing Mitchell.

Mitchel faltered, cracked him with that left hook again and Leonard staggered but regained his balance and pulled Mitchell into a clinch.

The round ended with the champion out of danger—and five rounds later Mitchell, blinded, bruised, bleeding, lay at his feet.

\* \* \*

A FEW years ago Leo Lomski came out of the Northwest hailed as another Ketchel, earned the right to fight for the light-heavyweight title and met Tommy Loughran at Madison Square Garden. At the bell, Lomski rushed from his corner, broke down Loughran's guard and belted him over with a right to the chin. Tommy struck on his shoulder blades, his heels in the air, and only the lower rope behind him kept him from going out of the ring.

"One-two-three-four—"

The new Assassin had the champion down! But at nine the champion was up, circling around the eager Lomski, holding him off with his marvelous defense. Lomski rushed and rushed, swinging leather for the champion's chin. Slowly the minutes ground away. With eight seconds to go, his right landed. This time Loughran sagged to the floor head first.

"One-two-three-four-five—"

Instinct pulled Loughran to his feet at the count of eight, just as the bell clanged. Two seconds more and Lomski would have been champion of the world!

With the opening of the second round, Lomski rushed again, but now Loughran stopped him with a straight left that tilted his head back, threw him off balance—and that blow changed the course of the fight. It went the limit, but in the remaining rounds, Lomski, throwing that right hand against Loughran's left, just couldn't connect with the target.

# Precious Seconds

REMEMBER Eddie Wallace of Brooklyn? Probably not, unless you have followed the game very closely over a period of at least twenty years—yet Wallace missed fame by two seconds. He was a nice looking little Jewish boy, who started to fight professionally when he was sixteen years old and was burned out before he was twenty, but one night in 1914, in a neighborhood fight club in Brooklyn he had Johnny Dundee on the floor.

"One - two - three - four - five - six - seven - eight—"

Dundee was up, closing in, strong again, ripping Wallace to pieces with his vicious body attack. Wallace managed to go the route and for some years thereafter pursued a ring career that brought him neither glory nor gold save in a meagre measure—yet he had been within two seconds of the fortune that later was showered on Willie Jackson as a reward for having knocked out the great Dundee.

There you have the stories of several thrilling fights in which only seconds separated the champion from his crown.

---

### IN AUSTRALIA
### With ARTHUR KELL

BY knocking out George Simpson in the third round of a fifteen-round contest at the Sydney Stadium, Maxie Rosenbloom threw a "bombshell" among the local critics, who said the "play boy" was through. The ex-light-heavyweight king proved he was far from it by giving a delightful exhibition of brilliant boxing, dropping his countryman to the resin on a number of occasions before adding the finishing touch. Simpson foolishly entered the ring with a heavily bandaged ankle, but it is doubtful if he would have done any better if not handicapped with the injury.

A well-known Melbourne sporting writer once said, "A Chinese hermit knows more about jazz bands than Jack Carroll knows about boxing." Jack has made that wise scribe "eat his words" by proving himself to be one of the greatest welters in the world by beating Bep Van Klaveren (twice), Wesley Ramey, Jack Portney and our middleweight champ, Fred Henneberry (twice).

Jack Carroll is a slaughter-man by trade in Melbourne, married, with two children. In his twenty-nine years, Carroll has had twelve years in the hemp square.

Not much is heard of Merv "Darkie" Blandon these days, and the pugnacious featherweight is sadly neglected by the National Sporting Club. Blandon is a great little fighter, although he may not come up to expectations as far as boxing ability is concerned.

After beating the veteran Jack Fitzgerald, Young Kimber, a product of Jack Dunlevy's gym, did not live up to expectations when he went down to a points decision to Jackie Sharpe at the Newtown Stadium.

Maxie Rosenbloom travelled to Melbourne and met Ambrose Palmer, stating he does not blame the ex-heavyweight champion of Australia for retiring.

Claude "Tiny" Nichols lost a golden opportunity to distinguish himself when Maxie Rosenbloom, whom the Western Australian was to have fought, contracted a cold, consequently the bout was called off.

For a fighter to come from comparative obscurity to be one of the leading bantamweights in the land overnight is something out of the ordinary. "Snowy" Clarke of Western Australia accomplished this feat by defeating Micky Miller in

---

## The Ring's Quiz Answers

Copyright, 1940—The Ring, Inc.

HERE are the answers to the questions printed on page 43:

1—Eligio Sardinas is Kid Chocolate; Christopher Battalino is Battling Battalino; Samuel Lazzaro is Joe Dundee; Jacob Finklestein is Jackie Fields and George Chipulonis is George Chip.

2—Leonard won the lightweight title from Freddie Welsh by a K.O. 9 rounds, N. Y. City, May 28, 1917. When he retired, an elimination was staged. Jimmy Goodrich stopped Stanislaus Loayaza in 2 rounds and Rockey Kansas beat Goodrich to gain international recognition. Sammy Mandell beat Kansas in 10 rounds in Chicago for the title.

3—"The Fighting Marine," Gene Tunney; "The Naval Cadet," James J. Corbett; "Honest Hearts and Willing Hands," John L. Sullivan; "The Prize Fighter and the Lady," Max Baer.

4—Armstrong stopped Sarron in the sixth round to win the world featherweight crown.

5—No. A fighter can take out a license as a pro for his first fight without ever having competed as an amateur.

6—The largest size of a boxing ring measures 24 by 24 feet.

7—The New Garden was opened on Dec. 11, 1925. The Delaney-Berlenbach fight featured on opening night.

8—The last star bout in the old Garden on closing night was that between Sid Terris and Johnny Dundee.

9—The N.B.A. is an organization composed of various boxing commissions throughout the country.

10—Dempsey, Toledo, O; Tunney, Philadelphia; Ritchie, San Francisco; Dundee, New York; Young Corbett, Hartford; James J. Corbett, New Orleans; Bob Fitzsimmons, Carson City; Joe Lynch, New York; Johnny Kilbane, Los Angeles; Barney Ross, Chicago; Mickey Walker, Chicago.

---

Melbourne after having given the national title-holder a sound thrashing. The Western Australian boy had a fight in Sydney but no attention was given him. He then travelled to Melbourne and is now sought after by many Southern promoters.

Although he was giving away twenty-five pounds, Ron Richards knocked out "Young" Acquinaldo in the third round in Brisbane. Acquinaldo was down seven times in the second round.

The previous week in Brisbane, "Young" Acquinaldo was disqualified for foul tactics in a contest with Les Pearson. After his defeat at the hands of Richards, Acquinaldo attacked the referee and Richards, but he was soon quieted and left the ring.

The referee for the Barney Ross-Jack Carroll title fight next December will not be announced until the contestants are in the ring on the night of the fight. Ross is taking care the official will be free to exercise his judgment when the time comes.

Charles Lucas, on returning from America, made

---

## The Ring's Quiz

Copyright, 1940—The Ring, Inc.

HOW much do you really know about fights and fighters? If you can come through with three out of five you can pat yourself on the back as an expert in the history of the game. The answers will be found on page 45.

1—Identify the following in boxing by giving their fighting names; each a former world title holder: Eligio Sardinas, Christopher Battalino, Samuel Lazzaro, Jacob Finklestein, George Chipulonis.

2—From whom did Benny Leonard win the lightweight title? How did Sammy Mandell gain the title vacated by Benny?

3—What fighters starred in the following plays: "The Fighting Marine"; "The Naval Cadet"; "Honest Hearts and Willing Hands"; "The Prize Fighter and the Lady."

4—From whom did Henry Armstrong win the featherweight title and in what manner?

5—Must a fighter be an amateur before he can become a professional?

6—What is the largest size a boxing ring can be?

7—When was the new Garden opened and with what feature attraction?

8—What was the last feature bout staged in the old Garden?

9—What is the National Boxing Association?

10—In what cities did the following famous fighters win their titles: Jack Dempsey, Gene Tunney, Willie Ritchie, Johnny Dundee, Young Corbett, Bob Fitzsimmons, Joe Lynch, Johnny Kilbane, Barney Ross (lightweight) and Mickey Walker?

---

a trip to Melbourne to interview Ambrose Palmer. He is hopeful of inducing the brilliant Palmer back into the ring. John Henry Lewis is said to be the bait.

Maxie Rosenbloom made a press announcement to the effect that he is fed up with boxing and will very soon retire and live a normal life. Many announcements like this one figure in the papers, but most of them are publicity stunts.

Leo Kelly has resumed training after his idle spell caused through an injury to his eye.

George Simpson wants to fight Rosenbloom again on a winner-take-all basis. He blames his ankle as the foundation of his defeat at the hands of "Slapskie" recently.

Hughie Meeghan, son of the famous Australian champion of that name, knocked out "Kid" Rooney in the sixth round of a ten-round contest at Leichhardt Stadium.

Bill Wooller, 133 pounds, knocked out George Lowe, 131 pounds, in the fourth round of the main ten-round contest at Leichhardt Stadium.

---

We regret to announce that the notes by Herb McHugh, our Australian correspondent, did not arrive in time to be used in this issue.

# FAMOUS FINISHERS

## By HYPE IGOE

**W**HEN Lew Jenkins popped Pete Lello on the "button" and knocked him out in the first defense of Lew's lightweight title, the old timers about the ring rubbed their chins and asked themselves if this skinny, hollow-cheeked Texas cavalryman didn't belong among the "quick finishers" of all time. It all happened in the second round.

No question about the Jenkins punch. Whether he finishes as quickly or slow, there is no doubt about his having earned the right to have his name enrolled among the best punchers of all lightweight history. Once Jenkins tags a man, cleanly, the show is over. All that remains is to come in and pick up the victim.

To look at Jenkins, before he goes into the ring, one would have a feeling of pity for the fellow. Nature has made him scrawny. He has dickey-bird legs and there isn't a wasted ounce of flesh on his bones.

In all my experience, I can't recall any one like him in structure unless it was "Spider" Welsh, the San Francisco "Pieman" who went to Butte, Montana, in 1904 to pick up a little easy money, disposing of an unknown named "Battling" Nelson. The "Spider" looked enough like Jenkins to be his twin brother. The unknown knocked the "Spider" out in sixteen rounds and it was he who came back to San Francisco telling sports writers that a "world beater knocked me out." Like Jenkins, the "Pieman" could punch and we couldn't believe our ears when "Red" Sammy McClintock, the manager, and the "Spider", sang such a startling duet over the prowess of the man who, as the Durable Dane, was destined to knock out Jimmy Britt and Joe Gans to establish himself as undisputed champion of the lightweight division.

*George K. O. Chaney, a portsider, who rolled up a record number of knockouts and was dubbed the "K. O. King."*

*Young Otto, an amazing one-round kayo artist.*

\* \* \*

**I**N my contemplation of the famous "quick finishers" of the ring, my mind wanders back to names which never will be erased from the honor roll of great hitters, yet all the great hitters were not necessarily "quick finishers".

There have been noted hitters who were content to go along, gradually wearing down their prey, methodically, carefully with the least possible danger to themselves.

There were other punchers who stalked a man all through a fight with the one thought of ending the fight in a punch. Joe Gans was that kind of a hitter. I watched him mince-step after Mike Twin Sullivan in the old Woodward's Pavilion in San Francisco, waiting for a chance to catch the sprightly Mr. Sullivan. The opening, which none of us saw, save Gans, came in the fifteenth and Sullivan was stretched out over the lower rope like a glass-eyed scarecrow.

I have seldom seen a more convincing knockout. If the subject before the house is "quick finishes", that one was greased lightning. All the men I saw Gans knock out, never moved after Joe nailed them, except Willie Fitzgerald. Gans stepped in with a short right to Willie's jaw and the Irishman went down in a sitting position his legs crossed under him like a tailor usually squats.

Willie wasn't unconscious. He sat there giggling up at Gans as the precious ten seconds were tolled over him. I don't think that Fitzgerald knew what hit him. Surely he didn't know he was on the floor in front of the great Gans, being counted out else he might have tried to get up.

Despite that Joe was a master workman and fought in the careful, yet convincing style of his day, I'd be more inclined to name Bob Fitzsimmons, Jack Dempsey, Young Otto, George Chaney, Joe Louis, Kid McCoy, Stanley Ketchel, Newark Patsy Kline, Sam Langford, Aurelio Herrera, Dal Hawkins, Peter Maher, Georges Carpentier, Tommy Ryan, Joe Walcott, or Charley White as quicker finishers.

\* \* \*

**O**F course the punch is back of all quick endings, Joe Louis landed hard, accurately and quickly when he f— Schmeling the second time. When they first — he had an old, washed up "has-be— try to block Max's early clout

Joe learned a great lesson in — ing nailed him with a hard righ of the first round and, that pun day was the one which really bro twelfth round. It drilled Louis to something like fifty-seven more ri a stretch of twelve rounds, Loui punishment.

He wasn't knocked unconscious. position against the ropes at first, tl

*Paul Berlenbach, a fighter who mowed 'em down early.*

his head resting on his right glove. Screaming from his corner was Jack Blackburn, Joe's trainer and coach, from the time he left the amateur ranks.

"Git up Chappie, git up, boy! Git up, Chappie!"

"Chappie", Blackburn's nickname for Joe, heard, yet couldn't respond. He lifted his head off his glove, looked toward Blackburn and shook his head, as much as to say:

"Jack, it can't be done!"

* * *

*A*H, but the second fight was different. That was one of the prize "quick finishes" of all time. Jack Dempsey had visited Joe at his Pompton Lakes training camp a day or two before the fight and Jack kept harping on a quick finish:

"Sail into him and don't let Schmeling get started! Belt him out before he gets a chance to measure you with a right as he did in that first fight. Fight him as I used to fight—go with the bell and never let up on him!"

That was pretty good advice. Joe may have had such an annihilating attack in mind, even before Dempsey spoke to him. In any case, the bell rang and it was over before the echo of the starting gong had died away.

It ever has been my contention that had Louis always fought with a rush, none of the men he has ever met would not have gotten out of the first round.

Perhaps he never would have been able to catch a fast-moving fellow like Bob Pastor in the first round. As a matter of fact, Joe did drop Pastor in the first round at Detroit and failed to keep him there. He dropped him in the second and yet Pastor went on to the eleventh round before Joe finally brought him down to stay.

That is one reason why I believe that Billy Conn, light as he is, will give Louis a lot of trouble if they meet in June. Speed has always bothered Joe. He likes to fight at his own pace and when Pastor set it, Joe was at a disadvantage.

* * *

E'S fourth round knockout of Tony Galento was a "quick-  
  " shambles. Joe had almost been knocked out in the  
   ound and was floored in the third. He got up and  
   to himself:

   has gone far enough!"

  urious, swift, devastating. Galento was punched  
  n in an attack which only went to prove that  
  much more quickly than has been his habit.

*B*OB FITZSIMMONS was a fast finisher. He was an all-time great hitter. Usually when he hit them right, they stayed put. Like Gans, Bob worked for a finale. He brought down Jim Corbett in fourteen rounds after taking an unmerciful licking, to become the heavyweight champion of the world. Fitz could make a quick finish when he wanted to bear down. While still champion Fitzsimmons knocked out Gus Ruhlin in six and Tom Sharkey in two rounds, classic in quick finishes when Bob got around to the final curtain.

Young Otto, whose real name was Arthur Susskind and who devotes his time these days in developing young "Diamond Belt" and "Golden Glove" amateur boxers, was an astonishing finisher when he was boxing. He holds a world record for knockouts in the first minute of the first round—some sixteen of them I believe it was! One punch and that was the end. There was no getting up to be flattened again and again. When Otto dropped them they "snored."

Were he to come along at the present day, he probably would be a greater sensation than Lew Jenkins. Any fellow who could stretch them out in that fashion, right now, would be wild fire at the box office.

When Jenkins first came to New York from Texas and began boffing the boys to sleep, it was certain that he would wind up as boss of the lightweight throne. Lou Ambers was the champion but he couldn't hit hard. Besides Lou was having trouble making the lightweight limit and when he came to defend his title against Jenkins he was not strong. The end was fast. Tagged, he couldn't escape and another "fast finish" was chalked up for Jenkins.

Otto was a harder hitter than Jenkins. So was Aurelio Herrera, the Mexican, who ran up eleven straight knockouts in 1903. They were mostly, one, two, three and four round finishes and they were swift when they came. Herrera could hit his man on top of the head and knock him out. Otto may have been a more accurate puncher though no harder hitter.

* * *

*G*EORGE CHANEY of Baltimore, a south-paw featherweight was a swift finisher. He was a body puncher and he was often charged with being a foul fighter simply because, his victims on receiving one of his left hooks to the body doubled and went to the floor. The fallen man's seconds and friends made sure there was a protest of "foul" registered, when the blow might have been perfectly legitimate.

Both Henry Armstrong and Billy Conn have come in for accusations along that line because they too are body fighters. It is unfair because usually it is the gambler who sets up a cry of foul, whose only hope is that either man will be penalized enough rounds to lose the fight, even when he actually has won.

Armstrong, at his best, was a pretty fast finisher if he got his man going. Not a great hitter, he was ruthless if he got a tired man on the run. Henry never clinches and when the other fellow holds to save himself, Henry's two fists beat a cruel tattoo on body and ribs.

* * *

*D*EMPSEY was a swifter finisher than Joe Louis, in my opinion. That's why I think that a fight between Joe and Jack would have ended in the first round, with Jack the winner. He hit savagely and in turn was most difficult to hit himself. Dempsey's speedy finish of Luis Angel Firpo was a good example of how swiftly Dempsey could end a bout. Jack didn't spend a second in clinching and he hit from any angle out of a "bob" and "weave," an exasperating, confusing attack and one which made him a most difficult target to hit.

Schmeling proved that Louis can be hit hard and so did Galento. When he was the real Dempsey, it was almost impossible to land a blow on Dempsey's jaw, so consistently was his head moving off the line of fire.

Jimmy McLarnin was a corking finisher. He was a superb boxer to start with, a will o' the wisp before he became celebrated as a puncher. If McLarnin got home with a solid punch to the jaw, the finish wasn't far away. At even weights, he would have whipped Jenkins by knocking Lew out.

## NORTHERN CALIFORNIA RATINGS
### By Sheridan Brown

**Heavyweights**—Max Baer, Buddy Baer, Lou Nova, Harold Blackshear, Pat Valentino.
**Light-heavyweights**—No activity.
**Middleweights**—Fred Apostoli and Young Corbett III, Little Tiger Wade, Eddie Booker, Billy Latka.
**Welterweights**—Little Tiger Wade, Joe Ybarra, Sheik Rangel, Flash Sebastian, Joe Gavras.
**Lightweights**—George Latka, Cecil Hudson, Verne Bybee, Danny LaVerne.
**Featherweights**—Verne Bybee, Chick Delaney, Danny LaVerne.
**Bantamweights**—Tony Olivera, Little Dado, Little Pancho, Rush Dalma, Jackie Jurich.
**Flyweights**—Little Pancho, Little Dado, Jackie Jurich.

## NEW ENGLAND RATINGS
### By "Doc" Almy
#### (Boston Post)

**Heavyweights**—Nathan Mann, Tony Shucco, Terry "Tiger" Warrington, Al McCoy, Johnny Shkor, Larry Lovett, George Fitch.
**Light-heavyweights**—Terry "Tiger" Warrington, Al Gainer.
**Middleweights**—Henry Chmielewski, Howell King, Coley Welch, Frankie Nelson, Ted Lowry, Babe Verilla, Frankie Britt.
**Welterweights**—Mike Kaplan, Jimmy Leto, Louis Kid Cocoa, George Martin, Irish Eddie Dolan, Ralph Zanelli, Ernest "Cat" Robinson, Fred Cabral, Red Moffet, George Henry, Buster Carroll, Oscar Suggs, Billy Tordiglione.
**Lightweights**—Dave Castilloux, Paul Junior, Pat Foley, Red Guggino, Johnny Bellus, Slugger White, George Salamone, Harry Gentile, Billy Lancaster, Al Gauthier.
**Featherweights**—Abe Denner, Larry Foley, Al Mancini, Sal Bartola, Bobby Ivy, Dom DiCiantis, Joey Archibald, Joe Iannotti, Sammy Garcia, Tony Costa.
No bantamweights or flyweights.

## PITTSBURGH RATINGS
### By Ray M. Todd

**Heavyweights**—Billy Conn, Harry Bobo, George Hughes, Charley Massera, Big Jim Thompson.
**Light-heavyweights**—Billy Conn, Irv Sarlin, Teddy Yarosz, Lloyd Marshall, Irish Jackie Haley, Ira Hughes, Mose Brown.
**Middleweights**—Billy Soose, Charley Burley, Ossie Harris, Freddie Lenn, Joey Mattis, Lou Pitts, Steve Kullich.
**Welterweights**—Fritzie Zivic, Charley Burley, Erv Hicks, George Silvaey, Tommy Yarosz, Johnny Cregan, Tommy Daniels, Billy Morris.
**Lightweights**—Sammy Angott, Tommy Speigal, Johnny Rucker, Sammy Adragna, Jiggs McKnight, Sammy Parotta.
**Featherweights**—Canada Lee, Billy Bates, Mimmie Adragna, Tony Roma, Eddie Tuscher, Bruno Pucci.
We haven't any fighters in the two lightest classes, bantamweight and flyweight.

## TEXAS RATINGS
### By Bill Davee

**Heavyweights**—Buddy Scott, Jack Marshall, Babe Ritchie.
**Light-heavyweights**—Jimmy Webb, Maxie Long, Carl Dalio.
**Middleweights**—Elby Pettaway, Augie Arellano, Robert "Pork Chops" Alexander.
**Welterweights**—Willie Neyland, Bill McDowell, Russell Ramirez.
**Lightweights**—Lew Jenkins, Nick Peters, Lee Harper.
**Featherweights**—Henry Hook, Johnny Ramos, K. O. Barrado.
**Bantamweights**—None.
**Flyweights**—None.

## CANADIAN RATINGS
### By Lawson Bampton

**Heavyweights**—Champion, Tiger Warrington; 1, Oliver Shank; 2, Larry Bouchard.
**Light-heavyweights**—Champion, Tiger Warrington; 1, Eddie Wenstob; 2, Bill Sparks.
**Middleweights**—Champion, Len Wadsworth; 1, Frankie Genovese.
**Welterweights**—Champion, Sammy Luftspring; 1, Maxie Berger; 2, Norman Hurdman.
**Lightweights**—Champion, Dave Castilloux; 1, Billy Marquart; 2, Harry Hurst.
**Featherweights**—Title vacant; 1, Jackie Callura; 2, Spider Armstrong; 3, Danny Webb.
**Bantamweights**—Title vacant; 1, Eddie Petrin; 2, Scotty Ramage.
**Flyweights**—Champion, Desse Greene; 1, Ken Lindsay; 2, Aurelien Lamothe.

## ILLINOIS RATINGS
### By Gene Engel

**Heavyweights**—Lem Franklin, Tony Musto, Altus Allen, Henry Wacker, Carl Vinciquerra.
**Light-heavyweights**—Eddie Campo, Booker Beckworth, Settimis Terricini, Star Harvey and Paul Frazier.
**Middleweights**—Tony Zale, Milt Aron, Natie Bolden, Johnny Barbara.
**Welterweights**—Holman Williams, Leonard Bennett, Jack Cooper, Tito Taylor, Tony Motisi.
**Lightweights**—Pete Lello, Davey Day, Nick Castiglione, Leo Rodak, Willie Joyce.

**Featherweights**—Frankie Covelli, Eddie Dempsey, Gene Ward, Henry Huerta, Armando Sicilia.
No bantams or flyweights.

## RATINGS OF WISCONSIN BOXERS
### By Matt Dougherty

**Heavyweights**—Billy Gillespie, Mickey Hayes.
**Middleweights**—Tony (Ciancola) Martin, Tony Bruno, Jimmy Pierce.
**Welterweights**—Indian Billy Lee, Ray McKnight, Ralph Leslie.
**Lightweights**—Annunzio Ferraro, Matt Mihalovich.
**Featherweights**—Phil Zwick, Frankie Gaudes.
**Bantamweight**—Johnny Gaudes.

## CLEVELAND RATINGS
### By Sparky Rudolph

**Heavyweights**—Patsy Perroni, Lem Franklin, Buddy Walker, Buddy Knox, Eddie Simms.
**Light-heavyweights**—Lloyd Marshall, Jimmy Reeves, Willie Muldune, Max Minnich.
**Middleweights**—Jimmy Bivins.
**Welterweights**—Frankie Wallace, Cleo McNeil.
**Lightweights**—Mike Gamiere, Georgie Toy, Lee Sheppard, Jimmy White.
**Featherweight**—Joe Marinelli.
**Bantamweights**—Freddie Pope, George Pace, Lou Laurie.

## PHILADELPHIA RATINGS
### By Nat Frank

**Heavyweights**—Gus Dorazio, Henry Taylor, Willie Reddish, Nick Fiorentino, Joe Downey.
**Light-heavyweights**—Tony Cisco, Eddie Miller, Bob Wilson, Wally Sears, Joe Barr.
**Middleweights**—Roxie Forgione, Young Gene Buffalo, Ossie Stewart, Johnny Carter, Georgie Miller.
**Welterweights**—Mayon Padlo, Reds Graber, Danny Falco, Buck Streator, Billy Mims.
**Lightweights**—Bob Montgomery, Jimmy Tygh, Billy Maher, Mike Evans, Tommy Cross.
**Featherweights**—Bobby Green, Al Brown, Johnny Forte, Johnny Marcelline, Tony Tedesco.
**Bantamweights**—Tommy Forte, Frankie Donato.

# Famous Finishers

Nat Lewis, the old time manager declares that Benny Leonard was the fastest finisher he ever saw.

Stanley Ketchel was a fast finisher. After he had fought Jack Sullivan a twenty round draw in Butte, Ketchel ran up a string of twenty-one knockouts. True, they were victims culled from the "sticks" around Butte, Mont., yet they were most part quick knockouts. Ketchel relished a fight over a distance. He liked to take his time if there was a twenty round fight in front of him. He could win quickly in the first or in the thirty-second round as he did when he knocked out Joe Thomas.

When the time came for the finish Ketchel fairly exploded with fury.

Sam Langford was a superb finisher. Often he could call the round and the punch. He knocked out big Harry Wills in Los Angeles in this fashion. Sam didn't like one of the scribes in that town and in a clinch, Sam leaned over the ropes and said to the writer he disliked:

"Get ready to ketch this Brown Panther! I'm gonna knock him into your lap with a right cross in the next round."

Remarkable prognostication! That's exactly how it ended, punch and all!

Paul Berlenbach, powerful, rather awkward, was a furious finisher when he got ready to "dress up" his victim. He was a cruel body puncher. Old Dan Hickey, hero of many Fitzsimmons camps and boxing instructor at the New York Athletic Club, found Paul in a wrestling squad and fancied that Paul would be a greater success as a fighter. He landed Paul on the light-heavyweight throne and woe betide the man Paul got in trouble!

He was the best body puncher to come along in a long stretch of years. If a man weakened in front of him, the end was quick, decisive.

Charley White of Chicago, with his peculiar, stiff-armed left uppercut to the jaw, was a deadly finisher. He stretched them with a single punch, just as Dal Hawkins did, with the exception that Hawkins dropped his left hook down instead of bringing it up like White did.

Both men followed the theory of surprise, contending that if you landed a jarring punch to the jaw without the other fellow's eye having seen it start or come, the element of surprise was there, the brain was shocked because the eye had not warned of its coming and the result was the same as if the hapless one had been hit from behind with a blackjack. Hawkins often "lost" his man after flattening him out like an old attic carpet. Hawkins was on the frail side, never weighing more than 128 at his best. He met the tough lightweights of his time, Gans, Erne, Owen Ziegler, Charley McKeever, Martin Flaherty, Kid McPartland, Elbows McFadden and Spike Sullivan.

Hawkins fought Martin Flaherty in Carson City on the day that Corbett lost his title to Fitzsimmons. The bell rang, they went quickly to the center and Hawkins dropped his left hook on Flaherty's chin, a fourteen-second knockout. Hawkins always disputed the quick knockout record with Battling Nelson. Bat claimed it, saying that he had knocked out Billy Rossiter in two seconds, plus the ten count, in Chicago.

Hawkins maintained that a slow-moving fellow like Nelson never could have got his man in two seconds for the simple reason that he couldn't have left his corner and got to the center of the ring to land the knockout punch in that time. I'll string along with Hawkins on that, having seen Nelson fight many times and knowing that he wasn't that speedy. Hawkins died in San Francisco recently and he went to his grave without ever having been accredited with the swiftest "finish" on record.

\* \* \*

TERRY McGOVERN blasted his way through to many quick finishes. He was a rusher and he could punch. Many old timers still vow he was the greatest fighting machine of all time and the fastest finisher.

Young Corbett, a hard hitter, could finish a man quickly when he got him going. Corbett's downfall was his dislike for training. He enjoyed life and never wanted to set aside the good things to eat and drink for the rigors of training. Inclined to be pudgy, he had the pudgy man's slant on life.

Kid McCoy could polish them off with breath-taking dispatch when he got a man in groggy condition. He was the trickiest fighter who ever lived and if he got a man in a fog that fellow never came out of it.

Some of the greatest fighters the ring has ever known failed when it came to finishing a man quickly because they lacked the punch. The punch is the basis for all speedy finales.

# SOCKING *the* REFEREE

## *"Playful"* Tactics of Al Davis in Bout With Fritzie Zivic Recall to Old Timers, the Days of Other Rough-and-Ready Glove Pushers

### *By* GEORGE T. PARDY

*Battling Nelson, who stands out as an example of a rough-house scrapper.*

THE recent rough-house fracas in Madison Square Garden between welter champ Fritzie Zivic and Al Davis, when the latter was disqualified after two minutes and thirty-four seconds of round two had elapsed for hitting Zivic below the belt thirteen times, gave the crowd a bit of a thrill such as fight fans are unaccustomed to under modern ring conditions. Especially when young Al, on being checked in his fouling frenzy, started what came near being a free-for-all mixup by kicking at Referee Billy Cavanagh and his erstwhile opponent.

As might be expected, the State Athletic Commission revoked the offender's license and Davis goes on the sidelines indefinitely so far as New York State is concerned. There was a good deal of speculation, psychological and otherwise, advanced by sport scribes in the daily press, as to the whys and wherefores of Davis's looney behavior. But it all sums up to this—he has an ungovernable temper, loses his head under fire and adopts the rip-roaring battle tactics of a mad mandril or goofy gorilla on the warpath.

Viewed from a strictly ethical standpoint, there is no room on the straight sports calendar for exciting entertainment of the kind furnished by Mr. Davis's spasmodic lapse into untamed savagery. If that sort of thing were permitted, the scrappy boys might as well be handed axes and sent in to hack each other up like Roman gladiators.

Just the same, while many folks were shocked on that auspicious occasion, one suspects that oldtimers among the spectators got a laugh out of the proceedings, as they recalled certain unorthodox doings of rough-and-ready glove pushers in a vanished era.

* * *

THE fact that the Zivic-Davis affair created such a public sensation is sufficient proof, if any were needed, of how thoroughly boxing is policed and kept within legitimate bounds of action nowadays. Before boxing commissions ruled, when the sport was conducted along happy-go-lucky lines, fouling an opponent or socking a referee, if not exactly rated as minor offenses, were not considered worth while making a big fuss about.

One of the roughest, toughest welterweights that ever lived was "Mysterious" Billy Smith. A hurricane, two-fisted slugger was Billy, a front-ranker in his class, and at the same time as unscrupulous and savage in his methods of attack as a timber-wolf. When fighting Joe Walcott in 1898, Smith not only abused the colored lad verbally, but repeatedly butted him, wrestled, and shoved an elbow into Joe's left eye.

The referee did nothing about it. Joe's manager, Tom O'Rourke, was in Walcott's corner, and instructed his man to foul Smith back. Joe did his best, but was no match for Smith at that game

and in the fifteenth round, Joe complained bitterly that the "Mysterious" one had bitten him in the shoulder as they clinched.

Smith yelled back an obscene insult relative to Joe's parentage, and added that he'd expect to get blood poison if he was fool enough to sink a tooth in the Barbadoes darky. And so the scrap went merrily on to the twentieth and final round. Walcott was so badly rattled that Smith got the decision that time, though subsequently Joe reversed the verdict.

* * *

SMITH and Tommy Ryan were outstanding rivals for welter honors. They fought repeatedly, with Ryan always having a shade the better of

*Al Davis, throwback to another rough, tough welterweight, Mysterious Billy Smith, who often bullied his way to victories.*

things. Tommy was a supreme scientist and a hard puncher as well, but Smith made him travel his best, whenever they coupled up. Their battles were epic affairs, contested with bulldog fierceness. They nursed a perpetual grudge, a fact of which the fans were well aware, with the result that packed houses were in order whenever the militant pair crossed arms.

One of their bouts took place before a Minneapolis club in 1894. Joe Choynski, then in his prime as a heavyweight contender, officiated as referee. Smith rushed Ryan continually, and his aggressive tactics won the spectators' applause. But Ryan's clever counter punches and superb generalship enabled Tommy to score up a winning margin of points, and the referee decided in his favor.

Smith considered he had a grievance. After the bout, he filled up on forty-rod whiskey, and went to the hotel where Choynski was staying, with the avowed intention of taking it out of Joe's hide. Choynski wasn't in, which was fortunate, so far as Smith was concerned, for game as the latter was, his chances in a rough-and-tumble combat with the blond young giant from the coast would have been woefully slim. Other times, other manners! One can scarcely visualize a top-notch boxer of today trailing a referee in such a fashion!

In fact, he wouldn't dare. It would be too costly a job, both by action of the commission and the police.

*W*HAT was by long odds the most vicious encounter in which Smith and Ryan engaged was a scheduled twenty-five round contest before the old Coney Island Club, on May 27, 1895. The memory of the Minneapolis battle still rankled in Smith's mind, and he told numerous admirers that this time he would knock out Tommy if he had to kill him to do the same!

There are plenty of veterans still around who saw that fight, and every one of them will tell you that for speed, fury and openly expressed hatred between the principals, it was never excelled, and perhaps never equalled. Smith tore into Ryan ferociously from the first bell, accompanying his punches with a blistering stream of blasphemy. Ryan met him half way, timed him with beautiful counters, blasted him with stinging lefts and rights, and cursed him vindictively. Said Referee Tim Hurst later on:

"It wasn't only a noble scrap, as a swearing-match it laid over anything I ever dreamed of. Some of the cuss words was bran-new to me, they must have invented 'em. As for fouls, Billy started fouling and Tommy got right back at him with his own stuff. I just let 'em go their own ways, they were out for little short of plain murder, and there was times when I sort of thought it would end up in work for the coroner!"

The love feast reached such fiery heights of exultation in the eleventh frame, with both men raging and mauling on the ropes, that the police entered the ring and halted the festivities. Then the blue coats retired and let 'em go at it again.

It was the same storm-session of oaths and piling wallops up to the eighteenth round, and at this juncture the pace was so hot and atmosphere so sulphur-clogged that the gallant law officers once more intervened, and this time choked off the frantic gladiators for keeps. There was nothing left for Referee Hurst to do but declare a draw. This he did, to everyone's satisfaction except Messrs. Smith and Ryan, whose appetites for blood and carnage were still unsatiated.

Smith was a rough customer both in and out of the ring. Ryan, on the contrary was a peaceable chap under ordinary circumstances, but Smith's insults got under his skin and drove him to retaliate in kind.

* * *

*R*YAN'S reputation as a cool and crafty boxer was well deserved. It was very unusual for him to lose his temper between the ropes, as he did with Smith, but there was one other occasion where his anger got the better of his judgment. That was when he met Kid McCoy in a six-round bout at the Tattersall's Athletic Club, Chicago, in 1900.

The story of how McCoy tricked Tommy Ryan in their first ring battle is familiar to most students of fistic history. Briefly, the astute Kid coaxed Ryan into a fifteen-round engagement at Maspeth, L. I., where McCoy was supposed to lie down. Ryan didn't train, came in the ring out of condition, and was given a masterly trimming with a kayo windup by the Kid.

It was a lovely double cross, put over in artistic style. Four years elapsed between the Maspeth incident and the Windy City bout. Malachy Hogan, one of the West's most prominent referees, was the third man in the ring. Ryan, keen for revenge, had worked himself into splendid fighting shape. McCoy was also trained to a hair, for he well knew what a dangerous proposition Tommy Ryan was when in condition.

The men fought the six rounds at top speed. It was a gorgeous exhibition of skill and clean, sharp hitting. The weight, 154 pounds, was easier for Ryan to make than McCoy. Honors were fairly even, but if there was a shade, it was in Ryan's favor, as McCoy seemed a trifle weak in the final round. However, Referee Hogan thought McCoy had won and proclaimed the Kid victor.

* * *

*S*CARCELY had the announcement been made, when Ryan sprang at Hogan. Tommy's gloves had not yet been removed, and a five ounce mitt collided with Hogan's jaw. Now Malachy was known to fame as a street and barroom scrapper who had never met his match in a go-as-you-please argument. Staggered for an instant, he recovered his balance quickly and lit into Ryan with true Celtic zeal.

Police and Pinkertons swarmed into the ring en masse, and a very pretty miniature riot was in the making, as partisans of Hogan and Ryan ducked under the ropes. Finally, the referee and gloveman were disentangled and quiet was restored. Then Ryan explained that, according to his agreement with the Tattersall Club, the bout was to be called a draw, provided that both men were on their feet at the conclusion of the sixth round. Naturally, when he heard McCoy named winner, he figured he was swindled by Hogan, and couldn't refrain from pasting the traitor!

However, Hogan claimed that he knew of no such arrangement being made, and had therefore given a verdict as his judgment directed.

All of which made a fine muddle in betting circles. In some cases, wagers were paid on a McCoy victory. In others, interested parties waited to see what the outcome might be.

What followed completely upset the old precedent that there can be no appeal from a referee's decision. For the Tattersall executives went into a huddle next morning and wound up by reversing Hogan's dictum. They pronounced the bout a draw, and it was thus listed in all the record books!

* * *

*I*N the same year that Hogan and Ryan staged their impromptu mill, Chicago ring patrons were treated to yet another act of the time-honored melodrama—"soak the referee." Clarence Forbes and Walter Bloom were matched in the windup of a boxing show at the Star Athletic Club. Although he never won a title, Clarence was rightly listed as one of the best featherweights of his day. His brother, Harry, later world's bantam champion, officiated as Clarence's chief second.

The match was considered important, and it was generally supposed that George Siler would referee. But at the last moment announcement was made that a Mr. Jake McGonigal of Omaha would fill the third man role. Where and how the Star officials dug up McGonigal, and why, were questions destined to remain unanswered. He was a perfect stranger to the Chicago fans. Later on most of them decided he ought to have remained a stranger.

Clarence Forbes gave Bloom an artistic trimming. He completely outclassed him at all stages of the bout. The sixth and final round found Bloom badly cut up, groggy and holding on to escape a kayo. To all appearances it was a cinch victory for Forbes.

But McGonigal had a surprise packet in store for the spectators. Smiling broadly, the stout person from Omaha waved his arms in an all-embracing gesture and announced:

"Both these boys have done well, gents, and I take pleasure in calling it a draw!"

A roar of indignation went up from the astonished crowd. The decision was so raw that even Bloom's adherents failed to greet it with enthusiasm. The Forbes brothers yelled madly in unison and charged the referee. Harry hit him on the left jaw, knocking him toward Clarence, who kept him from falling by belting him on the right jowl.

Jake McGonigal was in a bad spot. When the cops rescued him, his countenance was a red ruin. Each of his assailants was a fast worker, a fact that McGonigal was never known to deny.

There was never any attempt made to discipline the Forbes boys. They were wrong, of course, in thus taking the law into their own hands, but public sympathy was with them, and the universal opinion was that the blunderer from Omaha got just what was coming to him.

* * *

*A*MONG the lightweight kings of the past, Battling Nelson stands out as a sterling example of a real rough-house scrapper. Bat bulled his way, regardless, when in action, taking all the other fellow could dish out, and not being over-particular as to how he got home a telling punch.

If an opponent elected to slug with him, so much the better, if he dabbled in foul work, that too was Nelson's meat. In fact Bat was at a disadvantage when facing an absolutely clean, scientific boxer. He loved to mingle with the fellows who were willing to trade wallops in close.

When Nelson fought Joe Gans

# New Faces

### TOMMY ARDEN

THE middleweight division has a future star in Tommy Arden, former amateur champion from Fort Wayne, Indiana, who is making rapid strides in the professional ranks at Louisville, Kentucky.

Arden boxed as an amateur for two years and during that time engaged in 40 bouts and won several sectional titles in Northern Indiana in the vicinity of Fort Wayne and Auburn, Indiana, besides boxing in the Golden Gloves Tournament at Chicago.

After meeting with success in the amateurs, Arden moved to Louisville to start his professional career under the direction of Jimmy Dell, a former fighter and boxing promoter. At this writing, Tommy has had five pro fights, meeting experienced opponents, and with the exception of his first bout, all were six-round main events. Four were won by decisions and the other by a knockout. Arden holds decision wins over Billy Sparks, Jimmy Davis, Joe Murphy, and Tony Kramer and a three-round knockout over Bruce Atwell.

Arden is only 18 years of age and weighs about 158 pounds, but he boxes like a veteran with plenty of experience and packs a hard wallop in both hands.

At the present time, Jimmy Dell, Arden's trainer and manager, has been keeping the middleweight ace in six-round competition in local rings and bringing Tommy along step by step. Tommy is headed for the Kentucky middleweight championship.

\* \* \*

### CHUCK HIRST

WILLIE SHAW, former Michigan bantam and welterweight champion, had a good prospect in hand in a young, hard hitting Jewish welterweight, Chuck Hirst by name. Chuck tossed aside amateur boxing after three fights, to enter the pro ranks and since joining the money squad, he has been doing very nicely.

In his first three bouts he gained decisions over Gordon Drake, Art Neyman and Henry Higgins. Then he went into a knockout streak. He stopped Barney Ross in 1:40 of the first round; Sammy Ketts in 58 seconds; Larry Ray in the second round; Ernie Montroy in the second; Jimmy Harper in the fourth; and then he sent Len Nelson to sleep in 1:20 of the first.

Chuck is anxious to get a crack at Young Al McCoy to settle the matter of Detroit supremacy in their class, and he will have a lot of folk behind him if the match materializes.

\* \* \*

### GLENN GRAY

IN Mineral Springs, Texas, where there is a huge army encampment, boxing is an important sport. Hailing from that district is a lad, Glenn Gray, whose father, Chester, saw considerable service in the army and navy, and according to dad, his son has all the earmarks of a good fighter. Glenn has had upward of sixty fights as an amateur but only recently joined the ranks of the money chasers. As a pro, he hopes to fight frequently around the army camp sector. He lost only one fight in five starts, that to Roy Salomey of El Paso. Pop Thomas, promoter at Lubbock, thinks well of Gray's chances. Recently at one of Thomas's shows, which Dempsey refereed, Gray beat Sonny Smyer.

Young Gray still goes to school. He is a senior in Mineral Wells High School, where he is idolized by his schoolmates. Gray's father was a boxer in the army and navy. He served thirty years before retiring, four in the navy and 26 in the army.

All Mineral Springs is behind the efforts of young Gray to make good. His record to date as a pro, follows: Kid Leva, won 8 rounds; Kid Leva, won, 10 rounds; Fanzo White, won, 6 rounds; Ray Salomey, T.K.O., 4; Sonny Smyer, won, 6.

---

# Socking the Referee

at Goldfield, Nevada, in 1906 for the lightweight title, the battle went into the forty-second round before Referee George Siler declared Gans winner on a foul. The fight was notable for the colored champion's superb defense, and the wonderful precision with which he landed his punches; and the dogged persistence of Nelson, whose marvelous endurance was never exhibited to such a degree as in this gruelling contest.

Siler overlooked quite a number of fouling offenses by Nelson in the earlier stages of the contest. Referees weren't inclined to be squeamish in the days of long distance scraps, but as time went on Nelson got more and more impatient because of his failure to corner Gans and beat him down.

His impatience finally reached the breaking-point. In the forty-second session the Dane cut loose with all he had, using his elbows, wrestling in the clinches, butting like an enraged steer. When he tried to kick Gans, it was too much for Siler, and Bat was at last disqualified.

*Billy Smith butted, wrestled, and bit Joe Walcott on the way to his 1898 victory.*

# TERROR THRILL for JOE

### Louis' Crown Tottered in Balance When Buddy Baer's Dynamic Punch Drove Him Through the Ropes—Champion Lucky to Escape Disqualification When His Secretary Leaped Into Ring in Violation of Rules, While Bout Was Still On and Before Baer Struck the Canvas

## By DICK COX

THERE was glory enough and to spare for victor and vanquished, when Joe Louis, defending his world's heavyweight title for the seventeenth time, defeated Buddy Baer in the Griffith Stadium, Washington, D. C., on May 23, when Referee Arthur Donovan disqualified Baer upon the refusal of Manager Ancil Hoffman to leave the ring, or allow Buddy to answer the bell for the seventh round. The preceding session supplied unlimited ammunition for future fistic gabfests. The boys will be wrangling endlessly, even as in the case of the historic Tunney-Dempsey "long count" battle, over Louis's wallop on the chin, that landed just after the bell in the sixth, and dumped Buddy for a third and final knockdown.

They'll wrangle, for that's the immemorial privilege and style of the fight fans, although the basic facts in that startlingly sensational encounter are sufficiently plain on the record.

Buddy Baer had twice gone to the floor under a fusillade of paralyzing punches. He got up the first time as the count of six was tolled off. After his second fall, Buddy scrambled up at "nine!" He was weak and staggering, practically out on his feet.

The uproar was terrific, with 23,912 frenzied spectators yelling in leather-lunged unison. Louis had walked calmly to a neutral corner. The instant Buddy was erect, the colored panther leaped forward and shot a right to the jaw that sent the big chap crashing to the canvas.

The gong had clanged three seconds before Louis blitzed into his savage attack, but, owing to the ear-splitting tumult that prevailed, the champion never heard it. Referee Donovan insisted that the Louis punch landed just as the gong signalled the end of the sixth round, but the consensus of opinion was that the punch thudded home right after the gong clanged, and the pictures prove that to be correct. There were absolutely no grounds for accusing Louis of a deliberate foul. The champion is far too cool-headed and fair in his ring tactics to be intentionally guilty of such an action. His past record as a clean, conscientious fighter speaks for itself. The fault rests on the official timer who should have banged away at the gong to call attention to the round's termination.

Manager Ancil Hoffman argued vehemently that Baer should be declared winner on a foul. Donovan promptly denied this plea. Ten seconds before the seventh round was due to start, Donovan told Hoffman and the Baer handlers to leave the ring. They didn't obey. The gong rang. Louis walked forward. The referee halted him. Donovan again instructed Hoffman and his colleagues to leave the ring. They refused, and then came the disqualification of Buddy Baer!

* * *

THE referee acted precisely as his official position gave him the right to do. Had Baer been able to respond to the gong for the seventh frame, one of two things must inevitably have happened. Either Donovan would have been compelled to stop the contest to save Buddy from further punishment, or he wouldn't have lasted any longer than it would have taken the cool, sharp-shooting champion to hang a final kayo on him, for the plucky young giant was hopelessly beaten.

It was a melodramatic curtain-fall on a battle radiating thrills. The first big nerve-shock occurred in the opening round, when Baer drove the spectators frantic with excitement by landing a beautifully timed, dynamic left hook to the jaw that spun the champion sprawling through the ropes. Joe slumped head outside, but got to his feet, and was inside the ring, punching back, at the count of "four!"

Naturally, the minds of those present who had seen Firpo smash Jack Dempsey through the ropes, and come within an ace of uncrowning the then king of the heavies, reverted to that memorable occasion. But there was a wide difference in contrasts. The badly hurt Manassa Mauler was only just able to stall through and recover, after weathering a storm of devastating punches.

Louis, though dazed, recuperated with extraordinary swiftness, and had the situation well in hand, almost before the crowd had ceased shouting wildly over Buddy's surprising feat.

For it was an astonishing exploit, when you figure that the young Californian was generally considered an easy target on whom Joe would score a quick bullseye. Joe himself conceded that the blow which dropped him was no fluke, but a potent wallop, cleanly delivered, and landing with stunning accuracy.

* * *

BUT the colored marvel never demonstrated more clearly his possession of that subtle quality known as "class," than he did in the way he coped with momentary disaster after a short curtailment of action by returning coolly to the fray, tearing into Buddy with both fists, yet never for an instant fighting wildly, or leaving himself open for another counter-thunderbolt.

Briefly, he was Joe Louis, supreme scientist, fighting with canny generalship one of the toughest battles of his career, and coming through with flying colors over a dangerous trail. For danger there was in plenty during this Homeric combat with a lusty young foeman, infinitely his superior in advantages of height, weight, reach, and equipped with punching power equal to the blasting vigor of the Brown Bomber's own deadly deliveries.

Buddy Baer was unquestionably great in the hour of defeat, greater than in any of his ring victories. The younger of the Baer brothers not only gave Louis a real battle, and stamped his trademark in crimson letters on the champion's visage, but made Joe extend himself to the limit in order to win. Also, Buddy erased what has always been a blot on his escutcheon, the memory of the night when he quit before Gunnar Barlund. That fateful incident had established the general belief that a yellow taint marred his pugilistic makeup.

But he no longer belongs in the doubtful class as regards either courage or ability. Between the Buddy Baer of the Barlund episode, and he of the Washington thrill-opus, there is assuredly "a great gulf fixed!" Buddy has struck his fistic stride, and improved amazingly.

* * *

THOSE who have been clamoring for the scalp of Referee Donovan should take into consideration that while the bell did sound prior to the final knockout blow that placed Baer flat on the canvas, Arthur should be given the benefit of the doubt when he says he did not hear it. The arguments I have heard are based on one point—that the third man in the ring should be on the alert and hear the gong. But if the gong is weak, as the Washington bell was, and many scribes failed to hear it signal the end of the round, doesn't it follow that the referee, likewise, might not have heard it?

The only point at issue, so far as I can see, is that concerning a member of Joe Louis's staff, his secretary, Freddie Guinyard. By what authority did Freddie leap into the ring before any of the official seconds could get there! That has not yet been explained! The pictures clearly show that Freddie had heard the bell. He was in the ring even before Buddy Baer's big hulk had struck the canvas, and by his acts, had Donovan adhered to the letter of the code, Joe Louis could have been disqualified. Guinyard stood near the ropes and watched Joe land the final haymaker, thereby violating the rules.

Even though his motive was a good one, to call attention that the round had ended, he had no business within those ropes as he is not a second. But what he did adds to the accuracy of the claim that the bell had sounded, because the failure of the men to cease firing, is what caused Guinyard to jump into the ring as Baer was flopping to the canvas.

* * *

*H*ERE are a few of the highlights of the fight:

1. Louis was forced to throw more punches and fight harder than in all of his previous sixteen championship bouts put together. He hit Baer with more than 100 wallops before he could floor Buddy.

2. The Brown Bomber carried a most worried look following the first round.

3. Baer never held. He fought courageously and gave the spectators one of the greatest battles seen in years. His was an exhibition of gameness such as few carry into the ring.

4. The contest saw Louis at his best despite the knockdown he suffered. He gave the finest exhibition of boxing and punching that he has ever displayed.

5. Joe Louis shed his first blood from a face wound. Except for an occasional spurt of crimson from his nose, Joe has never felt the steady flow of claret or required a surgeon's needle, not even when he was flogged by Max Schmeling in their first engagement.

6. The world heavyweight king has one drawback which Dempsey didn't have—a weak jaw. He cannot take a heavy wallop to the chin. Max Schmeling first brought that to the attention of the public; then came Tony Galento, and now Buddy Baer has made the argument convincing.

7. Buddy proved that he has a heart as big as a mountain and made many of the so-called wise guys of the writing profession, who always try to belittle a fighter by dubbing him a "bum," eat their words.

8. The bout, like the Dempsey-Firpo, the Dempsey-Tunney second fight, the Dempsey-Sharkey and Sharkey-Schmeling bouts, takes its place among the world's most controversial contests in ring history.

9. The sportsmanship of the Washington gathering was all that could be desired.

10. Baer was not deprived of a victory by that foul punch landed after the bell had sounded. He was all in and even his mentor, Ancil Hoffman, speaking to scribes after the fight, said he didn't think Buddy could have continued another round. Hence, while Baer was knocked dizzy after the round had been finished, he probably would have been knocked cold a few minutes later had the seventh round gotten under way.

11. Baer rearranged the spelling of the word "bum," so frequently used against him, to the word "bomb."

12. Arthur Donovan held Baer away from the befuddled champion when Joe scrambled back into the ring, and the champion profited by that most valuable time.

13. Donovan failed to shoo Louis to a neutral corner after he had dropped Baer in the sixth round. He permitted Joe to stand right over the stricken gladiator. There could be no doubt but that the famed New York official had lost control of the bout as it progressed, possibly because he was suffering pain from an injured ankle that bothered him considerably. He was not his usual self in this cyclonic affair.

* * *

*A*FTER the fight was over, Ancil Hoffman placed many charges against the arbiter, among them his failure to count over Louis in the first round.

That is not necessary. Under commission rules, where there is an official knockdown timer, the referee picks up the count at five or more—as soon as he has the situation under control, and in the meantime, the timing is done by the knockdown official. That's why he is appointed. As a matter of fact, the knockdown timer did a good job. Those around the ringside and those listening in over the radio could distinctly hear him. Louis used four seconds going out and coming back.

Baer absorbed an unbelievable amount of punishment that reached its culmination in the sixth round

*Louis' gilded boxing crown came close to slipping from his kinky head as he did a back flip through the ropes when tagged by Buddy Baer's terrific left hook in the first round. The above was made as the champ's head hit the apron of the ring outside the ropes and Referee Donovan pulled back Baer who was entangled in Louis' legs. Fortunate for Joe this happened, as it offered him support.*

when he was sent sprawling to the canvas three times, for a count of six, a nine count and for what spelled his doom—the blow that landed after the bell had sounded, ending the session.

\* \* \*

THE gong-confusion that bewildered things considerably at the conclusion of the bout had an earlier inning at trouble-making. When Louis went into action again in the first session, after being propelled through the ropes, he and Buddy were mixing matters to the accompaniment of the steady roar of the crowd, when both scrappers thought they heard the gong clang. Simultaneously, they dropped their hands and began a retreat to their respective corners. Donovan was right on the job a few seconds later when he motioned them to continue hostilities. They did so with a vim, and shortly after the round ended with Louis scoring a terrific left hook to the head.

Whether Donovan can be blamed for that lull in action is problematical. It must be remembered that Louis was still dazed when he came back after that flop out of the ring and Buddy apparently was too amazed at his own feat to take advantage of his opportunity, sail in, and gamble on a few solid whacks to win the world crown. Whatever the reason for their temporary inactivity, they didn't seem to know whether to resume or to rest.

It was Buddy's great chance and he missed it by a mile. This is where Hoffman charges Donovan aided Louis, but that is highly debatable. Buddy was as much to blame for the lull as either Louis or Donovan.

\* \* \*

BUDDY opened the second frame with a headlong charge at the champion. The younger Baer was chockful of confidence, inspired by the fact that he had absorbed many of Joe's potent sockdolagers without going down, and had landed one of his own that opened the heavyweight monarch in truly undignified fashion. Buddy let go both hands for the body, but Joe straightened him up with three straight lefts to the face, and rocked him with a right to the head. Buddy was trying to get in close, and whenever they buckled into holds it was noticeable that he made good use of his superior bulk and height by leaning his weight on the champ as much as possible. The youngster was no longer a novice so far as ringcraft was concerned. But Louis changed his attack to the body, and the midsection battering checked Buddy's onset. Just as the bell sounded, Louis put a solid right to the head, but Baer stood up well under its impact.

Louis opened the third by shooting a hard left hook to the jaw. Buddy retreated, came in again, and drove a right to the ribs. Louis caught him with two more left hooks to the head, ducked a right return and missed with his own right. Joe tore in and drove in a volley of alternate rights and lefts to body and face. Buddy was taking punishment that would probably have stopped a fighter of less heart and stamina, but he stood to his guns gallantly, and clipped Louis with a right swing to the head at the close of the round.

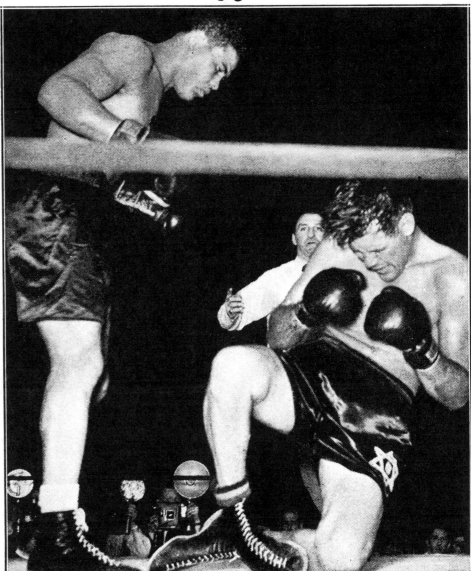

*A furious barrage sent Buddy to the canvas in the sixth round. Here is the first knockdown. Note Louis standing over Baer as did Dempsey over Willard. At the count of six Buddy got to his feet and the waiting champ tore into him to score the second knockdown.*

When Louis came out for the fourth there was a perceptible swelling over his left eye. The champion set grimly to work, taking a left to the body, but snapping back Buddy's head with a straight left jab that had a lot of force behind it. Joe's trenchant jabs were landing frequently but Buddy kept pressing in. Louis switched to the body assault again, and they mixed with a will.

Louis was landing the cleaner punches, but Buddy mauled steadily away, and connected with a couple of stiff rights to the stomach. Joe slammed a hard right over on the jaw, and as Buddy reeled back, put in three sharp left jabs on the face. The pace was fast, and both men seemed a trifle tired, as well they might. At the bell, Louis again reached Buddy's face with two smart left jabs.

\* \* \*

BOTH men seemed much refreshed by the minute's rest when they came up for the fifth, and a sizzling session followed. Joe batted Buddy with two furious left hooks to the jaw, but the youngster wouldn't retreat. Instead, he came in with a rush, and put a right cross on the jaw that made Louis clinch and hang on for a brief instant. Joe leaped in and sent a jolting left to the head. But a moment later Buddy smashed his own left twice in succession to Louis's puffed left eye.

These punches sliced the skin, and the crowd shouted madly, when a thin, crimson trickle of blood ebbed from the wound. This bothered the champion, and occasionally he rubbed the injured spot during the intervals when they boxed at long range.

# The Punch After the Bell

*In the Magic Eye series presented above, we see the sequence in the fateful sixth round. First we see Buddy Baer down, resting on his elbows and knees for a count of nine. This is the second knockdown in that round. Going down the left side panel, in the center, we see Buddy rising, obviously groggy. The third picture sees Referee Donovan starting toward the leg weary youngster. Note the smile on Arthur's face. Now, in the right side panel, comes the story of the blow after the bell. First we see Louis rushing in for the kill. Next, while Buddy is covering up, Joe aims with his right for an uppercut. As Buddy swerves forward, the blow connects and Baer begins to topple. Now follow the sequence on the next page.*

# A FOUL IS CLAIMED

*Here, note how Buddy falls to the canvas and Joe stands over him, watching eagerly. The center photo in the left panel shows that while the referee and Louis didn't hear the bell, Joe's secretary did, for he violates the rules by rushing into the ring, though not a second, to aid the champion. This, in itself, was sufficient cause for the disqualification of the title holder. The lower photo in the left panel shows the seconds of Baer rushing to his aid, while Donovan holds back Louis. Then comes the argument between Donovan and Ancil Hoffman, Baer's manager, who demanded the disqualification of Louis, first for hitting after the bell, and again because of the appearance in the ring of Louis' secretary, even before Buddy had struck the canvas.*

Buddy ploughed his way into close quarters. There were a couple of clinches, and then Louis flamed into fighting fury. His gloves showered a perfect barrage of lefts and rights to body and head, blows that Baer didn't seem to be able to block or evade. The Californian swayed under the murderous assault, staggered, but didn't go down. Driven toward his own corner, Buddy rallied and was fighting back at the bell.

Then came the spectacular sixth round. It found Louis still boiling over with concentrated rage, though outwardly he preserved an icy calm. But behind that deceitful calm lurked the grimly determined spirit of Kipling's "first-class fighting man!" The champion rushed his opponent and nailed him with two vicious rights and lefts to the head. Young Baer didn't flinch. He came back aggressively and they traded punches rapidly.

Suddenly Joe saw the opening he had been scouting for. His right glove shot through his opponent's guard to the chin and toppled him for a short count. Game as they make 'em, Buddy regained his feet. Joe stalked him with vigilant care and landed with lightning lefts and rights to the head. They were blows that would have felled an ox, and the only wonder is that Buddy recovered sufficiently from their stunning force to again struggle to his feet. But he did, just as "nine" was counted off. Then—the bell—and Louis's final wallop that stretched Buddy on the canvas, as already described!

\* \* \*

WELL, look at it any way you like, it was one whale of a scrap, and deserves an outstanding place in fistic annals. All the more so, because not one ring patron out of ten expected it to be anything but an exercise gallop for the champion.

# DEMPSEY-FIRPO SCENE REVIVED

*Buddy Baer, conceded one chance in ten to beat Joe Louis, uncorked a terrific left hook in the first round that dumped the champion over rope, to bounce on his shoulders on the canvas-covered apron, as did Dempsey in his fight with Firpo. Joe Louis took a count of four in returning to the ring, but gained an additional twenty-five seconds when both he and Baer thought the bell had sounded and ceased firing. Despite his auspicious start, Buddy found the going too tough and was hammered dizzy in the sixth, and disqualified in the seventh when he didn't answer the bell.*

Mike Jacobs has said that Buddy Baer will be rematched with Louis at Washington, probably in July. It goes without saying that the California youngster has richly earned another shot at his conqueror. A second meeting between the pair is the sort of attraction bound to draw a bumper house. Buddy Baer will be on the short end of the betting again. But there'll be lots of folks willing to back his chances of worsting Louis next time.

This doesn't mean that I am of the opinion that Buddy can turn the tables on his conqueror. I still rate Joe Louis as the peer of any heavyweight, white or colored, in the universe. And Joe's Washington performance furnishes ample evidence that he has not retrograded.

But the old maxim to the effect that "anything can happen in a fight," is as true today as it was when the bareknuckle gladiators acknowledged its wisdom. Any boxer who has proved his ability to punch and "take it," as young Baer did, must be accorded a chance of whipping any adversary, no matter how formidable.

If at any stage in the Washington battle Buddy Baer had shown signs of fear, if he had ever abandoned his bold offensive in favor of a cautious defense, thousands of fans wouldn't be voicing his praises today. But the lad made good. He "stood the gaff" like a Trojan, and battled like a veritable Achilles!

The performance of Buddy and the commotion that followed as a result of the disqualification and the foul strike, made the Conn-Louis fight the financial success it was.

If there is one thing the fight fan appreciates, it's a game fighter, and Buddy Baer proved all of that. He certainly made the scribes eat their words. He took more abuse than most of the opponents who have faced Louis in recent months, and all because, at one stage of his career, in the Barlund fight which he entered ill, he quit under fire. Long after Louis and Buddy will have retired, the fight fans will discuss the knockdown of the Brown Bomber and the punch after the bell that raised a storm around the world.

# IN FISTIC SPOTLIGHT

*Joey Peralta, Arizona Mexican, who has compiled a fine record.*

## JOEY PERALTA

LES KRELL is a long, thin guy out of Tamaqua, Pa., with a soft spoken voice and not given to the usual outbursts of temper which seem to engulf the average fight manager when their glove wielders become the topic of conversation.

But Krell has a legitimate complaint to register on the pugilistic status of Joey Peralta, and his well-modulated tones in defense of his fighter carry as much authority, if not more, than the wild eyed, mouthy complainants whose rantings are as ludicrous as some of the efforts of their muscle bound meal tickets when they get into the ring.

For the long, thin guy points with justifiable pride to the record compiled by the twenty-six-year-old Nogales, Arizona-born Mexican, Peralta, and pressures his point with convincing talk that when lightweight contenders for a crack at Sammy Angott's title are mentioned, it is unfair to omit the name of the smart-moving Joey who, Krell insists, belongs right up there bracketed with Allie Stolz, Beau Jack, Maxie Shapiro and Chester Rico.

Over a period of six years in this business of bashed beezers, Peralta has engaged in approximately one hundred and fifty fights and if his record of having lost only fifteen of these isn't as good as any that can be offered by the supposed leading titular pretenders, then Krell wants to be shown in black on white a more imposing escutcheon before backing water on his fighter's status.

Peralta has compiled an enviable list of victories.

The Tamaqua resident was the first fighter to whip Chalky Wright following the latter's winning of the world featherweight title, and had weaved a handsome carpet of consecutive triumphs before he lost to Lenny Mancini in his debut in Madison Square Garden.

Joey also holds victories over Cleo Shans, two-time conqueror of Maxie Shapiro, Baby Breese, Carmelo Fenoy, George Zengaras, Bill Speary, Billy Davis, and Howard Burton among others, and less than six months ago fought two draws with Bobby Ruffin in fights in which Peralta was entitled to the decision according to local newspapers.

Only last March, Peralta went ten gruelling rounds with Bob Montgomery in Philadelphia, and the chances are that had the fight been held anywhere but in the Bobcat's back yard, Joey might have fared better with the official award. At any rate, following the fight, Peralta, a distance fighter who oddly enough tired as the fight progressed, had three abscessed teeth abstracted.

Krell, a cattle dealer whose partner turned over Peralta to Les for managerial purposes, is confident that Joey can more than hold his own with the best in the division. He is anxious for a chance to pit Peralta, married and with two daughters, in a championship tilt with Sammy Angott.

*    *    *

## BUDDY MOORE

IN June, 1940, when Buddy Moore—winner of the Golden Gloves heavyweight title in 1939, the Inter-City, Atlantic Coast and National championships as well —turned pro, his manager had such confidence in Moore's boxing ability that he promptly matched him with first-rate fighters. As any expert will tell you, no boxer just out of the amateurs—his gameness and boxing skill and punching power notwithstanding—is ready for such competition as thoroughly seasoned professional scrappers. However, the promising young colored lad came through with knockouts over Ernie Petretti, Johnny Sionas, Steve Colucci, Tiger Harris, Maynard Daniels—and won over Al Blake in six heats.

These victories made Moore's manager grow even more confident; confident beyond reason. Because he matched his comparatively green protege against the rugged and experienced Wild Bill Boyd, who had defeated such battlers as Charley Massera, Chuck Crowell, Henry Cooper and Johnny Shkor; had knocked out Ford Smith, Sandy McDonald, Bob Nestell, Billy Nichy, Buck Everett, Big Boy Brackey, Joe Wagner, Al Boros, Jim Robinson, Dan Hassett, Harry Bobo and others.

Can you imagine a smart manager matching a young prospect with a kayo artist like Boyd? It seems almost inconceivable, but it was done. And so was Buddy Moore, after having stood under the terrific beating Boyd dealt out to him for ten furious rounds. Later, Buddy won a spiritless six-rounder over Frankie Willis and a dull one

*Buddy Moore, whose return to fistic warfare seems destined to meet with success.*

*Archie Moore, Coast middleweight star.*

*Indian Benny Deathpaine, popular in Mid-West.*

over Howard Williams.

Moore's confidence in himself was obviously broken. Being of the quiet, uncomplaining type, Buddy said nothing to his manager and continued his ring career. He lost to Johnny Shkor. And then was disposed of by the hard-hitting Al Hart in two rounds.

By that time the young Negro had become heartsick, and upon the advice of his guardian, Walter Clark, Buddy quit boxing. After Buddy had rested for eight months, Clark sent him to the country to rough it for a month. In the meantime, Clark began to look around for another manager and decided on Paul Damski who is now handling Moore.

Buddy was born Edward Moore, on December 18, 1921, in Jacksonville, Florida. His parents brought him to New York when he was seven. He is an only child. He had three years at high school. At 15 he began to box—"just for fun."

"I was later advised," explained the gentle-mannered and quiet-voiced young man, "to join the Salem Crescent A. C. I did so and was instructed in the finer points of boxing by George Gainsford. He later entered me in a Golden Gloves middleweight tournament. That was in 1938. I won four bouts by one-round kayoes, losing the fifth by decision. Out of my 51 contests as an amateur I lost eight. I reversed five of 'em by knockouts."

When Moore returned from roughing it in the country recently, he was introduced to Paul Damski, famous fight manager, and was told that Paul would be his new guide. After a four-weeks workout in the gym, Damski pronounced Moore ready to fight again. He matched him with Marty Clark. They battled to a thrilling draw. Buddy's next bout, with Jimmy Carollo, also ended in an exciting draw. Then Buddy trounced Al Smith.

Six-foot-seven-inches, 300-pound, Big Ben Moroz came next. Moore gave the giant a neat shellacking and had the fans limp with excitement in every round by rocking Moroz with terrific overhand wallops. Buddy almost punched holes through Big Ben's huge body.

After Moore had trimmed Odell Reiley, he had a six weeks' rest, then took on Big Ben Moroz again. The result was the same as in their previous meeting. Buddy took Ben's hammer-like wallops and came in with sharp punches to the head and cannon-like shots to the body. This time Moore succeeded in damaging Ben's face to some degree, cutting both his eyes with overhand wallops and making his body beet-red from body punishment.

Six feet tall and weighing 200 pounds, Moore is often mistaken for Joe Louis—so closely does Buddy resemble the great heavyweight champion—both in looks and manner. Married two years, Moore is the proud father of a fifteen-months' old son.

\* \* \*

## ARCHIE MOORE

CALIFORNIA boasts of one of the best middleweights in the game in Archie Moore, formerly of St. Louis but now making his home in San Diego. Archie, after several months of idleness due to four operations, has returned to the ring and hopes to be as successful in his comeback as he was before illness placed him on the shelf. In his first start since recovering, Archie scored a two rounds kayo over Shorty Hogue on October 31, at the San Diego Coliseum in a show put on by Promoter Linn Platner who

has been operating with success there for seventeen years. Prior to the Hogue battle, Moore fought twice this year, stopping Bobby Britton January 28 in three rounds and Jimmy Casino in five on St. Patrick's Day.

Moore has a fine record. Among his victories are those over Jack Coggins, Johnny Romero, Jimmy Casino, a draw with Eddie Booker, a decision in 12 rounds over Ron Richards in Australia and a knockout over Fred Henneberry in Australia in seven rounds. His friends are rooting hard for Archie to make good again.

\* \* \*

## SANTIAGO SOSA

CUBA has a young fighter who compares favorably with Kid Chocolate as a drawing card when the Keed was tops in the Pearl of the Antilles. The boy's name is Santiago Sosa and he holds the lightweight championship of the Islands. He is managed by Luis Gutierrez, who handled the affairs of Kid Chocolate and is trained by the latter.

Sosa started his amateur career in 1937 and in 1938 he competed in the amateur championship tournament which was sponsored by Nat Fleischer, and received from THE RING Editor a handsome belt when Sosa was returned the winner of the featherweight crown. The following year he turned semi-professional and has been making rapid progress since.

On November 4, 1939, he won the semi-professional featherweight championship of Cuba from Guillermo Barrios, winning the decision. Luis Gutierrez saw Santiago and knew the kid was good. He then took Santiago under his management and today Santiago Sosa, and Joe Legon, the Cuban Welterweight champion, are the two best drawing cards in Cuba.

In his fifth professional fight, in the summer of 1940, Sosa stopped Baby Oriental in 9 heats to win the Featherweight Crown of Cuba. After that, Santiago defended his title 3 times and successfully retained it. Baby Coullimber was his last challenger, but Sosa gave him a bad licking, winning the unanimous verdict in 12 rounds, after scoring 4 knockdowns. After that fight, he gave up his title to compete as a lightweight.

Santiago Sosa was in top form then and the promoters knew they had a real little star in the market. Simon Chavez, the South American featherweight title holder was imported to fight Sosa. Sosa knew that this same Simon Chavez held victories over *five world champions*—Kid Chocolate, Sixto Escobar, Petey Scalzo, Freddie Miller (twice) and Joey Archibald, as well as over Fillo Echevarria, Johnny King and Ginger Foran, yet accepted the bout.

The bout took place and Santiago was at his best. He gave a terrific lacing to Chavez. After that fight, Sosa lost his first professional bout to that Mexican *tornado*, Carlos Malacara. Malacara won a split verdict.

After Malacara, along came Carl

# In Fistic Spotlight

"Red" Guggino, and he was easily beaten by Sosa. Then Sosa stopped Gallardo in one round and left for Panama.

Santiago did not have a very successful trip. He lost to Battling Nelson and drew with Leo Torres, but Santiago was sick and returned to Cuba weighing only 122 pounds. After four months rest, he reappeared and weighing 139½ against Mexican Tony Mar, he started a new winning streak, and has yet to be stopped.

On December 13, last year, Santiago scored in 12 easy rounds, over Jose Pedroso, then the 135 pound king, and along with his Pedroso victory, came the lightweight crown of Cuba. This year Sosa has gone 12 times to the post losing but once. He has defended his title three times and stopped his only Panama conqueror, Battling Nelson, in two rounds. His last start found him off his feed, as he allowed Carmelo Fenoy, Spanish lightie, to take a decision from him.

Among his victories this year we find Juston Jimenez (K.O. 8 rounds), Panchon Martinez (K.O. 2 rounds), and decisions over Charley Varre, Matt Dougherty, Clarence Cotton King (twice), Juan Villalba, and Joey Peralta. Yes, he is the best lightweight in Latin America, including Juan Zurita, J. J. Fernandez, Carlos Malacara, Rodolfo Ramirez, Victor Castillo and all the other stars.

Cubans are eager to see him in a title bout with the world champion.

* * *

### INDIAN BENNY DEATHPAINE

*I*NDIAN BENNY DEATHPAINE, the Mighty Aztec who carries a wallop in either hand. The Indian, though he has been fighting for a number of years, gave his ace performances against Jimmy Webb, whom he stopped in 40 seconds of the first round and Allen Matthews, whom he knocked out twice, each time in the second round.

The Aztec is a popular fighter in the Mid-West where he has done almost all of his boxing. He scales around 170 pounds and is claimant of the Indian light heavyweight championship.

---

### THE RING QUESTION BOX

*Martin Sommers, Bangor, Maine.*

*Q—Was the Schmeling fight with Sharkey in which Jack was declared the loser on a foul, the only world heavyweight title fight ever decided on a foul? . When Louis fought Simon in Detroit, was that a twenty round fight? Are twenty round contests permitted any more? What was the last such a fight, title or non-title bout, scheduled at that distance?*

*A—Yes, it was. The Simon-Louis bout in Detroit was scheduled for twenty rounds. So was the Louis and Pastor in St. Louis. Several states permit distance fights, among them Nevada and Idaho. The most recent was that between Henry Davis and Harvey Woods in Boise.*

*Alphone Sombreil, Montreal, Can.*

*Q—Did Rex Layne and Ezzard Charles fight twice or three times?*

*A—Layne won the fight in Ogden in which Jack Dempsey was the referee but lost one fight in San Francisco and was stopped in another. They fought three times.*

---

# HALL OF FAME

## Henry Armstrong

## (HENRY JACKSON)

The only fighter in the history of boxing to hold three world titles simultaneously. Henry was born in St. Louis, Missouri December 12, 1912. He started to fight under the name of Dynamite Jackson in 1929 and did not use the name of Armstrong until 1932.

Known as Homicide Hank and Hammern' Hank he was a perpetual motion fighter who never stopped throwing punches.

He won the featherweight title by knocking out Petey Sarron in six rounds, Oct. 29, 1937. He won the welterweight title by outpointing Barney Ross in fifteen rounds on May 31, 1938 and the lightweight crown by decisioning Lou Ambers on Aug. 17th, 1938. This was the only time that a boxer fought two consecutive fights for two titles in different classes. Henry gave up the featherweight crown on December 5, 1938. He lost the lightweight title back to Ambers on August 22, 1939 and lost the welterweight crown to Fritzi Zivic on October 4, 1940, he failed in an attempt to regain the crown from Zivic, when he was stopped in 12 rounds on January 17, 1941. It was the only time in 192 fights that he was stopped.

On March 1, 1940 Henry boxed to a ten round draw with Ceferino Garcia in a bout for Garcia's middleweight title.

While welterweight champion Henry defended his title twenty times. From October ninth to thirty 1939 he defended it five times.

After losing to Zivic in the return fight Armstrong retired, but made a comeback in 1942 and boxed until 1945.

During his career Henry fought 14 men who held world championships. Henry scored 97 knockouts in his career.

He defeated, Mike Belloise, Lew Jenkins, Fritzie Zivic, Baby Arizmendi, Juan Zurita, Midget Wolgast, Aldo Spoldi, Ceferino Garcia, Ernie Roderick, Chalky Wright, Leo Rodak, Willie Joyce, Tippy Larkin, Al Davis, Sammy Angott, Enrico Venturi, Frankie Klick, Benny Bass, Eddie Brink, Pedro Montanez, and Wally Hally.

# Fighters as Thespians

*Joe Louis Is Devoid of Dramatic Aspirations But Most of the Heavyweight Champions Sought Fame Before the Footlights or Camera and the Majority Failed to Make Good—Best Stage Hits Were Scored by John L. Sullivan, James J. Corbett, Bob Fitzsimmons and Jim Jeffries*

## By THE VETERAN

WHEN Joe Louis was recently assigned to special duty with the movie cast of "This Is the Army," the world's heavyweight champion got his second fling in the cinema. Two years ago he was starred in a film, entitled "The Spirit of Youth," and when it was completed, the Brown Bomber swore he would never again strut under the Kleig lights. He just felt that he didn't belong in an actor role, and he kept his word as long as he remained a civilian.

But once you're "in the army now" things are different. Whatever vows you may have made regarding your future conduct go blooey when opposed to the will of your Uncle Sam.

So it came about that Joe had to do a camera stunt along with 350 other soldiers who formed the cast of Irving Berlin's war play. Well, that was okay, orders are orders and must be obeyed. Joe, like a good soldier, stepped into line with the rest of his comrades. But he did ask that he be kept clear of a speaking role, and this request was granted.

*John L. Sullivan, who was at his best in "Honest Hearts and Willing Hands" and in "Uncle Tom's Cabin."*

With the exception of a few lines which he orates, Louis plays a silent part. He does a tap dance while drumming in company to a fast tune on the punching bag, and sings with his comrades in the finale. Joe has absolutely no ambitions in the screen or stage amusements line. The Army stunt was something that had to be done as military duty, and he went through with it.

\* \* \*

FOLLOWING the completion of the picture, Louis reported at the War Department in Washington to help arrange details of a projected world tour to put on boxing shows for American soldiers overseas. The heavyweight champion is of the opinion that the projected boxing shows would place emphasis on the necessity of attaining perfect physical condition, and he believes that the net result of such a tour would be the forging to the front of many good prospects in the person of soldiers who might decide to take up a professional ring career after war is over.

\* \* \*

WELL, one thing is certain—that Louis doesn't have to worry about capitalizing on film appearances. As matters stand now under Army regulations, he won't be able to do any actual fighting for the duration, hence, whether he won out as an actor, or the contrary, doesn't affect his box office status as far as drawing power is concerned.

It wasn't thus with former champs. Most of them tried to use their drawing power in fisticuffs as an aid toward building them into big stage or movie attractions, and the majority failed in this respect. Louis still remains the ace attraction in boxing, and doesn't have to keep himself before the public through pictures. Once the Axis is licked and the champion is back in civil life, there's a

fruitful pugilistic plum waiting to be picked by him. That's a match with Billy Conn, also now a member of the armed forces, and I miss my guess badly if such a battle wouldn't turn out to be the first million dollar post-war gate!

The screen, both in the "silent" days, and in the "talkie" era has proved a lucrative source of income for fighters. Not always as stars, but in a variety of roles demanding the athletic type of talent. The list of adventurers on the silver sheet of romance is too long to give in detail. But, offhand, one remembers such names as Frank Moran, Young Corbett III, Fidel LaBarba, Bert Collins, Les Kennedy, Maxie Rosenberg, Jackie Fields, Joe Benjamin, Texas Kid, and others, as performers whose faces were familiar to thousands of movie fans.

Besides these better known ring gladiators, Hollywood has helped many a good old has-been to drive the starvation wolf away from his door. It's a fruitful field of exploitation for the pug fraternity, and who knows if, some day, a real honest-to-goodness film star may

*"Gentleman" Jim Corbett, the master boxer and king of all pugilist-actors.*

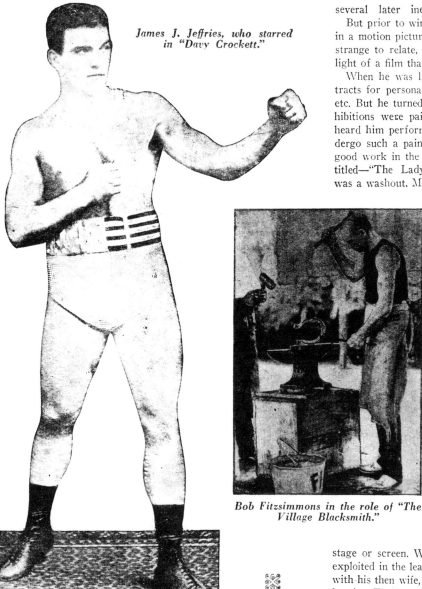

James J. Jeffries, who starred in "Davy Crockett."

Bob Fitzsimmons in the role of "The Village Blacksmith."

several later ineffectual attempts on the comeback route.

But prior to winning the title he was cast for a prominent role in a motion picture which had Primo Carnera for its hero. And, strange to relate, Baer's performance was the outstanding highlight of a film that was otherwise a good deal of a "dud."

When he was listed as fistic king he obtained numerous contracts for personal appearances at night clubs, vaudeville offers, etc. But he turned out to be a flop. His singing and dancing exhibitions were painfully mediocre, and those who watched and heard him perform went away from there resolved never to undergo such a painful ordeal again. Hollywood, remembering his good work in the Carnera picture, signed him up for a film entitled—"The Lady and the Fighter." This picture, however, was a washout. Max failed to click.

Max Schmeling, Jack Sharkey and Primo Carnera never filled roles in stage plays, nor had any of the trio the least ambition to become star actors. Each appeared in vaudeville, but only as boxers, displaying their skill with the gloves, but none fell for the dramatic lure.

Which was just as well for their respective peace of mind, for they all lacked the magnetic appeal which is such a necessary and vital asset to the achievement of success in drama. Gene Tunney, although a professed admirer and student of the Shakespearean drama, never had any hankering after the glories of a stage career. He wasn't much of a success in vaudeville sparring appearances after he defeated Dempsey, because his reserved attitude toward sport followers, and openly expressed contempt for the ring, except as a means of acquiring a fortune, killed whatever chances he may have had of attaining popularity.

* * *

JACK DEMPSEY, despite his popularity as a fighter, was unable to capitalize his popularity as an entertainer, either on stage or screen. When Jack was at the summit of fame he was exploited in the leading role of a melodrama entitled "The Fight," with his then wife, Estelle Taylor, once a film actress, cast as the heroine. The late David Belasco staged the show, but had nothing to do with financing it, and he had a hectic time trying to turn the Manassa Mauler into a pseudo Richard Mansfield.

He didn't succeed, because a whole army of Belascos could not have overcome the champion's handicap—the possession of a light, almost falsetto, voice, which, coming from a chap of such Herculean frame, sounded as startlingly comic as though an elephant were to squeak like a mouse.

When John L. Sullivan spoke his stage lines he roared like a hungry lion, and the echoing bellow of his bass vocal organ from that vast chest, delighted melodrama lovers. It was the kind of utterance expected from a slugging hero of gladiatorial mould. No matter how punk the play was, John L.'s rugged personality put it over.

There was a lot of money spent on "The Fight." Probably no other drama ever got the enormous amount of free advertising given it by New York's papers. Columnists and sport writers swam in oceans of space while plugging the Dempsey show. They really imagined that Jack would be as big a hit as Sullivan was in his day.

Mind you, the play wasn't half-bad of its type. Full of action, spilling melodrama in floods, with a swell scrap scene where Dempsey went into action in his colorful, dynamic style, and kayoed his man in a grand mauling spree, it seemed as though it should have been a box office success.

Not so, however! After the opening night, when throngs clamoring for admission blocked Broadway so that the police reserves had to be called out to get street traffic back to normal, "The Fight" didn't make good. It closed after a lamentably short run, and then took to the road, where its sponsors hoped that rural

yet be developed from the ranks of the hit-and-get-away brigade. Strange things have happened in the film world, where surprises are no novelty.

Looking back down the line of heavyweight champions, one observes that, on the whole, the transitions from ring to stage or pictures haven't been particularly successful. Jim Braddock, who preceded Louis as champion, hadn't any desire to be an actor. His talents didn't lie that way, and his only connection with the theatre was when he gave boxing exhibitions in vaudeville, after taking the heavyweight title from Max Baer.

Baer was an astonishing failure as a public entertainer, although, up to the time he became cock of the fistic roost by whipping Carnera, he seemed to be the most colorful product of pugilism in a decade.

Both in the ring and private life Max registered as an amusing clown par excellence, forever cutting up, getting a laugh out of everything, and so full of pep and vigor that he was the life of the party wherever he chanced to be. You'd have said, that, if ever there was a chap designed by nature as a stage hit—it was Max Baer.

But he was really superficial, all on the surface, as it were. Max was unreliable and had no genuine talent. That assertion goes for his ring work, as well as his ventures in the entertainment line. After he became champion he went to pieces as a fighter, as was clearly demonstrated by his poor showing against Braddock, and

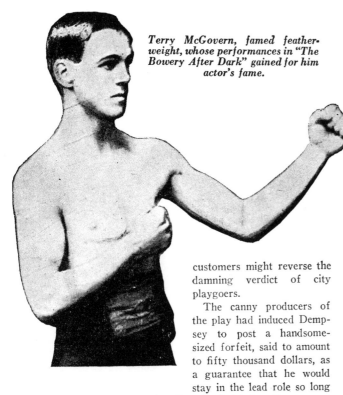

*Terry McGovern, famed feather-weight, whose performances in "The Bowery After Dark" gained for him actor's fame.*

customers might reverse the damning verdict of city playgoers.

The canny producers of the play had induced Dempsey to post a handsome-sized forfeit, said to amount to fifty thousand dollars, as a guarantee that he would stay in the lead role so long as "The Fight" was kept going. But the "sticks" audiences were also unappreciative of Jack's noble efforts to elevate the modern stage. After a few weeks, the drama was playing to a corporal's guard of spectators, and Dempsey, thoroughly disgusted, threw up his hands, let the forfeit go, and abandoned all dreams of a successful footlights career.

He was not a shining success in vaudeville or pictures, either. The cold fact was that his public didn't care for a hokum Dempsey. They wanted to see him knocking some bozo stiff in a genuine scrap, with a volley of his justly celebrated wallops—but that was all!

Even as Samson's strength lay in his abundant head of hair, so Jack's audience appeal rested in his punching ability. As a prizefighter, he rated 100 per cent. As a private citizen he had, and has today, a host of friends, whose members patronize the Broadway cafe of which he is the big show card.

But as an actor, his earning power was no greater than that of the veriest ham who ever wasted perfectly good grease paint on a face it was never meant to adorn!

\* \* \*

JACK DEMPSEY'S predecessor on the heavyweight throne—Jess Willard—was another woeful example of a misfit in the entertaining line. When Willard returned here after defeating Jack Johnson for the championship title in Havana, there were plenty of vaudeville bookings awaiting him.

But, as Mark Twain has written—"it's a solemn and awful thing to see a man persisting in an attempt to sing, when it is the will of God that he should confine himself to sawing wood!" And the initial appearances of Jess as an amusement purveyor to John Public were audience flops of such deadly inert nature that one disgruntled critic was driven to comment upon his debut as "an unforgivable insult to the human race!"

Which was playing it pretty low down on poor Jess, but the fact was no power on earth could have made even a mediocre actor out of him. His personality value was absolutely nil. He was a rather ungainly figure in the ring, and on the stage his movements were about as graceful as those of a cook stove trying to climb a tree. Also, he hated the whole business of the theatre and its atmosphere and was audience-shy in the bargain. For that matter, he had no liking for the ring either, except as a medium for making money.

In contrast to such dynamic scrappers as Dempsey and Terry McGovern, the giant Willard looked on his fighting career as a disagreeable necessity that he had to make the best of. He was originally a teamster in the far West. The publicity sharps exploited him as a cowboy, but though he could ride fairly well, he never punched cattle or took part in a roundup.

\* \* \*

A SHORT time before he lost the world title to Dempsey, a film was produced with Jess as its star. That was in the days of "silent" screen drama, and if memory serves correctly, it was entitled "The Champion." The public showing of the picture was held back until Willard's fight with Dempsey was decided. Its producers, who, like nine out of ten folks those days, thought Dempsey never had a chance with the big chap, felt that the drawing power of their investment would be increased considerably if they waited until Jess had added fresh lustre to his laurels.

But they gave a private showing of the film to a carefully selected and very limited number of guests. These latter came by special invitation, and I chanced to be included among the elect.

Willard was cast as a cowboy. His leading lady was Arline Pretty, who once played opposite Douglas Fairbanks in "silent" pictures. The days of the talkies had not yet arrived when Jess took this screen hurdle.

At first it had been intended to show Willard as Miss Arline's lover, but Jess wouldn't stand for this at any price. So another man was put in as the gallant squire of dames, and Willard appeared as a sort of protector of the amorous pair.

In this connection Jess performed heroic deeds by the score, which mostly consisted of slamming obnoxious people for a kayo, rescuing Miss Pretty from fiends in human form, and lending a helping hand to her sweetie, who never seemed to gather sense enough to keep from getting in Dutch.

Willard rode quite a bit in the action, and the picture being of the Western brand, participated in numerous bandit chases, etc. Taken on the whole the film was a hackneyed, stereotyped affair of the gun-shootin', hard ridin' sort that never projects a single original idea. But if Willard had whipped Dempsey at Toledo it might have been strong enough to pull its producers out of the red.

As it was—the latter were socked for a dead loss, for the picture was never shown to the public. It would have been perfectly futile to present Jess to the movie fans as a hero, after what happened to him in those fateful three rounds with the Manassa Mauler.

\* \* \*

JACK JOHNSON, from whom Willard took the title, made several vaudeville appearances after he became champion by beating Jeffries at Reno, Nevada. These stunts, however, were confined to sparring exhibitions. He wasn't a drawing card because racial prejudices turned "thumbs down" on him. There was no getting away from public resentment over the passing of the championship to a colored man.

It was unfair and unsportsmanlike, but the feeling persisted and there was no way of changing it. Oddly enough, after Johnson retired he scored as a public entertainer, making successful appearances at night clubs, and winning recognition as a band leader.

Jack, like most of his race, was a great music-lover. Those who know him best are aware of what musical miracles he can execute with his favorite instrument, the big "bull

*Jimmy Britt, California's contribution to fistic and thespian lore.*

# Fighters as Thespians

fiddle." In his band-leader capacity he was a welcome attraction in Seville and Paris, as well as Hollywood, although he never figured as a picture star.

Johnson had no desire to shine as an actor, although, in point of intellect and quick perception, to say nothing of his well developed sense of humor, he was probably better fitted to take the dramatic road than most of his fighting contemporaries.

\* \* \*

JIM JEFFRIES wasn't any great shakes as an actor, but he got by well in vaudeville because the public liked the lively sparring matches he gave in conjunction with his brother, Jack. Jeff boxed as he fought, roughly and with evident desire to do damage to his opponent.

Jack Jeffries was never a success in the ring. But it was a curious thing that he was never afraid of his champion brother, and when the two got together with the gloves, Jack sailed into the big fellow with tremendous vim.

Although less bulky than Jeff, the brother was a hefty cuss himself, and as strong as the proverbial ox. Jeff didn't spare him, and on one occasion, the two went on in a three round exhibition at Tattersalls, Chicago. In the last frame Jack ran into a clip on the jaw that laid him flat as a flounder.

Up he got in a hurry and sailed into Jeff with both fists flying. The champion was laughing, but when Jack threw a swing that landed on the nose, and started the claret flowing, the grin disappeared. Jeff was plainly riled, and went for brother Jack with the apparent intention of knocking his block off.

The applauding yells of the crowd must have warned him that he wasn't in there to commit murder, for he suddenly eased up, and contented himself with guarding off Jack's frenzied assaults until the round was ended.

They wrangled bitterly in the dressing-room afterwards, but Jack recovered his temper, and later they sat side by side in a ringside seat, watching the bouts, apparently on the best of terms.

\* \* \*

AFTER he won the heavyweight crown from Fitzsimmons, Jeffries went on the stage as Davy Crockett, in a melodrama of that title. He didn't have too much talking to do, which was a good thing, as his mental powers were not too heavily over-taxed.

The play was rich in scenes of physical violence in each of which Jeff scored okay, as might have been expected. It was oldtime border stuff, with lots of bullets flying, and here again, Jeff was right at home, for he was an enthusiastic hunter and good shot with either rifle or revolver.

Therefore his handling of those weapons was expert and realistic, and went far toward covering up his lack of dramatic knowledge. The real Davy Crockett as history records, was a dauntless frontiersman who shot to kill with unerring accuracy, and Jeff couldn't go very far wrong in impersonating a character so much akin to his own. Had he been cast in more polished roles, such as Jim Corbett played so well in "The Naval Cadet" and "Gentleman Jack," Jeff would have been a total loss.

As it was, "Davy Crockett" had successful runs in most of the key theatrical cities of the U. S. The scene in which Jeff, trapped with the "gal," in a log cabin, with wolves howling outside, finds the wooden door bar is missing, and thrusting his brawny arm through the iron staples holds it shut tight against the assaults of the wild beasts, never failed to bring down the house in a wild storm of applause.

Not quite in keeping with dramatic unities, perhaps, but none the less a highlight of the show, was the appearance of Jeff between the second and third acts in a sparring bout.

I have already said that Jeffries was a rough exhibitionist, and this was amply demonstrated during his "Davy Crockett" glove bouts. His sparring partner at the starting off of the show was Yank Kenny, a huge six-footer who bore an amazing facial resemblance to Jim Corbett.

Kenny at no time could be classed as a first-grade scrapper. But he had fought quite often, had several knockouts to his credit, and it might have been supposed that he would have filled the bill nicely as Jeff's sparring partner. But he couldn't get used to Jeff's heavy punching, and frequently threatened to throw up his job, unless the champ handled him more gently.

But Jeffries either couldn't or wouldn't play light. The upshot was that Kenny finally carried out his threat, swearing that one of his ribs had been broken by a hearty wallop, and quit the show. He was replaced by the ever faithful brother Jack, who always seemed to be immune to the effects of fraternal punching.

\* \* \*

BOB Fitzsimmons, like Jeffries, pleased the vaudeville crowds because his sparring bouts were always of an energetic nature. Fitz's sparring partners earned their salaries, for the lanky, freckled pugilist bruised them up considerably with jolts and jabs that carried a lot of force, even though Bob "pulled his punches" and never made an attempt to kayo a man who wasn't his match with the gloves.

He never shone in a regular play. Once an enterprising producer had a melodrama written under the title of "The Slugging Blacksmith," and persuaded Bob to fill the hero role. Fitz knew his limitations and didn't care about the proposition, but accepted a bonus in advance and the rehearsals started.

But it was "no go." Fitzsimmons felt himself altogether out of place as a wearer of the sock and buskin, and couldn't get interested in his prospective elevation to stage stardom.

The consequence was that he "went through the motions" listlessly, and drove the unfortunate director nearly crazy by his indifference to bawled instructions, and the air of humorous contempt with which he regarded the whole proceedings. In the long run the producer abandoned his idea of making a great heroic actor out of the matter-of-fact Fitz.

Perhaps Bob might have done better had he been cast in a comedy role. For he could sense a funny situation and make the most of it without half trying. After he retired from the ring he made his living for many years in a vaudeville monologue act that "went over" successfully.

He was in theatrical harness, appearing on a vaudeville bill in Chicago, when he contracted the cold that developed into pneumonia and caused his death in that city in 1918.

\* \* \*

OF all the fighters who transferred their activities from ring to stage, James J. Corbett proved to be the finest actor. Jim was just as much at home before the footlights as he was behind the ropes, perhaps even more so. He had a natural talent for the theatrical field, and his one-time manager, William Brady, has gone on record as stating that, quite outside the reputation he won as one of the most scientific boxers that ever donned the gloves, the young Californian who dethroned John L. Sullivan could have earned a good livelihood on the stage as a performer either in the legitimate or vaudeville.

Besides a handsome face and fine athletic figure, Jim Corbett possessed the gift of clear, accurate delivery in his speech and the ability to make good either in comedy or emotional scenes. It was a source of amazement as well as of gratification to Brady that Corbett required so little coaching as an actor.

Jim appeared as the good-looking hero of two melodramas—"Gentleman Jim" and the "Naval Cadet," while under Brady's management, and in both cases he scored decided hits. For years after he quit the ring he was a topliner in vaudeville, as a monologue artist. He was a born story-teller and never failed to keep his audiences interested and in good receptive humor.

In direct contrast to the polished, graceful Corbett, the man from whom he took the blue ribbon of the ring, John L. Sullivan, was a good deal of a joke considered as a Thespian. Sullivan was really no actor, nevertheless the Strong Boy from Boston was an acknowledged darling of the gallery gods.

When John, prior to losing the championship, used to stride forward before the footlights and announce in his thundering bass voice that—"I can lick any man in the house!" his hearers applauded frantically, for they believed him and were a unit in supporting that assertion.

He didn't need dramatic ability to put himself over with the public. It was just his personality that counted—he was John L., and that was enough. Whether as Simon Legree in "Uncle Tom's Cabin," or the slugging hero of "Honest Hearts and Willing Hands," John never lost his following of enthusiastic admirers.

Among the most celebrated boxer-Thespians of the old school were Jimmy Britt, Jack McAuliffe, and Terry McGovern. Britt and McAuliffe were noted monologists. They could keep a theatre gathering interested and amused no matter where they went. Their story telling was full of human interest. Britt's recitals were masterpieces.

As for McGovern, his work with the aid of Sam Harris, his manager, and Joe Humphreys, his co-manager, is too well known for repetition here. His greatest work was in "The Bowery After Dark."

# DEMPSEY'S TUMBLE TOP RING THRILL

*Jack's Backward Flip Out of the Ring in First Round of
Firpo Fight Made That the Most Dramatic*

## By DANIEL M. DANIEL

*Jack Dempsey training for Firpo bout.*

WATCHING Jack Dempsey wrest the heavyweight championship from Jess Willard in that sunbaked ring in Toledo was thrilling. Seeing Joe Louis batter Joe Schmeling and avenge his previous defeat by the German was a kick. But the thrill of thrills in so far as this writer's ring recollections are concerned came on the night of September 14, 1923, at the Polo Grounds in New York, where Dempsey stopped Luis Angel Firpo, the Wild Bull of the Pampas, in the second round, after the Argentinian had punched the American out of the ring in the first.

The Dempsey-Firpo battle lasted only 3 minutes, 57 seconds. But into that brief period were jammed more thrills than have been packed into several thousands of rounds of struggle by other heavyweights for the title now held by Louis.

A poll of the old timers of the ring unquestionably will establish the Dempsey-Firpo tussle as the most highly dramatic in their experiences. Nat Fleischer, publisher of THE RING, calls it his master thrill. So does Jim Dawson, boxing expert of the New York *Times*.

Dempsey himself designates the Firpo fight as the toughest of his career. "I was knocked out by the Argentinian's first punch and went right on fighting in my sleep," Jack confesses.

The high light of the fight in which a South American came so close to taking the world's heavyweight title for the first time of course was Dempsey's header out of the ring in the first round.

* * *

MORE has been written about that incident than about any other in the history of boxing. More articles have been built around this pulse-quickening development than any other similar happening in title competition. Charley White knocked Benny Leonard out of the ring in Benton Harbor, in circumstances somewhat like those which enveloped the Firpo exploit. And yet, ring history shows nothing exactly like the trip which Jack took out of that ring. It was an historic boxing incident.

It was a righthander that drove Dempsey through the ropes, and almost cost him his title.

It was a righthander that spilled Dempsey out of the ring, on the downtown side. Sitting together in the first row of the press box, right under Dempsey as he came their way, were Jack Lawrence, Miss Jane Dixon, and Bill McGeehan.

Some accounts of the incident insist that Jack fell into Bunk Macbeth's typewriter.

However, it was the trusty portable of Mr. Lawrence that suffered under the impact of 192 pounds of hurtling human as Jack landed in that press box.

Lawrence heard Dempsey gasp an epithet and shout, "Help me back in there."

Ring legalists still insist that if Firpo had had a handler thoroughly conversant with the rules, and had refused to continue the fight on the ground that he had knocked Dempsey out—that Jack had been aided back into the ring after he had been stopped—Firpo would have argued himself into the heavyweight championship of the world.

However, let's not wonder what would have happened that night. Too much did happen.

* * *

I DISCUSSED the fight with Dawson the other day and he said, "Dempsey got a terrific right on the shoulder blade when he was standing upright, without a crouch, for the first and perhaps the only time in his ring experience. I don't believe the punch itself hurt him. It was the impact. When he landed on Lawrence's typewriter he seemed to know exactly what was going on."

How does this jibe with Dempsey's own version of the backward flop out of the ring?

"First let me say that Lawrence's grabbing me to help me back into the ring did not assist me," Dempsey says.

"I know the writers meant well, but they hindered me. I was able to navigate and knew what I was doing.

"Firpo backed me to the ropes and was lashing away at me with both hands. I was trapped. I was trying to get back into the center of the ring, where I could let him have it.

"He shot a left at me, and I ducked it. I ran right into one of his sweeping right swings, and out I went.

"I was twisting my body to get away, and my head was bent, right back against the ropes. That left me off balance, and a sucker for a flight out of the ring, when he belted me with the right swing.

"The upper part of my body went through the ropes, and my legs flew up into the air. You cannot realize how I felt. I grabbed at anything that came along, and punched one of the officials in the eye.

"If the press box had not been built much higher than is customary, I could have suffered serious injury. I might have broken my neck.

"As I toppled into a typewriter, I saw the referee dash to the ropes and standing over me, start counting. I knew I had to get back in there quick or lose the title. But try to rescue yourself from a comparable position with boxing gloves on your hands!

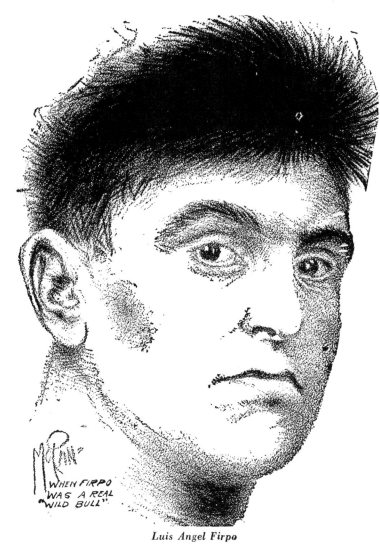

WHEN FIRPO WAS A REAL "WILD BULL"

*Luis Angel Firpo*

Well, I just about made it. The count was nine when I returned to action.

"I said to myself, 'Jack, this was much too close for comfort. This hombre hits too hard and you can't take any more chances.' So I let him have it in the second.'"

\* \* \*

*T*O the writer, one of the most amazing occurrences marked Dempsey's return to the ring.

Firpo was waiting for him, and threw a left and a right to the chin. Jack looked groggy.

But just when it looked as if the title were about to change hands, Dempsey turned the tide with one punch.

Jack crashed one of his super rights to the heart. Firpo winced. Soon the round ended.

That blow was one of the hardest struck by the world champion in that battle of giants. The marvel of it all is that the Argentinian didn't go down and remain down when that punch struck. The thud could be heard around the ringside. Firpo's mouth opened wide as the fist crashed and momentarily he couldn't catch his breath. But, being in perfect physical condition, he quickly recovered.

About a year after the fight, Dempsey discussed it with the late Bob Edgren, cartoonist and ring expert of the old *Evening World*.

"Bob, I would like to tell you something from the inside," Dempsey revealed. "Firpo actually stopped me with his first punch. My head was knocked out, but my legs were alive. I fought the rest of the fight in a daze."

As a matter of fact, the punch to which Dempsey referred was Firpo's third, not his first.

Luis's first was a right to the face. His second was a left to the

temple. Then he cut loose a right swing which Jack blocked with his arm.

Then Firpo whipped a right to the body, and Dempsey's knees sagged. That was the punch.

Jack's knees touched the canvas but he grabbed Firpo about the body and pulled himself erect.

Now Dempsey did something miraculous for a fighter who, as he insists, was out on his feet. He belted a left to the jaw and the tremendous man from the Argentine went down like a poled steer.

\* \* \*

*I*T was a terrific right to the jaw after 57 seconds of fighting in the second round that gave Firpo his quietus, and killed his title chances.

It was that first round, however, that furnished the classic touch. Before Firpo drove the Manassa Mauler out of the ring, he was knocked down seven times. Five times the referee, Johnny Gallagher, counted. Twice the Bull went to a knee and rose before Gallagher could say, "One."

Dempsey was knocked down twice and Firpo nine times —for a thrill total of eleven—in those 3 minutes, 57 seconds.

Dempsey says, "I went into the fight determined to win with one punch, if I could. The cheer that rang through the Polo Grounds when Joe Humphreys introduced me made me feel great. I said, 'Those people call on you as an American to knock this guy silly.'

"I remember that right at the start I cut loose with a left hook. Had it landed, the fight might have ended then and there. Though I will say that big guy could take it, and plenty.

"I missed that left hook, and then the grandstand hit me. Some of the reporters were charitable and said I slipped. I didn't slip. I was knocked silly.

"Next thing I knew, looking through a fog, I saw Firpo on the floor.

"I read the next day that I had knocked him down seven times. Well, you can't prove that by me, because I don't recollect anything about the first round except Doc Kearns' face, white, scared, as I sat in my corner after the first round. Doc gave me the smelling salts and said something about my having slipped. He meant I didn't have the old zing any more.

"Well, my head wasn't clear, but my instinct was operating. I said to myself, 'You let those cheers make a sucker out of you. You planned to let that guy miss and then let him have it. Well, go back to your plan—and don't let him hang around for any pictures because this man could stop you cold,'

"So in the second round I did what I should have done in the first place, and hung the old kayo on him.

"Funny, I don't remember having gone into any other fight so confident, so relaxed. On the afternoon of the contest I was walking down Riverside Drive, and I saw a lot of kids playing on the grass. I joined them. Now, if I had been tense, I never would have done that, would I?"

\* \* \*

*T*HE rise of Luis Angel Firpo to the place of a contender for the heavyweight championship of the world is a story not only dramatic. It is downright fantastic. Perhaps the most fantastic in the entire history of the roped arena.

Almost out of nowhere came this big hulk of a man with primordial instincts—out of nowhere to clamber through the ropes with Dempsey that September night in 1923.

There were some 85,000 persons in the ball park, and the take was $1,200,000, of which Dempsey got approximately $450,000 and Firpo $150,000.

This was one of the golden fights of the Million Dollar Gate era developed by Tex Rickard.

Jimmy Walker talked about this fight only recently. He discussed an angle which hitherto had not been discussed. Jimmy was the father of the boxing law in the state of New York. In 1923, this law was in its infancy. Every fight staged under it had some bearing on its continued life.

It seems that before the Dempsey-Firpo scrap, there was a report that it was not going to be on the up and up. However, let Walker tell about it:—

"I never have attended a fight in such fear as I watched the Dempsey-Firpo engagement. A few days before the fight I met Charley Murphy, of New York political fame, and he shook the Murphy finger at me with a warning, 'Senator Jim, there are a lot of folks gunning for you for having put through your boxing bill. I am told that this Dempsey-Firpo affair has been pre-arranged. I hope, for your sake, that it is on the level. Better watch out.'

"I got quite apprehensive, and decided to watch every move of the two fighters with the closest attention. I was out to detect larceny.

\* \* \*

"WELL, the two fighters climbed into the ring, and they looked honest enough to me. Then I felt a figure by my side. It was Jess Willard, from whom Dempsey had won the title in 1919, and who had fought Firpo.

"Willard said, 'Do you mind, sir, if I crouch alongside of you?' I replied, 'Jess, if you can squeeze in here by my side, you're welcome.'

"So Willard squeezed in, and then the bell rang and the warriors squared off. Dempsey missed with a left and then Firpo landed and Jack slipped down. Willard jumped to his feet and blocked my view. Jess shouted, 'I told Jack that man could hit. I warned him. I told him that man could punch.'

"Jess wouldn't sit down. In fact, he wouldn't even tell me what was happening. He just stood there and shouted.

"Well, sir, I want to confess that the Dempsey-Firpo fight was the only one I ever attended which I did not see.

"The contest lasted less than four minutes, but after the first knockdown, I saw nothing, and whatever I know about the contest I remember from having read about it in the papers the next day.

"Murphy never asked me about the fight because it was quite obvious even to the fiercest foes of boxing that no two fighters ever had been more earnest, or more desperately on the level."

The start of the fight was orthodox enough. The bell rang and Dempsey charged from his corner in the Dempsey manner. He was short with a left and grinned. Firpo took that right war club of his and let Jack have it in the face. Then Luis smote the Mauler on the left temple and before you could say Elmer Mickleweight, the Bull hauled off with a Pier One right to the body, and Dempsey looked like a dead pigeon.

Jack grabbed Firpo for all he was worth, and, on arising, smacked a left-hander to what the fancy calls the mush.

\* \* \*

FIRPO hit the canvas, but refused to take a count. Luis landed with right to the body and right to the jaw, and Dempsey was in trouble.

While the crowd was on its feet, shouting, screaming, gesticulating, Dempsey lashed a left uppercut to the Argen-

tinian's jaw and Luis sank to his knees.

As Firpo was rising, Dempsey, whom Referee Gallagher had forgotten to send to a neutral corner, cracked a right to the head. Firpo went back again, and Gallagher chased Dempsey away, with a warning.

Up came Firpo, wild as a bull, fire in his eye, muttering in his choicest Argentinian lingo.

Dempsey replied with a right to the jaw, and down went Firpo again!

Luis once again disdained a count and after getting up, let Jack have it with rights and lefts. Imagine the bedlam!

It was then that Dempsey went through the ropes. What a first round, and what a fight!

As the second heat got under way, Dempsey dashed out of his corner determined not to let the Bull last another minute, if he could help it.

They boxed around and then Firpo hit Jack with a thump thumping right to the body. Jack held tight. As they broke, Jack uncorked two red hot left hooks. Luis didn't like them. Two right uppercuts, a smack into the midriff, and Firpo was in dire straits.

A few short-arm punches, and Firpo went down. At the count of five, the South American arose, and it wasn't long thereafter that Jack uncorked that climactic right to the jaw which ended the fight.

Science? There was next to none in this contest. Art? Well, if a gigantic figure like Firpo lying on the canvas is art, if Dempsey hurtling out of the ring is art, then the battle was a Corot, a Correggio, a Raphael, a Rubens and a Bellows all painted into one thrilling panorama.

Drama? Nothing like it before, nothing like it since—and if the mere punch by punch story will help convince you, here it is:—

ROUND ONE—Dempsey whirled and glided across the ring like a panther. Firpo was scarcely out of his corner when Dempsey was on top of him. Jack lunged out with a left, but it was short.

Firpo lashed out with a right and it landed on Jack's face. Firpo's big boulderlike fist and hairy forearm landed clublike on Dempsey's left temple. The champion was partially stunned, but he blocked the next blow, a right swing that caught him on the forearm.

Firpo quickly whipped over a right to the body and Dempsey's knees sagged. It appeared he was ready to sink to the floor, but he saved himself by grasping Firpo's body and pulling himself to his feet. Dempsey's knees touched the canvas.

Dempsey arose and swung quickly into action. He hooked his left to Firpo's jaw. Down went Firpo. Luis disdained a count. He clambered to his feet, eyes blazing and rushed pell-mell into the champion. The Wild Bull crashed his right solidly to the body. Dempsey couldn't avoid it. Firpo shot his clublike right to the jaw and staggered *(Continued on page 38)*

*The third knockdown in the opening round. Luis was floored seven times in this session and gave a display of extraordinary gameness.*

*Firpo sends Dempsey out of the ring during the first round of their bout at the Polo Grounds.*

# Dempsey's Tumble

the titleholder. Dempsey stepped in with a left uppercut that stunned Firpo and the Argentinian sank slowly to his knees.

Dempsey arose and swung quickly into action. He hooked his left to Firpo's jaw. Down went Firpo. Luis disdained a count. He clambered to his feet, eyes blazing and rushed pell mell into the champion. The Wild Bull crashed his right solidly to the body. Dempsey couldn't avoid it. Firpo shot his club-like right to the jaw and staggered the title holder. Dempsey stepped in with a left uppercut that stunned Firpo and the Argentinian sank slowly to his knees.

Dempsey stood over him but Luis managed to get up, only to receive a cruel left followed by a terrific right to the body. Firpo was gone. He winced but didn't go down. He swung his ponderous right to Dempsey's ribs three times. Dempsey side-stepped a fourth attempt and let loose a swinging left that crashed to Firpo's jaw. Once again Firpo went down.

Dempsey stood directly over him in violation of the rules while Referee Gallagher began the count. Firpo attempted to rise and Dempsey lunged a right at him, the blow grazing Firpo's head just as he was getting off the canvas. The referee overlooked this unintentional violation of the rules. Firpo sank back again. The referee warned Dempsey to beat a retreat and as he did so, the Argentinian arose.

Dempsey was at him in a jiffy. He landed a left and right to the jaw, dropping Firpo in Jack's own corner. Again Firpo ignored a count. Eyes blazing and sullen features enraged, Luis rushed at Dempsey, swinging lefts and rights. He rushed

Dempsey across the ring. A right swing that came up almost from the floor, caught Dempsey and sent him hurtling through the ropes.

Several newspaper men threw up their hands and checked Dempsey's fall. They pushed him back into the ring, while the referee and the knockdown timekeeper were counting. The count of nine had just been reached when the champion got back into a fighting pose. Firpo was atop of him with a rush, flailing away with both hands. He shot out a left and then followed with a lusty right that caught Dempsey on the chin.

Dempsey suddenly rallied. He leaped at his foe and crashed a right solidly to the heart. Firpo winced under the force of impact. He exchanged blows with the champion and then worked Dempsey into Firpo's corner just as the bell sounded.

*Round Two*—Dempsey rushed out of his corner. The champion, highly excited, glided in close on the waiting Firpo and raked him with short-arm lefts and rights. Dempsey glided pantherlike after his prey but was met with a crashing right to the body and jumped into a clinch.

On the break, Dempsey stepped quickly back and landed two damaging left hooks. Dempsey dug his left into the body, then shot two right uppercuts and followed with a left to the body as Firpo jumped into a clinch. Dempsey shook him off and drove in short-arm blows. Firpo sank to the canvas.

The count reached five when Firpo arose. Luis lashed out a long right to the neck. Dempsey got inside a left lead with short-arm jolts. In close, Dempsey drove his left mauler deep into Firpo's midsection. On backing away, he crashed a short-arm right to the jaw.

Firpo went down like a poled steer. He lay motionless for two seconds then started to writhe and twist convulsively. He rolled over on his back. He drew up one knee in agony. The count reached five when Dempsey, instead of standing over his fallen foe, went to a neutral corner. Firpo was motionless as the count reached ten and Dempsey had successfully defended his title.

## MINNESOTA NEWS
### By SPIKE McCARTHY
#### (Pinch-hitting for Billy Colbert)

DAN SMITH, a St. Paul amateur boxer of 1939-40, and now a United States Marine, was wounded in the battle of Iwo Jima. Good luck, Dan, and a speedy recovery.

Roy Westphalinger, the Northwest's most prominent fight announcer, has just been promoted to a staff sergeant. Roy, a veteran of three years in the Army (18 months overseas), is now stationed at Camp Hood, Texas.

My best regards to Lt. Bill Bush, former Recreational Director at Camp Wolters, Texas, 1942-43. Bill was instrumental in putting over with a bang, the big Camp Boxing Tournaments held there every three months.

Augie Ratner, former Minneapolis boxer of the twenties, is now the proud owner of Augie's Lounge, one of the better night spots in the Flour City.

Phil Gallivan, former big league baseball pitcher, and now a St. Paul tavern proprietor, has been bit by the boxing bug and now wants to become a boxing promoter. Well, he should do all right as he is well known and is a very popular guy. Good luck to you, Phil.

Chuck Singer, one-time Minneapolis lightweight, and now a successful grocery store operator, is still looking for a heavyweight prospect. Who isn't?

Sgt. LeRoy Holmes, a St. Paul amateur boxer of five years ago, has been seriously wounded in action in Germany. Best of luck to you, LeRoy, and a full recovery from your wounds.

I wonder at what part of the universe my old pal, and good buddy of my Army days at Camp Wolters, Texas (Soft Shoe Louie Katz), is now stationed! Old Soft Shoe was for many years the program man for the boxing clubs here in St. Paul, Hibbing, and Duluth.

Floyd Hagen, St. Paul's crack lightweight, is now home on a furlough after being in the South Pacific for the past 18 months. Floyd is now a coxswain and has been in the Navy for the past two years.

Iron Mike Ferrozzo, one-time manager of Charley Ratzleff, the old heavyweight, and Fred Lenhart, has now taken over the managerial duties of Buzz Brown, Negro St. Paul welterweight.

If the following boys see this little item, will they please get in touch with the writer. Marcus (Al) Luna, Adam Delgado, and Jose Lanza. These boys are all in the infantry across the sea, and I would like very much to hear from them. They were all crack boxers down at Camp Wolters, Texas.

Dick Watzl, a former St. Paul middleweight boxer, now a member of the uniformed division of the local police department, and Smiling Bob Costello, a detective in the juvenile department, have charge of the police department's boxing team. They have a nice, modern, well-equipped gym where they can be found every night teaching the young boys the fundamentals of boxing, good sportsmanship, and the value of clean living. The boxing game could surely use more men like these two.

Charley Teirney, St. Paul's popular chief of police, is a boxing fan of the first water. He never misses a show in either town and can always be found in the press row with James Lynch, the Ramsey County prosecuting attorney.

Send all boxing news to this writer, care of the Mike Gibbons Gym, Hamm Bldg., St. Paul, Minnesota. If any boxers are seeking work in the Northwest part of the country, please get in touch with this writer or with Billy Colbert. Thank you, will be seeing you again next month.

# WOLGAST vs. RIVERS In Double Knockout Bout

### However, Referee Jack Welch Dragged Champion Upright and Held Him Up as He Counted Mexican into a Jobbing

### By DANIEL M. DANIEL

THE secret yearning of all steady patrons of the ring is the double knockout. It never happens, but that doesn't prevent the customers from hoping that some day it will be their good fortune to be around when two contestants land the double haymaker, and both hit the canvas for the full count.

The closest thing to the double knockout in the modern history of fistic championship competition was seen at Vernon, Cal., on July 4, 1912. The contestants were Ad Wolgast, lightweight champion of the world, and Joe Rivers, a Los Angeles Mexican, born Jose Ybarra.

This double socko came in the thirteenth round of one of the hottest scraps in the annals of lightweight struggle.

The referee, Jack Welch, could have ruled a double knockout and made no mistake. But he gave the decision to Wolgast by a knockout, and since has been held to have committed one of the biggest boners perpetrated in title fisticuffs. Rivers was jobbed.

The battle between the tough Wolgast and the hard-hitting Rivers is listed as the most dramatic in the lightweight class, even over the fight in which Charley White had Benny Leonard out of the ring at Benton Harbor.

Veterans who saw Jack Dempsey fight Firpo, who saw the Manassa Mauler stop Willard, pick the Wolgast-Rivers imbroglio over both of Jack's triumphs for thrills, sustained suspense, for the gamut of emotions a human can run through in watching two gloved gladiators belt each other all over the ring.

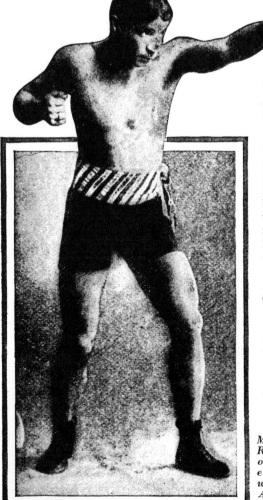

Mexican Joe Rivers, one of the greatest lightweights in American ring history.

The Wolgast of July, 1912, had taken the lightweight championship from Battling Nelson. A year previous to the Rivers fight, Ad had belted out the crafty Owen Moran, incidentally, also in the thirteenth.

In July, 1912, Rivers was very much on the rise. In 1911, he had been stopped in sixteen heats by Johnny Kilbane, but Joe did not let this discourage him. He fought a 20-round draw with Frank Conley, who at the time was one of the toughest lightweights in the world.

\* \* \*

IN 1912, Rivers stopped Conley in a dozen heats, and California began to clamor for a chance at the lightweight title. Vernon made a strong financial bid for the fight, and Wolgast eventually agreed.

However, the Wolgast camp made what turned out to be a very important stipulation. It would agree to the Rivers match only if Jack Welch of San Francisco—the poor guy is dead—were named the referee.

Perhaps it was something of the custom in those days for the man with the title to reserve the privilege of picking his own third man.

*Ad Wolgast, world lightweight king who was aided by referee in bout with Rivers.*

In any event, the Rivers camp was so delighted with the opportunity to sign with Wolgast that the referee stipulation was overlooked. Los Angeles went daffy. The title was as good as won by Rivers, w h o m it could see only as the conquering hero.

There were 11,000 fans in the arena on the outskirts of Los Angeles that hot sunny July afternoon in 1912.

Rivers was younger, m o r e fiery, more eager. It did not take the experts very long to discern that Wolgast was not in the best of shape. He was flatfooted, slow.

*The famous double knockdown in the Rivers-Wolgast battle for the world lightweight championship at Vernon, Cal., July 4, 1912. Note Referee Welch assisting Wolgast to his feet. It was the most sensational double knockdown ever recorded in this country.*

lefts to the face.

"There w a s a savage gleam in Wolgast's eyes as he came forward, his hands held low and his shoulders moving in readiness for a deadly swing from either left or right.

"Rivers shot out a left, measured his man, then stepped in to drive home a magnificent right to the jaw.

"At the very same i n s t a n t, the half crouched champion let fly a left swing that started from the canvas and caught the Mexican low.

"As Wolgast landed that foul punch,

Wolgast resorted to every trick known to the wily ringsters of his time. Not the least of his weapons was his nasty tongue. He taunted Rivers, he called him all the rotten names a champion in fear of defeat would sling at opposition.

They slugged each other all over the place for a dozen bruising, gruelling sessions, and then came that famous Thirteenth.

At this point, Rivers had the title on points. There was no doubt about it. The Wolgast corner was in a furore and a fury. Herman Stitzel, handling Ad, later said that Wolgast had refused to come out for the thirteenth and that he had been forced to threaten the tired champion with a beer bottle.

Time and again Wolgast had hit Rivers low, but every time Wolgast's handpicked referee had turned his eyes the other way. Let Rivers tell you what happened in the big round:

"Near the end of the thirteenth round I saw another low punch coming and, unable to avoid it, I tried to beat him to it with a left hook to the body and another to the jaw, which knocked him out.

"But in the meantime, this low punch of his had landed, and I went down, with Wolgast falling on top of me.

"At the count of six, I was on my feet. When the bell ending the round clanged at the count of eight, I was in my corner.

"Meanwhile, Welch dragged Wolgast to his feet. He held him upright as the bell closing the round sounded.

"Remember, he had counted only eight when the round closed. Yet that referee went right on counting up to ten, and said I had been knocked out."

\* \* \*

WELCH dashed out of the arena, jumped into a car and went to San Fernando, where he boarded the train for San Francisco, and locked himself in a drawing room.

When the crowd realized what had happened, a mob formed, and went in search of Welch. It boarded the train on which he was a passenger, but could not find him. Lucky for Welch!

Rivers' description of the thirteenth round agrees with that of most unbiased critics who were at the ringside that day. Harry A. Williams wrote his agreement with the Rivers version and added, "I recall that two rounds before the finish Wolgast seemed to be tiring and his handlers were feeding him brandy."

One of the ringside stories had it this way: "When the thirteenth round started, Rivers definitely was on top. Almost down, Wolgast recovered, and met the oncoming challenger with a left to the wind which went perilously near the danger line.

"The blow doubled up the Mexican. In his anxiety to finish his man, the champion missed badly as his opponent ducked from side to side, then straightened out and shot a succession of

Rivers hit him with that terrific right to the chin, and both fighters went down in a heap. It was a double knockout.

"The referee walked over to the champion, stooped down, lifted him up, lugged him to his corner, and then pointed to Wolgast as the winner. He jumped out of the ring and was out of the arena before the crowd could realize what Welch had done."

Wolgast was a discredited champion when he left the ring, while Rivers was cheered as a winner and, no matter what Welch had said, the true title holder.

In the Rivers dressing room three doctors examined the Mexican and said he had been fouled.

\* \* \*

SOME weeks later Welch had the temerity to show up as the referee in another Wolgast fight. And he had the guts to attempt to justify his decision.

Welch said that Wolgast had been the first to land. He added that he found no precedent in ring history for declaring both men knocked out, and decided that the man whose punch had struck first was entitled to the decision. That it happened to be Wolgast was just coincidence.

One of them had to beat the count, and Welch decided that it had to be Wolgast. A neat way of putting it. So he picked the champion off the floor and held him up while Rivers was being counted out.

The worst to which Rivers was entitled was an even break. There was nothing to prevent Welch's declaring a double knockout.

Rivers also could have been ruled the winner either on a foul or by a knockout.

Rivers got a second shot at the lightweight title, against Willie Ritchie, another Californian. It was a very queer-looking affair, and there were charges that the Mexican had quit.

However, years later Joe said that he had been doped. Not exactly a new slant, but interesting.

Rivers said that before the fight his handlers had insisted on his taking three slugs of brandy. He never had done it before, he insisted, and protested. But they said, "Don't be a dope, the brandy will carry you along."

In the eighth the booze began to slow him down, Rivers said, and in the eleventh, the final round, he could not lift his arms. Very interesting, but how about the first seven rounds? Dope doesn't work that slow.

\* \* \*

THIS man Welch, who refereed the Wolgast-Rivers bout, had an interesting history. He was an exponent of the theory that in the ring, roughhouse tactics were to be admired. He insisted that he was working for the spectators, and that they liked rough and tough battling.

However, came a time when two fighters produced too much rough stuff even for Welch.

Some months before the Wolgast-Rivers affair, Welch was the third man in the ring when Frank Klaus met Jack Dillon in San Francisco. They violated every rule in the book right from the start but Welch did not have the guts to throw one or the other out of the ring.

Finally Welch announced that he would not referee the fight any further. The two contestants went along minus Welch, and the fight lasted the limit. Then Welch had the audacity to announce that Klaus had won the fight on points!

When Freddie Welch was struggling for a shot at the title which he was to win and lose to Benny Leonard, Wolgast fought him off for a time and finally consented to meet Freddie, but only with Jack Welch as referee. Freddie refused and Wolgast would not change his conditions. Finally the Briton accepted Welch as the third man, but the fight never came off.

It is interesting to note that when Owen Moran was stopped in the thirteenth round by Wolgast at San Francisco on July 4, 1911, he shouted foul just as Rivers did a year later. Motion pictures of the fight tended to uphold the Moran contention.

* * *

WOLGAST was not a great fighter. He was a slugger and interesting enough to watch, but not exactly an ornament to the scientific side of the game. Much of what has been written about Adolph, in a dramatic and nostalgic vein, has been colored with that aurora which Time sheds on the rough lads of other years.

Wolgast, for example, wasn't the fighter Benny Leonard was, nor did Ad give anywhere near as much as Benny did to the title, the sport, and the public.

Rivers would have been an interesting fighter if his career had not been so inconsistent. Mexican and Indian, of a family going back to the old Spanish days in California, Rivers came to the fore in a tournament for featherweights, staged by Tom McCarey in Los Angeles.

Rivers charged through that competition, beating, among others, Johnny Kilbane, who later stopped Joe in 16 rounds.

Had Rivers won that title, he would have got the shot at Abe Attell and the title, and who knows? However, Kilbane got the shot at the fading Abe, and won the championship. Rivers was only nineteen when he met Wolgast. It was Joe's first fight as a lightweight.

That the Wolgast side of the argument had the "works" it was rumored around Los Angeles before the engagement with Rivers.

As the referee hopped out of the ring on his panicky way to the train, he was stopped by a Los Angeles lawyer named Earl Rogers, who said: "It was the most gigantic swindle and the most wholesale bit of robbery that ever came to my notice. As early as ten o'clock this morning it came to my ears that a plot was on foot whereby Wolgast was to be given the victory, no matter what the cost might be. I watched every move of the three men inside the ropes and was satisfied early in the bout that the referee was favoring Wolgast. I openly charge that the decision was a crooked one."

Al Harder, official timekeeper, announced that Rivers could not have been knocked out, as there were only nine seconds left of the thirteenth round when Joe dropped to the canvas.

* * *

IN the Lewis-Burke fight, a ten-rounder at the Fairmont Club of New York on August 13, 1909, there were several knockdowns. In the first round Burke dropped Willie with a right-hand to the chin for a count of six. In the second, Willie retaliated by putting Burke on his back for a count of nine with a left hook that raised him off the floor.

Then came the sensational third. Both were mixing it in the center of the ring with Lewis having a shade the better of the milling. They were hammering away with lefts and rights to body and jaw when suddenly Burke started a right hook and Willie tried to beat him to the punch with a similar blow. They both landed at the same time and each hit the canvas.

Referee Billy Joh was flabbergasted. He jumped between the fighters and looking down, he snapped out the count. Burke, who landed on his face, was trying to turn on his side, but Lewis in falling, toppled in such a position that part of his body was resting on the sailor's knees. Burke's efforts to rise were futile because the weight of Willie's body was keeping him down. Willie wriggled and was just getting to his knees when at the count of six, the bell sounded, saving the situation.

When the next round started, Lewis rushed his man and landed many telling punches, but Burke was strong and took the punishment without flinching. Thus the bout continued until the sixth, when Willie again crashed his right to the chin and this time Burke went down for keeps and was counted out.

* * *

DOUBLE knockouts are scarce as hen's teeth and when they do take place, they receive wide publicity. Back in 1896 Ed Hagen and George Skulky engaged in a private fight for a $5000 purse in Chicago. It was a humdinger with bloodshed from the third round on to the sixteenth session when the bout was ended by a double knockout. Each raised his left almost from the ground after a hectic session and the blows landed with terrific force. Both hit the canvas and were out cold. When revived, the officials decided to divide the purse.

Three years previously at the famous Olympic Club of New Orleans, George Dawson and Ed Greaney engaged in a similar bout. Both rights crossed to the chin in the third and the lights went out for each. The referee called off all bets and called the bout "no contest."

On February 19, 1939, a double kayo took place in Salt Lake City when Pete Giacoma and Dock Diamond fought at the McCullough Arena. Each was out of commission as the boys landed a right to the chin.

On April 3, 1941, such a spectacular ending was witnessed in the middle-west when Al Doriac and Pat Kissinger, welters, engaged in a stirring scrap in Kansas City. Referee Harry Corbett ruled that each man lost by a knockout and that's how that bout was recorded.

When you see a double kayo you've witnessed something in boxing that happens but "once in a lifetime."

## Here is the Round-by-Round Story of the Wolgast *vs.* Rivers Fight

*Round* 1—They went in close and exchanged rights to the face. Rivers stood erect and continued his pokes to the face, while Wolgast crouched, bored in and caught Joe a stiff right over the heart and a hard right swing to the jaw. Wolgast sent his right to the body. Rivers ripped a terrific right for the jaw, but fell short. Wolgast placed two lefts to the mouth, while Rivers played on the kidneys with his left mitt. They clinched and, in the break, Joe let loose two powerful rights to the jaw. He struck two blows after the gong for which he apologized.

*Round* 2—Wolgast's left ear was cut as he came up with a left to the wind. Joe retaliated with a left to the jaw and right to the stomach, which made Wolgast stagger. In several mix-ups Rivers scored right and left wallops. The crimson dropped from Wolgast's left ear.

*Round* 3—Rivers met the champion with stiff jabs over the heart and at close quarter mauled the body. Both missed rights. In the mix-up both were wild. Wolgast landing a few blows and Rivers missing frequently, Ad put a hard left to the wind and tore into his opponent, but the Mexican fought back viciously. The bell interrupted a good slugging round.

*Round* 4—They feinted and Wolgast bored in. In the break Rivers hooked a right to the jaw. The claret was flowing freely from his face, while Wolgast's left eye was swollen. Rivers pelted the optic with right and left, with Wolgast boring into the body. Adolph missed a left swing as Joe walloped the sore ear with a right swing and then shot a left hook to the jaw.

*Round* 5—Wolgast took two left swings to the

face in order to land one left to the body. They clinched. The champion started wrestling and was cautioned by the referee. Wolgast missed two vicious left swings for the teeth and the round closed.

*Round* 6—Most of this round was spent in uneventful sparring.

*Round* 7—Rivers met his opponent with a right to the heart and then Ad took another right to the stomach. Head to head they fought across the ring, Wolgast scoring well to the body. Joe then opened up and staggered the champion with a starboard wallop to the chin. He then landed a stiff right to the stomach and got a similar poke in his—the corresponding part of his own anatomy.

*Joe Rivers (left) and Ad Wolgast together years after the double knockout bout.*

## LATE BOXING RESULTS

Flyweights—Mickey Hill kayoed Frank Appo, 9.

Bantamweights—Mace Carey drew with Clarence Talbott, 3. Clem Stewart beat Pat Danahar, 4.

Featherweights—Sal Bartolo outpointed Al (Babyface) Pennino, 8. Bobby Polowitzer outpointed Billy Marcus, 8. Donald Scanlon outpointed Billy Commodore, 4. Reg Lawton and Joe Bissaker, drew. Billy Alexander kayoed Billy Tollis, 2.

Young Strikefoot knocked out Dean Davis, 3. Clint Miller outpointed Kudo Ortiz, 8; Gilberto Osario beat Benny May, 6. Joe Dell defeated Wendel Douglas, 4. Bobby English outpointed Art Gomes, 6.

Charley Cellers knocked out Ricky Silvia, 2. Eddie Thomas knocked out John Taylor, 1. Reg Lawton and Joe Bissaker drew, 12. Billy Alexander kayoed Billy Tollis, 11. Joe Weatherall beat Bill Porter, 4.

Lightweights—Johnny Cool outpointed Vince Dell 'Orto, 10. Pat Brady knocked out Rudy Rivera, 3. Johnny Villanueva knocked out Henry Pratt, 3. Nick Stato knocked out Lou Prince, 5. Lou Suliveres outpointed Ellsworth Simley, 4.

Al Victoria outpointed Jeff Holloway, 6. Al Wooster knocked out Babe Querion, 2. Charley Wooster knocked out Bernie Small, 2. Johnny Priest drew with Pedro Crivello, 6. Tee Hubert knocked out Bobby Giles, 2.

Ralph Walton outpointed Alex Doyle, 10. Ray Nulph outpointed Joe Trillo, 6. Charley Howard outpointed Carl Olsen, 4. Joey Kushner knocked out Little Palmo, 3. Charles Hall outpointed Vic Jade, 6. Patsy DuPont outpointed George McKinnery, 4.

Frankie Curry outpointed Tony Morin, 4. Chet Bossio knocked out Kid Tagg, 4. Jimmy Esposito knocked out Joe Henderson, 1. Young Gougga beat Bill Wilson, 4.

Welterweights — Chester Slider outpointed Genaro Rojo, 10. Jimmy Dundee kayoed Stan Wilkes, 4. Mick Craven beat Mick Halpin, 4. Billy Marsden defeated Al Watkins, 12. George Sands kayoed Bill Hibbard, 10. Sammy Mammone outpointed Joey Manfro, 8.

Charley Fusari knocked out Pat Scanlon, 6. Allen Faulkner outpointed Dave Viau, 6. Harry Preston knocked out Freddie Torres, 2. Kid Filipino outpointed Billy Harrison, 10.

Shiek Rangel knocked out Speedy Cannon, 6. Johnny Worthey knocked out Ken Thompson, 2. Lou King outpointed Joe Rondeau, 3. Julie Cross outpointed Miguel Arroya, 4. King Kong Walker drew with Mac Doggie, 4.

Middleweights—Holman Williams outpointed Charley Burley, 10. Vinnie Vines outpointed Jean Goumet, 8. Oscar Boyd outpointed Arthur Hardy, 6. Walter Cunningham outpointed Clem Fitzpatrick, 6.

Billy Walker outpointed Tony Gillo, 6. Harry Daniels outpointed Federico Chavez, 4. Bill Simmons knocked out Major Read, 2. Ernie Woods knocked out Major Eagle, 1.

Ossie Harris outpointed Fritzie Zivic, 10. Sgt. Mad Anthony Jones outpointed Coolidge Miller, 10. Tony Del Gatto outpointed Baudelio Valencia, 6. Don Anderson knocked out Joe Rossi, 4. Jimmy Murray knocked out Lorenzo Gill, 4.

Light-heavyweights—Eddie Turner knocked out Wally Rich, 2. Jack Young kayoed Young Richards, 7; Jackie Marr beat Alf Gallagher, 12; Willie Davis knocked out Freddie Bailey, 1.

Heavyweights—Jack Hannon Porter knocked out Leroy Bolden, 5. Alex Stanton kayoed Jim Edwards. Jack Simmons stopped Bill Huggett, 8. Al Ware knocked out Doug Ellison, 7. Gus Schlee knocked out Alex "Bearcat" Jones, 6. Robin Lee drew with Charley Johnson, 6.

## WITH OUR GI'S IN CHINA
### By T/SGT. LOUIS DE FICHY

IN KUNMING, CHINA (Special) — The first round of the All-China Armed Forces boxing tournament was held at the Kunming Hangar Playhouse this Monday before the largest boxing crowd of servicemen to ever witness a boxing tournament in China.

Eleven bouts filled the card, and every fight was a thriller from start to finish. The boxing shows now being conducted at Uncle Sugar cannot compare with the talent that is available in the ICD.

The China Division of the Air Transport Command again swept the card by grabbing three straight victories and advancing them to the semifinals. The ATC boxing team is favored to cop high honors in the tournament.

The show was highlighted by an open heavyweight bout in which Pfc. Roy Hawkins, 194, Portland, Oregon, former Pacific Coast AAU heavyweight champion, representing the 1342nd BU, pounded out a three-round decision over Corp. Wayne Choate, 210, Fort Smith, Ark., who has won heavy titles at Camp Claiborne, La., in 1943, and at the British-American Tourney at Ramgarh, India, last year.

It was a sensational fight, a slugfest throughout. Another ATC member, Sgt. Louis Boytik, 110, Galveston, Texas, of this base, won a three-round decision over Chen Shung, 120, hailing from Bangkok, Thailand. Boytik, spotting the Chinese boxer ten pounds, did not dim his chances. His ring generalship pulled him through with flying colors.

Keeping the ATC record intact, Sgt. Jimmy Whiteford, 150, Chicago, Ill., also representing the 1342nd BU, won on a T.K.O. in 1:40 of the second round over Sgt. Johnny Wooley, 152, Louisville, Ky. The referee awarded the bout to Whiteford when Wooley was ready to hit the canvas to slumberland.

## CLEVELAND BOXING NEWS
### By PHIL GOLDSTEIN

LARRY ATKINS and Bob Brickman presented their first outdoor show of the season at the Stadium on June 26 and Cleveland fans were given a real boxing treat by Archie Moore, 162, New York, who technically kayoed Lloyd Marshall, 166, in the tenth and final round.

The first three rounds were fairly even but thereafter Moore was in complete charge with the exception of a beautiful right on the chin exploded by Marshall in the fifth. Moore was badly hurt but manoeuvered himself out of danger. His margin of superiority increased as the fight progressed.

**In the tenth, he scored three knockdowns. Referee Jackie Davis wisely stepped in at this point and halted the bout.**

**In the eight-round semi-final Bobby Richardson, 157, beat Pete DeRuzza, 157, New York, in a tame bout.**

Leo Garrett, 135, won an unpopular six-round decision over Jackie Connelly, 136, New York. Connelly lost the last two rounds but won the first four.

Rudy Zadell, 138, Barberton, kayoed Johnny Virgo, 138, Rochester, in the third with a right cross and left hook to the jaw. Virgo was leading prior to the knockout.

Chuck Lloyd, 132, beat Jimmy Ainscough, 140, Akron, in a pleasing four-rounder.

In the opening four-rounder, Rudy Turner, 152, Buffalo, beat Lloyd Gullick, 157.

## ARENA RINK BOXING CARD IN EASTERN NOVA SCOTIA
### By CHESTER MACDONALD

EASTERN NOVA SCOTIA fight fans saw Charlie (Bearcat) Jackson, 195, of New Glasgow dispose of George Peck, 190, of the R.C.N. Halifax in the 8th round in the main go of a card staged in the Arena ring, New Glasgow. Jackson, a Negro clouter, displayed plenty of willingness to mix it in the first frame while Peck boxed cleverly, but Charlie had him on the floor for a no-count near the end of the round.

The fans were on their toes as the boys slugged toe to toe in round two. The following rounds saw both boys mixing it freely with Jackson's heavier punching gradually wearing down the Haligonian. Near the end of the 7th, Jackson threw an assortment of punches that had the visitor on queer street. The 8th wasn't far gone when the Bearcat ended the fray with smashing right and left hooks to the head.

Percy Paris, Negro, 125, of New Glasgow, scored a T.K.O. over Mickey DeCoste, 125, of New Glasgow in the fourth frame.

Joe Bellefontaine, registered a win over his fellow townsman, Mickey Melanson. Both boys were featherweights, Mickey was down three times.

Young McEwan, 135, of Westville, kayoed Johnny MacDonald, 135, of New Glasgow in the second. In the semi-final Sparky Paris, Negro, 148, stopped Alex Brown, 148, of New Glasgow and Halifax in three rounds after taking two no counts.

Danny Ellsworth put on the show.

# Wolgast vs. Rivers

*Round 8*—Ad blocked two attempts of Joe to land on his body and then tore in with sledgehammer rights and lefts to the jaw, switching to the body and forcing the Mexican to cover up.

*Round 9*—Wolgast crouched and covered. They clinched, after which Wolgast got two lefts to the wind. Rivers poked his left and then ripped a hard right to the kitchen. Next he sent a right uppercut to the mouth and a left to the body that almost lifted the Mexican off his feet. Ad again tore in ripping both hands to the jaw and continued his fusillade, which forced Joe around the ring, but did no damage.

*Round 10*—Ad kept on top of his man. Both landed light punches to the jaw, and Rivers did some good pummelling on the face. Ad tore in and unsuccessfully tried a right for the body. At close quarters Joe kicked through with some smacking wallops to the teeth.

*Round 11*—Rivers pranced around, placing his left frequently in Ad's face. In a terrific slugging match both boys fell through the ropes. They shook hands on being assisted back into the ring. They slugged again, honors being about even. The gong found them going at a great rate in one of the neutral corners.

*Round 12*—In a clinch the boys exchanged body blows. Wolgast swung a left for the jaw, and as he did so his left foot slipped. He missed another hard left. Joe kept shooting his southpaw to the face and then switched with a hard right to the jaw and landed several hard rights in a terrific slugging match.

*Round 13*—Rivers rushed. They clinched, both holding. Wolgast was nearly bowled over from a right to the jaw, but bored in with furious lefts to the wind. He missed twice. Joe continued his fusillade of lefts to head to head. Both boys were fighting head to head. Ad suddenly crouched and sent in a terrific left directly over Rivers' groin. At the same instant Rivers pounded his right to Wolgast's jaw and the champion went down and practically out. Rivers fell, writhing in pain, and Referee Welch began to count. Claims of foul in behalf of Rivers were made from all corners of the arena, but the claims were not heeded by Welch, who picked Ad up from the floor and declared him the winner. His seconds had to carry him from the ring. Rivers was lying on the floor, but in a moment arose unaided.

# POSTWAR OUTLOOK

## By IRVING RUDD

*Tommy Gomez, wounded sixteen times, but back in fistic fold.*

THE RABID ring enthusiast scanning his favorite sports section is beginning to note many familiar names creeping into the boxing headlines. Freddie "Red" Cochrane, Gus Lesnevich, Tommy Gomez, Patsy Giovanelli, Marty Servo, Reuben Shanks, Beau Jack and numerous other fistic favorites have been discharged from the service and are raring to go.

Although Gus H. Fan will chortle gleefully, "Now we'll see some *real* fighters," —he may be in for a big letdown. Some of the above-mentioned scrappers have been inactive for as long as three years and may never regain the keen edge they possessed before they wnt off to the wars. The most notable example, we feel, is Freddie "Red" Cochrane, the welterweight champion. An in-and-outer, albeit a topnotcher, the Jersey redhead won the welterweight title from Fritzie Zivic on July 29, 1941. Then, with many lucrative money shots in the offing Cochrane, nevertheless, threw away these literally golden opportunities to enlist in the Navy. His last recorded fight prior to his enlistment, was a loss in ten frames to Zivic on September 10, 1942.

For three years Cochrane served valiantly, survived many strafings, was a great morale booster and coach to the boys in blue, but failed to see sharp competitive ring action. Discharged recently, he began to train seriously to make up for the lost time and face one or two tough fighters before putting his hard-won, profitless title on the block. While Cochrane and others were away, the calibre of pug developed during the acute wartime shortage was far below the standard of some five years ago. Men who received huge sums of money for main bouts in the Garden and other clubs could not, by pre-war standards, rate a six-round or semi-final spot on most matchmakers' cards.

For example, a welterweight favorite who has been boxing close to ten years and although he feared no man and fought the best, was beaten as regularly as a rug on Friday afternoon, only recently turned away hundreds at a local club in New York and earned a purse of close to $2,000. This writer recalls the same fighter gladly signing a guarantee contract for $150 to tangle with a nationally known favorite in an eight-rounder at this same club four years ago!

\* \* \*

THERE have been exceptions and the most noteworthy was the fellow Red Cochrane signed to meet—Rock'em, Sock'em, Rocky Graziano. This tough East Sider has shown no favoritism as to the type of opponent selected for him. Tommy can belt, can take a hefty wallop in return, and even old-timers grudgingly admit Graziano "belongs." So, on June 29 of this year, almost three years since he last faced topflight opposition, Cochrane, with a few warm-ups under his belt set out to face the best battler brought out on the homefront during this war.

For nine rounds it was nip and tuck and the Garden crowd was hysterical and limp as first the plodding Rocky would shake Red up and then the ex-sailor would come roaring back to put forth the best fight of his career. Cochrane unfolded a bag of pre-war tricks that befuddled the Dead End Kid. Red speared him silly at times. He slipped wild leads and countered beautifully to befuddle the youngster who was just a kid in knee pants when Red was an established fighter.

Both men showed hearts as big as a catcher's mitt coming into the tenth and final frame. Cochrane especially, for he had been stung by the "cheese champ" and "bum" epithets of the sports writers. Suddenly, like an ancient "lizzy," the welterweight champion ran out of gas, and then Rocky really poured it on. Poor Red knew in his mind what he wanted to do to offset the rushing Graziano. The will was there, but the stamina and strength were all gone and as everyone knows, tough Tommy won on a K. O.

They met in a later bout and this time the game Cochrane was duck soup for Graziano who scored another ten-round knockout. Most boxing experts feel that Cochrane, should he attempt a title defense against a hard punching welter like Ray Robinson, would be shorn of his crown.

\* \* \*

IS THIS to be the fate of most returning servicemen? Not if you'll listen to Tommy Gomez, the heavyweight from Tampa, Florida, who flabbergasted reporters when he arrived from Europe on the *Queen Elizabeth* recently and said, "I believe that 16 bullet and shrapnel holes will make me a better fighter—perhaps heavyweight champion of the world!"

Gomez, who kayoed 36 out of 45 opponents, before entering the army, was shot up three times in less than 10 hours last February 6 during the crossing of the Ruhr. He said he was pleasantly surprised

*Lenny "Boom Boom" Mancini, wearer of the Purple Heart, who has returned to the ring and now scales 154 pounds.*

to discover that the wounds in his arms, back, chest and legs made him more "relaxed" when he was boxing. Tommy pointed out that tension always tightened him up previously and prevented him from putting forth his best efforts. He cites his last bout which he lost to Johnny Flynn in Madison Square Garden as an example. After more than a hundred exhibitions Tommy is raring to go and expects to face his first foe about the middle of December.

"I tried to arrange an exhibition with Billy Conn," Gomez declared, "but somehow it couldn't be managed. I can lick Conn right now," he emphasized. Tommy's list of victims is studded with top-flight names like Teddy Yarosz, the late Tommy Tucker, Tony Musto and Buddy Knox.

\* \* \*

GUS LESNEVICH, fresh out of the Coast Guard, has no qualms about meeting rugged opposition as soon as he is in shape. In fact, Lesnevich wants the toughest of 'em all, Joe Louis!

"I have never made much money with the title," the light-heavyweight champion declared. "I am going to try again and defend my crown within the six months as the boxing commission wants me to do. After that," Gus added, "I want the big fellows. After all, I went 30 close rounds with Billy Conn and you saw what Billy did to Louis."

Lesnevich, 29 years old, stated that his present weight is about 187 pounds but that he could make the 175 pound limit if he had to. However, when he tackles the heavies, Gus expects to tip the beam at the 180 mark. Lesnevich last faced sterling opposition when he dropped a ten rounder to Jimmy Bivins on March 11, 1942. Close to four years will have elapsd when the 175 pound kingpin next laces on the gloves. How he will fare against the best is problematical.

\* \* \*

MARTY SERVO, Al Weill's rugged little welter, is best remembered for his corking setto against Ray Robinson in New York when he came closest at that time to whipping the then unbeaten Harlemite. Servo's re-entry into the ranks of pugilism will serve once again to spotlight the activities of colorful Al Weill who always made good copy when his men were active.

Other well-known personalities have been obscured by the war, and it will be great to read of the antics of characters like Eddie Walker, Jack Barrett, Johnny Attell, Lew Burston, Chris Dundee, Lew Diamond, "the Honest Brakeman," Evil Eye Finkle, and so many others who in many cases were more newsworthy than the scrappers they guided. They have all kept busy during the war with the ordinary material at hand but will soon get back into stride with the kind of fighters they had been accustomed to handling. Barrett already has one war boxer in tow who is making good with a vengeance—Wildcat George Henry.

Lenny "Boom Boom" Mancini, a perpetual motion puncher who rated high on THE RING's list of contenders, showed great form in winning his first comeback start although he wears the Purple Heart for severe wounds received while soldiering. Another Purple Heart vet, Vinnie Rossano, who cleaned up all opposition in Europe, is flashing his old bolo wallop with pre-war accuracy, having won his first two starts since his discharge. Beau Jack is prancing around Stillman's Gym looking as formidable as ever.

\* \* \*

THERE is plenty of opposition ready and eager to face the returning servicemen in natural matches which should draw tremendous gates around the country.

Jimmy Bivins, for one, feels that he has been sidetracked for quite some time. Tami Mauriello feels the same way. Whether or not men like Joe Baksi and Lee Oma can stand up to stiffer opposition remains to be seen. Both have been exceedingly inactive. The former, a game plugger, may find himself baffled by the clever antics of the smoother boxers now in action. Oma, who has been batting about for ten years with very little success, captured the hearts of heavyweight followers during the past year and a half and if he can stay in shape and show the determination he is capable of, might fight his way to the very top. He has

*Marty Servo, back from the Coast Guard and rarin' to go.*

the experience and knowhow to test the best.

\* \* \*

AN INTERNATIONAL angle looms with Bruce Woodcock of England figuring quite prominently in postwar plans. He may visit this country, or a possibility exists that some of America's crackerjack clouters might cross the ocean to tackle big Bruce.

Freddie Mills rates highly, too. There is talk of Lesnevich visiting Europe to defend his title against the popular Mills.

Marcel Cerdan, although a ring veteran, must be considered with our crop of welterweights when one discusses international boxing matches. There are, no doubt, a few great fighters who have come along in Australia during the past few years.

With air travel now so fully developed, American boxers will easily travel to faroff lands to compete with the best the foreign countries can offer. The time element is most important, as previously, an American boxer, although well paid, had to sometimes give up as much as from six months to a year of his time travelling to Africa, Australia or Europe; during which interval he dropped out of the local limelight in America.

\* \* \*

RUGGED Jake LaMotta, the "One-Man Gang," is another civilian anxious to meet anyone, anywhere, anytime. A match talked about that would bulge the walls of any stadium is one featuring Jake with Rocky Graziano. What a slugfest that would be! It's strictly a case of the irresistible force meeting the immovable object. Jeeves, my digitalis, please.

As we go down the line, there's Ray Robinson, Jimmy Doyle, Tippy Larkin, Freddie Archer, and Willie Joyce, all good ringmen, who have served the public during war days and are now set for the big game that is in the offing.

The big fight between Joe Louis and Billy Conn is being discussed at great length and will gather voluminous reams of copy as the date draws nearer, but regardless of who stands up or falters in the keen competition sure to ensue in all divisions from now on, the little guy who plunks his hard-earned kale through the wicket can rest assured that from now on he'll see the kind of battles and battlers he never imagined possible in his wildest dreams.

# MECCA of MAYHEM

*Stillman's Gymnasium, Eighth Avenue's Emporium of Sock, New York's Fistic Landmark, the Training Place of World's Greatest Fighters*

## By IRVING RUDD

THE red-hot boxing fan or chance passerby who scurries up the long flight of stairs leading to Stillman's Gym on Eighth Avenue between 54th and 55th Streets in New York City, and plunks thirty-five cents into the outstretched palm of Jack Curley, who mans the turnstile, buys himself a grand afternoon's entertainment.

From 1 o'clock to 3 in the afternoon on any day including Sundays and holidays, the fan may sit back comfortably and watch a parade of pugs go through their training paces. Champions and near-champions, has-beens, and up-and-coming youngsters clamber in and out of the two large rings up front. A stairway at the rear of the gymnasium leads to the exercise floor where the fighters skip rope, punch the light or heavy bag, or go through loosening-up calisthenics.

It's an afternoon well-spent, but it's a pity that the customers can't be let in on the real entertainment supplied by many characters who play the leading roles in this scenario of sock. These include the boxers, managers, matchmakers, trainers, and publicity men. The belly laughs their authentic antics provoke, would put a top-flight Broadway musical to shame.

The lunch counter at the back of Stillman's is the center of the stage. You see a matchmaker of a boxing arena like Max Joss, Moe Fleischer (no relative of Nat's), or Joe McKenna, usually has an office for which he pays a fairly high rental but generally, when he wants to transact some very important business, he hies himself to the gym and haggles with the managers over terms for the use of a fighter. Many an important match has been closed over a cup of coffee and doughnuts, or in one of the numerous niches near the lunch counter.

* * *

SUDDENLY a voice attracts your attention. ". . . so I'm fighting in the semi-windup at the Broadway Arena the other night and this guy is a cutie and a pretty fair banger to the bargain. He puts me on the deck twice but I come back to win. It's a helluva fight so they put us back on top the follerin' week. I'm swingin' on the gate for twenty pernts. This time I'm in great shape, weigh only about

*Lou Stillman, proprietor of the gym that bears his name, enrolling a newcomer.*

43 pounds, and I'm hep to this gee. All I does is stick and move, stick and move. Soon, I'm givin' him a paint job and I cops the duke."

We know you're amazed because the speaker is a portly, pot-bellied gent of at least forty-five. We can't blame you if your jaw droops in dismay and you exclaim, "Ye gods! Is he a *fighter?*"

Well, the portly personality is Eddie Walker, a leading manager of fighters. The majority of fight managers always use the first person when describing a bout which any of their boxers have engaged in. It's never "my fighter" but more often "me" or "I." For example, when a match is offered, the average fight pilot will reply, "Sure, *I'll* fight your guy." Some of the more modest managers condescend to use "we" or "us."

However, when it comes to taking a punch on the chin, the manager usually refers to that "bum of mine, the blankety-blank stiff."

Translating the confusing jargon of the ring, fight manager Walker, one of America's outstanding figures in boxing, was simply explaining how his battler boxed in the semi-final at the Ridgewood Grove against a clever, hard puncher. His pug was on the floor twice but came back to win a sensational brawl.

The promoter at Ridgewood Grove put both men back in the main event the following week with Walker's charge drawing down twenty per cent of the net receipts. In the second encounter, our hero is in good condition, weighing 143 pounds, and wise to the tactics of his adversary. He jabs and moves cleverly throughout the fight, and smears his foe's face red with blood to win the decision.

* * *

SPEAKING of fighters reminded the boys of "Bat" Norfolk, a huge rubber, who stood well over six feet and weighed about 260 pounds. A mild-mannered Bible student who believed in constantly "turning the other cheek," poor "Bat" was set afire enough times via the hotfoot method to warm half the population of New York City. Although he possessed a massive pair of maulies that could stave in a brick wall, Norfolk managed to keep cool

*Johnny Dundee, who set a record for rope-skipping at Stillman's Gym.*

*This is the home of the famous Stillman's Gymnasium, where the world's greatest fistic stars prepare for their bouts.*

under the constant torment to which he was subjected.

The story goes that "Bat" Norfolk did lose his temper one day when he was a pretty fair heavyweight fighter. Bat was piloted by an unscrupulous individual who continually paid him off in peanuts. One night when Norfolk was scheduled to box, he found out that he was supposed to be getting $100 instead of the $50 his manager said was due him.

He cornered his pilot and in no uncertain terms let him know that he'd practice his bag-punching exercises upon that worthy's chin if the pay-off was incorrect. Norfolk's handler, without a murmur of protest, instantly acquiesced. This seemed strange to "Bat." The payoff was set to take place after the bout in a garage adjacent to the arena.

It was pitch black when the fight mentor stepped inside the garage and called, "Bat! Oh Bat! Where are you?"

"Heah Ah is," rumbled the Negro heavyweight who was standing beside him all the time!

"O.K. Norfolk. Here's the dough." Holding ten ONE dollar bills in his mitt the manager began to count: "Ten, twenty, thirty, forty, fifty dollars . . ." Norfolk interrupted the count.

"Jes' a moment, boss. Yo' is bein' too damn nice to ol' Bat. I'd like to see dis dough 'stead of feelin' it. Le's come outside heah where there is mo' light."

The manager sensed a murder and beat a hasty retreat. The scurrilous scoundrel is still among the missing.

\* \* \*

LITTLE CHARLIE GOLDMAN, an outstanding trainer, storms up the stairs and heads for the lunch counter. "What's this fight game comin' to?" he demands of no one in particular as he orders a "cuppa cawfee."

"Bunch of Johnny-Come-Latelys ruining this business. I'm up in Zunk's (Mike Jacobs' assistant matchmaker) office trying to

close for a match for this new preliminary kid of mine. Zunk says, 'Will yuh fight this McCormick kid? He's a beginner like your kid. Wait, I'll call his manager.'

"So he gets on the phone and dials a number," Goldman relates between sips and bites, "and the next thing he's asking 'is this Goldsmith's Department store? Well, I'd like to speak to Mr. Saunders of Ladies' Wear!'

"Ladies' Wear Department.

"A fine thing boxing comes to when a manager must be located in such a place!

"All we have today is cloak and suiters, buttonhole makers and ladies' underwear salesmen handling fighters. Ye Gods! What's boxing coming to! No wonder so many poor kids get socked around until they get punchy!"

\* \* \*

WHITEY BIMSTEIN, another greater trainer, joins the gab-fest. "Did I ever tell you about the time I managed a fighter with a floating rib?" he inquires.

"Well, it seems that this 'tiger' of mine had been hurt around the ribs in a previous fight, and before you knew it he was an honest to goodness hypochondriac about his rib. One night he was boxing in the Queensboro Arena and halfway through the third round he was clouted hard in the midsection. When he got back to the corner, he started complaining about his side and wanted to quit. I coaxed him to go out for the next round and he started out fine, but as soon as he was belted in the belly, he looked to quit again!

"He kept back-pedaling," Whitey related, "and when he reached my corner he hollered, 'Whitey throw in the towel!' I ignored him and he stayed on the bicycle, clinching and running. He came around to the corner again, and once more he shouted, 'Whitey, throw in the towel!' I acted as if I hadn't heard him. He was desperate and kept circling his man. Finally he came around to the corner for the third time in the round, and then he screamed, 'Whitey, you better throw in that towel, I ain't comin' around again!' "

\* \* \*

STILLMAN'S GYM is quiet and almost deserted now as the last sparring session comes to an end. The crowd of fight guys has thinned out to a mere handful.

Tex Sullivan, stellar publicity man for Jimmy Braddock when the latter was champ, and now a manager of several name fighters and a promoter, is discussing some publicity angles for his next show at the Ridgewood Grove. Someone asks him if he's heard from Braddock lately, and it isn't long before likeable Tex, manager of Lee Oma, George Kochan and Lee Q. Murray, is reminiscing about some experiences Braddock had on a barnstorming tour when he was at the peak of his popularity.

"You know," said Tex, "Jim once picked up an easy $200 just for chewing the fat.

"The champ was on a tour," Sullivan revealed, "and he received a wire offering him $200 to umpire the first inning of a baseball game in the backwoods of Kentucky. Braddock was in Louisville at the time and he wired back accepting the offer. Jim started out by car on a cold, gray morning with a threatening overcast sky above. As Mushky Jackson, the Malaprop King would have phrased it, 'Braddock and his gang arrived just in the knack of time 'cause it was grizzling furiously.'

"Although the ball game was probably called off because of the heavy rain," Sullivan went on, "the champ decided to drive down to the ball field. Braddock entered the deserted grandstand and was bemoaning his tough luck, when suddenly a tall stranger who looked as if he had just emerged from a Li'l Abner comic strip approached Jim.

" 'Yer the champ, ain'tcha?' he inquired. 'Muh name is Ezra Hawkins and I'm the promoter of this hyar baseball game. Sorry about the rain.'

"The hillbilly joined Braddock in his moody silence and then slapped his thigh as if struck with an inspiration. 'Say,' he beamed, 'my grandpappy is over to the house with a bunch of his pals. I wonder if yuh'd mind a-comin' down there and shake hands with the boys for the two hundred?'

# Mecca of Mayhem

"After that," Tex concluded, "Jim used to kid us and pester about some more of 'them thar handshakin' assignments."

A pall of silence envelops the now almost empty gymnasium. Only Lou Stillman and his efficient manager, Jack Curley, are present. Lou Stillman has been conducting a gymnasium in New York for over thirty years, or ever since Alpheus Geer and Hiram Mallinson induced him to run one for the Marshall Stillman Movement, an organization devoted to the rehabilitation of convicted men. Marshall and Stillman were the names of Geer's grandparents.

Stillman's real name is Louis Ingber, but everybody called him Mr. Stillman at the old place, and when it became necessary for him to take it over as a private undertaking the name was too valuable to be changed.

\* \* \*

*I* ASKED Stillman whether he ever took a vacation, since every time I have visited his boxing landmark I have seen him on the job.

"I'm afraid it can't be done. You see I run this gym as a personal problem. I personally take charge of everything here. I leave nothing to others when my attention should be given to it, and I play no favorites. The ordinary novice and palooka get the same treatment that I give to the top lads. A preliminary boy some day may become the champ, is the way I look upon the fighter and therefore I treat him with the same respect as I do the ranking men of the game.

"For thirty odd years I have been doing this and nothing can change me now. I stay on the job day after day—Saturdays, holidays, Sunday, rain, shine or snow. That gym is just me and I couldn't desert it for a vacation."

"Did Jack Dempsey do much training here?" I inquired of the master of Eighth Avenoo's Emporium of Sock.

"Yes, often. He was the greatest fellow in the history of the sport in my book. Often when I needed a friend badly, he was the one to come to the rescue. He would call up and ask: 'How are things, Lou?'

"Not so good, I would tell him. And he'd reply: 'Don't worry pal. Pass the word around that I'll be up to do some training today.'

"And before Jack got here, the place would be jammed with scribes and patrons who had learned of Dempsey's intention.

"How that fellow could draw 'em in! Only once in all my career did I see anyone who could pack 'em in here in greater numbers than did Jack and that was the day when Primo Carnera, led by Bill Duffy and Leon See, brought Primo Carnera here for his first workout. Italians came to the gym from all parts of the city. They flocked to Eighth Avenue in such numbers, I had to call upon the police to keep order. Even women with babes in their arms came to see Satchel Feet. The place was jammed as never before or since and I should judge that 2,000 persons were chased from the avenue by the bluecoats."

Stillman declares crowds attending workouts are the best barometer on attendance at a boxing show, and contends he can guess the size of the gate within a few hundred dollars after watching them for three or four days.

He never saw a fighter who enjoyed training as much as Dempsey, and names Johnny Dundee as the most extraordinary boxer he ever looked at in a gym. Several years back the renowned Scotch-Wop skipped rope an hour and ten minutes to beat Babe Herman in a contest. Lou timed the boys and did the counting.

There were many unique happenings in the old place, and one of the strangest was Soldier Bartfield and Frank Carbone winding up what started as a friendly workout kicking and biting each other on the floor. It was all half a dozen huskies could do to pull them apart.

"Boxing is a great sport," wound up Lou. "There is nothing wrong with it or the thousands who attend the shows all over the country wouldn't be spending millions per year to see the men in action."

# HOW LOUIS WRESTED TITLE *from* BRADDOCK

### Joe Stopped Jim in Eighth Round at Chicago on June 22, 1937, With a Right to the Jaw

### *By* DANIEL M. DANIEL

ELIMINATING Tommy Burns and his disputed right to consideration, we find that in a line started by John L. Sullivan with his 1889 triumph over Jake Kilrain, Joe Louis is the fourteenth holder of the heavyweight championship.

Will Billy Conn, of Pittsburgh, who tackles Joe for a second time at Yankee Stadium in New York on the night of June 19, be No. 15?

The experts already have decided that, irrespective of how far Louis may have deteriorated through his long layoff from competition—a recess which dates from his six-round triumph over Abe Simon for the Army Relief Fund in New York on March 27, 1942—the Negro title holder will prevail again over his white challenger.

However, with all that, there lies in this Louis-Conn situation a most intriguing element of suspense, and something-could-happen.

That you never can tell about horses, women and fights was accentuated on the night of June 18, 1941, at the Polo Grounds in New York, when Conn had the better of Louis right up to the knockout in the thirteenth round.

Had the impetuous Irishman kept a cool head, had he been content with coasting along on his advantage through the fifteen-round limit, Billy Conn would have been the fifteenth glove champion that very night.

However, all that is water over the dam—though we are going to come back to it later on in this series of flashbacks in the career of Joseph Barrow of Alabama, known as Joe Louis, in whose veins flows not only Negro but Caucasian and Cherokee Indian blood.

\* \* \*

MY immediate design is to trace Joe's rise to the championship, and to reconstruct for you the fight with Jim Braddock, in which Louis achieved a knockout in the eighth round.

Louis was crowned king of the realm of boxing on the night of June 22, 1937, in Chicago.

Joe weighed 197¼ pounds, Braddock tipped the beam at 197. And the third man in the ring was Tommy Thomas.

Braddock's story, the drama of the man who rose from poverty, from relief, from being a public charge, to the heavyweight championship of the world, is known to every follower of boxing. It is one of the most alluring yarns in the entire book of the ring.

Before going into details of the battle in which Louis won from Braddock, let us fill in the background.

Braddock became the champion on June 13, 1935, in the now non-existent arena in Long Island City, by beating Max Baer in 15 rounds, on points.

There was no question about supremacy that night. Baer was supposed to be the killer, Braddock was expected to be the victim. But with calm, relentless skill, with a clever antidote for the clowning Maxie, Jim piled up enough points in the 45 minutes of action to win the title without any chance for dispute or controversy.

Baer had taken the championship from Primo Carnera, one of the most tragic and pathetic figures in the annals of boxing, on June 14, 1934. Max stopped the Gargantuan Italian in the eleventh.

Carnera had won the title from Jack Sharkey, who had beaten Max Schmeling, who had become recognized as the leader by winning from Sharkey in four rounds on a foul. That was after the title had been left vacant through Gene Tunney's retirement following his none too brilliant victory over Tom Heeney.

\* \* \*

TUNNEY, as you know, had beaten Jack Dempsey, who had won from Jess Willard. Jess had knocked out Jack Johnson, who had stopped Jim Jeffries. The Boilermaker had taken the title from Bob Fitzsimmons, and the Blacksmith had stopped Jim Corbett. Gentleman Jim had punched the daylights out of poor old John L. Sullivan.

After Jeffries' retirement, in March, 1905, Tommy Burns beat Marvin Hart for what was supposed to be the heavyweight title. Burns was knocked out by Jack Johnson in the fourteenth round in Sydney, New South Wales, on December 26, 1908.

That completes the job of painting in the titular scenery for the approaching battle between Louis and Conn.

Now for the remarkable career of Joe Louis. Born at Lexington, Alabama, on May

*Louis completes a right hand swing as Braddock desperately backs away shortly before he was knocked out in the eighth round.*

13, 1914, Louis eventually landed in Detroit, and went to work in the Ford plant.

Joe began to fool around with amateur boxing, and after amazing successes in the Golden Gloves and other simon pure festivals, broke out as a pro on July 4, 1934, when he stopped Jack Kracken in one round, in Chicago.

Within one year, Louis was ready for the standout heavies of the world—an incredible development.

On June 25, 1935, Joe stopped Carnera in the sixth.

On September 24, 1935, Louis whaled the tar out of Max Baer in four rounds. Before the year was out, the Negro mauled Paulino in four. Joe was on his way.

On June 19, 1936, Louis suffered the one and only setback of his career. He was whipped, and knocked out, by Max Schmeling, the former champion, in twelve rounds in New York. In my next article, I will go back to Joe's defeat by the German, and the Negro's full measure of revenge on June 22, 1938, when he almost killed Max in a fight that lasted only two minutes, four seconds.

*Braddock's seconds rush to his rescue after he had been counted out in the eighth round.*

* * *

LOUIS refused to let the setback by Schmeling throttle his ambition or kill his determination.

Two months after his defeat by Schmeling, Louis started his comeback campaign with a triumph over Jack Sharkey, stopping the faded former champion in the third.

Al Ettore was whipped in five heats; Jorge Brescia in three; Eddie Simms in one; Stan Ketchel in two.

Then came that ten-rounder with Bob Pastor in New York, on January 27, 1937. Pastor did not do too much fighting that night. He did do considerable legging around the Garden ring, and, if he achieved nothing else, got the satisfaction of having lasted the limit.

This, of course, set up the later battle with Pastor in Detroit, in which Bob went into the eleventh.

After his New York quadrille with Pastor, Louis stopped Natie Brown in four heats.

Then came the match with Braddock. In this was involved a tremendous pother of ring politics and behind the scenes maneuvering.

Braddock had signed to fight Schmeling in New York. Tickets had been printed. The fight was postponed.

Once again tickets were printed. But for a second time the event was postponed. Finally it was scheduled for June 22, 1937, in New York.

Braddock did not tackle Schmeling, but chose, instead, to make a match with Louis.

First Braddock had pleaded arthritis. Then it was a bad thumb. Ultimately came the explanation from Joe Gould, Jim's manager, that Americans would not support a fight in which Schmeling, affiliated with the Nazi Party in Germany, was a participant.

Maybe Gould had something there. In any event, Braddock had been out of competition for two years. His tours had not been too successful financially.

Gould and Braddock were determined not to risk the title without absolute certainty of a truly opulent return. This could be Jim's one, big, last chance. He had come up the hard way, he just could not afford to take too many financial risks.

Schmeling howled. Germany howled. The New York Commission yammered. Max went to Speculator, N. Y., and punished

himself through a long training regimen.

Then Max came down to New York and went through a farcical weighing in. The idea was for the German to claim the title by default.

The idea was interesting enough, but the scheme did not work out. The Phantom Fight became a source of fun-poking in the sports pages, Schmeling had to admit defeat and flew back to Naziland on the ill-fated Hindenburg.

"I will win the title yet, and I will come back to America to demand justice from the American public," yodeled Max as he quit our terra firma.

He did come back, and his manager, Joe Jacobs, came very close to being forced to ship back what was left of Max in a little box. However, the one-rounder with Louis gave Schmeling a lot of phony marks, and a castle in Germany.

Tackling Louis on the very June night he was supposed to be fighting Schmeling in New York, Braddock made one of the most remarkable stands you will find in all the grand theatre of heavyweight championship competition.

* * *

THOSE who saw the 32-year-old campaigner wage his stubborn and game battle against the 23-year-old powerful Negro never will forget how Jim floored Joe in the first round; how Braddock staved off the inevitable in the fifth, sixth and seventh; and how Louis scored one of the most devastating knockouts in the history of the title in the eighth.

The end came after 1 minute, 10 seconds of fighting in that fateful eighth. The older man was very tired. He had taken a far more severe beating than even the closest ringsiders that night in Comiskey Park realized.

That's one of the strange things in every Louis appearance. The ringsiders never seem to appreciate how terrifically he hits and how tough it is to stand up against the Brown Bomber for even three minutes.

Braddock disdained running around the ring. He fought the kind of fight Louis liked—stand up and sock.

Soon after the gong in the eighth, Louis hooked a left to the head. That was the real finisher. Braddock was a goner.

"Wham!" went the Louis right! A straight crash to a wide open chin!

Braddock was lifted off the canvas. He whirled like a sick Dervish, then crumpled to the floor, face in the resin.

Referee Thomas counted, but it was a perfunctory process, demanded by boxing law. Tommy could have kept right on tolling up to a hundred in so far as Braddock was concerned.

It was one of the most convincing knockouts the game has seen, one of the most terrific punches that yet has gained the title in the heavyweight class.

* * *

AFTER the fight the experts were unanimous in the belief that Louis had achieved his crest in the sixth round. In that session the challenger incised a deep cut over Braddock's left eye anew and began to show serious signs of wilting.

However, good as Louis was in that hectic sixth, he did not come out of it unscathed. Braddock was tiring but still blazing, he was fading but still as game as they ever have come, fading out but still breathing defiance.

As the sixth got under way, Joe drove two lefts to the face

and followed with a sharp right to the jaw. That hurt.

Yet, Braddock did not back away. He tore in with a two-fisted attack and sent the Negro back to the ropes, quite satisfied not to press the point at the moment.

It was then that Louis sent the fistic scalpel deeper into the cut he had made over Braddock's eye as early as the second minute of the fight. Blood streamed down Jim's face, impairing his vision. The gore squirted over Joe. It was a carmine carnival.

Louis sensed that the end was nearing, so he charged in with a succession of right-handers that staggered the older fighter.

Louis then tore open Braddock's upper lip. But, did Jim back away? Not for a second. He lashed a right to the jaw and Joe's knees sagged. The bell came to his relief.

* * *

BRADDOCK was in real trouble even as early as the second round. His knockdown of Louis in the opening heat was accomplished with a red hot right. It tipped Joe over and he barely deigned to take the short count. Up he jumped and ripped into the champion with plenty.

In the second round, Louis had his troubles, too. But just before the bell he came through with a couple of specials—a right, then a left, and the good barkentine Braddock was flying signals of distress.

Braddock was none too spry coming out for the third, but once he had warmed to his task, he was still dangerous. As, for example, when he crossed a couple of rights to the jaw. Had Jim hit the mark with his third, that would have been a still better fight, for Louis's knees had sagged.

On they fought through the fourth, fifth and sixth. Then, in the seventh, Jim opened with a hot left that sent his challenger to the ropes.

Louis tore in and jabbed his left. Soon Joe was bleeding at the nose and Jim was ditto at the mouth.

As the eighth got under way, Braddock sent Joe into retreat with a couple to the noggin. However, a Louis attack on the body was murderous. As Jim lowered his guard to protect his stomach, Joe hooked for the jaw. A left, then a right, and down went Jim. A new champion had been crowned!

* * *

WITH that victory over Braddock, Louis became the second Negro to hold the world heavyweight title. The first was Jack Johnson.

Braddock received $262,000 for his 22 minutes of fighting. Louis was rewarded with the title and $110,000. Mike Jacobs cleared something like $150,000, net.

The house came to 48,000 paid, with a grand take of $715,000.

"I should have had a couple of tune-up fights," wailed Braddock the next day.

"And I should have made better use of the right uppercut with which I sent Louis down in the first round."

In the *Sun,* New York, Frank Graham wrote: "The end of Braddock as a champion was in keeping with his entire career. He fought as he always had. Ruggedly, dangerously and gamely.

"A majority of the experts conceded him only an outside chance

*The Brown Bomber is proclaimed the new world titleholder.*

to win, and thought the odds against him should have been longer than they were at ring time, when they were only 8 to 5, or thereabouts. But Braddock believed in himself. He wasn't in there just to take a beating and get as much as he could for relinquishing the title. He was in there to win, and he never stopped trying, even when it was obvious to those who looked on that he couldn't possibly stave off defeat.

"The picture that he left in the minds of those who were at the ringside will remain with them always. A picture of an old-time gladiator who walked unblinking into a raking fire. Who scorned to evade punishment by holding or running. Who sought only to trade punches with his foe and bring him down. Who must have known that defeat was inescapable. But who refused to admit it.

"Braddock, who never was a great fighter, exerted a great influence on those whom he touched in his passing as champion. And as long as prize fighting endures he will remain a symbol of that courage which is the highest form of expression that is given to a prize fighter.

"Johnny Broderick, who was at Braddock's side on the march from the dressing room to the ring, couldn't bear to see the finish, but left the ringside after the sixth round.

" 'I knew then what was coming,' Broderick said, 'and I didn't want to see it. Braddock gave his title to Louis. It is too bad he couldn't give him his heart.' "

* * *

LOUIS confessed that he owed something to Max Schmeling. "Schmeling taught me to climb into a shell when I got hit," said the champion. "When he dropped me in the first round, the first thing that came to my head was caution. I got hell from Chappie (Trainer Jack Blackburn) between rounds for not taking the count of nine, but I knew what I had to do. Instead of piling in, like I did after Schmeling hit me in the second round, I just boxed and took my time.

"From the middle of the second round, after I had managed to slip under Jim's lefts, I knew I only had to be careful to realize my greatest ambition. Since the Schmeling fight I always wanted to get knocked down to see if I could come back. I did, and I'm satisfied I can be a worthy champion. I'll fight any man any time they tell me to fight."

* * *

JOE WILLIAMS, of the New York *World-Telegram,* wrote: "As the fight was fought, Braddock was made to order for the Negro. The old champion was pitching right up his alley all night long. He carried the fight to Louis—and Louis always likes that. He stood up straight, shooting his punches from an erect position, instead of stepping around, as he had done against Max Baer, or weaving, as Schmeling had done to confuse Louis. Braddock did everything wrong to win the fight and everything right to lose it. He couldn't have played more completely into the hands of Louis if Louis' own handlers had been directing his tactics. Louis will murder any man who stands up straight and leads to him. That's what Braddock did and that's one of the reasons Louis looked so impressive.

"Louis showed, first against Schmeling, and later against Bob Pastor, that he is incapable of grappling

# How Louis Wrested Title from Braddock

with even slightly involved situations. It was impossible to tell in the Chicago fight whether Louis is still susceptible to mental confusion in new situations because Braddock didn't offer any.

"The Jersey Irisher fought like an old tintype. But maybe that's the only way he could fight at 31 and weighed down with thick layers of a two-year-old rust. He was around yesterday saying he wants another crack at the Negro.

"This moved Mr. Jack Kearns to remark: 'I guess the poor guy hasn't come to yet!'"

\* \* \*

THE blow by blow story of the battle follows:

### ROUND ONE

Braddock met Louis as he came out and threw a long right, but it was wild and they clinched. Jim tried another right and it was wild. Louis unleashed a terrific right but Jim blocked it. Jim sent two lefts to the face and Louis sent a left to the body. They sparred cautiously.

Louis missed a left to the head but he followed with a heavy right to the jaw. Jim sent a left to the body.

Jim sent a left and right to the body and Louis then hammered him in the body with both hands. Louis connected with a terrific right that staggered Jim, but Braddock staggered Louis with a sizzling right that upset Joe. Louis was up at the two count and was fighting back furiously at the bell. Braddock had a slight cut over his left eye.

### ROUND TWO

Braddock sent two lefts to the head but they were high. Jim then tossed a left to the head and Louis countered with a right to the jaw. Braddock sent another left to the head, then missed a hard right to the same spot.

Braddock drove two heavy rights to the head, but they were a trifle high. Louis sent two light lefts to the head and they sparred cautiously. Braddock drove two vicious lefts to the body. Louis missed a left and right to the head and Jim countered with a crisp right to the head.

Jim sent a hard left to the jaw and Louis backed away. Louis tried to hold Braddock off with his left, but Jim cracked him with a hard right. Louis staggered Braddock with a hard right and left to the head, and Jim was in distress as the bell rang.

### ROUND THREE

Jim was a little slow coming out, but when Louis got close enough he banged him with a short right to the head. Braddock was short with a heavy right to the head. Louis sent a series of lefts to the face. Braddock crossed two rights to the jaw that buckled Joe's knees, but he missed with a third one. Both missed rights to the head and then sparred at long range. Braddock missed a short right to the head and they exchanged lefts.

They sparred for several seconds before Louis sent a stiff left to the body. Braddock's right to the head was short, but he followed with two hard rights to the head. He followed with a right upper cut to the jaw but took a right to the head in exchange.

### ROUND FOUR

They sparred cautiously and Braddock whipped a left to the head. As they sparred again Braddock drove a left and right to the jaw. Joe then sent three lefts to the head. Louis sent another left to the face and Braddock whipped both hands to the body but missed two hard rights to the jaw.

They traded lefts to the head and Louis connected with a sharp right to the jaw. Braddock sent a short right to the jaw. Louis had the better of an exchange of lefts. Louis missed a right to the head and Jim shot a right uppercut to the head.

### ROUND FIVE

Jim cracked Louis on the head with two rights. Two lefts to the nose drew blood from Louis' nose. Louis countered with a heavy left to the jaw.

Braddock sent a sharp right to the jaw. Braddock sent a hard left and right to the jaw. Louis was doing more forcing now, but Braddock drove a jolting left to the head. Louis sent three lefts to the face and a hard right to the jaw. The blood dripping from Joe's nose seemed to be making him breathe with difficulty.

### ROUND SIX

Louis backed away as Jim swung an overhead right. Braddock landed two glancing rights on Louis' jaw. Louis drove two lefts to the face and followed with a hard right to the jaw, but the champion came back with a two-fisted barrage to the head that sent the challenger back into the ropes.

The cut over Jim's left eye was reopened as they came out of a clinch. A series of lefts sent the blood streaming from Louis' nose. A series of rights staggered the champion and one of these blows opened a cut in Jim's upper lip, but the champion refused to back up and he buckled Louis' knees with a right to the jaw at the bell.

### ROUND SEVEN

Braddock sent a left to the head that drove Louis to the ropes. He followed with rights to the head and body and sent three lefts to the head. Jim missed a right to the head and Louis stood off and stabbed him with a series of lefts.

Jim missed a left to the head but scored with a right to the body. Braddock scored with three uppercuts to the head. Braddock drove a left and right to the head but Louis countered with a left and right to the head.

Louis was bleeding at the nose and Braddock from the mouth. Braddock drove a heavy left to the head and followed with two rights to the jaw. Braddock's left eye was puffed and swollen as he went to his corner.

### ROUND EIGHT

Braddock drove Louis to the ropes with a left and right to the head but he took a left and right to the body. Louis drove a left to the head and a heavy left hook to the body.

Louis drove a left hook to the head and a short right to the jaw that dropped Braddock to the canvas and he was counted out.

Louis wins by a knockout.

The time was 1 minute, 10 seconds.

# A CHAMP RECALLS

## Jack Johnson Selects Jim Jeffries as Greatest Heavyweight of All Time— Says Fighters of His Period Were Far Superior to the Present Crop, Excepting Joe Louis

### By JACK JOHNSON
*(Former world heavyweight champion)*

THE Louis-Conn fight is the topic of the month.

Everywhere where sports fans congregate, the latest "Battle of the Century" is the topic of conversation.

Will the Brown Bomber retain his crown?

Will he win by a quick knockout?

Will Conn's cleverness offset Louis' wallop and enable Billy to come through with a victory?

What effect has four years of ring idleness had on champ and challenger?

Will Conn's added weight—he'll go into the ring scaling around 182 pounds—be a handicap or a help?

These and numerous other queries have been fired at me by fight fans who have attended my physical fitness lectures and talks on boxing at Huber's Museum on the gay Forty-second Street of New York City where I am now appearing. I have just passed my sixty-fifth birthday and I feel as young as I did when I was in my prime as world heavyweight champion because of my contact with these people who speak my language when they talk of fights and fighters with me. It is a tonic. It keeps my mind alert and I enjoy every minute of the time I spend in this museum arguing and listening to arguments about my favorite pastime.

Many persons have asked me how one learns to box or fight. To some it comes naturally. Others learn through practice and from teachings by competent instructors, and still others get into the sport by sheer accident.

The last named was true with me. I got into the game when I learned that I could hold my own in a fight after I had engaged in one with a railroad brakeman who attempted to toss me off a freight train on which I was stealing a ride. It was a rough-and-tumble battle down in Galveston, Texas, and when I emerged the victor I had attained the confidence that enabled me in years to come, to stand my ground against the world's greatest fistic warriors and eventually win the world heavyweight title.

\* \* \*

NAT FLEISCHER, Editor of this publication, thinks that during my fighting career I earned the right to be designated as the greatest heavyweight fighter, considering all assets of a first rate ringman, and for this I am extremely grateful. That designation is open for wide discussion.

Tex Rickard, the man whose gambling brought to boxing the first million dollar gate and who, with his lure of $120,000 in gold, got me to fight Jim Jeffries in the latter's comeback, didn't agree with Nat. He had his idol, the man whom I stopped in fifteen rounds—Jeffries, the great California Boilermaker. According to Tex they came no greater in fighting qualities.

That prediction was made a few months before Rickard's death, when Gene Tunney was the heavyweight king. Since then we have had several other champs, the greatest of whom is our present king, Joe Louis, and I doubt that Tex would have changed his mind were he alive today. I am inclined to agree with Rickard, strange as it might seem, but I'm proud to have THE RING Editor think of me in that vein.

*The start of the battle between Johnson and Jeffries which Tex Rickard refereed.*

Since I fought that rough-and-tumble fight with the brakeman, I have come to the conclusion that life is one great battle after another—in and out of the ring. I have my own philosophy about life. Keep in the pink—live naturally—eat moderately—exercise according to the strength of your body—treat your fellow men as you would have them treat you—and you can face any fight, big or small, in or out of the roped square, and feel that the odds are not against you. That is my philosophy and I live up to it. My greatest wish is that when I celebrate my sixty-sixth birthday, I will have the privilege of boxing four rounds with the heavyweight champion for a noteworthy charity, just to prove to the world what physical condition means.

Recently I was sitting in THE RING office discussing the coming Louis-Conn battle when THE RING Editor questioned me:

"Jack, what do you think of the present day heavies compared to those of your day?"

"They are a dime a dozen," I replied. Not that I want to throw cold water on the boxers of today, but because history proves that the men of my fighting era were giants in comparison to the best of today's fighters. There is only one man who stands out today, Joe Louis, and in my humble opinion, not only could I have whipped Joe when I was at my best, but I'll name Sam Langford, Jeffries, Corbett, Choynski, Tom Sharkey, Fitz and Tommy Ryan among some of the old timers who would have taken Joe into camp and Jack Dempsey among those who followed me.

Why? Because we had fighters who knew every angle of the game, knew how to stand properly to get the best leverage for a punch; knew the most important art in boxing—how to feint—

and could take a punch far better than can the Brown Bomber.

Very few of the present day heavyweights, or for that matter the men in any other class, can box. They stand awkwardly.

"Did you ever study the pictures on your wall," I asked the Editor, "of Corbett vs. Jackson; Johnson vs. Jeffries; Fitzsimmons vs. Corbett, to enjoy seeing the perfect stance?" He looked at the one to which I pointed and then I took off my coat, rolled up my sleeves, had him stand before me and I illustrated what I meant.

I asked him to toss his left at me, then counter with a right. He did, but as he countered, he went out of position. That's what I was looking for.

I then did the same stunt and the Editor soon saw what I meant by perfect stance. I purposely missed a punch and immediately let go one with the other hand, and brought my point out more clearly. How? By illustrating that when one has a perfect stance, as did the masters of my period, when they missed they were always in proper position to toss a punch with the other hand and land effectively.

Joe Louis can't do that. Billy Conn is the best of the present school in that respect because he boxes like the old timers and has the best stance of any fighter of this era. He counters well, has a beautiful jab and crosses his punches with the accuracy of the old school. But he lacks a great essential. His blows are comparatively weak.

Louis and Conn each have a good left hand, but how many more of the men of today can boast of that? Very few.

Few seem to know how to lead with a left and rip into the body with a right. That was my specialty. Tommy Burns can testify to that. Most of the present school, instead of shooting straight punches, keep swinging without doing any damage.

I recently listened to a discussion on the air between THE RING Editor and the man who was quizzing him on boxing and when the time to quit the air had come, I heard the quiz master say:

"Well, Nat, like most of the old timers you simply won't agree that progress has been made in boxing as in all other sports."

That's where the quiz master was wrong. Boxing has made progress so far as commercialism is concerned, in the class of individuals who take up boxing as a profession, in the class of fight patrons and the management of the sport through legalized commissions, but not in boxing itself. The men of the past, as Nat Fleischer pointed out in his arguments, far surpassed the present age leaders. There are no Abe Attells, Owen Morans, Jem Driscolls, Johnny Kilbanes, Benny Leonards, Jimmy Wildes, Jim Corbetts and fighters like Jim Jeffries, Bob Fitzsimmons, Tom Sharkey, Jack Root, Stanley Ketchel, Tommy Ryan, Joe Choynski, George Dixon, Joe Gans, Joe Walcott, Sam Langford, Sam McVey and loads of others I could name. They were masters of the art. They were kings in every branch.

Of course all old timers have such thoughts. But they cannot help possessing them since they saw what they saw and haven't met up with the likes of those fistic scientists since. I question that any one who knows boxing, who knows anything about ring history or famous fights, would say that Jim Jeffries, Bob Fitz-

simmons or Tommy Ryan in their prime, could not have waded through the present list of heavyweight championship contenders one after the other and rocked each to sleep. Frankly, and I say this without the least prejudice, it wouldn't have been any contest, that's how good these old timers were to the present crop.

I have been asked frequently what my toughest battle was. Many seem to think it was my fifteen round mill with Sam Langford at Chelsea, Mass., because of the many statements made by Joe Woodman, then manager of Sam, belittling my ability and praising Langford's to the skies. I'll admit that was a tough one but I had several far tougher.

Strange as it might appear, the toughest fight I ever had, was not in the ring. It was one I had with myself over a long stretch, my idea of dethroning an idol of the people. I refer to the pre-fight days of the Jeffries-Johnson battle. Yes, that was my toughest.

Before Jeffries came out with his defi, few persons paid any attention to me, but once our agreement to fight was signed, the bitter attacks I had to face were far greater than any I ever faced in my entire fighting career. The caustic remarks, the threats to injure me, the attempts to blacken my character—fighting those constituted my toughest battle.

My fight with Jim Jeffries actually started down at Rushcutter's Bay in New South Wales, when Jack London, famous writer, war correspondent, novelist, urged the world to find an opponent for Jack Johnson who will bring the heavyweight crown back to the white race. Before he left for America to rejoin the staff of the New York *Herald* for which he was a special correspondent for my fight with Burns, he remarked to me:

"Well Jack, that was a terrible beating you gave to Tommy. I'm sorry for your sake that you won so readily. The white race won't be satisfied now until they find someone to whip you as badly as you

*The final round—Sam Berger tossing in the sponge to save Jeffries from further punishment in fifteenth round.*

whipped Burns and that man will have to be Jim Jeffries."

Whereupon he stood and waited for me to answer. I hesitated for some time, because I was bitter at that remark coming from a great man like London, but when I could regain my equilibrium, I said:

"Jack, I won the championship according to the rules of the game. You'll admit I didn't use any foul means to gain it. I'm sorry you feel as you do, but I want you to go home with this thought in mind, and write it when you reach New York—I won the championship of the world by defeating Tommy Burns in a square and fair fight and I can whip Jim Jeffries just as easily. I feel that I can beat any man in the world and I hope, now that Jeffries has been retired for so long, that he won't be foolish and heed the call of those who think he can retake the title. I hope he'll remain retired."

London looked at me, held my hand as he bid me goodbye and parted with the remark:

"I disagree, Jack, and there are thousands in America who are on my side. I shall urge his return to the ring."

And he did. You remember his words as they appeared in the New York *Herald*:

"Jeffries must emerge from his

# A Champ Recalls

alfalfa farm and remove that golden smile from Johnson's face. It's up to you, Jeff, to bring the title back to the white race."

He started the movement in America for the return of Jeff, and you know what happened.

Recently in THE RING, a review of that fight was staged by Daniel M. Daniel in his excellent series on old time ring battles. Hence, I won't go into details here, but I will say that throughout the fight I kept my right glove on Jeff's left forehead. I kept it there and the powerful left of the Californian was merely an idle threat. He couldn't use it effectively on me while I hampered him as I did.

As I went into the ring that day to fight Jeff, I was amazed at the number of well wishers I had. I heard many cheers. That's more than took place in Australia where my entry brought lusty boos and hisses and being in a foreign land, you can well imagine my feelings as I faced Burns. Perhaps that's one reason why I gave him that terrible beating.

I have often heard it said that Rickard was most anxious for Jeff to win hence it might surprise my readers when I say that when I got into the ring for the fight with Jeff, Tex walked over to me and said:

"Jack, this is your greatest day. You're getting the opportunity of a life time. You're about to meet the man who most people say is the greatest heavyweight of all time. Folks are going to watch you. If anything goes wrong, they'll never forgive you.

"I want you to go right in when that bell sounds and go out to win. I want Jeff to do the same. Make this fight one that the public and you will be proud of. I want to promote some big heavyweight fights again and it all depends on what you do."

I didn't fall down on Tex. I gave my all and when that bout was over, Tex was the first to come and congratulate me.

When Tex placed his hand on my shoulder signifying that the bout had ended and he had declared me the victor, I was the happiest man in the world. Nothing I did since then or before, not even the winning of the heavyweight title from Burns, made me so joyous. I had settled forever the question of the right to the heavyweight crown.

A great fighter had fallen that day. A man whom I always cherished as a superhuman ringman, had been taken into tow by me and that was something to cherish.

When I walked to my dressing room, I stopped momentarily as a thought came to me—I wonder what Jeff was like in his prime?

I have been wondering ever since, especially when I see the stories that so frequently have come into print in recent months about great heavyweights.

Who was the greatest heavyweight of all time?

Could Louis have whipped Dempsey?

Could Jack Johnson have beaten Louis?

Was Jeffries a greater fighter than the present champ?

Yes, these queries on the air, in the writings of sports columnists and fired at me in Huber's Museum, still make me think.

Did I win from the Ghost of a Great Champion?

Was I a better all-around fighter than Jeffries?

Could I have whipped the Jeff who beat Fitzsimmons and Corbett and Sharkey?

Would that great left, which Tex Rickard always thought was the finest in all ring history, have stopped me as it did Gentleman Jim, Ruby Robert and Sailor Tom among others?

I wonder!

Time marches on and so long as people will discuss boxing, those queries will continue to be fired at the experts and the pros and cons will have their say while the public listens.

# The FIGHTER and the MAN

## By IRVING RUDD

*Jake LaMotta, one of the busiest of all fighters, a man of many vocations.*

HAVE you ever wondered what sort of fellow your favorite fighter is like outside the ring? Away from the tension and turmoil of training, or removed from the glare of the ring spotlight, many of the outstanding name fighters prove to be extremely interesting personalities who have hobbies and traits that are unique when one considers that too often the popular conception of a pugilist is that of a dumb, uneducated brute who knows nothing more than to hammer out a living with his fists.

To Jake LaMotta, leading contender for middleweight honors, must go the undisputed laurels as the busiest avocationist in boxing. In addition to pursuing his career as the No. 1 160 pounder, LaMotta finds time to dabble in real estate, train Doberman pinschers, teach the neighborhood kids how to box, and is on the Board of Directors of the Park Arena in the Bronx.

In fact it was LaMotta who first saw the possibilities of converting a deserted, ramshackle theatre known as the Blenheim into the modernistic Park Arena boxing club.

Ray Robinson plays the piano well and

can hold his own with any of the theatrical leaders when it comes to dancing and singing.

Jersey Joe Walcott made his living in a shipyard when he retired from boxing temporarily.

Bruce Woodcock, the English heavyweight champion, is still a railroad maintenance man.

Bob Boucher, a young middleweight, now campaigning in local rings, was an Army Air Force fighter pilot who temporarily laid aside his plans to finish medical school to become a boxer.

Georgie Abrams, outstanding middleweight contender, is an excellent cartoonist.

Archie Moore is a restaurateur with a huge establishment in California.

Jimmy Kidd Hatcher, the Southern lightweight, is an expert hair stylist and operates a beauty parlor in Sarasota, Florida.

\* \* \*

OUTSIDE the ring heavyweight champion Joe Louis is a modest, inconspicuous, dignified citizen. At one time phlegmatic, uncommunicative, almost distrustful of people, Joe, with many years of travel and army experience behind him, has developed into a more genial personality, a fellow who enjoys a good joke, and feels at ease in all types of company.

Louis has many hobbies and being a good example of a clean living American, his diversions run mostly to sports. Before the war Louis organized a Negro softball team, managed it, and played with the boys when training routine for a fight did not interfere. Joe rarely misses a game featuring his hometown favorites, the Detroit Tigers, if he can help it.

Horseback riding comes a close second on Louis' list of hobbies. The Brown Bomber owns an enormous ranch in Michigan. He breeds horses there and owns a small circular track for riding purposes. His love for horses was so great that he was the happiest man in the world when the army assigned him to the cavalry at Fort Riley, Kansas, when he enlisted in 1942.

A natural athlete, Louis has also mastered the game of golf and devotes a lot of his spare time to it. This year the great ambassador of the Negro race hopes to resume sponsorship of the Joe Louis National Negro Open Golf Tourney, an annual tournament he ran before the war intervened.

Joe loves to sleep and usually hits the hay for an average of fourteen hours per day. He gets a terrific kick out of the comic strips. Superman, Dick Tracy and Joe Palooka are his three favorites. He is intensely loyal to his pals, loves children, and also finds relaxation in the movies and radio. Bing Crosby and Bob Hope are his favorites.

\* \* \*

AS for Billy Conn he is exactly the opposite of Louis when it comes to temperament. Billy is the kind of fellow who likes crowds, boisterous fun, the race track, the Broadway mob, and a good game

*Ray Robinson, a pianist and tap dancer with extraordinary ability.*

of poker. He is a devout Catholic and a likeable happy-go-lucky guy. Billy has thousands of personal friends all over the country.

His relationship to his kid brother Jackie hasn't changed despite fame and popularity. Despite the Kilkenny cat attitude of both men, inwardly there is a deep feeling of mutual respect and admiration. Jackie still vows he can wallop the tar out of the handsome Pittsburgh challenger in a street fight and poor Johnny Ray, Conn's manager, has to be constantly on the alert to prevent Jackie from upsetting the applecart. Only a few weeks ago the kid brother almost caused a postponement of the fight with Louis when he played a prank while Conn's trainer was cutting the bandages from Billy's hands with the result that Conn was cut on the hand.

Billy will go all out for a fellow he likes. He searched all over for his old Irish sparmate, the veteran Mickey McAvoy, Brooklyn heavyweight, and found him driving a beer truck. Conn lured Mickey from behind the wheel by offering him three times as much as he was making as a driver. Conn not only desired McAvoy as a sparmate, but needed him badly, for Mickey is a good story teller, a great pal, and provides the Conn camp with lots of laughs. There's never a dull moment when you're in the company of William David Conn!

*Tippy Larkin, the only fighter who uses hunting as part of his training program.*

*I*T is extremely difficult to believe that the tigerish Rocky Graziano, who blasts his foes into submission with fearsome ferocity, is a jovial, hail-fellow-well-met when he pulls off his fighting togs.

The Rockem-Sockem Italian kid, whose given name is Thomas, is pretty much the same sort of fellow as when he was plodding along the small club circuit, a slugger without much future.

Today, with the possible exception of Louis and Conn, Graziano is the most popular pugilist in the world. He is cheered wherever he goes and is in great demand for appearances at charity functions and other affairs. Rocky never turns any of these requests down if he can help it. His bizarre, flamboyant, uninhibited taste for clothing is known to fight followers all over the country.

It is not unusual to see Graziano, who abhors neckties, appear in the ring when being introduced at Madison Square Garden in peg pants, sharpie sandals, a garish bright-colored sports jacket or sweater, and tousled black hair, rarely combed. On one occasion at a small club he climbed into the ring for an introduction with the usual tieless sports shirt, but wore a woolen skating hat of bright red!

Rocky is completely unaffected by the fame that has come to him. He still pals with his old cronies downtown. It is not unusual to see a tribe of kids accompanying the Rock wherever he goes. In Brooklyn where he recently bought a home, Mrs. Graziano is kept busy all day telling the youngsters when Rocky is expected home. His naturalness is so unbelievable as to be startling. A fight fan who had met Graziano casually several weeks earlier, was startled to see the dynamic middleweight contender approach him with a hearty handshake and backslap.

His mild manner is in direct contrast to his fighting fury in the ring. A reporter relates how Rocky, visiting Mike Jacobs' office, was accosted by a complete stranger who bellowed: "So you're the guy who never wears a necktie!" Then the pest, an utter unknown to Graziano, pawed at the ring killer's muffler, pushing it askew to reveal that Rocky did *not* wear a necktie! Whereas Graziano would have been perfectly justified in belting the nuisance, he gracefully grinned and passed it off as just another penalty of his new found fame.

* * *

*A*NTHONY FLORIAN ZALESKI, the world's middleweight champion, whom you know better as Tony Zale, the man who defends his title against Rocky Graziano in July, is another of our boxing champs who likes baseball. Zale proved his adaptability away from boxing by becoming a topnotch physical instructor for the Navy during the war. Although the remuneration would be far less than his earnings as a boxing champion, Zale can take his place tomorrow beside the best steel mill worker standing in front of the hot blast furnaces.

Tony went to work in the steel mills at Gary, Indiana, his hometown, at an early age. In July, 1935, he quit the ring after a few setbacks to go back to the steel mills. Tony Zale, although no man of letters, like other good fighters, has proved he can make his living at an ordinary trade like anyone else besides fighting for money.

* * *

*S*WITCHING the topic back to heavyweights one must not overlook the new Cinderella Man of Boxing, Jersey Joe Walcott. "The Brown Braddock" as he is now called, is like his Skeeter State predecessor, a graduate of the relief rolls, yet despite his new found fame as a leading heavyweight challenger he is still the same gracious individual.

Walcott is a qualified construction worker. During the war he worked in a shipyard. Father of six children, the 31-year-old Negro is a good family man and likes nothing better than to be home with his kiddies. Generous to a fault, Joe is always handing out good sums of money to any old buddy with a hard luck story—even in times like these.

Years ago in Merchantville, New Jersey High School, Walcott was a good all-around athlete. For a nice, gentle-mannered chap whose right name is Arnold Cream, Jersey Joe Walcott is quite a rough, tough, two-fisted terror in the ring.

Another fighter from New Jersey, Tippy Larkin, is probably one of the best huntsmen in the sports world. An expert shot with a rifle, Larkin is perhaps the only modern day fighter who uses hunting as part of his training regimen. Many of the old timers improved their wind, strengthened their legs, and built up their endurance with long treks through wooded lands in search of game.

Larkin once threw his camp into a turmoil when he suffered an accidental wound in the shoulder when a gun suddenly went off. Luckily the wound was superficial and Tippy escaped serious injury. Tippy still loves the outdoors and trains for every fight no matter how small or how very important at a training camp in the country where hunting plays a large part in his conditioning.

* * *

*R*AY ROBINSON, as noted earlier, is quite talented when it comes to entertaining, but of late, recognizing the seriousness of the problems that beset the youth of this country, and the current cases of juvenile delinquency, Ray has donated several thousands of dollars to various organizations which help youngsters and guide them properly.

Manuel Ortiz, the great little bantamweight champ, who takes on any and all challengers, could retire to-morrow to his huge truck farm at El Centro, California. A shrewd produce merchant, Manuel was making a living with his farm long before he became famous as a boxer. He too, is a family man, and with opposition in the 118 pound class dwindling more and more, the next year or two may see the El Centro farmer retire to the rustic comfort becoming a country squire.

*(Continued on page 35)*

*Georgie Abrams who will join the ranks of cartoonists when he hangs up his gloves.*

# IN OUR QUESTION BOX

**Peter Slobodian, Montreal, Canada**

Q.—Did Billy Pinti ever fight Sal Bartolo, and what was the result? How many fights did Pinti have during the years, 1940 to 1942?

A.—Billy Pinti lost an 8 round decision to Sal Bartolo in 1942.

The second part of your question will be answered in the 1946 record book now on sale at THE RING Book Shop.

**Pfc. Palmer, Ft. Hamilton, Indiana**

Q.—In what round did Schmeling knock out Louis? How did Jake LaMotta win over Ray Robinson?

A.—Louis was knocked out in the 12th round by Schmeling. LaMotta won a decision over Robinson in Ray's only loss.

**Wally Vanderpool, Council Bluffs, Iowa**

Q.—How old is Phil Terranova? How many times has he fought since he turned professional? How many has he lost? When did he turn pro?

A.—It would take a great deal of time to answer this question. All this information can be found in THE RING Record Book. You fans should buy this book.

**Arthur Tompkins, San Francisco, Cal.**

Q.—How many million dollar gates have there been in boxing? In how many was Joe Louis?

A.—There were five million dollar gates in all of which Dempsey was a participant. When Dempsey fought there were no special arrangements made for radio rights, and the movie contract called for a settlement prior to the bout. His million dollar receipts are from the sale of tickets only. His million dollar gates follow:

Dempsey vs. Tunney..........$1,895,733
Dempsey vs. Tunney (Chicago) $2,658,660
Dempsey vs. Carpentier.......$1,789,238
Dempsey vs. Firpo...........$1,188,603
Dempsey vs. Sharkey.........$1,083,530

The total receipts of the two fights in which Joe Louis is listed as having grossed more than a million dollars, included the radio and movie figures. In none of Louis' fights to date, has the actual gross at the gate reached the million dollar mark. Thus in the Schmeling-Louis second fight, the gross including the radio and movie contract was $1,015,012, and the actual gross at the gate was only $940,096.72.

The Louis-Max Baer fight, gross at the gate only $932,944, and the entire receipts, including movies and radio were $1,000,932.

Dempsey is the only fighter in ring history to have taken part in million dollar gates in which only the ticket receipts figured.

## "THE RING'S" RATINGS FOR THE MONTH

### Ending January 15, 1946

*Fighters who hitherto have been rated but are now in the armed forces and have become inactive, have been removed until such time as they* **resume boxing** *When those removed are again active, they will receive the recognition previously granted to them. Only active fighters, service men and civilians, will be rated monthly. In our ratings the position of champions now in the service is frozen for the duration. Inactive service men are kept in the ratings for four months before being removed until they resume boxing.*

| Heavyweights (Over 175 pounds) | Light-Heavyweights (Not exceeding 175 pounds) | Middleweights (Not exceeding 160 pounds) | Welterweights (Not exceeding 147 pounds) |
|---|---|---|---|
| World's Champion Joe Louis | World's Champion Gus Lesnevich | World's Champion Tony Zale | World's Champion Freddie Cochrane |
| 1—Billy Conn | Archie Moore | Jake LaMotta | Ray Robinson |
| 2—Jimmy Bivins | Lloyd Marshall | Holman Williams | Beau Jack |
| 3—Tami Mauriello | Phil Muscato | Charley Burley | Tippy Larkin |
| 4—Lee Oma | Nate Bolden | Rocky Graziano | Jimmy Doyle |
| 5—Elmer Ray | Billy Fox | Marcel Cerdan | Sammy Angott |
| 6—Bruce Woodcock | Herb Narvo | Bee Bee Washington | Marty Servo |
| 7—Jersey Joe Wolcott | Georgie Kochan | Steve Belloise | Tommy Bell |
| 8—Joe Baksi | Walter Woods | Sonny Horne | Johnny Greco |
| 9—Arturo Godoy | Fitzie Fitzpatrick | Marcus Lockman | Freddie Archer |
| 10—Freddie Schott | Joe Kahut | Jimmy Edgar | Nick Moran |

| Lightweights (Not exceeding 135 pounds) | Featherweights (Not exceeding 126 pounds) | Bantamweights (Not exceeding 118 pounds) | Flyweights (Not exceeding 112 pounds) |
|---|---|---|---|
| World's Champion International Title vacant | World's Champion Willie Pep | World's Champion Manuel Ortiz | World's Champion Jackie Paterson |
| 1—Chalky Wright | Sal Bartolo (N.B.A. Champion) | Benny Goldberg | Seaman Terry Allen |
| 2—Allie Stolz | Phil Terranova | Luis Castillo | Joe Curran |
| 3—Willie Joyce | Jackie Graves | Tony Olivera | Rinty Monaghan |
| 4—Bob Montgomery (Recognized by N.Y.) | Miguel Acevedo | Cliff Anderson | Bunty Doran |
| 5—Ike Williams (N.B.A. Champion) | Al Phillips | Simon Vergara | Stumpy Butwell |
| 6—Bobby Ruffin | Charley Cabey Lewis | Theo Medina | Tommy Burney |
| 7—Ronnie James | Nel Tarleton | Luis Galvani | Hugh Cameron |
| 8—Enrique Bolanos | Carlos Chavez | Sammy Reynolds | George Parks |
| 9—Wesley Mouzon | Kid Zefine | Jackie Jurich | Alec Murphy |
| 10—Freddie Dawson | Frankie Carto | Lorenzo Safora | Jimmy Gill |

# The Fighter and the Man

THUS we see that the men in boxing who make a living with their fists are no different than men in other walks of life who earn their daily bread in a variety of endeavors. Among pugilists there are bright, brainy individuals, many of them college men, well bred, and there are dullards.

Bible students, gamblers, longshoremen, precision machinists, students of law, medicine, liberal arts, and mechanics are numbered among the thousands of prize fighters who have taken to boxing for pay, either temporarily, or for a permanent money stake. Like your next door neighbor, they are witty, dull, happy-go-lucky, moody, bright conversationalists, well travelled and experienced, or silent introverts.

So as you sit at your favorite fight club and watch a muffin-eared, flat-nosed battle-scarred veteran like Fritzie Zivic, don't shake your head in dismay, for like Fritzie he may be one of the shrewdest business men in his city. Likewise don't misjudge the slashing, rip-tear merciless belter who pounds his foe into a state of helplessness. When he sheds the gloves you'll probably find him a grand, lively chap, a credit to any class of citizens. The pugilist proved his worth during the Great War that just ended. This business of boxing after all is just that—a business.

Tony ZALE ..TURNS BACK THE MARCH OF TIME at 34!..

1946..ZALE - 32 YR OLD.. WINNER..HAD TO BE ASSISTED FROM THE RING..

1948 ..ZALE.. LOOKING SHARPER THAN EVER REGAINS THE MIDDLE- WEIGHT TITLE!..

HE'S TOO TOUGH FOR ME!

FATHER TIME..

# *The* MODERN MIRACLE MAN

## By TED CARROLL

THERE probably isn't a man alive who, taking a look at Tony Zale following his win over Graziano the night of September 27, 1946, would have predicted that this badly used up battler would last two more years in the ring. It is doubtful that there has ever been a winning fighter as close to the verge of collapse as was the Gary Gladiator when his hand was raised in triumph that evening.

He had to be assisted from the ring. It was some time before he could leave his dressing room and his bruised features, drawn and taut, gave him the appearance of an old, old, man. Little wonder that Zale unhesitatingly admits that the first fight with Rocky Graziano despite his victory, was the toughest he ever fought!

Tony Zale was 32 years old then, his boxing career had begun 15 years before in the Golden Gloves and he had just come through a four year hitch in the Navy. Consequently when he caved in from exhaustion in the Turkish bath atmosphere of the steaming Stadium in Chicago last year, he looked as finished as any veteran pugilist possibly could.

Most observers doubted that he would hold the new titleholder, Rocky Graziano, to his return bout contract, but would call it quits. In fact some such idea seemed to be in Zale's mind but somewhere between July 16, 1947 and now, Tony Zale turned back the clock and discovered some new and vital source of energy.

\* \* \*

RINGSIDERS blinked their eyes as though in a dream at the rejuvenated Zale in the recent Zale-Graziano battle over in Newark.

The weight of the years which had clung so heavily to him in both the previous contests with the New York slugger seemed to have been discarded along with his bathrobe at the opening bell. Mid-westerners who had watched the Gary Man of Steel for years, swear he never looked sharper.

Save for a fleeting moment in the second round when he careened slightly under a Graziano cannonading. Zale's legs looked as spry and trustworthy as those of a sprightly two year old colt. His left hooks were never snappier, alternating to body and head.

With sure quick movements, he made Rocky miss crucial blows during Graziano's bid for victory in the second and from then on, it was just a matter of moments.

## QUERIES ANSWERED BY NAT FLEISCHER

### SERVIO TULIO LAY, COLON, PANAMA

Q—In a contest billed for the bantamweight championship of Panama, the title holder, Melvin Bourne, weighed 123 pounds and his challenger Claudio Martinez, 117. Since the champion failed to make the weight, 118 pounds or less, did he lose the title? He lost to Martinez. What I would like to know is if he had won, would he still retain his title? As a loser, would Martinez have become the new champion?

A—Bourne lost his title on the scales. Had he won the fight, he still would have been minus his crown. He can no longer be considered the champion. His conqueror, Martinez, is the leading contender for the crown. The fight must be registered as an overweight match and not a championship affair.

### GILBERT DRAKES, DEMERARA, BRITISH GUIANA.

Q—Which of the two between Joe Louis and Ray Robinson has given more to charity? What is meant by a cruiserweight?

A—Joe Louis by far. A Cruiserweight is equivalent to a light heavyweight in America. It is the class below the heavyweights.

### JACK STEVENS, JUDSONIA, ARKANSAS

Q—Please settle a dispute. Did Joe Giambra and Joey Giardello fight before or after Bobo Olson was knocked out by Archie Moore?

A—Before. Giardello and Giambra fought on October 13, 1952 and November 11, 1952, while the Olson-Moore fight took place on June 22, 1955.

### GERALD O'SULLIVAN, ALBANY, OREGON.

Q—Was Hurricane Tommy Jackson ever rated Number One by either the NBA or The Ring? What was his rating when he fought Floyd Patterson?

A—Yes, he was rated Number 1 by both at one time. The Ring had him Number One contender from January through July, up to the time he was knocked out by Patterson, July 29, 1957. He previously had been rated second, third and fourth by both NBA

and The Ring. Before the Patterson fight, the NBA also had him the top challenger.

### A. L. BARRS, HOLMGATE, CLAY CROSS, DERBYSHIRE, ENGLAND.

Q—Was Randy Turpin recognized as world champion when he boxed Bobo Olson in New York?

A—No, he was recognized as European champion and Olson as American title-holder. Turpin defeated Charley Humez, the French entry, in an elimination match for the European laurels. At the same time Olson qualified by beating Paddy Young in the final round of an American tourney. Olson then whipped Turpin for the world championship.

### PETER J. HARRIS, OAKLAND, CAL.

Q—In a state like New York, where rounds are the means for deciding a contest, is it possible for a world champion to lose his title if the rounds are even? Of course I refer to the fact that when the rounds are even, the officials may decide a bout by means of the Eagan four points system which is used in conjunction with the round by round scoring.

A—Yes. If the rounds are even, the officials, according to the New York Commission rules, are required to add their points and the one leading on points, wins the bout. If the points and rounds are even, the officials call the bout a draw. In the case of a draw, the champ, of course, retains his title.

### FRANK K. SINGLETON, KANSAS CITY, MO.

Q—I note on TV that frequently boxers hold and the referee steps in and tears them apart instead of ordering them to break as they do in England and on the European continent where I have seen many boxing bouts. Why do referees in America instruct the boxers to "be sure to break when I tell you," and then forget all about their instructions and rush pell-mell into the fray, often spoiling a fight that otherwise would be enjoyed?

A—Don't ask me. It is a matter that

can be handled only by commissions. Only incompetent referees interfere with the boxers. A warning with a penalty following further holding would soon break that style of fighting in America. Many US boxers have been disqualified in Europe for holding.

## The Modern Miracle Man

SUCH carryings on by some up and coming youngster are to be anticipated but for a 34-year-old family man, father of two, who first donned the mitts away back in 1931, it's almost unbelievable! Graziano almost ten years younger, seemed to have aged that much in two short years since his first fight with Zale, whereas Zale moved around like Rocky's junior. Since Graziano is a guy whose diet knows no limitations, plus liberal doses of long black stogies with varying bed times, which is in strong contrast to Zale's never out of shape routine, the answer might be here.

A silent individual, Zale if he has come upon any secrets of rejuvenation, isn't telling.

All Tony says is that he's just coming out of the effects of his long period of service and that accounts mainly for the difference in his performance in 1946, 1947, and 1948.

* * *

THERE is probably less fault to find with Tony Zale as world's middleweight champion than there is to almost any sports figure you can think of. From whatever angle he is viewed, whether it be war record, physical condition, deportment, or courage, Tony comes up with flying colors.

He's unusually well thought of by his managers and handlers, his neighbors in Gary, Ind., and by those who served with him in the Navy. Conservative in dress and manners, his only drawback is extreme quietness covering up a pleasant personality which comes to the surface during those rare occasions when he has something to say.

His resumption as world middleweight king, solves a lot of problems and gives boxing another champion for whom no apologies need be offered nor alibies advanced on any grounds whatsoever.

# GOOD CLUB FIGHTERS

## By HARVEY BRIGHT

*From New York City's East Side we have a Jewish welterweight, Hy Melzer.*

### HY MELZER

FROM the lower East-side of New York City where Benny Leonard, Ruby Goldstein, *et al.,* got their start in life comes a twenty-year-old Jewish lad who has begun the climb up the fistic ladder. He first tossed leather as a professional back in the summer of 1947 and since then he has entered the ring on thirty-five occasions, losing but one encounter.

The wavy-haired, clean-cut welterweight stands five foot nine sans shoes. He is a better than average boxer with a nice left and an ability to take a solid blow without folding.

Melzer has taken the duke over well touted opponents such as Tony LaBua, Joey Carkido, Chaforo Martinez, Freddie Monforte, Tony Bardoni, and on and on.

Today he is fighting main events and has a large following from the lower East-side

*And still another welter, Tommy Bazzano, from Middletown, Connecticut.*

where his friends and neighbors expect big things of their hero.

### MIKE SAAD

MIKE RYAN, who fights under the name of Mike Saad, is a Manchester, New Hampshire, lad. He has shown his wares all around New England, New York City and as far South as Miami.

Saad is another busy welterweight. He has averaged better than two fights a month this year and has won more than he has lost. The Granite State leather pusher has met some good boys in his pro career, including Walter Stevens, Al Couture, Roy Carter, Dom Sinibaldi, and Billy Graham, to mention but a few.

Mike goes all out in his endeavor to please the crowd and regardless of whether he wins or loses, those who pay the freight, the fans, are sure to witness a fight when the New England welter climbs between the ropes.

A good "club fighter," Saad is guided in his ring career by Joe Baker, the owner of Baker's Gym in Manchester.

### TOMMY BAZZANO

TOMMY "BUSY BEE" BAZZANO, youthful Middletown, Conn., welterweight, has made it a habit to climb into a ring for a fight at least once every two weeks since he turned pro in November, 1947.

A pleasing performer with well over 40 bouts in the New England area, Bazzano, who had fought as Jimmy Parlo in a few of his early fights, is not a one-punch artist but has a tendency to wear down his opponents with hard left hooks to the body.

He dropped his first pro bout to Jackie Armstrong but soon after came back to draw with and then kayo Armstrong. Others whom he has lost to and then defeated in return bouts are Billy Morris and Lenny Trader.

Among the good club fighters he has defeated are Eddie Richmond, Angel Chavez, Rolly Johns, Jimmy Milligan, Johnny Dudley, Whitey Kozey and Billy Patterson.

With his willingness to fight and be a crowd pleaser Manager Jim Higgins has little trouble keeping "Busy Bee" Bazzano busy.

### FELIX RAMIREZ

FELIX RAMIREZ, twenty - year - old Mexican youth hailing from San Jose, California, started a fistic career in the professionals back in 1947 by kayoing Hal Lee inside two rounds. He showed a good right and the makings of a superb left.

Recently at the Laurel Gardens in Newark Felix met the former featherweight champ of the world Sandy Saddler and although Ramirez lost the duke he extended Sandy to the limit and lasted the entire ten frames. Showing fine boxing ability and a left that was well rehearsed, the California youngster proved that he could take it as well as dish it out.

Of the thirty-five bouts that Felix has engaged in he has lost only five decisions and was knocked out but once in the early days of his career.

Since the Saddler affair Ramirez has con-

*Another welterweight, Mike Saad, hails from Manchester, New Hampshire.*

quered Jose Cardenas, Carlos Camacho and Ermano Bonetti, the Italian importation.

Ramirez, relatively unknown, made a name for himself in his fight with ex-featherweight champion, Sandy Saddler. Sandy had just narrowly lost his title to Willie Pep and was taking on a couple of tune-up fights before leaving for a bout in the British Isles. The first boy he met was the San Jose youngster, who, unawed by Saddler's reputation, took everything his opponent had and kept coming back. Ramirez was on the floor four times but only once as the result of a legitimate knockdown. Sandy was forced to travel at his fastest gait throughout the ten-rounder and though he decisively won the decision in the end, he knew he had been in a fight. He had cuts above and below his left eye and was forced to temporarily cancel his British trip.

*Felix Ramirez, Mexican lightweight, who calls Jan Jose, California, his home.*

# NEW FACES PROMISING

## Fine Crop of Youngsters Flashed Into Prominence During 1949, and They May Fill in Vital Gaps on Boxing's International Front in 1950

### By JERSEY JONES

*Enthusiastic New York followers are tabbing middleweight Jimmy Flood as another Rocky Graziano.*

AS THE Twentieth Century, Anno Domini, moves into its half-way mark, the American chapter of the fistic fraternity finds itself confronted by one of the most crucial periods it has known since the knuckle-dusting trade became Big Business.

Boxing is in a mighty precarious state of artistic and financial health at the moment. Three years ago it was estimated that some 750 professional clubs were operating regularly, and generally successfully, throughout the United States, but at this writing, it is doubtful that more than 300, if that many, are functioning, and the total continues to dwindle with every passing month. Divers and sundry have been the reasons offered for the steady decline in attendance and receipts. The main cause has been paucity of outstanding talent.

There has been no apparent falling-off in the public's interest in boxing. That interest seems to be as keen as it ever was. Give Gus Q. Fan what he wants, and he'll turn out in person—television or no. This was amply evidenced on several occasions during 1949 when attractions with the proper "appeal" set new all-time records in various American centers.

THE Ezzard Charles-Pat Valentino affair in San Francisco established two new marks for California. It drew the largest indoor crowd in the state's long, colorful ring history, and the re-

*George Kaplan of Brooklyn is a youngster with a lot of natural ring savvy.*

ceipts topped all previous boxing figures for a California production.

Four up-state New York communities reported new all-time local highs —Rochester with Joey DeJohn and Pete Mead, Syracuse with DeJohn and Lee Sala, Binghamton with Sala and Joe Taylor, and Schenectady with Sala and Sandy Saddler in a double windup with fair opposition.

The Rocky Castellani-Tony Janiro outing in Scranton attracted the second largest gate in Scranton's boxing archives—topped only by the Mickey Walker-Pete Latzo brawl for the world welterweight title in 1926.

Our Canadian neighbors also checked in with a new set of figures compiled by Laurent Dauthuille and Johnny Greco, whose scrap in Montreal shattered all existing marks for a clouting carnival in the Dominion.

No, there has been no decline in the public's interest in boxing. But, unfortunately, these developments were the exceptions rather than the rule in 1949. The scarcity of outstanding talent made it difficult, if not impossible, for even the most alert, enterprising promoter to come up regularly with the sort of attractions he needed.

Taken by and large, the year was a discouraging one for the American sock market—and a disastrous one for many of the promoters who tried to operate.

*Rocky Marciano of Brockton, Mass., a promising heavyweight.*

DURING the entire year, only seven bouts staged throughout the United States grossed $100,000.

The top gate was the $246,546 drawn by Ezzard Charles and Jersey Joe Walcott in their National Boxing Association heavyweight title bout in Chicago's Comiskey Park. The next best was the $177,128 reported for the Ray Robinson-Kid Gavilan outing in Philadelphia's Municipal Stadium.

The others to reach the six-figure mark in receipts were:

Ezzard Charles vs. Pat Valentino, San Francisco, $167,870.

Jake LaMotta vs. Marcel Cerdan, Detroit, $159,762.

Rocky Graziano vs. Charley Fusari, New York (Polo Grounds), $135,117.

Ray Robinson vs. Steve Belloise, New York (Yankee Stadium), $120,860.

Ike Williams vs. Enrique Bolanos, Los Angeles, $108,298.

OFFICIAL statistics released by Madison Square Garden for its 1949 boxing activities are significant. Only 20 shows were staged during the year in the House that Tex Built, compared to

*Scotland, long a specialist in top flyweights, has another good one in Vic Herman.*

*Considered one of America's best heavyweight prospects is Rex Layne of Utah.*

the usual annual production of from 28 to 32.

For the first year since the prewar era, the Garden's total receipts for boxing failed to hit $1,000,-000. (The figures were in the neighborhood of $800,-000, for a not too impressive average of $40,000 per show.)

Also for the first year in a decade, not one of the cards succeeded in drawing

flyweight classes are practically extinct.

The only division that offers any serious encouragement is the middleweight. Jake La-Motta and Rocky Graziano unquestionably would do big business, and Ray Robinson, moving up from his welterweight class to meet the LaMotta-Graziano winner, also would

represent prolific box-office activity.

There is an outside chance, of course, that some of the youngsters just beginning to attract attention may come along fast enough during 1950 to move into headline spots, and supply the "new blood" so vitally needed in the industry.

FOR one, there is Ross Virgo, a welterweight operating out of Rochester, N. Y.

Until he dropped a decision to the more experienced Lester Felton in Detroit recently, Virgo had been unbeaten in 19 bouts spread across less than 14 months of professional campaigning. And for a kid of his limited experience, he had whipped some pretty fair opposition. Among those he had beaten were Chester Rico, Ted Bussey,

Dave Andrews, Johnny Kaufman, Cliff Hart, Al Hersh and Tony Pellone. Virgo definitely is worth tabbing.

a gross of $100,000. The top mark was $95,865, set by Kid Gavilan and Ike Williams in the third and "rubber" chapter of their series. Willie Pep and Sandy Saddler, in their encore meeting, earned second spot, with $87,563.

Such other major fistic centers as the Chicago Stadium, the Detroit Olympia, the Boston Garden, the Cleveland Arena and Philadelphia's Convention Hall made no effort to operate on regular schedules during the year. There weren't enough topline attractions available, so they promoted on a "spot-show" basis—as and

*Joe Lindsay another young Brooklyn heavyweight prospect.*

when certain matches with local appeal materialized. It is doubtful if any of those arenas showed much in the way of financial profit for the year.

Many a club scattered around the landscape, which in lush times had been accustomed to drawing $4,000 to $5,000 as a regular thing, found itself doing business in 1949 on receipts of $1,000 and less. More than one instance was reported of gates hitting as low as $400.

And, as we remarked several paragraphs back, the main reason for it all was lack of talent. The paying populace couldn't work up the necessary enthusiasm for the generally poor quality of the cards offered.

WHAT will materialize in 1950 is something that remains to be seen. On the American scene, there is no heavyweight shaping up as a likely opponent for Ezzard Charles in a major promotion—unless, as seems likely, Joe Louis decides to stage a serious return to the ring.

Our light-heavyweight class starts and stops with Joey Maxim and Archie Moore.

Welterweight Ray Robinson and Lightweight Ike Williams are one-man parades in their respective divisions.

The only big-time match available among featherweights is a third and payoff meeting of Willie Pep and Sandy Saddler.

So far as the United States is concerned, the bantamweight and

An Irish southpaw, Bob Murphy of San Diego, also seems to be worth checking. Murphy is a light-heavyweight, and, from all accounts, packs a thunderous punch. Bob isn't exactly a freshman in the trade—he started tossing leather in 1945—but it wasn't until last year that folks beyond the environs of San Diego began to take heed of him, and he became a popular attraction in Los Angeles.

Murphy's record is loaded with knockouts—and there's nothing quite like the kayo wallop to excite the interest of the cash customers. As this is being written, the statistics credit Irish Bob with having flattened 36 of 43 opponents—and that's pretty fair clouting in any league. The young man hasn't stacked up against top opposition as yet, and his best performance probably was the four-round kayo he slipped over on the fading but cagey veteran, Lloyd Marshall, in Los Angeles.

A YOUNGSTER who may become another Rocky Graziano in box-office appeal is Irish Jimmy Flood, middleweight out of New York's Yorkville district. Flood has a lot to learn about boxing, but he has the sort of "exciting" style that made Graziano such a tremendous attraction. There's nothing fancy or flashy about Jimmy's modus operandi. He just walks in and whales away with both hands—and he hits with authority.

*A brilliant boxer, Johnny Williams is one of England's brightest heavy-weight prospects.*

That Flood is improving steadily with experience is indicated by his series with Herbie Kronowitz in New York and George LaRover in Philadelphia. Held to a draw by Kronowitz in their first meeting, Flood came back to edge out Herbie in the second, and win decisively in the third. LaRover also held Flood to an even split in their first clash,

*Ross Virgo, Rochester, N. Y., middleweight, ran off 19 straight wins before suffering defeat.*

Tommy Bell. From all accounts, Delaney not only is a good boxer, but a stiff puncher. His record is well studded with knockouts.

Smith, the 1948 National amateur lightweight champion, has done well in his first year as a pro. Confining his activities exclusively to Cincinnati rings, Bud's earlier accomplishments in-

*Another promising English heavy is Jack Gardner, with 17 kayoes in his first 19 starts.*

but Jimmy flattened the veteran in a hurry when they met again.

Two of the best young prospects in the nation are a pair of Ohio Negroes — welterweight Ron Delaney of Akron and lightweight Wallace (Bud) Smith of Cincinnati.

Fighting professionally less than two years, Delaney has already beaten such experienced campaigners as Eddie O'Neill, Willie Russell, Cecil Hudson and

cluded wins over the likes of Jesse Underwood and Joe Discepoli, and he capped his year's impressive record by coming through with a brilliant decision over the rated Tommy Campbell.

THE main hunt for "new talent" centers, of course, in heavyweights, but embryo Jack Dempseys and Joe Louises don't happen very often in this business.

The tugging-and-hauling affair between Roland LaStarza and Cesar Brion in Madison Square Garden recently was a keen disappointment to a lot of folks. LaStarza and Brion were rated two of the best of the younger crop of big 'uns, and there even had been talk that one or the other could be developed by next summer into an opponent for Ezzard Charles—even, possibly, for Joe Louis, if and when the old Bomber decided to announce his serious return to the ring.

Roland and Cesar still can be listed as "prospects," but neither, in his present form, can be considered seriously for major recognition in the more or less immediate future.

Rocky Marciano may be a possibility, but, first, we'd like to see the Brockton, Mass., slugger against real opposition. Marciano unquestionably can punch, but from the little we have seen of him so far, he'd have difficulty hitting anyone who knew anything about boxing. He fights out of an awkward crouch, doesn't seem to have much of a defense. He relies upon ponderous swings to win for him.

Probably the best of the younger heavyweights is Bob Baker, of Pittsburgh, who breezed through the Golden Gloves last year, and has since been breezing just as easily through professional competition in and around Smogtown. Baker is a smooth operator. He knows how to box, he knows how to punch, and he continues to improve with every start.

*Bob Murphy, San Diego middleweight, has piled up sensational knockout record.*

THE unwillingness of the other young heavyweights to meet them has put Joe Lindsay of Brooklyn and Maynard Jones of Wilmington, Del., in difficult spots. To get any sort of action, they've had to fight opponents who rate above them in the fistic scales. But they've done pretty well for themselves, all things considered. During 1949, Lindsay split a pair of decisions with the dangerous Omelio Agramonte, winning in Philadelphia, and losing in New York, and he also whipped Dusty Wilkerson twice in Philadelphia. The 21-year-old Jones, former All-Navy champion, had to fight such seasoned opposition as Joe Baksi in Newark, Abel Cestac in Baltimore and Arturo Godoy in Wilmington, and it was tough going for a kid of his limited experience.

It would be interesting to see what Lindsay and Jones could do with the LaStarzas, Brions and Marcianos, but there isn't much likelihood of any such matches materializing.

One of the finest young heavyweight prospects we have seen in some time is Georgie Kaplan of Brooklyn. He seems to have a lot of natural ring savvy. He moves

# THEY
# FAILED
## *to*
# PLEASE

When Roland LaStarza (left) and Cesar Brion of Argentina were matched for an appearance in Madison Square Garden, the fans figured that they would see the two best developments among the young heavyweights shoot the works to prove their right to recognition as top men in their class. But they proved a dud. Neither showed enough to warrant the praise that has been showered on them. Just ordinary—was the verdict of the spectators.

Rocky Marciano, the third member of the group of newcomers among the heavyweights who has gained national attention by piling up many victories, scored another "kayo" when he stopped Pat Richards of Columbus, Ohio, but that victory gained him nothing. Pat was a push-over, imported just to add to Marciano's list of "victims." Al Weill shouldn't feed his fighter, a good prospect, with such poor talent.

## NEW FACES PROMISING

around well, has an idea what boxing's all about, and punches fast and accurately with either hand. But he's still a year or two away from making a serious bid for headline recognition. Only 19, Kaplan hasn't fully developed physically, and needs time to acquire the necessary strength and ruggedness, as well as experience.

Another possible heavyweight bet for future circulation seems to be Rex Layne, youthful Utahan. For a yearling, Layne has done well for himself—though, naturally, he hasn't been up against too formidable opposition as yet. His handlers have been taking him along easily, giving him every opportunity to learn and improve. To date, Rex has run off 12 knockouts and one decision in 13 starts, and has given a good account of hmself in an exhibition with Ezzard Charles. Except for two quick hops to Hollywood, Layne has confined his fistic activities so far to his native Utah, but his managerial board feels it won't be long before he'll be ready to try his luck in New York and Chicago.

WHILE the American scene hasn't been too prolific with its development of young talent, quite a few good kids seem to have popped up in several sectors of the international front.

Britain, for instance, has become quite excited over the possibilities of two likely heavyweights—Johnny Williams and Jack Gardner.

Williams isn't exactly a freshman. He started fighting as a middleweight in 1946, but it wasn't until last year, when he became a heavyweight, that he rated headline status. Johnny isn't too rugged, but he is an exceptionally clever boxer.

Though lacking Williams' skill, Gardner has proved himself a good two-fisted puncher. He piled up a remarkable record for his first year of professional leather-pushing, 17 of his 19 opponents failing to go the distance with him. In the only bout that went its scheduled route, Gardner outpointed that tough Frenchman, Stephane Olek. Jack's only defeat was of the "technical" variety, inflicted by the cagey Canadian veteran, Vern Escoe, a nasty gash over the youngster's left eye prompting the referee to call a halt at the end of the fifth round.

Fellow-Canadian and stablemate of Escoe's, Earl Walls, also has become quite a favorite with the British public. A good boxer, and a vicious puncher, Walls has been having a merry time with his European opposition. He started by stopping the Scot, Ken Shaw, in three rounds. Since then he has run off three fast ones, requiring only a round apiece to stiffen Piet Wilde of Belgium, Kurt Schiegl of Austria, and Albert Coulbaly of Algeria.

ANOTHER heavyweight who has been stirring up considerable to-do in Europe is the American, Aaron Wilson, who has established headquarters in Paris. Wilson recently showed in England for the first time and celebrated the occasion by flattening the former British champion, Jack London, with one punch, in 27 seconds. Among Aaron's European accomplishments was the winning of an open heavyweight tournament in Brussels. He flattened his first three opponents, and whipped Stephane Olek in the finale.

Britishers are envisioning a possible world middleweight champion in Randolph Turpin, youngest of the three fighting brothers. The 21-year-old Randy hit headline rating during 1949 by running off seven straight wins, among them spectacular knockouts of the Belgian Cyrille Delannoit and the American Pete Mead.

Scotland, which seems to specialize in top flyweights—it produced two world champions in Benny Lynch and Jackie Paterson—came up during the year with three fine little fellows in Peter Keenan, Joe Murphy and Vic Herman.

Unbeaten since he turned professional late in 1947, Roger Baour crashed the top brackets in European lightweight ratings by knocking out Andre Gonnet for the vacant French title.

ONE of the finest fighting machines in Europe, the Italian Tiberio Mitri, established his status by annexing the continent's middleweight title. Mitri has been unbeaten in three years of pro fighting and 50 battles. His record shows wins over Cyrille Delannoit of Belgium, Laurent Dauthuille of France, Dick Turpin of England, Giovanni Manca of Italy and Jean Dobiasch of Poland. He's done a thorough job of cleaning up his main opposition.

Albert Yvel, the Algerian, who holds the French light-heavyweight title, is touted as a 175-pounder to watch.

Australia uncovered three native Aborigines for its main excitement during 1949—lightweights Jack Hassan and Alfie Clay and bantamweight Elley Bennett.

One of the top developments of the year was Vic Toweel of South Africa. Younger brother of lightweight Jimmy Toweel, 21-year-old Vic turned pro in January, after a brilliant amateur career and ran off a string of a dozen straight wins.

# IT'S GOLDEN GLOVES TIME

## *By* TED CARROLL

IT'S Golden Gloves time again in the good old U.S.A., meaning that for the next few months there will be more blows swung, landed and missed in boxing rings all across the country than during the remainder of the year. This is the time when many striplings find out whether their fighting ability has been real or fancied. The great amateur boxing tournament which long ago assumed countrywide proportions is in its 24th consecutive year of operation. Some might call it No. 23 since the magic words Golden Gloves were not coupled until 1927. It was Paul Gallico, at that time sports editor of the New York *Daily News,* who, learning of the newspaper sponsored tourney held by the Chicago *Tribune* in 1926 brain-childed this simple but fascinating title for the *Daily News* version of the amateur tournament.

Arch Ward, *Tribune* Sports Editor, is generally given credit for the original idea. The New York response was so overwhelming, that the Gloves have been gaining momentum ever since. It has now reached the point where nearly any kid with boxing ambitions tries them out for the first time in the Golden Gloves.

THE "sub-novice" class idea was a stroke of genius. The fighting instinct has always been present in most youngsters. But putting it to the test in real competition before the Gloves came along, was risky business. Beginners chanced injury and quick disillusionment if a direct plunge into the professional ranks was taken. The old style "amateurs" were not without dangers. Our able confrere, Mr. Jersey Jones, once suffered, vicariously of course, from such a disaster. Jersey once had a protege whose possibilities seemed excellent.

Since this was in the pre-Golden Glove era, Jersey entered his lad in an amateur tournament to get things started. Up in the ring, Jersey glanced over into the opposite corner and nearly fainted when he saw Canada Lee, the champion, sitting over there. Needless to say Jersey's novice, given such a foe for his first fight, didn't last the round and announced his retirement in the dressing room immediately afterwards.

Something like this happened to—of all people—Joe Louis, who in his very first bout tangled with an amateur champion, John Miler, who proceeded to have this all time great on the deck no less than seven times.

Such amateur mismatching was frequent in the old days. The "Gloves" halted all this with the "sub-novice" arrangement whereby beginner meets beginner in a fair and square test. Boxing is no sport for those who have nothing but the inclination, and the Golden Gloves have proven invaluable in swiftly weeding out inept aspirants with a minimum of risk to themselves.

Another Golden Gloves godsend has been the unusual completeness of the physical checkups. The old time amateur got himself an A.A.U. card, turned up at a tournament, was weighed, given a quick brushoff "examination" by somebody, and was tossed in there. Until recent years the professionals were given little better protection, particularly in small towns and outlying districts. Insurance companies don't check over applicants any more thoroughly than do the Golden Glove directors in the various cities today. This wise policy is reflected in the almost complete lack of serious injury in Golden Glove tournaments.

AS THE RING is primarily concerned with professional boxing, the relationship of the Golden Gloves to, and the effect upon, the professional side of the sport is the main object of this piece, rather than a history of the great amateur tournament itself. With a full generation of activity to cover, this would take a volume anyway. It should suffice to say, that from its limited Chicago beginnings, the tournament, usually under newspaper sponsorship, has spread out to include such cities as Detroit, Cleveland, Omaha, St. Paul, Columbus, Milwaukee, St. Louis, in the West, besides New York, Philadelphia, Washington, Atlanta, Miami, Baltimore, Boston, Trenton in the East.

With both Chicago and New York running tourneys some sort or inter-city series was inevitable. This came along in 1928. Eventually it became sectional—with "Chicago" coming to include almost everything west of Philadelphia, and "New York" taking in the Atlantic seaboard. Puerto Rico was also added to the eastern lineup.

The competition didn't even end there and international teams have been crossing the Atlantic to oppose American outfits. U.S. representatives have also journeyed overseas to engage the foreigners. Provisions have been made for service fighters to ease into Golden Gloves competition as well as for those from the far reaches of the Pacific.

The Golden Gloves have given many an "under-privileged" kid his first taste of a decent diet and healthful living conditions in the training camps to which all the tourney survivors are treated. Travel experiences, flurries of fame, and publicity have brightened many lives with drab beginnings.

Since its scope has been so all inclusive, almost every professional boxer active today might be called an ex-Golden Glover. Few of them missed participating in a G.G. tourney at one time or another. For the purposes of this article and to keep it within reasonable limits attention will be paid only to those prominent professionals, past and present, who were conspicuously successful as Golden Glovers.

LEADING the list of all those Glovers who were to succeed as pros, is an illustrious name, Barney Ross. Ross was the first Golden Glove champion to become a world's champion, a more worthy forerunner could hardly have been hoped for. When Ross won the lightweight title from Tony Canzoneri in 1933 the Golden Gloves had graduated its first titleholder.

Ross had been outstanding as an amateur, but oddly enough in the intercity contests between Chicago and New York he had his hands full with Al Santoro in Madison Square Garden in 1929. The boys appeared about evenly matched at that stage of the game, although Ross gained the three-round decision. Barney went on to win two world titles, Santoro never got out of the prelim class.

Nearly everyone knows that Joe Louis first attracted attention in the Golden Gloves. Joe was a light-heavy in those days in 1934. Few will question his right to be called the greatest Glover of them all, although Ray Robinson would probably get some support.

As good as Sugar Ray was in the Golden Gloves, he was overshadowed when he won the featherweight G.G. championship in 1939 by Buddy Moore, one of the most extravagantly ballyhooed G.G. heavyweights of them all. Curt Hoerrman, scion of a brewing clan, was hot on the trail of Moore. Robinson, who was handled by the same trainer who took care of Moore, George Gainsford, was tossed into the bargain as just something extra. The idea of Ray Robinson being excess baggage sounds funny today, especially since Moore petered out long ago, but that's the way it was.

Robinson was so good by the time he won the G.G. lightweight championship in 1940, that he started knocking out experienced pro fighters as soon as he turned professional.

The light-heavyweight class has been a happy hunting ground for the Golden Glove boys. A couple of them, Bob Olin in 1934, and Gus Lesnevich in 1941, won the title. Both of these were Golden Glove pioneers going way back to the beginnings of the idea.

Gus' great rival in his amateur days was a chap named Mark Hough. Both were middleweights then. Mark was another outstanding amateur who never gained similar status as a professional. Joe Maxim, a genuine Golden Glove great, is another old grad who has gone a long way in the pro field.

In selecting the top middleweight among the G.G. alumni, Tony Zale is given the nod over Solly

# IT'S GOLDEN GLOVES TIME

Krieger but it's a photo finish. Both held the middleweight professional championship, but Zale's claim was more universal. Zale was more colorful in the last stages of his career, but Krieger was always a vastly underrated boxer. In his amateur days way back in 1929, Krieger was known as Danny Auerbach, but switched monickers when he became a paid performer.

A SURPRISINGLY large number of boxing men rate Solly a better fighter than Zale. Billy Conn, who fought both and should know, is one of these. The Pittsburgher had no trouble at all with the smaller Zale. Krieger was one of the very few to earn a verdict over Sweet William in three tries.

On the other hand, Al Hostak was always easy picking for The Man of Steel from Gary, Ind., while the best Krieger could do with the Far Westerner was an even break in two skirmishes with him.

Billy Soose, also an ex-middleweight champ, was an ace "glover" too, but was more widely recognized as a college product in his amateur boxing days. Soose, much too good for the rah-rah boys, was responsible for the eastern intercollegiate rule barring Golden Glove champs from college meets.

NO time need be wasted or explanations advanced in picking the all time G.G. welterweight, just say Ray Robinson and the case is closed.

The same thing goes for our lightweight standout, previously mentioned Barney Ross.

Willie Pep won the Connecticut State amateur titles but apparently passed up Golden Gloves competition. This leaves Petey Scalzo, a real Golden Glove standout and former world's featherweight titleholder, as a solid choice as the all time G.G. featherweight.

Bantamweights Lou Salica and Georgie Pace were both ace Golden Glovers in their amateur days, Louis beat the little Clevelander for the title as pros so that gives him the edge as the kingpin bantamweight.

The flyweight class is just about nonexistent in the States so Harold Dade is best known as a bantamweight but he was a wiz wizard as a G.G. flyweight. This, plus a pro record, that includes the world's bantamweight title, puts him up front as our all time G.G. flyweight.

Most of the pro successes mentioned in the preceding paragraphs had as contemporaries in their Golden Glove days, rivals who sometimes outshone them, but never made the grade as professionals. Detroit had a long string of these, most of them boxing as simon pures around or about the same time as Joe Louis. Some of them

looked better and had more impressive amateur records than the Bomber.

Lorenzo Pack, Stanley Evans, Clinton Bridges, Johnny Whiters, Milton Shivers, Howell King, were all touted as sure shots to tear the professional ranks wide open when they were boxing in the Gloves out around Detroit. None of them lived up to expectations.

NEW YORK also had a long lineup of the same. Sedgewick Harvey, George Brothers, Sal Affinito, Al Santoro, Jimmy Carollo, Jim Howell, Johnny Clinton, had it all over many future pro stars as Golden Glovers but never got very far themselves as pros.

Max Marek, who beat Louis as an amateur, was a Chicago disappointment. Ill-fated Lem Franklin, Cleveland Gloves hero, made a promising start as a pro but fizzled out.

A real Golden Glove ace and one of the most underrated heavyweights of recent years was Bob Pastor. Had Joe Louis not been around the one-time New York University athlete might have won the world's heavyweight title, as he defeated practically everyone else.

Almost every pro prospect of the moment is an ex-Golden Glover. New York fans are looking for big things from Johnny Saxton, a 1949 G.G. winner, who is being taken along by vet Bill Miller, long-time Golden Glove coach and one of the most able of the boxing trainers. Out West, after a tough struggle, Keith Nuttall with a recent win over Harold Dade, may be about to fulfill all the fine things predicted for him when he was the boy wonder of the state of Utah.

With the G.G. tourneys as examples, the public has seen mass boxing conducted with little risk to youthful and unskilled participants. They have kept a steady stream of talent flowing into the pro ranks. They act as an annual tonic to the boxing game, keeping interest alive in spots where the pros have been lagging.

The crowds show no sign of diminishing as the years go by. Sellouts still are the rule rather than the exception in both the preliminary and final rounds.

All in all, the influence of the Golden Gloves upon the professional game has been very good.

## LEFT HOOKS FROM SCRANTON AND VICINITY
### By Ken (Duke) Stigner

SCRANTON, Pa.—The Scranton Armory was jammed with fight fans who came to witness the oft-postponed and widely publicized ten-round feature of Promoter Branker's Anthracite A. C. professional show between ex-Marine Rocky Castellani, 154, from Luzerne, Pa., and Harold Green, 160, Brooklyn. The Rock, fighting a careful, cautious battle, flicked and jabbed his way to victory over ten rounds.

In two heats, the fifth and seventh, Green caught up with Casty and had the Luzerne boy wobbly and in trouble.

The vast assemblage, despite the fact it was put on just ten days before Christmas and the mines

working on a three-day work week, bears out this writer's contention that there is nothing wrong with boxing that good matches can't cure, when a local boy is one of the principals. More than 4,000 fans paid $13,202.50 into the till.

This was the second meeting between the two boys. Casty won a split decision over Green in Madison Square Garden after both fighters were on the floor for nine-counts.

The second bout was definitely not sensational. It was simply another chapter in the book, boxer vs. slugger, and Castellini, a smart, sharp left-jabbing boxer, won with ease.

The six-round semi-windup didn't last long. But while it lasted, exactly three minutes, it was a dandy. Sonny Genelli caught more solid smashes than ever before in his glittering career. Bob Bowman, Lancaster, a crude yet effective belter, stood toe to toe with Sonny and they punched each other silly. Bowman suffered a deep cut over the right eye and couldn't go on. Genelli was awarded a second-round T.K.O. Bowman weighed 151¾, Genelli tipped the Fairbanks at 153¼.

Lou Pompey, South Scranton, the kid with all the tools of the trade, just seemed to be unable to get started and as most of his punches went astray he blew a decision to John Potenti, a plugger from Boston. Looks like Lou left his fight in the gym.

Dunmore heavyweight Joe Coviello, 210, outlasted Mike Barron, 190, Binghamton. Coviello boxed beautifully, however, and gained the nod of the officials. During the third round Mike nailed Joe with a stinging right and Joe's knees buckled. Coviello in his anxiety to score a K.O. missed repeatedly with sweeping hooks.

Youthful Mel Goldsmith, 149-pounder from New York City, attracted the attention of the crowd with his caged tactics. Only 18 years old, Mel outpointed John McKenzie, veteran from the Bronx, N. Y.

Carl Stritt, South Scranton, 152, was T.K.O.'ed in two minutes of the second round by Bobby Peck, Sunbury. Stritt had made two trips to the canvas before Referee Manny Gelb stopped the contest. Stritt had beaten Peck in a previous bout.

Waiting for the Bell—Billy Soose, ex-middleweight champ at the Cast-Green battle looking as fit as a fiddle. . . . Chairman Jones of the State Boxing Commission a ringside spectator. . . . Tony Baldoni, Wilkes-Barre scrapper, challenged the winner. . . . Might be an interesting bout if some promoter could get Casty and Jimmy King in the same ring. . . . Don't be surprised if Mullins, Wilkes-Barre, becomes the big office attraction around these parts the coming year. . . . Local fistic followers look with favor on the appointment by Governor James F. Duff of John "John Ox" DaGrosa to the State Athletic Commission in charge of the Quaker City district. . . . 'Tis rumored that Nat Branker, promoter of the Anthracite A. C., has peddled his 50 percent of stock of the club to Ernie Genell. . . . If Chairman Jones of the State Athletic Commission gives his permission, we're liable to see a new promoter here. . . . Branker, retiring because of ill health, will long be remembered as the most colorful head of a boxing syndicate of the post-war era.

## DENVER AND VICINITY
### By W. G. (Bill) Thomas, Jr.

PROFESSIONAL boxing in Denver is still hibernating. There were no pro shows in the state last month. Jack Kanner and George Zaharias, matchmaker and promoter, wanted very much to bring Sandy Saddler to the Mile High City, but had too much trouble securing an opponent.

Corky Gonzales, Denver featherweight, suffered the second defeat of his professional career by losing a vicious ten-rounder to Miguel Acevedo at St. Paul, Minn., December 14th. Acevedo managed to get by Corky's defense and score heavily to the body. Corky was knocked down in the sixth round but was not hurt. In the semi on the same card, Jesse Mongia, Denver, lost a close one to Featherweight Roy Higa, Honolulu. This makes the score one up, as Mongia copped the nod in their other torrid battle a few weeks ago.

Amateur teams throughout the region will compete in the Golden Gloves Tournament in Denver sometime late in January. The winners will go to Chicago for a try at the National Title. Many small tournaments have been held throughout the state, and the winners have been entered in the Denver Regional Meet.

The writer's address is 4313 Sheridan Boulevard, Denver, Colo.

# Fifty Years of Progress

*Jack Dempsey, Idol of Fistiana, Named by American Sports Writers "Boxing's Top Man" of Last Half Century*

## By AL BUCK

*Jack Dempsey, who brought million dollar gate to pugilism.*

AMONG other things, naming Jack Dempsey "Boxing's Man of the Half Century" has served to emphasize the tremendous progress made by the sport in the last 50 years. Starting with the first James J. Jeffries-James J. Corbett bout on May 11, 1900, and ending with the Ezzard Charles-Pat Valentino battle on Oct. 14, 1949, the game has advanced steadily until now it is a tremendous industry operating all over the world. An ancient sport, boxing came into its own in the first half of the 20th Century—the Golden Era of Pugilism.

Dempsey was the game's most exciting figure, but he alone was not responsible for boxing's growth. No one man was. Looking back over the years it is possible to single out this and that individual, men like Tex Rickard, Jimmy Coffroth, Bill Brady, Jim Corbett, Jimmy Walker and Joe Louis, among others who made major contributions to the sport. Rickard, for example, put boxing on Wall Street's big board, but it was Jim Coffroth who was largely responsible for placing the sport on the big-time circuit.

Tex had promoted the Battling Nelson-Joe Gans fight in Goldfield, Nev., in 1906, but that was a mining camp operation. It wasn't until Jeffries decided to come out of retirement and "redeem the honor of the white race" by fighting Jack Johnson that Rickard came into his own. Jack and Jim met at a hotel in Hoboken, N. J., to sign for the bout, and to allow promoters to bid for it.

Rickard's bid was $101,000 and he got the match. So there would be no doubt as to his sincerity, he brought the money to the meeting, and tossed it onto the table in front of Jeffries and Johnson. The other promoters thought he was crazy, but events proved otherwise.

WHY was the meeting held in Hoboken, across the harbor from New York City? Because in New York boxing was illegal. A man broke a law just by signing for a prizefight within the boundaries of the great Empire State in the year 1909.

Tex took the fight to California, and with the assurance of Gov. Gillett that he could stage the match, started building an arena in San Francisco. He reckoned without the reformers. The Governor weakened and the attorney general got out an injunction. Rickard was forced to retreat to Reno, Nev.

That Johnson beat Jeffries in 15 rounds on July 4, 1910, is a matter of record. There are those who believe Big Jeff was "Boxing's Man of the Half Century" nevertheless. Among them are Dan Morgan, the veteran boxing manager.

"Jeffries knocked out Bob Fitzsimmons, the hardest-hitting heavyweight champion, and he also knocked out Jim Corbett, the father of American boxing," is the way Morgan explains his belief that Jeffries was the greatest. The public, however, remember Jeff as the original hollow shell, the man who failed to come back.

From the standpoint of ability alone, Johnson may have been the game's greatest. Nat Fleischer does not hesitate to give him first place in his book, "The Heavyweight Championship." Unfortunately Johnson contributed nothing outside the ring. He hurt, rather than helped boxing.

IT WASN'T until he promoted the Dempsey-Jess Willard slaughter at Toledo that Rickard became a power. At last boxing had the perfect combination—the great promoter and the great champion. The million-dollar gate was just around the corner.

A guarantee of $300,000 to Dempsey and of $200,000 to Georges Carpentier set the stage for the "Battle of the Century." Tex was thinking in terms of 100 years, but his partners, alarmed by the large guarantees, withdrew. On his own, Rickard built Boyle's Thirty Acres in Jersey City, and on July 2, 1921, drew $1,789,238. Boxing was big business at last. Now to make it a respectable business.

Rickard liked to attract what he called "the best people." He liked having women attend his fights. He took steps to see that every one got the seat his or her ticket called for. He couldn't have done all this without Jimmy Walker.

James J. Walker, the playboy-statesman, will long be remembered for the Walker Law. It made boxing legal in New York, and has served as the model for boxing laws in nearly every state of the Union.

"I wanted to be sure of getting the seat my ticket called for," is the reason the late Senator Walker gave for sponsoring the boxing law. There was another reason of course. Jimmy Walker loved boxing, and was always at the ringside. His contribution to the sport cannot be overlooked in reviewing the first half century in boxing.

In fact Walker, Rickard and Dempsey made possible Madison Square Garden. With the Walker Law and Dempsey as an attraction, Tex was able to sell stock to raise the money necessary to build the famous arena. The Garden remains Rickard's monument. He might well have been "Boxing's Man of the Half Century," although he would no doubt have preferred to have the honor go to Dempsey.

The Manassa Mauler is more than a champion. He drew the first million-dollar gate and the largest gate of all time—$2,658,660—when he fought Gene Tunney a second time in Chicago. That was the Battle of the Long Count, and there are many who still consider Dempsey champion, although the decision went to Tunney.

JOE LOUIS made a contribution to boxing beyond his remarkable ability as a fighter. He broke down the "color line" and struck a powerful blow at racial discrimination. Like Dempsey he had a great promoter in Mike Jacobs to pave the way. Jacobs, an associate of Rickard, became Tex's successor. With Louis as his attraction he restored the million-dollar gates. The second Louis-Billy Conn bout in New York drew the second largest gate—$1,925,564.

Jacobs had both courage and vision. He challenged the Garden monopoly by persuading Braddock to risk the heavyweight title against Louis in Chicago. Then he set up his own monopoly with Louis as his attraction. Joe Louis defended the heavyweight title 25 times. In one year he risked the crown seven times.

The choice of Dempsey over Louis in the poll conducted by the Associated Press to name "Boxing's Man of the Half Century" has become a subject of debate. Nevertheless Dempsey's selection seems to justify a story written by Fleischer in another publication. In it the publisher of THE RING promoted a "dream fight" between Dempsey and Louis. Dempsey was the winner in Fleischer's mythical battle. It is my belief that had Jack and Joe clashed when both were at their peak, that Dempsey would have won, but that is something that can never be settled. Let the argument continue.

IN looking back 50 years consideration must be given to James A. Farley. He became Postmaster General of the United States, and chairman of the Democratic National Committee, but at the recent dinner of the Boxing Writers' Association, he said the thing he was most proud of was the no-foul rule.

The no-foul rule in boxing is Jim Farley's rule. He conceived it and wrote it into the boxing code. When he did, he saved boxing. For years the sure thing gamblers had stipulated that in case of a foul all bets were off. Heavily backed fighters, on discovering they couldn't win, were fouling out and saving their supporters' money.

Farley changed all that. He did it with the aid of Foulproof Taylor, inventor of the Taylor protector. Now no fight can be won and lost on a foul. Incidentally Foulproof Taylor has never been given full credit for the part he played in saving the sport. He conceived the idea of a foulproof protector, now universally used.

The first Jack Sharkey-Max Schmeling fight caused Farley to go into action. A careless left hook thrown by Sharkey was responsible. Jack was well on his way to the heavyweight championship. He had Schmeling outpointed from here to the Rhine.

*Tex Rickard, the man who ruled the roost during the Golden Era of Boxing.*

Then his punch went low. Joe Jacobs, Schmeling's American manager, leaped into the ring and claimed the championship.

In the confusion that followed, Referee Jim Crowley awarded the fight and the championship to Schmeling. He had no other choice. As for Schmeling, he gained the dubious distinction of becoming the first and only man to win the world heavyweight championship while sitting down.

THERE are others who must be remembered. Gene Tunney, for instance, retired as the undefeated world heavyweight champion. He never came back as did Jeffries. Louis has retired undefeated too, but his future activities are still a matter of speculation.

Henry Armstrong won three titles—featherweight, welterweight and lightweight—within a period of 12 months and held them all at the same time. There have been few greater champions than Armstrong.

Frank Erne, Willie Lewis and Dan McKetrick took boxing across the water and made it a popular sport in France in the early years of the 20th Century.

In one individual promotion, Mike Jacobs presented four championship bouts—Lou Ambers vs. Pedro Montanez; Barney Ross vs. Ceferino Garcia; Marcel Thil vs. Fred Apostoli, and Harry Jeffra vs. Sixto Escobar—in the same arena on the same night.

Shortly after the A.P. poll was announced Col. Heinie Miller, secretary of the National Boxing Association, went on record as favoring Joe Gans as "Boxing's Man of the Half Century." Others have raised their voices for Benny Leonard, Abe Attell, Stanley Ketchel and Sam Langford.

Two world wars were fought during the last 50 years, but boxing survived both, and is now entering what appears to be a period of renewed prosperity. Louis' successor as world heavyweight champion has yet to be crowned, but Ezzard Charles, recognized by the NBA as the titleholder, has been doing his part by meeting every challenger as he presents himself.

WHAT part television will play in the future of boxing has not been determined as yet, but the new medium is sure to be a factor. Ned Irish, executive vice-president of Madison Square Garden, is definitely in favor of television. He doesn't think sports attendances have been hurt by it.

At the moment Jack Solomons of London looms as the world's outstanding promoter, and the possible successor of Jacobs on the world-wide stage. Here at home the International Boxing Club, headed by Jim Norris, is operating successfully in New York, Detroit and Chicago.

Recently Gene Tunney said: "There is nothing the matter with boxing that another Jack Dempsey couldn't cure."

And there isn't. Boxing's Man of the Half Century was not only a great fighter. He was an exciting fighter and he remains a colorful personality. He is a successful businessman, with a restaurant on Broadway and a hotel in California. He continues in boxing as a referee, and with millions of others, he served in our armed forces during World War II. There is only one Dempsey—the most colorful figure in boxing in the past half century. To this day he remains "The Idol of Fistiana," as Nat Fleischer calls him in his book on Jack's career.

The boxing commissions played their part in the late years of the half century, too. They made great improvements in the conduct of boxing. Black tape on the hands

# NEW FACES

## LEON DAUGHTRY

HERBERT HARRIS a genial manager and trainer, who is a boxing instructor at the Police Boys' Club No. 2, Washington, D. C., was in to see us touting the praises of his newest find Leon Daughtry, a Washington, D. C., welterweight, who turned professional last year and since that time has rung up six wins out of seven fights.

Harris should know what he's talking about as he learned boxing from "The Old Master," Joe Gans. Harris used to work out with Gans and he hopes to impart to Leon many of the assets that made Gans one of the all time greats.

Daughtry was only thirteen when Harris noticed the youngster in a street brawl and was so impressed with the way the child handled himself that he took him under his wing and has been handling him ever since.

Only nineteen with forty amateur bouts under his belt the Washingtonian sports a good punch and his ring savvy is improving with every showing.

The lad was born in Rocky Mountain, North Carolina, and at an early age his family moved to Washington where he completed his schooling. At the Armstrong High School he was a standout star at track, basketball and boxing. Leon has shown marked aptitude at sketching and wants to use that ability when his fighting days are over. In his spare time, which isn't much, as he is a hard trainer, the youth studies history and furthers his artistic talents.

Keep a weather eye on Daughtry.

## PAT MARCUNE

THE big drought in the punch industry has been occasioned by the complete lack of adequate training. The young crop have a hard time finding anyone who can show them the ropes. It's a lucky lad indeed who can connect with a trainer who has it on the ball.

Those who remember Lou Nova and Bob Pastor will recall a gentleman who sparred with both of them. He was Al Braverman. Currently Al has teamed up with Artie Curley in a double endeavor, the running of one of New York City's most modern gymnasiums and the joint partnership of a stable of fighters.

One of the younger additions to their partnership is twenty-one year old Pat Marcune. Here is one lad who will have the benefit of a trainer who has the background necessary to teach boxing.

Marcune was born of Italian parentage and brought up in the Red Hook section of Brooklyn. He then moved to Coney Island where he now resides.

During the past war he served for two years in the Coast Guard and received citations for his participation in Asiatic action.

Considering that Pat never laced on a glove as an amateur, in fact had never entered a ring prior to his first fight last year, the ex-Gob has an enviable record.

He has iced eleven of his opponents and won three by decision while losing two.

It is reported that an altercation with a business associate in which Pat kayoed the other man, a heavyweight, is what first gave Pat an inkling of his punching power and gave him the idea of a ring career.

He looks like a lad to watch.

# FIFTY YEARS OF PROGRESS

of the fighters and dirty towels in the hands of the seconds have been eliminated. Medical care has been increased. The New York Commission's Medical Advisory Board has just started to function. Boxers are not allowed to fight every night, or every other night for that matter, as in past years.

All this represents steady progress obtained in the first half century. The game should grow stronger in the 50 years leading to 2000. Then they will be picking "Boxing's Man of the Century." Will his name be Jack Dempsey?

---

## ADDITIONAL GERMAN BOXING DIARY
### By J. A. Tree

FRITZ GRETZSCHEL put on a show at the Sporthalle, Berlin, that included Hans Stretz, middle champion and three other men of this division who have held the title at one time or the other with a 7,000 crowd.

Ex middle champion, Carl Schmidt, 71.5 kilo was far too good for Jackie Jakobsohn, 71.5, and won easily on points.

Ex European middle champion, Jupp Besselmann, beat Franz Schmidt, 71.5, on points in an exciting battle.

Champion middle Hans Stretz produced the form that won him the title and beat Robert Luma inside five rounds. Luma took counts of 8 and 9 before receiving a heavy right to the chin which put him down for the final count. Ex middle champion Peter Muller, 70.5 kilo, won on points against Fritz Gahrmeister.

The young welter Gustav Scholz knocked out the veteran Hasen Diekmann in the second round.

Sieb drew with Hans Spazierer.

A crowd of 3,500 turned up at Dusseldorf for the fight programme which was headed by the Sachs, 79 kilo, and Otto Bastian, 79 kilo, bout. The ex-amateur was too good for Bastian and took an easy win on points.

Cruywels, 76 kilo, drew with Junkuhn, 78 kilo.

Norbert Nettekoven drew with Winnfried Henne, both weighed 79.5 kilos.

Leo Starosch, 67.5 kilo, beat Alfred Herchenbach, 67.0, on points. Herchenbach had to take a count of eight in the fifth session from a body blow.

Buttermann, 67 kilo knocked out Walter Trittschack in four rounds. Trittschack took four counts in the first two rounds from good rights to the chin and in the fourth took a further two before receiving a liver punch that put him away for the final count.

In Koln a small crowd of 2,000 turned up for the welterweight championship of Germany between Hans Schmitz and Walter Schneider, the latter winning on points. This pair fought for this vacant welter title last December, the fight ending in a draw still left us without a champion. In the tenth session Schneider took over the fight and landed four or five good rights to the face and head and soon Schmitz' right eye was cut. Schneider was far the better man in the last round and showed that he was the champion.

Jimmy Lyggett, 66 kilo, beat Gottmann, 66, on points although he fought with an injured left hand which he received in the second heat.

Rudi Neumann lost on points to Sanger after taking counts of nine in the second round and the eighth heat.

Werner Handke beat the ex-lightweight champion Heinz Sander on points. Both men weighed 60 kilo each.

In Dortmund, Gerhard Tiedtke, 180, was knocked out in the third round by Neuhaus, 182, in the main event on the card. Neuhaus will certainly go places on this form. Tiedtke took a count of eight in the third and on getting up was caught by another right which brought a close to the fight.

Johann Sieben, 155, lost to Kemena, 141, on points.

Pinsdorf, 124, drew with Krafft, 122.

Zimmer, 128, was knocked out by Borner, 130, in four rounds.

The Hamburg promoter, Mr. Franz Hahn, in an effort to get back some of the 30,000 D. Marks he lost on his Hoff vs. Kleinholdermann promotion in November last, put on a show at the "Allotria." He did not meet with much success, for there were only some 500 people in attendance. The main bout was a heavy contest between Heinz Seelisch and Leo Hillers. It must have been the easiest cash that Seelisch has picked up, for in under 125 seconds he had earned himself some 600 D. Marks by knocking out his man. The punch was that of a hard right which landed directly under the heart and Hillers had to be carried from the ring. Two hours later he was still receiving treatment in his dressing room.

Paul Schirrmann light-heavy put up a grand fight against the tough Hermann Vermeulen and was given the verdict on points.

At the Slaughter House, Keil, some 3,500 fight fans forgot the cold when they were entertained with some grand all action bouts.

Gunter Nurnberg, 90 kilo, drew with Robert Warnbrunn, 90 kilo, over six threes in a heavy contest.

Jungverdorben, feather, put up a first class show to beat the fast moving Nierschack on points. Nierschack lost the second round when he landed a low punch.

It is certain that Joe Walcott will fight the German champion Hein Ten Hoff at Esslingen on the 7th May at three o'clock in the afternoon. The only uncertainty is that Hoff must fight Wilson Kohlbrecher in defense of his title before April, and should the champion sustain any injury in this bout it may well bring about a postponement in that of the international contest. Joachim Gottert, the matchmaker of that area, is putting the final touches to the contests which were left undone by Promoter Schuble and it is reported that all is in hand. Joe Walcott will not only receive a guaranteed purse of 7,500 dollars, but will also be on the receiving end of 40% of the gate receipts. It is expected that a crowd of 50,000 will be in attendance and this cut of the gate money will give Walcott a draw of some $10,000. The American troops in that area, which includes Stuttgart and Frankfurt, will pay to see the fight in dollars and this will provide the cash for Walcott's services. The Germans paying in D. Marks will enable Hein Ten Hoff to receive some 50,000 D. Marks as prize money.

For reader's interest. One kilo equals two pounds approximately. Any reader interested in this column and who would like to get in touch with the writer can do so at: 501.BSE.RASC.-GCLO.BAOR.3. Germany.

---

## RECORD BOOK CORRECTIONS

In 1950 RING Record Book make following corrections. Page 666, in Paddy Young's record, on February 21, 1949, change the loss to Nick Mistovich in 8 rounds to a victory for Young in 8 rounds. Page 30, in Heavyweight History on May 23, 1941, in Joe Louis' fight with Buddy Baer, Baer was disqualified in 7th round and not knocked out.

---

# INCOMPETENCY THE CAUSE

## Ray Arcel and Other Boxing Celebrities Blame Lack of Good Seconds for Injuries Suffered by Fighters

### By AL BUCK

*Whitey Bimstein, a recognized ace among seconds.*

WHEN boxing fans talk about the good old days "it ain't necessarily so." They were good all right, but the present era is better.

One recalls that Benny Leonard, ill with the grippe, traveled to Milwaukee with a doctor and went through with his bout against Richie Mitchell. And Abe Attell, suffering from yellow jaundice, didn't hesitate to take on Battling Nelson in Philadelphia. The late Joe Jacobs used to tell how Benny Valger postponed an appendectomy to fulfill an engagement in St. Louis. All this happened in "the good old days"?

Going over the records of the proofs of the latest *Ring Record Book,* we found many interesting results of fights in which some of the world's best talent were participants and in looking through THE RING files to read the accounts of some of these, we were amazed to note the number of contests which under today's strict commission regulation, would probably never have been permitted to have taken place, bouts in which one of the contestants was in such poor physical condition, he couldn't possibly have passed the medical tests.

There are hundreds of such stories about the old-time fights, particularly in days prior to commission regulations. They all go to prove that they were rugged men, and at the same time a trifle foolish. In tempting fate they were lucky, but all could have had a tragic ending. In this modern age, things are better, last year's casualty list and the serious injury suffered by Carmine Vingo, to the contrary. We have that on the authority of Ray Arcel, among other famous trainers of boxing.

ARCEL, a successful trainer since the first days of the Walker Law and before, concedes that there are some things wrong about boxing and suggests several remedies. Boxers now have better medical protection than ever before. This is particularly true of New York's nine-man medical advisory board, a doctor in attendance at each show, and low cost insurance.

When Vingo was knocked out by Rocky Marciano at the Garden recently, it was probably the prompt action of Dr. Vincent A. Nardiello that saved the defeated heavyweight's life. All over the world more and more care is being taken of the boxer's physical well being. When these efforts are defeated, it is usually due to the boxer himself.

"One of the troubles with boxing is what I call assembly line training," Arcel explained. "There are too few competent trainers, and most of them have too many fighters to train. For the most part the boxers look upon training as a necessary evil.

"When Whitey Bimstein and I were partners years ago, we had two men working for us. They did nothing but rub the fighters we handled. When a fighter got through working out, he returned to the dressing room and rested for a half hour. He dried off before he was rubbed, then took his shower, waited a little while longer, and left the gym.

"Now a kid gets through boxing, rushes to the showers, doesn't bother to dry off, gets dressed in a hurry and is on his way. He's too interested in something else to give boxing more than a passing thought.

"The trainers themselves have too much work to do. Many of them watch the boy box, and then send him on his way without advice and attention. It all adds up to a lot of colds and frequent postponements, with the fighters rarely in condition.

"In the old days a boxer didn't cancel out because he was usually in shape. He was in condition because he was interested in his work and trained properly," Arcel continued. "It is different today."

THERE is no doubt but that illness and injury have wrecked many a card. Since the indoor season started, for instance, Joe Baksi has twice cancelled bouts with Bernie Reynolds, once because of a cut eye and again because of a bruised hand. These injuries can be traced to carelessness.

In one week Walter Cartier, New York middleweight, pulled out of a match with Lee Sala at the Garden because of a cold, while Ernie Vigh came down with pneumonia and his bout with Johnny Bratton at the St. Nicholas Arena had to be cancelled.

Such things didn't happen in the old days it seems, but it is hard to imagine a Commission doctor okaying a sniffling Leonard to fight Mitchell, or allowing Attell to get into a ring with Nelson while sick from jaundice. That is all for the best, of course.

"I recall Leonard suffering a cut eye in winning from Andy Saviola in ten rounds, and less than two weeks later outpointing Young Billy Angelo in ten rounds. It wasn't a smart thing to do perhaps, but Benny, the master boxer, knew how to protect the eye," Arcel added.

"Take Charley (Phil) Rosenberg. He took off 39 pounds to make 118 and win the bantamweight title from Eddie (Cannonball) Martin. He took off 23 pounds for Eddie Shea and when he lost the title on the scales, he just refused to make weight for Bushy Graham. Abe Attell Goldstein, another bantamweight champion, was a strong durable fighter, who wanted to succeed in the ring. He was one of those neighborhood fighters, something that seems to be lacking today.

"There is still some neighborhood interest in boxers from the Bronx and Brownsville. Yorkville in New York City is excited about Jimmy Flood, but on the whole the neighborhood interest isn't what it used to be. Perhaps the race is going soft. I had to get out and hustle for a living when I was 12 years old. That doesn't happen any more.

"The young fighter today lives at home, often is managed by a member of his family, owns an automobile and usually has a girl friend," declared Arcel. "His interests are divided. And he doesn't get the attention he should from manager and trainer. Too often they have other interests."

WHAT then is the solution? Arcel thinks boxing commissions should do more about supervising the gymnasiums. "Most gyms are dirty to begin with. Often they are overcrowded,"

*Jimmy Johnston, one of the most competent handlers of boxers in recent years.*

Arcel pointed out. "Most fighters want to train between noon and two o'clock. Then they can rush off and see a movie.

"Instead of worrying whether a boxer wears white or black trunks, or whether a second has a white or green sweater, the deputy commissioners should be in the gyms.

"They should see that the gymnasiums are sanitary. They should make sure that the boxer is training properly," Ray insisted. "S u c h things should be part of a deputy commissioner's job. If he attended to it he could solve a lot of problems."

Izzy Kline, who operates the new Mid-West gym in Chicago, sees eye-to-eye with Arcel. Only Izzy would go a step further. He'd make the trainers and seconds qualify.

The late James J. Johnston used to say that boxing was the only sport or business in the world where a man could go in with nothing. He needed, according to Jimmy, neither money nor experience. All he had to do was dig up five dollars and the Boxing Commission would license him as a second. From then on he'd be on his own.

"**T**HEY don't even use the trial and error method in licensing seconds," Kline said. "A second should be made to pass an examination, both written and otherwise. He should be made to demonstrate that he knows his business.

"Experience should not be a qualification in itself. A young second may be highly qualified. Some of the fellows who've been around for years don't know what it is all about," Izzy continued. "We should all have to pass examinations."

Perhaps, Kline added, house seconds might be used. That is a second for each corner, furnished by the club, who would work with the boxer's regular handlers. That would only be a step away from having a doctor in each corner.

"I think having a doctor at the ringside is enough," Kline said. "A competent second is what is needed. There are all too few of them."

**K**LINE explained that in all Golden Glove bouts in Chicago an experienced second must be in each corner.

Like Arcel, Kline has trained many champions. He recalled that Ken Overlin had a severe cold just before he defended the middleweight title against Steve Belloise back before World War II. Overlin went to the extreme of taking electrical treatments for his sniffles, and the record book shows he won from the then youthful Belloise.

The second Barney Ross-Tony Canzoneri fight is vivid in the Chicago trainer's memory. Barney turned an ankle in training, and it looked as if the fight would have to be postponed. Manager Art Winch, however, was equal to the occasion. With Kline's help he fashioned a home-made cast. It consisted of strands of rope, whites of eggs and salt. They shaped it around Ross's ankle. He wore it in the fight and the eggs and salt had the further tendency to draw out the soreness.

Ross also defended the welterweight title against hard-hitting Ceferino Garcia with a broken left hand. That happened in the fight, and there was nothing anybody could do about it. Barney bluffed his way through.

Another fighter who was continually bothered by sore hands was Allie Stolz, according to Willie Ketchum, his manager and trainer. And yet Stolz never cancelled a fight.

**S**OME fighters, Leonard among them, often deadened the pain in their hands by the use of cocaine. Still Leonard was one of the greatest fighters of the ages. "They're not like that now. Take Irving Palefsky, a big strong kid," Ketchum said. "He always has a cold. Why? Because he runs out of the gym before he's taken the time to dry off."

"Another thing a fighter doesn't do today is wear a hat," remarked Whitey Bimstein. "The other day a kid was in a hurry to get out of the gym. When I asked him where he was going he told me there was a swell picture playing at the Rialto.

"They go out without a hat and they catch cold," Whitey concluded. "Then the manager blames the trainer."

"Too often the trainer hasn't control of the fighter," Arcel contended.

Often too the manager hasn't control. In many setups the final authority rests with a member or members of a boxer's family. Tami Mauriello's brothers all had more to say about Tami's activities than any of his several managers.

A quarter of a century ago a fine lightweight prospect was K.O. Phil Delmont, of New York's rugged Lower East Side. A terrific puncher, one of Phil's performances was to knock out Mickey Walker early in that great champion's career. But Delmont had too many brothers, who insisted on poking their collective noses into his fistic affairs, and because of family interference the youngster never fully cashed in on his natural talents.

Yes, many a fine prospect has been handicapped by meddlesome relatives, but, on the other glove, many another likely youngster has been helped by his kinfolk.

One notable case is that of Charley Fusari and his father. Mr. Fusari looks after his son's finances, and sees that the greater share of his purses are deposited in the bank. He leaves the matchmaking to Vic Marsillo, Charley's manager.

In another way Fusari, the fighter, is the exception. He never goes in the ring unless he is in top physical condition. Fusari is a clean living youth, and is always in shape.

**D**OWN through the years boxers managed by one or more members of their families have been successful. There were the Striblings—Pa, Ma and Young W. L. Sam Wallach managed all of his brothers—Leach, Dave, Phil and Marty Cross. Brother Clyde Hudkins did the business for brother Ace, and Sister Lena Levinsky handled the ring affairs of brother King.

One of the most successful family combinations the boxing world has known was the Mitchells of Milwaukee. Billy managed his brothers, Richie and Pinkey, and they were a popular big-time clan for a long time.

Harry Rappaport of Newark also did a fine job with his brother, Jack, a welterweight who fought the best of them a quarter of a century ago.

And Charley d'Angelo nursed his brother, Lou, along so well that the rugged Trenton youngster eventually became good enough to fight Champion Pete Herman and most of the other ranking bantamweights of his day.

Also there is Joey LaMotta, manager of his brother, Jake, the middleweight champion, and the Cartier twins, Vincent and Walter, are also in the manager-fighter business.

The danger in these kinds of setups is that it sometimes leads to syndicates. Then the control rests with a person unknown and the manager becomes little more than a messenger boy.

When Billy Gibson managed Leonard and Jack Kearns had Jack Dempsey they were the final authority. This was also true of Johnston, Dumb Dan Morgan, Dan McKetrick and other old-time managers. In a sense they were pioneers in a sport that is world wide in its appeal. It isn't a perfect sport, of course, but it is not as bad as it has been painted, and as Ray Arcel and others have pointed out it has improved with the years. Abuses can be corrected. In time they will be.

## SUCCESS

Mike Jacobs, who formally retired as a promoter on May 20, 1949, staged 320 shows at Madison Square Garden since his start in that arena on October 29, 1937. Four million persons paid close to $15,000,000 dollars to see his shows.

# FIGHTS TO REMEMBER

## By ED VAN EVERY

THE Jack Dempsey-Luis Angel Firpo contest, fought in the Polo Grounds on the night of September 14, 1923, has been voted the greatest fight the prize ring has seen in the past fifty years. This accolade, the consensus arrived at in a nation-wide Associated Press poll of the sports writers, can hardly be disputed, notwithstanding few of those who cast votes have been in touch with fistic doings as far back as the turn of the century.

This writer's ringside experience dates back to October 12, 1895, when Young Griffo and George Kid Lavigne went twenty rounds to a draw at Maspeth, L. I. But even though that match pitted against each other two of the world's best lightweights, the real fight on the card was not the main event—it was the semi-final in which Billy Ernst, the Fighting Dutchman and local hero from Brooklyn's Williamsburg sector, beat Arthur Valentine of England. For years, that battle rated as THE Fight of Fights in our book.

Since then a lot of water has gone under a lot of bridges and we've seen the bridges of a lot of noses dented and we are ready, on mature consideration, to concede that not only was the Dempsey kayo over Firpo more thrilling than even the Ernst triumph over the Briton, but was the standout scrap of them all.

*Dempsey going through the ropes in Firpo bout.*

THOUGH it lasted three seconds under four minutes, the 80,000 spectators certainly got their fill of fistic drama. In sixty of those 237 seconds of battling, one or the other of the contestants was on the canvas or out of the ring. There were eleven knockdowns in all, with Firpo hitting the deck seven times in the first round and with the heavyweight crown in the balance when Dempsey was pounded through the ropes before the stanza was over for the thrill of thrills, and the Argentine Giant going down and out for the grand climax in the second.

Yes, that was the tops—the pugilistic saga. Still, one can recall a fight here and there that was not so far behind even the Dempsey-Firpo joust, capital "T" terrific though it was. There was the affair between Benny Leonard, the lightweight champion, and Richie Mitchell of Milwaukee in the Garden when the Garden was on Madison Square, and which happened about two and one-half years before the Dempsey-Firpo epic.

Though the Leonard encounter of January 14, 1921, lasted into the sixth and was highlighted by three fewer knockdowns than the Dempsey-Firpo embroglio, the lightweight setto was, in some details, the more interesting thriller. In the Wild Bull, the Manassa Mauler opposed a rival with little besides tremendous physical power and courage. He knew nothing about boxing. He was so lacking in boxing skill that Bill Brennan, after he had been stowed away by Firpo, remarked: "That guy must have learned boxing in a stone yard."

The Leonard exchange of wallops with Mitchell was one between a ring master and a glove artist of superior grade. Leonard was among the greatest who ever pulled on a glove—the greatest in some books—and as for Mitchell he might have become the lightweight king had Leonard not been the head of the class.

Benny, influenced, some say, by the fact close friends of his had wagered heavily on Benny to score a one-round victory, tried for a quick kayo and he almost made it, but came close to losing his laurels in trying to gain his objective. The bout was underway but a few seconds when Leonard whipped over a right cross that landed on the cheek bone and down went Richie. He came up groggy at nine and it seemed that he was through. Mitchell was quickly dropped again and this time was reeling drunkenly when he just beat the count. He got to his feet with a crimson trickle from an ugly gash opened under his right eye.

THOUGH Mitchell was soon floored again and was unsteady on his pins as he rose at eight, Leonard was not fighting with his accustomed coolness. He was over anxious to stop his man before the round ended. Benny's punching lost something of its accuracy as he tore in, and he was wide open for a desperation left thrown by Richie. It caught Benny over the heart and Leonard stiffened in his tracks momentarily. Like a flash, the challenger crossed a right flush to the jaw and Leonard pitched over to the floor, where he lay, not moving.

Leonard was hurt and not till the referee signalled three did the champion try to roll to his knees. His corner was in a panic as his seconds yelled advice. The spectators were stunned at the sudden turn of the battle. The house was packed to capacity as the program, arranged for the benefit of the Devastated France Fund under the sponsorship of Miss Ann Morgan, had drawn many notables of every walk in addition to the regulars among the fight fans. The late Alfred E. Smith, then Governor of the State of New York, was an interested ringsider, one of the few fights he ever saw.

As the count reached six Leonard was poised on his knees and hiding his hurt with apparent calm like the superb ring general he was. He nodded to his manager, Billy Gibson, assuring Billy that he was capable of carrying on, though his smiling lips were blood-flecked as he came up. Instead of retreating or trying to fall into a clinch, Benny made a menacing gesture with his fists as though about to charge his antagonist. Mitchell came to an uncertain pause, somewhat puzzled by Benny's action, and as he did so, the Leonard attack was suddenly unleashed. Benny was fighting fast but expertly as the bell ended this stirring round.

From here on Leonard was "The Leonard." He gave his opponent no quarter, yet took no reckless chances. He was caught with one jarring cross in the second, but was quickly in command again and beat Mitchell to the punch with a mechanical perfection that was a treat to behold.

In the sixth, he had Richie primed for the kill and, though the challenger fought valiantly to the end, he was felled three times more before the seventh knockdown proved the finisher.

High though the Leonard-Mitchell match rates in the annals of modern puglisia, to this reporter the second of the Leonard meetings with Lew Tendler, fought two and one-half years later, deserves an even loftier niche. For here was that rarity of duels with nature's weapons, the perfect fight.

For the entire fifteen rounds on that occasion Leonard made not one false move of hand or foot in

## IN SYRACUSE RINGS
### By Billy Shaw

NICK (BULL) BARONE, 176, Syracuse's light-heavyweight star, fell victim to what was described as a "reverse hometown decision," when he met up with Reuben Jones, 175, tough and willing Norfolk, Va., boxer, in a ten-round star bout at the Coliseum. The Bull, a hot favorite to win, actually did outpoint Jones, but Referee Tony Petta gave Jones seven rounds; while Judge Harvey Smith saw it six for Jones, three for the Bull, and one even. Judge Dick Albino, veteran official, liked Barone for seven rounds and gave Jonesy three.

Some of the oldtimers at the ringside differed with the officials. They figured the Bull won the first five rounds handily and should have gotten the verdict or at least a draw. The seventh, eighth and ninth were hard fought with Barone outscored by his rival. The tenth was even as both let fly with hammer blows in close to make the fight a fast and interesting affair, all the way. The bout drew only 2,145 fans for a gate of $3,775.00.

Results of the other bouts follow: Ted Calaman, Philadelphia, 178, knocked out Elliott Beckham, 199, Yonkers, in the third round of the scheduled six-round semi-final. Calaman looked very impressive. Vernon Williams, 193, Atlantic City, knocked out Earl Mathews, 221, Wilkes-Barre, Pa., in the second; Joe Trofe, 153, Philadelphia, defeated Gilly Williams, 153, Rome, in a slow sixer. Glen Schmitte, 161, Liverpool comer, stopped Young Spinner, 164, in the first round. Jimmy DiMura, 126½, Syracuse, won the decision over Johnny Howard, 122, Cleveland, in a one-sided four.

Carmen Basilio, young Syracuse welterweight, who has been winning regularly, trekked to New York City where he lost a point decision to Mike Koballa, Chris Dundee's scrapper, from Pittsburgh, at the Eastern Parkway Arena. Prior to the Gotham tilt, Basilio stopped Adrian Mogart of France, in seven rounds, in the feature bout at Buffalo. Basilio is likely to face Koballa in a Syracuse match as the fans would really go for that one. Beating Carmen today, is quite a task, indeed.

What do you think Joey DeJohn is doing? The Syracuse-Buffalo thunder-puncher is addressing boys in Syracuse schools, under the sponsorship of the Ptimits Club. Joey is doing talks on boxing, and a very good speaker he is, too.

The State Athletic Commission decided DeJohn should take an additional three months' rest to recover from the effects of a jaw fracture received in his thriller with Lee Sala. X-ray examination of DeJohn's jaw showed it had not healed completely. Being a clean fracture, Commission physicians claim such an injury takes longer to heal.

Amateur boxing under the sponsorship of the Disabled American Veterans, got underway last month. . . . Louis Amendola, is Director of Bouts. . . . The best looking amateur prospect in these parts is Mike DeJohn, younger brother of Joey, a heavyweight. . . . Nick Barone has three return matches that will make him money, providing he wins them all. . . . Local bouts with Bob Satterfield, Dave Whitlock and Reuben Jones would pull good gates. . . . A Basilio-Koballa return fight would pull a good crowd too. . . . The big fight of the summer season outdoors, the one that will draw the most money, is a return match between Lee Sala and Joey DeJohn.

## FIGHTS TO REMEMBER

the judgment of such fistic wiseacres as Kid McPartland and Patsy Haley. Talking of the fight with Tendler recently in his restaurant, a well-known Philadelphia sports center, Lew had this to say:

"It was like being in there with a mind reader. It seemed Benny knew everything I was going to do before I did it. He was always a thought ahead of me."

"THE fight of the year of any year," was the tag put on the Rocky Graziano-Tony Zale conflict fought on September 27, 1946, in the Yankee Stadium, New York, by many fight enthusiasts. And its encore out in Chicago the following July, in which Rocky wrested the middleweight title from Tony, was almost equally sen-

sational. In each clash the apparent loser came back when on the verge of a knock-out to put the crusher on his opponent. Each of these tilts left the onlookers limp.

There have been few more savage brawls than that between Billy Petrolle and Justin Suarez 19 years ago this coming summer in the Queensboro Arena, Long Island City, and Petrolle's Garden go with Jimmy McLarnin.

The Garden fight was a story book battle for the reason that Billy, deemed a 10 to 1 underdog, had Jimmy in trouble in the very first round, flat on his back in the fourth, and had the baby face of the favorite all but punched out of shape for an amazing victory. It was a real war, that one, yet did not compare in punching intensity with the tussle which the Queensboro fans saw between Billy and Justin.

WAS there ever a scene in the Garden, old or new, such as was witnessed the night of May 10, 1929, at the end of the first round between Jackie (Kid) Berg and Bruce Flowers? Flowers made a specialty of taking a signal from his corner and turning on a leather fusillade that was a veritable hurricane for the last half-minute of the round. But this time when Bruce cut loose against the London lad the visitor not only met the Negro speedster at his own game but let loose a glove tempest that all but swept Flowers through the ropes as the two blazed away for the entire 30 seconds. It was a whirlwind exchange the like of which was beyond the memory of the ringsiders. So excited was the Garden throng that newspapers were torn to shreds and sent floating down toward the ring like giant snowflakes.

Going only as far back as February of last year, how about Willie Pep's comeback to regain the featherweight championship from Sandy Saddler, the hard-punching Harlemite, who had belted out the Connecticut pride a few months earlier? Surely this was as brilliant a performance as one could hope to see.

Close to being kayoed for the second time in his career no fewer than three times and his face a gruesome sight from the blows of his dynamite-fisted conqueror, Pep, with uncanny skill and a fighting heart, weathered 15 blistering rounds that stamped the true champion in a fashion that brought even the most rabid of old-timers out of their seats. It was as fine an exhibition as ever has been seen in New York or elsewhere.

Some of the old-timers will, of course, bring up the name of Stanley Ketchel, the Michigan Assassin, and his fights with Billy Papke, the Illinois Thunderbolt. Especially the one of September 7, 1908, at Vernon, Calif., as a result of which Papke wore the middleweight mantle for slightly over two months and one-half.

The writer was not privileged to see that one, but examination of the voluminous data compiled by Nat Fleischer, editor of THE RING, in his book on Ketchel, reveals that the fighting heart of the Michigan lad alone made this a fight out of the ordinary. Ketchel was the victim of a deliberate sneak punch on the handshake from which he never recovered. How he managed to survive until the 12th round is something not easy to explain. But Ketchel was every inch the champion, and that accounts for his great performance. He had sweet revenge

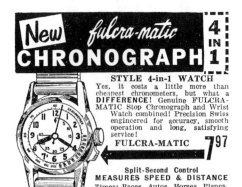

and the title back in their next meeting when he disposed of Papke in 11 rounds.

WHICH fight did the writer cast his vote for in the A.P. poll? This may be a surprise, but our vote went to the second Joe Louis-Max Schmeling fight. Not so much for the fight it was, but rather for something we saw that night that will probably never be seen again. And that was the look of hatred that glinted in Louis' eyes and was written in the expression of the ordinarily impassive-visaged Brown Bomber.

It was the one and only time Joe ever went into a ring with deep ill-feeling for an opponent. His spleen had nothing to do with the fact he had been humbled by his foe in being subjected to the only knock-out of his career. This was a thing inspired by an unfair article written by a former newspaperman for a national weekly and were words probably put into Schmeling's mouth by the author of the piece.

In the article Schmeling declared that Louis had deliberately struck a foul blow to save himself from being knocked out. This, despite the fact that Max, when discussing his victory in his dressing room after the fight and asked if he thought the low punch by Louis had been deliberate, replied:

"Ach, no. The poor fellow was so badly punished he did not know what he was doing."

Joe and his managers were incensed. They threatened legal action against the publication responsible for the story.

"If you sue," advised Mike Jacobs, "I'm certain you'll win your case. But if you sue, you'll never get Schmeling in the ring again in this country."

"I'd rather get that man back in the ring," Joe said, "than get all the money in the world. Get him for me."

Jacobs got him, and so did Joe. And when he did, for the only time in his life, there was murder in his heart. You could see it in the expression of his face as he came from his corner and it said: "Tonight I'll kill you or you'll kill me!"

# FIGHTERS ARE PEOPLE

## By BARNEY NAGLER

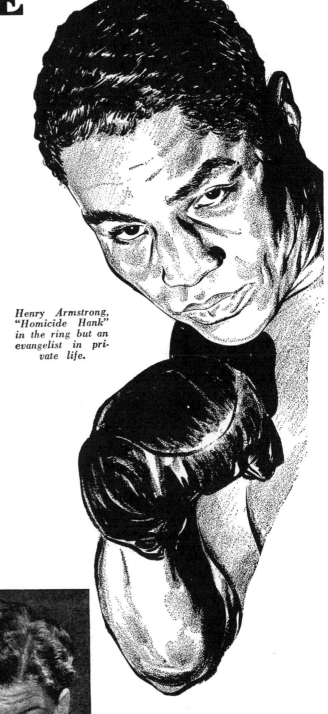

Henry Armstrong, "Homicide Hank" in the ring but an evangelist in private life.

I REMEMBER sitting in the living room of a little house on a tree-lined street in Detroit. It was quiet, except for the hesitant words of the woman in the rocker on the far side of the room.

"No," she said, "Joe wasn't always quick like they say. He was a clumsy one, Joe was, always falling over the butter churn when he was a little one."

The open-faced woman was the mother of Joe Louis Barrow and her description of Louis, as a young 'un, hit right at the experts. For a long time they had described Louis' grace of motion in the ring as a natural instinct inherited from his forbears.

The quiet words of a humble woman had exploded that theory. Louis had been taught. He was hand-made, molded by a man named Jack Blackburn, who had taken the quiet, awkward boy and had turned him into a fighting machine.

They were thought-provoking, were these words by Joe's mother, and now, years later, it comes to mind that here's a point for study: How much are fighters' styles dependent on their personalities?

THERE'S Henry Armstrong, for example. Hammerin' Hank, Homicidal Henry, the only man ever to hold three championships at the same time. Here was a fighter of furious instinct, a relentless man out for the kill.

Seeing Armstrong at work was a revelation. Here was stark, unharnessed fury on the jungle prowl. The conclusion to be drawn from this was that Armstrong must be such a man outside the ring, living at a pace aimed at setting a new world record for the distance.

No, it wasn't so. Armstrong was an introvert. He would sit by himself, hour upon hour, in the quiet of a Harlem room, and write poetry. Nice, pleasant poetry of a mystic turn, deep-thought and heavily worded.

Once I asked Armstrong what had turned him to the tender business of setting down his psyche in rhyme and he smiled: "Guess," he said, "I'm atoning for all those things I do in the ring. Some fellows call it compensation for something or other."

Homicidal Henry was that way and it came as no surprise, recently, to find that this great former fighter, this man of fury, had become an evangelist. It was a natural turn. He was using the words out of The Book to express himself, just as once he had used the rhyme. In his case, at least, his fighting style was a far cry from his inner feelings. He was a ring contradiction.

SO, for that matter, was Billy Conn, the Pittsburgh kid. Sartorially, Conn was a flash. He dressed in a manner that best represented money in the bank. He was, in a word, loud.

He was a brash fellow too, this good-looking guy from the Liberty section of Pittsburgh, a slum-strewn section wherein lived the hard-working honest folk of a city of toil.

Conn had come up from this section, but he had overcome his early beginning by proving a fine ring workman. Yet, from his background, from his manner outside the working platform, from his unwillingness to consider other people's feelings you would expect that Billy the Kid would be a slam-bang kind within the ring.

Al Davis, nicknamed "Bummy" and made a villain of as a fighter crossed up the dopesters by dying a hero.

It wasn't so. Conn was a master boxer, possessed of a skill and manner that escapes 999 out of every thousand kids who try the ring for a career.

He was slick and quick, possessed a fine left hand, and a competent right. He was skill on the march in the ring. No haphazard give-and-take for Conn. He calculated every move—every one but the suicidal surge against Louis in their first fight—and won money and fame in the prize ring.

Yet, knowing him outside the ring you would never believe he would be the way he was while giving a boxing lesson to an antagonist. Truly, Conn was a contradiction.

NOT so, however, was another standout heavyweight, the German, Max Schmeling, who grabbed himself a piece of the world championship by the margin of a low blow. Did you ever see Schmeling at work? He

# FIGHTERS ARE PEOPLE

was calm and detached, occupied only with the business at hand. He was cold and arrogant in manner, devoid of any purpose but victory.

He was the same outside the ring, never once permitting himself the luxury of not knowing his next move, and what it meant to him in terms of success—and money, American money.

Once, before his second fight with Louis, an event which produced a one-round knockout of the German, I saw Schmeling underline his singleness of purpose at his training camp at Speculator, N. Y.

Schmeling lived in a house on the road just above the hotel in which the fight reporters covering his camp were quartered. It was a privilege, permitted by appointment only, to visit Schmeling at his house. At least, so he thought.

One night, however, a bunch of the boys walked up the road and invaded Schmeling's parlor. He was not there. He had gone for a walk. The reporters decided to sit around and swap lies for a time.

A SHORT time later Schmeling returned, accompanied by Max Machon, his constant companion. Schmeling almost put the reporters in a deep freeze by his manner. He looked around the room, in which the writers sprawled in a dozen easy chairs, and snickered:

"Fine! Nice! I'm glad you boys are having a good time. I would like you to go now. I've got to go to sleep. I'm here for work, not fun. Goodnight."

Schmeling turned and sauntered from the room. The thick-skinned reporters were chilled beyond recovery. They left in a hurry. All ended well, however, because not one writer was felled by pneumonia.

Schmeling never gave this episode another thought. He was that kind of a personality. To him boxing was a business, to be lived and learned 24 hours a day.

He took time out for recreation, but only on a whim. He was as coldly calculating inside the ring as out.

Remember Al (Bummy) Davis? They hung a tag on him, those who believed he could be worth more at the gate if he were presented as a free-wheeling hoodlum. What's more, they could point to his family background to prove he was rough and tough.

Inside the ring, Davis was trapped by the buildup imposed on him and, on the night he let loose at Fritzie Zivic in the Garden ring and kicked away, everybody said: "What could you expect?"

THE truth was that Davis was a quiet-spoken boy of sensitive nature. They put a bum rap on him early and when he lived up to the standard they had applied to him all were happy.

When he died under the hail of bandit bullets in a Brooklyn tavern those who had built him up as a bad boy were disappointed to learn he had given his life in a hero's role.

You can't set up a pattern. After all, fighters are people, too.

# The RING TEST

*Copyright, 1950,* THE RING *Magazine*

## CAN YOU KO THIS QUIZ?

EACH question correctly answered adds points to your score. Ten points for a knockout; six or more gives you the decision; five earns you a draw; less than five calls for more workouts with THE RING Magazine and Record Books. Experts average six points on this quiz!

*Opening Bell!* Pile up an early lead! Each round worth ½ point. (Mark True or False.)

1—The height of a fighter, as well as his weight, determines the class a fighter will be in.

2—The shortest heavyweight championship fight on record was Joe Louis' knockout of Max Schmeling in 2:04 of the first round.

3—The originator of the corkscrew punch was Kid McCoy.

4—The rest period between rounds today is one minute, while in bare knuckle days it was one-half minute.

5—Arthur Donovan has refereed more heavyweight championship bouts than any other referee, past or present.

*Mid Way!* Watch your step, opponent is fighting back. Each round worth 1 point. (Underline correct answer.)

6—He fought in more title bouts than any other fighter: (George Dixon), (Joe Louis), (Henry Armstrong).

7—The greatest weight difference in a world championship fight was that in the bout between: (Jack Johnson and Tommy Burns), (Tommy Loughran and Primo

*Here's your hint for round ten.*

Carnera), (Jim Jeffries and Bob Fitzsimmons).

8—Comes from Cuba and is known as the HAWK: (Kid Chocolate), (Kid Gavilan), (Luis Galvani).

9—What fighter was given two cracks at the world lightweight championships on successive July Fourths and was knocked out both times? (Joe Rivers), (Joe Gans), (Rocky Kansas).

*The Big Round!* Worth 3½ points.

10—Name the contestants who competed in the first main event in the present Madison Square Garden on May 5, 1925.

## IOWA-SOUTH DAKOTA SPARKS
### By Bill Hawkins

OTTUMWA, IA.—Jesse Turner, St. Louis middleweight, punched out a unanimous 10-round decision over Jackie Parks, Iowa's middleweight champion. Turner, a master ring general used a short, choppy left hand that had the Iowan covered with sundry cuts and abrasions about the face. Several times he used a hard right that dug into the Iowa champ's mid-section.

Russell Tague, Eldridge, featherweight, and a former member of the Chicago G. G. team of recent international bouts, halted Henry Martinez, Des Moines, in the final round of their four-rounder. Ronnie Snibbing, Cedar Rapids featherweight, won a six-round decision over Paul Martinez, Omaha. Jack McGinnis, Cedar Rapids welterweight, received a strained ligament in his left shoulder in his bout with Eddie Morrow in their four-rounder. The bout was stopped in the second round. Burrell Smith of Oskaloosa, Ia., won over Joey Nathan of Omaha in four rounds.

Our Mail Bag—To J. C. L. at Spokane. Mail the results of your bouts to THE RING correspondent in your section. To carry your results would only be a repeat of boxing news from one column to another. This in order to save much needed space. George Coleman of Fort Wayne, Ind., would like to show his heavyweight, Bud Hershey, around the middlewest. . . . He is six feet tall and scales 185 pounds. . . . Jim Brady of Newark, N. J., is now looking after Budd Farrell, 158, and is seeking bouts around the middlewest. . . . He can be reached at 30 Marshall Street, Newark, N. J. . . . To J. L. at Rapid City, S. D. Get the new 1950 RING Record Book and you will find the records you mention. To Ken L. at Sioux Falls, S. D., Earl Puryear is now living in Omaha. Look over THE RING Book Shop. To H. L. at Yankton, S. D. No record of such a fighter in my files or any record book. To Jay M. at Worthington, Minn., Mail the boxing news to the correspondent in your section. Buy the Record Book direct from THE RING. To Bud G. at Chicago, Ill., Harry Pegg is the Editor of the *Veteran Boxer* and it has news of the old timers. To Jake, Clinton, Ia. RING Magazine has a list of these books and I suggest you write them.

Jim McKay of Norfolk, Nebr., would like to move into Iowa and other boxing points with his youngster Billy Tannehill who is entering the professional ranks. He has been boxing three years as amateur. He fought 24 bouts, won 11 decisions, scored two kayos, and two T.K.O.'s; fought two no-decision bouts. Entered in nine tournaments, and won five titles. He is a featherweight, crowd pleaser and can box and punch.

Last Minute Sparks . . . Mildred Burke, who claims the women's wrestling title has been showing her talents around Iowa. . . . News for this column must be in my hands by the fifth of each month. . . . Mail same to Bill Hawkins, 2206 North Lafayette St., Sioux City, Iowa. Our phone number is 8-6849. Boxers and managers are urged to keep us informed when they change their addresses, as we are in constant contact with promoters seeking talent. . . . Promoters seeking talent are asked to list their address with us. . . . Paul Anthony, promoter at South Bend, Ind., and former Sioux Cityan is making plans to visit his old friends in Sioux City around the middlewest this summer.

**Soldiers — Sailors — Marines
Read THE RING for
Boxing News from Your Home City
Subscribe for It at Your Army Post**

# BOXING PLAYBOYS

## By TED CARROLL

**A**NY afternoon in Stillman's Gym in New York you'll find fighters of every size, shape and description jamming all available floor and ring space, bustling through the training routine. The majority are ambitious and conscientious, early-to-bed boys who try as hard as is humanly possible to grab the gold and glory that ring success stands for.

It seems that the ones who take things most seriously are those who'll never make the grade. All too often among the fun loving few who can't wait to get out of the gym and into some escapade or other, you'll find the really gifted prospect.

Among such is the talented Lee Oma, Tex Sullivan's handsome heavyweight, who might be world's champion today had he really applied himself to developing his great natural abilities. Only a few weeks ago the clowning Lee and Bill Weinberg were disqualified for fouling and clowning in a bout in Ohio. Joe Louis, himself, is among those who rate the Detroiter as the only man who might have been given a real chance with the Brown Bomber.

When Tex Sullivan almost threw a fit over the idea of having Oma oppose Louis in an exhibition last winter, Joe, expressing surprise, drawled, "Dunno what his manager is worried about. That Oma is one fighter who really knows how to take care of himself in there."

For natural skill, Oma has been compared favorably with the likes of Tunney and Johnson, and by such a competent veteran authority as Joe Woodman. On his good nights, light-hearted Lee can vanish from punches as if by magic. Had he been of a more serious frame of mind, he would unquestionably have made his mark as one of the really superlative boxers of all time.

**E**VERY now and then Oma arouses hopes that he may at last have seen the light and is ready to lay off the monkey business and get down to real business. Right now he is the rage of Buffalo, where enthusiasts see him as a probable winner over any heavyweight active today. Such a build-up is nothing new for Lee. The same sort of talk swept through the boxing world as far back as 1944 when he handed tough Tami Mauriello as nifty a boxing lesson as anybody ever received.

Shortly afterwards, Lee decided it was a lot more fun being a Broadway playboy and that took care of him. Oma's basic skill is so great, he has boxed his way back into heavyweight contention in spite of himself. Although he's been doing it for years now, boxers of his style usually wear well and there is still hope for him despite his Ohio setback.

With rings and gyms the country over crammed with the clumsy and the incompetent, it seems a pity that such artistry as Oma is capable of should be so lightly tossed away. To say nothing of the vast financial rewards it may still possibly bring.

**B**OXERS today are generally a lot more serious and take better care of themselves than they did in past years. The gay blades are few in number now. Tony Janiro, the doll-faced fisticuffer from Youngstown, O., seemed headed in that direction, but he has had his fling and is now back on the straight and narrow. With Tony it has been a case of being too good-looking for his own good.

"Give me a homely fighter every time," muses Manager Eddie Walker. "The girls won't leave them good-looking guys alone. They're only human, and it drives you nuts," Walker remarked as he discussed several cases with me.

Oma is tall, dark and handsome; Janiro has a pink and white complexion, big baby blue eyes, curly blond locks and a kiddish grin. Add to these a Fancy Dan fighting style and you have a perfect foil for feminine attraction.

Janiro, again like Oma, was loaded with natural talent when he started out. He looked like a refugee from a kindergarten when he won the Golden Gloves title back in 1943. Losses were few and far between for him during the first three years of his pro career from 1944 to 1947.

A terrific Madison Square Garden card during the war years, three bouts with Canadian Johnny Greco lured thousands of customers through the Garden turnstiles. The Garden is just one block from the bright lights of Broadway and by 1948 the good-looker from the Mid-West had found the going much more pleasurable on the big town's main stem than was good for him.

Janiro may have gotten off the Broadway beat just in time to salvage a promising career. It looked that way in his Detroit scuffle with Charley Fusari, who had taken on the reformed playboy as a breather in between his middleweight forays. Manager Frankie Jay, who rates a break, has been keeping his fingers crossed that the Fusari win and the Graziano draw gained by his Tony portend the reawakening of his fighter's ambitions and possibilities.

**A**MONG the sober-sided modern fighters, Cuban Kid Gavilan has been known to do most of his training on the dance floor for some of his recent fights, but for fun-making and carryings-on between bouts, the old-timers had it all over the newcomers.

Maxie Rosenbloom didn't smoke or drink, but harried Manager Frank Bachman seldom knew where he was between fights. Maxie's memory was never too sharp, and it is true that he got his days mixed for the James J. Braddock fight and had to be run down and hustled out of a night club to get to the Garden in time for his meeting with Jersey James.

Maxie was one of the busiest fighters of all time. He'd fight anybody anywhere, and his purses were usually spent before he received them. But, profiting by his experience as a pugilist, Rosenbloom as an actor has saved his money and is said to be quite well off today.

That fabulous period in our history known as the Roaring Twenties is also often referred to as the Era of Wonderful Nonsense. Obviously the fighters, like everybody else in those delirious days, careened along at a dizzy pace.

Mickey Walker not only went along, he came close to leading the parade that splurged through those tumultuous times. Along with Jack Kearns, no slouch himself, Mickey caroused not only from coast to coast but overseas as well. The British press 20 years later still dwells at great length upon the riotous revelry with which Kearns and Walker had become synonymous on the occasion of their invasion of England back in 1929.

Walker squandered a fortune many times over. Only a middleweight, no fighter was too heavy for Mickey when he was good, and by the same token, no check was too heavy for him to pick up when the fight was over.

Curiously enough, while Walker didn't miss a minute of the madness that took over the country during his heyday, it didn't seem to affect his fighting. He was a great fighter for many years!

His frivolities didn't prevent him from winning two championships and knocking out heavyweights, although his best weight seldom exceeded 165 pounds. A slugging fighter, he shows little effects of a career that was a veritable frenzy of furious fighting and frolicking.

Harry Greb was pretty much the same as Walker, since the Torrid Twenties spanned his career also. Greb's dashing doings outside the ring apparently took none of the edge off his brilliant efforts in it, but could have exacted a toll in other ways. Harry's death on an operating table was most untimely.

A volume might be written about Battling Siki's capers, excluding his ring exploits. The jungle-born Siki's life would be rejected as too improbable were it fiction, but it all really happened.

The African's saga took him from

# BOXING PLAYBOYS

the steaming jungles of his native Senegal to his finish in a gutter of New York's Hell's Kitchen.

In between Siki did about everything that could be imagined. Typical of the Jungle Boy was his parading a young lion up and down the Paris boulevards.

Little Jack Sharkey, Pancho Villa, Jimmy Slattery, Kid Chocolate, Ace Hudkins, hit all the high spots during meteoric flashes on top of the world. Bantam Jack Sharkey was a colorful little fellow. Although Tunney was boxing at the same time, Little Jack was the hero of the Greenwich Village section of New York, from which both hailed. Wearing a derby hat over one eye, a flower in his lapel, cloth top shoes and a cane, Little Jack strutted his stuff through the hectic night life of the Prohibition era.

The great little Filipino, Pancho Villa, loved a good time. His passion was clothes. Since he couldn't show them off sitting at home, he was always on the go.

THE Harlem hotspots fascinated Kid Chocolate, but the finishing touch that actually curtailed this dazzling boxer's career came from a jaunt he took to Europe. Stopping off at Madrid, the Cuban Dandy hit a pace that left him just a reasonable facsimile of his former self.

The late Jim Buckley, who managed him, always claimed that Canada Lee should have been one of the greatest fighters of all time.

"He won't go home nights. He wants to be an actor and he trails around with those dancers and musicians until all hours up in Harlem," gruff old Jim would complain.

Today Canada admits that this was so. He is now one of America's greatest Thespians and has appeared in many Broadway hits.

Oma had a counterpart many years ago in Newark Charley Weinert. Like Lee, a handsome fellow and a shifty boxer, the blond Jerseyman couldn't resist the lure of Broadway.

Still France's greatest boxing hero, Georges Carpentier enjoyed his days as the darling of the Paris boulevards to the fullest. Hi-jinks with high society over here as well as in Paris and London occupied much of the flashing Frenchman's time outside the ring.

One of the late Jack Curley's favorite yarns recalled the time he was awakened in the middle of the night out at his Great Neck, L. I., mansion by an enormous racket downstairs. Upon investigation, who should it turn out to be but Carpentier, for whom Mons. Curley acted as a sort of agent, and a pal introduced by Gorgeous Georges as H.R.H. the Prince of Wales, now known as the Duke of Windsor.

MAX BAER played the clown to the vast delight of press and public during his reign as heavyweight champion of the world. But Maxie differed from the other merry maulers in that, while he thought nothing of tossing his dignity to the four winds, he kept a tight grip on his dough, and is today independently well off.

Except where his money was concerned, Baer lacked the stability to get the most out of his unusual equipment as a heavyweight fighter.

Like Baer, many smart boxing people insist that Lew Jenkins had everything it takes to become a standout lightweight champion. It's a cinch that few men his weight could hit any harder. Once Lew had won the title, a locoed bronk back in his native Texas had nothing on him for general deportment.

Tiger Jack Fox had much in common with Jenkins. Back in 1938 Tiger Jack was an exceptional light-heavyweight. The Tiger's disdain for all the conventional conditioning a boxer is supposed to undergo was startling. He only went home and to bed when there was no other place to go and there always seemed to be some other place. In spite of this, he was so good that he was named leading aspirant for the 175-pound crown and ordered to meet Melio Bettina to decide the championship.

This golden opportunity mattered little to Fox. In his ceaseless nocturnal prowling through Harlem, he met up with a recalcitrant lady who punctuated a difference of opinion with a carving job on the Tiger which landed him in the hospital.

The wound was no mere scratch, but Fox was back in there fighting Bettina before the medicos told him he was ready. He was an easy victim for the Beacon, N. Y., southpaw.

Here was a case when a fighter's folly had cost him a championship.

MEXICAN BOBBY GARCIA, a top line featherweight, was another one whose digressions cost him dearly. At least the equal of Louis "Kid" Kaplan, who eventually won the featherweight crown, the swarthy ex-soldier led our own Jersey Jones a merry chase trying to keep tabs on him while at the same time sorely trying the even disposition of patient Manager Jimmy Bronson.

There haven't been many twin boxers in action, but when the twins are playboys, too, as were the Perlick boys, Herman and Henry, that's really something. "Those guys made an old man out of me," reminisces Tex Sullivan. "I was only 19 when I was managing them, but two years later I was ready for a wheel chair."

Years ago Englishman Owen Moran's reputation for cain-raising was as great as his renown as a fighter—and that's saying plenty.

Old Jack Johnson romanced his way through life with little ill results to his superlative skill.

Those fast-living middleweights seemed to do pretty well, though. Stanley Ketchel, who was in the same class with Greb and Walker as a fighter, set the style for them outside the ring as well.

You can find malcontents around who trace the humdrum drabness of the boxing business today to the disappearance of the fun-loving fighters of yore. They point at John L. Sullivan, who was a prime example of a fighter who had his fling and at the same time made boxing really popular in America.

Times change and the post war era of World War II is funereal in contrast to the wild and wooly goings-on that followed World War I.

The boxers now simply go along with the times and if their new attitude leads to safeguarding their health and money most of the old-time playboy boxers would probably agree that they have the right dope.

## THE RING QUESTION BOX

**C. Fleming, St. Johns, Newfoundland**

Q.—Was it in a championship bout that Firpo hit Dempsey out of the ring? Was the bout won by a knockout or did it go the distance? Did the contestants ever fight a return bout?

A.—The Dempsey-Firpo bout, Sept. 14, 1923, was fought for Dempsey's world heavyweight title. The champion stopped Firpo in the second round. That was their only fight.

**A Ring Reader, Bridgeport, Conn.**

Q.—Did Tommy Farr ever fight in the U. S. after being defeated by Joe Louis? If so, whom did he fight and what was the result?

A.—Tommy Farr had four other bouts in the U. S. after losing to Joe Louis. His opponents were Jimmy Braddock, Max Baer, Lou Nova and Red Burman, with the Welshman losing all decisions.

**Ernie and Bill, Bayonne, New Jersey**

Q.—Was the first Zale-Graziano bout televised? We remember seeing the fight but we are not sure if it was a movie film or actual television.

A.—The first Zale-Graziano fight was televised and motion pictures were taken of the bout.

**A Reader, Brookwick, Pa.**

Q.—Against whom did Jim Corbett defend his title?

A.—Charlie Mitchell, whom he stopped in three rounds, and Bob Fitzsimmons to whom he lost the title.

Q.—In what round did Jim Jeffries beat Tom Sharkey and Gus Ruhlin? Where and what were the dates of each fight?

A.—Jeffries fought Sharkey twice, winning a 20-round decision on May 6, 1898, at San Francisco, and after winning the title, he took a twenty-five round decision from Sharkey on November 3, 1899, at Coney Island. He stopped Ruhlin in the fifth round of a title bout on November 15, 1901. All such questions can be answered by the 1950 Ring Record Book.

**Wilfred Beaudette, Hooksett, N. H.**

Q.—Was Ken Overlin ever middleweight champion of the world? If so, during what years did he hold the crown?

A.—Overlin was champion. See the 1950 RING Record Book.

**Harry Johnson, Montreal, Que.**

Q.—What is the official decision in the Woodcock-Savold fight?

A.—Savold won by a knockout in the fourth round. Woodcock retired because of a deep cut between the fourth and fifth rounds and the official verdict is a fourth round knockout.

**Art Wagoner, Toronto**

Q.—Can a world championship fight end in a draw?

A.—Yes. Nothing to prevent it. If all the officials differ in the score, then it is a draw. If two call it a draw, it ends in a draw. In places where there is only a referee, he has the authority to term the battle a draw.

**ESF, Denver, Colo.**

Q.—Was there ever a fighter called the Kentucky Rosebud? Was his real name Walter Edgerton. Is it true that he fought such stars as George Dixon, McGovern, among others?

A.—Yes. That was his name, Edgerton. He fought Dixon five times in great battles. He engaged in contests with the cream of his time. He beat Joe Gans a number of times at the start of Gans' career.

**Jackie Adams, Denver, Colo.**

Q.—The late Otto Floto said that in his opinion Peter Jackson was the greatest of all heavyweights and next to him he placed Jim Jeffries and then Jack Dempsey. In THE RING Record Book we find that Jeffries, as you stated in your interesting series on his life, fought more top men than any of his successors or predecessors. Among them were such great fighters as Joe Choynski, Gus Ruhlin, Joe Goddard, Peter Jackson, Bob Armstrong, Bob Fitzsimmons and Jim Corbett—a truly great list. What is your opinion about Jeff? Doesn't he belong on top? Would Peter Jackson have whipped John L. Sullivan had they met each in their prime?

A.—I have always placed Jeff in second place. He was a great fighter and his record shows it. As for your other query, I cannot say. Your guess is as good as mine. Each was a marvel.

# FOR THRILLS—IT'S BOXING

## By NAT LOUBET

FOR thrills, there is no sport that excels boxing. There were sufficient thrills in the Dempsey-Willard, Dempsey-Firpo and the second Louis-Schmeling bouts to enable sports scribes the world over to write millions of words about those fights. The stories of those historic contests will never die.

The heavyweight division is one that abounds in "Fights that Never Will Be Forgotten."

The big boys of the roped square are the main thrill providers. That's why, when the top men of that division are booked, especially in a world heavyweight championship bout, they draw the biggest gates and the largest attendances. The million-dollar gates may not come back again for many years, but it is safe to predict that the heavyweights will continue to be the best gate attractions when colorful fighting men are in the opposite corners. Sullivan, Corbett, Fitzsimmons, Jeffries, Johnson, Dempsey, Tunney, Louis—they hit the jackpot because they possessed what it takes to bring out the fight fans in droves.

"Fights that Will Never Be Forgotten" list among the contestants all of the above names.

Back in 1889, John L. Sullivan engaged Jake Kilrain in an historic battle, the last bare knuckle fight for the heavyweight championship, a contest in which Sullivan stopped his man in the 75th round.

That was the start of a long series of fistic encounters in which history - making fights were recorded.

There was the first battle for a world heavyweight title with gloves, one in which John L. Sullivan clashed with James J. Corbett at New Orleans. That affair has so often been reviewed that we won't go into details, but suffice it to say that it was a thrill provider.

Then came the three-round knockout of Charley Mitchell, claimant of the British heavyweight crown, by Corbett, the Dancing Master, and that was followed by still another contest that aroused world-wide interest, the one in which the historic "solar plexus" punch was born. It was in that contest that Corbett was kayoed in the 14th round to lose the world crown.

ANOTHER great battle took place at Coney Island in 1899 when Fitzsimmons lost the championship to the California Grizzly Bear, James J. Jeffries. It was Fitz's first title defense and in two subsequent contests Freckled Bob tried to regain the throne but failed in equally interesting mills.

The turn of the century saw one of the most dramatic spectacles of the prize ring when Corbett, old as fighters go—like Louis today—decided on returning to the ring in an attempt to regain the crown he had lost to Fitzsimmons. But at the age of 34, it was not Ruby Robert whom he was to face, but the husky Jeffries. Corbett wasn't given a chance. The sports critics ridiculed the audacity of Gentleman Jim making a comeback against one of the greatest, and often referred to as the outstanding heavyweight of all time.

But Corbett fooled 'em. Had he continued to box Jeffries instead of pulling the same stunt that enabled Joe Louis to knock

out Billy Conn after the Pennsylvanian had rolled up a good lead, Corbett would have been the first to win back his title. He had a tight grip on the throne when Jeffries suddenly exploded and the bombardment put Gentleman Jim out of the running.

But he went part way into the 23rd round before he was battered into submission. A short left hook to the body turned the trick. What a moment before had looked like certain triumph for the former bank clerk, suddenly turned into bitter defeat.

Lack of opposition forced Jeff into retirement shortly after that mill and after cleaning house in many parts of the world, disposing of all pretenders to the throne left vacant by Jeff, Tommy Burns was universally recognized as world heavyweight king. He set a world record for a K.O. in a heavyweight title bout. He put Bill Squires away in 1:27 of the opening round, a mark that still stands. Joe Louis came closest to it when he stopped Max Schmeling in their second encounter in 2:04.

Figuring in the dramatic and sensational bouts of the century was that between Jack Johnson and Jeffries after Johnson had dethroned Burns in Australia to gain the purple robe. It was Johnson's rise to fistic heights that brought about the era of White Hopes, a period in which the world was combed for white heavyweights who might bring the title back to the Caucasian race.

Jeff was urged to make a comeback—much against his will—and after six years of idleness, during which he lived the life of Reilly, he was no match for the stalwart Negro from Galveston, Tex. Jeff, who had prevented Fitz and Corbett from regaining the crown, became a chopping block for Johnson, who halted him in the 15th round.

Then along came another giant, Jess Willard, who put an end to Johnson's reign in Havana, Cuba, by stopping "Li'l Arthur" in 26 rounds. That bout ended the White Hope era.

Dempsey zoomed into the scene with his bludgeon body attack that put Willard into such a helpless state he had to call it quits at Toledo at the end of the third round. With Dempsey's rise came into being the million dollar gates, the first of which was the bout with Georges Carpentier in Jersey City, in which the Frenchman was knocked out in the fourth round.

Luis Firpo provided a never-to-be-forgotten thriller when he put Manassa Jack over the ropes at the Polo Grounds and then was dropped seven times before the Argentinian was counted out by Referee Johnny Gallagher in the second round.

Dempsey's stunning upset at the hands of Gene Tunney in Philadelphia and their return bout, the "Battle of the Long Count," were among other famous ring contests that go into the category of "bouts to be remembered." They drew the throngs and huge gates.

It was not until 1930 that another historic ring encounter was recorded, the one in which Max Schmeling won the world title while sitting on the canvas, claiming a foul in his fight with Jack Sharkey.

The spectacular Max Baer,

*Who will forget this comedy scene—the giant Primo Carnera entangled with Max Baer in their title bout in the Garden Bowl of Long Island City.*

## FOR THRILLS—IT'S BOXING

pounding Primo Carnera into submission after sending the Italian Goliath to the canvas for 12 trips, furnished still another of the many thrilling fights among heavyweights—bouts that cannot be forgotten—as did the bout in which Jimmy Braddock, the Cinderella Man of boxing, relieved Baer of the crown via the decision route in 15 rounds.

No one can forget the fine battle Braddock put up against Joe Louis in Chicago before he was kayoed to lose the crown to the Brown Bomber, who, with that contest, started a reign that lasted 11 years before Joe retired and during which period Louis defended his crown successfully 25 times for a world record.

Down the line we go and find several more thrillers in the knockout of Max Schmeling in the opening round by Joe Louis in their return engagement and Louis' knockout of Billy Conn in their first bout, a mill in which, had Billy not been too cocksure of the result, he would have won via the decision route as he was well ahead on points on the official score cards.

Then we have the title bout in which Jersey Joe Walcott came within a whisker of winning the crown from Louis, who scored the victory on a split decision, and the quick knockout of Tami Mauriello by the Bomber after the champ had been sent on his heels and looked like a goner shortly after the bout got under way.

Those contests will be fought over and over again by the fistic enthusiasts who, gathered on a dull winter's day, engage in hot stove league talk.

Though the second Walcott-Louis fight and the return affair between Joe and Conn and the N.B.A. title tilt between Ezzard Charles and Walcott were not of the type over which one can grow enthusiastic, they have a place among those most frequently discussed because of the bearing each had on Louis' future.

Even the Woodcock-Savold battle in England takes its place among the most-talked-of battles of the century. This one primarily because it was given world title recognition by the British Board of Boxing Control and because it was a bloody mill with the American halting the Empire champion.

*Joe Louis (right) has Tami Mauriello in trouble early.*

# When Is A Boy A Man?

## Patterson Case Poses Problem.

### By TED CARROLL

IN most parts of the civilized world 21 is the magic age which transforms an adolescent into an adult, although many a teen-ager makes the sudden transition from childhood to maturity by way of a military uniform. The argument that if an 18-year-old is ripe enough to be shot at, he should be old enough for anything else is always cropping up here and there. A similar situation has plagued the boxing overseers for many years. Namely, should an underage contender be allowed to meet the sternest competition in long contests?

The New York Commission and other official boxing bodies have in the case of Floyd Patterson, teen age pugilistic prodigy from Brooklyn, a puzzler which figures to keep them awake nights. The undefeated 1953 Rookie of the Year, is obviously ready for the best of the lightheavyweights, but he is only 18, which means that if the New York rules are adhered to, he won't be allowed to fight a ten rounder for two more years.

Under the Empire State boxing bylaws, 6 rounds is the longest any 18-year-old can box professionally, 8 rounds is the limit for a boy of 19, and he must have passed his 20th birthday before he can box a ten round bout.

Technically 6 of Patterson's bouts have been 'illegal' as they were of 8 rounds duration, and it now turns out that instead of being legally old enough to go that distance, he was 18 instead. Jacking up a fighter's age is a time honored trick in the boxing business, and there have even been cases where birth records of older persons were used by under-age applicants for licenses.

● ● ●

While the intent of the 20 year rule in New York is very good, being clearly designed to protect the physical development of the youngster, and also to prevent his being subjected to pressure too great for such tender years, its idea runs contrary to the careers of most of the great boxers of the past.

Patterson is far from being the first teen-ager to show the kind of promise he is showing. That all-time great of the featherweights, Terry McGovern, would have been in a tight spot had such an edict been operative when he was fighting. The old Brooklyn Terror, was World Bantamweight Champion at 19, World Featherweight Champion at 20 and was past his prime at 21! The natural conclusion here would be that such an early finish makes the modern ruling look very good, but in contradiction to that opinion, consider the case of the old Phantom of Philadelphia Tommy Loughran.

In 1922, at 19, Loughran was tangling with such titans as Harry Greb and Gene Tunney. Every bout he had that year was against a champion or near-champion. Besides Greb and Tunney, such names as Mike McTigue, Lou Bogash and Bryan Downey were included in his list of foes of 32 years ago.

A year later, Loughran made his first appearance in New York. His opponent, none other than Harry Greb! When Loughran climbed through the ropes, the old Madison Sq. Garden crowd gasped in amazement. "What—there must be some mistake! This choir boy can't be the fellow who's been fighting guys like Greb!" said a startled old-timer.

Before he had reached his 21st milestone, Loughran had been through five scuffles with Greb, three with McTigue, two with Jeff Smith, and has also boxed Young Stribling, Ted Moore, and the great Jack Delaney.

How did such rugged early years affect Loughran's career? In strong contrast to McGovern, Tommy thrived

on it, remained in the ring for 18 years and in 1942, at the age of 40, was in such remarkable physical condition he was accepted for service in the U. S. Marines.

Loughran's career would seem to be a boost for the "tougher-the better-" school of thought, which argues that a kid either has it or hasn't, so toss him in there with the tough ones as soon a possible and get it over with.

Loughran himself is inclined to believe this, using his own history as Exhibit A.

Unlike McGovern, who was all offense, Loughran took the Art of Self Defense literally, and he was geared to withstand his rugged youthful campaigning. By concentrating on superb boxing Tommy was able to remain undamaged in his tough early bouts. Tommy mastered the fine points of defensive boxing so well, he added years to his career. His early battles against the big timers helped rather than hurt him.

● ● ●

Those old time California aces, Eddie Hanlon and Abe Attell, had experiences paralleling those of McGovern and Loughran. Hanlon, like Terrible Terry was the dynamic type battler, while still in his teens he was engaging topnotchers in gruelling twenty round contests and he was through at 21.

Attell, also got a very early start, but soon realized that to last in the business, you had to learn something about avoiding punishment. In 1900 at the age of 18 he was meeting the great but fading George Dixon for the vacated featherweight title. Attell credits Dixon for making him see the light, and he began to really work on his cleverness. Abe got so good at it, he went on to become one of the greatest boxers of them all, and lasted 13 years as a topnotcher.

Georges Carpentier was one of the boy wonders of the ring. At 15 he was meeting Charles Ledoux for the bantamweight championship of France. At 18 he was European welterweight champion, at 19 he was meeting men like Willie Lewis and former middleweight champions Billy Papke, and Frank Klaus.

He was only 21 at the outbreak of World War I and was already heavyweight champion of Europe, with remarkable showings against U. S. heavies Joe Jeannette and Gunboat Smith behind him, although he was still only a middleweight.

In 1927, 19 years after his first bout, the Orchid Man campaigned in the States, performing creditably for a man of his years.

In his last visit to this country in 1948 Georges looked surprisingly well preserved, youthful, and handsome at 54.

● ● ●

A QUARTER century ago the New York Boxing Commission was putting restrictions on the fighting routes of the teeners. The two bouts with Jack Delaney which made Jimmy Slattery a reigning fistic sensation for a time were both limited to 6 rounds because the Buffalo boy was underage. The deliberate Delaney couldn't catch up with the flashy 19-year-older the first time they met in 1925, and 5 months later, Slattery's speed carried him to another victory over the hard hitting Bridgeporter.

Being exposed to tough competition at an early age didn't particularly harm Slattery. Young Stribling and Harry Greb were among his rivals when he was only 18. Slattery won a claim to the light heavy title later on and boxed for 12 years. A performer of fantastic grace and skill, Jimmy had the potential to have scaled even greater heights had he taken things more seriously, and conditioned himself more thoroughly.

The famous New York neighborhood classic between Sid Terris and Ruby Goldstein at the Polo Grounds in 1927 had to be cut to 6 heats because Ruby was only 19, and there were numerous other such cases back in those days.

Some far-seeing souls got around this age restriction by adding a few years on the boxer's original application. Tony Canzoneri is said to have been only 16, instead of the required 18, when he made his professional bow. If this is so, and the record book confirms it, by the time he

# NEW FACES

### Billy Wade Mayo

SIX-FOOT-TWO light-heavyweight Billy Mayo sprung a surprise upset at Madison Square Garden recently by trouncing Gary Garafola—a Rocky Marciano type fisticuffer who'd lost but two out of 15 pro fights. The lanky lad, undismayed by Garafola's looping wallops, stood his ground and traded socks with his powerful foe. The victory has endowed Mayo with prestige and much-needed confidence. The somewhat shy southerner seeks, to gain friends via his walloping fists; also to find a place for himself in the fistic circle.

The stork delivered Billy Wade Mayo in Oglethrope, Ga., on March 15, 1932. At 16, he quit high school to work as a timber cutter. "Reason I became a boxer," he explains with a boyish smile and a delightful southern drawl, "is ah simple one: Ah like to fight. In 1949, after having three amateur bouts, Ah enlisted in the Army. During my 3 and a half years in the service—two of them on the Korean battlefront—Ah took part in 27 bouts, winning twenty-two of them."

Discharged in August, 1952, Mayo returned home and went back to felling trees—and resumed his fistic career as a pro. After a few fights he decided to try his luck in New York rings. But that was only a far-off dream. So he continued to topple timber around Oglethorpe. Finally, he got in touch with Ralph Como, manager of Jimmy Herring, who agreed to handle him. After winning six pro fights by knockouts, Billy came to New York.

"With more experience," observes Como, "Mayo'll chop down opponents, the same way he cuts down trees."

---

# WHEN IS A BOY A MAN?

was 19 Tony was boxing Bud Taylor for the world's bantam title and was already recognized as one of the outstanding boxers of the period. Canzoneri fought for 15 years.

Tami Mauriello, who was only 16, got around the ruling, by simply presenting an older brother's name and birth certificate. Tami's teens were taken up fighting people like Billy Soose, Gus Lesnevich, Steve Belloise, and other high ranking battlers of the time. He was over the hill at 24.

Tony Janiro, who still looks cherubic after all these years, was another who got around the underage rulings in one way or another. A sparkling performer in his kid days too, Janiro like Slattery, loved fun more than fighting and this rather than being rushed along, crimped his career.

Jimmy McLarnin looked so young boxing the likes of Bud Taylor and Pancho Villa on the coast, he was tagged "Babyface".

There is a unanimity of opinion among the various boxing bodies relative to restricting the operations of "under-21" boxers. Down in New Orleans, 18 year old Ralph Dupas, is only permitted to go 8 rounds, in New York 6 rounds would be his limit. This flashy youngster, like Patterson, is going to give the bigwigs something to think about very soon, as he is closing in on the topnotchers, and since he won't be eligible to fight ten rounds for a couple of years, some exception will probably have to be made in his case as well as Patterson's.

• • •

A quick riffle through the *Ring Record Book* reveals that many famous fighters ranging all the way back to the last century were knocking on the champions' door long before their 21st birthday. Decades ago, the great George Dixon had established himself as the best little man in the U. S. while still in his teens. Dixon was a world's champion, before he reached the age of 20. Despite his early maturity in the ring, Dixon fought for 20 years. Lasting this long even though he could have taken far better care of himself. There were no restrictions on age or the distances of bouts in that long-gone era and Dixon engaged in a bout lasting 26 rounds while still 18 years of age! Such a contest today, involving a boy of this age, would bring the cops on the run, with life suspensions or even jail sentences handed out to all implicated.

Billy Conn, according to the records had whipped 3 former worlds Middleweight kings before reaching his 20th birthday, Babe Risko, Teddy Yarosz, and Vince Dundee.

Back in the Twenties, one time lightweight king, Sammy Mandell, had gained national prominence, and top ranking as a contender, at just 19 years of age.

Pugilistic prodigies are much more frequent among the littler fellows as bigger men mature much more slowly as a rule. Heavyweight champion Rocky Marciano, who started out at 24, wasn't even thinking about being a fighter, at an age when many small men had already seen their best days.

Patterson's manager Cus D'Amato is naturally wary of hurrying things along too fast, thereby risking the ruination of a rare prospect. The commission is in a real dilemma, since the only opponents capable of meeting him are the topliners, with those of lesser merit being unacceptable. To curtail his activities for the next two years, or until he reaches 20, would probably hamper his progress.

It seems that the only solution here is to forget regulations in his case and taking him at face value, regard him as any other contender, a contender of such unusual qualifications, that exceptions must be made in his case.

The precedent here is the success gained by such prodigies as Loughran, Canzoneri, Dixon, Attell, Carpentier, Conn and others in the past. None of them suffered through being given premature tests of fire.

# I Believe

## By EZZARD CHARLES

### (Former world heavyweight champion)

IF I get the opportunity to fight Rocky Marciano for the the world heavyweight championship next summer— and I believe I will, God willing—I will be only the second man in my division to have received two chances to regain the crown. James J. Corbett had two chances. After losing the title to Bob Fitzsimmons by a knockout in the fourteenth round at Carson City, Corbett faced James J. Jeffries at Coney Island in what almost resulted in victory for Gentleman Jim. He was knocked out in the twenty-third round after leading the champion most of the distance. Not satisfied that Jeffries was his master, Corbett tried again, this time in San Francisco where he was stopped in the tenth round in 1903.

Other former kings of the division have attempted to re-win the championship, but as history records it, no one has succeeded. But those other than Corbett, had only one fling at it, and now, from all indications, I shall have another try to regain the crown I lost by a knockout to Jersey Joe Walcott in seven rounds in Pittsburgh in 1951. Down the line we find that Jeffries, Dempsey, Schmeling, Louis and Walcott all made their pitch, but without success. Perhaps the Fates will favor me when I get my chance again.

I firmly believe I can turn the trick, I feel confident that I can overcome the jinx that has ruled over all former title holders among the heavyweights who tried to regain the crown. I think I can beat Marciano. In fact, I was never more confident of winning a fight than I am of taking the measure of Rocky.

● ● ●

I was born on July 7, 1921. In June, 1954, I will be approaching my thirty-third birthday. Walcott was at least 37 when he hit me that left hook in Pittsburgh on July 18, 1951 that stripped me of the title I held so dearly. Louis was 36 when he tried to beat me in 1950. Rocky Marciano

*Ezzard Charles, former heavyweight champion, after losing decisions to Nino Valdes and Harold Johnson, came back strongly to kayo Coley Wallace and then clinch a June title bout by flattening Bob Satterfield.*

will be approaching his 30th birthday in June of 1954.

Age means nothing if you're not too old and you're always in condition. The three year difference between me and Rocky is nothing because I have been an active fighter and he has had no more than five major fights in almost three years.

I'm not going into the hogwash about being destiny's baby. Destiny won't help me when I get into the ring. But I believe I can beat Marciano. If I didn't think so, I wouldn't be fighting any more.

Friends and fans have asked me why I continue fighting. I have saved my money and if I hung up my gloves tomorrow, I would have little to worry about financially. I am not rich but neither am I poor. I keep fighting and will keep on fighting as long as I believe that I am capable of winning back the title.

Tom Tannis, my manager, has often said that when the time comes that I feel that I want to quit the ring, he will make no move to stop me. He will leave it to me entirely to make that decision. But until I really find that the field of heavyweights is such that I have no chance, I will continue. I have had my ups-and-downs, but as of today, I think I am superior in fighting ability to any one in the heavyweight division, and that includes the champion whose greatest asset is his punching power. I'll admit that he has it on me in that respect, but I have proved in my last contests against Coley Wallace and Bob Satterfield, that I have developed a punch, which is not as devastating perhaps as is that of Rocky, but has been sufficiently powerful to halt Wallace, a pretty good boxer, in ten rounds and put away Satterfield, one of the hardest hitters in the division, in the second round.

● ● ●

There was a time in 1951 when I had a few doubts. When Walcott knocked me out, I began to wonder even though I knew that I had trained down too fine for the fight.

I don't want to take anything away from Walcott but I took that fight as just another contest. I had already beaten Joe twice. The third one was a favor to help Walcott retire with money in his pocket. It was also a favor to the Dapper Dan Club in Pittsburgh.

That's the last boxing favor I ever want to do. Joe gave me a chance to get the title back and I just couldn't get going against him in Philadelphia that June 5th of 1952. I thought I won the fight and so did most of those who saw it, but, I will admit I didn't deserve to win it. Anyway, he got the decision. I have lost a few since, too.

Rex Layne got a decision over me in 1952. It happened in Ogden, Utah, on August 8th and that was one year Christmas came quite early. This is no reflection on Jack Dempsey, the referee whom I have always admired, but he called

## I BELIEVE

seven rounds even and Layne got credit for two of the other three rounds. I was dumbfounded when the verdict was given. I couldn't understand it.

Harold Johnson was given a decision over me in Philadelphia in 1953 and that was another year Santa Claus arrived without snow and before Winter. I'm positive I won that, too.

Nino Valdes caught me on the worst night of my entire career and gave me a licking. I deserved it for taking too much for granted. But that's all in the past. I won't take any credit from the Cuban. He beat me fairly. I know

I lost that one, but blame myself. I'd like a return bout. I've tried to get it but without success. His manager demanded too much.

● ● ●

I have never kidded myself. Fighting has been my profession and though I have fought great fighters and great punchers, I have never been hurt. I have been boxing, as amateur and professional since 1937 and know my strength and my limitations.

I have always vowed not to make the mistakes of some of the champions who preceded me. I have always said that I would not fight if I didn't have the faith in myself any more.

I not only have faith, I feel that I am now a better fighter than I have been in some years. I felt it when I fought Coley Wallace and I knew I had it when I came back off some terrific wallops by Bob Satterfield to knock him out in the second round.

I have faith in the knowledge that in Tom Tannas and Jake Mintz and my trainer, Jimmy Brown, I have three men who have my interests at heart. They will not push me forward for the sake of money. They have faith in me. It helps. I have found myself for the first time in a long time and I know where I am headed if I get the chance.

I have seen Marciano fight. He is strong and is a much better fighter than they give him credit for being. I have fought strong men before. I have fought great punchers before.

Lloyd Marshall, the only other man besides Walcott ever to knock me out, was one of the best punchers I ever

fought. Archie Moore, Jimmy Bivins, Walter Hafer and Walcott, were terrific punchers. I'd hate to be in there with Satterfield on an off night.

I am not afraid of punchers. The left hook of Walcott's has not become the nightmare some critics think it has. It has just taught me to be more careful.

● ● ●

I am a better boxer than Marciano and certainly on the basis of experience, there is no comparison. I have no plans for him in advance, if and when they make our fight. I just plan to be in the greatest shape of my career. I anticipate a tough, rough fight. I know he can hurt but he's human and he can be hurt, too.

For twelve rounds Walcott gave him a tremendous going over and it is remarkable that Rocky stood up under the beating he took. Then Joe got tired and careless and was knocked out. That, in my opinion, was the only tough major fight Rocky ever had.

There are no easy fights, ever. How well, I have learned that lesson in recent years!

Rocky Marciano will be far from an easy fight. I have never been a boastful guy nor have I ever made rash predictions about the outcome of any of my fights. I'm making no prediction now, either.

I am stating what I sincerely believe —that I think I can beat Rocky Marciano. I think I can be the first to get that heavyweight title back and will be thanking God for that second chance that nobody ever got before.

*Ezzard Charles blocks a left thrown by Joe Walcott during their heavyweight championship bout on June 22, 1949. Charles won the 15-round decision and became heavyweight champion.*

Berra (Right, inset) isn't alone as a catcher. Rocky Marciano (circled) starred in that position and had a trial with the Chicago Cubs.

# by Yogi Berra

## YANKEE CATCHER AND ONE OF BASEBALL'S MOST VALUABLE PLAYERS MAKES HIS DEBUT AS A RING EXPERT.

THIS Bobo guy is quite a fighter, and I am very glad that he beat Kid Gavilan and kept the middleweight championship. This made me a real expert. I told the Gavilan fans on our ball club that the Cuban didn't have enough of what it took, and the way the fight went, I sure was right.

I don't want to take all the credit for myself. I got some hot dope on Bobo Olson even before he beat Paddy Young. I ran into Sugar Ray Robinson and he told me to go with Bobo, right through.

Ray said that Olson always would have a great advantage over any opponent, in his fine condition.

Being a ball player, I know exactly how important condition is, no matter if you are a fighter, a jai alai player, a track athlete, a soccer player or baseball pro.

I played a lot of soccer around St. Louis before I came into the Yankee chain, and if you haven't got condition in that game, you sure are out of luck,—and out of wind.

Robinson told me, "Olson is a great fighter. He is in shape, he keeps on punching, and he never lets his backers down. Stick with Bobo, all the way."

So when all the Gavilan boosters come along, I remember what Ray tells me, and could be I put a thin dime on Olson. Only don't tell Commissioner Frick. He doesn't like ball players to be betting plungers.

THE Gavilan boys holler that he had a bad hand against Olson, and the next time will be punching two fisted instead of saving the right for relief duty.

I watched the fight very close on television, and Gavilan sure saved that right. But I don't think it was hurt. Keeping one hand in the bullpen fighting Olson is not very smart stuff. But that's what the Cuban did.

If Olson gives Gavilan another fight, and so far as I am concerned it should be Giardello, in preference, I will go for Bobo again, even if Gavilan is ready with two right hands.

I have no objection to Gavilan, as I hear he is a right guy, and I know he is a good fighter. But before they go back to anybody in any class, I think they should give other candidates a fair shot. That means Giardello.

I do not pick Giardello to beat Bobo. But could be this

paysan will give Bobo a very interesting evening for 45 minutes. That's a long time to be fighting one guy in any ring, and I congratulate myself that in baseball we play only nine innings, not fifteen.

I am very much interested in Rocky Marciano, who is a friend of mine and a grand guy. You know, I have seen Rocky in only one fight, that scrap in which he knocked out Roland La Starza. Between Marciano and La Starza it was very tough to choose on a basis of good guys.

On a basis of punching,—well, this Rock can hit. He reminds me of Joe Di Maggio in his prime, of Ted Williams, of what Babe Ruth must have been.

One good, well-timed swing, and BOOM. The whole shindig is over. This thing called timing is terrific both in baseball and in fighting. If you are off your timing, it's just too bad. You can be the greatest batter in the world with the greatest average. But let your timing be off and a bush pitcher will make you look silly. I saw that worked out on our Spring training trip in April.

THEY say that Marciano can't box too well. I don't agree with that. I know he is not one of the most graceful fighters we have had, but he is no bum for science, the way I read in some stories in the New York papers.

We who make a living playing baseball know how important it is to be able to hit that home run when you need it. That's why all of us ball players admire Home Run Marciano. The other guy may make him look bad for a round here and a round there. But when the time comes, it's socko! The game is over. One swing.

I wonder how this Marciano makes out if he sticks to baseball. He tells me he was a fine catcher, and would have gone on in the Cub farm system if he had not injured his arm. A receiver with a bum arm is no bargain, believe me.

The way things break, Marciano certainly is very lucky he goes into the fight game.

But suppose Rocco sticks to baseball, and comes up in the National League, as a hitter with that four base punch? I like to think about that.

People now and then ask me if I ever had any thoughts of going into boxing, and I laugh that off. But the fact is, I was approached by some prominent boxing people in St. Louis, when I was a middleweight.

They said that if I would do what they wanted, I would get rich. I told them that I was not the fighting type. I just had turned down the hockey promoter in St. Louis, who also promised me a little private gold mine if I would become an expert skater. He said that he would guarantee that I would become a great hockey star and land in New York with the Rangers.

WELL, I did not like getting cut up on the ice, any more than I cared about getting cut up in the ring. But I did get to New York.

So I went in for baseball, landed with the Yankees, have been doing okeh in salary and World Series money, and get a lot of fun out of going to the Garden and watching the fighters and the hockey players.

The basketball guys, too, because I could move around a court, as well as on a soccer field, when I was in high school in St. Louis, and besides, I am a St. Louis University fan, heart and soul. They turn out great basketball teams there, year after year, with a ten season average which could be the best in the country. They are always good.

To be a first grade fighter, you have to have the willingness, and the ability, to hurt a guy.

Now, don't get me wrong. Being willing to hurt a guy is okeh if the man you want to hurt is out to get you, and he has as much chance to belt you as you have to sock him.

I am not putting the ring business on trial for being cruel. I often figure that I am better off if I can hurt certain birds which are out to hurt me. I don't want to mention names, but you know who these guys are.

A catcher, especially in the big leagues, and more especially on a championship club, gets a going over. He is fair game for anybody coming into the plate. It doesn't matter if the runner hasn't a ghost of a chance to score. But he will try to kick the ball out of your hand, or throw a hard block on you, or in some way hurt you, cut you, kick you in the head or stomach.

The fans like that sort of thing, and some of it which isn't strictly legal is okehed by the umpires. A lot of that rough stuff is hidden because of the jumble at the plate, where you have the catcher, the runner and the umpire in a small area.

If I was to pull some of that rough stuff on guys out in the open, say at third base, there would be a howl which is heard from the Bronx to Oakland, Cal. But I am not kicking.

THIS brings me back to Home Run Marciano. He is fighting Ezzard Charles, and I have been asked to expertize on that one, too.

Irv Noren, our outfielder, is the Yankee ring expert. He knows a lot about boxing. He reads every line of The Ring Magazine, he watches live fights and TV fights, and I think could handle himself with the gloves, even though he has no rep as a scrapper.

Noren says it is Marciano by a knockout, and I have to go along with Irv.

Has Charles got a chance? Sure he has. Who knows what will happen when two fighters get into the ring? Look that up in the Record Book. Leave us not forget that this Charles used to be the champion of the world.

However, barring a big break, Marciano belts this Charles out, and is ready for another big gate in September.

The unexplainable break, like a Charles victory over Marciano would be, happens in baseball all the time.

Like in 1949, when Casey Stengel has his first season with the Yankees. We are going through Texas, and play a Class B team in Greenville. The Yankees are 100 to 1, but, of course, there is no betting. There never is on such games.

Well, we could do nothing right, and that Big State League club gave us a whacking which none of us ever will forget.

## NAT FLEISCHER SAYS:

SINCE we last went to press the eleventh Marquess of Queensberry passed away. The grandson of the man who lent his name to the modern rules of boxing he was in his own right greatly interested in the sport of men.

During World War II the late Marquess put on boxing shows all over England for the troops and was noted for his disappointment of the growing commercialism in boxing. On several occasions he indicated his dislike of the growing interest by boxers in money and stated his belief that where money is God, the game is not always conducted on as high a plane as it might be.

(ED. NOTE) One of the main reasons that when commercialism creeps in boxing is hurt, stems from the urge of the athlete to jump into the professional ranks where he can get paid long before he has learned his trade. This means that pugilists turning pro are often given inadequate performances and are washed up long before they should be. The need by TV for new faces is expediting this trend that is drying up the pool of talent.

If all boxing promoters don't take cognizance of this situation and attempt to incubate a few worthy youngsters the game may be in for hard times ahead.

● ● ●

TO veteran boxing authorities, there was nothing surprising in Gil Turner's two so-called "upset" defeats by journeyman Bobby Jones. It was inevitable that something of the sort would happen to Turner sooner or later. If Jones hadn't done it, somebody else would have. Turner had been steadily declining since Kid Gavilan knocked him out in their welterweight title bout, and in each succeeding match it became more and more obvious that too many tough battles were exacting their toll.

Both in actual years and in ring experience, Turner still is a comparative youngster. He is not yet 24, and has been fighting professionally only four years. Yet now, which he should just about be hitting his peak, he is finished as a big-time competitor.

The Philadelphian's case is not exceptional these days. In fact, it is merely another instance of what is becoming the usual thing. Fighters storm out of nowhere, become sensations overnight, are rushed into gruelling battles before they're ready, then fade away almost as quickly as they come. The demand for "new faces" in a profession scarce in top line talent is responsible for many promising youngsters being ruined. They get "punched out" in a hurry and are washed-up veterans when they should still be learning the trade. Irish Bob Murphy is a notable case.

Two of the brighest young middleweights to come along in recent months, Willie Troy and Moses Ward, may have ruined each other in their savage brawl in Detroit. Both boys absorbed terrific punishment before Ward finally collapsed. Lickings of that sort don't do youngsters any good, and the performances of Troy and Ward since then would seem to indicate that both boys suffered serious damages in that battle. In his next start, Troy was demolished by Joey Giardello in Madison Square Garden. Ward collected another lacing from Holly Mims in Detroit, then was knocked out by Georgie Johnson at St. Nicholas Arena in New York. These are only a few of the many cases of promising ring futures being jeopardized by the exigencies of the moment.

Television is largely responsible for the unhappy conditions. TV dates must be filled; there aren't enough good attractions available. Likely-looking kids are rushed ahead of schedule, before they have learned more than the basic ABC's of the trade. They have some natural talent to star with, and maybe exciting styles, but they aren't ringwise enough to know how to take care of themselves properly. They sop up too much punishment. For a while their youth and strength may carry them through, but every tough fight takes something out of them, and it doesn't require very many tough fights to reduce a strong, rugged, ambitious youngster to a weary-legged, arm-heavy, soft-chinned has-been.

● ● ●

FRANK MENKE, a brother writer and a dear friend for more than forty years, recently passed away.

Menke, who was noted for his "Encyclopedia of Sports" and "All Sports Record Book" also collaborated with a number of sports celebrities on their autobiographies. He began his newspaper career with the Cleveland Press and in 1911 came to New York to work for the newly-formed National News Association, now known as the International News Service. He ultimately became the sports editor for King Features, International News and Universal Service.

Menke, annoyed by the large number of clippings, diaries and books he had to carry as reference when on assignment, came up with the idea of incorporating them into an all-sports record book which, through the years, grew to immense proportions. The latest edition of "Encyclopedia of Sports" contained over 1,000 pages and covered more than 75 sports. The Ring Editor assisted Menke in preparing the section on boxing.

————

## YOGI BERRA

IN baseball, there are nine men on a side, and one of the nine might get hot and win for you. In the ring one guy faces one other guy, and maybe the champion has an off night.

I was asked to do this piece about a favorite sport,—this piece, for just this once.

I want to promise the readers of The Ring Magazine that I will not do this again, and will not horn in on the staff.

In the meantime, I am going along with Bobo and the Rock, and want to say how lucky the boxing game is to have two such great fighters to interest the fans.

Coming up from the South, all of us Yanks promised one thing when we got back to New York. We were going to see this Tommy Jackson guy, who belts the stuffing out of Dan Bucceroni.

Jackson may be only a kid, but anybody who can sock experienced guys around is worth looking at.

Too bad I wasn't around when Lou Nova was fighting. They tell me he was another Yogi, and maybe we'd have had something in common, even if I don't know much about "dynamic stances" and "cosmic punches."

Anyway, good luck to the fight game, the Ring Magazine, and to Rocky and Bobo.

# Money Against the Title

## By MURRAY GOODMAN

THERE'S a check for some $5, and change, hanging in a frame in the office of Paul Damski that once threw the accounting office of Madison Square Garden into complete confusion.

The check, made payable to Walter Neusel, a heavyweight fighter from Germany, represented Neusel's pay for fighting Ray Impellitieri, the huge Italian in Madison Square Garden on December 29, 1933. Neusel won the decision over the 6 foot, 7 inch, 272-pounder, in a bout that was supposed to lead him to a title fight with the then champion, Primo Canera. Neusel not only didn't get the title fight but the payoff check was never cashed. It became the souvenir of Damski and his partner, Jimmy Bronson. They had guaranteed Impellitieri $7500. The fight drew a little over $12,000. When they got through paying out, there was nothing left for Neusel and his managers.

This prelude comes about because Alvin A. Naiman, a boxing hobbyist from Cleveland, Ohio, has guaranteed Carl "Bobo" Olson the tidy sum of $125,000 for the defense of the world middleweight championship against Rocky Castellani in San Francisco. Naiman's offer, in behalf of his charge, Castellani, was not only gratefully and quickly accepted by Olson and pilot Sid Flaherty, but constitutes

↑ *Walter Neusel, German heavyweight, gets a poke in the nose from Ray Impelletiere during bout which Neusel won but had only $5 left for himself after The Imp collected big guarantee.*

*After several deals in which he lost money by guaranteeing opponent too much, Felix Bocchicchio got it all back, with interest, when he collected $250,000 for Jersey Joe Walcott's return match with Rocky Marciano in Chicago. Left to right— Bocchicchio, Walcott and Joe Louis.*

a record guarantee by a manager for a chance at the championship.

Naiman, who boxed as an amateur in his youth, was guided in this by the fine hand of Jack "Doc" Kearns, and it got him the title shot, by-passing Joe Giardello, who was waiting patiently in line. Naiman is taking the financial risk of gambling for the crown and the gate.

It doesn't matter that he can well afford it since he is reportedly comfortable with a Steel Company and a Wrecking Company, among a few other investments, going for him in and about Cleveland. It does matter that Naiman, led by the experienced and expert hand of the good Doctor, has brought back one of the most interesting practices of boxing.

PROMOTERS have gone to great lengths to make certain matches the largest being Tex Rickard's flat guarantee of $450,000 to Jack Dempsey for the second fight with Gene Tunney, in Chicago. But managers have, and occasionally still do, come forth with tempting bait to get their fighters the cracks at bouts for or toward the title.

Kearns, the master, only as recently as December 17, 1953, demanded and got a guarantee of $100,000 for Joey Maxim to fight Archie Moore for the lightheavyweight title in St. Louis. Moore had to tak a lowly ten per cent for the privilege of wining the title. In three fights with Moore with the title at stake, only once did he get the better of the purse or percentage.

The story of how Kearns exacted a $200,000 advance, with the guaranty of an additional $100,000 from the gate for Dempsey's fight with Tom Gibbons in Shelby, Mont., on July 4, 1923, is one of the famous tales of boxing. Gibbons, needless to say, got nothing for his efforts because the town went completely bankrupt as Kearns fled with the dough.

Kearns was also the key in the strange contract that Tommy Loughran had for his lightheavyweight title defense against Mickey Walker in Chicago on March 25, 1929. Loughran had signed a contract with the newly-formed Chicago Stadium Corporation. He was paid a bonus of $25,000, agreeing to fight any one the Stadium picked for him to fight for one year.

When they made the Walker match, Kearns insisted on $50,000 if Walker lost, and only $10,000 if he won. Loughran was to get 55 per cent of the net receipts. He also agreed to pay the semil-final of Tuffy Griffith and Leo Lomski $12,750. Loughran figured on a $300,000 sellout. The net turned out to be $141,890. Loughran's share was $78,039. He won and was stuck for the $50,000 plus the semi-final—a total of $15,289. And he still had his contract to fill out.

"I'll have more fighting to do here," he moaned. "And if the rate of pay doesn't improve, I'll grow poorer every time I fight."

Loughran's luck with guarantees was nothing but bad. On September 27, 1933, he assured Jack Sharkey $25,000 for Philadelphia's first 15-round fight. The bout grossed $28,000. Loughran got nothing for his efforts and also lost the fight.

FELIX BOCCHICCHIO, manager of Jersey Joe Walcott, learned the hard way about guarantees. In 1946, when he was building Walcott to title proportions, he gave Lee Oma $35,000 to fight Walcott in the Garden and lost $4,500 on the deal. That fight, however, and others, got ancient Joe the shot with Joe Louis in 1947.

It cost Marty Servo a big bundle of cash to win welterweight title from Red Cochrane. He guaranteed Cochrane $50,000 for the chance, and he lost about $8,000. With Servo is trainer Charley Goldman (left) and Manager Weill.

Tommy Loughran starred in many contracts that contained guarantees. His luck was nothing but bad when it came to collecting.

Al Naiman (seated), manager of Rocky Castellani, looks over contract he signed with Rocky (left) and Truman Gibson of International Boxing Club, guaranteeing Bobo Olson $125,000 for championship match in San Francisco.

And in May of 1953, Felix the financier, completed the coup that would do credit to the King of Wall Street. He insisted on a guaranty of $250,000 for the return bout with Marciano and got it. Walcott, kayoed in 2:25 of the first round, got paid at the rate of some $1750 a second.

There is nothing like the proverbial ready green to make stubborn champions put their baubles on the line against challengers they would otherwise ignore. Sammy Mandell guaranteed Rocky Kansas $50,000 for the shot at the lightweight title he won in 1926.

Jimmy Carter had to assure Ike Williams $25,000 and lost $19,000 in taking the 135-pound robe in 1951.

Sandy Saddler had to take 10% with Willie Pep in 1948 to get his opportunity at the featherweight title.

Louis, in order to get at Jimmy Braddock, had to give up a percentage of his ring earnings for a period of ten years. Mike Jacobs tried to break the agreement, but the case was settled out of court and Braddock and his man-

## BOXING NEWS FROM HAWAII
### By Ted Yamachika

CARL "BOBO" OLSON, middleweight champion of the world, impressed his home town fans by disposing of Jesse Turner of St. Louis, Mo., in the eighth of a scheduled ten round non-title fight at the Honolulu Stadium. The fight was stopped by Referee Louis Freitas in 1.09 of this round when Turner, almost unable to defend himself, was taking a merciless pounding. While Olson was unable to floor the game St. Louis battler. Turner had taken such a severe beating that had the fight been stopped a round or two earlier, it wouldn't have met with disapproval by the majority of the fans.

Olson's display of boxing skill and sharp-shooting by a big man was classier than anything seen in these parts. He dictated the course of the battle and had things so much in his favor, he was as relaxed as a fighter working out in the gym. His versatile, educated left was at its best.

Olson first hurt Turner in the second round when he caught him with several hard rights and lefts to the head. Turner started bleeding from his mouth and nose from this round on and his face was a bloody mess at the end of each round hereafter. He opened up again in the fourth and in the seventh and had Turner in such a bad way in the latter frame that Turner had nothing left when he came out for the eighth. Olson weighed 166¼ to Turner's 161.

The fight was promoted by the Tommy Miles, Sam Ichinose-Ralph Yempuku combine and drew a small crowd of 5,159 fans. Gross gate receipt amounted to $15,067.40.

Bull Halsey, 160, stablemate of Olson, knocked out Dalfus Brown, 156¼, in the tenth and final round of the semi-final. The finisher was a left and a right to the jaw.

## BOXING IN PUERTO RICO
### by Mario Rivera

EFRAIN (CYCLONE) SANTIAGO, 117¾, encountered a tornado when Black Pico of Cuba, 117½, scored a seven round keyo over the local boy in a bout scheduled for ten rounds at the Sixto Escobar Stadium in San Juan.

Santiago fought well during the first five heats despite the fact that a right cross dropped him for an eight count in the second round. In the sixth round Black Pico opened up and dazzled the fans with his ring skill. Due credit must be given Santiago for accepting this bout, knowing all along that

Pico was a much superior man in every department but he was willing to gamble for a chance to obtain national recognition in a division where talent is scarce here.

In the semi-final Elias Valentin Viruet, 129, lost the first round to Emilio Gonzalez Perea, 130, then came along to win. He dropped Emilio eight times in the process. The bout was stopped at 1:27 of the fifth.

In another six rounder Ernesto Pumarejo, 130, and Lou Carmona, 130, fought a draw.

Victor M. Hernandez, 143, was the hit of the show when he scored a kayo in 2:37 of the third of a scheduled four rounder over Juan Rodriguez Llanos, 146. Wild-eyed Hernandez brought back memories of Rocky Graziano in his hey-day as he proceeded to pummel his opponent before the referee called a halt to save Juan from further punishment. It was the third consecutive victory for Hernandez.

In the opening four, Juan Ortiz Perez, 131, scored over Felix Fines, 128.

Fighters interested in seeing action down here should contact me, Mario Rivera Martino, Hermanas Davila 321, Bayamon, P. R.

Bobby Rosado, 150, supplied the big July 4th fireworks in Puerto Rico when he scored a knockout in 18 seconds of the third round over Walter Haines, 146.

Making his first appearance in Puerto Rico. Rosado, who left the island when he was only two years old, endeared himself to the hearts of the fans by his sensational kayo. The long awaited native boxing idol seemed to have arrived!

The third round was short lived. Rosado rushed out of his corner and with one punch, a left hook, which dropped Haines flat on his back.

Pastor Casado, 125½, scored a very close eight round verdict over Elias Valentin Viruet, 125, in the semi-final bout. There was very little to choose from between them.

In four round bouts: Victor M. Hernandez, 147, clearly outpointed William Palou, 146; Enrique Velez, 125, scored a TKO over Juan Ortiz Perez in the third; Ramon Mendez, 118, kayoed Carmelo Cepeda, 119, in the second heat.

# MONEY AGAINST THE TITLE

ager Joe Gould collected in full.

Al Weill, one of the cagiest of managers, plunked $50,000 on the line to

Red Cochrane for the welterweight title bout with his Marty Servo in 1946. Weill dropped $8,000 in the venture and won the crown. Earlier, with Lou Ambers, Weill demanded a guaranty of $80,000 for Ambers against Pedro Montanez of the Carnival of Champions show, with the privilege of a percentage. The show lost a lot of money but Weill got $84,000 for Ambers, the extra being training expenses. Mike Jacobs tried hard to get Weill to accept less, but he refused.

AND the guaranty can have two sides, too. Sam Golden, manager of George Ward, was all but signed to fight Jack Britton for the welterweight title back in 1922. He agreed to pay Dan Morgan, Britton's manager, and Britton, $25,000 if Ward lost, $30,000 if Ward won. He had $10,000 in his pocket as a down payment. He had contracts from the Old Garden giving Ward 55% of the gate. Golden walked in to close the deal and discovered that Mickey Walker and his then manager, Jack Bolger, had walked in with an offer of $60,000 for Britton. They forgot Ward, who had beaten Walker twice, and Walker won the title from a fading Britton.

No story on guarantees would be complete without the tale of Mushky Jackson, as a fighter. Mushky was managed at one time by Weill. Weill got a fight for Jackson and asked him whether he wanted a guaranty or a percentage. Mushky always liked the feel of money in hand. He took $50. The 20 per cent he had a chance to take instead would have netted him five times as much.

"How did I know?" he asked afterward, "That I was such a drawing card. And anyway, $50 is better than nuttin.'"

# BOXING SLANG

Followers of various branches of sport use terms which, to the layman, often as understandable as Sanskrit. Baseball has its "bingles", its "grass-cutters" etc. Golf has its "foozles" and its "stymies". Billiards has its "English" and its "freezes". And so on, down the line.

A special argot is used by sports critics for every sport. Racing and boxing lead the field in this respect. The first slang expressions used in sports writing were devised by turf writers in England and they were quickly followed by those who reported fistic events. The man who popularized slang in boxing was Pierce Egan, British author of 'Boxiana' and he in turn, picked up many expressions from journalists who used them half a century or more previous!

It was Egan, however, who kept adding to the list until his boxing reports were loaded with expressions that eventually found their way into the common tongue.

William Shakespeare, though he never had gone in for pugilism, anticipated the terms of the prize ring for he uses many words that in later years were adopted in sports reporting. Thus the word "pay" which he used to signify "to beat" or to thrash".

Most of our sport slang can be traced to boxing. There is little original to-day in the use of slang expressions, not even the word racket, which even Shakespeare used and about which we hear so much to-day.

If you turn to Egan's "Boxiana" Volume I, 1812, you will find "racket" used in a fight report indicating a "fraud" or "robbery". Not much different from what we describe as a "racket" to-day. Most of the slang terms so frequently used by present day writers may be found in "Egan's Dictionary of Slang", 1843. Here are a few of the many slang expressions one sees in print following an important ring battle:

"Bruiser"—a fighter
"Pug"—a fighter
"A cross"—a fake
"Bettors were cleaned out"—They went broke
"He acts like a yokel"—He doesn't know his way around.
"The conk"—the head
"The beezer"—the nose
"The smeller"—the nose
"Chopping block"—a glutton for punishment
"Sharpshooter"—a clever fighter who can hit the mark with consistency.
"Claret"—blood
"Putting the lug on"—borrowing money
"Peepers"—eyes
"Flop"—a failure
"A ham"—a poor fighter
"Sap"—a brainless fighter
"Thief"—a manager
"Sold himself"—made a good public showing
"Got his nanny"—angered his opponent
"A Whizz"—a sensational fighter
"Busted smeller"—a broken nose
"Bunch of fives"—the fists
"Mug"—the face
"A teaser"—a light punch
"Double cross"—failure to abide by an agreement

MARY ANN

"A poke"—a straight blow to the face

"Biffs"—punches

"Battered him for a loop"—hit him from all angles

"Landed a haymaker"—scored a knockout punch

"Hit him with a Mary Ann"—hit him with a punch that came up almost from the floor. A blow made famous by Frank Moran

"Sent to the cleaners"—knocked out

"Palooka"—mediocre boxer

"Dead as a doornail"—knocked unconscious

"Can't put a dent in a pound of butter"—cannot hit with force

"A chopper"—downward punch

"The dukes"—the fists

"The lug"—the heart

"The breadbasket"—the stomach or abdominal region

"Humdinger"—a beautiful, effective punch

"Annie Oakley"—a free ticket—one that is punched full of holes

"Moocher"—one who seeks free tickets, as a habit

"A tramp"—poor fighter

"The suckers"—paying spectators at a poor contest

"Put to sleep"—knocked out

"Punchy"—a condition of a fighter brought about by repeated head blows

"Horizontal fighter"—one frequently knocked out

"Pasting"—a bad beating

"Flop"—a failure

"A scream"—a fighter whose antics please the fans

"A whizz-bang fighter"—one who is sensational in his actions

"A knockout"—Terrific fighter—a pleasing one—a hot favorite

"Went haywire"—lost control of his punches

"Went cuckoo"—lost control of his senses

"Lam him one"—land a solid punch

"The kisser"—the face

"Taking the count"—remaining down for a count of nine

# HALL OF FAME
## Jack Dempsey

## (WILLIAM HARRISON DEMPSEY)
### ELECTED TO HALL OF FAME 1954

"The Manassa Mauler", the most glamorous figure in the long history of boxing, the first fighter to draw a million dollar gate and the only man to take part in a fight that drew two million dollars. Born in Manassa, Colorado June 24, 1895, he first started fighting in 1914 under the name of Kid Blackie. Won the heavyweight title by knocking out Jess Willard in three rounds at Toledo, Ohio on July 4, 1919. Lost the title to Gene Tunney on a ten round decision at Philadelphia, Pa. on Sept. 23, 1926. Failed to regain title when he was again outpointed in ten rounds by Tunney in Chicago, Ill. on Sept. 22, 1927 in the famous battle of the long count. While champion he defended his title six times.

His fight with Georges Carpentier at Jersey City, N. J. on July 2, 1921 drew boxing's first million dollar gate. His fight with Luis Firpo was the first million dollar gate in New York and his fight with Jack Sharkey on July 21, 1927 was the first fight in which a champion did not fight that drew over a million dollars. His fight with Tunney in Philadelphia drew just under two million dollars, but the crowd of 120,757 was the largest paid attendance at a fight.

The fight with Gene Tunney at Chicago drew over two and a half million dollars, the largest gate of any fight.

After retiring as an active fighter in 1927 Jack continued to barnstorm and box exhibitions all over the world until he went into service in 1941 as a Lieut. Commander in the U. S. Coast Guard.

Dempsey during his career defeated Gunboat Smith, Carl Morris, Jim Flynn, Arthur Pelkey, Battling Levinsky, Billy Miske, Bill Brennan, Tommy Gibbons, Fred Fulton, Porky Flynn and Homer Smith.

# Saved by the Bell

A knockout that wasn't. Blasted through the ropes by Floyd Patterson's furious closing drive, Joe Gannon, Washington light-heavyweight, was dead to the world when bell ended Madison Square Garden fight.

## By JERSEY JONES

NEITHER in actual years nor in ring experience could Joe Gannon have been listed as a "youngster." He was 27, and his ring carer had begun ten years before in his native Washington, D. C. But his efforts—interrupted for a couple of years by army service—had been confined to "small time" operations, and he was practically a total stranger to the nation's masses of fight followers.

A clever lad, and a consistent winner in the minor circuits—his record showed thirty-one wins in thirty-three starts, and he'd been unbeaten in his last seventeen—Joe was certain that all he needed to make good in major competition was the chance. His confidence was shared by his manager, Al Weill, pilot of Rocky Marciano, and regarded as one of the shrewdest judges of talent in the trade.

Now Gannon was getting his big chance. Weill had maneuvered him into a top spot in Madison Square Garden. His opponent was youthful but highly-ranked Floyd Patterson. Normally, a main event in the Garden is scheduled for ten rounds, but in this instance, because Patterson was not yet 20, the distance was limited to eight.

The New York sock market, not knowing much about Gannon, was inclined to tab him a soft touch for Patterson. But Weill wasn't noted for overmatching his fighters, even for robust TV paydays, and if The Vest thought Gannon good enough for Patterson, the Washingtonian must have had the stuff.

For two rounds it looked as though Weill had calculated well. Gannon gave a neat exhibition of shifty boxing and snappy punching. With a fast left jab and a jolting right, he actually outfought Patterson in the second, and the surprised onlookers were beginning to envision a startling upset.

But Gannon couldn't maintain the pace. Patterson had too much speed, too much aggressiveness, and too many combinations. Gannon began to slow down. His shifty defensive skill kept him away from serious trouble for a while, but by the end of the seventh, as he trudged back to his corner, he was a weary, disillusioned young man. He knew he couldn't win now, but with only one more round to go, he'd at least have the satisfaction of saying he had gone the distance with the spectacular Patterson.

For two and a half minutes of that final frame, Gannon back-pedaled frantically to avoid Patterson's blazing finish. Only thirty seconds remained. Then, suddenly, a vicious right crashed against Gannon's jaw. Joe's knees buckled. Patterson gave him no chance to recover. Flailing away with both hands, Floyd poured rights and lefts in on his hapless opponent. Gannon reeled back. A final Patterson left hook to the chin sent him collapsing against the ropes. He crumbled to the floor, half inside, half outside, the ring, shoulders flattened on the apron, legs draped across the lower rope.

Gannon was completely out, but just as the timekeeper started the count, the gong clanged, ending the round and the fight.

The bell had saved Joe Gannon from being officially knocked out.

INCIDENTS of this sort are not unusual in this rugged trade. Ring annals are loaded with accounts of bouts ending with fighters unconscious on the canvas but rescued by the bell from being counted out.

Perhaps the most historic case was the one involving Stanley Ketchel and Philadelphia Jack O'Brien at the National Athletic Club, which held forth in the old Fiss, Doerr & Carroll horse mart in New York's East 24th Street.

It was in March, 1909, and the spectacular Ketchel, world middleweight champion, was appearing for the first time in a New York ring. His opponent, O'Brien, a light-heavy-weight, was a wily, ringwise campaigner, rated as one of the cleverest boxers in the business. The bout was over the ten-round no-decision distance.

For five rounds the aggressive Ketchel could make little headway against O'Brien's shifty boxing. Philadelphia Jack was like a phantom, darting here and there, slipping away from Ketchel's dynamic rushes, and scoring often with his educated left to the champion's face.

But the youthful Ketchel was not to be denied too long. He reached O'Brien with a couple of pulverizing swings to the body in the sixth, and the veteran was hurt. Jack seemed in pain as he went to his corner at the end of the round.

From then on, Ketchel was boss, but O'Brien fought back gallantly, using every trick and strategem in his vast repertoire to hold off the savage slugging Michigander.

By the end of the eighth, O'Brien was near exhaustion, and the only question remaining to be answered was whether he'd be able to last the two remaining rounds.

Ketchel came plunging out of his corner at the start of the ninth, and drove a terrific left to O'Brien's mid-section. The veteran hurtled back to the ropes and sagged to the floor. At nine, he stumbled up, and by desperate clinching and stalling, managed to finish the round.

Then came the tenth. Ketchel, thirsting for the kill, cut

been blazing a merry trail in the professional arena, and was being touted as a certain world champion in another year or so.

This night Eddie was paired with a rugged, experienced heavyweight, Cap'n Bob Roper, at the Commonwealth Club in Harlem.

The heavier but slower Roper couldn't compete with the speed and brilliant boxing of the youngster. Round after round Cap'n Bob plodded forward, swinging away with both hands, but he couldn't catch the elusive Greenwich Villager. It seemed that wherever Roper moved, O'Hare's darting left hand was popping into his face.

Going into the last round, O'Hare was far out in front. Roper hadn't landed a solid punch in the fight.

Maybe Eddie, winning so easily, became overconfident and careless. Perhaps Roper's determination was finally due to pay off. Whatever it was, the bout had only seconds to go when Roper suddenly nailed O'Hare with a wild left. Eddie reeled. Roper stepped in with a right. O'Hare collapsed. He was completely out when the count reached four or five—and the bell rang.

The officials could do nothing but give O'Hare the decision. But it was somewhat ironical to have the announcer bellow: "Winner, Eddie O'Hare"—and the winner was unconscious in his corner, his handlers working feverishly to revive him.

That experience must have taken something out of O'Hare.

*Final bell also saved Tony Janiro from being counted out in battle with Jake LaMotta in Madison Square Garden in 1947. An exhausted Janiro was flat on his back when gong clanged as timekeeper tolled four.*

loose with everything he had. O'Brien, battered and weary, had nothing now to hold him off. Snarling and snorting, the champion ripped a left, then a right, to the jaw. O'Brien careened to the floor with such force that he rolled over when he hit the canvas. Gamely, Jack staggered up at nine, and tried to keep Ketchel away with his left, but Stanley brushed the feeble jabs aside and drove both hands to the body. As O'Brien sagged Ketchel nailed him with a right to the jaw and Jack again toppled downward.

O'Brien appeared to be finished this time, but the old fighting instinct once more brought him, tottering, to his feet. He groped blindly toward Ketchel. Stanley dove at him, driving to the body with a right and hooking to the jaw with a left.

Both punches landed. O'Brien, lifted off his feet, fell backward and crashed to the canvas, his head landing in the sawdust box, just outside the ropes. This time there was no doubt that the veteran was finished. He was stretched stiff on his back when Referee Tim Hurst began the count.

In the excitement of that dramatic finale, reports conflicted on just how far the count had reached. Hurst himself said later he had tolled six when the bell rang, ending the fight—and saving a gallant old warrior from being counted out.

BACK in 1921 one of the finest prospects in the light-heavy-weight ranks was Eddie O'Hare, a tall, lanky kid out of New York's Greenwich Village, and managed by the astute Leo P. Flynn. O'Hare, a standout as an amateur, had

He seemed to lose some of his confidence and cockiness. A few months later he was knocked out in four rounds in Madison Square Garden by another promising light-heavy-weight, and a Greenwich Village neighbor, Gene Tunney by name.

Disgusted, O'Hare decided to get away from New York for a while and try to "reorganize" himself. Toting along a few of his cronies for company, Eddie hied himself to the Maine woods. It was mid-winter, and the snows were heavy. One day, while he and his pals were horsing around, diving off the roof of their cabin into a deep snowdrift, O'Hare broke his neck.

WHEN Ernie Schaaf, one of the nation's top heavyweights, suddenly collapsed in the thirteenth round of a scheduled fifteen-rounder with Primo Carnera in Madison Square Garden early in 1932, a lusty chorus of hoots and catcalls promptly swept through the big arena. The bout had been a dull, boring thing, and neither fighter had absorbed anything in the way of heavy punishment. Despite his massive proportions, Carnera was not regarded as a particularly hard hitter. He was too muscle-bound. Press and public howled "Fake!" as Schaaf was counted out.

When Schaaf, failing to regain consciousness, was rushed across the street to Polyclinic Hospital, it was considered part of the "act"—another episode in the strange build-up of Carnera for a shot at the world heavyweight title.

But it was no "act." Schaaf died in the hospital.

In trying to find the reason for Ernie's tragic ending,

## SAVED BY THE BELL

authorities checked back and decided that it must have been an aftermath of a gruelling brawl, five months before, with Max Baer in Chicago. It was theorized that Schaaf, who had suffered severe head injuries in that bout, hadn't fully recovered.

Schaaf did absorb a brutal lacing in those closing rounds with Baer, and he was flat on his face, completely out, when the final bell rang at the count of two.

The Chicago affair was a return ten-rounder between Schaaf and Baer. Ernie had outfought Madcap Max in their previous tussle, a rugged sockfest in Madison Square Garden a year and a half before. It was Baer's first appearance in New York, and Schaaf had been a bit too experienced for him.

Although Baer had supposedly improved in the meantime, it looked at the end of the eighth round in Chicago as though Schaaf would repeat his New York triumph. He was slightly ahead in points. But he ran into trouble in the ninth, when Baer rocked him several times with thunderous clouts to the jaw.

Midway through the tenth and final round Baer clipped Schaaf with a right. Ernie shivered from stem to stern. Three more rights in succession sent him stumbling drunkenly toward the ropes. Baer tore in with a savage two-handed bombardment of the head and body. Schaaf started to sag to the canvas. Another right to the jaw finished him. He collapsed, landing face down on the floor. Two seconds later the bell rang.

OF more recent vintage, fans will recall the **Jake LaMotta-Tony** Janiro "handicap" match in Madison Square Garden during the summer of 1947.

Janiro was a welterweight, but LaMotta, a full-blown middle, agreed to "make" 155 pounds, and Janiro's handlers reasoned that Jake would weaken himself doing it.

LaMotta "made" the weight, coming in at 154½. Janiro scaled 149¼.

Tony's speed and clever boxing got him off to a big early lead. The plodding LaMotta was too slow for him. Had Janiro been content to continue his hit-and-run tactics, he probably would have won. But he was too cocky for his own good. Winning the early rounds so handily, Tony became puffed up with himself, and decided to beat Jake at his own slugging game. It was a bad blunder. Janiro had neither the strength nor the punch to swap with the rugged Bronxite, and if LaMotta had weakened himself making the weight, it wasn't in evidence. Jake seemed as strong as he'd ever been, and his vicious body punches gradually slowed Janiro down.

Now the tenth and final round was coming up. Weary Janiro's one hope was to last through it. His instructions were to "keep moving; stay away from him." Tony tried, but his speed and strength had gone. The aggressive LaMotta had no trouble catching him and smashing past his feeble jabs. Then, with only seconds remaining, LaMotta exploded a violent left hook against his chin. This was it! Flat on his back toppled Janiro. Utterly exhausted, he couldn't have beaten the count—but he didn't have to. The bell rang at four!

## MICHIGAN FISTIC FACTS

**By Jack Waina**

THE turn of the New Year found several major developments in fistic events to come here. First, the Motor City Arena and its brewery sponsor have parted and the weekly televised shows will subside January 18th. Second, Nick Londes has announced that his club at the Olympia Stadium, will try to promote every two or three weeks, with or without video.

The falling out with it's sponsor has brought to an end, at least temporarily, three consective years of promotion at the MCA. Reluctant to continue on a weekly basis without television, the group announced it planned to continue with upstate promotions and an occasional show on a larger scale at possibly the Fairgrounds.

In the meantime the announcement of the Olympia to run more frequently has brought out hope of more competition and that may give the sport some of the injection it has so sorely needed for some time!

During the month of December, six shows were offered and the combined paid attendence totals reached a mere 5,425, an average of less than 1,000 spectators per show. Of these shows, one was a nationally televised offering, four locally TV'd, and one a club promotion at Saginaw without TV which drew the most of 1,091 fans.

---

Motor City Arena, Televised locally, paid attendance 860 fans: Johnny Summerlin, 196, Detroit, put on one of his better efforts in drubbing Toxie Hall, 196¾, Chicago, in the eight round feature bout. So impressive was Summerlin that referee Jackie Swartz scored all eight rounds on his card in favor of John.

Bud Baker, Detroit light-heavy, stopped Bill Curro, also of Detroit, in three; Al Adams, 189, Detroit, defeated Syl Wagner, 198, Bay City, in five; and Syl Armstrong, 173½, Chicago, KO'd Kenny Lovegrove, 176½, Hamilton, Ontario, in five.

---

Saginaw Auditorium, paid attendance 1,091 fans, gross $2,481.06.

Allan Kennedy, defeated Young Chico, 153, Detroit, in six; Jay Watkins, 139½, Flint, stopped Frank O'Neal 139, at :53 of the fourth; Eli Legett, 139, Detroit, drew with Ralph Capone, 134½, Chicago, in six; Chuck Coleman 165, Detroit, drew with Larue Harvey, 165, Detroit, in six; and Larry Boaz, 159½, Detroit, bested Lou Barry, 159, Detroit, in six.

Embrel Davidson, 209, Detroit, defeated veteran Henry Hall, 186, Milwaukee, in the feature eight rounder. Ray Mizzi, 158¾, Detroit, beat Dolph Miller, 150, Flint, in four; Larry Watkins, 133½, Flint, bested Ron Dash, 140, Detroit, in five; Willie Coleman, 190½, Detroit, KO'd Chuck Church, 188½, Owosso, in three; and Eddie Lee Walker, 178, Detroit, KO'd Richard Garrett, 178, Detroit, in one.

---

MCA, Televised locally, 852 paid attendance.

Jimmy Perrault, 149¼, St. Paul, Minn., upset Allan Kennedy, 148½, Bay City, in a six; Eli Leggett, 136½, Detroit, bested Ronnie Stribling, 136½, Chicago, in six; Bobby Evans, 155½, Detroit, best Henry Bronko, 155¾, Detroit, in five; and Al Adams, 189, Detroit, won over Rex Traux, 187, Grand Rapids, in five.

---

Olympia Stadium, televised nationally, paid attendence 560 fans.

Harold Johnson, 175, Philadelphia, had very little trouble with gangling Marty Marshall, 179, Detroit, in a ten. Marshall was down for a nine count in the eighth and was fortunate to finish on his feet.

Clinton Beacon, 174, Toledo, KO'd Jimmy Davis, 179½, Detroit, in two; Eddie Smith, 164, Detroit, stopped Sherman Williams, 160½, Indianapolis, in two; Frank DeGazio, 180, Niagara Falls, halted Petey Graham, 195, Detroit, in two; Vic Brown, 154 Detroit, bested Mickey Warner, 158¼, in four; Eddie Troy, 157, Detroit, won over Jimmy Godbolt, 155, Detroit; and Ted Wright, 146½, Detroit, best Adrian Hefel, 146½, Detroit, in four.

---

MCA, televised locally, 1,064 fans, attending. Clarence "Duke" Harris, 146, Detroit, won over Waldo Fusaro, 145, Italy, in eight. Bud Baker, 175, Detroit, KO'd Eddie Lee Walker, 176, Detroit, in three; Dick Ramizetti, 128¾, Detroit, KO'd Nelson Ludy, 135½, Detroit, in three; Leo Desjardin, 145, Windsor, stopped Farmer Wright, 146, Jackson, in four; and Yama Bahama, 151, Bimini, Fla., bested Jasper Hall, 148½, Detroit, in five.

By
**LESTER BROMBERG**

# LOOKING BACKWARDS FROM 1985

*They'll probably be saying of "Bubby" Olson (right) that he never stopped moving in and throwing punches and especially that he could take it, as remembered from his battle with "a boy named Cartier"*

*(Editor's note—We wondered how today's fighters would look from the vantage of 30 years later. So we put the writer on a "time ship" and he's looking backwards as if it were the past)*

SOME old-time fight managers were sitting around the other day in this year of 1985, wondering how the champions of the mid-1950s would have compared with those of today. One veteran handler wisely said: "What are you knocking yourselves out for? Every great fighter belongs in his own generation. Let's just talk about each champion in his time."

"All right," one fellow agreed, "I used to get a kick out of that middleweight champion, Bubby Olson. Now I remember—"

"Wait a minute," another manager interrupted, "he wasn't called Bubby, he was called Bobo."

"You're right," rejoined the first, "there was another middleweight in the book, a German fighter by the name of Bubby Scholz. But, whatever they called him, that Olson, he wasn't anything spectacular but he never stopped moving in and throwing punches."

"Plenty of guts," said still another in the group. "I saw him the first time he fought in New York, long before he won the title.

"It was out at Eastern Parkway Arena and he boxed a boy named Cartier. Now this Cartier, he could punch, a terrific right hand he had when he caught you right with it.

"In the fourth round I think it was, Cartier caught Olson coming in. It was a flush shot and you could tell the force of the punch by the expression on Olson's face but he didn't clinch, he didn't back off, he hesitated for a fraction of a second and then stepped in, going back to his busy routine.

"The next round Olson backed this Cartier against the ropes near the side where I was sitting. He hit him a right to the head and a left to the body and Cartier went down. Cartier must have twisted his ankle landing because he got up fast enough but with a look of pain and he hobbled around so bad it was stopped in that round."

"I wasn't there that night," confirmed one of the old timers, "but I heard about it. And they tell me he never

got shook up that hard again."

"Not again," corrected the fellow who had been talking about Olson, "but before that, a couple of years before, he got nailed good by this other great middleweight champ... what was his name? Oh, yeah, Sugar Ray Robinson. Robinson knocked him out in Philadelphia."

"From what I've been told," another manager said, "he was a scared kid then, they brought him on from Hawaii and all the people here warned him, 'that Robinson, he'll kill you,' and when he got into the ring, he was believing it, he didn't fight his fight at all."

"That's true," somebody chipped in, "you know they boxed in San Francisco not too long before Robinson retired. By that time, Olson had gotten some confidence and Sugar was beginning to skid, although not too many people realized it. It went 15 and Robinson never had Olson hurt. Robinson only won it by putting on a tremendous spurt in the last five rounds."

A mere boy, who liked to hang around with the vets, inquired: "You say he never stopped moving in, what was he, a club fighter?"

An older chap laughed. "No, kid, he could box, he had great judgment of distance, he made you miss, he could slip punches and he could block. He wasn't spectacular because he mostly punched with a half-open glove and didn't get real power. But he could knock you out by cutting you up or running you out of gas."

"Say," volunteered the youngster, "what was this Rocky Marciano like? I saw his picture in The Ring Record Book. He looked tough, rugged. . . . I see he won the title without losing a fight. And I see he knocked out this great Joe Louis."

"Don't get it wrong now," urged a real old timer, "he didn't win the title from Louis, he fought Louis when Louis was an old man, in fact Louis was on a comeback, he knocked out an old Louis who couldn't punch with his right hand any more. Louis was through, he was—"

"Quit mixing the kid up," challenged another veteran,

"sure, Louis was through then but was that Marciano's fault? It's always that way—young fighters get a chance at an old fighter when the match comes along and, whatever they do, nobody gives them credit."

"Don't tell me Marciano could have knocked out Louis when Louis was flattening everybody!" responded the man who had first commented on Marciano, "Louis was a knock-'em-dead puncher, Marciano would have made one mistake—and bang, he would have been out."

"You know so much," said his protagonist, "you don't know that Marciano had a great chin. Why, that guy he won the championship from, I mean that Jersey Joe Walcott, he dropped Marciano in the first round with a beautiful shot, Marciano got up and was hurting him before the round was over.

"Another thing—Louis had trouble with funny styles. And Marciano, he was bent over, in sort of a half crouch. It was hard to get a clean shot at him, although he wasn't too much of a boxer. But what difference did it make? A heavyweight never needed more than a punch, a chin and condition and Marciano had all three."

The very first handler in on the discussion, who had been listening, observed: "What's the matter with you guys? At the start, you agreed with me, everybody belonged in his generation. They crossed generations—and Marciano won, so why the talk?"

"Well," said the Louis supporter stubbornly, "Louis met better fighters than Marciano and he fought more often."

"I'll grant you that," said the Marciano man, "but they did fight and Marciano knocked him out, didn't he?"

"Quit it, will you?" begged the fellow who had assumed the role of a moderator, "let's talk about something else."

"Did any of you managers see that light heavyweight champion, Moore, Archie Moore?" said the youngest of the group hopefully.

There was a chorus of "sure, sure, a lot of times."

"Every time you looked up it seemed like he was fighting that Joey Maxim," offered one manager.

"It was only three times," insisted another manager.

"It seemed like 10 or 12 times," persisted a fellow manager.

"No, there were three fights and they might not have been too exciting," it was admitted, "because Maxim was one of the smartest around at the time and he wouldn't let Moore do too much with him. But Moore always beat him.

"I remember one of Moore's title fights that was a real thriller, though. That was with Harold Johnson, if I got the name right, a pretty good boxer from Philadelphia."

A couple of heads nodded affirmation. . . . "Johnson, that was his name."

"Well," he continued, "Johnson would have won if it was 10 rounds, he had a good jab and a right cross and he was well ahead going into the 11th—it was a 15-round fight, of course.

"Funny, Moore wasn't rattled about being behind, he was a cool one, not even after Johnson caught him off balance and dropped him. The thing was that, after the 10th, Johnson was getting tired and losing his confidence and everybody who knew boxing knew it—including Moore, naturally.

"You could see Moore moving on him in the 13th, opening up with nice combinations, and in the 14th he took Johnson out like a real champion."

"I read that Moore had been boxing 20 years before he got a chance at a title," the kid said, "how come?"

"There were reasons," an old timer reported, "when he was young, in line for a middleweight title fight he got sick. Then, when he was ready for the light heavy title, one champion after another ducked him, they feared his ability and they weren't sure he could draw."

"Another thing I wanted to ask you fellows about," the youth resumed, "what was this Kid Gavilan like? I read about his bolo punch, was that what he won the welterweight title with?"

One of the ancients chuckled. "No, son, that was his window-dressing. The bolo was nothing more than a right uppercut but thrown from 'way back with a windup so's the crowd would have something to yell about. His best punch was a left hook. He could double up and triple up with it—when he still had it."

Another old timer testified: "But, when he started to slow down, he wasn't the same fighter. I was down in Philadelphia the night he blew the title to that Sexton—"

"You mean Saxton, Johnny Saxton," an associate reminded.

"'Scuse me, you're right," said the man, "anyway, here he was with Saxton, who backed away and wouldn't fight, except in the clinches, and he wouldn't, or couldn't, step out with a fast pace. I thought he won the fight but it was Saxton's town and Saxton got the decision."

"Who was lightweight champion at the time?" inquired the lad.

"Carter, Jimmy Carter, didn't you ever hear of him?" a vet countered.

"I know that name," the kid admitted, "I remember reading about him but it didn't stick."

"I could understand that," a manager said, "Carter was a real good belter but he wasn't consistent, he twice lost his title to ordinary fighters—a fighter you probably never heard of, Lauro Salas, and a game rough guy who couldn't punch, Paddy DeMarco. He got it back both times and some people had the idea he hadn't been doing his best. I never thought so, I just thought it was part of his nature, some nights he was hot, some nights he couldn't pull himself together.

"It wasn't only in title fights. Even, when he was boxing over the weight, with no worries on his mind, he used

*Looking backwards, from 1985, it seemed that everytime you looked up there was Archie Moore, (right) world light heavyweight champion, fighting "that Joey Maxim" (left). It was only three times—but it seemed like 10 or 12.*

## LOOKING BACKWARDS FROM 1985

to goof. He'd get licked or fight a draw. Of course, I'll say he went into other guys' home towns in these over-the-weight fights. Still, he wasn't on the ball at all times and you couldn't forget that."

"Did they pay much attention to the little fellows in those days?" the youth asked.

"In this country there weren't too many fighters below the featherweights," one old timer replied, "that Sandy Saddler was a stringbean with a wicked left uppercut and his title fights with a real all-time great, Willie Pep, kept the featherweights in the news for several years. When Pep faded away, Saddler missed him plenty."

"I'll take you 'way, 'way back," offered another ancient, "I remember when I was a lot younger than this boy here, I must have been no more than 12, my father took me to see Tony Canzoneri fight Benny Bass, that was in 1928, 57 years ago . . . no, I'm not telling you my exact age . . . believe me, this Canzoneri, he was fast, could box and could punch. And right while we were sitting there, my father said to a friend, 'Did you ever see anybody like this Canzoneri tonight?' All of a sudden a guy in back turned around with a look of disgust on his face. 'Why don't you shut up?' he said to my father, 'you never saw Abe Attell.' And he was right, my father never saw Abe Attell.'"

At this point, the kid in the crowd said: "Yes, who was Abe Attell?" The old timers of 1985 looked at each other. That was digging back a little too far, even for them. The meeting was promptly adjourned.

---

*"Carter was a real good belter but he wasn't consistent, he twice lost his title to ordinary fighters..."*

*In 1985, the argument whether Rocky Marciano could have beaten Joe Louis in his prime is still being waged.*

# It appears that the path to the heavyweight title is open to any heavyweight who can do any one of several things well enough.

## By TED CARROLL

REVIEWING the careers of heavyweight champions of bygone years, there seems to be no set formula for gaining the top of the heap. Two of the greatest, Jack Dempsey and Jack Johnson were as opposite as it is possible to be in boxing techniques. Still both of them are always rated among the best of all time.

The old Manassa Mauler was the living proof of the old crack "The best defense is a good offense." He tore into all opponents at the opening bell and kept punching until something gave.

Dempsey possessed the natural gifts of unusual quickness, inborn savagery, ruggedness, and punching power required by his fighting style. His attack was tigerlike in its intensity.

Johnson was the other extreme. Boxing was originally the Art of Self Defense, and the man from Galveston, Tex. took good care of himself inside the ropes. He was as catlike in movement as Dempsey was, but used his incredible reflexes to avoid punishment rather than to inflict it. His eyes popping, he did a flat-footed shuffle about the ring, picking off his opponent's leads in the air, and smothering his attempts in close.

Johnson reduced Boxing to a science of self protection. As far as is known, he never suffered any facial damage in 20 years of battling. The cut eyes and damaged features so prevalent in his profession, were unknown to him. Not as spectacular as Dempsey, he was equally effective. Johnson's attack was moulded around his defensive pattern. Swift, sharp counters followed the blocking of his opponents blows. He seldom led himself but once his opponents did, his retaliation was sudden and decisive.

JOHN L. SULLIVAN the idol of the late 19th century was strictly the Dempsey type. He was a brawling, slambanging fellow who excited the public in his day as much as Dempsey did a generation later.

Corbett, his successor was the first of the Fancy Dans among the big boys. The contrast between him and John L. was as marked as that between Tunney and Dempsey.

According to oldtimers James J. Jeffries' assets were a bear-like resistance to punishment, and strength. Jeff must have had these in excess, for heavyweights with such qualifications have come and gone without getting anywhere.

Bob Fitzsimmons rode to fame on what the imaginative sports scribes of the Gay Nineties called the "solar plexus" punch. This was obviously nothing more than an ordinary punch to the body but the term fascinated the guys and dolls of those days and Fitz' "solar plexus" punch was a household word for years thereafter.

The old Boy must have been a mighty walloper, since Jack Johnson years later always insisted that the freckled Englishman hit him harder than anybody ever did. Fitz was ancient when Johnson got around to him but to hear Jack tell it he still packed a wallop.

Willard was unique in that he was one of few to make headway in the ring aided mainly by size. The Tall Pine of the Pottawatomie differed from most of the other ring giants in that he was almost immune to punishment when in top shape. Nearly all the other ring giants turned to be collapsible when hit on the chin, but not Willard. He sopped up enough punishment to flatten a ring full of ordinary heavies when he met Dempsey in Toledo. 6 feet 6 ins. tall and 250 lbs, he was a towering specimen and the first real giant to win a modern heavyweight championship.

TUNNEY was very much of the Johnson-Corbett school. He applied the methods of a student to his boxing. He carefully diagnosed the ring styles of his foes, came to certain conclusions and then acted accordingly.

Completely befuddled by Harry Greb at first, he went into conference with himself and finally solved the Greb problem. He reasoned that Georges Carpentier was too frail to stand body punishment and concentrated on the Frenchman's mid-section.

He figured the way to halt Dempsey was to take the steam out of Jack's opening burst by getting in the first punch. Going on from there he analyzed Dempsey's style and discovered Jack could be nailed by a right hand punch when he made his opening charge. Once arriving at a decision Tunney acted upon it with automatic precision. His coldly methodical methods paid off with the heavyweight championship of the world.

In Louis at his peak could be found traces of several other outstanding heavyweight champions. Only Dempsey could fire them as fast or as hard. At times he shuffled and countered as adeptly as Johnson.

Only Tunney studied an opponent any more thoroughly. Louis' quality as a student of boxing styles is brought out by the disaster that befell all his opponents the second time they tried it with Joe. Joe invariably had the correct answers for maneuvers and tactics that befuddled him the first time, the next time they were tried by an opponent.

In his two-handed punching power could be found the key to Louis greatness. He was a great hitter with either his left or his right. Added to this his left jab was an offensive weapon, unlike the lefts of Tunney or Corbett which were mainly defensive.

Old George Nicholson, long time sparmate for the Bomber always insisted Louis' left jab was his best punch. "It feels like any other heavyweight's straight right," George disclosed.

MANY a big fellow has set sail for the heavyweight title with only a wild right hand punch but Max Baer is the only one who ever made it. Max had what most of the other wild swingers lacked—a cast iron chin—but he staked his all on that looping blockbuster and cashed his chips when he won the world's title. If Maxie landed solidly only a fighter of unusual quality would not have all the fight taken out of him.

Schmeling was in a fog after Baer nailed him in the first.

Carnera floundered and flopped for eleven rounds but was actually through the first time Maxie tagged him.

Pat Comiskey, the country's heavyweight hope at the time, got hit just once in the first round, leaned over the ropes, and called it an evening.

Schmeling was another one who went a long way on a right hand. Schmeling was a one handed fighter if ever there was one. He made little use of his left hand in the ring. The German laid back, fighting in a stance which Joe Louis called "sideways" and waited for a chance to send over his right. He was a needle point sharpshooter with it, and when it landed it packed plenty of power.

Carnera would come apart at the seams when belted solidly, but to give the big fellow his due, he was a lot better boxer than he was given credit for being. Joe Louis among others is authority for this. Primo also had a ramrod left jab which was an effective weapon. Heavier than Willard Carnera lacked Big Jess ruggedness but moved much faster than was to be expected from a man of his 260 lb. bulk.

Ezzard Charles fitted neatly into the Corbett-Tunney school. No punchers, they had a scientific approach towards winning the big title. Charles boxed well enough to win the world's heavyweight crown although only a light heavyweight, a notable feat.

# NAT FLEISCHER SAYS:

### SETS BAD PRECEDENT

Rules are made to be obeyed but sometimes it pays, even though the penalty may be high, to turn the eyes the other way. As for example in the case of Dr. Swetnick, the New York Boxing Commission medico in charge at the Eastern Parkway Arena. In the fifth round of the fight between Danny Giovanelli and Jimmy Martinez of Glendale, Arizona, Danny dropped his man with a left to the body and a right to the head and Jimmy appeared to be in poor condition as he was taking a count.

When he got to his feet, he was shaky and as Giovanelli came forward to launch another attack, Dr. Swetnick, sensing danger, despite the rule which prohibits the doctor from stopping a bout, got into the ring and halted the contest. The rules stipulate that when a doctor sees danger approaching, he must recommend to the referee to halt the bout, not to interfere with the progress of the bout. But Dr. Swetnick decided to do the job himself and was severely critized by the press but was praised by the commission for his quick action.

Perhaps it was in the best interests of the sport and Martinez but the action sets a bad precedent. It is a simple matter for the medico to instruct the referee act, but even better if the officials showed alertness by acting on their own.

### BAKER STRENGTHENS POSITION

When Bob Baker added Julio Mederos to his list of victims in their Garden bout, he strengthened his position among the top rated heavyweights and eliminated the hard hitting Cuban who has been touted to the skies as a top contender. Maderos showed a lack of science and a lack of boxing skill, but he does possess a good sock. Perhaps with additional experience and training he will duplicate the feat of Agromonte and Valdes, countrymen who hit the high spot.

### GRAZIANO'S LIFE STORY

There is more to the story of boxing than the skill and the power behind one's punches. Too frequently we forget to investigate the human side of the quaint characters in pugilism. Boxers, like the rest of us are human and often the human side of the individual far surpasses in interest his fighting qualities.

Such was the story of Max Baer, Maxie Rosenbloom and Battling Siki among others who headlined the sports pages for many years and now we have another in the latest "thespian" among pugilists, a boy who made his way from rags to riches, from the slum area of New York to the movies and the theatre, from hoodlumisn, juvenile delinyuency and prison cells to a post of honor in the new profession to which he has been graduated.

Let's introduce to you the former world middleweight champion, Rocky Graziano, one time gangster whose bare fists enabled him to gain the leadership of an East Side mob, made life miserable for the minions of the law and who as he grew into young manhood turned the power of his punches into almost a million dollars and a world championship. And to-day, following his ring retirement, he is Martha Raye's leading man on a weekly television show which is seen by millions.

In the book, "Somebody Up There Likes Me," his life story written with the help of Rowland Barber, (Simon and Shuster—$3.95), we get the full background of the East Side Kid who went sour on the world twenty years ago and pummelled all who stood in his path including an army officer for which assault he served time in a military prison. It is a story exceedingly well told by his ghost writer, reproduced in the vocabulary of the inarticulate Rocky. It is a dramatic story of juvenile gangsterism, an intimate picture of the sordid life tough kids lead.

Step by step Barber takes the reader along the "Rags to Riches" road, one which like all of the Horatio Alger tales, leads our hero to the pinnacle of fame.

The only difference between the Alger hero and the hero of Rowland Barber's book is that the latter deals with a real character, not a make-believe one. There's plenty of kick in "Somebody Up There Likes Me", a kick such as Rocky Graziano exhibited in his three great fights with Tony Zale.

The book may be obtained through "The Ring Book Shop."

# PATH TO THE HEAVYWEIGHT TITLE

Jersey Joe Walcott was a hitter who retained his punch at an age when knockout power and sharp reflexes have long deserted most fighters. A cagy boxer with it he finally got his wallop over after years of trying, and wound up the heavyweight champion of the world.

THE heavyweight throne has been occupied at one time or another by men of varied styles and methods. Hitting power may entrance the customers but a look backwards over the list of the successful, shows the boxers have done very well.

Corbett, Tunney, Jack Sharkey, Charles, none noted as knockout punchers all made the grade. As might be expected, the blasters, John L. Sullivan, Dempsey and Louis—proved most magnetic and the greatest public idols.

A couple of giants eased into the big spot, Carnera and Willard.

James J. Braddock made it on faith and courage.

Schmeling did most of his fighting using only one hand as did Max Baer but both wound up worlds champions.

Strength and ruggedness turned the trick for Jim Jeffries. Pure Defense put Jack Johnson up there.

It appears that the path to the heavyweight title is open to any heavyweight who can do anyone of several things well enough.

---

## IN SYRACUSE RINGS
### By Billy Shaw

A GATHERING of only 2,650 fans turned out at War Memorial Auditorium for the 10 round return battle between Chico Vejar and Billy Graham, the very popular New Yorker. Televised nationally and surprisingly not "blacked out" locally, although it was not announced, the bout would be seen on a local station, the fight proved one thing—Graham apparently is at the end of the fistic trail. Billy's reflexes are away off kilter. Countless times he saw openings in Vejar's defense, but seldom was able to score. The ever-plodding Chico punched Graham around pretty much as he pleased to win the unanimous decision of Referee: Ray Miller, 5-4-1, and Judges: Jack Kimball, 6-3-1, Ted Shiels, 8-1-1. Only the referee had it close.

The gross gate of $8,500 fell far below expectations. Each fighter received $4,000 from T-V and the promoter, Norm Rothschild who combined with the IBC to present the show, is said to have hauled down $2,000 from the sponsor.

Vejar's youth, speed and aggressiveness, offset the scientific assault of Graham. Billy scored several times with jarring hooks and right-crosses, but never fazed the busy Chico, who kept belting them in from all angles. Vejar scaled 154½ pounds, which is too much poundage for this youngster. Graham, a natural middleweight, at 156½ pounds.

---

A rough miller, Ray Drake, 156½, Brooklyn, won a heavily booed decision from Eddie Prince, 152, Poughkeepsie, in the 8-round semi-final. Sammy Jackson, 170, Syracuse, compiled an easy one-sided win over Johnny Johnson, 176½, Buffalo, in 4 rounds. Mickey Savage, 153, Detroit, now managed by the Amos boys, won by a clean knockout over Harry Budniewski, 158, Dunkirk, in the third round of a scheduled sixer. Bobby Jackson, 162, Cleveland, outpointed Leo Owens, 162½, Syracuse, in the opening six. Jimmy DiMura, 132, Syracuse, won from Elmo Miller, 132, Chicago, in a fast six rounder, which was staged after the main event.

## BOXING IN PUERTO RICO
### By Mario Rivera Martino

FOR the first time in my association with boxing as a reporter, both here and in the states, this correspondent had to pay his way in to report a professional boxing program. The stupidity of it all is magnified when you consider that this reporter was covering the event for The Ring Magazine, a publication of world renown and international coverage unmatched in its class.

The feature event of the program, which was held at the Sixto Escobar Stadium, saw Francisco Colon Garcia, 134½, Puerto Rico, score a 10-0 shut-out over George La Malza, 135, Philadelphia, in ten heats. There is no doubt that Colon-Garcia would have scored a knockout if it were not for the fact that he suffered a fracture of his left hand in the third round. Being a south-paw, Francisco was denied his best weapon, due to this fracture, but had enough on the ball to cop all ten rounds over his inexperienced rival.

The semi-final saw Pastor Casado, 126, score a decision in six rounds over Felix Hernandez Carrion, 126, in the best bout of the evening. In another six rounder Elias Valentin, 132, outpointed Ernesto Pumarejo, 136.

Pablo Casado was awarded an unpopular four round decision over Felix Fines. They are featherweights.

In the opening four Ramon Carmona scored a four round TKO over Rivera. They are featherweights.

# PRESS PHOTOGRAPHER

*A top camera clicker of the Fourth Estate for over three decades gives Ring readers the low down on how fights are covered by the magic eyes.*

## By SAM ANDRE

THE Press photographer is a strange bird. He'll bruise ribs, pull leg muscles and wrack his body with pain so that he can record the exciting fight pictures you're accustomed to seeing in newspapers and every issue of "The Ring."

Either in attendance or via television, you've seen photographers jammed into each corner of the ring during important fights. In championship matches, jammed is putting it mildly. Yet this condition has grown steadily worse each year much to the annoyance of spectators, boxing writers and somebody's favorite tailor who has a seat in the press row.

In the late 20's only three photographers covered the usual weighing-in and the fight. I was there for the N. Y. American, the late Izzy Kaplan for the N. Y. Daily Mirror and Hank Olin for the Daily News. For a championship fight, two or three more would appear. But today the weighing-in ceremonies for a championship fight is a fantastic madhouse, topped only by a super madhouse called the winner's dressing room. It gets as much photographic coverage as the President taking oath.

No, photographers don't enjoy going through this ordeal. It's an assignment and they must do it, then go through the final stages at ringside for the fight. Here, the ring apron is a few feet beyond the ring ropes to protect a boxer knocked out of the ring. To get a clear shot of the action, a photographer in the first row must lay on his stomach on the ring apron and get his camera under the ropes. Since the photo syndicates and some newspapers have at least two photographers working from the first row, the crowding in each corner makes it almost impossible for more than two men to work with reasonable efficiency.

In the second row working press, photographers must try to clear those in the first row. To do this they must stand, lean forward and hope for an opening now and then for a shot. Photographers in the third row might just as well give up, watch the fight if they can for they can't make a shot unless the knockout occurs on the ropes in front of them. And then, only because the front row photographers must get off the apron in order to reset the camera distance.

With this obstruction and confusion before them, the boxing writers seated behind photographers just have to wait and view the motion pictures of the fight to find

This photo of Jimmy Braddock's kayo over Tuffy Griffiths in the second round at Madison Square Garden in 1928 was taken from the press mezzanine, shooting down at the ring. Today most of the photographers work at the ringside and shoot up at the action.

Above photo shows Pancho Villa kayoing Jimmy Wilde in the seventh round at New York's Polo Grounds in 1923. Notice how foggy picture is compared with one directly below.

This picture shot in England two years before the above shot shows the same Jimmy Wilde, being halted by Pete Herman in the 17th round at London. Sharpness and light shows how far ahead in press work were the English cameramen at that time.

The end of the fight between Sam Langford and Ian Hague in the fourth round at London. You wouldn't guess from the quality of this photo that it was taken way back in 1909.

out what actually happened in the ring. As for the tailors, who incidently are loudest to protest in such a spot, somehow they always manage to have good seats.

Getting back to "Years ago", photographers in England were far ahead of their American brethren in equipment. They had better lenses, cameras, faster plates (film) and above all, expert darkroom technique in the use of chemicals. A perfect example is to compare the two photos, one showing Pete Herman knocking out Jimmy Wilde in a London ring in 1921 and the other made two years later, 1923, in New York when Pancho Villa KO'd Wilde. Both were made under the same conditions, that is, by use of the ring lights only. Flashlight bulbs did not come into use until 1927 and were seldom used during boxing bouts. Actually, England's photographers were making great fight pictures as early as 1909 as can be seen in the photo of Sam Langford's K.O. of Ian Hague. However it's a different story today. The equipment available to American photographers, now puts them far out in front throughout the world.

When the new Madison Square Garden opened in 1925, the Circus people had a few five by five feet balconies installed, overhanging the mezzanine's center section for placing spotlights. This made an ideal cage for covering boxing matches, after the Circus left. Two were on the 49th Street side with Izzy Kaplan using one and I used the other while the Daily News worked out of one on the 50th Street side.

Working from the cage with a 4x5 Graflex and 12 inch lens, the ring canvas from that angle acted as a backdrop. This enabled the art department to do a minimum of retouching in sharpening up the figures of the boxers.

This is clearly noted in the photo of Jim Braddock's knockout of Tuffy Griffiths. Some fine pictures were made considering the slow film (glass plates) then in use. A

## PRESS PHOTOGRAPHER

knockdown was the best bet for a good picture as the action slowed up enough to conform with the slow speed in which the camera had to be operated. Eventually glass plates were discarded and replaced by the faster panchromatic film which improved fight pictures greatly.

The late William Randolph Hearst had a small camera with a fast lens, called "Cyclops", imported from England. It was to be tried out at ringside for something different in fight pictures. A test was made from the first row ringside but the camera proved too small and impractical. The next camera tried was the German made "Erneman" with a 1.9 lens, the fastest made. This was the camera that started photographers working ringside, but I worked from a third row seat on the aisle at ring center. Soon, others joined the ringside trend and within a short time photographers started working from the sacred working press row. Jimmy Powers, sports editor of the Daily News, started

it by getting Hank Olin a seat next to his. When I mentioned it to my sports editor, the late Ed Frayne, I was given a seat too.

The "Erneman" was a tough camera to use in that the focus had to be right on the target. If the lens was set for say 10 feet distance and the shutter was snapped when the boxers were either 9 or 11 feet, the picture would be out of focus and could not be enlarged to any great extent. The camera had a perfectly ground lens and when properly used, the results were outstanding. Its use faded when the Strobe light came into being. With this speed light now in use, it is no longer necessary to have a special camera and lens or even high speed film. The light itself makes the picture and with the many experienced news photographers using it, outstanding fight pictures are being made. It's not the equipment that worries the photographer now, it's that morning after the fight backache, sore ribs and the echo of "sidowninfront".

## NAT FLEISCHER SAYS:

### MOORE CONGRATULATED BY PRESIDENT EISENHOWER

Boxing received a big lift when Archie Moore posed with President Eisenhower and other sports celebrities at a luncheon in Washington to discuss juvenile delinquency. Archie, who has done much to aid boys' clubs, was congratulated by The Chief Executive for his sportsmanship.

In his recent appearance on "The Masquerade Party", a top rated TV show with Peter Donald as master of ceremonies, Moore made a hit. So clever was he that the reviews on his part in the show were highly commendable—another boost for the sport in which Archie earns his livelihood.

### 'TWO TON TONY' CHANGES ROLE TO THESPIAN

Two Ton Tony Galento has joined the thespians. Former pugilist and wrestler, Galento is now trying his hand on something new. In his debut on the legitimate stage, he played the part of "Big Jule" in the cast of "Guys and Dolls", a play based on the story written by the late Damon Runyon. Tony has been appearing with a sum-

mer stock company and his start was made in Valley Forge, Pa., where he made a hit.

Asked after the performance how he liked his new role, Tony replied: "Gee, this is tougher than meeting Joe Louis."

### SANGOR, FORMER BOXER MAKES GOOD AS A COMMISSIONER

Joey Sangor, the West Allis, Wisconsin druggist who as a featherweight rolled up an excellent record between 1921 and 1930, is piling up as fine a record as chairman of the Wisconsin Boxing Commission to which he was recently elected. Joey knows the needs of boxing and has used his knowledge of the sport to the benefit of those over whom his commission rules. Men of the Sangor type are sadly needed in boxing to-day. Since he was appointed by Governor Kohler in 1951, boxing has improved greatly in his state and much of the improvement can be traced to his efforts.

Sangor's latest move on behalf of boxers was to have Senator Harry Frank introduce a bill in the State legislature for compulsory insurance for all pugilists, something that should be done by every commission in our country that lacks that protection for those who box within its domain. New York was the first to pass such legislation and Pennsylvania, New Jersey, Massachusetts, Connecticut and California quickly followed.

### KETCHUM: "I MANAGE CARTER"

Willie Ketchum, manager of Jimmy Carter who lost his lightweight crown to Buddy Smith, takes issue with the statement that he is not the sole owner of the contract on Carter. Says Ketchum, "I have been accused often of having partners in the management of Jimmy Carter and want to go on record with the statement that I am the sole owner of the former title holder. He and I have an agreement on file with the boxing commission and no one has any agreement with me sharing my management of Carter. As for the reports that on occasions when he has lost on close decisions to fighters who are rated his inferior, he has not tried to win, all I can say is that Carter has had his off days and has given the best in him every time he has fought.

# SKILL — ASSET OF GREATNESS

### By NAT FLEISCHER

## Greatness is Measured in Terms of All-Around Ability; Marciano One of Most Powerful Punchers in History, Lacks Other Essentials for All-Time Ranking

STAMINA, endurance, ceaseless firing, a powerful sock and determination.

Those words have appeared in almost every story in praise of Rocky Marciano's knockout victory over Archie Moore.

They describe the qualities possessed by the world heavyweight king and have been picked up by many of Rocky's followers who have condemned the attitude of the majority of sports writers who, according to these critics, fail to recognize Marciano as a great fighting machine.

What's wrong they ask?

What must a champion accomplish to win public acclaim?

How much longer must an undefeated heavyweight king who has taken the measure of every opponent he has faced, play second fiddle to his whipped adversary in the reports of the contests in which he engages? Those queries have repeatedly been asked since Rocky's latest triumph.

Apparently there are two schools of thought on the matter of what constitutes greatness—those who regard hitting power as the chief asset and those who figure that greatness rests in all-around ability.

What are the qualifications for greatness? Definitely Marciano possesses a measure of

ROCKY MARCIANO ..HAS BLASTED ALL THE CLEVER BOXERS...

JACK
JOHNSON.

greatness if we are to ignore clevernes, accuracy in delivery and base our verdict upon the few assets the Brockton Blockbuster does possess.

Overall, if one is a student of boxing, he realizes that Marciano lacks many essentials that are necessary before one can be classed in the category of greatness. Analyze his fighting qualities with those of such masters as Benny Leonard, Jack Johnson, Joe Gans among many others, and one soon realizes why the heavyweight king fails to receive the acclaim his followers believe is due him.

ROCKY has been the central figure in three thrilling contests—the Walcott bout in Philadelphia, the first Charles battle and the Moore affair.

He has proved that he is one of the most powerful punchers of all time.

He is unceasing in his offense.

He has won 49 fights in a row, 43 of them by knockouts.

He can down a man with one blow if he lands it properly as he did in Philadelphia.

Yet the post-bout applause has always been for the man whom he whipped. That it seems, is what irks his supporters judging by the basketful of letters received by "The Ring" following his kayo of Moore, all of which centered on the above points.

Ring savvy, defensive skill, excellent countering, beautiful blocking, they argue are wonderful assets. But have these, they ask, prevented the crude, wild swinging, awkward, heavy missing Marciano from reaching his goal?

They have something there. The win and loss columns are what count most in summing up success in boxing and so far there are none in the latter in Rocky's career. He was knocked down by Jersey Joe Walcott and again by

Moore, but he got up and eventually mowed down his opponent.

Hence it is obvious that the world heavyweight king's backers rest their claim primarily on Rocky's tremendous power in his fists, his durability and the will to win.

Those who believe that he lacks the necessary qualifications for gaining a niche in the fistic Hall of fame as one of the greatest heavyweights of all time, won't argue that as a puncher, he takes his place with such greats as Fitzsimmons, Jeffries, Louis and Dempsey. They limit his qualifications for greatness to the category of "hitting power", strength and durability all of which Rocky possesses to a high degree but which assets they stress are insufficient to gain for him a place among the greats of the past.

In his case, they have proved ample fighting qualities to enable him to win the crown and to defend it successfully six times. But what about cleverness, the art of feinting, sidestepping, blocking, counter attacking and measuring an opponent? They certainly are not part of his fighting make-up. Without those, how can one place him alongside the masters?

NO one belittles the fighting ability of Marciano.

What the scribes have done, is to tear apart the argument of his ardent supporters that he. is the greatest or close to it, of all the heavyweights who preceded him because he has won every bout since turning pro. They fail to take into consideration his many shortcomings.

Granted that he finally clouts his adversary into submission, do they take into account the fact that in the bout with Moore, for example, he missed almost two-thirds of the fifty odd punches he tossed when he had Archie against the ropes, a perfect target for the kill?

One must consider that, plus the ease with which he can be hit, in attempting to rank the Brockton Blockbuster.

He's a charming fellow. He has sincerity and humility. He never stops trying. When downed, he gets up and fights with more viciousness. That's all in his favor.

Despite his ring crudeness, he can move about at a pretty fast gait and can toss more punches than any heavyweight of recent years. But misses more frequently than any champion I've ever seen.

He's a rough, tough, awkward fighter who gets there eventually and because of that, his supporters ask, isn't a pugilist of that type equal in greatness to the polished fighter who outpoints his opponent and reaches his goal without the aid of T.N.T. blows?

There you have both sides of the

argument-take your choice. If greatness, an attribute every pugilist aims to acquire, is to be measured by what we know Rocky possesses, then he must be classed as a great fighter. But if the true qualities of greatness are considered, he is outranked by many of his predecessors. What are such qualities?

1—Ability to outbox boxers, to outpunch punchers.

2—Ring, generalship.

3—Durability.

Marciano cannot outbox anyone. He must rely entirely on durability to outlast smarter and frailer opponents. He's too easy to hit, too easy to cut.

His arms are too short for him to be a boxer. He knows nothing about the art of feinting and counter-punching, assets possessed to a high degree by such masters as Jack Johnson, Gene Tunney and Tommy Loughran.

He has faced very few real punchers during his career. The two best, Walcott and Moore—both thirty-eight years old at the time—had Rocky on the canvas. Joe Louis is not included since when he met Rocky, the Brown Bomber had long since lost his once devestating punch.

The calibre of opponents is most important in evaluating greatness.

A Billy Graham or a Lulu Constantino looked like great boxers against lesser opponents but pitted against the top men of their class, their short comings in other assets were shown up and their boxing ability alone was offset by the attributes other, better opponents of theirs possessed.

Is Rocky Marciano a great fighter who can take his place as one of the ten ranking heavyweights of all time?

Based on the above analysis, the answer is no. He's one of the greatest since Corbett defeated Sullivan, in hitting power only. Beyond that he lacks the essentials that add up to greatness.

**Benny Leonard, lightweight champion of several decades ago, had the all-around ability that added up to greatness.**

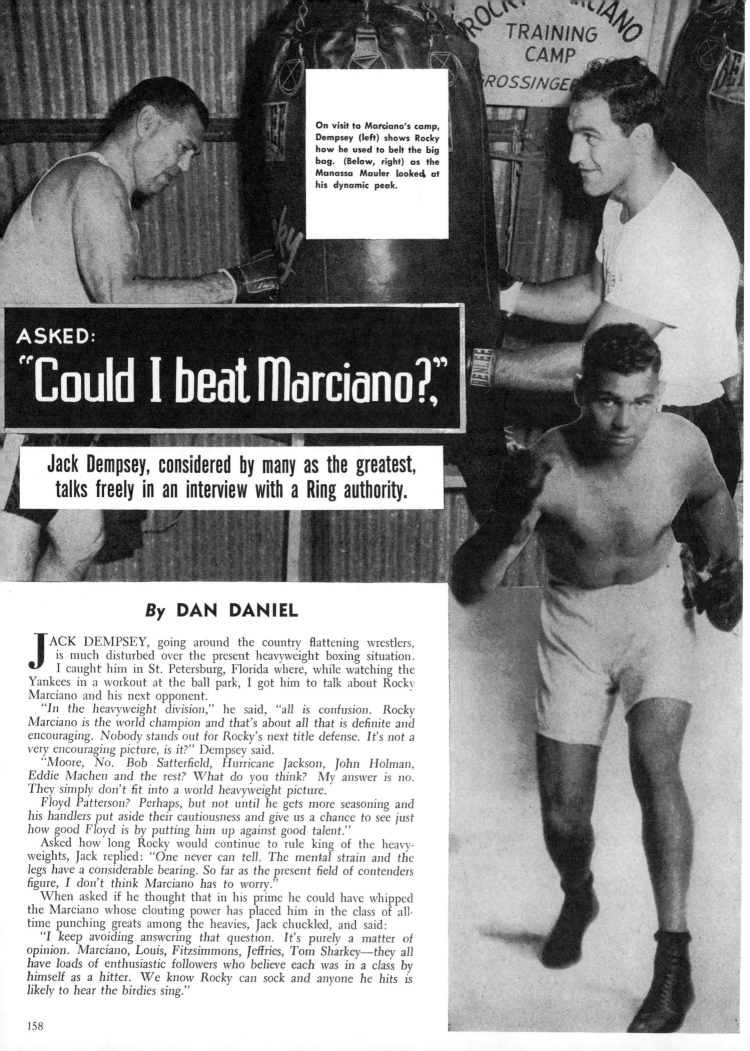

On visit to Marciano's camp, Dempsey (left) shows Rocky how he used to belt the big bag. (Below, right) as the Manassa Mauler looked at his dynamic peak.

# ASKED:
# "Could I beat Marciano?,"

Jack Dempsey, considered by many as the greatest, talks freely in an interview with a Ring authority.

## By DAN DANIEL

JACK DEMPSEY, going around the country flattening wrestlers, is much disturbed over the present heavyweight boxing situation. I caught him in St. Petersburg, Florida where, while watching the Yankees in a workout at the ball park, I got him to talk about Rocky Marciano and his next opponent.

"In the heavyweight division," he said, "all is confusion. Rocky Marciano is the world champion and that's about all that is definite and encouraging. Nobody stands out for Rocky's next title defense. It's not a very encouraging picture, is it?" Dempsey said.

"Moore, No. Bob Satterfield, Hurricane Jackson, John Holman, Eddie Machen and the rest? What do you think? My answer is no. They simply don't fit into a world heavyweight picture.

Floyd Patterson? Perhaps, but not until he gets more seasoning and his handlers put aside their cautiousness and give us a chance to see just how good Floyd is by putting him up against good talent."

Asked how long Rocky would continue to rule king of the heavyweights, Jack replied: "One never can tell. The mental strain and the legs have a considerable bearing. So far as the present field of contenders figure, I don't think Marciano has to worry."

When asked if he thought that in his prime he could have whipped the Marciano whose clouting power has placed him in the class of all-time punching greats among the heavies, Jack chuckled, and said:

"I keep avoiding answering that question. It's purely a matter of opinion. Marciano, Louis, Fitzsimmons, Jeffries, Tom Sharkey—they all have loads of enthusiastic followers who believe each was in a class by himself as a hitter. We know Rocky can sock and anyone he hits is likely to hear the birdies sing."

What type fighter did he think could whip Rocky, I countered. A hitter like Jack? A clever boxer like Tommy Loughran or Gene Tunney?

Again, a chuckle.

"The kind I'm thinking about is not on the fistic market today," said Jack. "It's the combination fighter, the kind I met when I faced Gene Tunney. It will require a combination boxer with cleverness, hitting power and one who can match Rocky's excellent physical condition to beat him," said the old champ.

And then Dempsey reminisced. He seemed to be thinking of the days when he was in his prime and probably what might have happened had he and Marciano fought. He spoke of Tunney and compared the physical condition of Gene with that which Rocky possesses every time he faces an opponent in the ring.

"You know, every time I see Rocky in action, he reminds me of Gene."

"In what way," I asked.

"Mostly conditioning. There wasn't a fighter in my days who trained so hard, perfected himself so thoroughly and entered the ring so fit as did Gene. Visualize him in the two battles we fought and you quickly get your answer on why he won the title from me and then repeated his victory when we met in Chicago," he answered.

Then he continued: "Marciano has set an example for the youth who have taken up boxing as a profession. Those who want to get to the top must be hard as nails, have a clear picture of what they hope to accomplish and must avoid the pitfalls that so often mean the difference between success and defeat. That's where Rocky shines and if he continues to remain in the field, I doubt that any of the present crop, newcomers or veterans, can hold a candle up before him. Like Gene Tunney, Rocky has mastered conditioning—a most important factor in boxing," said Jack.

### INTEREST IN DEMPSEY AT AMAZING PEAK

Interest in Dempsey personally is at a very high level. Perhaps this has something to do with the lack of outstanding class among the contenders, so called, for Marciano's title. When the current picture becomes drab, the fans turn for solace to their idols of the past. And the old Mauler still is very much an idol.

The customers have revived the old dispute as to whether Dempsey, in his prime, could have whipped Joe Louis.

It is strange, but yet the truth. As time rolls on, Louis and his superlatives recede into the background, and Dempsey's skills become more and more impressive.

This traces, in part, to the fact that Louis is the more recent fighter. So many thousands of fans have seen Joe swinging hot leather. But how many actually saw Dempsey in action the day he took the title from Jess Willard in Toledo in 1919? How many watched him lose to Gene Tunney at Philadelphia, and again at Chicago?

Dempsey is not a man with an inflated ego. He is a realist if ever there was one in the ring. He believes that he could have whipped any man who ever climbed through the ropes. How correct is this belief? Who can say?

Dempsey is not backward about saying that he could have stopped Louis. He agrees that Joe and his drive would have presented very serious problems. But Jack is sure that he could have tagged Louis with enough before the Brown Bomber could have got to him with sufficient.

"Joe probably will apply one to my whiskers next time I see him," Dempsey chuckled. "But I think I could have taken him, and who is there to tell me 'NO.'"

### JACK DODGES QUESTION OF MARCIANO'S CLASS

On the subject of Marciano, Dempsey is reticent. Jack likes Rocky. Also, Rocky is in competition, making a living

Dempsey, ex-heavyweight champ of the world, seen leaving for another tour of the United States as a wrestling referee.

out of the ring, and Jack is not one to demean a ruling champion.

It is one of Marciano's fine distinctions that he attracts friends, friendly attitudes. He is something of a fistic Babe Ruth. The home run king was everybody's friend, and everybody was his pal. He never ran anybody down, and nobody ever blasted him.

That's Marciano, and Dempsey would be the last one to utter one sentence aspersing Rocky's class, his place in the all time rating.

Could he have taken Marciano? Dempsey chuckled. "I don't want Rocky to walk up to me one of these days and lay me out. Rocky is a terrific puncher, a fine guy, a good fighter, our current standout."

There are things which Marciano could do better if he followed Dempsey's advice. What things? There, again, Dempsey begged off.

"Marciano has a fine coach in Charley Goldman, and this man Weill knows a few things, too. Marciano is a fine fighter. He has been taught much by Goldman since he started his climb to the top. It takes time. Rocky has gone a long way in perfecting his faults."

I saw Dempsey win the title at Toledo. I saw Louis defend his championship on numerous occasions and I've seen Rocky often. I don't believe that Marciano rates him-

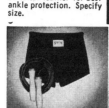

## "COULD I BEAT MARCIANO?"

self over these two.

Dempsey would have stopped Rocky because Marciano would have taken too long to hurt the Mauler. Rocco warms to his task slowly, and usually doesn't get to the point until the eighth round. Once he has worn down his man, Rocky hurts plenty.

Dempsey was no feeler-outer. The bell rang, and he went right to work, no dilly-dallying. He gave everything he had, all the way.

**INDUSTRY VS. RING ONE-SIDED FIGHT**

Dempsey came up in a very tough school. There were more fighters, better ones, than we have today, and that is no aspersion on the men who now make their livings in the ring. The times have changed and no one realizes that better than the Maussa Mauler.

"I have great confidence in Julius Helfand, chairman of the New York Commission," Dempsey continued, in discussing the boxing situation. "New York is the leader and what happens there in boxing is reflected around the country.

"I think Helfand will bring back some of the small clubs. They are so

important. The small clubs were the minor leagues of boxing. Suppose all the minors in baseball shut down? Where would the club owners get the players? In studio television? How funny that is! Studio fights.

"Big, strong kids don't want to fight under present conditions. The competition between industry and the fight game today is too tough for the ring.

"A youngster becomes a fighter. He can't develop in some small club, and go on to another small club. There are no small clubs. He has to wait for his chance on the television schedule of some bigger club, and the waiting list is long.

"So he gets hungry, and goes to a factory and gets a union card and $80 or $100 a week, with a pay check every week. That's important. In boxing, you have hungry weeks. In industry, salary every week.

"Well, if conditions in boxing do not attempt to fight against that weekly pay check, what's the answer? Nothing but what you have today."

**NOBODY IS HUNGRY TODAY, JACK SAYS**

"Nobody has to go hungry today," Dempsey went on. "There is plenty of work for the man who wants to work. A kid can make plenty of dough for himself doing almost anything.

"I was hungry. I had to fight my way along. Freights and the like, fight, fight all the time. The life was tough, but it hardened you.

"I liked to fight. I think that today there are a lot of professional boxers who do not like the ring.

"However, this is America. We will make out. Especially if the New York commissioner keeps up the battle for the right thing."

Dempsey insists that the IBC has ruined free enterprise in boxing and has killed off the small clubs.

Jack seems to overlook the fact that the times have changed, the television has produced conditions which favor the bigger clubs and make it impossible for the litte ones, minus TV revenues, to breathe.

"Kids are discouraged from going into boxing because of conditions. Also, because of the bad name the sport has got for itself, temporarily. I know things will clear up. I'm sure of it," said Jack.

Dempsey fails to see that conditions eventually made it impossible for the smaller promoter to go on doing business and that the professional fight industry had to move into strong hands backed by big money.

Bad? Yes. In many ways. But that is the trend in these United States. The small business man is being gobbled up by the big corporations in every field, not alone boxing.

Will boxing ever fight off this powerful competition? Dempsey remarked. "No. Not entirely," he answered. "But the things Helfand is trying to do should help rehabilitate the sport."

Meanwhile, the fans of the nation flock to see Dempsey flatten scrappy wrestlers in those mock fights, and boxing followers wonder, all over again, if the old Mauler wasn't the greatest the game has produced.

Could Dempsey have flattened Louis? Could Dempsey have stopped Marciano?

These are intriguing questions for us to mull over while we wait for the situation among the heavyweights to jell, and produce a contender whom we would be willing to watch on TV for free, let alone with a $50 top in Yankee Stadium.

## RATINGS

Young Martin, 1, and kayoed Billy Morris, 2.
Leo Espinosa defeated Keiichi Komuro, 12.
Dai Dower outpointed Robert Meunier, 8.
Cliff Eskridge kayoed Johnny Martin, 9.
Mario de Leon stopped bantamweight Rudy Coronado, 6. Unable to make the weight, Frankie Bennett relinquished Australian title and lost decision in non-title bout to Bindi Jack, 12.
Mario Ruiz and Cheto Fernandez drew, 10.
Vic Angeles kayoed Frank Cruz, 5, and drew with Joe Cruz, 6.
Blackie Robinson whipped Vic Campo, 8.
Guiseppe Gaviano whipped Renato Denti, 8.
Lud Giordano kayoed Pee Wee Pollard, 2.
Ray Valadez kayoed Juanito Miranda, 1, and bested Jorge Correa, 6. Manuel Alcala kayoed Zurdo Castillo, 3, and Manolo Ortiz, 2.
Chico Argaez kayoed Pedro Cortes, 1.

# The Gold Rush

(Upper scene)—A few rude shacks comprised Goldfield, Nev., in 1904, and (below) as booming mining town looked two years later when it awaited Gans-Nelson bout.

## 50 Years Ago, The Fabulous Purse for Gans-Nelson Bout Put Desert Mining Town on Map and Began Tex Rickard's Colorful Career as a Fight Promoter

**By JERSEY JONES**

IN his New York office, Sam Harris squinted again at the telegram, then handed it over to Joe Humphries, his associate in the management of Terry McGovern. "What do you think, Joe?" he asked.

Humphries read the wire. It was from Goldfield, Nevada, offering McGovern $5,000 to fight a Jack Clifford there. The name of the

Box offices in new stadium did thriving business as miners, cowboys and town's leading citizens (yes, women, too) lined up for tickets to the Big Fight.

sender was George L. Rickard.

Humphries snorted. "Who in blazes is George L. Rickard and whereinell is Goldfield, Nevada? This must be somebody's silly idea of a joke, offering McGovern that much money to fight a mugg in a town I never heard of."

The telegram, unanswered, ended in the waste basket.

Across the continent, in San Francisco, two other managers received similar offers for their charges to box Clifford. Willus Britt, handling his brother Jimmy, reacted as had Harris and Humphries. Refusing to consider the thing seriously, Britt tossed the telegram away.

For a few fleeting moments, Billy Nolan, managing Battling Nelson, was tempted to do likewise. On second thought, however, Nolan decided to investigate. Billy hadn't heard of Goldfield or Rickard, but he'd had some experience promoting fights in western mining centers, and thought this Rickard-Goldfield thing might be worth looking into. What could he lose? Goldfield couldn't be much more than a day's jaunt from 'Frisco.

Billy made the trip and was well rewarded. A shrewd individual, it didn't take him long, after landing in Goldfield, to size up the situation. Pay dirt had been discovered there and the town was booming. Rickard, proprietor of The Northern, the community's leading saloon and gambling hall, was chairman of a local citizens' committee. News traveled slowly in those days—this was in 1906—and Goldfield's newly-found prosperity had yet to become known to the outside world. It was the task of Rickard and his colleagues to promote an event that would attract immediate attention to the town. Someone suggested a prizefight.

None of the committee members knew much about boxing promotions, but the suggestion met with enthusiastic approval. Rickard, as chairman, was delegated to handle the details.

George Lewis Rickard, dubbed "Tex", was a colorful character. At 35, he'd had an adventurous life. Born in Kansas City while his parents were emigrating southward from Illinois, he was only 12 when his father, an itinerant millwright and farmer, died in Sherman, Texas. The youngster had to quit school and find work to support himself and his mother. He became a cowpuncher in the Texas Panhandle, then town marshall of Henrietta. When the gold rush started for Alaska and the Klondike, he was in it. From prospecting he shifted to saloon and gambling operations, first in Dawson, then in Nome. Although doing well for himself, restlessness caught up with him. He headed back to the United States and ended up in Goldfield.

Now he was in the unfamiliar role of boxing promoter. In his first venture he received a liberal "education" from the glib-tongued opportunist, Nolan.

"Listen," said Billy, to Rickard and the committee. "You gentlemen want a big event that will put Goldfield on the map. You don't care what it costs. Fine. Then don't bother with Nelson and Clifford. It wouldn't mean anything. Nelson is the leading contender for the world lightweight championship. Clifford is nobody, an ordinary fighter bouncing around the mining circuit. Get after a real big-time attraction, an important fight that will get you the attention you want. Put up a real purse, and maybe you can get Joe Gans to meet Nelson for the title."

(Left) Copy of articles of agreement for Gans-Nelson bout, and (above) rivals shaking hands before start of gruelling brawl, which ended with Nelson's disqualification in 42nd round.

What did Nolan mean by a "real purse"?

"Oh," said Billy casually, "something like $30,000. That would be cheap for the publicity you'd get all over the world."

To an experienced promoter, a $30,000 purse in those days would have been fantastic, even for an outstanding match like Gans vs. Nelson, but Rickard and his associates were not experienced promoters. They knew little of boxing purses, and Nolan's suggestion seemed reasonable. It was, indeed, a cheap gamble to take for the tremendous advertising the fight would bring them, and, after all, that was the main purpose of the promotion. So they agreed upon the purse and Labor Day, September 3, was set as the date.

Nolan was a hard bargainer. First, he demanded to see the $30,000. It was collected, converted into $20 gold pieces, and put on display in the window of the shack used by the committee for its headquarters.

Although Nelson was the challenger, Nolan then demanded that Bat's contract call for $20,000, or two-thirds of the purse. Next, he insisted on a "bonus" of $2,500 for signing, and another $500 for Nelson's training expenses.

Gans, the champion, realized he was getting the short end of the deal, but he didn't argue the point too strenuously. Joe had parted from his manager, Al Herford of Baltimore, and was doing his own business, with a Frank McDonald as adviser. Nelson may have been getting twice as much out of the fight as Gans, but $10,000, plus another $1,000 for expenses, represented an exceptional payday for Joe, probably the biggest of his career. Confident of beating Nelson, Gans lost no time signing.

Nolan wasn't entirely satisfied. He'd won the financial battle, and now concentrated on the fight itself. He stipulated a ringside weigh-in, at the class limit, 133 pounds, with the fighters wearing all ring togs. This was supposed to favor Nelson, a natural lightweight. Gans had been scaling 140 and more for recent non-title bouts, and the

belief was prevalent that Joe would weaken himself getting down to the lightweight mark. When Gans reluctantly agreed to weighing-in ringside, instead of four or five hours before the fight, Nolan still wasn't content. He demanded the rivals scale in three times the day of the bout, first at 12 noon, then at 1:30, and finally at ringtime, 3 o'clock.

Gans protested the unfair demand. He'd have to go all day without food or liquid. Nolan was adamant. Either Joe would agree or the fight was off. It was strictly a bluff on Nolan's part, but it succeeded. Gans agreed.

The next move was to decide upon the referee. George Siler of Chicago, recognized as one of the ring's most fearless, competent officials, was satisfactory to both camps. Siler accepted the assignment. Ed Graney of San Francisco was invited as alternate.

Meanwhile, a big, wooden outdoor arena, seating 7,861, was running up another robust item of expense for the promoters. The reported cost was about $10,000. Rickard was, indeed, getting a liberal education in fight promoting. Another $1,000 had to be paid the State of Nevada for a license, and along with various incidentals, such as printing, help and one preliminary bout, the entire expense of the venture represented about $60,000, a fabulous figure for a prizefight in that era.

Ticket prices were scaled from $25 for ringside down to $5 for general admission.

Jack Clifford, the opponent Rickard had originally offered to McGovern, Britt and Nelson, appeared in the preliminary. He had an easy time disposing of Bobby Lendil, a Nelson sparring partner, in two rounds.

Gans and Nelson experienced no difficulty with any of their weighings-in. At the final one, neither moved the beam at 133 pounds, and it was announced the rivals scaled the same, 132¼.

The officials, besides Referee Siler, were Jack Welch, timekeeper for both Gans and the club, and Charley Dixon,

## THE GOLD RUSH

Tex Rickard, who promoted the Gans-Nelson fight at Goldfield.

timekeeper for Nelson. Larry Sullivan, a local banker, and associate of Rickard's, was announcer.

Gan's handlers were Frank McDonald, Bob Turner, Kid Simms and Eddie Hanlon. Nelson's seconds were Nolan, Tim McGrath, Johnny Reide, Jim Griffin and Young Kid McCoy.

The attendance, somewhat short of the arena's capacity, was estimated at 5,500, including 200 women. The gate receipts were $69,715, assuring the promoters about a $10,000 profit on their spectacular gamble.

Because of the intense interest in the fight and heavy wagering on the result (Gans was a 10 to 7 favorite at the start), Sullivan announced that the arena was policed by the sheriff and an army of deputies, and any sign of disorder would be summarily dealt with.

It was 3:22 p.m. when Siler called the fighters to the center of the ring for instructions. Gans, winning the toss for corners, chose the northwest, where he'd have the blazing desert sun at his back. During instructions from the referee, Gans interrupted to offer Nolan a bet of $2,000 to $1,200. Billy declined.

Lack of space prohibits a detailed round-by-round account of the fight but, briefly, here is how it progressed:

Gans, too clever and ringwise for the rugged but comparatively crude Nelson, had the better of the early milling. Several times Nelson was warned for butting. In the fourteenth, Bat fell through the ropes and Gans pulled him back into the ring. At the end of the round Nelson kicked Gans and Joe promptly kicked back.

Nelson was warned again by Siler for elbowing and butting in the fifteenth, and in this stanza Gans scored the first knockdown of the fight, dropping Bat with a right to the chin.

In the sixteenth, the rivals wrestled in a clinch and tumbled through the ropes. Gans was bleeding slightly from the mouth as he went to his corner.

Nelson seemed to be taking charge of operations at this point, and when he won the next three rounds it looked

as though Gans' weight-making ordeal and Bat's stamina were beginning to tell. Joe had particularly rough going in the 23rd when Nelson had him wincing and retreating from savage body punches. Gans weathered the storm, however, and by the 30th round he was again dominating the action.

By now both rivals had slowed down, and the bout was degenerating into a clutching, mauling affair.

In the 32nd, Gans cracked his right hand on Nelson's head.

By the 40th round both seemed near exhaustion, but Gans appeared in slightly better condition than Nelson. Bat, warned repeatedly for rough tactics, was bleeding from an assortment of facial cuts, and both eyes were nearly closed.

During the 41st round Gans, in a clinch, looked over Nelson's shoulder, toward Bat's corner, and grinned as he taunted Nolan: "Hey, what time is it?"

At the start of the 42nd a desperate Nelson lunged out of his corner, charged head first into Gans and began roughing Joe around. A couple of times he hit low. Pulling out of a clinch, Bat fired a right squarely into Gans' groin. Joe sank to his knees and doubled over on the canvas.

Siler, without hesitation, stepped in, ordered Nelson to his corner and declared Gans winner and still champion. The foul was so obvious not even those who had wagered on Nelson disputed the decision.

All this was just fifty years, a half-century, ago. An obscure gambler and a desert mining town had been suddenly catapulted into world-wide prominence. As the years moved on, Goldfield gradually drifted back to obscurity but the gambler, George L. (Tex) Rickard, went on to become one of the most spectacular promoters boxing has ever known.

## TEXAS BOXING NEWS
### By Harlan Haas

**Beaumont, Texas, W. W. Farris, Promoter:** Joe Brown, world's ranking lightweight from New Orleans, scored a four round technical knockout over veteran Eddie Brant, Dayton, Ohio, in the ten round feature attraction at the Sportatorium. Brown scaled 136, Brant, 140.

Floyd East, 136, Lake Charles, stopped Hector Bacuetes, 134, New Orleans, in a couple. Stanley Jones, 160, Houston, proved that his first knockout over Harold Redman, 159, Beaumont, was no fluke as he again put the skids under Redman, this time in five rounds. Lorenzo Hainsworth, 134, Orange, decisioned Lil' Bobby Flores, 139, Houston, in another six rounder.

▶ Corpus Christi, Texas, Benny Lozano, Promoter: Eloy Tellez Vann, 173, Corpus Christi, kayoed Harold Woodson, 177, San Antonio, in the fourth round. Juan "Lefty" Perez, 124, Corpus Christi, hammered out a six round win over Roy Hernandez, 128, Houston. Gilbert Hinojosa, 148, Corpus Christi, beat Dennis Woodbury, 150, San Antonio, in another six. Anthony Beasley, 141, Houston, made his pro debut by whipping Andrew Villareal, 143, Corpus Christi. In the four round opener, Salvador Villegas, 125, Corpus Christi, defeated Frankie Chacon, 135, San Antonio, by virtue of a two round tko.

▶ Corpus Christi, Texas, Benny Lozano, Promoter: Paul Jorgensen, the world's sixth ranked featherweight from Port Arthur, appeared in Corpus Christi for the first time, and won a ten round decision over Mexico City's Kid Campeche. Jorgy won the fight easily enough, but the courageous little Mexican with the bob and weave style kept boring in all the way to make it interesting. Jorgensen weighed 129, Campeche, 130.

## RATINGS

Cesar Morales kayoed Baby Lizarraga, 6. Joe Gonzalez stopped Gregorio Medina, 10. Rudy Garcia stopped Collier Cox, 8. Humberto Carillo whipped Roy Hernandez, 10. Roy stopped Americo Rivera, 7. Billy Evans stopped Paul Armstead, 4. Luis Contreras kayoed Otilio Galvan, 6. Brian Bennett outpointed Darcy Carr, 10. Emilio dela Rosa and Beto Couray no contest, 6. Barry Hatcher stopped Herb Pittman, 10. Carlos Ortiz kayoed Miguel Cardenas, 3. Freddy Fuller kayoed Ray Powell, 4. Herman Duncan defeated Dom Sacco, 6. Luis Trujeque stopped Gregorio Santos, 8. Already bantam champion, Kevin James became double Australian titleholder by stopping Bobby Sinn, 9, and adding feather laurels to his collection. Jesus Santamaria won over Manuel Prescott, 6. Felix Cervantes defeated Torito Olivares, 8. Ricky Miner koyaed Puyas Boy, 7. Baby Yucatan beat Felipe Nevole, 10. Harold Piper defeated Nestor Reyes, 10. Pantera de Champoton II kayoed Zurdo Sanchez, 7. Roberto Garcia beat Gildardo Bacho, 10. Paul Lee won from Johnny Juliano, 6. Enrique de la Cruz and Ramon Gonzalez drew, 2. Dave Rodriguez whipped Chebo de la Torre, 10. Reyes Castanon kayoed Eduardo Santos, 5. Eduardo also lost to Sammy Serrano, 10. Luis Espinosa whipped Lauro Garcia, 8. Ray DeLeon won from Rodrigo Duenas, 6. Joaquin Carrillo bested Memo Baltazares, 10, and Beto Rodriguez, 10. Pepe Montes and Alfredo Mijangos drew, 10. Roberto Hernandez kayoed Raul Duran, 5, and bested Sal Fierro, 8. Tony Vazquez stopped Chino Padilla, 4. Joey Reyes kayoed Raul Sanchez, 3. Al Olivera defeated Dan Silva, 8. Jesus St. Maria kayoed Enrique Perez, 2. Frankie Gifueroa kayoed Pedro Figueroa, 2.

### BANTAMWEIGHTS
Mario D'Agata became world champion by stopping Robert Cohen, 6. Leo Espinosa retained his Orient bantamweight title by outpointing Orient flyweight champion Hitoshi Misako, 12. Kevin James, Australian bantam champ lost in 12 to Fedrico Scarponi. Raton Macias outpointed Tanny Campo, 10. Ricardo Moreno kayoed Frankie Campos, 4. Cris Miranda beat Rudy Alcantara, 8, and drew with Fighting Gorio, 8. Juan Cardenas stopped Pierre DeSouza, 8. Joe Medel stopped Mike Cruz, 2. Larry Bataan stopped Baby Comacho, 8, and whipped Tommy Umeda, 10, while the Baby kayoed Jess Martinez, 4. Lucio Gonzalez kayoed Apolinar Huerta, 8. Baby Ross and Buddy DeMarco drew, 8, Buddy kayoed Rica Jr., 4. Claudio Martinez scored over Byron Cumberbatch, 10. Rudy Coronado kayoed Henry Morales, 1, and Otilio Galvan, 4. Miguel Lazu scored over Manuel Perdomo, 8. Australian Champion Kevin James halted featherweight Bobby Sinn, 9. Raul Leanos whipped Babe Ruiz, 10. German Ohm kayoed Jorge Gabino, 7. Wally Livingston bested Prince Johnson, 6. Pulga Herrera kayoed Eddie Luna, 1, and Gallito del Rio, 6. Federico Scarponi outpointed Teddy Rainbow, 12. Cheto Fernandez kayoed Kid San Martin, 4. Joe Becerra defeated Mario Ruiz, 10. Chocolate Barrera won from Chiquilin Torres, 8. Manuel Rodrigeuz and Chuy Rodriguez, 10. Arab Jr. defeated Ben Dayrit, 10. Marcial Galica kayoed Tony Alamillio, 3. Chango Ceballos kayoed Bobby Johnson, 3. James Hardman bested Fireman Kid, 8. Nacho Paredes won from Pepe Chavarria, 8.

### FLYWEIGHTS
World Champion Pascual Perez retained his title by halting Oscar Suarez, 11. British Empire Champion Dai Dower defeated Stanis Sobolak, 10. Memo Diez stopped Tony Mesa, 5. Hitoshi Misako was outpointed by Bantamweight Leo Espinosa, 12. Danny Kid outpointed Keiichi Komuro, 10. Bindi Jack won vacant Australian title by stopping Alan Gibbards, 6. Ramon Cruz defeated Chucho Hernandez, 8. Tibico Torres and Luis Gallegos drew, 6.

By DANIEL M. DANIEL

# DID JOHNSON TAKE DIVE?
# JACK SWORE HE DID!

Jack Johnson, as he looked when he was the heavyweight champion of the world.

**B**OXING history is full of mysteries which never have been cleared up. These "**whodunnits**" of the ring are no less interesting, dramatic and intriguing than their counterparts outside of the roped arena.

It is the plan of The Ring Magazine to publish a series of these unsolved riddles, revealing many details which have come to light in recent years, and, in many cases, are available only to this publication.

Standing out pre-eminently in the list of fistic "whodunnits" is the fight in which Jess Willard acquired the heavyweight championship of the world from Jack Johnson in 26 rounds at Havana on Easter Monday, April 5, 1915.

It will be recollected that Johnson acquired the title first by knocking out Tommy Burns, and later by stopping Jim Jeffries, who had retired and then had been persuaded to come back and face Jack at Reno in 1910.

Willard was to lose his championship to Jack Dempsey at Toledo on July 4, 1919, and that fight, too, will have to be included in our series of the Mysteries of the Roped Arena.

Johnson was a 7 to 5 favorite over Willard. In condition, and in earnest, at ease instead of being hounded and harassed and kept out of the United States because of a Mann Act indictment, Jack would have been 4 to 1. But the onetime stevedore from Galveston was a man enveloped in difficulties and worries that hot, sunny afternoon in Havana, and something happened.

## WAS JOHNSON BEATEN
## OR DID HE TAKE A DIVE?

The question is—Was Johnson beaten in a fair and honest fight? Or was it a fake? Did the defending champion do everything he could to retain the title, or did he make a deal to let Willard win, with the understanding that as a non-champion he no longer would be sought by the Federal authorities on the Mann Act indictment?

In the vast majority of the ring "**whodunnits**" the boxing detective is forced to reach conclusions solely from the evidence at hand, without direct support of suspicion from one of the principals.

The Johnson Case, however, finds the suspicion of skullduggery and connivance backed up by Johnson himself.

This would seem to clear up the mystery and leave the fight on the books as a plain phony. But competent ring critics have doubted the authenticity of Johnson's confession. This makes it a double barreled "**whodunnit**" with a multiplicity of embellishments found in no other ring mystery.

According to the story which Johnson gave to Nat

# DID JOHNSON TAKE DIVE?

Fleischer, editor and publisher of The Ring Magazine, who paid $250 to the hardup former champion, he took a dive.

Here is yet another strange facet. Fleischer paid Johnson for a story which he refuses to accept as authentic. He continues to insist that Willard actually was the better man.

## WILLARD WAS NOT IN ON POSSIBLE COLLUSION

However, there are many competent judges of fights who accept Johnson's confession, pitiful as it is, and who are forced to cast a shadow on Willard's title.

Let us hasten to say this—if the fight was a fake, Jess had no knowledge of collusion, no involvement in the plot with Jack Curley and Harry Frazee, theatrical producer and onetime owner of the Red Sox.

According to Johnson's confession, he was to receive $30,000 to quit any time after the tenth round. Those who were putting up the money refused to shell out until they saw Willard the champion, but Jack says he refused to quit until Mrs. Lucille Cameron Johnson, his wife, signalled from the ringside that she had been paid off.

The plotters held off giving the money to Mrs. Johnson because they felt that the longer Jack remained in action the stronger would be the chance of his being stopped on the level.

But when Johnson fought on and got no signal from his wife, he got sore. In the eighteenth or nineteenth round he issued a sound warning to the plotters by wading into Willard and breaking one of his ribs.

This scared the conspirators, who brought the money to Mrs. Johnson at the end of the twenty-second round.

## PICTURE OF BEATEN JACK SHOWS SUSPICIOUS DETAILS

Even those who still insist that there were no suspicious circumstances in the Willard success admit that the picture of Johnson lieing down in that sunbaked ring, his title gone, reveals some peculiar details.

The photograph is reproduced on page 8. Take a good look at it. Does it impress you as being a picture of an unconscious fighter?

In the first place, Johnson's right arm is shielding his eyes from the sun.

In the second place, Johnson's thighs and legs are lifted from the red hot canvas, hardly a reflex.

## FLEISCHER TELLS WHY HE DISBELIEVES FAKERY

Now let us take a look at Fleischer's explanation of his belief that Johnson

was whipped on the level. He says:—

"After Jack Johnson had won the world heavyweight title from Tommy Burns in Sydney, Australia, he became a voluntary exile from his native land. Having become convicted and sentenced to a year in jail for violation of the Mann Act, he forfeited his bail and fled abroad. At the time Johnson twice had been married to white women. An affair with a third white woman got him into a jam with the Federal authorities. He was another victim of the law that had been passed years before to prevent the wholesale transportation of prostitutes from one section of the United States to another.

"While Johnson was a fugitive from justice, the hunt for a "white hope", so long unsuccessfully, came to an end with the discovery of a man from the wide-open spaces, Jess Willard from Pottowatomie, Kansas. Since Johnson could not enter the United States, an arrangement was made by Jack Curley and Harry Frazee to promote the bout at Oriental Park, Havana, home of the Cuban Race Track Association.

The Negro was not knocked senseless, but he failed to rise after being floored in the twenty-sixth round while on his back, one arm thrown across his face as though to shield his eyes from the flaming Cuban sun.

That position while being counted out, gave rise to rumors that he had thrown the fight.

## JOHNSON EXPLAINED HE RATED WILLARD LOW

"Preceding his fight with Willard, Johnson did little training. That aroused considerable concern in his camp. When I purchased his confession, I said:—

"Jack, remember my asking you why you didn't engage in more boxing at your camp in view of your long layoff." You then told me that you didn't think it necessary because of the poor calibre of the opposition you were going to face in Big Jess.

"He laughingly replied: "Yes, I remember, Nat. But the truth is that I didn't engage in much boxing because I had no wish to undergo the ordeal of strict training, knowing as I did that the fight would terminate with me on the losing end by way of a knockout."

"When Johnson reached his hotel in Havana after the fight, he said nothing about the bout being a fake. In fact, in my interview with him at the Palace Hotel he said:

"The heat, the worries I have had, and inactivity, caused me to lose the title. Willard proved the better man today and he won the championship fairly.

"Months later, when he found that Curley couldn't make good his promise to have the United States Government

quash the Mann Act indictment, he cut loose with hot shots at both Curley and Frazee. He accused the pair of double crossing him in getting his consent to fight Willard and asserting that he had been paid a handsome sum to throw the fight.

## FLEISCHER DID IT "IN GOOD OF BOXING"

"At the time, an agent for the "Peoples" of London, in New York, was hot on the story. He informed me of his mission and pleaded with me to obtain the consent of Johnson for the publication of his story in London. Instead, to cut out both him and the "New York Morning World", I decided on a little strategem. I did so with the intention of helping boxing.

"Johnson had borrowed some money from me. I knew he was in financial distress. He had his confession typed and I asked to see it. When I read it, I asked how much he intended to ask for it.

"The "Morning World" is willing to give me $100 and I'll take it, he said.

"If you really are serious about giving out this phoney story," I replied, "I can get you more for it. I'll publish it in "The Ring" and give you $250, but only if you agree to sign away all rights for future publication to me. It may not be used by anyone without my consent," I concluded.

"It's a deal, Nat," he replied. "Write what you want me to sign, and keep the story."

"That's how I got possession of the confession and it has never been used by me or any other publication, though reference to it has been made quite frequently. Now, for the first time, I am releasing the entire confession."

(Above) One the most controversial boxing pictures of all time was taken when Jess Willard knocked out Jack Johnson in twenty-six rounds in Havana on April 15, 1915. *"Did Johnson throw fight to Willard?"* Those who insist he did point to Johnson on the deck protecting his eyes from the sun. (Right) Jack Curley, who promoted the world championship fight and was accused by Johnson of being responsible for his action.

# JACK JOHNSON'S CONFESSION

Exclusive Property of Nat Fleischer, Ring Publisher

THIS confession of mine, is God's honest, Gospel truth. I swear by the Holiness of my Maker and my dear beloved mother, because of whom I consented to face Jess Willard in the ring, that I'm telling the truth and nothing but the truth. The confession that I told you about a week ago, was only half of what I really had to tell but now that you are being so friendly to me, I want to dictate to you the entire story as it should be printed.

I'm tired of being hounded. I accepted Curley's and Frazee's offer to let Willard win by a knockout, because they had promised that I would not be molested any more by the U.S. Government, and that I would be allowed to return home to see my dear, beloved mother—the one thing dearest to my heart. But as soon as Willard won, Curley and Frazee forgot their promise. They made me the goat. Sure, I got paid well for what I did, but they never would have got me to go through with this for any amount of money, had I not believed they would get me out of my difficulties and enable me to go back to my native land.

No one but Curley, Frazee and I knew what arrangements had been made by us. I didn't tell my wife about it until the morning of the fight and then I confided in her and informed her of her part of the plot—the collection of the money still due me, and the signals that would enable me to know that she had been paid in full and that I could let Willard win. I can never forget how sad she was, but she went through with it.

Curley had paid me my fight percentage before I had left the hotel. No one knew the money was there for safe keeping. I told my wife to watch at the ringside and that when I signalled her, she should go to the box office to collect from Curley the remainder of what was due me. Then she was to return and nod to me after which I would finish the plot.

Delay in paying the promised extra money was due to an incomplete count at the box office but at the end of the twenty-fourth round, Mrs. Johnson nodded that all was well and at the end of the twenty-fifth I signalled for her to leave the arena. When I saw her go down the aisle, I decided this was the round to end it, and so it happened.

I was happy when it was all over. I didn't mind losing as I did so long as I knew that the loss would enable me to see my mother. But it didn't. I was double-crossed by the men I had trusted.

During one of my conversations with Curley, he told me, **"Don't you know if you weren't champion you would not have all this trouble?"** I told him that perhaps he was right in saying so. I said to him, What is your idea about the fight with Willard and myself, let me hear from you. He said to me, **"How many rounds do you want to fight Willard."**

I told Curley that the amount of rounds did not matter with me, as I could set the number of rounds, being the champion. I said, **as far as I am concerned it can be 25, 50 or a finish fight.** He said to me. **"Do you think you can go that far."** I said, **if necessary I could go even further. A finish fight is alright with me.**

Then he asked me how much money I wanted. I told

him I wanted all the money I could possibly get. Curley told me that he thought he could collect a lot of money for me and also straighten my affairs with the United States Government if I should win. The next drift of conversation was that of what a great mother I had and how she loved and worshipped me.

He told me that I should see her as soon as possible. All the time I was listening to Curley and thinking to myself, I should see my mother. This night Curley and I was talking, it was in the middle part of the week. I remember telling him that I would pick him up that Saturday. Curley then told me it was necessary that he should come back to the United States very quick because he had two men in the states that would back him, Jack Gleason and Webber.

Anyway, I said, you must wait until Saturday. We met on a Saturday evening and I went to a theatre with him. We talked all through the show on the subject of the Willard-Johnson fight. I did not decide then that I would lose. I did not speak a word even to my wife on the subject. Curley did not leave as was scheduled and we were around together quite a bit. He nursed me like a baby. **He tried to show me all great things that would be done for me after the Willard fight, if Willard was the winner.** He said that, time and time again. Curley did not have much cash then. We talked about expenses etc., and I agreed to pay my own way to wherever the fight was to take place. Curley left London and came to America, and then I started my trip. I had to leave England on a ship bound for Buenos Aires, South America. After I got to South America, I could not cross the Andes Mountains on account of the snow, then I had to turn back from Buenos Aires.

We set sail for Barbados, West Indian Island. Then from there we went to Havana, Cuba. Immediately upon our arrival I cabled Jack Curley, and he cabled me back to stay in Havana and wait for him. I stayed at the Trocadaro Hotel. Curley came over, he told me that I could not get through to Mexico. It was impossible to get through Carranza's soldiers, Pancho Villa was the man that was backing Curley. He, Pancho is the great outlaw of Mexico. He withdrew from the combination, and that left Curley flat at the time being. I opened a bank account in Havana, Cuba, to enable Curley to do some things that he wanted to do and could not do without the cash.

Curley was a cunning fellow, at least, he tried to be. After my working with him and doing most everything that he asked me to do concerning the fight, he tried to double cross me. After the fight was over I was to get a film to take along with me to Europe. He stalled through this session until the day came that I had to sail for Spain, and he tells me the pictures were not finished, and that he would send me a film on the first boat that left New York, or wherever he should be. I waited, and no film came. I went to a certain express company in London. I done a little private detective work myself. The day when Al Weill came to the express office for the films, I was standing behind the post in the express office close to the window in which Al Weill received the films.

As soon as the cashier took his hands off of the films, and Weill had them in his hands, I certainly grabbed the films and said. "These are mine." Weill said "Nothing doing you cannot do that." And I said "Well I did it, and I am going to keep them," meaning the films. Then Weill went to see his lawyers, and I went to see my lawyers, which was myself, and I sold the rights and the film to Jack Mailer. The lawyers tried to prohibit me from selling them but I had the lead on them and I sold them to Mailer. Then I put the films out on commission in England. This was a negative that I snatched from Weill in the express office. That is how I got the films.

I was to get so much of Willard's earnings, because after the fight I had to take it on the cuff from Frazee and Curley because if they paid me the lump sum, they didn't have any cash left. So, therefore, I trusted them to send me a certain percentage of Willard's earnings, and if I was not smart enough to get the cash money, I would have been up against it for payment. I was to have lost after the 10th round, namely the 11th.

**I fought on for a couple of rounds then I said to them if they didn't come through quick, I was going to do my best to win the fight. So that stalled for a couple of rounds, and they was counting the money, they had an idea in their heads that after 12 rounds Willard might accidentally wear me down, but not so. About the 18th or 19th round I gave a couple of hard punches breaking one of his ribs, and then about the 22nd round everything was O. K. and I gave my wife a nod, and she went out of the arena.**

**After she left I began to feel happy and glad, believing I was going to see my mother again, and that Curley would arrange and fix matters for me.**

I did not tell my wife just what I was going to do until the morning of the fight. I can never forget how sad she was, and how she cried and didn't want things to go that way.

I told her it was best for all concerned, because I had been framed in America, and Curley would fix and arrange everything so that I could come back home. It was a drama, a very sad drama for some, a very happy drama for me at the moment, knowing that I would not be tantalized and pushed about after the championship had left me.

Never mind what Curley may say in the future, but he arranged for Johnson to lose the fight. I always know I lost to a man that could not beat me. There are many people that say when one is traveling abroad in Europe and can come home any time he likes, he may never wish to come home when he is free to come.

But when you are not free to go home, you are always wanting to go back to your home. That feeling goes with the most quiet man, and also the most desperate man, when he can't do as he wants to. Jack Curley never proved to be a genuine sport. I have read different articles in magazines where he said horrible things against me.

I have often wondered if he has forgotten the $5000 I let him take in Las Vegas. At the time, we were in Mexico with this writer, if I could only mention his name without causing a disturbance. That same writer once wrote a story telling the public how kind I was to my friends, because he lived in the camp we me, saw me at all times, and he knows just how kind I was to every human being. I still say that I lost through pressure to a man who could not beat me."

*once wrote a story telling the public how kind I was to my friends, because he lived in the camp with me, saw me at all times, and he knows just how kind I was to every human being. I still say that I lost through pressure to a man who could not beat me.*

*This is a true account of what happened in my fight with Jess. Willard. I put the blame just it belongs. yours truly*
*Former Champion*
*Jan—27—1916    Jack Johnson*

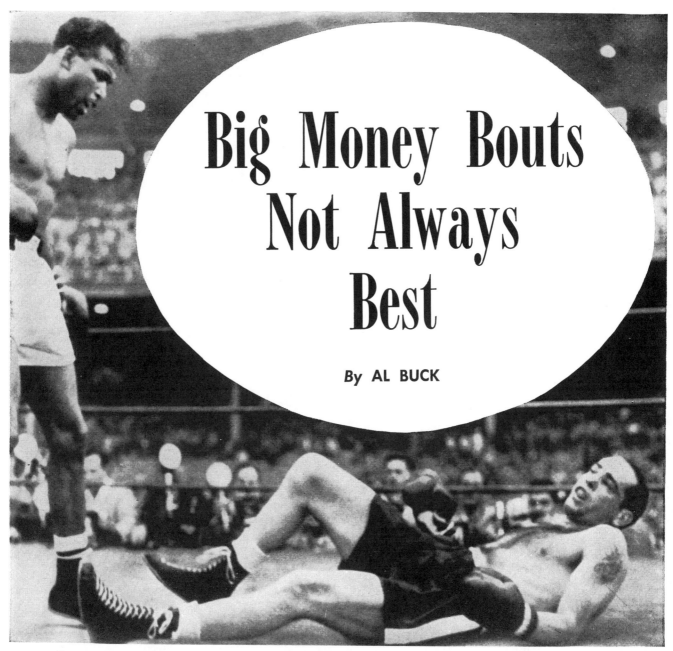

# Big Money Bouts Not Always Best

### By AL BUCK

The largest gate of 1956 was paid by the loyal California following of Bobo Olson. However, they were disappointed as Bobo was kayoed in four rounds by Ray Robinson in a rather tame fight.

EVEN in the electronic age a gate exceeding $100,000 is common in boxing. Five fights last year, four of which involved world titles, touched six figures, and two of these exceeded $200,000. What was there about these contests that lured the customers to the box office? What sold 'em, and once in the area did the fans get value received for their money?

Boxing is an ancient sport. These questions could have been asked 10 or even 20 years ago. Today television sponsors must ask themselves the same questions as they pay fees ranging from $30,000 to $200,000 to bring both a fight and their products into your living room.

The largest gate last year was $233,456 paid to see Sugar Ray Robinson score a quick knockout over Bobo Olson in defense of the middleweight title at Wrigley Field, Los Angeles. The fight, as seen in the ring, wasn't worth that kind of money. Neither was the $100,000 kicked in by the sponsor.

Why then did they buy? There are a number of answers to the question.

First a title fight in Los Angeles was a novelty. Second there was a TV blackout over a 100 mile radius. Robinson's exciting comeback, when he knocked out Olson to regain the title in Chicago captured the public's imagination, and in California Bobo was still a local hero. The Hollywood American Legion Stadium, associated with the International Boxing Club, gave the show a great promotion.

For days prior to the fight little else appeared on the sports pages of the Los Angeles newspapers. The build-up drew the fans. Olson stayed around for four rounds. It wasn't a $200,000 fight. I'm sure Eddie Leonard, Hollywood matchmaker, has put on many better ones at the weekly shows in the Legion Stadium.

Going back to the Golden Age, Tex Rickard was the master of ballyhoo. Rickard had the imagination to see Georges Carpentier, war hero of France, but only a middleweight, as an opponent for Jack Dempsey in a world heavyweight title fight. He had a plan too. First Carpentier was to fight King Levinsky for the world light-heavyweight title. When Georges knocked out Levinsky in four rounds Tex signed him to fight Dempsey.

Rickard gambled again in building a huge wooden bowl in Jersey City that was known as Boyle's 30 Acres. Then came the slogan: "*The Battle of the Century.*" The result was boxing's first million dollar gate, $1,895,733 to be exact.

Was it worth the money? Yes, if only for the right hand that staggered Dempsey in the second round. The year was 1921, and Georges was the popular favorite. He crumbled in the fourth round. As a spectacle the Dempsey-Carpentier show is hard to beat. The ring has had few more dramatic moments.

Rickard's greatest promotion, the second Gene Tunney-Jack Dempsey bout at Chicago, drew the record gate, $2,658,660. By Illinois law the bout was limited to 10 rounds, but it will be remembered for the 14-second long count, brought on by Dempsey's refusal to go to a neutral corner after knocking Tunney down. Later Gene dropped Jack to his knees. After it was over the customers had something to talk about. In fact people are still talking. The fans got full value.

Getting back to present day activities neither Floyd Patterson nor Archie Moore was champion when they fought for the heavyweight title in Chicago last November. The throne had been vacated by Rocky Marciano, and yet the TV sponsor paid $200,000 to put the two contenders on the air. Why?

One reason for the high fee was the fact no heavyweight title fight had been on television since 1953 when Marciano knocked out Jersey Joe Walcott in the first round. Marciano always insisted on theatre network TV, feeling that so called home television would kill the gate. In addition to paying $200,000, the sponsor also agreed to black out the Chicago area.

The result was a gate of $233,456, second largest of 1956. The fight went five rounds, ending with Patterson knocking out Ancient Archie to be crowned world heavyweight champion. Did the customers get what they paid for? Those in the Chicago Stadium did. Patterson's speed was the deciding factor after he had taken Moore's best punch, a right to the jaw, in the first round.

Obviously the fight lost something in transmission. Judging from the questions I've been asked and the comments I have heard the TV audience was not impressed. If this is so, the sponsor got less than what he paid for, but of course there was the prestige of telecasting the first heavyweight title fight in more than three years.

The situation that existed when Marciano retired was similar to the one created by Gene Tunney's retirement. The year 1930 brought Jack Sharkey and Max Schmeling together for the world heavyweight championship at the Yankee Stadium. There was $749,935 in the box office when Sharkey, with the American flag drapped over his shoulders, was booed as he climbed into the ring.

Sharkey was a picture fighter that night. For three rounds he was the German's master. Suddenly in the fourth round Jack hooked low and Schmeling went down. Joe Jacobs, Max's manager, was in the ring shouting "*foul.*" Referee Jim Crowley hesitated and then appealed to the judges. Judge Charley Mathison hadn't seen the punch. Judge Harold Barnes had and called it. Schmeling was declared heavyweight champion on a foul.

The result left a sour taste. The fans felt they had been cheated. Sharkey's low left was a factor in Commissioner Jim Farley installing the "no foul" rule. Now all boxers are required to wear foul-proof protectors. This rule alone was worth the money spent to see Schmeling win the title while on the canvas.

There have been times when the fans have been given a bargain. Such an occasion was the Italian Hospital Fund show promoted by Humbert J. Fugazy at the Yankee Sta-

TV's Darlin' Chuck Davey drew a packed house to see him battle Kid Gavilan for The Keed's 147 pound title back in 1953. Gavilan toyed with Chuck for a few rounds then went to work and stopped him in the tenth.

After the thrill-packed Philadelphia fight, a large crowd turned out for the second Marciano-Walcott go. Rocky ended matters with one punch to the dismay of the fans.

The large turn out for the all star Italian Relief show in 1925 got their money's worth as Dave Shade kayoed Jimmy Slattery (above) in a big upset. On the same card the great Harry Greb vs Mickey Walker duel took place in which Greb gave the "Toy Bulldog" a licking.

## ARUBA, N.W.I. RING NEWS
### By Jimmy Lambert

**Although many local fight fans expected Sugar Boy Nando,** 152, Aruba, to defeat Jimmy Ford, 147, Nassau, in the main 10-round event at the Swingsters Square Garden, they were surprised to see the easy manner in which Nando swarmed all over Jimmy to win the unanimous decision.

In the 8-round semi-final which was fought in a tropical rainstorm, Young Quick Silver, 153, Aruba, fought gamely for the first part of the bout but faded during the last half with the result that Kid Fenton, 152, Aruba, came from behind to win a very close decision.

Buddy Baer, 153, St. Martin, gained a 6-round decision easily over Kid Colorado, 153, Curacao. Kid Telefonito, 143, Aruba, won a close decision over El Negrito del Batey, 147, Aruba, in another 6-rounder, and Kid Godoy, 123, Colombia, easily defeated Kid Spider, 126, Aruba, in a 4-rounder.

## PITTSBURGH PUNCHES
### By Mickey Davies

**Arnold (Pa.) High School Gym—Before a packed house, young Garvan Sawyer** of Cincinnati, Tom Tannas' new heavyweight aspirant, on the brink of getting stretched himself, came roaring back to knock out big Embrel Davidson of Detroit. The finish came in the fifth frame. This marked Sawyer's tenth fight, of which he has won nine.

Felix Antonio, 173, Dayton, beat Emil Brtko, 199, Pittsburgh, six rounds. Art Mayorga, 217, edged Frankie Williams, 192, six rounds. Johnny Morris, 162, Pittsburgh, stopped Skippy Green, 160, Pittsburgh (I) Eugene Tippett, 144, McKeesport, won six round decision over Willie Epps 142, Youngstown.

Alonzo Johnson, 180, Rankin, scored a TKO over Tony Sinibaldi, Youngstown in the second round.

## LEFT HOOKS FROM SCRANTON AND VICINITY
### By Kenneth (Duke) Stigner

**On one of the coldest nights of the year, more than 700 fans braved the snow** storm to witness the second slam bang amateur card at Wilkes-Barre's Grananda Ballroom, in which a pair of highly-touted ring generals met defeat. The unexpected losers were Stanley "Corkey" Seigal, Pottsville and Joe "Doc" Vosefski of Carbondale.

In the feature attraction, a five rounder, Vosefski was matched against Frank Dudley, Wilkes-Barre YMCA, and in the second heat Dudley found the range, dropped Vosefski for a two count with a left hook, and pounded "Doc" with rights and lefts until he sank to the canvas. Vosefski got up at the count of eight, but the referee stopped the bout.

In the semi windup "Corkey" Seigal, a welterweight, three times fleet champion in the Navy and a couple of times the Middle Atlantic champion in the AAU, was defeated by Zaleski.

In the 160-pound class Mike Lucas, Pottsville YMCA, lost to Herbert White of the South Side Boys' Club, Philly, on a TKO in the second round. Ray Burke, Pottsville gained a second round TKO over George Smith, Schuylkill.

Leo Rindgen, Newtown Boys' Club lost an unanimous decision to George Washington. They are in the 147-pound division.

Dave Coates, Pottsville, took on Walter Smith of the Newtown Boys' Club in a pier six brawl, Coates winning. Frank Russo, featherweight, took a popular decision over Robert Johnson of the South Branch "Y" Philadelphia.

▶ The Veterans Professional Boxing Association of Lackawanna elected the following officers for the year: Tom Joseps, President; Jack Downy, Vice-president; Sonny Genell, Secretary; Joe Rabiego, Treasurer; Billy Palumbo, Ty Coleman, Billy Pollock; Mickey Barron and Al Jackson, board of directors. Mickey Barron, long a regional favorite will be in charge of boxing at the Ukrainian Center. . . . Amateur boxing is going over big at Binghamton, N. Y. and Endicott-Johnson City. . . . Write me 109 Robinson St., Chinchilla, Pa.

How much rest can a fighter take before Ring Rust sets in? Read the May RING.

## BIG MONEY BOUTS NOT ALWAYS BEST

dium in 1925. The top attraction was the Harry Greb-Mickey Walker middleweight title fight. Mickey was welterweight champion at the time. The decision went to Greb after 15 rounds of terrific, and at times sensational fighting.

For an opener Promoter Fugazy had Joe Lynch, former bantamweight champion, and little Jack Sharkey in a four round bout. The decision was a draw. On the same card Harry Wills, then No. 1 heavyweight contender, knocked out clever Charley Weinert in two rounds, but the big surprise was the two round knockout scored by Dave Shade over the then promising Jimmy Slattery. A slam-bang evening and worth the $339,040 contributed by the cash customers.

Another bargain was the Carnival of Champions promoted by Mike Jacobs in 1937. It grossed $232,644, and while four title bouts were on the card it was a dull evening. Even the gate was disappointing. The only good fight was Barney Ross defending the welterweight title against Ceferino Garcia. With his right hand broken Barney came from behind to win. Lou Ambers was content to box and play it safe to win from Pedro Montanez in defense of the lightweight title. The bantamweight bout went all the way too with Harry Jeffra winning the crown from Sixto Escobar. Fred Apostoli cut up Marcel Thil and stopped the veteran Frenchman in the 10th round.

Apostoli and Thil were supposed to be fighting for the middleweight championship, but Gen. John J. Phelan, chairman of the N. Y. Commission, refused to give the contest formal recognition. The 55 rounds fought bored the fans, but the fact that four champions were on the card impressed the Madison Square Garden directors. They fired James J. Johnston as promoter and took in Jacobs as a partner.

Joe Louis received a big build-up before he was brought into New York to fight Primo Carnera, but Bomber Joe was always worth what people paid to see him. Jacobs took a train load of New York sports writers to Detroit to see the young wonder of the west against Natie Brown. Natie refused to cooperate, and the fight went the 10 rounds. That was the tip-off. No tankers were numbered among Louis' opponents. He never required them to wear handcuffs.

The second Louis-Max Schmeling bout, grossing $1,015,012, lasted less than a round, but the fans were more than satisfied. Louis was at his peak that night. He was over the hill after

four years in the Army when he fought Billy Conn a second time. So was Conn, but the match had been a long time in building.

During the war years when anybody, even two stray dogs, could draw $100,000 at the Garden, the fans talked of Louis and Conn meeting again. Billy was leading going into the 13th round of their first fight when Louis knocked him out. That was in 1941. Five years had elapsed since then and when they fought again. Conn had lost much of his speed, but Louis could still punch. The knockout came in the eighth round.

The howl that went up was to be expected. Jacobs charged $100 for a ringside seat, and the take was $1,925,564, second highest in boxing history. Congressmen made speeches about the $100 tab, but the fight wasn't that bad. You might call it ordinary, and that was the trouble. The fans felt like suckers.

Big gates mean big crowds and only a big fight will draw the customers and cash. The fact Sugar Ray Robinson lost the middleweight title to Randy Turpin in London was enough to pack the Polo Grounds for the return bout. For reasons not easy to explain an international flavor always sweetens the gate. Turpin and Sugar Ray packed 'em in. The gate was $767,625, largest ever drawn except for a heavyweight fight.

The thrill came in the 10th when Robinson badly cut, realized he would have to win quickly. Sugar Ray didn't hesitate. He turned it on. In a matter of seconds Randy was limp and helpless against the ropes. Referee Ruby Goldstein called a halt, and Robinson was champion again. The fans felt well rewarded as they started for the exits.

The same can't be said for those who paid $274,451 to see Kid Gavilan slaughter Chuck Davey in the Chicago Stadium. Davey, a southpaw, had been built-up on TV. Few thought he could fight, but the video public was convinced Chuck was a champion in the making. Gavilan changed their minds. He played with Davey, waiting until the 10th to finish the job.

Other fights in '56 that drew better than $100,000 were Moore and James J. Parker at Toronto, a formal black tie affair promoted by England's Jack Solomons, and the two Carmen Basilio-Johnny Saxton bouts, one in Chicago and the other in Syracuse. Already Robinson and Gene Fullmer, fighting at the Garden in January have topped $100,000. These were good, though hardly great fights. I've seen as good, and sometimes better ones on Monday nights at the St. Nick.

# KNACK FOR NICKNAMING

## Jennings, Runyon, Igoe Excel at Taglining

### By TED CARROLL

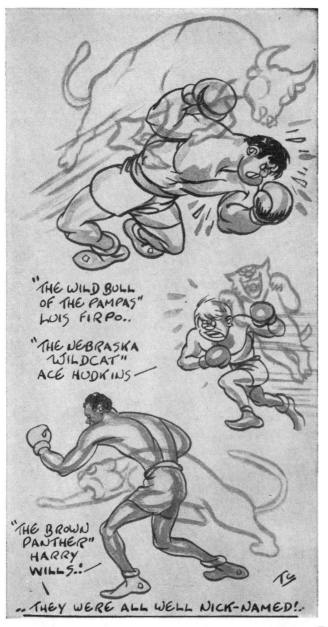

"THE WILD BULL OF THE PAMPAS" LUIS FIRPO..

"THE NEBRASKA WILDCAT" ACE HUDKINS —

"THE BROWN PANTHER" HARRY WILLS..!

.. THEY WERE ALL WELL NICK-NAMED!..

A FEW months ago columnist Bill Corum of the N. Y. Journal-American decided that the time had come to give current heavyweight champion Floyd Patterson, a nickname. Major Bill asked his readers for suggestions and after all the returns were in, who should bob up as the winner of the naming contest, but ex-lightweight king, Ike Williams, whose brainchild **"The Young Master"** struck Mr. Corum's fancy. To say that the name of Floyd Patterson has now become synonymous with Ike's selection, would be a little less than accurate. In fact, it is understood that Mr. Corum is still in the market for a nickname for Patterson that will stick.

Nicknames are funny things, they are as much a part of boxing as the gloves or the ring. They date back to bare-knuckle times when such identifications as "The Benecia Boy" and the **"Tipton Slasher"** were applied to ancient battlers. Why some nicknames gain such rapid popular favor, leaving an indelible imprint, has always been most intriguing.

Why, for example, should his fellow townsmen in Cincinnati call former world heavyweight champion Ezzard Charles, **"Snocks"**?

Who first tagged Ray Robinson, **"Sugar Ray"**? A nickname of such fame it has been translated into the French "le sucre" and anglicized into "His Sugarship" in Merrie England.

Who first referred to Joe Louis as the **"Brown Bomber"**?

And what would be wrong with referring to the agile, atomic age, Patterson as the **"Jet Bomber"**?

The late Damon Runyon, who had a flair for that sort of thing, is generally credited with coining the cognomen **"Manassa Mauler"** in describing Jack Dempsey. The tagline **"Toy Bulldog"** he hung upon Mickey Walker, still brings a glow of satisfaction to ailing Francis Albertanti, in the dreary confines of his hospital room. Jim Jennings of the N. Y. Mirror is usually given the call as having first tabbed Rocky Marciano **"The Brockton Blockbuster"** although there are other claimants.

No fighter was ever more aptly nicknamed than old Ace Hudkins, **"The Nebraska Wildcat"** of the Roaring Twenties. This colorful appellation perfectly described the clawing, cantankerous, wild and wooly westerner.

Although a native of Schenectady, N. Y. which is a long way from Fargo, North Dakota, Billy Petrolle became famous as the **"Fargo Express."**

A half century ago **"Brooklyn Tommy"** Sullivan belied his nickname by hailing from St. Louis, Mo.

Old George Godfrey came from way down in Georgia, but because his manager, Jim Dougherty was nationally known as the **"Baron of Leipersville, Pa.,"** Godfrey automatically became the **"Dark Shadow of Leiperville."**

In his younger days, old Harry Wills had not only the coloration, but the sleek movements and lithe, powerful physique of a jungle cat. So it was as **"The Brown Panther of New Orleans"** that he became known to a generation of fight fans.

It was inevitable that massive, charging Luis Angel Firpo would be called **"The Wild Bull of the Pampas."** The late Hype Igoe is said to have been the first to note the resemblance, and so describe the shaggy-haired Argentinian.

To Sid Terris, old time lightweight star, go the alliterative honors. Sid was known as the **"Galloping Ghost of the Ghetto."** His great rival for neighborhood affections, Ruby Goldstein, was the **"Ghetto Jewel."**

The late great, cartoonist-writer T. A. "Tad" Dorgan, dubbed Joe Gans **"The Old Master"** more than fifty years ago. Tad also called big Jack Johnson **"Lil' Artha"** after the ex-heavy king's middle name, and this proved popular for a long time.

There have been two "phantoms" of great reputation, the late Mike Gibbons **"The St. Paul Phantom"** and Tommy Loughran **"The Phantom of Philly."**

Being of Jewish parentage and a native of New York's East Side didn't prevent old time featherweight Benny Valgar from being called **"The French Flash"** thirty-five years ago.

For many years, Young Stribling was known as the **"Georgia Schoolboy"** until Jim Jennings, who also has a knack for nicknaming, sadly observing Strib's safety-first tactics in a fight with Paul Berlenbach, called him **"Willie-the-Clutch."** Unfortunately for him, this phrase soon supplanted Stribling's earlier nickname.

In the later part of the 19th century, such appellations, as **"The Boston Strong Boy"** for John L. Sullivan, **"Gentleman Jim"** for James J. Corbett, and **"Terrible Terry"** for Terry M'Govern, were household words.

..FROM NOW ON.. YOU'RE THE TOY BULLDOG!

MICKEY WALKER     FRANCIS ALBERTANTI

George Dixon was widely known as **"Little Chocolate"** although his complexion was more cafe-au-lait in tintage. The name **"Gentleman Jim"** fitted Corbett's general appearance and dress, but was hardly consistent with the bitter feuds the clever Californian carried on with his rivals.

One of the unsolved mysteries of the boxing game has been the immunity of some fistic greats to "nom-de-guerres." The late, great Benny Leonard was always just plain Benny Leonard, Gene Tunney, Barney Ross, and Tony Canzoneri were others in the same boat. Willie Pep was occasionally called **"Willie the Wisp"** but never consistently or universally.

Although they were among the most famous in boxing, such nicknames as the **"Scotch Wop"** for Johnny Dundee—and the **"Boston Tar Baby"** for Sam Langford are no longer socially acceptable or even printable in many quarters.

The late great columnist W. O. M'Geehan, tagged eccentric Battling Siki **"The Singular Senegalese."** A long time ago columnist Joe Williams called Maxie Rosenbloom the **"Harlem Harlequin"** but this artistic designation soon deteriorated into the more familiar **"Slapsie Maxie"**—another Jennings contribution to the boxing glossary.

Not all the identifications which attach themselves to fighters can be called complimentary, **"Willie-the-Clutch"** certainly wasn't, and sensitive Tommy Loughran was keenly hurt when M'Geehan took to tagging him **"Tanglefoot Tommy"** years ago, the descriptive **"Brooklyn Billygoat"** does not make Paddy De Marco happy, and ex-heavyweight champ Boston Jack Sharkey, reserved his sternest stares for writers who called him the **"Gabby Gob."**

Although he's now flirting with the half century mark,

Jimmy McLarnin is still **"Baby Face"** when he is recognized by old admirers or makes a public appearance.

He antedated the atomic age, but the great British flyweight, Jimmy Wilde, was tagged **"England's Mighty Atom"** by a prophetic admirer years ago.

Old time Negro boxers really went in for fancy nomenclature, quite often giving themselves these odd sounding nicknames. Such fantastic titles as **"The Harlem Coffee Cooler"** (Frank Craig), **"The Trenton Tea Warmer"** (George Cole), **"Kentucky Rosebud"** (Walter Edgerton), **"Birdlegs"** Collins, **"Klondike"** and **"Steamboat Bill"** Scott were typical of the names in which the boys took great pride.

There are two prominent "assassins" in the Ring Record Book, Stanley Ketchel **"The Michigan Assassin"** and the **"Astoria Assassin"** of the Twenties, Paul Berlenbach.

Maxie Baer had so many nicknames **"Livermore Larruper,"** **"Madcap Maxie"** etc., none of them really took hold. The same thing goes for Primo Carnera who was called **"Da Preem"** **"The Ambling Alp"**, among many of them occurring to imaginative writers of the time.

The fragile appearance of good looking Georges Carpentier so impressed an observer of years ago, and the contrast between **"Gorgeous Georges"** and the rugged ringmen of his time was so pronounced, that this writer likened the Frenchman to an orchid in a thorny thicket. From that time on, Georges Carpentier was known as **"The Orchid Man."**

The coal black hair and beetling brows of Max Schmeling, caused U. S. scribes to stamp him **"The Black Uhlan"** when he first showed up in the States.

Nicknaming tendencies among the fourth estate to-day, are but a shadow of what they were in the more romantic unsophisticated early years of this century, but it is a custom which will never entirely disappear. Few fight fans know or care that Tommy is the real first name of **"Hurricane"** Jackson. Teddy Brenner, promoter of the New York Sporting Club tagged Tommy with that one. With the exception of **"Sugar Ray"** this is the most widely recognized nickname in the ring today. Yama Bahama is a name worthy of inclusion among the most fantastic of all times, as is that of **"Tombstone"** Smith, west coast fighter. **"Cyclone"** is becoming more and more a part of Gene Fullmer's identification, another Brenner brainstorm, and the catchy **"Shasta Blaster"** tacked on Eddie Machen by Nat Loubet, managing editor of the Ring.

Boxing is a colorful business, and with that in mind, the more nicknames the merrier.

I CALL HIM THE OLD MASTER!

JOE GANS

"TAD"

# They Wouldn't Stay Down

Knocked out by Bobby Boyd at St. Nicholas Arena, this appeared to be the end of Tony Anthony's ring ambitions. But Tony refused to become discouraged and today is considered almost certain light-heavyweight champion.

## Great Fighters Refused to Become Discouraged by Defeat

### By JERSEY JONES

Joe Louis on one of his many trips to canvas before being knocked out by Max Schmeling. Another who refused to become discouraged, Louis went on to win heavyweight title and annihilate Schmeling in return match.

ALONG about 10:25 p.m. on August 1, 1955, a discouraged Ernie Braca probably would have been willing to peddle his managerial interest in Tony Anthony for a cancelled two-cent postage stamp.

Anthony had just been flattened in the third round by Bobby Boyd at the St. Nicholas Arena. It's no disgrace for any fighter to be knocked out, but it was the fourth time it had happened to Tony in twenty-eight professional starts, and by now Braca wondered if it could be developing into a habit.

That was less than two years ago. Today it is doubtful if anything less than an outright gift of the Empire State Building would induce an enthusiastic Braca to consider parting with the stylish young Harlemite.

The "chump" of 1955 shapes up as a "champ" of 1957. Not only does Anthony seem almost certain to annex the light-heavyweight title before the current year runs its allotted course, but he looms as a strong future contender for heavyweight laurels.

At the comparatively youthful age of 22, Anthony is one of the finest fighting machines in the ring. He has speed, skill and a pair of sharpshooting fists, while increasing weight has given him strength and ruggedness and an impressive string of wins has loaded him with confidence.

Tony is one fighter who learned to shake off the effects of discouraging early setbacks, and to learn and profit from them.

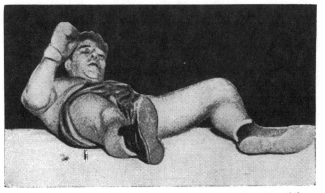

(Above)—Mickey Walker, flattened in one round by K.O. Phil Delmont, went on to win two titles and become strong contender for two others.
(Left)—Tiger Flowers was knocked out eight times before winning middleweight title. Here he is seen being polished off by Jack Delaney in old Madison Square Garden.

The most crucial stage of any ambitious young fighter's ring career is when he is overtaken by disaster. How he rebounds from it can often determine the success or failure of future operations.

Many a promising youngster has been ruined by one stunning setback. He has become so accustomed to winning that when he crashes into sudden, unexpected defeat, he doesn't know how to accept it. Instead of trying to benefit from bitter experience, he loses confidence in himself, and without confidence no ringster can expect to travel very far in his quest for glory.

The ability to take the bitter with the sweet is an important item in the psychological equipment of a young fighter. Boxing is a rugged give-and-take trade, and an aspiring hopeful must be prepared to absorb a few unpleasant jolts along the way if he expects eventually to be a success.

Check through the records of the ring's all-time greats, and you'll find that most of them had to overcome discouraging setbacks early in their careers.

Benny Leonard was a notable case. Before he was 17, Benny had been knocked out by Frankie Fleming and Joe Shugrue. Had Leonard quit the ring, deciding it was too rough for him, his action would have been understandable. But Benny refused to become disheartened. If anything, those defeats served as added fuel to the fires of his determination. Realizing he didn't have the strength or ruggedness for slugging, Leonard concentrated on developing speed and skill. He became one of the finest mechanics the ring ever has known—a brilliant boxer, deadly sharpshooter and shrewd strategist. Benny was world lightweight champion at 21, and still champion seven and a half years later when he announced his retirement.

No fighter had more discouraging early years than Jack Johnson, but the burly Galveston ex-stevedore went on to become what many veteran authorities regard as the No. 1 heavyweight champion of all time.

Then there was Theodore (Tiger) Flowers, the Georgia southpaw, who was knocked out EIGHT times before he became world middleweight champion.

His first amateur bout should have been enough for Joe Louis. Opposed to a Johnny Miler in Detroit, Shufflin' Joe must have thought he was sponsored by the Otis Elevator Company. He spent most of the three rounds going down and getting up. He was on the canvas seven times! Then, a few years later, as a professional,

there was the gosh-awful lacing Max Schmeling tossed into him before knocking him out in their first meeting in New York's Yankee Stadium. Many witnesses that night predicted that Louis never would recover from that demoralizing defeat. But history records that Joe went on to win the world heavyweight title a year later, and the following year annihilated Schmeling in one devastating round in their return meeting in the Stadium.

Jersey Joe Walcott was another case of persistency paying off for a fighter. There certainly was nothing in Pappy Joe's early record to indicate that he'd ever rise above the mediocre in the fistic scale. He was knocked out at least three times—by Al Ettore, Tiger Jack Fox and Abe Simon. Yet Walcott kept plugging along and eventually earned two cracks at Louis for the title. Loser on a disputed decision in their first bout in Madison Square Garden, he was knocked out by the Bomber in their return match in Yankee Stadium. Walcott still wasn't finished. Beaten twice in title matches by Louis' sucessor, Ezzard Charles, first in Chicago, then in Detroit, he finally scored on the third try when he knocked Charles out in a surprising upset in Pittsburgh.

The fight that actually started Gene Tunney on his drive to the heavyweight title was the only bout he ever lost. Gene wasn't knocked out but he absorbed such a brutal lacing from Harry Greb in their first meeting in old Madison Square Garden that it would have created no surprise if he had announced his retirement from the ring. Rather than discourage him, however, that vicious shellacking only served to rouse Tunney's fighting spirit and determination. In his dressing room after the bout Gene, through torn, bleeding lips, demanded another bout with Greb. "I know I can beat him," he said. He did—not once but four times.

It's all of thirty-eight years ago, but we still recall vividly the disastrous experience of a promising Irish kid in Elizabeth, N. J., in 1919. Then scaling around 130 pounds, he'd been fighting about six months and was becoming something of a local sensation. This night his opponent reported ill and was replaced by a substitute rushed over from New York. The substitute, Phil Delmont, was fighting his first professional bout, and the Elizabeth citizenry, not knowing anything about him, figured him a soft touch for their latest favorite. But something miscalculated, and in one round the local entry was spread out, unconscious, on the canvas. It was a catastrophe to the youthful Elizabethan, but it didn't discourage him from continuing his ring career. He went on to win two world titles—welterweight and middleweight—and become a strong contender for two others—light-heavyweight and heavyweight. He was Mickey Walker.

# PROMOTING IS RISKY BUSINESS

## By JOHNNY SALAK

YOU'VE got to spend a million bucks to put on a million dollar fight and the margin of profit, if any, is based on too many ifs, ands and buts to make life a pleasant stroll down to a ringside seat.

In our quest for information on the take-home pay of a big-time fight promoter this discouraging news came to light. After investing a hog-sized bankroll in such a production a promoter still must have luck riding with him all the way to make a big killing and more often than not he will breathe more easily when all the bills have been paid and he has broken even.

The Ray Robinson-Carmen Basilio world middleweight title bout at Yankee Stadium, New York, on September 23 is one of the biggest and most appealing fights in years. Between the actual receipts and revenue from theatre-TV the fight featuring two world champions should go over the million dollar mark.

What does the promoter hope to clear on this? He only shakes his head and says "See me after the fight. But I'll tell you one thing now. Whatever it is, if anything, it will be much less than most people suppose."

And he had figures to prove his point. A whole mess of fistic, financial and fiscal reports and statements on the Rocky Marciano-Archie Moore fight at the Yankee Stadium in 1955.

"That was the last big fight," he said. "Between the ticket sales, the radio rights and the theatre-TV revenue the fight did better than one and a quarter million dollars. We cleared about $97,000. But remember, we had everything going for us and we got all the breaks. There was a one day postponement but it helped us and the weather was right, theatre-TV, still pretty much in the experimental stages, did a fantastic gross in the movie houses and drive-ins throughout the country, Rocky Marciano was always a

splendid drawing attraction and Archie Moore did an incredible job of selling himself. Everything was ideal and yet one bad break along the way and that hundred grand profit could have been wiped out."

There are two things which will stun a promoter into icy silence. One is talk by a fighter of a guarantee. The other is talk by the weatherman of the threat of rain on the night of a fight. Not rain. Just the threat of it. If it rains and the fight is postponed you've got a fighting chance. But if it just looks as if it might get uncomfortable, hordes of potential ticket buyers won't venture out.

### ROBINSON-BASILIO GET 65%

For the middleweight title bout, Robinson is getting 45%, Basilio 20%, a combined total higher than that usually allowed. But it is safer than a guarantee. By way of example, Floyd Patterson, defending his title against Tommy Jackson for Emil Lence, had a guarantee of $175,000. It broke the back of the promotion and sent it into the losing side of the ledger. Cus D'Amato, Floyd's manager, benevolently kicked back $50,000 which, despite reports of making a $20,000 profit for Lence, probably saw him break even. Again, Patterson had a guarantee of $250,000 against Pete Rademacher in Seattle, Wash. It is doubtful that, under the conditions, the promotion could make a profit.

The public is familiar with the set of figures usually released to the newspapers after a big fight, which give the gross receipts, federal tax, net receipts, the share received by each fighter, the rental of the arena and what, ostensibly, is the promoter's profit.

But there are scores of expenses involved that never see

their way into print, some of which seem astonishingly high and yet are very real.

Taking the Marciano-Moore fight, the gross receipts from ticket sales came to $947,927.95. Federal tax immediately lopped off $83,298.09, which left net receipts at $864,629.86.

Add to that the radio broadcasting rights which brought in $35,000, theatre-TV swelling the receipts by $282,461.75 and service fees bringing in $9,608.66. The total income became $1,191,700.27.

Now we come to direct expenses! New York State receipts tax came to $59,732.60 and New York City receipts tax $2,979.25. Compensation for boxers saw the two main event fighters take a total of $672,373.22 and the preliminaries costing $11,150, with travel and training allowance eating up $511.90. There is usually another expense for stand-by boxers which comes to about $1,000. In this case it was unnecessary and there was no cost involved.

Next comes the payment by the promoters to the ring officials, referees, judges, deputies, etc., etc., etc. It totalled $1,612.

The special force personnel needed at Yankee Stadium

See all those chairs? They were erected for a recent outdoor fight at the Yankee Stadium in New York. The cost was $1 per chair. Count them . . . just another small expense.

that night, ushers, ticket sellers and takers, policing, etc., cost $13,159.40.

For preparation and cleaning up of the ballpark after the fight the figure came to an astonishingly $51,200.01. Depreciation on the outdoor ring used was $1,732.85.

Rental of the Stadium took a huge bite of $85,416.74. For the erection of the theatre-TV stand, where the cameras were mounted, a bill for $527.88 came in. The commentator cost $500.

Publicity and advertising is a major item in any big fight and for this one the amount of $59,861.68 was disbursed.

Printing of the tickets ran to $6,330.38. The boxing license and bond cost $275. Payroll taxes came to $8.06. Boxers' insurance was an even $80, while compensation insurance totalled $29.02. Along the same line, outdoor ring and equipment insurance was $192.50 and public liability insurance ran the promoter a check for $4,750. Travel expense for the management cost $5,356.67.

A color film of the fight cost $754.99 and general expenses were listed as $10,960.16. The boxing department salaries and expenses of the I. B. C. took $7,500.

The participation co-promoter of the fight, the Chicago Stadium Corporation came in for $97,352.98.

Totalling all the above items, we find that the direct expense involved in promoting the fight came to $1,094,-347.29, with the direct profit a modest $97,352.98, less

Here we see electricians putting the finishing touches to the ring lights. Cost of erecting the ring and working press, seen in this photo, and then dismantling after the fight cost $5,199, a small part of a promoter's expense.

than a ten percent return on what can be a very risky investment.

Breaking down some of the more interesting expenses listed above, we find that for photos and cartoons alone $1,873 was spent; for posters, cards, billposting, etc., a figure of $3,501 was laid out; rental of the chairs (at a dollar a throw) which were set up on the infield came to $3,347; to erect the ramp it cost $3,747; for the raised ringside lumber the bill was $9,082; erecting and dismantling the set-up came to $17,559; erecting and dismantling the ring and working press section cost $5,199. A bill for trucking alone was $1,472.

## TAXES TAKES BIG BITE

Taxes, as with all of us, takes a major share of the money involved in a boxing promotion. For instance the Dempsey-Carpentier fight in 1921 drew the record breaking sum of $1,623,380, the first bout ever in the million dollar class. It was estimated that a million dollars of the promotion went to the federal government in taxes, and it is well to bear in mind that the internal revenue rates were much lower in those days.

Dempsey's purse was $300,000 and the tax on his share was estimated at $161,000. Carpentier received $200,000 and kicked back $93,000. Rickard's estimated taxes on profits from the promotion (it was a big money maker for him) were $250,000. Amusement tax on tickets took $150,000 and taxes from the railroad, contractor concessionaire, referee, preliminary boxers· and others receiving remuneration in connection with the bout approximated $346,000.

It would be interesting to figure out the total tax collected from a bout such as the Robinson-Basilio affair.

The second Tunney-Dempsey fight paid off on an all-time record gross of $2,658,660. The net receipts were $2,151,-134.57. Tunney's share was a fabulous $990,445 and Dempsey received a comfortable $425,000 from the fight, plus $25,000 from film rights. The federal tax on this fight was better than a quarter of a million dollars, $265,866, and the Illinois state tax totalled $241,659.43. The rental for Soldiers' Field, where the bout was held, was $100,000. Expenses listed by promoter Tex Rickard were $150,000 and his profit was an impressive $551,134.57.

Probably the biggest loss ever sustained by a promoter in connection with a fight came in the Gene Tunney-Tom Heeney heavyweight title fight at Yankee Stadium on July 26, 1928, Tunney's last fight before retiring. And it was the guarantee bugbear that busted the bout. The gross receipts for the fight came to $691,014.50, good

## PROMOTING IS RISKY BUSINESS

money any way you look at it and ordinarily a profit-making venture. But Tunney received a guarantee of $525,-000 and Heeney, also on guarantee, got an even $100,000. The net receipts, after $139,483.77 federal tax and $30,-108.55 state tax, came to $521,422.23. At this point not even Tunney's share was covered.

Motion picture revenue brought in $20,000 and radio revenue added another $15,000, which brought the total receipts to $556,422.23. In addition to the $625,000 in purses, Yankee Stadium rental was $52,142 and general expenses came to $35,000. The total cost of the promotion was $712,-142, leaving the Madison Square Garden Corporation with a staggering loss of $155,719.77.

For the Dempsey-Willard fight in 1919, Rickard and his partner, Frank Flournoy, had the Bay View Park Arena in Toledo built, with a seating capacity of 97,000. The official attendance was only 19,650. Cost of construction of the arena was $100,000 a total of 2,000,000 feet of lumber being used. As a sporting arena the property was worthless after the bout, so the promoters sold the entire set-up to the American House Wrecking Company, the highest bidder, for $25,000.

Promoting, at best (with one eye on the weather), is a risky business where after all expenses are estimated little margin is left for error and the profit, if any, nowadays coming from the revenue derived from television.

"As one promoter, the day before his big fight, said *"Please God, if you want it should, let it rain, but* DON'T THREATEN ME!"*

## NAT FLEISCHER SAYS

### EXHIBITION TOUR FOR HEAVYWEIGHT CHAMP

Cus D'Amato, manager of Floyd Patterson, world heavyweight champion, intends to keep his fighter busy this winter. Not only is he dickering with Lou Viscusi for a fight with Roy Harris of Cut-and-Shoot, Texas, to be staged during the winter in the oil territory, but through the veteran Charley Rose, an exhibition tour has been signed beginning shortly after the title bout with Peter Rademacher. Rose it will be recalled, has in the past booked many champions on tours. The one in which Patterson will appear, is confined wholly to Canada.

Sam Taub, an old timer in the publicity and reporting field, has been hired as private secretary for Floyd and D'Amato. The veteran New Yorker, one of the first to broadcast national boxing matches, worked at Patterson's Greenwood Lake camp as public relations director for the Patterson-Jackson bout and did the same for Patterson for his bout with Rademacher.

### INTERNATIONAL DIAMOND BELT BOXING TOURNAMENT
### staged at Seattle, Washington August 1-3.

Heavyweight
   John Stewart, Far East Air Force
Light heavyweight
   Willie Richardson, Portland, Oregon
Middleweight
   Antone Pascua, Hawaii
Light middleweight
   Terry Smith, Seattle, Washington
Welterweight
   Servilio Fuentes, Cuba
Light welterweight
   Antonio Zaldivar, Cuba
Lightweight
   Jorge Garcia, Mexico
Featherweight
   Douglas Valliant, Cuba
Bantamweight
   Heiji Shimibukuro, Hawaii
Flyweight
   Ray Perez, Hawaii

### WEST VIRGINIA WALLOPS
### By Mickey Davies

PROMOTER Dick Deutsch showed Nino Valdes to the fistic faithful of the Mountain State, at his Radio Center Arena, and the big fellow gave the fans an example of his ringmanship by slipping, feinting, stabbing, and finally tossing a good right hand to the head of Jack Flood of Spokane, spilling him for the full count. Flood, displaying a pretty fair left hook, drew blood from Nino's nose in the third chukker, but needless to say, he was never in the fight, despite his efforts to score over the rated Cuban. The end came in the seventh. Valdes weighed 212, Flood, 202.

In a good semi-final six, Bob Jackson, 185, Dayton, Ohio, edged Herman Harris, 175, Asheville. Harris is now a sparmate of Nino Valdes.

A real alley brawl between lightheavies saw Billy Carter, 165, Charleston, taking the measure of Dick Vess, 172, Dayton, Ohio, in round four. In still another lively tilt, Al Berry, 147, Columbus, lambasted veteran Eddie Brant, 145, Dayton, in six action packed rounds.

Short Socks—Remember big Babe Hunt, the Ponca City, Okla., heavyweight of yesteryear . . . He is now hale and hearty and employed at the Pike County Atomic Plant in Ohio . . . Joe Luvura will run boxing at Jeannette, Pa. . . . Things in this territory seem to be perking up a bit, thanks to Dick Deutsch and Bobby Gleason . . . Address: 2224 Seventh St.. Phone 9-3051, Portsmouth, Ohio.

### SWINGS AND HOOKS FROM CENTRAL OHIO
### By Less Huffman

JOHNNY BROWN a local welterweight who was in his prime in the forties, lost his life when he fell while engaged as an iron worker on the new arena in the Ohio State University grounds.

The Lucal County Veterans of Foreign Wars have opened their gymnasium to all local boxers who have been invited to train there.

Charles Phiefer, in charge of boxing at the Dayton Gymnastic Club, has been putting on a few shows to see if the public will patronize them.

Big George Harrison, bother of Tommy, has turned pro. I am managing him. He is a fine prospect. He is six feet tall and a good puncher.

L. C. Morgan, Youngstown, O., lightweight, stopped Ron Stribling of Cedar Rapids in Chicago in the first by a T.K.O.

That's all for now. Write to me at PO Box 611, Station G, Columbus, Ohio.

### NEBRASKA BOXING
### By Floyd Hayes

OMAHA. Nebraska—The Omaha Golden Gloves tournament sponsored by the Omaha World-Herald was staged in Omaha's new seven million dollar auditorium, the first boxing event in the new arena. It was the 22nd annual tournament. The following gained the championships:
Leo Gaglio—Flyweight
Wendell Stewart—Bantamweight
Henry Moran—Featherweight
Joe Parks—Lightweight
Elmer Perry—Welterweight
Eddie Anderson—Middleweight
Russell Grothe—Light Heavyweight
Wayne Womochil—Heavyweight

Lincoln, Nebraska—A bill has been presented to the Nebraska Legislature to legalize 15 round boxing matches in Nebraska. The present law places a limit of 10 rounds on any bout. Another section to the bill asks that the state tax on boxing and wrestling tickets be raised from five percent to ten percent.

Bill Tannehill, Norfolk, Nebraska lightweight is making his home in Omaha since his Army discharge and is ready for action. . . . Benny Mason, Omahan who fought in the middleweight division in the Golden Gloves tournaments, has joined the pro ranks and had his first fight in Minneapolis recently. . . . Wendell Stewart is debating whether to join the pro ranks or attend Wisconsin University. My advice is go to college and box on the boxing team there.

# FLEISCHER FIRST TO DEVISE RING RATINGS

## By DAN DANIEL

As professional boxing and the years roll along, ratings, both annual and periodical, take on increasing importance. Ratings tell the ring fan who is who, and what's going on. Ratings guide the matchmakers. Ratings are the things boxers fight for, in addition to the financial considerations and available titles. Ratings contribute to the very life blood of the sport.

In view of this, many spurious claims about ratings have been advanced. Various self-enthroned authorities have insisted that they devised the idea of ranking the boxers of the world. The time has come to deal with the pretenders.

The first ratings in the history of boxing appeared in The Ring Magazine, issue of February 1925.

The idea of rating the fighters originated with Nat Fleischer, editor and publisher of The Ring Magazine, which with that February edition was celebrating its fourth anniversary.

Some time before Christmas, 1924, Fleischer came into The Ring office quite excited. "I have an interesting idea," he said. "Walter Camp's All America football selections are awaited annually with the keenest interest. Why can't we adapt that idea for boxing?

"In boxing, ratings would be even more authentic because we would have definite results with which to work. We know that A beat B, C and D and thus stands No. 1 behind the champion. How about it?"

The idea had a tremendous appeal for me. Here was something brand new in a sport which had been going on since the early 18th century, since the Roman cestus days, if one wanted to give it real antiquity.

Here was a powerful medium for increasing popular interest, and for strengthening boxer incentive.

So it was decided that morning to spring the ratings in the February 1925 issue.

Then came the question as to who would get behind the rankings, and how deep they would go into the ranks of the nine divisions—we had a junior lightweight class in those days.

Finally we decided to ask "Tex" Rickard to lend his name to the enterprise. "Tex" was the outstanding boxing figure outside of competition. He was the world's No. 1 promoter, the man who had made Jack Dempsey, then the heavyweight champion.

So up to Rickard's office we went, and "Tex" grabbed the invitation faster than jobless cousin Louie seizes a dinner bid.

It was agreed that Fleischer should make up the ratings, and that Rickard should have the right of review. It is interesting and significant that "Tex" did not make a single change.

How the first page of the ratings story looked, what the rankings were, are revealed in the accompanying reproduction of Page 6 of The Ring Magazine of February 1925.

Publication of the ratings created a tremendous stir in boxing the world over. Discussion as to the compiler's judgment broke out everywhere. The ratings took boxing by storm. The question arose, "Why wasn't this thought of long ago?"

Note the headline, " 'Tex' Rickard Ranks Boxers for 1924. Famous Promoter issues First List of Its Kind. Gives Dempsey and Leonard Only Complimentary Rating."

On the next page, The Ring Magazine ran a box in which it said, " 'Tex' Rickard's ranking of the boxers of the world for the year 1924, which appears in this issue of The Ring, is only one of the many striking features which this magazine will print during the current year. With this issue The Ring enters on a policy of expansion which will make it the most talked about sports magazine in the world."

The Ring Magazine, its editor and publisher, and its growing staff certainly made good on that promise. It still is doing that.

When the time came for publishing the second annual ratings, in February 1926, a national weekly offered Rickard $5,000 for the story. He accepted. Somehow, "Tex" got the odd notion that the idea belonged to him.

Fleischer was in Europe and I was in charge of The Ring. I notified Rickard and the national magazine that if they stole the feature, I would get a Supreme Court injunction, and The Ring Magazine would follow with suits for damages.

Rickard thought I was fooling. But I persuaded him to see the light and he signed a new authorization for use of his name.

On the death of Rickard, Jimmy Johnston sponsored the ratings. Then Fleischer came out as the sole author. Later, the staff and correspondents the world over moved into the enterprise and the ratings, growing year by year in length and authority, took on their current scope.

In time, too, Fleischer began to run monthly as well as annual ratings.

In time, too, the National Boxing Association picked up the enterprise, which, as an idea and not an invention, could not be patented or copyrighted. But the NBA lays no claim to having originated the important scheme.

Back in 1924, the job of ranking the top ten in each division presented some difficulties for Fleischer. But, as I recollect it, he finished the job within a week.

Now the monthly ratings require days and days of conferences, and the annual rankings take weeks to compile.

Let there be no mistake about where the idea was born, where it was developed, and where it has been worked out best.

# REPRODUCTION OF PAGE FROM THE RING MAGAZINE SHOWING FIRST BOXING RATINGS PRINTED ANYWHERE IN THE WORLD

Page 6        THE RING        February, 1925

## Boxers of World Ranked in 1924 by "Tex" Rickard

*Copyright, 1925, The Ring*

**FLYWEIGHTS**
1.—Pancho Villa, Manila.
2.—Frankie Genaro, New York.
3.—Al Brown, Panama.
4.—Jimmy Russo, Grand Rapids, Mich.
5.—Tommy Milton, New York.
6.—Corp. Izzy Schwartz, New York.
7.—Lew Perfetti, New York.
8.—Emil Paluso, Salt Lake City.
9.—Young Dencio, Manila.
10.—Kid Wolfe, Philadelphia.

**BANTAMWEIGHTS**
1.—Eddie Martin, New York.
2.—Abe Goldstein, New York.
3.—Bud Taylor, Chicago.
4.—Carl Tremaine, Cleveland.
5.—Amos Carlin, New Orleans.
6.—Harold Smith, Chicago.
7.—Pete Sarmiento, Manila.
8.—Vic Foley, Vancouver.
9.—Bushy Graham, Utica, N. Y.
10.—Johnny Brown, England.

**FEATHERWEIGHTS**
1.—Louis Kaplan, Meriden, Conn.
2.—Babe Herman, San Francisco.
3.—Mike Dundee, Rock Island, Ills.
4.—Danny Kramer, Philadelphia.
5.—Jose Lombardo, Panama.
6.—Bobby Garcia, Camp Holabird.
7.—"Red" Chapman, Boston.
8.—Joey Sanger, Milwaukee.
9.—Ray Miller, Chicago.
10.—Bud Ridley, Seattle.

**JUNIOR LIGHTWEIGHTS**
1.—Kid Sullivan, New York.
2.—Jack Bernstein, Yonkers, N. Y.
3.—Solly Seaman, New York.
4.—Lew Paluso, Salt Lake City.
5.—Eddie Wagner, Philadelphia.
6.—Joey Silvers, New York.
7.—Mike Ballerino, New York.
8.—Tony Vaccarelli, New York.
9.—Johnny Leonard, Allentown, Pa.
10.—"Pepper" Martin, New York.

**LIGHTWEIGHTS**
1.—Benny Leonard, New York.
2.—Sid Terris, New York.
3.—Sammy Mandell, Chicago.
4.—Sid Barbarian, Detroit.
5.—Johnny Dundee, New York.
6.—Louis Vicentini, Chile.
7.—Tommy O'Brien, Milwaukee.
8.—Charley O'Connell, Cleveland.
9.—Basil Galiano, New Orleans.
10.—Archie Walker, New York.

**WELTERWEIGHTS**
1.—Mickey Walker, Elizabeth, N. J.
2.—Dave Shade, San Francisco.
3.—Willie Harmon, New York.
4.—Lew Tendler, Philadelphia.
5.—Pete Latzo, Scranton, Pa.
6.—Morrie Schlaiffer, Omaha, Neb.
7.—Billy Wells, England.
8.—Jimmy Jones, Youngstown, Pa.
9.—Eddie Shevlin, Boston.
10.—Jack Zivic, Pittsburgh.

**MIDDLEWEIGHTS**
1.—Harry Greb, Pittsburgh.
2.—"Tiger" Flowers, Atlanta, Ga.
3.—Jimmy Slattery, Buffalo.
4.—Jack Delaney, Bridgeport, Conn.
5.—Johnny Wilson, New York.
6.—Frankie Schoell, Buffalo.
7.—Jock Malone, St. Paul, Minn.
8.—Bert Colima, Oakland, Cal.
9.—"Allentown" Joe Gans (Joe Hicks), Allentown, Pa.
10.—Ted Moore, England.

**LIGHT HEAVYWEIGHTS**
1.—Gene Tunney, New York.
2.—Young Stribling, Atlanta, Ga.
3.—Kid Norfolk, New York.
4.—Mike McTigue, New York.
5.—Ad Stone, Philadelphia.
6.—Jeff Smith, Bayonne, N. J.
7.—Paul Berlenbach, New York.
8.—Tony Marullo, New Orleans.
9.—Tommy Loughran, Philadelphia.
10.—Jimmy Delaney, St. Paul, Minn.

**HEAVYWEIGHTS**
1.—Jack Dempsey, Salt Lake City.
2.—Harry Wills, New York.
3.—Tom Gibbons, St. Paul, Minn.
4.—Charley Weinert, Newark, N. J.
5.—Quintin Romero-Rojas, Chile.
6.—Jack Renault, Montreal.
7.—Luis Angel Firpo, Argentina.
8.—George Godfrey, Philadelphia.
9.—Jim Maloney, Boston.
10.—Erminio Spalla, Italy.

## "Tex" Rickard Ranks Boxers for 1924

### Famous Promoter Issues First List of Its Kind,—Gives Dempsey and Leonard Only Complimentary Rating

*It is the exclusive privilege of* THE RING *to present to the boxing followers of the world "Tex" Rickard's ranking of ring performers for the year 1924. Coming from the leading promoter in the sport and the impresario at Madison Square Garden in New York the tabulation and the accompanying article are of unusual importance and vital interest. It is the intention of Mr. Rickard to make the ranking an annual feature in* THE RING. *It is intended to make the Rickard list each year on a relative parity with Walter Camb's All-America team in* ... *... United States*

titles and the total eclipse of foreign contenders for world supremacy. In tabulating the best ten in each class I was guided not so much by the ~~~~ eral impression as to wh~~ boxer deserved for his ~ his entire career, b~ complished in 192 this clear—the r basis of achiev~

Had I ad^ plan I wou¹ both T~ cha~

is No. 1—but that Harry Wills is No. 1, too. Dempsey is the champion, but Will~ ~ ~~~ on re-

# PAYMENT DEFERRED?

## By JOHNNY SALAK

AS far as subscription TV goes it may be later than you think. You'll probably be paying for your programs sooner than you imagine. But sooner or later it is bound to come.

Interest in this new form of video is, strangely enough, very high considering that the general public knows very little of subscription TV. Experiments, in which the public has participated, have been run but on very limited scales. What the average owner of a TV set knows he has mainly learned through articles in newspapers and magazines.

The initial fear of having invested a considerable sum of money in a television set that would merely act as a box office which would cut you off without entertainment unless you paid an exorbitant fee has been replaced with a sounder understanding and an intelligent outlook.

Subscription TV is necessary. It's necessary if bigger and better shows are to be televised. It's necessary if many of the top, large budget programs now viewed are to remain on television. The general viewer now realizes that, as far as quality is concerned, he is better off paying anywhere from ten cents to a dollar, depending on the show, to see what he wants rather than being at the mercy of sponsors and having to accept whatever they decide on or can afford.

Several companies have been working to perfect subscription TV and are now waiting for approval from the Federal Communications Commission. Among them are the Zenith Radio Corporation with their Phonevision, the International Telemeter Corporation and the Skiatron Corporation with Subscriber-vision.

A number of methods might be used to unscramble the coded, jumpy, uncertain image that would shift back and forth across the TV screen. The decoding signal can go through the air to the receiver. When the air code translator is set by means of a small card purchased at a conveniently located vending machine it utilizes the decoding signal to clear up both the picture and sound in the receivers. This method also lends itself to the sale of decoder cards, by mail or on monthly billing.

Another method is to have the decoding signal sent over the subscriber's regular telephone line and into the TV set. The decoding signal does not interfere with the use of the telephone nor does use of the telephone interfere with the picture. Collections under this method can be by monthly billing or through a coin box in the home.

Or the subscriber can pay for his program by dropping the proper amount for the program into a coin box attached to his receiver.

A decoding unit can be easily installed in any regular television set, regardless of age or make, for about the cost of an average table model radio.

IT is common knowledge that virtually all stadium and arena sports have suffered from television and even some of the best sports events have been banned from TV because of the absence of a home box office. For many events, the loss of gate receipts is greater than advertising sponsors can pay. Boxing has been trying to circumvent that by blacking out the area in which the bout is taking place, usually a 70 mile radius.

But that is only a "stop gap" experiment. Some events have been televised exclusively to theatres but the audience is limited and only a handful of the millions of fans who might want to see, say, a world championship fight can be accommodated. Subscription television would make it possible for all these sports events to be seen in the home. With a home box office all sports would gain needed economic support.

The problems the television industry have brought not only to sports but our entire way of living are many. They eventually will be ironed out, presumably to the satisfaction of all. The period we are going through now is merely the experimental stages of any new and large industry. The benefits of subscription TV to sports are many.

But more than just sports, subscription TV is a solution to the short run problem of putting the best feature motion pictures on TV, and also the long run problem of producing more and better motion pictures for all types of exhibition.

It is also a solution to the shrinking status of the legitimate stage and a return to the theatre from a few "houses" in major cities to virtually all of the homes in America. It solves the similar economic problems that have even further reduced the status of the opera and symphony, and, of course, the unsolved problem of how to develop the obviously great educational uses of television.

The public is always paying. But this is one time when it will be a pleasure to pay.

# D'AMATO GENIUS, OR

SOMEBODY had an extra newspaper and Sugar Ray Robinson, sitting moodily in the tourist section of this jet that was taking him to New York, ran through the sports pages. One story was about the Floyd Patterson-Tom McNeeley travesty and down at the bottom the writer speculated on Patterson's next opponent. It would be, the story said, either Henry Cooper's brother or Pete Rademacher's father. Robinson read it, then folded the paper and shook his head.

*"Cus Amato,"* he said. *"Man, he got to be the greatest fight manager. Look what he's done for his fighter. He gets him McNeeley. And he gets paid for it. Cus Amato got to be the greatest."*

*"Where did you get that one from?"* somebody sitting with Robinson said with sarcasm.

*"I don't have to get it from nowhere,"* Robinson said. *"Common sense makes him the best. Look at the thing. I had to fight an Artie Levine, and a Jake LaMotta and a Tommy Bell. Then they give me a Turpin and Joey Maxim."*

He shook his head. *"Look what Cus Amato gets for Patterson. He gets him Rademacher, Brian London and that boy Roy Harris. And now McNeeley. A manager is supposed to protect his fighter. That's all Cus Amato is doing.*

*"Don't tell me about fight managers. He got to be the greatest. All I know is I had to fight guys that could kill you and Patterson has to fight hardly nobody. And he gets paid money for it, too. I'm going to tell you something—I wish Cus Amato managed me."*

This seemed to be, at first, as strange a theory as has been advanced in boxing for some time. For "Cus Amato," or, to give him his correct name, Constantine (Cus) D'Amato, has become a stereotyped villain in the game. He is most everybody in boxing agrees, an oddball. They say he is also ruining the game.

Yet here was Sugar Ray Robinson telling you that as a fight manager Cus makes them all look like amateurs!

But as the plane kept swooshing towards Idlewild Airport and Robinson kept talking, you began to think about it and after awhile there could be no possible room for disagreement.

**Cus D'Amato, manager of heavyweight champion Floyd Patterson.**

# ODDBALL?

## "Cus D'Amato is the greatest," Ray Robinson says of Patterson's Manager

Ray Robinson, who acts as his own manager.

Let the old-timers knock Cus. Let the sportswriters take him apart at every opportunity. Say what you want about him. But don't ever try to say Cus D'Amato is not the best fight manager of our time.

It was nearly 10 years ago—on September 12, 1952—that D'Amato, wearing those blue gym pants of his, put his foot on the rope at St. Nicholas Arena and kept it there until Patterson was through and into the ring for the first professional prize fight of his career. It was against one Eddie Godbold and Patterson took him out in four.

Since then, Cus had managed to alienate almost every known person in boxing or around boxing and at one time, back in June of 1960, he seemed to have lost touch with his fighter, too. He has been ridiculed. He has been brazen and weird. But his record is astounding.

There are two points, and only two points, on which the ability of a manager of fighters can be measured. The important one is the condition of the fighter he handles. After this, you see how much money has the fighter earned. Everything else, the newspaper headlines and the recognition and the excitement; none of it counts.

And on these two points, Cus D'Amato, fight manager, is untouchable. Floyd Patterson has two slight scars—over his right eye if memory is correct—that came from a fight in 1953 with somebody like Westbury Bascom. Floyd had rubbed his face with coca butter for some time before the fight—somebody had told him it was good—and the grease-softened skin busted open when Bascom got going.

Otherwise, Floyd has about the same face today that he had before he was a fighter. He shows absolutely no wear and tear beyond this. He has a great pair of legs. His body is strong.

He ran into one terrible night, against Ingemar Johansson in June of 1959, but you can count the punches he was hit with in most of his other fights. Patterson comes with a chin that has to be weak. The notion here always has been that D'Amato, above everybody, knew of it. And he matched his fighter accordingly. All he was able to do, with this cautious matching, was to get his man to the heavyweight championship of the world!

## PATTERSON'S MONEY RECORD
## MAKES INCREDIBLE STORY

As for the money. Well, on Page 66 of Nat Fleischer's Ring Record Book and Boxing Encyclopedia, there is a table of Floyd Patterson's ring earnings. It begins with the Godbold bout. Patterson got $75 for the fight. It then goes on to show that Patterson received $250,000 for boxing Pete Rademacher at Sick's Stadium, Seattle. It shows Patterson earned $301,382.41 for taking on Roy Harris at Wrigley Field, Los Angeles. It shows he was paid $170,000 for a workout with Brian London in Indianapolis. And he took down something close to $300,000 for the McNeeley affair in Toronto.

This gives him a gross of over one million dollars for taking on four fighters who were, at their best, nothing more than average six-round boys.

You now throw in the staggering two million or so that Floyd was paid for the three Ingemar Johansson bouts and you have a financial picture that is positively awesome. If everything goes according to present plans, and Patterson meets Sonny Liston at Yankee Stadium in June, you can add another million to this figure.

So Patterson's earnings are tremendous. To go further, he has kept every quarter of the money that was possible to keep under today's tax structure.

Under the rules, then, Mr. Cus D'Amato comes out as simply one helluva manager of a fighter.

When you begin to think of this, there comes to mind one bleak Sunday afternoon in March of 1954 when D'Amato sat at a table in the bar of Luchow's Restaurant, a couple of doors down from his gymnasium on 14th Street in New York, and over some good, cold German beer, he talked about Patterson.

*"Floyd Patterson is going to weigh 184 pounds the night he wins the heavyweight championship,"* Cus was saying.

*"Drink the beer,"* we told him. At this time Patterson barely weighed 165 pounds and he was fighting such as Bascom and Dick Wagner and Tommy Harrison at Eastern Parkway Arena. The champion was Rocky Marciano. You had to be a wild man to picture Patterson even walking on the same side of the street with Marciano or Ezzard Charles or any of the other

"Sugar Ray" gave Floyd a bit of advice while they chat at Patterson's training camp before the McNeeley fight.

top heavyweights.

But on November 30, 1956, weighing 182 pounds, Patterson was chasing Archie Moore around the ring at Chicago Stadium and he was the fastest heavyweight, foot and hand, you ever wanted to see. In the sixth round he hurt Moore with a couple of hooks to the middle, then kept after him and loaded up with a big left hook and he was the heavyweight champion of the world.

Between 1954 and 1956, Patterson had been nursed to the championship. D'Amato howled about Jim Norris and Frankie Carbo and the International Boxing Club. He refused to fight for them until he was given a ton of money, $45,000, for taking on Tommy (Hurricane) Jackson in the Garden.

Once he had the title, Cus ran away from the Garden and launched his crusade against the *bad elements in the business."*

While he was at it, he dug up the Rademachers and Roy Harris' for his man. He made exactly one mistake. To this day, it is hard to believe Cus thought Ingemar Johansson was as dangerous as he turned out to be. It was one of the great jobs of protecting a fighter while making money for him. It is all that counts.

Why, then, with this record, is D'Amato so roundly disliked by just about everybody?

He is not liked because he takes advantage of matters and forces a Rademacher or a McNeeley on the public, they say. Cus also talks in circles. He even tried to ram through one of his own men, Harry Davidow, as a manager of Ingemar Johansson. He has turned the heavyweight championship into a farce and all of boxing is suffering because of it.

All of which is true. And all of which is to D'Amato's credit and everybody else's shame. For when somebody starts knocking Patterson and D'Amato for fighting Pete Rademacher, then they better ask, too, what Jack Hurley was doing as promoter of that farce and how in the name of anything could a boxing commission tolerate such a match. For it is the politicians who sanction matches, and the public who accepts them and pays money to see them, who are to be blamed for these terrible matches D'Amato digs up.

## TORONTO'S OKEH OF
## MCNEELEY WAS SINFUL

To pay anything the far side of 50 cents to see Patterson, on closed circuit television or in the flesh, going against McNeeley, qualifies a spectator as a prime sucker. For the Toronto boxing commission to allow the match to go on was a sin.

But let it proceed—they did. And pay to see it on television—the people did.

The fight nearly killed what is left of boxing. But you can't blame D'Amato for it. If everybody else is foolish enough to stand still for his moves, then he would be at fault to go out and dig up some tiger for Patterson.

His first loyalty is to the fighter. In this, he is impeccable. He gets the easiest matches for the

## D'AMATO GENIUS OR ODDBALL?

best of money. That always has been the name of the game, gentlemen.

Or have we forgotten Jack Dempsey meeting a washed-out, underweight Georges Carpentier in Jersey City and getting $300,000 for it? And Rocky Marciano going in with Don Cockell in San Francisco and getting $115,000? In fact, D'Amato never would have accepted anything as low as $115,000 for the Cockell match.

If all of this reads as if it is an accolade for D'Amato, you may be sure it is. This is an intense, white-haired guy who sleeps on a couch in an office on 53rd Street and Broadway. He gives away money as if he hates it. He insists his version of things is the only true one. Through his maneuverings around the first Johansson bout—which caused his suspension as a licensed manager and, for a good time, had Patterson standing away from him, Cus completely lost public opinion. His harrangues against racket guys became a bore.

But his fighter has the title. Frankie Carbo and Blinky Palermo have been convicted of a Federal crime and their trial showed they had every bit of power and influence that Cus always yelled they had.

By the time Patterson gets through flattening Liston—he is most certainly going to give Sonny a terrible beating in six or seven rounds, it says here—Cus's record may well be the finest of any fight manager we have had in the last 30 years.

### D'AMATO WILL CONTINUE
### TO GET AWAY WITH IT

All of which is not going to change him. For Cus D'Amato mistrusts the world. And he will keep digging up Rademachers for just as long as the public and the Commissions are silly enough to tolerate the idea. Meanwhile, D'Amato also will carry on his one man battle against the American press.

There was the night, back in the Summer of 1960, when Cus was scheduled to sail for Europe. He does not fly and he and George Lattimore, his companion, and one of their boxers were leaving ahead of Patterson, who would fly several days later.

Cus was walking around his apartment, talking and waving his arms as usual when a visitor came in.

*"Aren't you packed yet?"* the guy said.
*"The boat leaves in a couple of hours."*
*"It leaves to-morrow,"* Cus said.

*"You mean to-night,"* the guy said.
*"The ticket says it leaves to-morrow,"* Cus insisted.

The guy picked up a copy of the New York Times, turned to its page of shipping news, and looked up the departure time for Cus' ship. The agate table said the ship was to sail at 12:01 A.M.

*"That means to-night,"* the guy said.

*"You got that out of the paper?"* Cus said. *"How many times did I tell you not to believe anything you read in the newspapers!"*

Somehow, they got him on the ship. And somehow, out of all the yelling and the turmoil and the blasts at him, Cus D'Amato has managed to do one of the creditable managing jobs.

Gene Tunney, on right, is beating Jack Dempsey in their first encounter, in Philadelphia. Jack went into ring an 8 to 5 choice.

# LONG SHOTS GALORE HAVE SCORED IN BATTLES FOR HEAVY TITLE

## By JERSEY JONES

ADVANCE speculation made Cassius Clay a top-heavy choice to dispose of George Chuvalo in their Toronto get-together. The musty archives of boxing reveal many another challenger going into a heavyweight title match with the odds predominantly against his chances. But it has been said that nothing in boxing is more certain than its uncertainty, and many a long-shot has come through a winner.

With the possible exceptions of his manager, Bill Brady, and trainer, Bob Delaney, it is doubtful if any one conceded Jim Corbett much of a chance of dethroning the mighty John L. Sullivan in New Orleans in 1892. The prevailing price was 4 to 1 against Corbett. But Gentleman Jim, with his shifty foot-work and hit-and-run tactics, gradually wore down the aging, dissipated hulk of what had been the Boston Strong Boy and knocked him out in the 21st round.

Corbett, in turn, was a slight favorite when he hooked up with Bob Fitzsimmons in Carson City, Nevada, in 1897. It was a short price at 3 to 5, and it seemed well justified until Fitz drove that left hook into Corbett's mid-section (the historic Solar Plexus Punch) and flattened him in the 14th round.

Fitz was a pronounced 2 to 1 choice over Jim Jeffries two years later in Coney Island, but Jeff proved too strong and durable for the Cornishman and after absorbing everything Fitz could toss at him, registered a knockout in the 11th session.

When Tommy Burns, succeeding Jeffries as champion when Big Jim retired, finally was cornered by Jack Johnson in Sydney, Australia, in 1908, he ruled a slight 3-2 favorite with the wagering gentry. But Johnson was too big and shifty for him and won when the bout was halted by the police in the 14th round.

Johnson was a 10 to 7 favorite in his meeting with Jess Willard in Havana in 1915, but the Kansas giant outlasted him. Had the bout been limited to 20 rounds, Johnson would have won, but he gradually weakened and collapsed in the 26th frame of a scheduled 45-rounder. There are other versions of the climax.

With tremendous advantages in height, reach and weight, Willard was 6 to 5 against Jack Dempsey in Toledo in 1919, but Manassa Jack, with his speed and savage two-handed punching, wrecked him in three rounds.

Dempsey was 11 to 5 to turn back Gene Tunney's bid in their Philadelphia squabble in 1926. The Coloradoan was rusty from three years of ring activity and a determined, confident Tunney won decisively. A year later, when they put on their encore in Chicago, the advance speculation was at even money. Tunney, surviving the Long Count in the eighth round, again was winner.

Jim Corbett, on right, is getting hurt by John L. Sullivan early in their New Orleans fight. But Gentleman Jim, a 4 to 1 underdog, stopped the one-time Boston Strong Boy in the twenty-first. Referee, Honest John Kelly.

Bob Fitzsimmons, title holder, on right, and Jim Jeffries, with George Siler, referee, are about to go at it in Coney Island in 1899. The champion was a 2 to 1 favorite but the Boilermaker won in eleven.

Here we see Cassius Clay taking the title from Sonny Liston at Miami Beach in 1964, after Muhammad Ali had come into the ring a poor second choice, at 7 to 1 but surprised everyone by winning in six.

The year is 1935 and Max Baer, the champion, on left, is defending the title against Jim Braddock. Baer went into the fight a 10 to 1 favorite, but Jim got the decision after 15 rounds at Long Island City, N.Y.

Following Tunney's retirement, after beating Tom Heeney in New York's Yankee Stadium in 1928, an international elimination tournament to determine his successor resulted in American Jack Sharkey and German Max Schmeling tangling in the grand finale, also in the Yankee Stadium in 1930.

Sharkey was a 9 to 5 selection in advance, but messed up his chances when he fouled out in the 4th round. In the return match three years later, in Madison Square Garden's Long Island Bowl, Schmeling was favored at 6 to 5, and this time Sharkey won the decision.

Having beaten Primo Carnera in Brooklyn, Sharkey was installed a 5 to 4 favorite when he essayed to defend the title against the Ambling Alp in the Long Island Bowl in 1933. Carnera knocked him out in the 4th round.

Despite his champion's status, Carnera was on the short end of 7 to 5 when he hooked up with Max Baer, also in the Long Island Bowl, in 1934.

The price should have been longer. Baer handed the Leaning Tower of Pizza a thorough going-over, flooring him a dozen times before finishing him in the eleventh round.

Baer himself was a top-heavy selection against Jim Braddock in the Bowl in 1935. The price was 10 to 1 against Braddock, but Jimmy, accounting for one of the ring's most stunning upsets, won the decision and the title.

The first challenger to enter the ring favorite in a heavyweight championship match was Joe Louis when he met Braddock in Chicago in 1937. Shufflin' Joe was quoted at 2 to 5, and he justified the price by kayoing Braddock in the eighth round.

Louis was the busiest heavyweight champion the ring has known. During his reign of nearly fourteen years with four years out during Army service in World War II, he engaged in no fewer than 26 successful defenses of the title.

During the stretch from late '37 through 1941, the Bomber engaged in what the late Jack Miley of the New York *Daily News* dubbed the "Bum-of-the-Month-Club," and he didn't miss many of his challengers.

His industrious campaign carried from all over the United States, from Boston to Los Angeles. In every bout the Bomber was the "peoples' cherce," as they would express it in Brooklyn, and he won them all, but he had a couple of real scares en route, particularly with "little" Billy Conn in New York's Polo Grounds in 1941. Despite every physical disadvantage, Conn seemed well on his way to the title when he became careless and crashed into disaster in the 13th round.

Louis had another rough jolt in Washington when Buddy

Here we see Braddock after the Baer fight, none the worse for wear after the 45 minutes of action in the Long Island City Bowl in New York.

Baer, Max's younger but bigger brother, drove him out of the ring early in the bout. Joe climbed back and went on to win on a disqualification in the seventh.

Louis also ran into unexpected opposition from Abe Simon in Detroit. He needed thirteen rounds to stop Big Abe.

Arturo Godoy was another tough one for Louis in their first meeting. The rugged Chilean, bobbing and weaving, went the ten round route with him in Madison Square Garden. In a return match in the Yankee Stadium, Godoy absorbed a terrific lacing and was disposed of in the eighth round.

In his first defense of the title, late in '37, Louis had anything but a soft time with the rugged Welsh visitor, Tommy Farr, in the Yankee Stadium. Louis won the decision in fifteen rounds, but couldn't put Farr off his feet at any time, and Tommy was still in there, doing the best he could, when the final bell clanged. The price against Farr had been 5 to 2.

Still another scare was tossed into Louis when he hooked up with Tony Galento in the Stadium. Joe was shaken up by Tony's opening onslaught, and was dropped on the seat of his pants in the second session. He survived to demolish Two-Ton Tony in the fourth.

Louis' other victims (all by k.o.'s) in that "Bum-of-the-Month" campaign were Nathan Mann, New York (3), Harry Thomas, Chicago (5), Max Schmeling, New York (1), John Henry Lewis, New York (1), Jack Roper, Los Angeles (1), Bob Pastor, Detroit (11), Johnny Paychek, New York (2), Al McCoy, Boston (6), Red Burman, New York (1), Gus Dorazio, Philadelphia (2) and Tony Musto, St. Louis (9).

While in the Army, Louis fought twice in Madison Square Garden for service organizations, knocking out Buddy Baer in one round for the Navy's Relief Fund and stopping Abe Simon in six for the Army's Relief Fund.

Following his discharge from the Army in 1944, Louis embarked on a busy exhibition schedule for two years before risking his title again. His first opponent was Billy Conn, who had come so close to beating him in their first meeting. The return,

This is a camera shot of a character not seen often. It shows Joe Louis, heavyweight champion of the world, on the floor. The occasion is the first fight with Jersey Joe Walcott on December 5, 1947. Walcott, at 10 to 1, came within an ace of gaining the title. Referee Ruby Goldstein voted for him, but the two judges balloted for Louis.

in the Yankee Stadium was held in 1946, but this time a poorly conditioned and ring rusty Conn was no match for the champion. Louis stopped him in eight rounds.

Joe had a few rough moments in his next start, when he stacked up against Tami Mauriello, also in the Stadium. With his opening rush, Tami nailed Louis on the chin and drove him back to the ropes. The champion was hurt but recovered quickly, and his devastating assault finished Mauriello two minutes later. Time of one round: 2:09.

Following this performance, Louis

## LONG SHOTS GALORE HAVE SCORED IN BATTLES FOR HEAVY TITLE

embarked on another extensive exhibition tour, this one taking him throughout the United States and to Hawaii, Mexico, Central America, South America and Cuba before he returned late in '47 to defend his title again. The opponent was the veteran Jersey Joe Walcott, and the bout was held in Madison Square Garden.

The betting boys didn't think much of Walcott's chances. The odds were 10 to 1 against him. But Jersey Joe turned in a real surprise. He knocked Louis down twice during the bout, and was credited with outpointing him in several rounds, but the champion retained the title on a split 2-1 decision.

The verdict was hotly disputed, many of the witnesses contending that Walcott had won, and the hectic controversy resulted in a return match the following year in Yankee Stadium. This time the price against Walcott dropped to 13 to 5.

Once again Jersey Joe had the satisfaction of flooring Louis, but the champion was not to be denied. He knocked Walcott out in the eleventh round.

Following another busy exhibition tour throughout the United States, which carried into 1949, Louis announced his retirement, voluntarily relinquished his championship, and resumed his exhibition junket, whch was extended to Brazil.

Reconsidering his decision to quit, Shufflin' Joe returned in 1950 to face Ezzard Charles in Yankee Stadium. After Louis's announced retirement, Charles had beaten Jersey Joe Walcott in Chicago, for what had been advertised as a fight for the vacant title.

The aging, balding Louis, only a faint memory of his former great self, was badly beaten by Charles, but he elected to continue his ring operations until he was knocked out by up-and-coming Rocky Marciano in Madison Square Garden in 1951.

During his comparatively brief reign as champion, Charles was an industrious campaigner. Sandwiched in between exhibition bouts, the Cincinnatian stopped Gus Lesnevich in New York (7), Pat Valentino in San Francisco (8), Freddie Beshore in Buffalo (14), Nick Barone in Cincinnati (11) and Lee Oma in New York (10). He decisioned Joey Maxim in Chicago (15) as well as Louis in New York, and whipped Walcott again in Detroit (15). But he came a cropper in a third meeting with Walcott when Jersey Joe knocked him out in the seventh round in Pittsburgh.

Walcott, as champion, wasn't too active. In two years he engaged in only two title bouts, both in Philadelphia. He decisioned Charles, but was knocked out by Marciano in the 13th session.

Marciano, after taking the title from Walcott, was fairly industrious. He repulsed the assaults of Walcott in Chicago ('53), Roland LaStarza in New York ('53), Charles twice in New York ('54), Don Cockell in San Francisco ('55) and Archie Moore in New York ('55). Rocky was the choice of the wagering gentry in all his bouts.

With no other challengers in view, Marciano retired in '56.

In an elimination match in Chicago, to determine Rocky's successor, Floyd Patterson knocked out Archie Moore. Floyd was an erratic performer as champion, although he enjoyed the favor of the specu-

lative crowd in every instance with the one exception of his second match with Ingemar Johansson in New York ('60).

Johansson, on the strength of his spectacular knockout of Patterson in New York the previous year, was favored in the return, but Floyd evened the score by flattening the Swede. Patterson's record as champion included knockouts of Tommy (Hurricane) Jackson in New York (10), Pete Rademacher in Seattle (6), Roy Harris in Los Angeles (12), Brian London in Indianapolis (11), another over Johansson in Miami Beach (6), and Tom McNeeley in Toronto (4).

Although a winner, Patterson gave indications of having none too rugged a chin.

Patterson's fragile chin eventually proved his undoing, Sonny Liston demolishing him twice, each time in one round, first in Chicago ('62), then in Las Vegas the following year.

Liston didn't linger long as champion. After a brief exhibition jaunt in Europe, he returned to the United States to tangle with Cassius Clay in Miami Beach in '64, and lost the title when he retired in his corner between the sixth and seventh rounds. The next year he hooked up with Clay again, this time in Lewiston, Maine, but was polished off in one round. In both bouts, Liston was favored, first by a lopsided 7 to 1, and despite that defeat he ruled a 7-5 choice in the return.

Up to his affair with Chuvalo in Toronto, Clay had made only one other defense of his laurels, and that was against former title-holder Patterson in Las Vegas toward the end of 1965. The mouthy Kentuckian was the advance choice, odds of 3 to 1 being quoted against Patterson. Clay won in the twelfth round, all the way.

# How Would Done Against

CLAY VS. LOUIS

CLAY VS. DEMPSEY

## AN ANALYSIS OF CASSIUS' CHANCES IN SOME MYTHICAL EMBROGLIOS

### By TED CARROLL

IN LINE with his new "humility", the war cry of Cassius Clay, "I am the greatest", does not ring out as loud and clear as it once did. But let no man believe that this unfamiliar restraint on the champion's part betokens a lessening of confidence.

Although the volume has been muted Muhammad is no less definite in his opinion that no heavyweight champion of the past could have beaten him. Clay capsules his critique of all the one-time ring kings in one simple sentence. "They were all either too slow or too small!"

Harkening back just a few short years to the time of Sonny Liston, when many fistic observers went overboard on the "invincibility" of the since deflated Big Bear, critics have become wary of tabbing the outstanding champions of other days as inferior to Clay. Still it is becoming obvious that compared to titleholders of yore, Muhammad Ali has a lot going for him.

Everyone concedes that no man his size ever possessed such speed of hand and foot. But it is equally evident that the better champions of the past had assets of their own which Clay hasn't shown.

The first and most important of these is punch. Cassius hasn't flashed firepower comparable to that of such blasters as Joe Louis, Rocky Marciano and Jack Dempsey. Max Baer, Max Schmeling, Jersey Joe Walcott, even Ingemar Johannson and Floyd Patterson packed more power than Clay has shown thus far.

Clay is quick to point out that Louis, for all his greatness, was

# Clay Have Stars of Past?

**CLAY VS. MARCIANO**

**CLAY VS. JOHNSON**

slow on his feet. It is true that Joe was no fancy Dan for footwork but the old Brown Bomber could unleash lightning fast punch combinations with devastating effect.

In his younger days, Louis had one of the fastest right hands ever seen in the ring. It boomed out of his slow moving gait with the speed and suddenness of a striking rattler. Joe was also capable of following it up with a double left hook to body and head with great rapidity. Against a foe such as Louis, Clay would have undoubtedly tried to use his leg speed to its utmost with a lot of dancing about as he did with Liston.

He would have succeeded in making Louis look cumbersome and plodding for a time, but Clay's defensive technique relies greatly upon leaning backwards out of range of his opponent's blows. Against a right hand of Louis's speed and power, this would have been a highly dangerous maneuver and the current champion would have been flirting with disaster every time he tried it.

Clay does not give the impression of extreme ruggedness, and just one of Joe's right hand bombs finding the target could have meant curtains for Cassius. On the credit side for Muhammad, it should be recalled that Billy Conn, a boxer of the Clay stripe, and only a light heavyweight, at that—gave Louis trouble before falling in a late round. Bob Pastor, a crafty boxer, survived ten rounds with Louis.

It is possible to conceive of Clay getting a decision over Louis in a bout lasting the full fifteen rounds. But it is not so easy to imagine his going that distance without getting tagged by Louis's fast hands somewhere along the way. When that happened it could mean the end of everything right then and there for Muhammad Ali.

There are those who saw in Clay's adept handling of George Chuvalo a similar dose for Rocky Marciano had fate ever brought the undefeated retired champion into the ring against Muhammad Ali. Both Rocky and the rugged Canadian are charter members of the old line school of sluggers. But there are important differences between the two, all of them in Marciano's favor.

First there is the matter of punch. Chuvalo isn't in the same class with the Brockton Blockbuster in this vital department. In the matter of defense, Chuvalo stood up straight against Clay. Rocky fought in a crouch which would have made him a much more difficult target than the upright Canadian.

Although Rocky wasn't clever he still was the type of foe "you had to look for", in the words of Ray Robinson. He fought close to the ground, his head barricaded by his heavy forearms and elbows. Clean shots at him were not easy to get.

Clay insists Rocky would have been easy for him because he was too small, his arms were too short, and he was too slow. This may be true but Cassius forgets that there are ropes around the ring. Chuvalo did his best work when he jammed the elusive champion into them.

At trapping a rival against the ropes, or in a corner, and then bludgeoning him mercilessly Rocky Marciano was in a class by himself. Rocky would have staked his victory hopes against Cassius on such tactics. Whether such demolition methods would have succeeded against the bigger, faster and

## HOW WOULD CLAY HAVE DONE AGAINST PAST STARS?

smarter Clay is anyone's guess. The opinion here is that Rocky, who was a bleeder, might have been too hampered by cuts by the sharpshooting Clay to get the full mileage out of his blasting attack.

Of the mythical opponents here discussed Jack Dempsey is the only one in a class with Clay for both hand and foot speed. Clay dismisses the Manassa Mauler as too little. There would have been besides a height advantage, a thirty pound disparity in Clay's favor.

At his peak Dempsey was quick as a cat on his feet. He was not called the Tiger Man for nothing. He would rip a left hook to the body and to the head, followed by a right in a blur of fast action. He relied so much upon his offense as a defense that the great middleweight Harry Greb challenged him frequently because, as Greb put it, "Dempsey checks his brains in the dressing room".

The crafty Tunney proved there was something to Greb's analysis. Clay is a thinking fighter. His comments on boxing and boxers prove that. Against Dempsey he would have had all the advantage of cleverness that Tunney possessed.

On the other hand, he would have been spotting Jack—as in the cases of Marciano and Louis—punching power, and this never can be discounted, especially among the heavyweights.

Regardless of result Dempsey and Clay would have made a great fight, bringing together a high octane rapid-fire offense against an equally fast moving defense.

While Clay's chin is not exactly suspect, no one knows how rugged he really is. Against Englishman Henry Cooper he was down and in shaky condition at the bell ending the fourth round.

Liston, the only other hitter he has faced, never landed a worthwhile blow in their two fiascoes. Until the matter of Clay's ruggedness has been settled more to the satisfaction of the afficiandos it is

still somewhat premature to rate him as a probable victor over blasters such as Dempsey, Louis and Marciano despite the distinct advantages in speed and skill he would have had over them.

In answer to a query as to how he thought he would have fared against Jack Johnson after viewing an old film of this all-time master in action, Cassius Clay said, "Johnson was a talker. He keeps talking in the ring all the time."

A mythical match between the loquacious lad from Louisville and the garrulous giant from Galveston would have settled the all-time conversational championship within the ropes. In this Cassius would have had to be favored. He has been quoted as refusing to play the role of Johnson in a movie because of the old champion's interracial marriages and what he would have had to say to Johnson on this subject probably would have topped any rejoinder the glib Johnson could have voiced. Cassius might even have angered Johnson to such a pass that Jack's fabled poise and skill would have been affected allowing Muhammad Ali to find openings in his airtight defense.

Although time is decimating their ranks, adherents of Johnson as the best of them all remain uswerving. They base their superlative assessments of the Texan on his unpenetrable defense.

"Johnson would have caught Clay's jabs like Willie Mays catches a baseball," declaims the indestructible octogenarian Charlie Rose, a relic of the Johnson era. He may well have done so, but how much landing of punches could he have done from his flat footed stance against the swift stepping, mobile, Clay?

A fight between Clay and Johnson can hardly be visualized as an exciting affair. Cassius, taller, and with a vast edge in legwork, could well have sprinted his way to a 15 round verdict over the blocking, countering Johnson, who preferred the kind of foes who came to him, thereby setting themselves up for his swift retaliatory counters.

Much the same analysis could be made of a match between Clay and Gene Tun-

ney had these two been contemporaries. After Johnson and Jim Corbett Tunney usually gets the call as the cleverest boxer among the heavyweight kings. Like most boxers Gene was more at home as a counter fighter but he was also adept at the left jab and right cross one-two, with the trailing right packing considerable power. Like Dempsey and Marciano he would have been conceding to the present champion height and weight. Gene stepped about smartly in action but Clay's unusual fleetnees gives him an edge here.

A Clay-Tunney match would never figure to set the crowd roaring but would have provided an interesting duel of skill. In such a contest Cassius, as the bigger and faster of the two, would have to be given the edge in the odds.

Comparisons such as these between Cassius Clay and champions of the past are intriguing but are not without danger to the comparer since, as in the drab denouement of Sonny Liston, the future may make such analyses seem ridiculous.

Were Henry Cooper to land a lucky one or Doug Jones get the official nod over Clay next time, a conjectural piece like this would become a mere flight of fancy.

On the other hand no one has beaten Cassius Clay. Only one man has even come close in the bouts he has had since turning pro. Nor does anyone figure to do so in the near future.

With a situation such as this all that is left is speculation on how well the fast stepping, fast punching present kingpin would have done with the giants of the past.

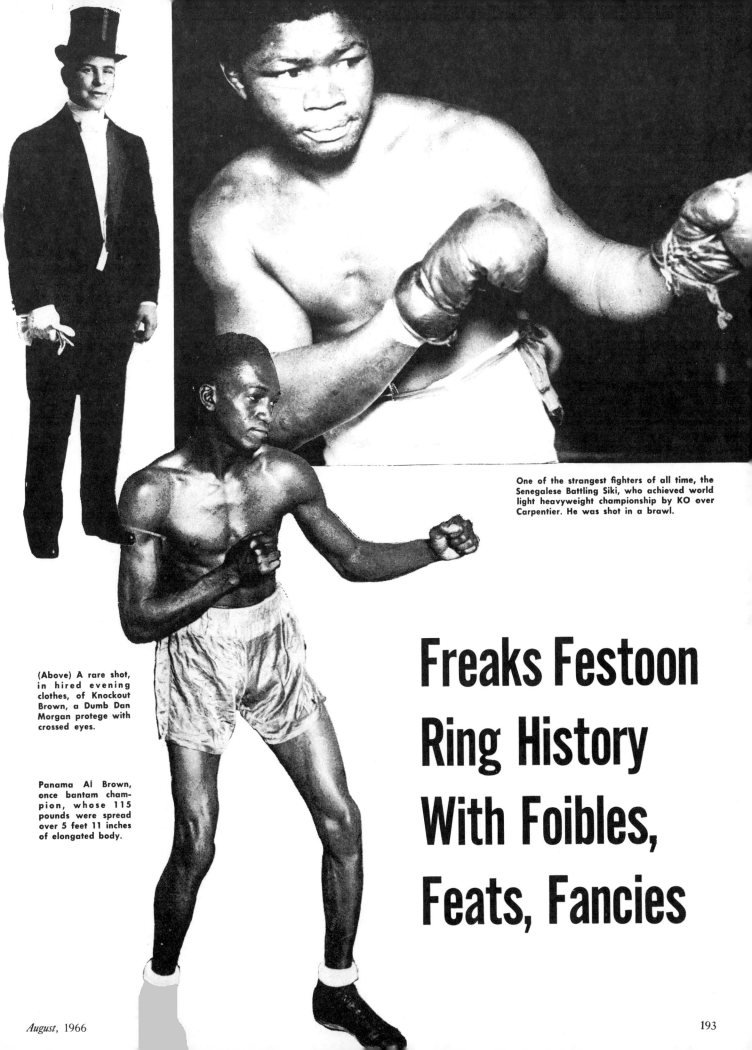

One of the strangest fighters of all time, the Senegalese Battling Siki, who achieved world light heavyweight championship by KO over Carpentier. He was shot in a brawl.

(Above) A rare shot, in hired evening clothes, of Knockout Brown, a Dumb Dan Morgan protege with crossed eyes.

Panama Al Brown, once bantam champion, whose 115 pounds were spread over 5 feet 11 inches of elongated body.

# Freaks Festoon Ring History With Foibles, Feats, Fancies

# Clay Tops List With Many Claims To Top Rating Among Oddities

### By DAN DANIEL

NO WALK in life, no profession, is free of freaks. Quite often they add spice and interest to the particular effort in which they are engaged. Boxing is no exception.

You might develop the notion that for a professional fighter to make his mark he must present a 100 percent physique, a psychology devoid of extreme quirks, a high percentage of victories, and a sensible approach to public relations.

However, our boxers aren't always able to meet the most exacting requirements. Quite often they make what appear to be their handicaps produce for them.

When this story first was projected it was ruled that Cassius Clay did not qualify as a fit subject.

However, on second consideration it was discovered that Muhammad Ali did rate as a freak.

How? Well, here is a heavyweight champion of the world who, in this era of the knockout fetich, goes for points.

Here is a heavyweight champion of the world who was born an American in Kentucky, bearing a famous Kentucky name, but renouncing American connections as a professed convert to Islam, and a practicing member of the Black Muslims.

Here is a heavyweight champion of the world who announces that he has conscientious objections to fighting, a man of combat who wants nothing to do with more serious combat, a fighter who doesn't want to be enlisted with the fighters.

Here is a heavyweight title holder who, more than any other holder of a world championship in any classification, has a predilection for talk, gab, more talk, boasting, and out and out tomfoolery.

Here is an American who doesn't wish to be an American, a fighter who doesn't wish to be a fighter for American patriotism. Now, if this man Clay isn't a genuine freak, one of the freakiest of all time despite his ideal physical proportions and ring skills, then we haven't had a real freak in boxing.

Foraging among the other heavyweight champions who qualify for the freak category we find a striking case in Primo Carnera. This onetime circus performer of Italy weighed 260 pounds,

Usually talkative Cassius Muhammad Ali Clay, world champion heavyweight, is forced to stick his fist into his mouth to accomplish a stoppage of vocal production.

On the left is Ed Dunkhorst, who stood 6 feet 3 in his socks, tipped the beam at 290, and had the distinction of being kayoed by Fitzsimmons. The dude on the right is Tommy Burns, who was top heavyweight despite his being only 5 feet 7 in height.

had a couple of hams for hands, and stood 6 feet 5¾ inches in height.

Apparently a pronounced gland case, with the typical prognathous jaw of such men, Carnera emphatically was not the heavyweight championship image. Yet this giant won the world title on June 29, 1933, when he knocked out Jack Sharkey in six rounds. A right uppercut finished off the Boston Gob, who just had landed a couple of his best punches, rights to the chin.

Carnera's ring skills, never respected as being of classic character, ultimately faded out and he went into the wrestling business, where his physical contours were more along standard lines.

In startling contrast with Carnera's proportions were those of heavyweight freak champion Tommy Burns, the Canadian

who was a none too formidable stopgap between Jim Jeffries and Jack Johnson. Burns was no taller than 5 feet 7 inches and gave no impression of the invincible model long associated with heavyweight title tenure.

No bigger than Burns, never weighing more than 160 pounds even as the heavyweight champion of England back in the bare knuckle days, circa 1790, was Daniel Mendoza, of Spanish Jewish descent. Daniel was the first polished boxer, a philosopher and a linguist.

Hardly heavier than Mendoza was the beaten contender from France, Georges Carpentier, who was stopped in the fourth round by Jack Dempsey on July 2, 1921. The Orchid Man was supposed to weigh 172 pounds but he tipped the beam at 164.

A physical freak who gained the title was Bob Fitzimmons, who had the torso of a giant and the underpinning of a lightweight. Ruby Robert was a 167 pounder who took the title from 183 pound Jim Corbett, and lost it to the 206 pound Jim Jeffries.

In addition to Carnera the over-size freaks include Ed Dunkhorst, a hulk of a man who could not fight a lick, and whom Fitz stopped in two rounds in jolly old Brooklyn in 1900.

If size really were the paramount factor in the establishment of heavyweight class Dunkhorst would have been a super champion. Ed weighed 290 pounds, much of it commercial lard, spread over a frame of 6 feet 3.

Charley Freeman, 6 feet 10½ inches,

**Whom have we here? The onetime flyweight champion Jimmy Wilde, who scored 77 knockouts and looked like a walking skeleton.**

**Mario D'Agata, pictured below, found that his being a mute did not prevent him from becoming world bantam champion in 1956.**

**Now, ladies and gentlemen, we come to a real freak, Joe Grim. He was knocked down more often than any other battler in ring history, yet he was stopped only thrice in 300 starts. He loved the floor.**

Upper left, Harry Greb, one of the greatest fighters of all time, whose total disregard for training regulations made him a freak. Above right, oddity Bob Fitzsimmons, who had the torso of a blacksmith and the underpinning of a lightweight. He is shown with Philadelphia Jack O'Brien. Below, Two Ton Tony Galento, who just has been starched by Joe Louis in the fourth round of a fight in which he had floored the champ.

320 pounds, was a Behemoth in an age in which, oddly enough, those bare knuckle brawlers were not famous for size.

Other fighters who belong in the list of freaks tracing to extreme height and poundage were Jess Willard, 252 pounds, 6 feet 6¼ inches; Ewart Potgieter, the South African, 326 pounds, 7 feet 2; Ray Impellitierre, 270 and 6 feet 7½; Buddy Baer, 245 and 6 feet 6½ inches; Harry Plaacke, 235 and 6 feet 5¾ inches; Gil Anderson, 250 and 7 feet; and Abe Simon, 252 and 6 feet 4 inches.

The legion of the large would not be complete without the current performers Ernie Terrell, who is 6 feet 6 inches tall and weighed 206 pounds for the Chuvalo fight, and Buster Mathis, who stands 6 feet 3 in height and whose weight has ranged between 320 and his current 242.

Among the heavyweights who join the smaller freaks are fat Willie Meehan and fatter Tony Galento.

Meehan was a roly-poly character who resembled a fighter just about as much as Carnera looked like a pole vaulter. Wee Willie had the distinction of gaining two four-round decisions over Jack Dempsey

before the Mauler became champion, in 1917 and 1918, and boxing two draw battles with Jack over similar distances, in 1917.

Dempsey managed to beat Fat William just once in five tries, at San Francisco in 1917. At the time four rounds was the legal limit in California. Conceivably this was all for the best for Meehan.

Galento was—well when you take a look at his picture as a fighter you decide that he was nothing more than a hoax. He never existed.

However, the fact remains that on the night of June 28, 1939, in Yankee Stadium, before 34,852 enthusiasts who paid $333,308 for the privilege, Two-Ton tumbled the heavyweight champion in the third round.

For Galento to have stopped Joe and become the champion would have been the all-time joke. However, the knockdown did not leave Joe in serious shape. In the fourth round, Galento was belted out.

Galento now revels as a disciplinarian among the Playboy Club bunnies and enjoys the scenery and his memories. Suppose he had hit Louis a bit harder? Boxing

The giant who is pushing the ceiling up is Ewart Potgieter, the South African who weighed 326 pounds and stood 7 feet 2 in height.

This is Eugene Criqui, the Frenchman who, despite a silver plate in his jaw, acquired in World War One, gained the world feather title in 1923 by stopping Johnny Kilbane.

shudders at the thought.

Eugene Criqui, the French feather who won the title by stopping Johnny Kilbane, belongs among the unusual ones because he carried on as a boxer despite the silver plate in his jaw, result of an injury in the first World War.

Jimmy Wilde, onetime world flyweight champion, 1916, looked as much like a professional boxer as Cassius Clay resembles Director of the Draft Gen. Hershey.

Wilde gave the impression that he was suffering from a complication of ills which might end his existence within the hour. But when the Mighty Atom got into the ring he was a package of dynamite. In his 139 fights Jimmy scored 77 knockouts.

While on the subject of the physically handicapped in the punching profession we find Howard Winstone, British featherweight leader, who lacks a couple of fingers on his right hand; Silent Martin, who was a deaf mute and Mart Mario D'Agata, former world bantamweight, similarly luckless.

One of the freakiest of the freaks was the unpredictable, colorful, incredible, undisciplined Battling Siki, the Senegalese who rose to the world light heavyweight championship by stopping Georges

Was Primo Carnera a freak? Well, you be the judge. Height, 6 feet 5³⁄₄ inches. Weight, 260 pounds. He became the world heavyweight champion in 1933, when he kayoed Jack Sharkey in six. Now Primo sells salami.

The roly-poly guy on the right is Willie Meehan, who despite his pudgy proportions lost only once in five meetings with Jack Dempsey, who is the other guy in the ring.

## FREAKS FESTOON RING HISTORY WITH FOIBLES, FEATS, FANCIES

Carpentier in Sept. 1922 in six rounds.

Siki lived the kind of life which is not conducive to good health and longevity. He got into a final brawl in December 1925 in New York and was shot to death.

Harry Greb was a freak in that he had freak ideas about training, discipline and condition.

Panama Al Brown, who weighed about 115 pounds and was only an inch short of six feet in height, looked like a walking cadaver. But, like Wilde, he was a dynamo in the ring. Brown won the bantam title in 1929.

Now we come to one Joe Grim. Here was a freak of museum quality. Joe delighted in stopping hard punches. He was floored more often than any other battler in a career which covered more than 300 fights, from 1902 to 1913, at weights ranging from 130 to 165.

Only four times was Grim knocked out but on each occasion he was greatly outweighed, by Sailor Burke, Luther Mc Carty, Sam McVey and 'way, 'way back, in 1904, by Young Zeringer, whoever he might have been.

Gene Tunney was something of a freak. From the Hudson River docks to lecturing on Shakespeare at Yale had to be freakish development.

### KNOCKED OUT MOST TIMES

| NAMES | HOME TOWN | WEIGHTS | Ko'ed By | Lost Dec. | Draws | Won | Total Bouts |
|---|---|---|---|---|---|---|---|
| Hatcher, Tommy | Tampa, Fla. | Welterweight | 9 | 2 | 1 | 2 | 13 |
| Horton, Al | Louisville, Ky. | Middleweight | 6 | 2 | 0 | 2 | 10 |
| Castillo, Tony | San Antonio, Tex. | Welterweight | 6 | 0 | 0 | 2 | 8 |

### MOST ACTIVE CHAMPIONS

| NAMES | HOMETOWN | WEIGHTS | Title Bouts | Ko's | Won Dec. | Non-Title Bouts | KO'S | Won Dec. | Lost | Total Bouts |
|---|---|---|---|---|---|---|---|---|---|---|
| Gavilan, Kid | Cuba | Welterweight | 3 | 1 | 2 | 7 | 0 | 6 | 1 | 10 |
| Moore, Archie | San Diego, Cal | Light Heavyweight | 1 | 0 | 1 | 8 | 6 | 2 | 0 | 9 |
| Carter, James | New York, N. Y. | Lightweight | 3 | 3 | 0 | 5 | 2 | 0 | 3 | 8 |

### MOST DEFEATS, MAIN BOUTS

| | | | | | | | |
|---|---|---|---|---|---|---|---|
| Womber, Danny | Chicago, Ill. | Welterweight | 9 | 0 | 1 | 9 | 12 |
| Williams, Charley | Newark, N. J. | Middleweight | 6 | 2 | 0 | 8 | 8 |
| Mathieu, Marcel | French Africa | Welterweight | 6 | 2 | 0 | 8 | 8 |
| Davis, Henry | Los Angeles, Cal | Lightweight | 6 | 1 | 0 | 7 | 10 |
| Herman, Freddy (Babe) | Los Angeles, Cal | Lightweight | 6 | 1 | 3 | 7 | 16 |

### MOST FIGHTS

| NAMES | HOME TOWN | WEIGHTS | Won | Lost | Draws | KO's | Ko'ed By | Total |
|---|---|---|---|---|---|---|---|---|
| Smith, Terry | Detroit, Mich. | Welterweight | 8 | 14 | 5 | 1 | 2 | 27 |
| Randell, Rocky | Rome, Ga. | Lightweight | 21 | 4 | 0 | 12 | 2 | 25 |
| Cockrell, Frankie | Los Angeles, Cal. | Welterweight | 12 | 9 | 4 | 3 | 1 | 25 |
| Butcher, Emerson | Rock Island, Ill. | Welterweight | 12 | 7 | 4 | 3 | 0 | 23 |
| Dennis, Earl | New York, N. Y. | Lightweight | 12 | 6 | 3 | 6 | 0 | 21 |
| Yantis, Bobby | Daytona Beach, Fla | Lightweight | 10 | 6 | 5 | 5 | 5 | 21 |
| Sligar, Otho | Houston, Tex. | Welterweight | 10 | 10 | 1 | 3 | 1 | 21 |
| Trevino, Roger | Houston, Tex. | Welterweight | 6 | 10 | 4 | 1 | 0 | 20 |
| Washington, Ulysse | Daytona Beach, Fla | Welterweight | 8 | 8 | 4 | 2 | 1 | 20 |
| Evans, Billy | Hollywood, Calif. | Featherweight | 4 | 11 | 5 | 0 | 0 | 20 |

### MOST MAIN BOUTS

| | | | | | | | | |
|---|---|---|---|---|---|---|---|---|
| Gault, Henry (Pappy) | Spartanburg, S. C. | Bantamweight | 13 | 3 | 0 | 8 | 0 | 16 |
| Valignat, Andre | France | Bantamweight | 11 | 1 | 4 | 3 | 0 | 16 |
| Herman, Freddy (Babe) | Los Angeles, Cal. | Lightweight | 6 | 7 | 3 | 2 | 1 | 16 |

### MOST WINS

| | | | | | | | | |
|---|---|---|---|---|---|---|---|---|
| Randell, Rocky | Rome, Ga. | Lightweight | 21 | 4 | 0 | 12 | 2 | 25 |
| Black, Jed | Janesville, Wisc. | Welterweight | 16 | 0 | 0 | 7 | 0 | 16 |
| Lane, Kenny | Muskegon, Mich. | Lightweight | 15 | 1 | 0 | 3 | 1 | 16 |
| Bickle, Bobby | Topeka, Kan. | Lightweight | 15 | 1 | 1 | 8 | 0 | 17 |
| Anthony, Tony | New York, N. Y. | Middleweight | 15 | 1 | 0 | 11 | 1 | 16 |
| Andrews, Al | Superior, Wisc. | Middleweight | 15 | 2 | 1 | 1 | 1 | 18 |
| Edwards, Phil | Wales | Welterweight | 15 | 2 | 0 | 2 | 0 | 17 |

An interesting early shot of Jack the Giant Killer, taken at the time of his spectacular title triumph over Jess Willard, Kansas Behemoth.

# 40 YEARS LATER, LONG COUNT STILL PROMPTS PROBE BY RING DETECTIVE

## Dempsey Insisted on Rule Which He Flouted at Chi; Could Tunney Have Risen Inside 10-Second Limit?

### By DAN DANIEL

FORTY years ago! It hardly appears to be possible. But the calendar doesn't lie. The current issue of The Ring is dated January 1967. Gene Tunney beat Jack Dempsey for the second time in the Battle of the Long Count on September 22, 1927, in Chicago. So it is forty years, after all. As Mushky Jackson, the Garden Immortal, so aptly has expressed it, "Whoda thunk it?"

Noting that the Long Count was celebrating its four decades anniversary, the Ring Detective was impressed with the availability of the fight as a subject for fresh investigation.

Not that there was a scintilla of doubt as to the authenticity of either of Tunney's victories, on ten round decisions, before 120,757 in the Sesqui-Centennial Stadium in Philadelphia, and at Soldier's Field in the Windy City before 104,943 paying guests, who pitched a record $2,658,660 into Tex Rickard's pot.

The first battle, on September 23, 1926, was a Tunney triumph all the way. In a driving rain, the Marine battered the Tiger all over the ring and in the tenth round appeared to have him on the verge of a knockout. Dempsey was an 11 to 5 favorite that dismal night. At Chicago, it was even money and take your pick.

The second fight developed many facets which will be talked about, and written about, just so long as there is interest in boxing and ring history.

Why the Battle of the Long Count? What was the Long Count? How did it come about in a world heavyweight championship contest? Under what set of rules did Referee Dave Barry refuse to go on counting over the fallen Tunney until Jack had gone to a far corner?

Before going into the details of that exciting seventh round,

Tunney is on the floor, watching referee Dave Barry and the time keeper. Barry has picked up the count from the timer. Gene does not look as if he could get up fast. Time hasn't helped to answer that question, which is being argued about to this day.

The shot above shows how the excitement in the historic seventh round got started. Gene let his guard go down and Jack clipped him with a terrific left. Then the fun began. The photograph to the left shows how Dempsey conceivably blew the championship. He stands over Tunney and stops the count by refusing to go to the far corner.

Tunney has regained his feet after the Long Count, which has been estimated at from 14 to 17 seconds. Gene appears to be in trouble. He is on his bicycle. But Jack hasn't too much left. He had passed his prime as a Great Fighter.

and a count estimated, variously, at from fourteen to seventeen seconds, let us go into a couple of intriguing might-have-beens.

Suppose Leo P. Flynn and Bill Duffy, who represented Dempsey in the conference on rules, had not held out for the stipulation that if either fighter scored a knockdown, the aggressor had to go to a far corner?

Leo's emphatic insistence on that rule, which was not in the code of the Illinois Boxing Commission, conceivably cost Dempsey the title, and the prestige of being the first beaten title holder to recover the heavyweight crown, 33 years before Floyd Patterson achieved that feat against Ingemar Johansson.

Suppose Dempsey had put up a strong and successful fight against the naming of Dave Barry? Would the other referee have enforced the rules so rigidly and rigorously? Would he have disregarded the stipulation that the fighter doing the decking had to move to a far corner, or no count?

In 1951, Ed Sullivan, who lived with the Dempsey entourage at Lincoln Fields while Jack was training for the fight, wrote a revealing column in the New York News about an offer by five Chicago hoods to have the "right man" referee the battle if the Dempsey camp fought for its choice. The fee was to be $50,000.

Of course, Dempsey refused to have anything to do with the thugs and their larcenous scheme.

Jack pointed out that no referee could help him regain the title because he could not hope to outpoint Tunney. "I've got to rely on these," the Mauler said, holding up his fists. "I have got to knock him out."

The rule on which Flynn and Bill Duffy insisted so strongly, and which made the Long Count possible, read like this:

"When a knockdown occurs, the timekeeper shall immediately arise and announce the seconds audibly as they elapse. The referee shall see first that the opponent retires to the farthest corner and then, turning to the timekeeper, shall pick up the count in unison with him, announcing the seconds to the boxer on the floor.

"Should the boxer on his feet fail to go, or stay in the corner, the referee and timekeeper shall cease counting until he has so retired."

It has been Tunney's contention, down through the years, that he could have regained his feet before a nine count. But examination of pictures of the knockdown tend to controvert the man who retired as champion undefeated.

In the New York Journal Bill Corum wrote that three years earlier Dempsey would have regained the title.

"Dempsey is through as a great fighter," Corum continued. The fight had emphasized that point with tremendous effect.

In the same newspaper, Tunney said that while he had won the title from Dempsey by boxing, he had retained it by fighting. "He gave me a harder fight than he had given me in Philadelphia," Gene added.

"I knew after the first round that I had Dempsey. I knew, further, that it would be only a question of time when I would knock him out. Twelve rounds would have done it.

"Twice I thought I had him. But he escaped, more from his tired slouch than anything else."

## 40 YEARS LATER, LONG COUNT STILL PROMPTS PROBE BY RING DETECTIVE

Now let us examine that historic and hysterical seventh round in Chicago's huge stadium.

Tunney appeared to be slow in getting the round under way. Gene, for some reason, was sluggish while Jack was stalking him like a tiger. Dempsey was driving the champion before him.

There was about a minute of this, and Tunney's legs appeared to be slowing. Jack unleashed a long, sweeping left and drove Tunney back to the ropes.

Tunney's jaw was unprotected and Dempsey hooked his left to the target.

Gene was crumpling. Like a flash came a terrific right which landed on the other side of his jaw. Then another left hook.

Gene slumped to the floor, scarcely six feet from Dempsey's corner. The champion reached for the low rope and pulled himself around to a sitting posture, facing the time keeper.

Referee Dave Barry motioned Dempsey to stop standing over his fallen rival, and go to the far corner, as stipulated in the rules which had been accepted for the fight.

Dempsey took some time in getting over to the far corner. His bullheaded attitude doubtless lost the title for him.

Some of the reporters insisted that Barry had picked up the knockdown timekeeper at one. Some said it was at five. By the time Tunney regained his feet the Long Count had occurred. Some said it was fourteen seconds, some made it seventeen.

Most of the reporters got the impression that had there been a normal course of events, Tunney could not have got up before a ten count. George Lytton, one of the judges, disagreed.

Gene was very cautious in the eighth round, and in the last two heats Dempsey did not have enough left to resume the stalking and the initiative. Jack hit the deck for a two count in the eighth. That was foolhardy. He should have taken nine.

Jack left the ring with both eyes swollen.

His left eye began to swell as early as the fourth round from Gene's unremitting righthanded attack.

With blood dripping from his face, Dempsey took a severe shellacking in the tenth round and it looked as if he just would have to hit the deck. But the former champion's dogged determination and gameness kept him on his feet. He could not recover the initiative and discount the big backlog of points Tunney had accumulated, despite the Long Count.

Dempsey left the battle scene with only three of the ten rounds, the big seventh, the third and, by a shade, the sixth. Tunney had seven heats and a firmer hold on the heavyweight championship of the world, and a radiant place in fistic history.

Lytton and Sheldon Clark, judges of the fight, both supported the actions of the referee.

Lytton's story, as told to Charles Collins, appeared in Liberty Magazine dated August 18, 1928. George was quoted as having said that the Illinois Commission had urged him to be the referee and he had declined. He gave the grand accolade to Barry, "for a splendid job, and a just one."

Lytton let neither Tunney nor Dempsey get off Scott free. He said that Dempsey had been guilty of foul tactics, in hitting low and using the rabbit punch. But he also indicted Gene for holding—keeping Jack's gloves captives in his arm pits.

However, Barry would have been remiss had he disqualified either fighter on the flimsy basis of the evidence. Dempsey's low blows were not hard enough to figure in the result. Dave did warn both fighters, and both more or less ignored him.

Barry, who admitted that he had counted 14 over Tunney, is dead. He succumbed on August 26, 1936. He is not around to explain what he did, for the hundredth time, or to offer a defense, were one needed, of his adherence to an accepted rule on which the Dempsey side had insisted.

Dempsey, past 70, says he lost the title to Tunney because of ring rust. He does not attribute his second defeat by Gene to a similar reason.

Tunney and Dempsey now are close friends, content to let history stand as it is. They refuse to delve again into the past and items which open the way to heated controversy.

Tunney was born on May 25, 1898, Dempsey on June 24, 1895. Thus Gene had an advantage of three years on Jack. This, in itself, should not have been a telling factor. But Jack was fading, Tunney was to retire, unbeaten, after knocking out Tom Heeney in eleven rounds on July 26, 1928.

Dempsey continued to make ring appearances through 1940. But the Battle of the Long Count was his last real fight.

Did the heavyweight class ever present two more skilled and formidable antagonists than the battlers of the Long Count?

Down through the corridors of Time, Echo answers, "Did it?"

---

## ● KANSAS CITY AND VICINITY ●
### By Max Yeargain

Over 3,000 fans paid $5,200 to see two 10-round main events in Memorial Hall, Kansas City, Kansas.

Ronnie Marsh, 187, young Kansas City heavyweight, now fighting out of Minneapolis, scored a TKO in 1:45 of the seventh round over Tommy (Hurricane) Sims, 182, Houston, when the Texan was knocked through the ropes and referee Sammy Anch halted the match.

Kelly Burden, 162, Kansas City Irishman, now has a 12-0 record. He knocked out Smiley Johnson, 165, Chicago, Ill., in 1:05 of the second round.

Bobby (Frenchy) Cauvin, 150, Kansas City won a tough fight over Chief Charlie Sacks, 152, rugged Indian veteran from Muskogee, Okla., in the 6-round semi windup.

In the opening 6-rounder, Carlos Che, 135, Chicago, Ill., looked impressive in decisioning Nick Haywood, 129, Kansas City.

▶ Ruby Goldstein, the George Jessel of the boxing toastmasters, the day following the fight did a tremendous job in speaking to advertising executives at their downtown club in Kansas City.

# "How I Would Have Clobbered Clay"
## By Joe Louis
### AS TOLD TO GEORGE WHITING

CASSIUS CLAY'S got lots of ability, but he is not The Greatest. He's a guy with a million dollars worth of confidence and a dimes worth of courage. I could have whipped him. In all honesty, I feel it in my bones. Clay can be clobbered, and if you'll pardon an old-timer talking, I am certain I know how.

These days, I get to the fights in most parts of the world, especially when Clay is defending my old heavyweight title. We kid around the training camps a little, and Clay makes speeches and goes into his act, telling the folks how he would have fought Joe Louis. I play along.

It don't harm nobody. Maybe helps the action, puts a few dollars on the take.

Fellows come up, asking for autographs, that kind of thing, and tell me I could have licked Clay with the Empire State Building tied to my feet. I don't say anything.

But a man gets thoughts sitting there watching Clay. I seen him fooling in the gym, and I seen nearly all his fights, right through from Willie Besmancff, way back in Louisville, to Cleveland Williams in Houston. Sometimes Clay fights good and sometimes he pulls rhubarbs that should get his head knocked off if the other guy knew his trade like they made me learn mine.

Trouble with Clay, he thinks he knows it all. Fights with his mouth. He won't listen. Me, first thing I learned in the fight game was to keep my trap shut and my ears wide open, especially when my wise old trainer, Chappie Blackburn, was telling me things for my own good.

We did all right. Seems like I won a championship, so maybe I'm entitled to speak up a word or two of truth after all these years. And the truth in my book is I'm sure I could've put Clay away, and also know how.

Clay says he's got the fastest hands and the fastest feet of any heavyweight who ever was born. That's his opinion and he's entitled to it. The kid has speed and can surely box when he has to. There's nobody around to outbox him, and the op-

Joe Louis at Houston, joining in horse play with Cassius Clay (on right) and Cleveland Williams before the fighters undergo the Texas Commission's official physical examination.

ponent who tries is in his grave.

Especially in the middle of the ring. With room to move, Clay's a champion, real dangerous. But he doesn't know a thing about fighting on the ropes, which is where he would be if he were in there with me. He's all confused, his feet in knots, and his body wide open to everything.

I didn't see Henry Cooper put Clay down in their first fight in London, but I'd like to bet Clay was coming off the ropes when he got caught with that left hook.

I certainly saw that German southpaw, Mildenberger, bang him good in a corner, and that was when Mildenberger had been battered into a hopeless, beat-up hulk in the 10th round. Clay did not appreciate that punch one bit, but if Mildenberger had known enough to send it over when he was fresh, I figure Clay would have appreciated it a whole lot less.

Sure, Clay's got fancy feet in the middle of the ring, faster even than Billy Conn or Bob Pastor, two of the quickest men who

ever gave me a run-around till I caught up. But Clay wastes his footwork, stumbling around like Conn and Pastor never did from where I was looking.

There's a couple of other things about Clay. He drops his left hand when he should be protecting that pretty face he's always talking about. Doing a fool thing like that in a championship fight, he could wind up looking like a meat wagon, or maybe riding in one.

Dropping your left hand ain't healthy. It was a weakness of my own till Max Schmeling taught me the hard way in our first fight.

If I were fighting Clay, I would start licking him at least five weeks before the bell, right in the training camp . . . some place like my old stand at Pompton Lakes.

There wouldn't be too much of the fancy fixin's and show-biz routines they give you in the gymnasiums these days, but there sure would be some murder going on. I never fooled around in work-outs.

I would pay top wages for the five fastest

## "HOW I WOULD HAVE CLOBBERED CLAY"

sparring partners I could buy. I would need quick targets to speed up my hands for a fast opponent like Clay, and I would feel real sorry for those boys by the time we were through.

Clay has his own ideas about sparring. Me too. There would be no horsing around. I never did pull punches with sparmates. Fighting was my business, and a man shouldn't play games in business hours. If I were training to whip Clay, my partners would go home bruised and busted up round the body, even from big gloves. Anyone who couldn't take it would be out, long before fight night.

And if I was boss in camp I'd aim to be boss in the ring, where the gloves come smaller. Any man who fights Clay's fight is crazy. With me, Clay would have to fight a Joe Louis fight, my way, all the way.

Which means I would go in to outpunch him rather than try to outbox him. I once thought I could keep up with Billy Conn, and for a long time it didn't take.

I'd see to it that Clay did not stay in ring-centre. Out there, I could be the Patsy on the wrong end of the punishment. No, he'd be hit into those ropes as near a corner as I could get him . . . some place where, from all I've seen, he just does not know how to fight.

If he stayed on the ropes, he'd get hurt. Sooner or later he'd try to bounce off, and when he did he would get hurt more. That's what the fight game is all about.

I'd press him, bang him around, claw him, clobber him with all I'd got, cut down his speed, belt him round the ribs. I'd punish the body, where the pain comes real bad. I know I can still feel the triphammers Rocky Marciano hit me with when he knocked me out when he was on the way up and I was on the way out.

Clay would have welts on his body like I did. He would ache, like I did. His mouth would shut tight against the pain and there would be tears burning his eyes. It is not very funny being under fire from body punches, and it wouldn't help Clay any looking for his trainer, Angelo Dundee, to come riding into the ring with a rescue posse.

Those guys in the corner fight good during the intervals, but they can't give you any more fists or any more heart when some guy's caving your ribs in.

"Kill the body and the head will die" Chappie used to tell me. It figures.

Sooner or later, I think Clay would get the message. Get it so good that he'd stop worrying about that face of his and drop his left hand like he did against Mildenberger and George Chuvalo. Those fellows got their opening by accident, and then fouled it up. I would work for it, and I wouldn't reckon to miss when it arrived.

If I goofed with a world title and a million dollars or so in the pot—plus all that television money these days—then I would not have any right to be in there with a smart fighter like Cassius Clay.

But only smart so far. Clay coming out of a corner all confused, busted up from body punches, would be a sucker for any opponent waiting for him with a shot in the locker. I'd be waiting, ready with something hot.

I haven't got around to figuring what kind of punch I'd send in for the pay-roll, but I learned several in my day. A one-punch fighter is only half a fighter. Take away his hammer and he's nothing. You have to be properly equipped.

When I won my title from Jim Braddock, I cut Jim's lip with a left hook, but that was only by way of preparation for the pay-off. When his legs began to wobble, I put my whole body behind a right to the jaw and Jim dropped on his face for good-bye.

Maybe I could hit Clay with that kind of right. It takes all sorts, like in my second fight with Max Schmeling. A right to the jaw gave Max a three-count; he took two more from a one-two combination; then I threw a straight left jab and a right cross for keeps. But all these counts started from a right to the ribs after Max had bounced off the ropes with his legs in a mess.

I owed Max a thing or two. After he beat me two years earlier, I spent lots of time studying his style before I discovered he was a sucker for a left jab.

I honestly feel I could have turned the same kind of trick against Clay, but my feelings don't predict which round. Only poets go around predicting.

I was prepared to travel all the way against Schmeling, but I got my chance to tag him in one. Contrariwise. I was hoping for a quick kill in my first fight with Billy Conn on the New York Polo Grounds.

But I came in too light, and Billy breezed along so fast he nearly took my title. Too bad he finally decided to slug it out, like

I hoped he would, and got his face all mixed up with my right in the 13th.

If I was fighting Clay, I would aim to be ready with the big one any time, from Round One to Round Fifteen.

In London and most other places I go, people always ask me how Clay would have come through against my old opponents, and we kick the thing around, arguing this way and that.

I think Jersey Joe Walcott would have outgeneralled him. Clay is faster, but old Joe had better style and better brains. When he dropped his left hand it wasn't a mistake. It was to feint you on to a right hand that could bring the roof on your head.

Billy Conn was like lightning. He learned his trade in the small clubs, from welter right through to heavyweight. He could have kept up with Clay because his legs knew where they were going. Only thing is Clay and Conn would have been running away from each other so fast that there would have been no fight.

Clay I think would have hit too fast for Jim Braddock and would have had too many moves for Max Baer. Maxie packed a punch but never paid enough attention to learning his business the hard way; in camp and round the clubs.

Schmeling could have taken Clay with his right, same way he took me when I forgot to keep my left up after I'd jabbed with it in our first fight.

But, of all my old opponents, the one to give Clay the worst time, would have been Rocky Marciano. The Rock didn't know too much about the boxing book, but it wasn't a book he hit me with. It was a whole library of bone crushers.

If Marciano caught up with him, I figure Clay would get discouraged and start looking for Angie Dundee to cut his gloves off.

Nobody ever beat Marciano, and I was wrong when I thought I was still young enough to know how. I could be wrong about Clay as well, but it's good to forget the calendar once in a while and dream up ways of whipping the man who wears your old crown.

Once I happened to walk along when Clay was hollering "I am The Greatest!" to some fellows outside the Theresa Hotel in Harlem. When he saw me, Clay came over and shouted to the crowd: "This is Joe Louis. *WE* is The Greatest!"

That was nice. Cassius Clay is a nice boy and a smart fighter. But I'm sure Joe Louis could have licked him.

# LISTON CARRIED MANY SECRETS TO HIS GRAVE

## By JERSEY JONES

NEVER before in the history of the heavyweight championship did the vital statistics concerning a world titleholder present the mysteries which attached to Charles Sonny Liston, who took the crown from Floyd Patterson on September 25, 1962 in Chicago, and lost it to Cassius Clay on February 25, 1964, at Miami Beach.

The exact dates of Liston's birth and his demise are not known. He carried these secrets, and many others, to the grave with him.

Liston kept insisting that he was only 38 years of age, and placed the date of his birth in St. Francis County, Arkansas, on May 8, 1932.

Since Liston was found dead in his Las Vegas home days after he had passed away, the date of his farewell cannot be arrived at with certainty.

And so it was that one of the most controversial figures in the annals of the ring was wiped out of the ratings by the inexorable blows of the ever victorious foe.

Liston died with one public distinction, if distinction it was. He was the only heavyweight champion barred from New York State.

Mike Parkhurst, who says he handled Charley's fistic and other affairs these last several years, told THE RING that Liston definitely was only 38 years of age, and that his recorded date of birth, May 8, 1832, was correct.

"There is a possibility that Sonny was confused with his boxer cousin, Sailor Liston, who fought around 1934," Parkhurst added.

"The report that he is survived by a daughter 25 years of age is erroneous. She is the daughter of Mrs. Liston by an earlier marriage.

(Left) The late Sonny Liston in his familiar fighting pose. (Above) Floyd Patterson falls into the ropes after taking a hard left from Liston. It was all over in a very few moments as Liston put Floyd away in the first round to win the heavyweight title in one round at Chicago in 1962.

Liston is presented with his heavyweight championship belt by Nat Fleischer, editor and publisher of The Ring, back in 1963, when he was training for his second contest with Patterson, in Las Vegas.

Patterson is about to hit the canvas for the second time in the first round of his second encounter with Liston. After three knockdowns, it was all over after 2 minutes, 10 seconds of action.

"I will say that many rated fighters would have none of Sonny. The leader of this crew was Jerry Quarry.

"One thing is definite. Sonny was not a narcotics addict."

At no time could Liston obtain a license in the Empire State.

Gen. Melvin Krulewitch, chairman of the New York Commission, said that he had evidence of Liston's association with men of questionable reputation and, in denying him a license, the New York Commission was acting in protection of boxing.

There was a lot of support for Liston. Hundreds of letters to THE RING pleaded that he had "paid his debt to society."

But Charley had to go to Miami Beach to defend his title against Clay. He had won the championship in Chicago and beaten Patterson a second time in Las Vegas.

Whether he was 38, or 44, as most boxing authorities believed him to be, the mysterious passing of Liston in his $50,-000 home in Las Vegas supplied further confirmation to the contention that world heavyweight champions enjoy a longer life than do competitors in other athletic fields.

One would assume that in a violent contact profession such as fist-tossing, terrestrial existence would be comparatively brief. But the records tend to prove otherwise. Of the many heavyweight champions dating back to John L. Sullivan, eleven are still up and about, with Jack Dempsey the senior survivor at the age of 75.

Those who've had the final counts droned over them were John L. Sullivan at 60; Jim Corbett 67, Bob Fitzsimmons 79, Jim Jeffries 78, Marvin Hart 57, Tommy Burns 74, Jack Johnson 68, Jess Willard 88, Max Baer 50, and Rocky Marciano 46. Marciano and Johnson died in accidents.

Thus, even at 44, Liston was the youngest heavyweight champion to have the final curtain dropped on him.

The age question had long plagued the Big Ugly Bear, as Clay dubbed him. Some years ago, when Sonny was training in a Las Vegas gymnasium, a reporter asked him how old he actually was. An annoyed Liston blasted him with: "Anybody who says I'm more than 35 is making my mother a liar."

Sonny was the 24th of 25 offspring born to a father married for the second time. He arrived on this mundane sphere on a dilapidated cotton farm near Little Rock. From an impoverished childhood, filled with hatred, insecurity and distrust, he became a juvenile delinquent.

By the time Charley was 18 he had been convicted of six mugging and was en route to Missouri State Penitentiary for robbing a gas station in St. Louis. It was the first of two prison sentences he served.

Liston's last bout was a nine-round TKO over Chuck Wepner in Jersey City last June 29. Here is a scene from the bloody brawl, the blood all flowing from the cut-prone Wepner.

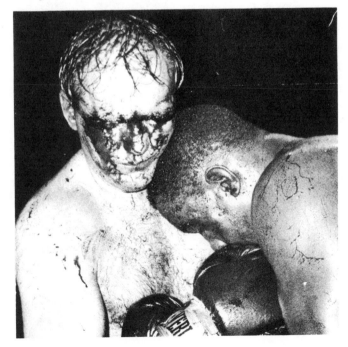

## LISTON CARRIED MANY SECRETS TO HIS GRAVE

In St. Louis he had been an anti-labor goon, an armed robber and an alleged rapist. A hulking, menacing figure (6 feet, 1 inch, 200 pounds) he was encouraged to try boxing by a Roman Catholic chaplain in prison, and fought his first fight on September 2, 1953, flattening one Don Smith in one round in St. Louis.

That win started a string of six victories, mostly in and around St. Louis. He began to spread his activities, with Detroit as his next port of call. Two wins over highly touted John Summerlin in the automobile capital followed, but also in Detroit he suffered his first defeat when his jaw was fractured by Marty Marshall. It happened in the fourth round of a scheduled eight. Liston finished the bout, but lost the decision.

Liston subsequently evened the score with Marshall by stopping him in six rounds in St. Louis, and closed the series by beating Marshall again, this time in ten rounds in Pittsburgh.

For the next five years—from 1958 through 1962—Sonny's ring career was one of continued success. He ran off 21 consecutive victories, all but three by knockouts, and he established himself as a popular attraction on national television.

His power was seen in Chicago, Miami Beach, Cleveland, Houston, Denver, Seattle, Philadelphia and Las Vegas, where his victims included Julio Maderos, Wayne Bethea, Billy Hunter, Frankie Daniels, Ernie Cab, Mike DeJohn, Cleveland Williams, Willi Besmanoff, Howard King, Roy Harris, Zora Folley and Albert Westphal.

The only opponents who managed to avoid knockouts and to last the scheduled routes with Liston were Bert Whitehurst (twice) and the crafty veteran Eddie Machen.

By this time Liston had established himself as a dangerous contender for the world championship, and on September 25, 1962, he was accommodated with a crack at Floyd Patterson and the title. The bout was held in Chicago, and Patterson failed to last one full round with him.

It was the following July 22 that Patterson was given the opportunity to regain his lost laurels, but he fared no better than he had in his first tussle with Liston. The return match was held in Las Vegas and again one round was all Sonny needed to dispose of the former champion.

Aside from a brief tour of Europe, Liston was inactive fistically until February 25, 1964, when he stacked up against a young upstart from Louisville, Kentucky. The youngster was Cassius Marcellus Clay, also known as Muhammad Ali.

The bout was staged in Miami Beach, and Liston quit in his corner at the end of the sixth round, insisting that he had injured his left shoulder.

The unsatisfactory ending of that affair resulted in a return match with Clay the following May 25, in Lewiston, Me.

This meeting also produced an unsatisfactory finish, with much confusion. The bout lasted only 1 minute, 42 seconds of one round, the shortest heavyweight championship bout on record.

Liston's quick defeat stirred up all sorts of suspicion and speculation. There were charges that Sonny had gone down from a phantom right-hand punch, but ringsiders concluded that his chin had been softened by too many grueling brawls on his way to the championship, and that the punch was legitimate.

Seemingly his poor showing in that bout spelled finis to Sonny's ring career. But he refused to be convinced. Following a year's retirement, he returned to action in Sweden, where he registered knockouts over Gerhard Zech in Stockholm, and Amos Johnson in Gothenburg.

In 1967 Charley made another junket to Sweden, disposing of two other Americans, Dave Bailey in Gothenburg and Elmer Rush in Stockholm.

In 1968 Liston did his brawling in the United States and Mexico, running off seven more knockouts, his victims including Bill McMurray in Reno, Billy Joiner in Los Angeles, Henry Clark in San Francisco, Sonny Moore in Phoenix, Willie Earls in Juarez, Roger Rischer in Pittsburgh and Amos Lincoln in Baltimore.

Meanwhile, Liston had established Las Vegas as his headquarters.

His "comeback" was unceremoniously wrecked on December 6, 1968, when an apparently decisive victory was suddenly turned into disaster by Leotis Martin, of Philadelphia, in the ninth round in Las Vegas.

But Sonny still wasn't ready to concede that he was finished. Last June 29 he appeared in the Jersey City Armory to belabor the much-battered Chuck Wepner into a gory mess and a 9th-round KO.

Through the years Liston occasionally filled in bit roles in motion pictures, invariably portraying mean, surly bad guys, an image he had conveyed to his opponents and the public.

Actually, Sonny was hardly "mean and surly." He wasn't too talkative, usually limiting his answers to curt "yeahs" and "noes." On occasion, however, he could be a pleasant conversationalist.

Aside from his wife, Geraldine, Sonny's main interests in life were youth programs, his interest stemming from his own impoverished and underprivileged childhood in Arkansas.

Sonny never learned to read, and his writing was confined to his name. But his fists earned him nearly $4,000,000 in paydays during his exciting, if erratic, career.

Sonny Liston is gone, and now will know the peace and tranquility he seldow knew in life.

# HANDWRITING EXPERT REPORTS —

## TOP FIGHTERS SIGNATURES REVEAL TRAITS, CHARACTERS

### By SALLY DRELL

THE crowds that clamor for a fighter's autograph get more than just a souvenir when he signs his name. A man's signature is part of him, a most revealing part. Just as his clothes or speech or body language telegraph messages to us, a man's handwriting can be a penetrating key to his character.

Great boxing champions have been analyzed from every point of view. Their styles, strengths and weaknesses have been rehashed until nothing new can be said. But let's look beneath the outward clues,

GEORGE FOREMAN—He's got persistence, curiosity, and aggressiveness. The F-stroke is like a slashing sword through the F-stem. He's got a bit of ego, but it's not as exaggerated as Muhammad Ali's ego. This man is more reserved. He makes decisions based on his head, not his heart, but he's also got strong intuition. He can be quite blunt and abrupt, and may even appear unfriendly at times.

JOE FRAZIER—Look at the F with the very long upper horizontal stroke. Usually, people who make long strokes in the upper zone want to be known for their intellectual prowess and accomplishments having to do with the mind. Joe Frazier may plan to do things in the future that are less physical than boxing. There's a huge lower loop in the J. You see these large loops in the handwriting of many boxers. It indicates he subscribes to the theory of traditional masculinity. He'd never go for a liberated woman. The man's role, to him, means strength and aggression and force. Joe is not secretive; he's outgoing.

MUHAMMAD ALI—There's a long drawn-out h in the middle of the word Muhammad, with an almost Arabic look to it. He may be deliberately striving to make it look Arabic as a bow to Islam. He's interested in cultural things—art, music. He's a cultivated person. There are signs of altruism in this handwriting, of being associated with a cause larger than just his own immediate family. He's a bit of a strategist, sometimes getting involved in a bit of chicanery, but he knows how to get himself out of it. There are signs of vanity and the erratic size of his letters indicates moodiness.

He may fly off the handle at times. His handwriting indicates he may do things he'd like to cover up. There's family pride and sensitivity. He's guarded; he's no 'open book' no matter how big a mouth he seems to have.

*[signature: Floyd Patterson]*

FLOYD PATTERSON—The first thing you notice about Patterson's signature is the odd looking F. It looks like a little sentry guarding the rest of the signature. He is probably quite reserved and self-protective, even defensive. He wants to shut out the world, so he puts up a strong facade. The very large F (compared to the rest of the name) is a sign of ego. It's a complicated formation, not easy to make. It's like he's winding up before getting ready to throw a punch.

He's a proud man, and he lives in a world of reality. He's capable of tact and diplomacy, being closed-mouthed. He likes to do things fast, can do things quickly, and with considerable imagination. He's impatient, eager to get things done. I think once you got past this man's defenses he would be cooperative, but it would be quite a job to reach him.

*[signature: Best Wishes, Sugar Ray Robinson]*

SUGAR RAY ROBINSON—Dynamic. He's much flashier than Griffith. Griffith has a light touch, he's got style. Robinson has a style of his own, but it's more typically "boxer." Robinson's handwriting has an outward hook on the top of the S and the R, kind of jutting forward. He probably had a very fast punch, surprised his opponents with unexpected shots. His timing was unpredictable in the ring. A tenacious man, he stays in the ring until the bitter end.

*[signature: Emile Griffith]*

EMILE GRIFFITH—Griffith's handwriting looks foreign and he was probably educated outside the United States. Notice the sweeping E, a long stem upward and a very graceful sweep down. That E would indicate gentleness and it protectively hovers over the rest of the name. The G does the same thing to Griffith, a protective cover. He probably knows that he's sensitive and gentle and tries to protect himself from people who might want to hurt him. There are great signs of intuition in his handwriting. He's very strongly influenced by his feelings. His t-bar is a heavy stroke, so we know that although he is sensitive, he can be aggressive when the occasion demands. He's intuitive, he's imaginative, and he's gentle. It's an artistic handwriting, not like the handwriting of a boxer. This is a man of the mind. Not an earthy type at all.

BENNY LEONARD—His handwriting stands out of all the boxing handwritings because of its simplicity. First, he was selective in his friendships and highly independent. Second, there is no trace of the egotism we see in most other fighter's handwriting. He was intelligent. His letters are easy to read and they're all connected, showing a logical mind. He's somewhat opinionated, indicated by the downstroke of the d. There's an aggressive quality to it, because the pressure is heavy, but it's not the typical signature of a fighter at all—no underscoring, no flourishes, no big capital letters. He's got a good grip on reality. His approach to boxing would have definitely been scientific; He would not be a glamour boy. He was probably analytical in the ring; a scientific fighter. The money, rather than the glory or ego satisfaction, would lure him to the ring.

JOSE TORRES—The first thing that strikes you about Torres' signature is the size of the capital letters. They're large, and large capitals indicate a larger-than-average ego. The loops indicate sensitivity. We see the underscoring found frequently in boxers' writing. He sees things on a large scale, and is not concerned with details. He sees the total picture, and that's what interests him. There's also a spiritual quality to Jose Torres. He's probably got an active fantasy life, and I would say he's quite idealistic. He may be interested in art, cultural things. It's a flashy signature, but it indicates good things—spirituality, sensitivity; a good guy.

ROCKY GRAZIANO—Rocky is surprisingly choosy when it comes to picking his friends. He's quite an independent guy. The Z becomes his particular interpretation of the familiar underscore. There's the usual flamboyance, the desire for attention, the ego. He's clear thinking, gets right to the point, is direct. He's got good coordination, and he's a realist.

JOE LOUIS—Joe's handwriting is interesting for the loops. He's quite sensitive and very generous. Not very well-educated, Louis sees things on a large scale. Not terribly analytical, details bore him. With an attitude like that, he should live a long time.

BENNY KID PARET—This man was repressed, and had strong guilt feelings. Health problems are indicated and it would be interesting to know when this was written. It may have been at a time when his brain was damaged already, which many boxing people are convinced took place before he fought Griffith.

HENRY ARMSTRONG—His handwriting has so many superfluous strokes that I suspect he may have clouded up his life in a similar way. The lines overlap so much they almost obscure what he's written. Probably his own worst enemy, Armstrong may have a tendency toward fuzzy thinking. He probably tends to dress in a distinctive, even flashy way; he's definitely a bit of a dandy. Loves the limelight.

*Good luck "Champ"*
*your pal Max Baer*
*8-3-57*

MAX BAER—The unusual thing about Max Baer's signature is the windup on the top of the M and the top of the B. Like Floyd Patterson's F, it's an extra, useless stroke. The formation of Max's M reveals an 'old world' attitude, a deep respect for old traditions. The L in luck and pal indicates some health problems. It was signed two years before Baer died of a heart attack, and the signature indicates there was something wrong with his heart. He was even-tempered, outgoing.

*Jack Johnson Former*
*Heavy Champion of the*
*World  Good luck*

JACK JOHNSON—Intelligent. Had unusual sexual preferences. His handwriting indicates a combination of the phallic symbol and the feminine symbol. The d in World is strong, showing self-confidence. The way it sweeps down at the end means he was opinionated and willful. He was not a direct person. A bit of a strategist and wheeler-dealer.

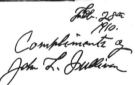

*Feb. 28th 1910.*
*Compliments of*
*John L. Sullivan*

JOHN L. SULLIVAN—His handwriting is quite pointy, a sign of mental development. His i-dot formation is a sign of critical ability. This handwriting was written ages ago, so you see the old style formations taught in school at the time.

JOSE NAPOLES—Very much likes to be a mystery to other people. Jose is a self-contained person. He isolates the word Napoles like a little island. He circles it as if he's closing himself off to the world. A very critical man, he may be too much so. He can be hypercritical of others, and of himself as well. He has good physical coordination; is introspective to the extremes; closed off.

GEORGES CARPENTIER—His handwriting has that foreign look. He is a cultured, stylish, independent person. He underscores in a distinctive way. He's got the usual desire to be center-stage, but he expresses it in a much more subtle way. He wouldn't be the type to pick out flashy clothes, but would wear well-made, understated, expensive ones. Not a precipitous person, he was patient and slow. Look at the delicate pen pressure, showing sensitivity. He is very much a Frenchman.

DICK TIGER—He was a flirt; the D shows capriciousness. He had a sense of humor, making him very attractive to women. The curves in D and T look like little smiles. He was charming and intuitive.

If we were to create a signature that combined the qualities found most frequently in boxers' handwriting, the result would look very much like the imaginary Billy "The Kid" O'Shea signature I created for this story. Eight out of ten fighters underscore their names, showing a desire to be the center of attention. It may also be a sign of an inferiority complex that is hidden by a show of personality force. Most begin their signatures with large capital letters, showing large egos. Their pen pressure is heavy, indicating aggressiveness, and the majority dip their "y" and "p" way down in what handwriting experts call the 'lower zone.' This dip, like the y in Billy, reveals strong physical desires, and emphasis on the physical, or a flair for the dramatic.

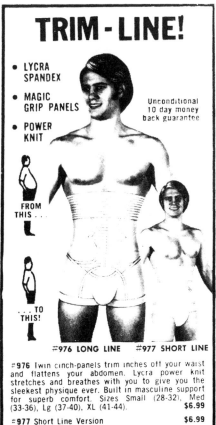
## HANDWRITING EXPERT REPORTS

through handwriting analysis, and see the real man.

Peter Heller, author of "In This Corner," published by Simon & Schuster, let me use his extensive boxing autograph collection as the basis for what I will say. As I gazed at the dozens of autographs Peter provided, I began to see definite patterns emerge. Some of the most common: the almost universally large size of the signatures; the frequently underscored, or under-lined, names; the heavy pen pressure.

Let's take a look at some of the most interesting fighters' signatures, along with what I was able to determine about each man based solely on an analysis of his handwriting patterns.

# What I'll Do When I'm Through

**By MUHAMMAD ALI**

## AS TOLD TO MURRAY GOODMAN

Muhammad Ali is one of the most strongly opinionated men to ever hold the heavyweight crown. His ideas on how to live or retire are well thought out.

WHEN and if I hang up the competitive gloves—and everybody in athletic competition must face that day—I'll have a full blue print for the future. It will, however, be a flexible blue print, subject to the changes of events and conditions.

I have always maintained that a man who has no imagination has no wings and cannot fly. I do not want to set the world on fire but neither do I have to roll over and disappear from the face of the earth.

The people will not let Muhammad Ali die. It will long remain a legendary name in boxing not because I'm just pretty and charming but because I earned that right to be loved by many. I gave the people what they wanted. I fought for minorities and their rights in this world. I have travelled the world urging people to see that their children were encouraged to become better educated to seek the many freedoms they now don't have. I will never cease in that fight to do the best for my people.

I have been fortunate to be able in my lectures to relate to all peoples, young and old. They listen to me and believe me because what I say is both down to earth and common sense. That is why I will devote a good part of my time as a Moslem Minister, preaching the teachings of Elijah Muhammad. By the time this is written, I may have already sold my home in Cherry Hill, N.J., and moved to Chicago to be closer to the Moslem scene.

There will be no financial problems for Muhammad Ali and his family. I will be either world champion again or will have done my best to win the title when I'm ready to quit fighting. The fight for the championship with either George Foreman or Ken Norton, depending on who wins the pending fight, will constitute the biggest purse in the history of boxing. That will give me well over $3,000,000 in the bank in money alone and all my children and my wife will have nothing to worry about. I will see to it that the children are given the best possible education so that they can all meet the challenges of life.

My training camp in Deer Lake, Pa., which I call a "Fighter's Heaven", will remain active. It is possible that I may decide to sell it but that, at this writing, is remote. I plan to use it myself to maintain my own physical condition. I don't ever again want to become fat and flabby. It is so easy to maintain condition once you've learned the secret.

My camp will be made available to all youth groups to religious sects for special days and outings and to other fighters who want to use it for training. There is no finer camp for an athlete to get into condition. I have even given thought to expanding a part of it into a day camp.

I will continue to lecture at colleges where I can fit the bookings in without interfering with my work as a minister. I will also box exhibitions in the many foreign countries that have long been trying to get me to come over. My earning capacity in retirement will be as great, if not greater, than it was as a boxer.

I have even entertained the idea of managing, training and developing young fighters. The thought intrigues me since I have my own methods of training and teaching. Just think of it, the one and only Muhammad Ali creating another fighter in his own image. Can the world be ready for another Ali?

The boxing world should begin preparing even now for my departure from the active fight picture. It is not conceit. Boxing will miss Muhammad Ali. The promoters should begin developing new faces and new talents. The champion of the world, whoever he is, must be a leader who fights often and helps the sport. There should be a worldwide search for heavyweights. Promoters should spend some money to keep boxing alive. They should start thinking in terms of giving young athletes an incentive to become fighters—guaranteed pay while learning, pensions, health insurance. Unlike any other sport, boxing is far behind in fringe benefits.

I will retire some day, perhaps soon, but I will never forsake boxing. Let us hope that the people in boxing don't forsake it after I'm gone.

Ali relaxing at his Deer Lake, Pa., training camp in which everything is on the rustic side. Ali is great on the "back to nature" bit. Admittedly, he also enjoys the better things of life.

Consistent with his love of children Ali is seen with Young Tiger, a boxing hopeful.

Keeping in top physical condition will always be serious stuff for Ali.

# FIGHTS THAT SHOULD NOT HAVE BEEN MADE TURNED HISTORY IN ODD DIRECTIONS

## By BOB GOODMAN

Heavyweight champ Muhammad Ali, as seen in his defeat by Norton in the twelve round split decision where he fought with a broken jaw. The date: March 31, 1973, San Diego, California.

Gus Lesnevich, light heavyweight champ looks up from canvas as Freddie Mills waits referee count in London, July 26, 1948. Freddie won in 15 and became the light heavyweight champ.

(Left) Ken Norton raises his gloves in victory after defeating Jerry Quarry, March 24, 1975. Norton won by a TKO in the fifth round at Madison Square Garden, N.Y.
(Below) Jimmy Braddock upsets Max Baer at Madison Square Garden, June 13, 1935. During their heavyweight fight Bear is cornered against the ropes in one of the most startling upsets in boxing history.

READ the headlines — "Lyle Next for Ali", "Lyle To Prep For Ali Against Jimmy Young", "Young Upsets Lyle", — they've told the story of the blunders of boxing.

Denver's Ron Lyle, beaten only once in his pro career, was assured of a heavyweight title shot with the man with the motor mouth. Naturally, Lyle wanted to stay in fighting trim while Ali was disposing of Chuck Wepner, and sought a couple of tuneup fights during the interim.

Jimmy Young, a Philadelphia heavyweight with no reputation, was offered up as the opponent for the "Hawaiian Affair." Those who have spent any time around the gymnasiums in Philadelphia know that Young has talent. He can box, has good movement and hand speed. Motivation and confidence were all that Young needed. Exit Ron Lyle.

It's happened this way throughout history. There always has been, "the tuneup" or "the payday" for the old man, that have thrown the monkey wrench into some of the best laid plans.

It happened to the great one himself. Ali was pretty well set for the second Frazier fight and would have pulled in millions for the effort. But he did have time for one little "home television" show before going into training for 'Smokin Joe'.

Enter Ken Norton — exit Muhammad Ali. It's history. March 31, 1973. Dateline San Diego, Calif. "Norton Breaks Ali'S Jaw In Upset".

Sure, Frazier-Ali had it out in Super Fight II, but that wasn't until January 1974.

It did let the world discover Ken Norton, who was devastating in his recent victory over Jerry Quarry in five rounds at Madison Square Garden. Norton, who has yet to settle the score with Ali, is currently looking for a title shot.

It's not only the top heavyweight blunders that have caused promoters and managers to choke on their cigars. Many plans have gone down the drain in other divisions with the matchmaker's plea, "He's ordinary," or "just a club fighter but he'll stand up," in their descriptions of opponents.

Tony Licata, undefeated in over fifty fights, ventured to Milan, Italy to meet a described "club fighter," one Ramon Mendez from Argentina. Licata, in line for quite some time now for a middleweight title shot, took the fight just to keep busy.

Nobody mentioned to Lou Viscusi, Licata's manager, that Mendez' record is as long as your arm in Argentina and the reason he's fighting elsewhere is that he's gone through everyone. Licata got over to Italy a few days before the fight and was caught cold via the decision route — the only blemish on an impressive record.

Who knows? It might be easier for Licata to get the title shot now that he has one loss. It's certainly no disgrace and possibly a plus for the New Orleans born Licata.

Speaking of middleweights, how many remember when champ George Chip fought against substitute Al McCoy on April 6, 1914

Jersey "Joe" Walcott moves back from a right thrown by Ezzard Charles. Walcott KO'ed Charles in the seventh round to win the world's heavyweight title on July 19, 1951.

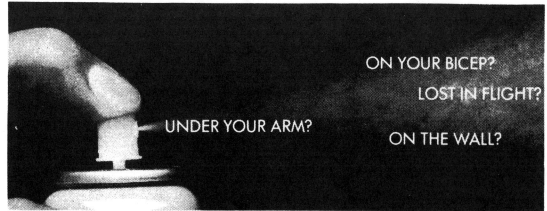

## FIGHTS THAT SHOULD NOT HAVE BEEN MADE TURNED HISTORY IN ODD DIRECTIONS

in Brooklyn? George's brother was ill.

"McCoy KO's Chip In First To Win Crown" was the headline.

In 1946, light heavyweight king Gus Lesnevich was all set to meet Joe Louis for the heavyweight title. It was a fight that would have made Lesnevich a wealthy man.

Gus and manager Joe Vella decided that they would hop over to London and thrash their 175-pounder, Freddie Mills in a quick title fight before they cashed in with Louis.

The result, as you can guess, was that Mills stopped Lesnevich in the tenth and Gus blew the title and the Louis fight with it.

And who can ever forget the night they were going to give "old man" Jersey Joe Walcott a last payday?

Ezzard Charles had already beaten Walcott twice in title fights and had done it over the decision route in pretty good fashion. The fight had absolutely no meaning or purpose and didn't figure to break all-time records at the gate in Pittsburgh's Forbes Field.

"Walcott New Champ — Charles Falls In Seventh" could be read in the papers across the land.

James J. Braddock, a struggling light heavyweight inflated a bit, was on relief, not being able to get work on the Jersey docks. His record of 19 wins, 21 losses with 3 draws, certainly didn't qualify him for any major shots. The powers were breeding a youngster by the name of Corn Griffin for a future championship fight. It wouldn't be long, one more fight, and he'd be ready.

"How about Jim Braddock?" asked one of the managers. "He's been out of work and gives a good show without hurting anyone."

Right again! Braddock was so hungry, he knocked out Griffin in two rounds in New York.

That was June 14, 1934. That was all Braddock needed. Within a year, he shocked the world with one of the greatest upsets in boxing history to gain the nickname "The Cinderella Man" by upsetting Max Baer to become the world heavyweight champion.

More recently, Don King, who has been able to keep recent heavyweight title bouts together, was moving his hard-punching but oft troublesome heavyweight Jeff Merritt, toward a title shot. He had knocked out Terrell and was in the ratings.

They took him to California to meet veteran campaigner Henry Clark, to do a favor for the well-liked promoter, Joe Gagliardi.

Jeff was caught with his pantaloon's down and stopped in one round by the well-conditioned Clark. Exit Jeff Merritt.

Rocky Mattioli of Melbourne, Australia, the world's number 5 rated welterweight, was scheduled to meet Billy Backus, the former world champion, as the semi-final to the Frazier-Ellis bout in Melbourne this past March. It would have been his biggest fight and his biggest purse with a world-wide television audience.

The local promoters made a match, which Mattioli's handlers figured would be a cinch and just what Rocky needed two weeks before his big fight. Besides, who ever head of Ali Afakasi?

They made the fight for the Australian title against the wishes of Kevin Watterson, Rocky's trainer. Mattioli was three pounds over the limit and had to sweat it off. Sin number two.

Weak from the weight loss, Rocky fought a decent fight but got cut under the eye and on the forehead. Even though he was winning, he just flattened out and it was stopped in the twelfth.

Mattioli blew his big shot and his Australian crown in a meaningless fight that attracted about 3,000 of Mattioli's relatives for the total gate.

# BAREKNUCKLE HEAVYWEIGHTS FROM JAMES FIGG TO JOHN L. SULLIVAN

## By DAN DANIEL

GREAT Britain never has had a world heavyweight champion during the Glove Era, which set in with the Sulliven - Corbett fight in New Orleans in 1892.

The British lay claim to Bob Fitzsimmons, who beat Corbett. But, while Fitz was born in Cornwall, he did almost all of his fighting in the United States and has been designated as an American fighter.

However, to the British belongs the credit for setting up the foundation of the Glove Era with the Bare Knuckle Era. This ran from 1719 to the Sullivan heyday.

The foremost exemplar of early bare knuckle days was Jim Figg, whose London Amphitheatre was the first locale for gloveless fisticuffs.

Bare knuckle fighting grew out of single

**Fight between Heenan and Sayers in England was first world title effort.**

**Father of Boxing, James Figg, was the first Briton to openly teach boxing and advertise exhibitions of the skill.**

stick competition and sword play.

The young bloods of old London town went strong for fisticuffs, and it wasn't long before the punching cult had its heroes and its champions.

The first bare knuckle battler with cleverness was Dan Mendoza, a Jew of Spanish descent. It is certain that Mendoza was the cleverest boxer of the early gloveless era. Dan suffered from the handicap of lack of weight. He tipped the beam at less than 160 pounds and stood only 5 feet 7 inches in height.

Mendoza was the first fighter to play up speed and introduce strategy. Some authorities give credit to Dan for inventing the jab. But there is a lot of fable about the early knucklers.

The rules of bare knuckle fighting were far different from those of the early glove days.

The bare knucklers did a lot of tugging and grappling, and a round ended when one of the fighters hit the turf or the floor. Length of fight went on minutes.

These rules were in force even as late as the Sullivan heyday. He and Charley Mitchell spent a lot of time in the mud in their 39 round draw at Chantilly, France. They fought in a driving rain.

Undoubtedly the most famous fight of the bare knuckle days was the 42 round draw between John C. Heenan, of the U.S., and Tom Sayers, of Britain, at Farnborough, En-

Jack Broughton gained the title "Father of boxing rules" when, in 1743, he codified the first set of boxing guidelines. He also originated the boxing glove.

land. It was the first major attempt to establish a world championship, and was fought in April, 1860. Heenan outweighed Tom, but the Briton put up an even fight.

American bare knuckle fighting was featured by father and son competition. Tom Hyer was the first American champion and his son Jake was a leading performer of a later date. The Hyers were of old Dutch New York stock. In those days pugilism and politics lived together a lot. The Hyers were important among the Know Nothing Party, infamous for a brawly existence.

Both in the United States and Great Britain, leading fighters contributed their acumen to parliamentary effort, among them, John Morrissey, who went to Congress, and John Gully, who served in a similar capacity in Britain. Morrissey played an important role in furthering gambling and horse racing interests at Saratoga, N.Y.

The earliest black invaders of ring competition were Tom Molineux, of Virginia, and Boill Richmond, who was servant to General Lord Percy during the Revolution. Both found little competition in the Colonies, and went to England, where they appeared in important fights.

Not one of the social elect among the bare knucklers was a character named "Yankee" Sullivan.

In 1856 the Vigilante Committee in San Francisco picked him up for misdemeanors, felonies and murders and threw him into jail.

That night he was found hanged in his cell. Rumor had it

Otherwise known as the Norwich Butcher, Jack Slack's early wins were said to be due more to fearlessness than ability.

# BAREKNUCKLE HEAVYWEIGHTS FROM JAMES FIGG TO JOHN L. SULLIVAN

that the Vigilantes had done it.

The list of bare knuckle champions, starting with Figg, includes: George Taylor, Jack Broughton, Jack Slack, Tom Johnson, Sam Martin, Dan Mendoza, John Jackson, Richard Humphries, Tom Owens Tom Cribb, George Meggs (known as the Collier), Harry Sellers, Jem Ward, Peter Crawley, Nick Ward, Jem Belcher, Bill Stevens, Ben Brain, Dan Donnelly, John Gully, Tom Paddock, Tom Faulkner, Bill Darts, Jemry Pearce, Tom Oliver, Bill Perry, Ben Caunt, Tom Spring, Jack Langan, Harry Broome, Simon Byrne, James (Deaf) Burke, Bold Bendigo (Boll Thompson), Tom Molyneaux, Bill Richmond, Ned O'Baldwin, Bob Travers, Tom Sayers, Aaron Jones, Jem Mace, Tom King, Jake Hyer, Tom Hyer, Yankee Sullivan, Joe Coburn, Mike McCoole, Tom Allen, Ben Hogan, Jim Dunne, Tom Cannon, John Morrissey, John C. Heenan, Charley Gallagher, Jim Elliott, John L. Dwyer, Joe Wormald, Paddy Ryan and John L. Sullivan.

It will be noted that near the close, the list includes many fighters whose title claims were not clear.

**(Above)** Scientific boxing, rather than merely brute strength and endurance, were developed with the advent of Daniel Mendoza, reigning champion from 1791–1795.

**(Left)** The "Gentleman Fighter," Richard Humphreys, beat Mendoza twice before becoming champion himself.

**(Right)** One of England's most celebrated champions, Tom Cribb, worked as a stevedore and then a coal heaver before his first fight in 1805.

(Left) Grandson of Jack Slack and called "Napoleon of the Ring," Jem Belcher was one of early pugilism's more colorful champions, being the first known man to sport an ascot or attach colors to the ring posts.

With the defeat of Benjamin Brain went the pioneer period of boxing, where brawn and endurance were the primary criteria for success in the ring.

(Left) Dan Donnelly was the first Irish champion, and his victory over George Cooper, in 1815, depicted here, is said to be his greatest fight.

(Above left) John Gully, released from debtors prison on condition that he box, became champion when he beat Bob Gregson over 36 rounds.

(Above right) When William Perry fought Charles Freeman, they fought 70 rounds, halted for nightfall, and continued the next day.

A giant of a man, Ben Caunt won the title from "Bold Bendigo" on an alledged foul in the 75th round of their April 3, 1838, encounter.

The championship contest between Tom Spring and Jack Langan in 1824 marked the first time in boxing history that a grandstand was erected.

"Bold Bendigo," born William Thompson, became a Methodist parson upon retiring from the ring after a rough and tough career.

To "Deaf" James Burke belongs the honor of having fought the longest championship bout on record, a gruelling 99 rounds against Simon Byrne.

(Above) Molineaux's predecessor, and first Negro ringman, was Bill Richmond, who was said to have whipped several British soldiers in succession when they fell upon him in a tavern back in 1777.

(Right) Only a middleweight by today's standards, Tom Sayers rose to the top and became heavyweight champion on June 15, 1858, when he beat Tom Paddock.

One of the Negro pioneers in the ring was Virginian Tom Molineaux, born March 23, 1784.

(Right) Jem Mace was probably the greatest pugilist England ever produced, and is considered the Father of the Modern School of British Scientific Boxing.

Although Tom Hyer's father, Jacob, was considered the leading American heavyweight. Tom was the first American to gain press and public recognition as champion of the U.S., on Feb. 7, 1849.

(Above) A top man in Tammany Hall, John Morrissey was not terribly skilled as a boxer, but would wear down his opponents with his remarkable endurance.

(Left) A power in politics and the ring, "Yankee" Sullivan ultimately lost the crown to Tom Hyer, moved west, and met a mysterious death in a California jail.

Known as a clever boxer with great punching power, John C. Heenan, born in New York in 1833, is seen dressed for his wedding.

Johnny Dwyer, of Brooklyn, fought a brutal bout with the tough ring veteran Jimmy Elliott for the American championship, on May 9, 1879. Elliot was finally stopped in the 12th round.

Champion for one fight, Paddy Ryan won the American heavyweight title by defeating Joe Goss in 87 rounds, on May 30, 1880, and lost his next fight to John L. Sullivan in 9.

John L. Sullivan was to many "the Champion of Champions." Fierce, powerful, and fast, John L. caught the public's imagination, and marked the beginning of a new era in boxing.

# GREAT FIGHTERS NOT ALWAYS GREATEST REFEREES

Ruby Goldstein (above left) was a well known boxer, and a highly successful referee, while ex-featherweight champion Willie Pep (below left), though competent, found third man jobs to be scarce.

## By MURRAY GOODMAN

**B**OB FOSTER, retired undefeated light heavyweight champion of the world, moved around the ring with an effortless grace that seemed natural.

"Don't hold, Jimmy," he said softly.

"Keep them up, Joe," he admonished gently.

Jimmy Ellis and Joe Frazier paid attention. Foster was the referee of this fight at 4:30 P.M., in the blazing heat of Melbourne, Australia. It was Foster's first major refereeing job.

"I was thinking seriously of making a comeback as a fighter," he declared. "Now, I've got a good new career. How long has this been going on? I was afraid to take this assignment at the beginning. I have been friendly with Ellis, and even though Frazier and I fought, we have been close friends. It was a little scary at the start, but I had no problems, and it was a good, clean fight as long as it lasted."

The bout ended in the 8th round.

"You get a funny feeling when you're not used to it," he added. "All your life you've been in there throwing punches, now you're watching them. I don't remember what round it was, but one of Frazier's punches missed my chin by a fraction of an inch. I came close to forgetting myself."

Foster has since returned to the ring, but his venture into refereeing is not unusual for former champions and greats of the ring. Some have been exceptionally good and have established outstanding reputations. Others, hired solely for the value of their respective names, have turned out to rate between ordinary and dismal.

Jim Jeffries was the first of the big-name former champ referees. He had retired as champion for lack of competition, and he himself established Marvin Hart and Jack Root as the logical contenders. They met in Reno in 1905, with Jeffries as the referee. The following year, he refereed the battle between Hart and Tommy Burns, then Burns and Philadelphia Jack O'Brien, and in 1907, the fight between Burns and Bill Squires.

Gorgeous Georges Carpentier, the French light heavyweight who went on to fight Jack Dempsey, was the third man in the ring for three fights that Jack Johnson had in Paris in 1913 and 1914. Johnson, having gotten into trouble with the U.S. Government in 1912, was in virtual exile in Europe. He was still recognized by most as the world heavyweight champion, however. He knocked out Andre Sproul in two rounds, and then fought Battling Jim Johnson (no relation). Carpentier called the fight a draw after 10 rounds, when Jack Johnson declared he had broken his arm. Under today's rules, Battling Jim would have won the title on a technical knockout. Johnson came back six months later to defeat Frank Moran in 20 rounds.

Few will recall that Gunboat Smith, who became the white heavyweight champion by knocking out Arthur Pelkey in 15 rounds on New Year's Day, 1914, in San Francisco, refereed the Jack Sharkey-Max Schmeling world heavyweight title fight in the Long Island Bowl on June 21, 1932. It is interesting to note that Smith lost that white title to Carpentier on a foul in London, England, in 1914.

Jack Dempsey, Jersey Joe Walcott, Jim Braddock, Joe Louis, Jack Sharkey and Max Baer were other world heavyweight champions who accepted reasonably big fees for refereeing chores. In the lesser weights, in addition to the new entry of Foster, the more prominent were Tommy Loughran, Benny Leonard, Willie Pep,

One of the more embarrassing moments for any referee was this one in Lewiston, Maine, which saw referee Jersey Joe Walcott, ex-heavyweight champ, seen restraining Ali, failing to pick up the count on downed Sonny Liston.

(right) Gunboat Smith, claimant of the "White Hope" title back in the early 1900's, far right, keeps an attentive eye on Sharkey, center, and Schmeling, left, during their January 1, 1914, encounter.

## GREAT FIGHTERS NOT ALWAYS GREATEST REFEREES

Mushy Callahan and Ruby Goldstein.

Dempsey demanded and received what was then the highest fee ever paid a referee, $5,000, and of course, expenses. He handled the Ceferina Garcia-Glen Lee middleweight title fight, the Chavez-Escobar bantamweight title bout, and a 10-round battle between Rex Layne and Ezzard Charles, in Ogden, Utah, in 1952, in which he called eight rounds even and awarded the fight to Layne.

Sharkey's biggest job was the Archie Moore-Yvon Durelle light heavyweight title fight, in Montreal, on December 10, 1958. Durelle had Moore bouncing up and down like the proverbial yoyo, until he ran out of gas from overexertion and succumbed in the 11th round. There are those who voiced the opinion that some of Sharkey's counts over Moore appeared a little longer than the allotted 10 seconds.

The dignified gentleman, Tommy Loughran, was called in to referee the Floyd Patterson-Pete Rademacher title fight in Seattle, but that was a rare public occasion for the former light heavyweight champion.

Jersey Joe Walcott, who did occasional refereeing jobs around the world, made the mistake of accepting the third man theme in the Sonny Liston-Cassius Clay return that ultimately wound up in Lewiston, Maine. Jersey Joe became somewhat confused when Liston went down in the first round. The timer, Francis McDonough, counted 12 but couldn't get Walcott's attention, and finally, it was Nat Fleischer who relayed the message to Jersey Joe that the count had already reached 22 and that Liston had been counted out twice. It was an embarrassing moment for the former world champion.

Braddock and Baer were competent referees, the Cinderella Man working occasionally, and Baer more frequently, on the West Coast. Baer, with a bad heart, succumbed in 1959 in a Hollywood hotel between refereeing jobs.

Willie Pep, Mushy Callahan, Benny Leonard, among the lesser weighted champions, were competent referees when they found work. Leonard, who had tried a comeback after a seven year absence from the ring, became a licensed referee in 1943. He died of a heart attack in 1947.

The most prominent of the fistic referees was a non-champion by the name of Ruby Goldstein. Ruby refereed many outstanding fights in New York, the most prominent being the Louis-Walcott fight in the Garden and the Joey Maxim-Ray Robinson light heavyweight title bout in the Yankee Stadium. Goldstein wilted in the heat in that latter one, and had to be helped. Robinson, ahead all the way, yielded to the bursting thermometer in the 14th round.

The critics say a referee should never score a fight because the boxer is unconsciously partial to the clever ones and the puncher to the "killers". A look at history may only prove that some are good, some bad and a few, just awful.

# First Round Knockouts in Title Fights Began with Jim Jeffries

SINCE the advent of modern boxing with John L. Sullivan, there have been only 37 first round knockouts in world championship bouts in the eight major divisions of boxing, these being heavyweights, light heavyweights, middleweights, welterweights, lightweights, featherweights, bantamweights and flyweights.

The first kayo in one was scored by heavyweight champ James J. Jeffries on April 6, 1900, when he halted Jack Finnegan in detroit, Michigan. With that kayo, the heavyweights took the lead, and have since kept it by a wide margin, in this sphere of boxing. Heavyweight champions have scored 13 first round kayoes in title bouts over a 76 year period. The lightweights follow with five kayoes, and after them come the bantamweights and flyweights with 4, middleweights, welterweights and featherweights with 3, and light heavies with 2.

The kayo leader in the group is heavyweight king Joe Louis, who scored five. Next is a three way tie among heavyweight Tommy Burns, heavyweight Sonny Liston, and current lightweight champion Roberto Duran, all with two kayoes. Fighters with one KO cut across the divisions. The heavyweights boast Rocky Marciano, Muhammad Ali and George Foreman, while the light heavyweights claim Gus Lesnevich and Bob Foster. In other classes there were middleweights Stanley Ketchel, Al McCoy and Al Hostak; welters Ted Kid Lewis, Jimmy McLarnin and Henry Armstrong; lightweights Joe Gans, Al Singer and Tony Canzoneri; featherweights Freddie

(Above) Chunky little Tommy Burns was the smallest man ever to win the heavyweight title, but he packed a kayo wallop. He stopped Jem Roche in just 1:28 of the first at Dublin, Ireland, March 17, 1908.

Joe Louis was the all-time one-round kayo king of the champions. (Above) Joe is in the process of scoring his most sensational knockout, putting away Max Schmeling in New York's Yankee Stadium on April 17, 1938. Time was 2:04.

Jack Roper outweighed Louis when they met in Los Angeles, April 17, 1939, but it didn't mean a thing. The Brown Bomber finished off Roper in 2:20 of the first.

They used to say that if you were late to a Louis fight you'd probably miss the whole thing. John Henry Lewis, en route to dreamland, was clouted out in just 2:29 of the January 25, 1939, Madison Square Garden title match.

The Brown Bomber wasted little time in teeing off against Tami Mauriello on September 18, 1946, at Yankee Stadium. Tami did his best to tie up Joe, but Louis kayoed Tami in 2:09, quickest of his five title bout knockouts.

Buddy Baer is chopped down by a sizzling punch to the jaw for the second of three trips to the canvas he made in his second meeting with Louis, at Madison Square Garden, January 9, 1942. It ended in 2:56 of the first.

No, there weren't three Rocky Marcianos against Jersey Joe Walcott in Chicago Stadium, May 15, 1953, but the trick photo shows how Joe must have felt. The right by heavy king Marciano put Joe away at 2:25.

Sonny Liston wasted no time with Floyd Patterson. (Left) Liston wins the heavyweight title in Chicago's Comiskey Park on September 25, 1962, in 2:06, and (above) he keeps it with a Las Vegas demolition job that took just four seconds longer. The date, July 22, 1963.

236

(Above) George Foreman's pulverizing right is an unnecessary coup de grace with challenger Jose Roman already on the deck. Roman was counted out in 2:00 at Tokyo, Japan, September 1, 1973.

(Left) Heavyweight champ Cassius Clay challenges Sonny Liston to get up, but Sonny doesn't. Official time of the May 25, 1965, KO in Lewiston, Maine, was 1:00, but TV films revealed the fight was stopped at 2:12.

Champion Gus Lesnevich, left, staggers Billy Fox before halting him in 1:58 of the light heavyweight title bout in Madison Square Garden, March 5, 1948.

Bob Foster's three knockdowns of Frankie De-Paula brought an automatic end to their 175-pound title match on January 23, 1969, in the Garden.

Stanley Ketchel knocked out Mike (Twin) Sullivan in 1:48 at Colma, California, on February 22, 1908 to gain full recognition as middleweight champion.

It was billed as a "no decision" bout in the little Broadway A.C. in Brooklyn on April 6, 1914, when Al McCoy (above left) faced middleweight champ George Chip (above right). Forty-five seconds later, McCoy was the new champion via a one punch knockout.

Referee Jack Dempsey sends Al Hostak to a neutral corner after NBA middleweight champ Freddie Steele goes down. The July 26, 1938, match at Seattle, Washington, ended in 1:43.

Welterweight champion Ted (Kid) Lewis watches Albert Badoud hit the canvas in their August 31, 1917, bout in New York. It ended in 2:45.

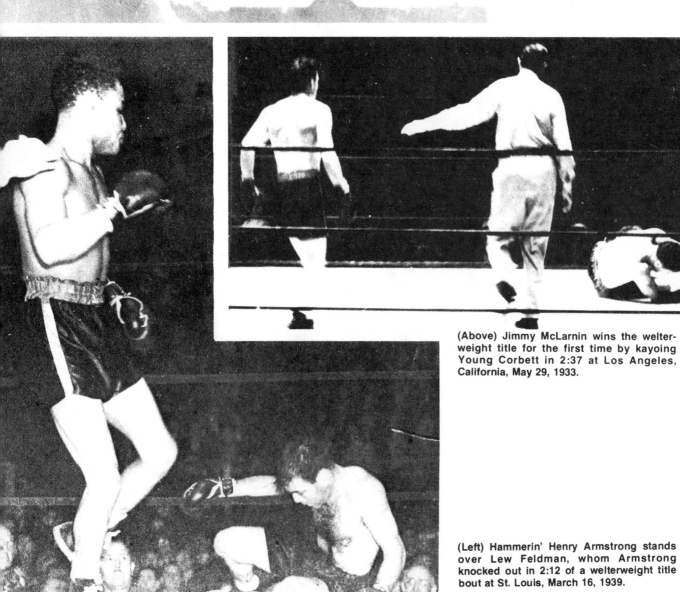

(Above) Jimmy McLarnin wins the welterweight title for the first time by kayoing Young Corbett in 2:37 at Los Angeles, California, May 29, 1933.

(Left) Hammerin' Henry Armstrong stands over Lew Feldman, whom Armstrong knocked out in 2:12 of a welterweight title bout at St. Louis, March 16, 1939.

Joe Gans lands the right that won him the lightweight title on May 12, 1902. He knocked out Frank Erne in 1:40 at Fort Erie, Canada.

Al Singer walks away as Sammy Mandell is counted out at 1:46 of lightweight title match July 17, 1930, in New York's Yankee Stadium.

Lightweight champion Roberto Duran stands over Masataka Takayama after flooring the Japanese challenger for the third time on December 21, 1974. The San Jose, Costa Rica, bout was over in 1:40.

Duran surveys his most recent KO in one. He flattened Alvaro Rojas of Costa Rica in 2:17 of round one at Hollywood, Florida, last October 14. The ref is Carlos Berrocal.

Featherweight champion Freddie Miller floors Spain's Jose Girones in the February 17, 1935 title bout at Barcelona which was over in 2:30 of the first.

(Above) Davey Moore watches featherweight challenger Danny Valdez go down and out in 2:48 of their title go in Los Angeles' Olympic Auditorium on April 8, 1961.

Raul Cruz, of Mexico, gets medical aid while featherweight champion Kuniaki Shibata acknowledges cheers from Tokyo fans on June 3, 1971. Cruz was counted out four seconds after first round ended.

Pedlar Palmer, left, and Terry McGovern square off before their fight for the vacant bantamweight title at Tuckahoe, New York, on September 12, 1899. McGovern knocked out Palmer in one minute and fifteen seconds.

Panama Al Brown (right) disposed of Emile "Spider" Pladner (left) in 2:21 of the first at Toronto, Canada, on September 19, 1932, to retain the world bantamweight title.

Bantam champion Sixto Escobar, of Puerto Rico, makes short work of challenger Carlos (Indian) Quintana, of Panama, in Madison Square Garden, October 13, 1936. The ten-count was completed at 1:49 of the first.

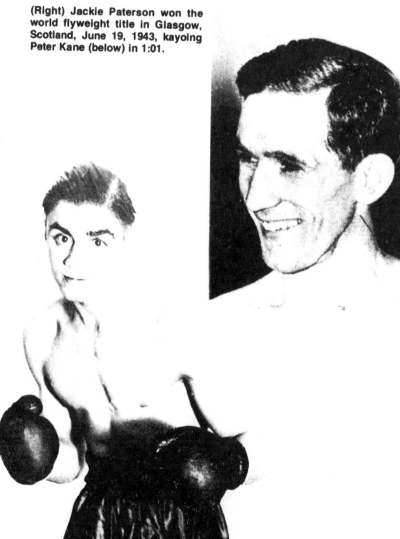

(Right) Jackie Paterson won the world flyweight title in Glasgow, Scotland, June 19, 1943, kayoing Peter Kane (below) in 1:01.

Jimmy Carruthers, of Australia, sends South Africa's Vic Toweel to dreamland at 2:19 of the first to win the bantam title at Johannesburg on November 15, 1952.

243

Spider Pladner's 58-second kayo of Frankie Genaro in Paris, March 2, 1929, enabled him to claim the world flyweight title.

Happy fan rushes to congratulate Pascual Perez, of Argentina, who kept the flyweight title with a two minute KO of Dai Dower in Buenos Aires, March 30, 1957.

(Left) It's all over for Pone Kingpetch at 2:07 of round one as Japan's Hiroyuki Ebihara captures the flyweight title in Tokyo, September 18, 1963.

**Q.** There was a young Mexican fighter in the 1968 Olympics who won a fight by disqualification over an American named Al Robinson after he suffered a serious eye cut from a butt. Can you tell me his name, amateur record and whether he ever turned pro. Also, did he win a medal in the '68 Games?

F. Santoni
Bronx, N.Y.

**A.** Antonio Roldan did win the Gold Medal when Robinson was disqualified for butting in the second round of their featherweight final. Robinson, at first denied the Silver Medal, got it after films showed that there had been no contact of heads. Roldan had six pro fights in 1969-70, while attending college. He had a 4-1-1 record with 3 KOs. Robinson's story is tragic. Considered a highly promising lightweight with only one loss in a dozen fights, he collapsed after a gym workout in April 1971. Despite several brain operations, he never regained consciousness, and on January 24, 1974, he died in an Oakland, California, hospital.

**Q.** Regarding the story on Artie Levine in THE RING (December 1975) a friend of mine says Artie is Jewish and I say he's French. Could you please straighten the matter out for us.

Russ Bernstein
Holyoke, Massachusetts

**A.** Artie informs us that on his father's side his lineage is French-Jewish, and on his mother's, German-Italian. And actually, the family name is Levien, and not Levine, though that's the handle Artie always used.

**Q.** Of all the world champions, including all weight classes, were any fighters besides Rocky Marciano undefeated through their entire pro careers?

Mike Fredrickson
Bellingham, Washington

**A.** Marciano is the only one in the modern era. Gene Tunney retired as undefeated heavyweight champion after his knockout of Tom Heeney in 1928, but Tunney lost one of his seventy-six pro fights, defending his American light heavyweight title in 1922 against Harry Greb. Jack McAuliffe, American lightweight champion in the bare-knuckle 1890s, was unbeaten in fifty-two bouts.

**Q.** What ever happened to the idea of sewing up cuts around the eyes between rounds? I thought it was tried out a few years back and found to be a practical thing.

John M. Rice
Beaumont, Texas

**A.** Quick stitching jobs have been successfully done in the hockey leagues, but as far as is known here the boxing commissions have gotten no further than talking about it.

**Q.** Is Paul Venti, who referees fights in New Jersey and sometimes in New York, related to the Sammy Venti who was a good lightweight in the late thirties?

Clarence Church
Lake Carmel, N.Y.

**A.** Paul is Sammy's younger brother, and he also fought as a lightweight. Sammy, of course, is the president of the World Boxing Historians' Association.

**Q.** I understand that Dick and Ed Modzeleski, who were big name college and pro football players some years back, had a brother who boxed pro in the late forties and early fifties. The family came from a coal-mining town in Pennsylvania.

George J. Zaleski
Pittsburgh, Pennsylvania

**A.** The oldest of the Modzelewski brothers, Joe Jr., was a heavyweight stablemate of Ezzard Charles, out of West Natrona, Pennsylvania. He fought under the name of Joe Modzele. Had twenty-four fights, winning sixteen, with six knockouts, plus some exhibitions with Ezz. Leading contender Bob Baker broke Joe's jaw and kayoed him in September 1949, and a year later, after a one round kayo by Sonny Parisi, he hung up the gloves. Today, Joe's living and working (as a chef) in Cleveland, Ohio.

## FIRST ROUND KNOCKOUTS IN TITLE FIGHTS

Miller, Davey Moore and Kuniaki Shibata; bantamweights Terry McGovern, Panama Al Brown, Sixto Escobar and Jimmy Carruthers; and flyweights Jackie Paterson, Spider Pladner, Pascual Perez and Hiroyuki Ebihara.

The totals by countries in first round title-fight knockouts has the United States ahead with 27, the British Commonwealth second with 3, Panama and Japan, third with 2, and France and Argentina fourth with one.

The last one round knockout scored was by Panama's Roberto Duran. He kayoed Costa Rica's Alvaro Rojas in Hollywood, Florida, on October 15, 1976, in a lightweight title defense.

Major one rounders in the heavyweight class include Joe Louis over Max Schmeling on June 22, 1938, in New York City; Rocky Marciano over Jersey Joe Walcott, Chicago, May 15, 1953; Sonny Liston twice over Floyd Patterson, once in Chicago, the other Las Vegas; Muhammad Ali over Liston, May 25, 1965, Lewiston, Maine; and last in the heavyweights, George Foreman over Jose Roman, Tokyo, September 1, 1973.

In the light heavies there were Gus Lesnevich over Billy Fox, March 5, 1948, and Bob Foster over Frankie DePaula, January 23, 1969. Both fights were held in New York.

Middleweight bouts had Stanley Ketchel stopping Mike Twin Sullivan, February 22, 1908, Al McCoy knocking out George Chip, April 6, 1914, and Al Hostak halting Freddie Steele.

Welterweight first rounders had Ted Kid Lewis over Albert Badoud, Jimmy McLarnin over Young Corbett III and Henry Armstrong over Lew Feldman.

Other's scoring wins in the lightweight, featherweight, bantamweight and flyweight division are Joe Gans, Al Singer and Tony Canzoneri, lights; Freddie Miller, Davey Moore and Kuniaki Shibata, featherweights; Terry McGovern, Panama Al Brown, Sixto Escobar and Jimmy Carruthers, bantams, and Jackie Paterson, Spider Pladner, Pascual Perez and Hiroyuki Ebihara, flys.

## By MARSHALL REED

*Legend—One having a special status as a result of possessing or being held to possess extraordinary qualities that are usually partly real and partly mythical.*

—Webster's Third New International Dictionary

THE RING is, among many other things, the keeper of boxing's legends.

Were one to go through a month's mail at random, or tap the wires of a week's telephone calls, it would quickly become apparent that among the champions of past and present, there are legends and there are non-legends.

Never mind the chemistry that makes Jack Dempsey a legend and Gene Tunney, his two-time conqueror, something less in public esteem.

Never mind the unique blend of blarney and ability that has made Muhammad Ali a legend in his own time.

Never mind the certainty with which fight fans who never even saw him will tell you that Sugar Ray Robinson, pound for pound, is the greatest ever to grind his ring shoes

# PHOTO STORY:
# RING LEGEND
# ROCKY MARCIANO

into resin-dusted canvas.

The fact is that there are legends and ordinary mortals.

And Rocky Marciano must be placed in the former category. Rocky's popularity today transcends what it was when he was heavyweight champion.

The Italian-American community, in particular, has a deep and abiding affection for this son of a poor Brockton, Massachusetts, cobbler; this one-time pick-and-shovel worker who sweated and toiled and eventually won boxing's biggest prize.

He was a champion with which the people could identify. He was strong, and he could punch hard. There was nothing of the fancy dan, the slick boxer, in him. He would have laughed if his trainer, Charley Goldman, had ever suggested he ought to learn something called a "shuffle." There was no show biz in Rocky. He was just a guy who worked

with his hands. And how he worked!

Mind-pictures of Marciano are frozen in the memory of every fan who ever saw him in action. Rocky mashing Jersey Joe Walcott's face as if it were a piece of silly putty. Rocky spouting blood from a horrendous cut on his nose before he came on to knock out Ezzard Charles. Rocky breaking the blood vessels in Roland LaStarza's arms so that the challenger could hardly lift them afterwards. Rocky punching, and the other men falling, falling. What a puncher he was!

All that brute force stayed inside the ring. Outside of it Rocky was warm, friendly, a family-loving man with simple tastes. After he retired, he spent much time amid the tinsel and glitter of movieland and TV studios, but when he'd happen to run into someone he'd known from the old days it was to talk wistfully of the family and of the fun he

"The Rock" was the peoples' champ--a boxer and person with which the average man could identify.

(Above) Rocky Marciano fires away at Muhammad Ali, but the 1969 meeting of the two legendary fighters was just a stunt for a filmed, computerized "super fight" which Rocky won. (Right) This was for real, with Ezzard Charles on the deck in second round of their 1954 title bout. Marciano scored an eight-round KO.

(Below) The Brockton Rock has Briton Don Cockell doing an involuntary rope-a-dope in the seventh round at San Francisco. Two rounds later the referee stopped it.

Rocky uncorks a haymaker against Roland LaStarza in their 1953 title match. The fight in New York's Polo Grounds ended in the eleventh.

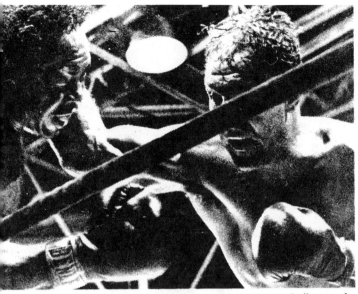

Rocky ends his work, landing the right that sent challenger Ar-chie Moore down for the full count in the ninth round of their 1955 clash. It was Marciano's 49th straight win, his 43rd KO. Seven months later he retired.

Although Rocky was retired, he wasn't idle. With a movie role in "College Confidential," he gives star actress Mamie Van Doren some tips on the way to strike the speed bag, and appears to be enjoying his work.

The retired undefeated heavyweight champ shows TV's late Ed Sullivan how it feels to be on the receiving end of his famed "Suzy-Q" right-hand punch.

A training camp visit from Jack Dempsey is a fun time for both Rocky and his trainer, Charley Goldman.

Hollywood's Cathy Crosby, Jayne Meadows and Steve Allen admire "Deputy Sheriff" Marciano.

Jersey Joe Walcott makes an unforgettable picture as he crumples against the ropes and Marciano strides away, having landed the punch in 13th round that won him the title on September 23, 1952.

(Below) Nat Fleischer, the late editor and publisher of THE RING, presents Marciano with the first of three Fighter of the Year awards that he won.

Rocky glad-hands Swedish heavyweight Ingemar Johansson, who was training for his 1959 bout with Floyd Patterson, then the champion. Ingo's right polished off Floyd in the third round.

Rocky was at home among celebrities from all walks of life. (Right) He hams it up with comedian Red Skelton. (Above) He visits with the late Chicago Mayor, Richard Daley.

## PHOTO STORY:
## ROCKY MARCIANO

used to have just kidding with the rest of the fellows as they'd sit around the kitchen table of the cottage where he lived when he was training.

And then, on August 31, 1969, the day before his 46th birthday, a plane crashed in an Iowa corn field and Marciano's life was snuffed out. There is little doubt that this untimely end had an effect on the Legend of Rocky Marciano, though what that effect has been is open to argument.

There are some who think that had Rocky lived out his years, his popularity would have continued to grow. Others feel that his tragic end may have magnified his stature, in the morbid way that movie actors James Dean and Rudolph Valentino became "bigger than life" after they departed from this sphere.

Whatever, the Marciano legend is secure. No one ever has matched his ring record: forty-nine fights, forty-nine wins, forty-three knockouts. RING magazine lists him as number five among the all-time heavyweight greats. Nat Fleischer, THE RING's founder, and its editor and publisher for fifty years until his death in 1972, placed Rocky tenth in his all-time ratings.

But whether you rate him first, or fifth, or tenth, one thing is certain. . .Rocky Marciano never will be forgotten. And deservedly so.

*Marciano digs a right hook into the bag as he works out for his title re-match with ex-champ Joe Walcott on April 10, 1953.*

# HEAVYWEIGHT CHAMPIONS AND THEIR KNOCKDOWNS

## By DAN DANIEL

**B**OXING historians of late have turned their attention to knockdowns suffered by heavyweight champions both previous to and during their title tenures.

A lot of attention has fallen on the knockdown suffered by Muhammad Ali in the fourth round of his 15-rounder with Chuck Wepner in Cleveland.

Tony Perez, the referee, ruled it an official knockdown. Ali has insisted that it was a mere slip produced by a stray shoe lace.

Into the records it has gone as a knockdown; No. 4 in the career of onetime Cassius Clay.

Two of his knockdowns came before Ali got to be heavyweight champion.

The first KD came in St. Nicholas Rink in New York, in the fourth round against Sonny Banks, whom he stopped in the fifth.

The next KD happened in London, at the hands of Henry Cooper, longtime British champion. This incident was featured by the Ripped Glove affair, which gave Ali some time to recover from the knockdown.

The third Ali KD came in Madison Square Garden, when Joe Frazier sent Ali down in the fifteenth round of their second meet-

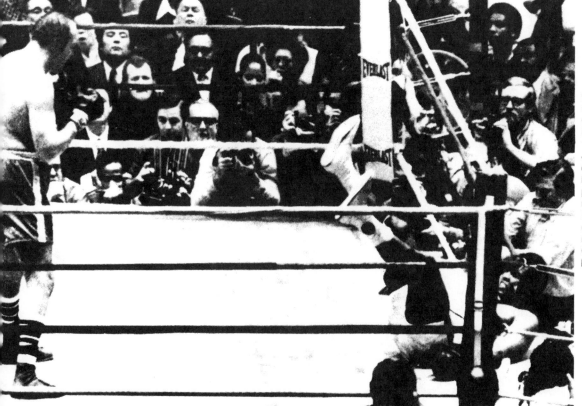

(Above) George Foreman towers over fallen defending champion Joe Frazier, on January 22, 1973, in Kingston, Jamaica. Foreman downed Frazier six times in the course of stopping him at 1:35 of round two. (Left) This knockdown, #4 in Ali's career, came in round nine of his title bout with Chuck Wepner, in Cleveland, on March 24, 1975.

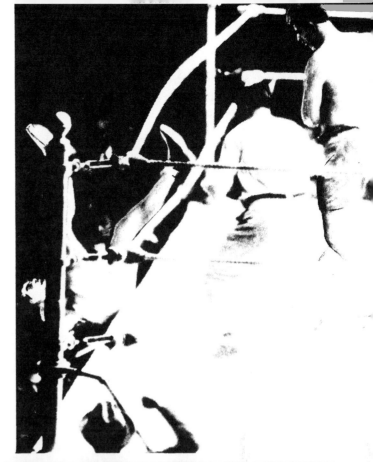

(Above) With sixteen knockdowns, Floyd Patterson remains the most frequently decked champion. Here, Ruby Goldstein counts out Floyd at 2:03 of the third round, on June 26, 1959, ending his match with Ingemar Johansson. (Right) Jack Dempsey is knocked through the ropes by Luis Firpo in the first round, on September 14, 1923.

ing.

Considering the length of Ali's career in the ring and nature of the knockdowns, his record in KD recovery is an interesting one. The Cooper and Frazier knockdowns were important and interesting.

Much more serious than the four Ali trips downward were the eight KDs suffered by Frazier; six the day George Foreman decked him in taking the heavyweight title away from Joe.

A seldom referred to knockdown is the one suffered by Joe Louis in the first round of the fight in which he stopped Jimmy Braddock in eight rounds in Chicago in 1937.

An historic tidbit is the Dempsey fight with Luis Firpo, the Wild Bull of the Pampas, in the now gone Polo Grounds in New York. This fight lasted only two rounds. In the first, Dempsey was knocked out of the ring. In the second, Firpo hit the deck seven times for a heavyweight record.

Standing out, too, is the feat of Max Baer, who in the process of stopping Primo Carnera in eleven rounds, knocked him down eleven times.

In sharp contrast are the two Liston-Patterson fights, both ended by KO of Floyd in the first round.

Liston, himself, was the victim of a one-round KO, by Ali at Lewiston, Me., in a small hockey rink. The real story of that so-called fight never will be set out in actual detail.

Ali's stopping Liston in seven was not a notable trick. There was something very wrong with Charles knocking out Cooper in

(Above) Max Schmelling is on the mat, put there by Max Baer, on June 8, 1933, in N.Y.C. Baer won that match by a 10th-round KO. (Left) Round four, June 19, 1936, Joe Louis is sent to the canvas by Schmelling, who went on to KO the Brown Bomber in the 12th.

## HEAVYWEIGHT CHAMPIONS AND THEIR KNOCKDOWNS

five rounds. It was a more noteworthy achievement.

I never will forget the Dempsey-Willard near-murder on July 4, 1919, in Toledo. I was there. Jess was mauled mercilessly. Out in three rounds. Out sitting in his corner with his face a mass of welts and bruises.

Not to be forgotten, too, is the brief encounter between Joe Louis and Max Schmelling for the title. The German was hurt seriously, more seriously than anybody outside of his corner realized. Joe truly avenged his 12-round KO by Schmelling before Louis became the world champion.

The most frequently decked former champion was Floyd Patterson, who hit the ·canvas 16 times. He got the reputation of being handicapped by a glass jaw.

Joe Louis was knocked down six times and George Foreman only once—the time he was dumped by Ali in Zaire.

The most frequently knocked down fighter of any class was the famous Joe Grim. He hit the floor 21 times against Jack J. Johnson in six rounds in Philadelphia.

It was a cruel match. Grim had no chance except to set that record. The all time yo yo.

Of the eight knockdowns registered against Joe Frazier, two were achieved by Oscar Bonavena on the night of his heyday in the Garden. Bonavena had the chance of his life. But he did not have the capacity to take advantage of those knockdowns.

One of the most written about knockdowns of all time was the KD of the Long Count in the seventh round of the second Dempsey-Tunney fight, in Chicago.

Jack had the Marine on the floor. Maybe he had him out. But Dempsey refused to obey their agreement to go to a neutral corner in the event of a knockdown, and he may have lost the chance to recover the title he had lost to Gene in Philadelphia a year earlier.

Because so many early Dempsey fights are lost in obscurity, the Mauler's KD record is not available.

Nor do we have an authentic KD record on John L. Sullivan, who had many bare-knuckle scraps replete with wrestling.

# HALL OF FAME
## *Bob Fitzsimmons*

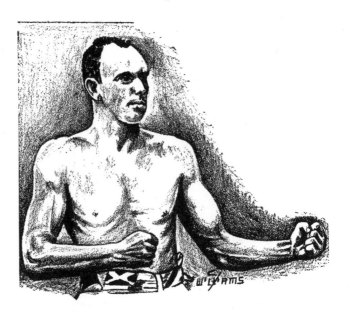

## ROBERT FITZSIMMONS
### *(ELECTED TO THE HALL OF FAME 1954)*

Fitzsimmons was the first fighter to win three world boxing championships, the middleweight, heavyweight and light heavyweight, in that order.

He was born on June 4, 1862, at Elston, Cornwall, England, and began his ring career in New Zealand in 1880. In 1890 he arrived in America and the following year knocked out Nonpareil Jack Dempsey in five rounds at Galveston, Texas, for the world middleweight title.

On March 17, 1897 he knocked out Jim Corbett in 14 rounds at Carson City, Nev., to gain his second championship, the heavyweight crown. Jim Jeffries took that title away from him on June 9, 1899, at Coney Island, N. Y., when he halted Fitzsimmons in eleven rounds. Three years later he was unsuccessful in trying to regain that championship from Jeffries, being knocked out in eight rounds in San Francisco.

It was on November 25, 1903, that he accomplished the unique feat of winning his third title, gaining a twenty round decision over George Gardner, at San Francisco, for the world light heavyweight title.

Heavyweight champion John L. Sullivan captured the American public's imagination. To pay tribute to their hero, the people of Boston contributed 8,000 dollars for a championship belt to be awarded to the Boston Strong Boy.

# The History of Championship Belts

By SAM ANDRE

**Tom Cribb's belt was the first documented, John L. Sullivan's stirred the most controversy.**

**The John L. Sullivan Championship belt was made of 12 karat gold and was studded with 397 diamonds and other precious stones. After a long search, it was finally discovered that this beautiful piece of workmanship had been melted down for its value in gold.**

SOON after the presentation of The Ring's 267th championship belt to Alexis Arguello by editor Nat Loubet at a Madison Square Garden luncheon a question arose concerning the recipient of The Ring's first belt.

Since *The Ring Encyclopedia* lists names only of the champs awarded a belt since 1952, a search through The Ring files show that the late Nat Fleischer, founder and editor, presented Jack Dempsey with the first championship belt in September of 1921 following Dempsey's four-round knockout of Georges Carpenter on July 2, at Jersey City, N.J.

Further research reveals that England's Tom Cribb was the first champion on record to whom a belt was presented, after defeating Jem Belcher 168 years ago.

There were many battles in which a belt was involved, but none could match the exciting saga of the most famous pugilistic belt of all—the John L. Sullivan diamond belt.

In 1887 John L.'s popularity was at its height. It was a time when boxing was the main topic in sports; baseball was struggling to draw fans and football was running a distant third for recognition.

Throughout the country and parts of the world, the 29-year-old Boston Strong Boy was considered invincible. He had compiled a sensational record, won the American bare-knuckles title in 1882 when he annihilated Paddy Ryan at Mississippi City, Mississippi and was preparing a tour of the country.

Aware of Sullivan's popularity, Pet Sheedy, a flamboyant promoter from New York, mapped out an exhibition tour that opened in Racine, Wisconsin, on March 28, went through the Northwest and down the Pacific Coast.

Before leaving, Sheedy and a few Boston sporting men conceived the idea for a trophy to be sponsored by the people of Boston and presented to their native son. Two Boston jewelers were asked to prepare a design for an outstanding championship belt.

A month after the tour had started, Sheedy returned to Boston and advised the jewelers

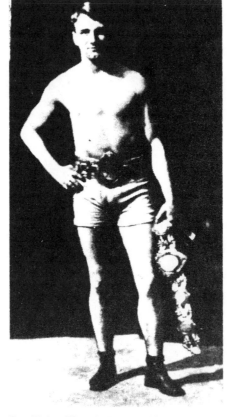

**The Welsh Wizard, Freddie Welsh, won the lightweight title from Willie Ritchie on July 7, 1914, and lost it to Benny Leonard, who stopped him in nine rounds in New York on May 28, 1917.**

to start working on the belt they said would take three months to complete. Next, Sheedy agitated the belt scheme through Boston's sports pages. It caught on at once.

Capt. Cook, editor of the Police News, the Police Gazette's rival publication, started the ball rolling with $200. Amounts from fifty cents to checks for $300 poured in. In the final counting the contributions came to slightly over $8000.

The belt started as a 12-inch square of 12 karat gold weighing about 2800 pennyweights. Rolled out it became the largest piece of flat gold ever seen at that time.

It was then fashioned into a belt 48 inches

long, 10½ inches tall and studded with 397 diamonds and other precious stones. The design represented the boxing ring with eight gold posts, through which ran three gold ropes. Between each two posts was a gold plate held in position by the ropes.

The center plate was surmounted with a large wing-spread eagle, with American, British and Irish flags on either side. The inscription read "Presented to the Champion of Champions, John L. Sullivan, by the citizens of the United States, July 4, 1887." The champion's name was set with 250 diamonds, a large diamond was set below the eagle and others distributed within stars on each plate. Inscribed on the back of the center plate were the names of 35 prominent persons.

The smaller plates on each side consisted of colorful enamel displays of the shield of the United States, characteristic fighting poses of John L. and an Irish harp. On the left panel, a formal photo of Sullivan, on the right, a photo of Sheedy. All panels were cluttered with the remaining diamonds. Officially the belt was valued at $8,000, but soon afterwards it became known as "Sullivan's $10,000 diamond belt."

It was a dazzling piece of workmanship and worthy of a champion.

On Monday evening, August 8, 1887, over 4,000 admirers of this great champion overflowed the old Boston Theatre to pay him hommage. The huge stage was occupied by 200 notables representing the State and City governments and various sports celebreties.

Prominent in the front row was Michael Sullivan, father of the hero, a small man sporting side whiskers (known as sluggers). seated next to Boston's Mayor, Hugh O'Brien.

Also in the front row was John L.'s brother Mike; Dave Blanchard, author of the old-time boxing code "Blanchard's Fair Play Rules" and Elmer Chickering, Boston's well known photographer for whom George Dixon worked as an office boy in 1884. Six years later Dixon knocked out England's Nune Wallace in 18 rounds for the world bantamweight championship.

**Richard K. Fox, publisher of the Police Gazette, presented heavyweight Jake Kilrain with a belt "Emblematic of the pugilistic supremacy of the world." John L. said of that belt as compared to his own, "Alongside this one, the Police Gazette belt is just a dog collar."**

Following the preliminary proceedings, John L., escorted by councilman William P. F. Whall, strode out on stage amid thundrous applause. Whall introduced the champ, and following a brief presentation speech, clasped the sparkling trophy around Sullivan's 46-inch waist.

Next came a series of boxing exhibitions between Bill Bushy, manufacturer of skin-tight and boxing gloves; George Godfrey, the black heavyweight champ; leading boxers Joe Lannon and George LaBlanch; Mike Donovan, former middleweight champ and, in the final, John L. stripped for a three-rounder with Steve Taylor.

The gift of the sporting public to its greatest idol, had two meanings for Sullivan. First, it was the world's most beautiful and costly pugilistic belt that belonged only to him and was not to be fought for and turned over to any possible victor.

Second, it put to shame the heavyweight championship belt that Richard K. Fox, publisher of the Police Gazette, presented to Jake Kilrain, a powerful heavyweight who had never won a fight.

During Sullivan's acceptance speech, he raised the famous belt over his head and said, "Alongside this one, the Police Gazette belt is just a dog collar."

On October 27, the Boston Strong Boy sailed for an extended exhibition tour of England to accommodate any British fighters abroad "who think they can lick me," as Sullivan put it. He meant Jem Smith, the British champ, and especially "that loud-mouth, Charley Mitchell." Aboard the SS Cephalonia was Harry S. Phillips, his new manager and the diamond studded belt.

Upon his arrival at Liverpool it seemed like all of England turned out to cheer him. All except the customs officers who demanded $600 import duty for the belt. When John L. refused, it was temporarily deposited in the Queen's bonded warehouse for safekeeping.

Sullivan carried the belt in a long velvet lined box and had intended to display it wherever British crowds gathered. Perhaps it was fortunate the belt was in the warehouse, for his train was mobbed at every stop from liverpool to London causing it to arrive many hours later. Then, so many people hung on to his coach on the way to the hotel, it collapsed, spilling everyone including Sullivan onto the street.

At his first exhibition before British boxing officials at St. James Hall, Mitchell taunted Sullivan with snide remarks. John L. was so riled he signed for a match on Mitchell's terms: a bare-knuckles fight to a finish in a 24-foot ring on turf, according to London Prize Ring Rules.

The fight took place on a rainy afternoon, March 10, 1888, at Chantilly, France, on the estate of Baron Rothschild before a few trusted people from both sides.

Mitchell's plan was to fall continuously, even without being hit, so that when Sullivan showed signs of fatigue, he could come on strong for the kill.

As the rain continued, the bout became slower and it was getting dark. After more than three hours sloshing in mud, with Mitchell down 38 times, both sides agreed to a draw at the start of the 39th round.

After the battle the fighters were arrested by the French Police and jailed. Mitchell served a couple of days, but Sullivan forfeited his bond, returned to England where he recovered his diamond belt and sailed for America.

Mitchell's backers were so certain he would have defeated Sullivan had the fight continued, they engaged the firm of Mappin and Webb to design a massive belt in his honor.

The finished product, containing 300 ounces of pure sterling silver and weighing 17½ pounds, consists of 11 small panels and three large ones with colored enamel flags of the United States and Britain and is embossed with heads of Sullivan, Mitchell, an eagle and lion.

Mitchell brought the belt to the United States, and it was on exhibition during his various tours. Americans were not impressed; there was only one belt—John L's.

In 1903, Mitchell, nine years retired, presented the belt to the London Museum for Antiquity. During World War I, the director often allowed the belt to be auctioned off to raise funds for wounded British soldiers, and each time the winning bidder returned it to the museum. More than $1.2 million was realized for the wounded.

**The late Nat Fleischer, founder and editor of Ring Magazine, poses with part of the Ring Museum collection of belts.**

(Left) England's 19th boxing champion, Tom Cribb, was the first champ to receive a championship belt. (Above) John L. Sullivan sailed to England in 1888 to defend his diamond studded belt against Charlie Mitchell. The fight took place in Chantilly, France, and went to 39 rounds before it was called a draw. Sullivan kept the belt.

Ted Broadribb, a popular British fight manager, bought the Mitchell belt in 1924 from Sir Harry Preston who had auctioned it off at a charity affair at Brighton for $2000. Two years later, editor Nat Fleischer purchased it for the same amount from Broadribb and placed it in the Ring Museum where it has since been on display.

John L.'s proudest possession was the diamond belt. Whatever his failings, including an enormous capacity for whiskey and the joy of spending his money, he considered the belt the greatest of all ring trophies and it was never out of his possession, even after he lost the title he held for ten years to Jim Corbett at New Orleans, Louisiana, on September 7, 1892.

Around 1895, Sullivan began loaning his belt to old friends for exhibition purposes. It was put on display in many of Boston's famous saloons, among them the flashy bar in Gay's Hotel, conducted by Jim Shea and George Gay at the corner at Washington and Dover Streets. Wherever it appeared the belt acted like a magnet bringing in customers.

The belt was passed around quite often and slowly diamonds began to disappear. Legend has it that Sullivan, when in need of quick money, would pick out a few diamonds to sell.

During that period, Sullivan was touring the country making a lot of money. His tour in 1895 netted him $85,900, in 1896 it was $91,000 and the next two years, $67,300. Though he spent it almost as soon as he

earned it money was available; therefore, it is more likely that some so-called "old pals" were the first to pick out a few diamonds.

Sullivan seemed to have lost interest in the belt after it was returned to him early in 1899 minus some diamonds. Finding himself in need of cash after a drinking binge, he borrowed $5000 from a Boston pawnbroker, for the first time.

The second time, with more diamonds missing he was loaned $3000. It was pawned twice more for the same amount, later to be regained by Sullivan or his friends.

In 1900, the belt was pawned in New York for $2000. Bill Muldoon, a wrestling champion and trainer for John L.'s fierce 75-round championship bare-knuckles fight with Jake Kilrain in 1889, redeemed the belt and returned it to Sullivan who had possession of his famous belt for the last time.

John L. swore off drinking in 1905, then toured the country to preach against the evils of liquor.

Interviewed on his farm at North Abingdon, Massachusetts, in 1917, his last recollections of the belt was that it was lost or stolen somewhere in the midwest. "The shop which was showing it" he said, "was broken into and the belt stolen."

On February 2, 1918, John L., a beefy old man of 57, died of a heart attack.

Now it was 1931. It was the heavyweight era of Max Schmeling, Jack Sharkey, Young Stribling, Primo Carnera, Max Baer and a

strong promising 23-year-old heavyweight, Ernie Schaaf.

Born in Elizabeth, New Jersey, Schaaf had adopted Boston as his home. His ring career started in 1925, and in the ensuing years he scored 28 knockouts, lost four and won 26 decisions (two over the clever Tommy Loughran) then went on to score six straight KO's. A great future was ahead.

Somehow, an idea developed in Boston to locate Sullivan's famous belt, shine it up and present it to Ernie with accompanying publicity as another John L. in the Boston Irish championship tradition. The fact that Ernie was of German stock didn't matter.

The idea was great up to a point—there was no Sullivan belt. It had disappeared.

George "Doc" Almy, boxing writer for the "Boston Post," followed every lead available in search of the belt in the Boston area but always drew blanks. The most promising of these leads placed the belt in the possession of a resident of North Abington, Massachusetts, in which town the old warrior had passed his declining years. However, it turned out to be a silk American flag once worn around John L.'s waist in one of his bouts. It was a gift from the old champ.

Exhausted, Almy contacted Nat Fleischer at New York's Madison Square Garden for help. Since 1922 when Fleischer first dreamed of buying the famous belt for the future Ring Museum, he traced every possible clue that might lead him to the owner.

The earliest published clue appeared in

Aside from receiving boxing's first championship belt, Tom Cribb was presented with a huge silver cup with the inscription, "In honor of your many brave battles," specifically mentioning Cribb's two defeats over Molineaux. Cribb is seen above with his cup at the Union Arms in Holborn.

1903. On November 25, Simpson's, a pawnshop in New York, after repeatedly asking Sullivan to redeem his belt, put it up for auction. Mr Simpson said he had loaned the old champ $1,800 on it in 1901 and had held on to it for a year of grace.

"No more bids?" shouted the auctioneer, "well then, sold for $2,900. The so-called "$10,000 diamond belt" passed into the hands of an unnamed dealer in precious stones who said it would be broken up.

Apparently some diamonds still remained, for the bidder, aware of the gold content must have considered the value of the remaining diamonds to have bid so high.

A small clipping from the "Baltimore News" on January 4, 1918, stated that "James King, the Baltimore horse dealer, has the big diamond belt of John L. Sullivan, the former champion who died Saturday. It was turned over to King by Sullivan about ten years ago and is now in a safety deposit box."

The article ended with an inflationary note. "The value at the time of the presentation to John L. was placed at $40,000, and with the rise in value of precious stones in the past 10 years, its value should be upwards of $70,000 now." Unfortunately for Mr. King, he didn't have the belt.

Another clue involved Jimmy Barry, a retired hard-punching heavyweight who had scored 30 KO's and was KO'd five times, four by the great Sam Langford, during a nine year career ending in 1913.

Knowing of Fleischer's interest in the belt, a fight manager, just returned from the Panama Canal Zone, told Fleischer that while having a few drinks with Barry and some of his friends, Barry mentioned that Sullivan had given him the belt and that he had pawned it in Stockton, California.

The manager returned to the saloon the

Promising heavyweight Ernie Schaaf, seen after being KO'd in the 13th round at New York's Madison Square Garden by Primo Carnera, had adopted Boston as his home, and for a while there were those in that city who tried to locate John L.'s title belt to award to Schaaf.

next day to get further information, but when he arrived he was told that Barry was shot dead during a brawl.

Fleischer contacted a Stockton sports writer friend and asked him to search all hockshops, jewelry and antique stores for the

Tom Sayers was presented with the above belt by Lord Drumlanrig, father of the Marquis of Queensberry, after Sayers beat Bill Perry, "The Tipton Slasher," on June 16, 1857, in 11 rounds.

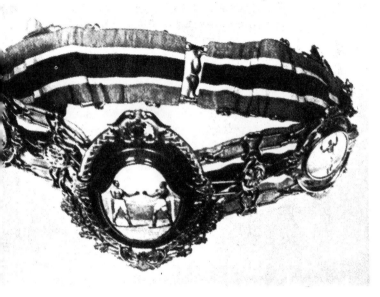

(Above) The Lonsdale Championship Challenge Belt, first awarded in 1909. (Right) Tom Cribb's silver trophy, much prized by its owner.

trophy. It was not in Stockton.

Finally, in 1926, Fleischer followed a lead that paid off. He went to Baltimore with a large and sharp photograph (now in The Ring Museum) of the original belt to meet his contact.

In The Ring files, an obscure folder contained the following, written by Fleischer:

"Back in 1926 a chap named Ed McGuire in Baltimore, owned the belt, but would not discuss how he got it. He said he had sold it to an "old gold" junk dealer in that City whose name I do not recall. I tried hard to purchase it from the dealer.

"I offered him $500, but he wanted $2000 and I could not afford it. My offer was all the money I owned after having bought the Charley Mitchell belt a few weeks earlier.

"Someone had told the dealer if he had it melted at the U.S. Mint in Philadelphia, Pennsylvania, he would get far more out of it in the value of gold. I told him it would be a shame to destroy such a relic. He wanted time to think it over.

"Shortly afterward I returned to

Baltimore after raising more money. I offered $750 for it, but he again refused, insisting on $2000. Perhaps someone told him that amount was what I had paid for the Mitchell belt.

"I tried again later, but he had taken the belt to the Mint where it was melted down. He received from Uncle Sam $812 for the gold. That was in 1927. When I saw the belt it compared with the photograph in every detail. I know it was the original belt, except for the missing diamonds and other stones which had been removed."

Such was the fate of the most beautiful and famous pugilistic belt, once the proud possession of the world's most renowned pugilist; John L. Sullivan, a two-fisted drinker and rule-breaking idol who stirred the imagination of a growing America.

Thirty years later, on November 5, a five-column photo of the belt appeared on the front page of the "Hammond Times," with a startling headline: "Long Lost John L. Sullivan Championship Belt Goes On Display Friday In Hammond."

The publisher, James S. De Laurier, pur-

chased the belt from Melvin Herman of Hammond, Indiana who offered it for sale in a Times classified advertisement. No mention of the price was made. The belt bore imitations called Zircons in place of the missing diamonds.

The 84-year-old Herman, living in a Hammond Rest Home, claimed he received the trophy in the will of his brother, Urbine (Sport) Herrmann upon his death in 1939. Herman had kept the belt in a vault for many years and now wanted to dispose of it.

The Times article, written by sports writer Loren Tate, stated: "It has been confirmed that (Sport) Herrmann, a wealthy sports-loving Chicagoan had a Sullivan belt at one time.

"But it is more likely that Melvin Herman got the belt from Charles West, former owner of the Indiana Hotel in Hammond, shortly before West's death in March of 1945. West reportedly came into possession of the belt in his Chicago saloon before he bought the Indiana Hotel in 1927."

A photo of the Herman belt was sent to Fleischer who remarked it looked very much like the original according to the photo.

Herman had much background material on Sullivan including a six-column "reproduction" of the original belt that appeared in the 1910 Dayton, Ohio, Journal. The word "reproduction" raised a doubt, but there were also a number of other questions that needed answers.

The then sports editor John Whitaker and current sports editor Dave Kennedy were quite certain at that time that the belt was a replica. Publisher DeLaurier, however, thought otherwise.

Tate's article concluded with a question and a partial answer: "Is it a hoax? If so, someone went to a great deal of trouble."

It was a hoax, and someone did go through a great deal of trouble to manufacture a replica which went to Florida when its owner, publisher DeLaurier, retired ten years ago.

The replica first made its appearance during the Pan American Exposition in Buffalo, New York, in 1901. The gentleman who displayed it made upwards of $200 per week until the fraud was brought to the attention of the authorities..

To go back to the beginning with boxing's first champion, James Figg 1719, there was no mention of a trophy until England crowned her 19th champion, Tom Cribb, following his two smashing victories over Tom Molineaus, the American challenger, in 1810

and 1811. A powerful 5-10, 195-pounder, Cribb was known as the "Gamest of the Game" and possessed enormous strength.

He was recognized as champion after defeating the former champion, Jem Belcher, for the second time, on February 1, 1809, on Epsom Race Course in a 30-foot ring. Blinded, bruised and covered with blood, Belcher was forced to admit defeat at the end of 31 rounds and 40 minutes.

On December 18, 1810, a rainy cold day at Copthall Commons, Cribb defended his title with a crushing victory over Molineaux, a powerful black who was reared in Virginia.

Molineaux flailed away without letup and appeared to have the fight won when he floored the champion in the 23rd round. Cribb survived the knockdown and forced the battle when Molineaux showed signs of exhaustion from his early efforts.

Siezed with a fit of shuddering, Molineaux seemed to weaken suddenly. In the 33rd round Cribb landed a punishing blow on Molineaux's throat. Before he could lash out again, Molineaux's legs gave way. He fell and was carried senseless from the ring.

In a return battle, September 28, 1811, at Thistleton, Cribb again won by a knockout in only 11 rounds. Molineaux started fast and was overpowering with rushes and sweeping swings. Cribb weathered the storm

of blows, except for one which completely closed his left eye.

Cribb kept pounding Molineaux's body with solid blows. Desperately, Molineaux landed a glancing blow to the head that sent the champion sprawling. But, Molineaux had shot his bolt.

After having his eye lanced, Cribb pressed the attack. A powerful left doubled up Molineaux, who was finished in less than 20 minutes.

For his two victories, the champion was presented with the first belt ever recorded in boxing history as a token of his fistic supremacy. The belt was made of lion skin and ornamented with large silver lion claws.

At a banquet at Castle Tavern, London, on December 11 that year, he was presented with a huge silver cup, "In honor of your many brave battles" and his most memorable, "the defeat of the American Challenger, Molineaux." In that era, a cup was the most highly prized trophy for it could be filled with Ale and passed around for a toast and a swig.

Forty seven years later, that cup was presented to the champion, Tom Sayers, on the stage of London's Victoria Theatre where Sayers received the stakes won by his victory over Tom Paddock, June 15, 1858.

Cribb held the title 11 years without a

**Then heavyweight champ Ingemar Johansson tries on the championship belt which had just been presented to him by the late Nat Fleischer, right. Left of Johansson is promoter Humbert J. Fugazy.**

## CHAMPIONSHIP BELTS

challange. His protege, Tom Spring, a clever boxer, who defeated some good men, attracted serious attention when he beat Tom Oliver in 25 rounds near London on February 20, 1821.

When Cribb retired he awarded the championship belt to Spring, the first heavyweight champion to adopt a fighting name. His real name was Thomas Winter.

After two grueling 77 and 76-round victories over Nat Langham in 1824, Spring retired, but did not give up the belt. The first battle, on January 27, at Worcester, was witnessed by an estimated 30,000 people, including many distinguished notables of the time.

Jem Ward claimed the vacant title after destroying Tom Cannon in 10 minutes on July 10, 1825. The victory included a championship belt. Ward defended the crown twice, the second bout being a knockout victory over Simon Byrne in 33 rounds of brutal exchanges, on July 12, 1831. The year before, Byrne defeated Sandy McKay in 47 rounds with McKay so badly punished he died as the result of injuries.

Ward retired in 1832 and announced he would present a championship belt to the first man to prove worthy of it.

James "Deaf" Burke, a vicious slugger, claimed the title and was challenged by Byrne. They met on May 30, 1833, at St. Albans, near London, for $500 a side. Ward refused to offer a belt to the winner.

The battle, a brutal encounter, lasted three hours, 16 minutes, during which time 99 rounds were fought. Byrne was so badly beaten he died three days later.

While Burke was in America looking for action, Ben Caunt and Bold Bendigo (William Thompson) fought for the title on April 3, 1838. Caunt was on the verge of defeat, but was declared winner on a foul in the 75th round.

When Burke returned to England, Ward, after seven years trying to make up his mind as to who should wear the championship belt, decided upon the winner of a Burke-Bendigo match. Burke was favored in the fight that was held on February 12 for a stake of $600 to $500, but he couldn't cope with Bendigo and lost the battle in the 10th round on a foul.

After a speech by Ward, the large silver champion of England belt, adorned with engraved figures and battle scenes, was girded around Bendigo's waist. The "Bold One" considered the belt his personal property and never gave it up.

In 1855, through subscription that raised $500, a new championship belt was manufactured by Mr. R. Hancock, head of a London silver establishment on New Bond Street.

The belt, about four inches deep, bore the inscription "Champion of England" and was ornamented with the British lion and emblematic designs of the prize ring. Strict rules were set down, among them: the belt could not change hands except in a fight, no fight to be less that $1000 a side and any pugilist having held it against all comers for three years without defeat, should become absolute possessor.

With the belt up for grabs, the best bruisers in England challenged for it. Two men survived the competition—Bill Perry, "The Tipton Slasher," and the celebrated Tom Sayers.

On June 16, 1857, Sayers beat Perry in 11 rounds in one hour, 42 minutes and was formerly presented with the belt by Lord Drumlanrig, father of the Marquis of Queensberry.

Meanwhile, in America, John C. Heenan, a boxer with deadly punching power, fought John Morrissey for the American title at Long Point, Canada, and lost. Heenan suffered a broken hand early in the battle and had to quit in the 11th round. When Morrissey ignored demands for a return bout, Heenan claimed the title and challenged Sayers for the world title.

Sayers accepted, and the international contest took place on April 17, 1860, at Farnborough, England.

After two hours, six minutes, the bruising battle ended when the ropes were cut in the 37th round. But five more so-called rounds were fought with the ring half-filled with

*U.S. Army private Willie Pep, who also happens to be featherweight champion of the world, proudly accepts The Ring Magazine's championship belt from publisher Nat Fleischer at a special ceremony in New York City, January 1943.*

spectators. The referee, unable to control the fight, declared it a draw.

Both men claimed victory. When Heenan demanded the championship belt and Sayers refused to give it up, a bitter feud developed.

One British publication "Punch," proposed that Heenan accept half the belt and Sayers the other half. Frank Dowling, editor of Bell's Life, suggested both receive a belt, paid for by public subscription provided the true belt remained in the hands of the editor, to be fought for in a return match.

Heenan maintained he was told the belt would be presented to him if he defeated Sayers, but Sayers denied this.

After much discussion on both sides of the Atlantic, it was decided to present each man with a facsimile of the championship belt. The presentation between the rival champions took place on May 31, 1860, before a cheering audience in the Alhambra Palace at Leicester Square, London.

Sayer announced his retirement and died five years later. Heenan lost to Tom King at Kent, England, in 1863 in 24 rounds, lasting only 35 minutes. He retired and died ten years later.

When Sayers retired in 1860 he offered his belt for competition. Sam Hurst won it, knocking out Tom Paddock that year in five rounds.

On June 18, 1861, Jem Mace, the originator of the modern school of scientific boxing, defeated Hurst in eight rounds and was awarded the championship belt.

Tom King won the belt from Mace in a 43-round victory on November 26, 1862, and when King refused a return fight, the British acknowledged Mace as champion (last champion under London Prize Ring Rules) and awarded him the belt.

In a battle for the world title on May 10, 1870, at Kennerville, Louisiana, Mace knocked out the American champion, Tom Allen in 10 rounds. He retired in 1890 after losing to Charley Mitchell in three rounds. Twenty years later he passed away at the age of 79. Mace's championship belt was purchased by Nat Fleischer in 1930 for The Ring Museum.

After Mace, British boxing fell into a rut until 1909 when Lord Lonsdale offered championship belts to be fought for at fixed weights in each class. Competition was keen and many new boxers soon developed into championship calibre.

The tournament established the flyweight class at 108 pounds and from it emerged one of the world's greatest, Jimmy Wilde from Pontypridd, Wales.

Starting in 1911, Wilde went on to score 64 KOs, won 42 decisions and won the world title on Dec. 18, 1916, with an 11-round KO over Young Zulu Kid, the American champion, in London.

He defended the crown 23 times, losing only to two American bantamweights, Pal Moore and bantam champ Pete Herman who won on a 17-round KO on Jan. 13, 1921. Two years later, on June 18, Jimmy lost the title to Pancho Villa of the Philippines at New York's Polo grounds via a 7-round KO.

Three weeks later, Villa was presented with the second Ring belt by The Ring editor Nat Fleischer, who had started the new era of championship belts when he awarded the first Ring belt to Dempsey in 1921.

Since then, The Ring has presented championship belts to 175 champions from all parts of the world and will continue to carry on the tradition in the future.

## IN SUNNY CALIFORNIA

**LOS ANGELES**—Unbeaten and untiled Alberto Sandoval, 113¼, Pomona, stretched his record to 20 with an easy knockout over Tony Moreno, 112½, San Antonio, at the Olympic Auditorium.

Sandoval, a former national AAU flyweight champ, dominated the fight from the offset. He dropped Moreno with a left hook in the first, staggered him twice in the second.

Moreno was out on his feet when referee Rudy Jordan halted the fight at 2:08 of the third. The victory gave young Sandoval his 13th KO.

The co-feature 10-rounder lasted just 59 seconds into the first. Hector Rivera, 130, Puerto Rico, blasted Eulogio Bojorquez, 138, Mexico, with a perfect left-right combination.

Other results: David Barrera, 119½, Los Angeles, decisioned Jose Luis Diaz, 120½, Mexico, (4); Antonio Adame, 149, East Los Angeles, KO'd James Bella, 145½, Los Angeles, (5).

The gate was $12,145.

*Heavyweight champion Floyd Patterson receives Ring belt from Nat Fleischer at 1956 Boxing Writers' banquet (above). Featherweight champ Hogan "Kid" Bassey and middleweight king Ray Robinson were awarded Ring belts in 1958 (below).*

*In 1937, the great Henry Armstrong received the first of what would be his three Ring championship belts from Nat Fleischer after he won the featherweight title. Armstrong's manager, Eddie Meade, looks on approvingly.*

# SUGAR RAY LEONARD—

## FROM PALMER PARK TO BOXING'S NEW SUPERSTAR

### PUGILISM'S PEAK

**BY GEORGE CLIFFORD**

There isn't much about Prince Georges County, Maryland, that hints of success. Although it wraps around the eastern half of Washington, D.C., it still has managed to avoid most of the affluence the capital bestows on its neighbors. Prince Georges has been limping for a long time, and things haven't been getting better.

At the end of World War II, most of the county's land was planted in corn and tobacco, and despite the occasional epidemics of blue mold, was considerably more inviting than its current crop—two-story apartment buildings, shopping and a bumper harvest of maca parking lots—make it. A frie once set out to build a quality community in Prince Georges. He went bankrupt.

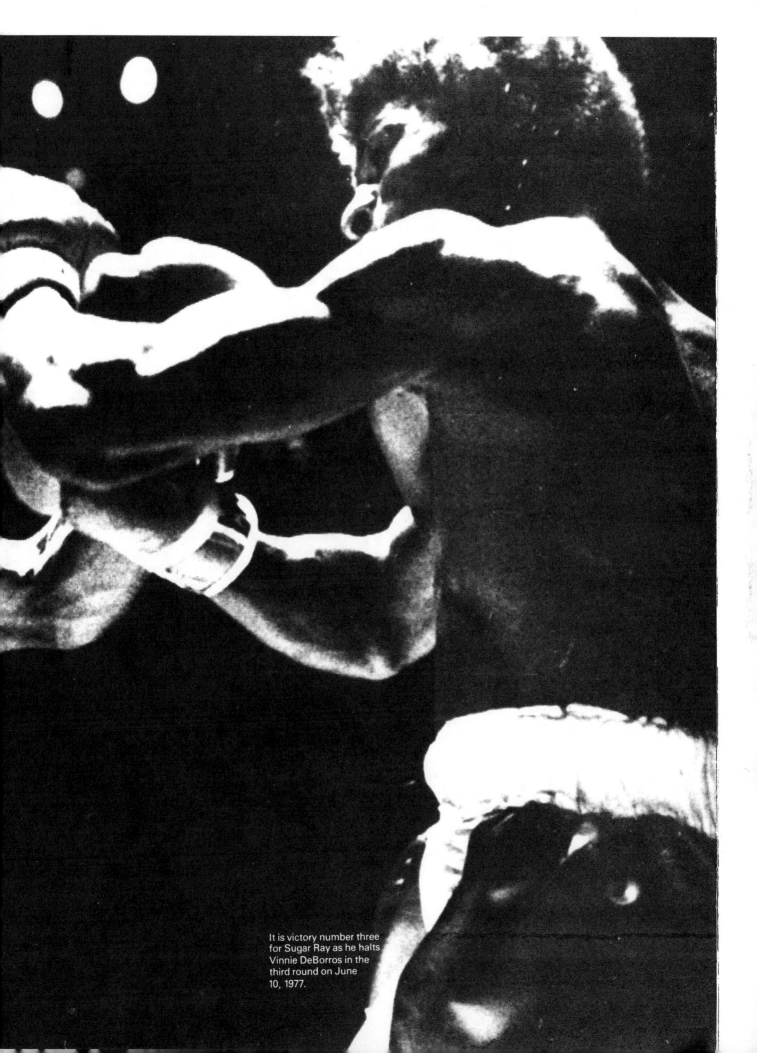

It is victory number three for Sugar Ray as he halts Vinnie DeBorros in the third round on June 10, 1977.

I t is a place where lower income whites moved in the 1950's to escape the influx of blacks who came to Washington, and where blacks, seeking a better life for their children, moved later. They were all disappointed. It has the blues—blue mold, blue collars and Monday morning blues that last all week. It is Washington's Newark. It needs a massive infusion of self-confidence.

At last it seems to have found one.

Locked in an avalanche of 1000-power smiles and a maelstrom of whirling fists is the county's best known citizen, the darling of the 1976 Olympics, and, quite probably, the next welterweight champion of the world (WBC version), Sugar Ray Leonard. While Washington, Baltimore, and now, Las Vegas, claim him as their own, Leonard not only lives in Prince Georges, he likes it there.

The sonorous voices of television like to remind their captives that Pennsylvania Avenue is the "Avenue of Presidents." It stretches from the glamor and glitter of Georgetown past the White House and the bastions of the bureaucracy to the Capitol and the restored elegance of the Hill. That's about as far as the sonorous voices are likely to follow it. But it keeps going. Over the Anacostia River, through the city's shame, Anacostia, and on into Prince Georges County.

That's the way you go to see Sugar Ray Leonard. You turn at a giant warehouse, follow another road past carry-outs and parking lots, and turn right just past a drive-in theater.

The Oakcrest Community Center doesn't look exciting from the outside. What grass there is needs cutting. The buildings, painted white, look a little tired, and so do most of the cars in the parking lot. Right in front of the door, however, is a cream Mercedes Benz 450 SL, with a black convertible top. It seems out of place.

This is where Leonard worked out as an amateur, where he learned to pound out 150 amateur victories and nine world titles, including the gold medal from Montreal. It is also the place where the now-professional Leonard, who could live and train anywhere on the face of the earth, chooses to pound the bags and pound his sparring partners.

It is an unlikely place for a fighter. Especially a great one. The inside is clean and well ventilated and remarkably well equipped. There are folding chairs around the ring, and the room seems to have the dusted and polished feel of a church hall. You feel that anyone could come there and be at ease.

They do come. Small children and men

---

Leonard makes his professional debut on February 5, 1977, in Baltimore, and wins a one-sided six-round decision over Luis "The Bull" Vega.

torso, a good but not great record in the ring, and a shyness that seems to be exaggerated by Sugar Ray's gregariousness.

Sugar Ray and Odell work well together, probing each other although, after years of sparring together, each can accurately anticipate even the breaths the other will take. Odell seems to give as good as he takes.

"Keep that head moving," Jacobs yells. "There you are. . . Side-to-side . . . there you are."

Leonard spars in five minute rounds, and a thin young man in a T-shirt that says "Caesar's Palace" watches the clock. "One minute," he calls out, and the rhythm of Leonard's punches picks up. "Thirty seconds," and Ray's fists move even faster. "Fifteen seconds," and Ray's fists move on his cousin's face like B.B. King's fingers on a guitar string. "Time."

It's that way through every round. You can hear Sugar Ray's fists. "Thump. Thump. Thump, thump, thump, thump." Then the voice yells "thirty seconds," and the fists go "thump-thump-thump-thump-thump."

It is more than a workout. Sugar Ray is trying out tactics as surely as an actor tries out moves during a rehearsal. He deliberately backs into the corner, and Odell comes after him, swinging. Sugar Ray blasts his way out, and Odell is left shaking his head to stop the ringing.

(In his victory over Pete Ranzany in Las Vegas in mid-August, Sugar Ray tried it again. He backed into the corner and cocked his right hand. Ranzany wisely backed off.)

The boy with the shaved head and the others at the Oakcrest gym got a better show than most spectators do at Sugar Ray's fights. There is more action, and it goes on longer.

"Time," the thin man says at the end of the workout.

"Beautiful," says Jacobs.

The entourage closes in around Sugar Ray, and walks with him to a corner of the room, where hands with towels gently wipe off the oil and the sweat, and Jacobs' loving fingers offer a massage. The audience is quiet as Leonard goes back to the locker room for his shower.

He looks fit and confident as he goes across the room. Odell Leonard doesn't fare so well. His eyes are puffed and squinting, like Kid Gavilan's were at the end of his career. And Odell has just started.

Boxing, as Ray Leonard well knows, is a dangerous business. He has said frequently, even after one-sided triumphs, "One punch can end a career." He makes plans against the end of his career.

Most of his unbelievable earnings have

Tough Jose Bernardo Prada loses a 10-round decision (bottom left) to Leonard in November, 1978. Two months later, Johnny Gant was decisively beaten in eight rounds (above left).

Above: A long right to the face is about to make Fernand Marcotte an eighth round technical knockout victim in February, 1979. Right: The darling of the '76 Olympics has become the '80s greatest attraction.

been invested wisely. He bought his parents a split-level brick home. His lawyer has set up a retirement plan, funded with government bonds and bank certificates of deposit. There are other investments he hopes will grow.

Most important, he owns all the shares in Sugar Ray Leonard, Inc., a business that, like Prince Georges County, has one great asset—Sugar Ray Leonard. Jacobs and Morton and even Angelo Dundee, his manager of record, are all employees. All but Dundee are on the payroll. He, like the good salesman he is, gets fifteen percent.

Leonard and Dundee seldom see each other except in the days immediately preceeding a fight and, of course, during the bout. Dundee makes the matches, in the beginning bringing Leonard along slowly, then, fight-by-fight, increasing the skills of his opponents. It is a process like going to school. Leonard had to get through the elementary classes before he could go to high school. Now he is ready for the university of pugilism—a championship fight. Some of the courses along the way, after all, were tough ones.

By most measures, Pete Ranzany was one of the tough ones. In the first round of that bout, Ranzany landed most of the punches, but it was Leonard who walked back to his corner at the bell with a smile. He had studied the man, and he knew he could beat him. It took Leonard most of four rounds.

Throughout his success in the ring, and the phenomenal economic success and publicity that have accompanied it, Leonard has managed to keep his perspective. Through it all, he is still the kid from Prince Georges County.

At the time of the first Floyd Patterson - Sonny Liston fight in Chicago, in September, 1962, most of the talking was done by a young heavyweight named Cassius Clay. He scoffed at the champion and the contender, and when the name of either was mentioned, he trumpeted, "If I can't beat him, I'll quit. I am the greatest."

It was a good act, and it certainly attracted attention, but by the third day, it was wearing thin. Even then. When he sat next to me in the hotel coffee shop the night before the fight, and ordered an ice cream sundae, it seemed worth talking about. Why, I wondered, did he do it?

"Do you ever watch boxing on TV?" the young heavyweight asked.

"Sure."

"Do you notice that there is no one out there in all those seats, beyond the first couple of rows? The fighters, they just go out there and fight, and they don't say nothing. Do you ever watch wrestling?"

"Not if I can help it."

"But you see these guys come out and say, 'I am the greatest. If I can't beat him, I'll quit.' And you look, and all those seats are filled. That's all I'm trying to do."

It seems reasonable that a fighter should do everything in his power to make every cent he can out of every fight. The game is too hard, and the risks too great, to do it for less. As Leonard so often says, "One punch can end a career."

It is probable that Muhammad Ali was the greatest, both in the ring and as a promoter. He deserves what he made, but his promotional spiels were more interesting when he looked at his audience, rather than looking over their heads, as he seemed to be doing in later years.

It is pleasant that Ali's successor as boxing's biggest drawing card is a nice young man who brings the people in with a big smile and soft words. And he still looks people straight in the eye.

Perhaps he is just lucky. Or perhaps America is ready for the return of the decent, pleasant, clean-cut hero, the All-American boy. Whatever, Leonard and Wilfred Benitez, the WBC welterweight champion, will gross over $1 million each for their bout in December. It seems safe to presume that most of that money is not coming on the basis of Benitez's strength as a drawing card.

Leonard came out of the dressing room and was surrounded by his admirers. He grinned his 1000-power grin, and posed with each of the small boys who stood around him, while a man with an Instamatic popped flash cubes. When it was the boy with the shaved head's turn—he was the smallest and the last—Leonard told the man with the camera to wait until the boy had his hand clenched in a fist, and Leonard held the boy in his arms for the picture.

The man with the camera wanted to be in a picture, too, and found someone to hold the camera while he posed.

"Take your time," Leonard said, reassuringly, and his smile in the picture was as wide as it had been with the kids.

A visitor suggested that all of this must be tiring for Leonard, particularly after a workout on a hot, humid day.

"I enjoy it," he said, his smile lighting up his face. "Particularly the time with the kids. I always have time for that. I want them to be able to look up to me. I'm glad they can look up to me. I want to be an example. I'd like to work with kids when I

stop boxing. Maybe counseling, that would be good."

His smile is as radiant as the Fourth of July, and you have to wonder if he is really happy, or is he just putting it on.

"I want to be happy," he said. "Now, I'm happy for what I can do for my mother and father, and I'm happy that I'm getting someplace. When I fight for the championship, I'll be one of the first little guys to box for more than $1 million. They say only heavyweights can do that."

And that Mercedes outside. Does that make him happy?

"Do you like it?" he asks. "I've only had it six months. I bought an El Dorado, and I had it for about a month, but I got tired of it. Then I got the Mercedes. Did you see the spoke wheels? I told the dealer I wanted spoke wheels and he said he had never seen a Mercedes with spoke wheels. I said to him, 'That's the reason I want them.'

"But happy . . . I guess I won't be really happy until I stop boxing. I hope I'll have money in the bank and a bunch of apartment houses. Then I'll be able to help people without hurting myself. And the most important thing, I can just be Ray Leonard."

No "Sugar"?

"I'll put the sugar in the jar." ∎

*George Clifford is the former sports columnist for the Washington* Daily News.

## LEONARD'S RING RECORD

| 1977 | | | |
|---|---|---|---|
| **DATE** | **OPPONENT** | **SITE** | **RESULT** |
| Feb. 5 | Luis Vega | Baltimore | W 6 |
| May 14 | Willie Rodriguez | Baltimore | W 6 |
| June 10 | Vinnie DeBorros | Hartford | KO 3 |
| Sept. 24 | Frankie Santore | Baltimore | KO 5 |
| Nov. 5 | Augustine Estrada | Las Vegas | KO 6 |

| 1978 | | | |
|---|---|---|---|
| **DATE** | **OPPONENT** | **SITE** | **RESULT** |
| Feb. 4 | Rocky Ramon | Baltimore | W 8 |
| March 1 | Art McKnight | Dayton | KO 7 |
| March 19 | Javier Muniz | New Haven | KO 1 |
| April 13 | Bobby Haymon | Landover, Md. | KO 3 |
| May 13 | Randy Milton | Utica | KO 8 |
| June 3 | Rafael Rodriguez | Baltimore | W 10 |
| July 18 | Dick Ecklund | Boston | W 10 |
| Sept. 9 | Floyd Mayweather | Providence | KO 10 |
| Oct. 6 | Randy Shields | Baltimore | W 10 |
| Nov. 3 | Jose Bernardo Prada | Portland, Me. | W 10 |
| Dec. 9 | Armando Muniz | Springfield, Mass. | KO 7 |

| 1979 | | | |
|---|---|---|---|
| **DATE** | **OPPONENT** | **SITE** | **RESULT** |
| Jan. 11 | Johnny Gant | Landover, Md. | KO 8 |
| Feb. 11 | Fernand Marcotte | Miami Beach | KO 8 |
| March 24 | Daniel Gonzales | Tucson | KO 1 |
| April 21 | Adolfo Viruet | Las Vegas | W 10 |
| May 20 | Marcos Geraldo | New Orleans | W 10 |
| June 24 | Tony Chiaverini | Las Vegas | KO 4 |
| Aug. 12 | Pete Ranzany | Las Vegas | KO 4 |

## Summary

| BOUTS | WINS | LOSSES | DRAWS | KO'S |
|---|---|---|---|---|
| 23 | 23 | 0 | 0 | 14 |

*from* The Ring Record Book

---

# SUGAR RAY R. ON SUGAR RAY L.

Ever since boxing began, fighters have taken the names of other more famous figures. There was a fighter by the name of "Babe Ruth" during the '20s, another who called himself "King Tut", and scores of Young something-or-others, so labeled after more famous namesakes.

Now, there is a new "Sugar Ray," named by the media in an obvious reference to the original Sugarman, Ray Robinson. There have been other "Sugars" — Bryant, Hammond, Hart and Seales, to name just a few — but few have acquitted their use of the name as admirably as the current "Sugar," Ray Charles Leonard, originally named for the composer-pianist.

What does the original "Sugar" — who was dubbed "Sugar" Ray Robinson after Jack Case, a sportswriter for a Waterville, New York, paper saw him in an amateur fight and commented "This Robinson is as sweet as sugar . . . " — think of the man currently wearing his name?

"I'm gratified he's using my name," said "Sugar" Ray. "I think it's great when kids think enough of you to use your name."

And what about Leonard's ring skills? "He's learning every time he fights. He's putting it together well. He'll go a long way. He's pretty good and he's coming along well. He's not great yet — but I know one thing . . . he wins!"

## WIN, LOSE AND DRAW By CHARLIE McGILL

# AN ADMAN LOOKS AT BOXING

**BEING** an ad man, my professional interest in athletes (boxers included) has always been to use them as a tool to sell products. In 1967 I used the late Joe Louis as a "spokesman" for a stock broker. He stared into the camera and said "Edwards and Hanly, where were you when I needed you?!", an obvious reference to his being taken advantage of financially when he was earning his purses. This first "image" commercial for a stock broker on American TV was so successful in exploding the business of Edwards & Hanly that the SEC put the screws on the brokerage firm with the ringing words "we won't tolerate a *negro* being a symbol of Wall Street."

I "packaged" the release of Rubin Hurricane Carter in his fight for a retrial which he got. And lost. (His second trial was a worse frame than the original, and, undaunted—and more important, innocent—he will, ultimately get out of jail after already serving a lifetime for a crime he did not commit.) I enlisted Muhammad Ali, and he was a champion in his work for the retrial, making speeches, leading marches, appearing at Bob Dylan concert benefits, etc.

Previously I had done three covers for *Esquire* championing Ali's right to the crown which was stripped from him for his refusal to be inducted into the army during Nam. For one cover, I enlisted Floyd Patterson, terribly humiliated by Ali in their championship fight, to pose with Ali (with Ali's hand over his big mouth) as Patterson defended Ali's right to the championship. Still another cover showed important people from Senators to artists to writers in a boxing ring, demanding Ali to be given his title back. The third Esquire cover showed Muhammad Ali as Saint Sebastian, modeled after the 15th century painting by Castagno that hangs in the Metropolitan. I explained the idea to Ali, and he agreed to pose. At the studio, I showed him a museum postcard of the Castagno painting to illustrate the stance. He studied it with enormous concentration. Suddenly he blurted out, "This cat's a Christian!" I blurted back, "Holy Moses, you're right, Champ!" And before we could affix any arrows to Ali, he got on the phone with his manager and religious coach, Herbert Muhammad (a son of Elijah Muhammad). Ali explained the painting in excruciating detail.

He was concerned about the propriety of using a Christian source for the portrayal of his martyrdom. I held my breath during their long, involved theological discussion. Finally, Ali hung up and said it was okay. I exhaled and we shot this portrait of a man against the authorities. When I saw the first transparency, I believe my exact words were "Jesus Christ, it's a masterpiece." *Esquire* had a sensational cover (and it was reproduced and sold as a protest poster). Three years later the Supreme Court unanimously threw out Ali's conviction. Allah be praised!

But my zaniest connection with the fight game came when I helped package a middleweight elimination bout. In 1966 Joey Archer was a lesser-ranked middleweight contender who wanted a shot at the crown. The champion was the Nigerian Dick Tiger, but Tiger wanted nothing to do with Archer, who happened to be a very good boxer with the reputation of being a spoiler. Tiger was planning a title match with Emile Griffith, a former champion. Poor Joey was out in the cold. Archer was a Bronx buddy of Ed Rohan, my production

> George Lois has been called "One of the cleverest inhabitants of that mystical street (Madison Avenue) . . ." by the Wall Street Journal, "Nearly as great a genius of mass communication as he acclaims himself to be . . ." by the New York Times and "art director, idea man, copywriter—advertising guru extraordinaire . . ." by the Erie, Pa. Times-News. In short, George Lois is one of—if not the—top advertising man around. Here's his account of how he has "packaged" boxing.

manager. When Rohan mentioned to me one day that Archer was going nuts trying to force a title shot, I figured we just might pull it off if we used some ingenuity. We did these two ads. You're looking at the entire campaign, actual size. They were minuscule ads, but they knocked fight fans dead. The first ad started the commotion, the second ad churned it into a furor. The public and the media were ensnared. *The Daily News* put Joey on the front page, challenging a snarling tiger through the bars at the Bronx Zoo. He became a hot property on the talk show circuit. Sportswriters attacked the nonplussed Dick Tiger. We had gone right to the target with Joey Archer's Irish chutzpah. The pressure on Tiger mounted. And before long, before my very eyes, Archer was given his chance to win the title by having an immediate, big money elimination bout. The Griffith-Archer match was set for the Garden. You know what happened? 1. The fight was a sellout. 2. I wasn't able to get free tickets. 3. I had to buy them from a scalper and paid through the nose. 4. I bet a bundle on Archer. 5. He lost.

# BY GEORGE LOIS

THE DATE WAS JUNE 16, 1983. THE SETTING was Madison Square Garden, once the mecca of boxing, but for almost a decade now an empty shrine to what used to be. But for one night it came alive again, taking on the appearance of a religious revival meeting as the Garden teemed with the devoted who had flocked to see the high priest of *machismo* come back to claim what was rightfully his. They were all there, all singing his praises in Spanish: his fellow Panamanians; Puerto Ricans who came ready to forget Roberto Duran's insult to them before the Nino Gonzalez fight; Dominicans and Mexicans who wanted to help their brother redeem himself and his Hispanic heritage; and Cubans, especially

# THE RETURN OF ROBERTO —AND MACHISMO

BY JOSE "CHEQUI" TORRES

those from Miami, who Duran believed never abandoned him. They were there to exhort Roberto Duran to rise to the heights he had once scaled, to make the world forget the disgrace of "No Mas".

They had come 20,061 strong to cheer for their idol. And any others presented to them on their night of nights. They had cheered the celebrities introduced in the ring before the main event: celebrities like Sugar Ray Leonard and Marvin Hagler, Floyd Patterson and Bobby Chacon, Hector Camacho and Jake LaMotta. But they saved their biggest cheers for the specter of their once-great hero, Muhammad Ali, and their fallen hero, Jack Dempsey. They booed lustily when heavyweight contender Gerry

Cooney was introduced to the huge crowd as the tall, clumsy heavyweight walked around the ring expecting to receive the adulation he normally receives from people of the Caucasian race. This was not to be his tonight; the Latin crowd was having none of his posturing, thirsting only for the real thing.

And then, suddenly, there it was. It swirled up the aisles behind an oversized Panamanian flag: Roberto Duran's entourage, heading for the ring. Among those leading the serpentine parade was a tall, slender, beautiful woman, black as pitch, dressed in white with a red kerchief wrapped around her neck and a white-tiered hat that, appropriately, resembled the fancy top

of a birthday cake on this, Roberto Duran's thirty-second birthday. While 40,122 eyes were on Duran, this woman, seen by only a few interested onlookers, walked unnoticed around the ring several times, touching each of its four corners and mumbling unheard words. She then walked slowly, deliberately, towards Duran, who was gyrating his body continuously, stopping only at times to shadow box. Oblivious of the noise 20,061 throats were making, she smiled and nodded at the once-and-future champ. Her smile seemed to say, "There! I did my job; Now it's up to you." She was a Cuban spiritualist from Guanabacoa.

"She represents tonight," said a black Cuban man sitting behind me—what Ray

272

Charles represented to Ray Leonard the night he made Duran quit like a dog. Memories of the blind, black singer interpreting America preceding the second Leonard-Duran encounter in New Orleans came to mind, followed by that unforgettable eighth round when Duran humiliated himself and shocked his fans with the infamous "No Mas, No Mas," signaling to the world that he wanted Leonard no more.

Ever since, Duran has been besieged by accusations that have driven the once-great Panamanian pugilist to the edge of a breakdown. Theories have overwhelmed the boxing community as to the forces that made Duran resign his crown to the modern Sugar Man without a struggle. Perhaps, no

one will ever know; not even Duran. But the fighter began a struggle to redeem himself, to get his macho-man reputation back, to erase the idea from the minds of millions who thought he was a coward. He was attempting to recapture his old image, to save his manhood, an effort that many, including some of his closest friends, thought was a put-on, a farce, to justify his reincorporation into a society that repudiated him.

When Duran defeated Nino Gonzalez and Luigi Minchillo in 1981, all he received from his friends was advice to quit the game that had made him one of the most prominent figures in the world of pugilism. "Stop," he was told, "before you make things worse." He had made things worse, as a matter of

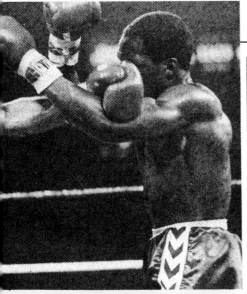

fact, when, in a pre-fight press conference, he accused Gonzalez of being just one of many Puerto Ricans who came to the U.S. to live off the welfare rolls. When he suffered a loss at the hands of WBC welterweight king Wilfred Benitez on January 20, 1980, his dreams of becoming champion once more seemed to be an unattainable fantasy. It was further sealed eight months later when unknown Kirkland Laing got the best of him in a 10-round pseudo fight in Detroit. Close friends abandoned the poor, defeated, ex-macho man. A lousy, unexciting victory that same year over another unknown, Jimmy Batten, didn't do much for Duran. This one should have sent him home for good. Instead, the man persisted.

fight seriously for a world's championship?

Besides, the trauma of the constant humiliation from his people in Panama and the majority of the boxing community was a heavy burden for Duran to carry. At home he could not walk the streets without being harassed. Journalists there made fun of him and called on their countryman to quit the game before he wound up punch-drunk or dead in a back alley.

When Duran was matched to fight former WBA welterweight king Pipino Cuevas in a junior middleweight fight earlier this year, Arum thought it was a good test for the Panamanian. Perhaps his last chance at convincing some of his old fans that Duran could come back and make them proud

Only one man believed in him: promoter Bob Arum, who could not conceive that a fighter as great as Duran had been until that miserable No Mas night, could collapse wholly in one single fight. Impossible! So, when promoter Don King jettisoned Duran, Arum took it upon himself to bring back the former great. If he couldn't reach the greatness of yesteryear, then why not try to bring out his best of today? Eighty percent of the old Duran was certainly better than 100 percent of many of today's welter and junior middleweight fighters. But, how could he motivate Duran to reach his best of today? How could anyone convince a man to suffer and to sacrifice for many months the hard training to get back in tip-top shape? How could a rich, fat man with 16 years of boxing experience, almost 32 years of age, 79 professional fights and 30 pounds of added weight pull himself together to

once again. He knocked out Cuevas in four rounds. And although many skeptics insisted that the two fighters were burned out, one being more so than the other, still people were talking again about Duran.

The pieces had come together: Duran was once again saleable, Tony Ayala had effectively removed himself from the junior middleweight picture, and the Mancini-Bogner, Moore-Duran double-header originally scheduled for South Africa had broken up with the breakage in Boom Boom Mancini's collar bone. Now the Roberto Duran-Davey Moore fight stood alone; and Madison Square Garden stood empty. The *matrimonio* was obvious, especially to a man of Bob Arum's marketing acumen.

And so, on that night of nights, as Roberto Duran answered the bell for the first round, his fate—and the future of *machismo* as well—lay firmly in his once-talented hands.

At the bell, Duran walked straight to Moore and they met in the center of the ring. Duran jabbed and moved; Moore did the same. There was a semi-smile on Moore's face. Duran's eyes were impersonal, cold, detached, hungry. His attitude was that of the old, lightweight Duran. He jabbed and jabbed in the first round and, at one point, Moore moved his head slightly to his left to evade one of Duran's jabs, and Duran's thumb met Moore's right eye. The inexperienced champ could not hide the accident. He showed all of us, including Duran, that his eye was hurt.

By the time the fourth round had begun, Duran, who by then was not sure if Moore was really that vulnerable, tested the champ by throwing a couple of combinations to his body. Moore responded by involuntarily lifting his right foot, unable to hide flinches of pain on his face. Indeed, Moore was that easy. Right then and there Duran realized that, in his 80th fight, he was to become the eighth man—and only the third Hispanic—to win three different world titles. No young kid with only 12 professional fights and 46 pro rounds could begin to think he could beat Duran.

Round four found Duran in complete control of the bout. By round four, "I began to try to give him confidence," said Duran later of Moore, "by not punching much and by letting him get off more." But Moore had been taken apart little by little, and had already lost his strength and his hope. Realizing this, Duran gave up any type of strategy and instead started to throw bombs at the eroding champ. The end became a matter of time.

After two minutes of fighting in the seventh round the Hispanic crowd stood up, waiting for the inevitable end. They screamed at the top of their lungs in anticipation of the soon-to-come victory. But referee Erenesto Magana, imported from Mexico, could not see that Moore's entire being was so seriously wounded that it could go on no more. Then, as Moore reared

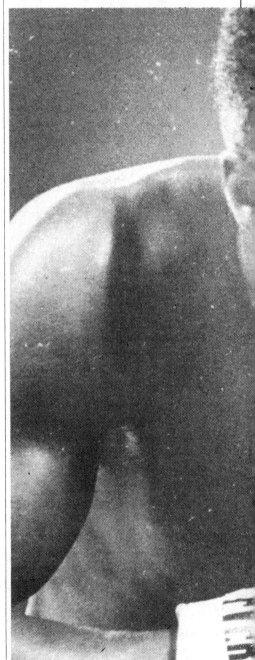

backwards, his right eye closed, his liver, ribs and stomach begging for compassion, Duran, cold as ever, walked in and threw a straight right to Moore's face. The champ, the crown no longer his, went down slowly. Unfortunately, he was saved by the bell.

Moore's trainer, Leon Washington, struggled with his defeated champion in the corner and thoughts of stopping the fight came to his mind. The one minute rest period was too short, and when the bell sounded for round eight, Duran went for the kill.

It was a pathetic two minutes. Referee Magana stared at the incredible pounding Duran was giving a defenseless and beaten Moore and simply froze. Yells from the press

row to stop the fight went unheard. Finally, after Magana ignored a towel that had been thrown into the ring from Moore's corner signalling surrender, Jay Edson, a former referee and now a Top Rank official, jumped into the ring, provoking the referee to wake up and put a stop to the one-sided fight.

**PANAMA.—ONE WORLD CHAMpion and twelve former world champions traveled to New York to see Roberto "Mano de Piedra" Duran beat Davey Moore on the night of June 16 for the junior middleweight championship.**

After the fight, Duran said he had plans: "I'll go to Panama for half a day to see General Paredes and a few close friends," he said. "Then I'll go to Miami to see *mis amigos cubanos...*" And the Cuban woman, black and beautiful, came to mind. So did Marvelous Marvin Hagler.

**The champion was Eusebio Pedroza, WBA featherweight titleholder, who will defend his crown for the 17th time against Dominican contender Jose Caba on August 13, at Saint Vincent, Italy.**
**The former champions who**

Photos by Jack Goodman

attended the fight, invited by National Guard Commander General Ruben Dario Parades, included featherweights Ernesto Marcel and Rafael Ortega; lightweight Ismael Laguna; junior welter Alfonso Frazer; bantamweights Enrique Pinder and Jorge Lujan; junior featherweight Rigoberto Riasco; junior bantamweight Rafael Pedroza; flyweights Alfonso Lopez and Luis Ibarra; and junior flyweights Jaime Rios and Hilario Zapata.

Of them, only Pedroza Zapata, Lujan and Lopez are still active in boxing activites.

Besides, two former world contenders, junior lightweight Antonio Amaya and flyweight Orlando Amores, also were in the group invited by Paredes.

From the group, only Marcel was an opponent of Duran, who beat Marcel by T.K.O. in 10 rounds on May 16, 1970 in Panama City. TOMAS A. CUPAS

### DURAN-MOORE SCORECARDS

|  | 1 | 2 | 3 | 4 | 5 | 6 | 7 | . | Tot. |
|---|---|---|---|---|---|---|---|---|---|
| **Judge Y. Yusako** | | | | | | | | | |
| MOORE | 10 | 9 | 9 | 10 | 10 | 10 | 7 | . | 65 |
| DURAN | 10 | 10 | 10 | 10 | 10 | 10 | 10 | . | 70 |
| **Judge Fernand Viso** | | | | | | | | | |
| MOORE | 9 | 9 | 10 | 9 | 10 | 9 | 8 | . | 64 |
| DURAN | 10 | 10 | 10 | 10 | 10 | 10 | 10 | . | 70 |
| **Judge Kasumasa Kuwata** | | | | | | | | | |
| MOORE | 10 | 9 | 10 | 10 | 9 | 10 | 7 | . | 65 |
| DURAN | 10 | 10 | 10 | 10 | 10 | 10 | 10 | . | 70 |

*"The only reason he wasn't defending himself was that he couldn't see."*
—Leon Washington, "justifying" his sending a battered Davey Moore out for the eighth round.
*"If I hadn't jumped into the ring, I don't think Magaña ever would have stopped the fight."*—Top Rank co-ordinator, Jay Edson.

Duran gave Moore a thorough going-over through the entire fight, methodically pounding the champion's rock-hard body and connecting repeatedly to the head. When Duran landed the big right hand near the end of the seventh round that sent the dazed and weakened champion bouncing to the canvas on the seat of his pants, it seemed the fight might be over. But Moore made it up on guts and staggered to his corner as the bell sounded, ending the round.

"Davey Moore wanted to go on,"

Washington said later. "I know he fights well when hurt and has great recuperative powers." But Moore was clearly beyond recuperating. Duran was fresher and Davey was handicapped by obstructed vision. The only thing accomplished by allowing Moore out for the eighth round was to soften him up for his next opponent.

If Washington's lack of good judgment was imprudent, then the referee's ineptness was criminal. Duran picked up in the eighth round right where he had left off in the seventh. Feet planted firmly, he teed off on the virtually defenseless Moore. Magaña ("M-A-G-A-N with a little thing over it-A," Bob Arum enunciated afterward, so all would get it right) stood indifferently, intervening only once, *to warn Moore for holding*. When the towel finally came from Moore's corner, after Roberto landed a vicious right that sent Davey falling into the turnbucle nearly two minutes into the round, Magaña stood by lackadaisically.

It's a good thing for Moore that Jay Edson, a former referee, acted instinctively without stopping to think of the propriety of climbing into the ring. If he hadn't, Duran might still be hitting Davey now.

---

The World Boxing Association outdid itself in providing a collection of the most incompetent officials ever assigned to a world title fight in recent years.

Originally, the WBA selected South African Stanely Christodoulou to referee, an inspired choice, given the anti-South Africa protests that were promised for the fight.

Christodoulou was disqualified on Wednesday afternoon. Ratings chairman Elias Cordova announced at the rules meeting at the New York Statler that Magaña of Mexico would be the referee and that the three judges would be Y. Yusako and Kasumasa Kuwata of Japan and Fernand Viso of Venezuela.

Moore's manager, Leon Washington, protested that as champion, Moore should be entitled to a "black referee," or at the very least, "neutral, non-Latin officials."

"The WBA does not assign officials by race," the affable Cordova said after rejecting Washington's demands. "Mr. Washington does not understand that Latin America is not a country. We have neutral officials."

The two Japanese judges carried the concept of "neutrality" to comical extremes, scoring four even rounds apiece. Duran pounded Moore in rounds 5 and 6, setting up the near-knockout in the next frame; Yusako called round 5 even and both he and Kuwata tabbed the sixth round even.

*BEN SHARAV*

# MIKE TYSON: THE LEGACY OF CUS D'AMATO

MIKE TYSON WAS SITTING IN A DARK room watching a video tape of Jack Johnson when a visitor arrived and suggested they watch the tape of Mike's 10-month career next. It didn't take long. Since his professional debut on March 6, 1985, Tyson has captured the imagination of the boxing world by streaking to 13 consecutive knockouts—and still counting. Nine of his victims have exited in the opening round. And while the debate continues as to whether he is a legend in the making, or just another built-up palooka who'll fall apart the first time he faces a top-notch fighter, nobody is accusing Mike Tyson of being dull.

Tyson watched the tape impassively, and for the most part, refrained from comment. One victory (over Donnie Long) was judged particularly pleasing because "everybody said he would give me trouble," and another because "I heard he was a cop." But as most of the knockouts flickered by, Mike was mute. In the time honored tradition of strong, silent men from Samson to Sylvester Stallone, he let his fists do the talking.

There is somewhat of a comic book quality about Tyson's fights. When he hits opponents, they just don't fall or slump to the mat. They fly across the ring, often

## Shaken By The Death Of His Mentor, Tyson Continues His Quest For The Heavyweight Championship

by Nigel Collins

bouncing off the floor or ropes before crashing to the canvas. It's a little like watching Popeye belt Brutus, or Batman plaster the Penguin. The violence is so exaggerated, it seems slightly surreal.

The spectacular manner in which Tyson disposes of his ring adversaries is not the only thing that makes him something out of the ordinary. Mike looks more like an NFL fullback than a fighter. He is 220 pounds of muscle crammed into a 5-foot-

ious to pass on their knowledge. D'Amato could only show the protege of his waning years the path to glory. Mike had to do the fighting. And fight he has, averaging a match every couple of weeks since his pro debut.

Tyson's whirlwind march through the John Does of the heavyweight division was hardly interrupted by the recent death of D'Amato. Although Mike was one of Cus' pallbearers, he was back in the ring

goes on, but it's tough when you lose two important people."

The heavyweight dreadnought seemed paradoxically vulnerable in his grief, but Tyson didn't always have such faith in D'Amato. It took time. When the State of New York first released Mike into Cus' custody, he couldn't quite figure out where the old man was coming from.

"I didn't know what was going on. I didn't trust him," recalled Tyson when

The winning team (from left to right) of Jim Jacobs, Mike Tyson and Bill Cayton.

11 frame. His 19½-inch neck is larger than any heavyweight champion's this side of Primo Carnera. He is, in a way, boxing's equivalent of William (The Refrigerator) Perry—sans fat. And he's only 19 years old.

But numbers, whether they relate to knockouts or biceps, are not the stuff that legends are made of. No, what makes Tyson something special is his lasting relationship with the late Cus D'Amato. It is the story of how D'Amato took a troubled young man under his wing, delivered him from the mean streets of New York City's Brownsville section, and gave him an opportunity to fulfill his destiny. A destiny that D'Amato was positive would lead to the heavyweight championship of the world.

However, the road to sport's greatest prize is not paved by wise old men, anx-

a week after the funeral.

"I don't know who made up the saying, but 'the show must go on,' " said Mike softly. "That's what Cus believed."

Nevertheless, D'Amato's death was a staggering blow, one that still brings a quiver to Mike's voice when he speaks of his beloved mentor.

"Cus was more than a father to me. Anyone can be a father and it doesn't really mean anything. Cus was my backbone. I'm not over it (D'Amato's death) at all. The things we practiced (in the gym) for years and years . . . now I'm starting to do them and he's not around to see it.

"As a person, I'm just not happy. I'm not in a state where I hate the world and want to commit suicide. Far from it. It's just that although I'm somewhat successful, the people I enjoy the most, like Cus and my mother, aren't here. I know life

asked about his early days in D'Amato's Catskill Mountain retreat. "The real objective for me was to get out of that place I was in (Tryon School in Johnstown, New York, a penal institution for incorrigible boys). I wanted to get the hell out of there."

Tyson downplays his wild years on the streets, saying: "I wasn't really a bad kid. I used to rob and steal. Other people may consider that bad, but in my atmosphere and neighborhood, it wasn't shit. Other guys did worse things. They murdered people."

At first, D'Amato's home was just another prison to Tyson, but slowly the child of the ghetto was won over by Cus's kindness and understanding. According to Mike, it took the better part of two years, but eventually, he grew to trust and love the man who had, in a different era, taken both Floyd Patterson and Jose Torres to world championships.

"He did everything for my best interest," said Tyson. "It sounds funny, but when I was late for dinner, he'd always make sure nobody touched my food. And he wouldn't let anybody go in my room. We used to talk all the time. I was young, 14 or 15 years old. The things he was saying didn't always mean that much to me. Then an hour after we would finish talking he would ask me, 'Mike, do you remember anything that I told you?' And I would say, 'Yeah, yeah,' and go outside. He told me so many things I would forget them. But then, I'd be walking down the street later and I would remember.

"Cus used to tell me mostly about how to be a successful person. I used to tell him how I would like to meet famous people like actors, and he would tell me to keep doing what I was doing and one day they'd be breaking their necks trying to meet me. And he was right."

One of the things D'Amato strongly believed was that boxing was a form of entertainment, and that in order to be successful, a professional fighter has to also be entertaining. About six months before his death, Cus told *The Ring*, "From the beginning, Mike has been taught to be exciting." In an effort to show exactly just how well Mike learned this particular lesson, we recently traveled to Albany, New York—the site of his 13th consecutive victory.

IT WAS A COLD, RAINY NIGHT, BUT ALmost 3,000 fans braved the elements, filling the Colonie Coliseum to capacity. Many among them proudly wore their Mike Tyson t-shirts. Basketball may have its "Dr.J" and baseball its "Dr.K," but a couple of kids at the Coliseum had a handmade sign proclaiming Tyson "Dr. Knockout." The posters already billed him as the "Future Heavyweight Champion."

The customers tolerated two inept prelims and then it was time for Tyson to do his thing. Whenever possible, Mike's bouts start around 9 p.m., so that the tape of his latest triumph is ready in time for the nightly newscasts across the nation.

The designated victim was Canadian Conroy Nelson, a tall lanky boxer, who entered the ring amidst a scattering of boos. When Mike came down the runway the arena erupted into a wall of noise that seldom subsided until the hero was on his way to the shower.

It was a typical Tyson fight. Mike exploded from his corner and immediately

took the fight to Nelson, who meekly covered up and retreated. Seeing that Nelson was protecting his head at all costs, Tyson wisely concentrated his attack to the body. As wicked hooks from both hands sunk into Nelson's sides, he grimaced and tried his best to survive.

Midway into the round, Tyson paused momentarily, and Nelson landed his only decent punch of the evening—a sharp right uppercut to the chin. The punch brought no adverse effects and Mike quickly resumed his assault. On two occasions, left hooks to Nelson's body almost ended the fight, but Conroy was still on his feet when the bell signaled the end of his three-minutes in Tyson's meat grinder.

Thirty seconds into the second, it was all over. It took just one brutal left hook to the head to take the rest of the fight out of the shell-shocked Canadian. The punch caught Nelson on the side of his nose, sending him tumbling to the floor. He rolled towards the ropes where he lay, one foot and one arm draped over the bottom rope. When referee Sidney Rubenstein's count reached seven, Nelson made an attempt to struggle to his feet. He appeared to just beat the count, but Rubenstein counted him out anyway. There was no argument from any quarter.

Shortly after his easy win, Tyson was seated on a couch in the trailer that served as his dressing room, surrounded by the flower of the provincial press. He politely

answered the same old questions he's already answered a hundred times before, but it was co-manager Jim Jacobs who really shined during the question-and-answer session. Jacobs parried probing questions into the quality of Mike's opponents with the skill of a career diplomat. When asked about Tyson's next scheduled opponent (the hapless Sammy Scaff), Jacobs made sure to emphasize his size (around 250 lbs.), but astutely avoided mentioning just how many of those pounds were pure blubber. It was a virtuoso performance by all concerned—and another step along the trail that Cus D'Amato had so carefully laid out for both manager and fighter.

It is the relationship between D'Amato and Jacobs that ties the Mike Tyson story together in such a neat package. Jacobs, a precise man who chooses his words carefully, is highly respected in boxing circles for both his knowledge of the sport and his association with outstanding fighters. Jacobs and his partner, Bill Cayton, have already handled two world champions in Wilfred Benitez and Edwin Rosario. The fact that they are also partners in the fight film business is another bonus. When it comes to researching opponents, or marketing a fighter, they have few peers. But it was Jim's almost lifelong friendship with D'Amato that brought them together with Tyson.

"There is no one in the world whose judgment I trust more than Cus

**Mike Tyson poses with trainers Kevin Rooney (right) and Matt Baranski. Rooney, the former fighter, was also trained by Cus D'Amato and is well versed in Cus' methods.**

D'Amato's,'' said Jacobs. ''If a thousand people, and I mean this literally, told me a fighter was ''A,'' and Cus told me he was ''B,'' he *was* ''B.'' And Cus D'Amato told me that in his opinion Mike Tyson was going to be the heavyweight champion of the world. That's all I had to hear.''

What has ensued goes far beyond the normal fighter/manager relationship.

''There is an incredible difference between our relationship with Mike and other fighters we've managed,'' said Jacobs. ''When Bill and I got involved with Wilfred Benitez and Edwin Rosario, it was exciting, but it was business. It is completely different with Mike. Our relationship with Mike is, first and foremost, a family relationship. It just so happens that he is a professional boxer. Cus adored Mike and that love and affection is contagious.''

> **"Cus was more than a father to me. Anyone can be a father and it doesn't really mean anything. Cus was my backbone."**

Despite Tyson's remarkable transformation from street punk to a young man on the threshold of possible athletic greatness, he remains partially hidden behind a screen of suspicion.

''I don't trust anyone,'' claims Mike. ''People want to do me favors. They want to take me out to dinner. But they didn't want to buy me dinner five years ago when I didn't have any food.

''Every day of my life I look in the mirror and I know I'm not Mr. Black America. I don't have the most charming personality in the world. But girls continue to call and want to go out with me. And eventually, they're gonna look for something in return.''

This bitter residue from the past will probably benefit Tyson as he swims boxing's shark-infested waters. It certainly doesn't sound like any camp followers will be draining Tyson's coffers. And those gnawing memories of his deprived childhood just might provide the catalyst to make D'Amato's formula bear fruit.

As Tyson's knockouts continue to mount, so does the number of people who tend to agree with Jacobs' glowing assessment.

''Right now I think he's the best young heavyweight I've seen in years,'' said veteran matchmaker Teddy Brenner. ''He's a great offensive fighter, highly competitive. He doesn't know about 'feeling out' an opponent in the first round. He goes for the kayo right away. He's a good puncher and a good finisher.

''I only have two questions that remain to be answered,'' continued Brenner. ''One, how will he do when someone takes him five or six rounds? Is he musclebound? If you remember, George Foreman was great in the early rounds, but then he used to run out of gas. Two, how well can Tyson take a punch?''

Brenner also helped put into perspective the sometimes questionable quality of Mike's opponents.

''Some of the guys he's beaten have been bums, but guys like Donnie Long and Conroy Nelson usually give you rounds. Tyson took them out early. I have problems getting him opponents for Atlantic City because guys know that if they get knocked out, they'll be suspended and have to take a lot of expensive medical tests before they can fight in New Jersey again.''

Others are not so charitable in their evaluation.

''In the way he's been handled, it's almost like he's a ''white hope'' in a black man's skin,'' opined *The Ring*'s own Jack Obermayer, who has had several opportunities to observe Tyson in action in Atlantic City. ''Tyson has an honorable man behind him in Jim Jacobs, but I think everyone is making far too much of him, far too soon.''

Jacobs would be the first to agree that it is premature to start talking about a title fight.

''Take a look at any fighter who comes to your mind, Joe Louis, Ray Robinson, anybody, and look at what they did in the first 10 months of their careers,'' challenged Jacobs. ''They weren't even in the embryo stage of their careers. They weren't even getting started in the first 10 months. That's why Bill and I get hysterical when people ask us when Mike is fighting for the world title.''

Jacobs also has an answer for those who criticize the calibre of opposition Tyson sees when he looks across the ring on fight night.

''I take that as a supreme compliment. The more we are criticized, the more I read in the papers that we are moving Mike too slowly, the more I'm pleased. I look on it as a badge of honor. The people who try to suggest the pace a young, 19-year-

old fighter with enormous talent should be moved at, are probably brilliant sports writers, probably excellent television commentators, but whether or not they are qualified to be boxing managers is a different question.''

''I find it amusing,'' adds Cayton, whose production *The Legendary Champions* was nominated for an Academy Award.

Part of D'Amato's method of building a fighter is predicated on never, never allowing one of his fighters to face a man Cus wasn't absolutely sure he could beat. Needless to say, D'Amato was less than enthralled when Patterson finally decided

> **"I wasn't really a bad kid. I used to rob and steal. Other people may consider that bad, but in my atmosphere and neighborhood, it wasn't shit. Other guys did worse things. They murdered people."**

to defend his title against Sonny Liston. And you had better believe that Jacobs and Cayton are following the D'Amato method with Tyson.

''I talked to Cus for thousands of hours about Mike,'' revealed Jacobs. ''Cus would repeat himself. He would tell me, in great detail, over and over, every step to take with Mike. When I think about what I'm doing, I just press a button in my head and I can hear Cus talking to me. What I am doing is precisely and exactly what Cus told me to do.''

But in the final analysis, it doesn't really matter what Jacobs does, or what anybody says or writes about Tyson. We have come full circle in our search for the answer to the riddle the untested Tyson presents—back to the fighter himself. Eventually, Tyson will step into the ring with someone capable of administering the final exam, and then, and only then, will we know whether Cus D'Amato was right.    □

**Robert Colay (left) reels under the fury of Mike Tyson's attack in a bout held in Atlantic City. Colay lasted exactly 37 seconds.**

**Mike Tyson poses in the gloves worn by Floyd Patterson when he won the heavyweight championship with a fifth round knockout over Archie Moore on November 30, 1956. Patterson, who was also guided by Cus D'Amato, was the youngest man to ever win the heavyweight title. Floyd says he is "pulling" for Mike to beat his record.**

# ANOTHER KIND OF PUNCH-DRUNK

by
Joseph D'O'Brian

*The closer a heavyweight comes to the championship, the more natural it is for him to be a little bit insane, secretly insane, for the heavyweight champion of the world is either the toughest man in the world or he is not, but there is a real possibility he is. It is like being the big toe of God.*

—*Norman Mailer*

NOT TOO LONG AGO, SOME FRIENDS and I got into a discussion of how there are so many top-flight boxers today who are getting into terrible trouble outside the ring. We weren't concerned with the odd barroom brawl, or the occasional one drink too many, or any of the little scrapes a healthy young man can get into now and then. We were talking about the guys who are ending up in prison, or in mental institutions, or with severe drug habits or other life-threatening emotional problems.

We came up with quite a list of names and incidents, all of them from the past three or four years.

Middleweight contender Tony Ayala, after a long series of problems with the law, is now serving a 20-year prison sentence for rape.

Bruce Curry, former WBC junior welterweight champ, was recently confined to a mental institution after displaying violently psychotic behavior.

Aaron Pryor, the *real* junior welterweight champ, is rumored to now weigh less than 120 lbs. Since it can't actually be proven. I had better not say how he got so fashionably slender.

Alexis Arguello, former lightweight champ, recently admitted to a problem with cocaine.

Former WBA heavyweight champ Mike Weaver attempted suicide following his loss to Michael Dokes in 1983.

And those are only a few that I remember off the top of my head. We must have come up with at least a dozen more.

Now, it may well be that on a percentage basis, boxers are no more likely than

*Joe Louis, pictured here posing with comedian Rodney Dangerfield, suffered from a severe mental disorder for many years after he retired from boxing.*

any other group of people to commit crimes, abuse drugs or become emotionally disturbed. But it did seem to us that boxing has always been an unsafe profession in that respect. Former world champs Joe Louis, Johnny Bratton, Mike McTigue, Ad Wolgast and Battling Nelson became insane. Freddie Mills, Randy Turpin and Billy Papke were suicides, Papke taking his wife with him. Mickey Walker, Benny Lynch, Sonny Liston and countless others died of alcohol or drug abuse. And the boxers who were what my mother called ''tortured souls'' must number in the thousands.

There might be any number of theories as to why so many boxers end up this way, and probably none of them are entirely correct. But this is a subject we had better think about. Boxing's reputation in the world at large couldn't be worse than it is right now, and it wouldn't hurt our standing at all if we were to start looking after our own a little more. So in the interest of debate, as usual, I present a few ideas and opinions. (I welcome, nay, require your comments on this, by the way. Write me c/o *The Ring*.)

The simplest answer to the problem is that boxers are overpaid. I will say right up front that I think this is nonsense. Most boxers are forced to work another job besides boxing, and those who can actually make their livings in the ring deserve to make as much as they can get. But it is true that if a fairly naive young man is making more money than he knows what to do with, it's easy for him to buy a lot of heartache. This has always been a problem: Lots of fighters today blow their money on cocaine; a few years ago they blew it at the racetrack.

Joe Louis, of course, is the classic example of a man who let money drive him over the edge. Louis made millions in the ring, but by the end of his career he was several hundred thousand dollars in debt. As far as anyone can figure it, Louis simply failed to realize that he wasn't always going to have such tremendous earning power. When he had it, he spent it; ''security'' was a word he didn't know. As a result, Louis ended up destitute, living on handouts. Perhaps it was this that drove him insane.

Shortly before Louis died, someone told him, ''It's too bad you're not fighting today; you'd have made so much more money.'' Louis replied, ''That doesn't matter. I still would have blown it all.''

That's probably true. It's human nature to want to blow money. I know I spend like a sailor when I have it, and if I had more, I'd spend more. My friend Herb Goldman once told me about a former welterweight champ (still alive) who was in the habit of buying cars, then simply abandoned them when he got tired of them. It's hard to get rid of several million dollars, but it can be done. At any rate, this fellow ended up broke, went through a long period of emotional turmoil, and only now seems to be pulling himself together. There are a lot of similar stories I could tell.

But money in itself doesn't make a man crazy. Look at Larry Holmes or Ray Leonard. They each made millions, and they each seem to like the nice things that money can buy. But they were careful. They'll never go broke, and thus it's unlikely that money will ever drive them to destruction. So you can't say that making money makes boxers do crazy things.

Losing money will make anyone crazy. I should imagine it would be easy enough to keep most boxers from ending up broke. Many businesses offer financial counseling to their employees; why can't boxing's governing bodies do the same for boxers? If the WBA, WBC and IBF really wanted to make themselves useful, they could offer seminars on investments, or on basic

*Sonny Liston and his wife Geraldine relax in a Chicago hotel room in 1963 shortly after his second fight with Floyd Patterson. Seven years later Mrs. Liston discovered Sonny's body in their home in Las Vegas, dead of a drug overdose.*

principles of business administration, or they might recommend brokers and financial advisers to boxers who need them. Something like this would be useful to any boxer, whether he was making $200 per fight or $2 million.

Another theory is that drugs are too readily available these days. This, too, is too simplistic an answer, I believe. Booze, heroin, cocaine and what have you have been around forever, and people have always abused them. But it is true that when you have a lot of career pressures—as what boxer doesn't?—mixed with a good deal of free time, the temptation to abuse drugs becomes greater.

Very often, a drug abuser who is well-known finds it harder to get satisfactory treatment than a drug abuser who is just Joe Average. If a celebrity checks himself into a drug clinic, he'll be hounded to death by the news media, and this is common knowledge. Therefore, a good many well-known athletes avoid treatment for

might want to get to the top and stay there, but wouldn't go all to pieces if he didn't succeed.

That's not the way it is now. A fighter *must* get to the top today; if he doesn't, he's nothing. And even if he does get to the top, if ever he falls, he falls forever. I won't go into a long sociological discussion of how this has happened, but it has happened: Great isn't good enough. Best is the only thing that matters, and best doesn't last forever. And when it's driven home to you that you're no longer the best, or even that you might not be the best, it's going to hurt.

It's interesting to note that you seldom see spectacularly self-destructive behavior on the parts of boxers who aren't world-class. I've known a few fighters, and I've found that the really great ones are a nice enough bunch of guys, but the ones I really admire as men are the club fighters, the ones who are going nowhere fast, and know it. They're the guys you want to sit

*Ad Wolgast, once world lightweight champion, dressed in his hospital gown while a patient in the psychopathic ward of Los Angeles General Hospital in 1927.*

*England's Freddie Mills prepares for his title-winning bout with Gus Lesnevitch for the light heavyweight title. Mills only held onto the 175-pound belt until his first defense, when he was stopped by Joey Maxim. Fifteen years later, Mills committed suicide.*

*Flyweight champion Benny Lynch was a great fighter but also a hopeless alcoholic.*

fear of publicity, with the result that the problem gets worse.

Here, again, the Alphabet Boys could help—if they wanted to. They're good at doing things in secret: Why couldn't they offer strictly confidential treatment to boxers who abuse drugs, in a compassionate, non-judgmental atmosphere? They're pretty good at calling for punishment of boxers who are caught failing the urine test: Why not help them to pass the test in the first place?

But this is not a problem for which the Alphabet Boys should be blamed. It's a problem that's been around for many years, ever since boxing became a big-money sport at the end of the last century.

The reason why so many fighters go over the edge, I'm pretty sure, is pressure. There was a time, when boxing wasn't so lucrative, when it was controlled by the it's-just-a-game British instead of the win-at-all-costs Americans—when a fighter

*The fury of "The Hawk," Aaron Pryor, who has been stripped of the IBF junior welterweight title for inactivity, is restrained by a member of the New Jersey Athletic Commission prior to his 1985 match with Gary Hinton. The still undefeated Pryor is alleged to have a serious drug problem.*

Photo by Pete Goldfield

down with, have a few beers and discuss the nature of the universe.

The club fighters are balanced: They know they're not the best, and maybe they've realized that they don't have to drive themselves crazy over it.

For the really first-class fighters, though, it's different. They are being tested every time they breathe. They're standing on top of a hill, with a hundred other guys trying to knock them off. Remember when you played king-of-the-hill when you were little? Remember how it was fun trying to get up the hill, but when you became king, you were suddenly under too much pressure to enjoy yourself? Now imagine that pressure multiplied by ten thousand. What's surprising is that so many great fighters manage to stay sane.

It's interesting to look at the various forms insanity takes when it strikes a fighter. Joe Louis, for instance, became convinced that a group of faceless men were trying to kill him. He took to sleeping behind flimsy barricades of furniture and clothing, and refusing to eat any food that his wife hadn't prepared. It doesn't take a psychiatrist to figure this out. When he was champ, Louis had to live with the fact that sooner or later, someone—he didn't know who—would come along and take his title away. When life became too much for him, he naturally reverted to what must have been his greatest fear.

Ad Wolgast, the lightweight champ, lost his mind a couple of years after he lost the title to Willie Ritchie in 1912. Long after, he would be seen on the streets in the early morning, running, throwing punches at the air. If a passerby asked him what he was doing, Wolgast would reply, "I'm fighting Joe Gans in a few weeks. Gotta get in shape." Gans had died in 1910.

Unlike Louis, who reverted to his great fear, Wolgast reverted to what must have been his great joy: the days before he won the title, when he was trying to claw his way up the hill. And that was where he stayed: an old man, still training for his phantom match with Gans.

If you want a modern example, look at Gerry Cooney. Following his loss to Holmes, he went into a deep depression, brooding like Achilles in his tent over his great failure. Now, this wasn't entirely Cooney's fault. If this had been an ordinary heavyweight title fight, Cooney would have been congratulated for a good try (which it was), then he might have fought his way back up and landed a rematch. As it was, he had the pride of all white America riding on his left hand, and that's a big load for one hand to carry. No wonder he was reduced to a quivering jelly that sat around saying "I'm sorry." We do it to our fighters, just as much as they do it to themselves.

I will admit that I don't have a ready solution to all this. I don't know if the boxing world needs a major attitude adjustment, or if this is by nature a sport that eats its own children, or if the problem lies in society as a whole.

But whatever the answer might be, we have to discuss the question. Not all great fighters mess themselves up, but if enough of them do that eventually, this problem may be more dangerous than the AMA and the Alphabet Boys put together. □